New York City SHSAT Prep
2020 & 2021

Lead Editor
Katy Haynicz-Smith, MA

Contributing Editor
Laura Aitcheson, MLIS

Special thanks to our writers and reviewers on this edition: Becky Berthiaume, Patrick Cox, Amy Craddock, Michael Collins, Thomas Darragh, Jonathan Habermacher, Mark Feery, Jennifer Land, Jo L'Abbate, Karen McCulloch, Laila Sahir, Anne Marie Salloum, Kathryn Sollenberger, Bonnie Wang, and Ethan Weber

Additional special thanks to the following for their contributions to this text: Naomi Beesen, Kelly Black, Connell Boyle, Matthew Callan, Megan Dusenbery, Joanna Graham, Adam Grey, Peter Haynicz-Smith, Jesika Islam, Rebecca Knauer, Mandy Luk, Jenn Moore, Camellia Mukherjee, Kristin Murner, Monica Ostolaza, Chris Ryan, Alexandra Strelka, Rebecca Truong, Oscar Velazquez, Shayna Webb-Dray, and Amy Zarkos

SHSAT (Specialized High Schools Admissions Test) is a test administered by the New York City Department of Education, which was not involved in the production of, and does not endorse, this product.

10 9 8 7 6 5 4 3 2 1

ISBN-13: 978-1-5062-5094-6

Kaplan Publishing print books are available at special quantity discounts to use for sales promotions, employee premiums, or educational purposes. For more information or to purchase books, please call the Simon & Schuster special sales department at 866-506-1949.

TABLE OF CONTENTS

PART ONE

Getting Started

CHAPTER 1

SHSAT Basics

CHAPTER OBJECTIVES

By the end of this chapter, you will be able to:

- Answer common questions about the Specialized High Schools Admissions Test
- Take advantage of the test's structure
- Approach the questions strategically

Common Questions About the SHSAT

You're using this book because you're serious about attending high school at Brooklyn Latin, Stuyvesant, Bronx Science, Brooklyn Tech, City College, Lehman College, Staten Island Tech, or York College. You probably already know that if you want to go to one of these specialized high schools, you have to take the Specialized High Schools Admissions Test (SHSAT). Fortunately, there are some steps you can take to maximize your score. Essentially, you need to:

- Understand the structure of the test
- Hone your Math and English Language Arts skills
- Develop strategies and test-taking techniques
- Practice what you've learned

The Specialized High Schools Admissions Test (SHSAT) is a standardized test. It's certainly not easy, but it is a fairly predictable test. This means that you can prepare for the content and question types that you'll see on Test Day.

Before delving into the specific content and strategies you will need to perform well on the SHSAT, you should know some basic information about the test. Here are answers to some common questions about the SHSAT.

Why Should I Take the SHSAT?

If you want to attend high school at Brooklyn Latin, Stuyvesant, Bronx Science, Brooklyn Tech, City College, Lehman College, Staten Island Tech, or York College, you must take the SHSAT. It is the sole criterion for admission. This means that your grades, extracurricular activities, and so on play no role in the admissions process. **Do not take the test if you are not serious about attending one of the schools!** If you score high enough to be accepted at a school, you will be expected to attend.

Who Administers the Test?

The New York City Department of Education administers the test. The Department of Education is composed of teachers and administrators who decide what students at New York City high schools need to learn.

SHSAT EXPERT NOTE

What Does the SHSAT Stand for?

The full name of the test is the Specialized High Schools Admissions Test. SHSAT is just a bit easier to say.

How Is the Test Scored?

Composite Score

The Composite Score is based on 800 points. The number of correct answers from the Math and English Language Arts (ELA) sections determines the Composite Score. In calculating the Composite Score, the Math and ELA sections are weighted equally.

Raw Score

The Raw Score is the sum of the correct answers from each section. There are 57 questions per section; however, 10 questions per section are experimental. The experimental questions are not scored. Therefore, the maximum number of scored answers per section is 47. Overall, the highest Raw Score for the total test is 94. The Raw Score is converted to the 800-point scale to determine the Composite Score.

Experimental Questions

The 10 experimental questions per section are mixed in with the scored questions. You will not know if a question is experimental or scored. Therefore, you should answer all questions as if they will be scored.

What Is a "Good Score"?

That's a good question, but there is no magic number that will guarantee admission. Admission to each specialized high school works like this: the Department of Education identifies the number of places available at each school. If there are 500 spaces available at Stuyvesant, the Board of Education accepts the top 500 scorers who identified Stuyvesant as their first choice. Therefore, you should just work to get the best score you can.

What Should I Bring to the Test?

You need your admissions ticket, two or more No. 2 pencils, an eraser, and a watch that does not contain a calculator. You may not bring a calculator to the test.

Taking Advantage of the SHSAT's Structure

You can be confident that the test will look very similar to the test-like practice in this book. Therefore, you can take advantage of the test's predictability and use what you know about the structure to raise your score.

You Do Not Need to Answer the Questions in Order

Usually, when taking a test, you automatically answer the questions in the order that they're written. However, there are a lot of questions on the SHSAT, and you may be able to make it easier on yourself by doing the questions you find easier first. For example, if you're good at Reading Comprehension questions, build your confidence and grab some quick points by doing them first. Or if you have a tough time with coordinate geometry, skip the coordinate geometry questions and go back to them when you have time.

You Can Move Between Sections

Most standardized tests don't let you move between sections or go back and check your work on a section you've already completed. On the SHSAT, however, you can go back to the English Language Arts section after you've finished the Math section.

There Is No Penalty for Wrong Answers

A correct answer is a correct answer. It makes no difference to your score if you get the question correct by solving the question or by guessing. Of course, you should solve the questions you know, but there's no harm in guessing when you don't know how to answer a question or are running out of time. Remember, you have a 0 percent chance of getting a question correct if you leave it blank. Your chances of getting a multiple-choice question correct if you guess are at least 25 percent. Go with the odds.

Answer Grid Tips

Don't lose valuable points on the test by misgridding! The answer choices are labeled A–D and E–H to help you keep track of answers.

Always circle questions you skip in your test book.

Whenever you choose not to answer a question, circle the entire question in your test book. This can help you in two ways. The first is that it will be easier to find the questions you skipped if they're circled. The second is that you are less likely to misgrid when you skip questions if you clearly mark the ones you skip. Anything that will help you approach the test efficiently is worth doing. Circling questions that you skip is relatively effortless and can save you time. Just make sure to go back and erase any extra marks on your answer grid before you're done.

Always circle the answer you choose in your test book.

A great way to avoid careless gridding errors is to circle your answers in the test book. If you circle your answers, you can quickly check your circled answers against your gridded answers to make sure that you did not misgrid. Additionally, if you have time to recheck your answers, it's easier to do this if the answers are circled.

Grid your answers in blocks of five.

Don't grid in each answer after you answer each question. Instead, grid in your answers after every five questions. As you're entering the answers into the grid, think to yourself, "1, A," "2, G," and so on. This will help you to avoid any omissions. Since questions alternate between A–D choices and E–H choices, you should be able to catch a mistake if you have skipped a question or entered answers onto the wrong line.

Approaching SHSAT Questions Strategically

As important as it is to know the setup of the SHSAT, it is equally important to have a system for attacking the questions. You wouldn't venture onto the subway for the first time without looking at a map, and you shouldn't approach the SHSAT without a plan. Remember, the more knowledge you have about the test and the questions, the better you'll be able to take control of the test. The following is the best way to approach SHSAT questions systematically.

Think About the Questions Before You Look at the Answers

It's hard to emphasize strenuously enough precisely how important this strategy is. Basically, it's *really, really* important! One of the most damaging mistakes that students make when taking the SHSAT is that they jump immediately from the question to the answer choices without stopping to think first. This is particularly true with the Reading Comprehension questions, but it is a problem with most question types. Here's what will happen if you read the questions and then go directly to the answer choices: you will be confronted with very tempting, but very wrong, answer choices. If you take the time to think before looking at the choices, you will be much less likely to fall for the traps.

> **SHSAT EXPERT NOTE**
>
> **Predict before you peek**
>
> Try to predict the answer—or at least think about it—before you look at the answer choices. If nothing else, you may realize what the answer won't be. This will help you to avoid the tempting "traps" set by the test maker.

Use Strategies and Guess Strategically

You'll learn more about Kaplan's strategies later, but the gist of them is that sometimes there are shortcuts to solving problems and guessing strategically. No one sees your work, so you do not have to solve problems the way you would in school. Any method that gets you the correct answer is the "right" way on the SHSAT. Additionally, because there is no penalty for wrong answers, don't leave any questions blank!

Pace Yourself

The SHSAT gives you a lot of questions in a relatively short period of time. To get through the test, you need to be in control of your pace. Remember, although you should enter an answer for every question, you don't have to answer *every* question correctly to score well. There are a few strategies you can employ to take control of your pace.

- Don't spend too much time on any one question. You can always circle a question and come back to it later.
- Give yourself a rough time limit for each question—move on if you run out of time.
- Be flexible—you can answer questions out of order.
- Don't spend more than 5 minutes on any one Reading passage—keep reading and move on. Remember, your points come from answering the questions.
- Practice under timed conditions.

SHSAT EXPERT NOTE

Take control

Taking control of your pace and practicing test-like timing will help improve your testing experience.

Locate Quick Points If You're Running Out of Time

Some questions can be answered more quickly than others. Some are simply amenable to shortcuts. For example, a Reading question that contains a line number or asks for the meaning of a specific phrase may be easier to answer more quickly than one that does not give you such a clue. Other questions will be easier because of your particular strengths. For example, if you're comfortable with geometry and are running out of time, look for the geometry questions.

SHSAT EXPERT NOTE

Play to your strengths and know your weaknesses

You know your strengths and weaknesses better than anyone else. Use this knowledge to work through the test efficiently.

CHAPTER 2

Inside the SHSAT

CHAPTER OBJECTIVES

By the end of this chapter, you will be able to:

- Describe the structure of the test, how it is scored, and the timing of each section
- Pace yourself effectively during the test

Structure of the Test

The SHSAT is a standardized test, which means that it is predictable. Therefore, you can take control and build your confidence by knowing what to expect. When you sit down to take the test, you should know what the test will look like, how it will be scored, and how long you'll have to complete it.

On the SHSAT, You'll see 57 English Language Arts and 57 Math questions on the test. The English Language Arts and Math sections are equally weighted.

English Language Arts Section

The English Language Arts section is the first section on the test. It contains 57 questions and accounts for one-half of your total points on the SHSAT. The suggested time for the section is 90 minutes, or 1 hour and 30 minutes. All 57 questions are multiple-choice questions.

The breakdown of the English Language Arts section is as follows:

English Language Arts Subsection	Subsection Breakdown	Total Number of Questions
Revising/Editing Stand-Alone Questions	3–5 questions	9–11 questions
Revising/Editing Passages	1 passage with 5–8 questions	
Reading Comprehension	6 passages with 6–10 questions each	46–48 questions

Math

The Math section is the second section on the test. It contains 57 questions and accounts for one-half of your total points on the SHSAT. The suggested time for the section is 90 minutes, or 1 hour and 30 minutes.

The breakdown of the Math section is as follows:

Math Subsection	Total Number of Questions
Grid-In Questions	5 questions
Multiple-Choice Questions	52 questions

Scoring

Scoring for the SHSAT is a little different. It's not that the scoring is difficult to understand; it's just that individual scores matter only to the extent that they are above or below a cutoff line, and that cutoff changes each year depending on how that group of students performs on the test.

Here's how the scoring works. First, you get a Raw Score based on the number of questions you answer correctly. The test contains 114 questions. 94 of the questions are worth 1 "raw" point, and 20 are experimental questions that aren't scored. The maximum Raw Score is therefore 94.

Next, your Raw Score is multiplied by a formula known only to the Department of Education to arrive at a scaled score. You receive a scaled score for each section and a Composite Score for the entire test. The highest possible Composite Score is 800.

Admission to all specialized high schools (except LaGuardia) is based solely on your Composite Score. The way this works is that all of the students are ranked from high score to low score and then assigned to the school of their first preference until all the available seats are filled. For example, if Stuyvesant had exactly 500 spaces available and the top 500 scorers all picked Stuyvesant as their first choice, all 500 scorers would be admitted. If the 501st scorer listed Stuyvesant as her first choice and Bronx Science as her second choice, she would be assigned to Bronx Science. Therefore, scores are relative; it matters only whether they are above the cutoff, but there is no way of accurately knowing what the cutoff score will be. All you know is that you should do your best to get the highest score possible and increase your chances.

Timing

Here's the way timing works on the SHSAT, which is different from a lot of other standardized tests. You'll have 180 minutes to complete the entire test. It is recommended that you spend approximately half the time (90 minutes, or 1 hour and 30 minutes) on each section. However, if you finish the English Language Arts section early, you can move on to the Math section without waiting for the 90 minutes to end. Similarly, if you finish the Math section with time to spare, you can go back over both the Math and English Language Arts sections of the test.

What this means is that you have both the freedom to structure your time and the responsibility to use your time wisely. While you can spend more than 90 minutes working on the first section, it may not be wise to do so. However, the flexibility you have in skipping around and going back to one section after finishing the other gives you ample opportunity to play to your strengths.

The Schools

In addition to preparing for the test, you should be doing some research about the schools. Remember, if you get accepted into a school, you will be expected to attend. Therefore, you want to make an informed decision here. The best way to get information about the schools is to contact them or check out their websites. Here's the contact information for each school:

The Bronx High School of Science

75 West 205th Street
Bronx, NY 10468
(718) 817-7700
www.bxscience.edu

The Brooklyn Latin School

223 Graham Avenue
Brooklyn, NY 11206
(718) 366-0154
www.brooklynlatin.org

Brooklyn Technical High School

29 Fort Greene Place
Brooklyn, NY 11217
(718) 804-6400
www.bths.edu

Fiorello H. LaGuardia High School of Music & Art and Performing Arts

100 Amsterdam Avenue
New York, NY 10023
(212) 496-0700
www.laguardiahs.org

High School for Math, Science, and Engineering at the City College of New York

240 Convent Avenue
New York, NY 10031
(212) 281-6490
www.hsmse.org

High School of American Studies at Lehman College

2925 Goulden Avenue
Bronx, NY 10468
(718) 329-2144
www.hsas-lehman.org

Queens High School for the Sciences at York College

94-50 159th Street
Jamaica, NY 11451
(718) 657-3181
www.qhss.org

Staten Island Technical High School

485 Clawson Street
Staten Island, NY 10306
(718) 667-3222
www.siths.org

Stuyvesant High School

345 Chambers Street
New York, NY 10282
(212) 312-4800
www.stuy.edu

Do some research. Talk to your parents, teachers, and guidance counselor. Some factors that you may want to consider are these:

- Location
- Condition of facilities
- Class size
- School size
- Areas of concentration
- Advanced Placement courses
- Research programs
- Availability of hands-on tech courses
- College courses offered
- Extracurricular activities

Test Dates

The test is administered on specific weekend dates in late October and early November.

Log on to schools.nyc.gov for updated information.

PART TWO

SHSAT English Language Arts

CHAPTER 3

Introducing SHSAT English Language Arts

CHAPTER OBJECTIVES

By the end of this chapter, you will be able to:

- Identify the format and timing of the SHSAT English Language Arts section
- Apply tips and strategies to the SHSAT English Language Arts section

English Language Arts Overview

The English Language Arts section is the first section on the test. It contains 57 questions and accounts for one-half of your total points on the SHSAT. The suggested time for the section is 90 minutes, or 1 hour and 30 minutes.

The breakdown of the English Language Arts section is as follows:

English Language Arts Subsection	Subsection Breakdown	Total Number of Questions	Pacing
Revising/Editing Stand-Alone Questions	3–5 questions	9–11 questions	1 minute per stand-alone question, $1\frac{1}{2}$ minutes per passage-based question
Revising/Editing Passages	1 passage with 5–8 questions		
Reading Comprehension	6 passages with 6–10 questions each	46–48 questions	Up to 5 minutes reading each passage, 1 minute per question

The Question Types

Revising/Editing Stand-Alone Questions

The beginning of the Revising/Editing section will look like this:

REVISING/EDITING

QUESTIONS 1–9

IMPORTANT NOTE

The Revising/Editing section includes Part A and Part B.

REVISING/EDITING Part A

Directions: Answer the following questions, recognizing and correcting errors so that the sentences or paragraphs are grammatically correct. Re-read relevant parts of the text before choosing the best answer for each question, but be mindful of time. You may write in your test booklet to take notes.

The SHSAT English Language Arts section includes 3–5 stand-alone questions. You will be asked to apply your knowledge of sentence structure, punctuation, usage, knowledge of language, organization, and topic development to answer questions.

Revising/Editing Passages

The beginning of the Revising/Editing Part B section will look like this:

> ### REVISING/EDITING Part B
>
> **DIRECTIONS:** Read the passage and answer the questions following it, improving the writing quality and correcting grammatical errors. Re-read relevant parts of the text before choosing the best answer for each question, but be mindful of time. You may write in your test booklet to take notes.

There is one Revising/Editing Passage with 5–8 questions. You will be asked to improve the organization and topic development within the passage in addition to correcting grammatical errors.

Reading

The beginning of the Reading section will look like this:

> ### READING COMPREHENSION
>
> #### QUESTIONS 10–57
>
> **DIRECTIONS:** Read the six passages and answer the corresponding questions. Re-read relevant parts of the text before choosing the best answer for each question, but be mindful of time. Base your answers only on the content within each passage. You may write in your test booklet to take notes.

The Reading Comprehension questions test your ability to understand what you've read. You'll have six passages, each of which will be followed by 6–10 questions.

The passages will appear on a variety of topics such as science, social studies, humanities, poetry, and literary fiction. The Reading Comprehension questions will test your understanding of what you've read in the passages as well as information provided in accompanying tables, charts, or graphs.

How to Approach SHSAT English Language Arts

To do well on the SHSAT English Language Arts (ELA) section, you need to be systematic in your approach. In other words, you need to know how you are going to deal with each question type and the section as a whole before you open the test booklet. Knowing your strengths ahead of time is an important part of using a strategic approach. For example, if you find the Revising/Editing questions more difficult than Reading Comprehension, you can leave them for last. It's up to you.

In addition, pacing is crucial. Reading six passages is a lot. You have to be aware of your time and plan it well. In general, you want to spend no more than 15 minutes answering Revising/Editing questions and use at least 75 minutes for Reading passages and questions. That gives you about 12 minutes for each of the six passages and accompanying questions.

CHAPTER 4

The Kaplan Method for Revising/Editing Text & Sentence Structure

CHAPTER OBJECTIVES

By the end of this chapter, you will be able to:

- Efficiently apply the Kaplan Method for Revising/Editing Text
- Determine the correct punctuation and/or conjunctions to form a complete sentence
- Identify and correct inappropriate modifier placement

The Kaplan Method for Revising/Editing Text

You will use the Kaplan Method for Revising/Editing Text to optimize your score on the SHSAT English Language Arts section. Be sure to use this method for every Revising/Editing question you encounter, whether practicing, completing your homework, working on a Practice Test, or taking the official exam. The more you use the Kaplan Method, the more it will become second nature in time for Test Day.

The Kaplan Method for Revising/Editing Text has three steps:

Step 1: Examine the question

Step 2: Read the text

Step 3: Select the most correct, concise, and relevant choice

Let's take a closer look at each step.

Step 1: Examine the Question

Revising/Editing questions test sentence structure, usage, knowledge of language, organization, and topic development issues. Identifying what the question is asking *before* you read the accompanying text will help you pinpoint your focus and will save you valuable time on Test Day.

For example, a question may ask, "Which sentence contains an error in its construction and should be revised?" The question stem itself tells you that there is a grammatical error you need to locate, so the best approach is to evaluate each sentence systematically.

Additionally, scan the answer choices for clues. If all of the choices involve comma use, or if they include both punctuation and verb corrections, you can hone your focus to read for just those types of errors.

A different question may ask, "Which transitional phrase should be added to the beginning of sentence 5?" In this case, the question stem tells you that the text is grammatically correct but would be improved by adding a transition. If the passage highlights a contrast or provides an opposing opinion, a phrase such as "On the other hand" is the best choice.

Identifying what a question requires of you is an important first step to answering the question correctly. Once you know what you're looking for, you're ready to move on to the next step and read the text.

Step 2: Read the Text

For Step 2, focus on the portion of the text to which the question is referring. For stand-alone questions, you will simply read the text in the box above the question.

When you are answering questions that accompany a passage, it is tempting to read the whole passage first and take notes, like you would for a Reading passage. However, this is not the best use of your time. For Revising/Editing passages, you should read only as far as is necessary to answer the question. (Keep in mind that this could include reading the sentence before and/or after a specific part in order to fully understand the context.) Once you have enough information, pause and answer that question before you move on to the next one.

Step 3: Select the Most Correct, Concise, and Relevant Choice

Your goal is to select the text that creates the most **correct**, **concise**, and **relevant** response. This means that the text:

- Has no grammatical errors
- Is brief, while retaining the writer's intended meaning
- Is appropriate for the surrounding text

All three of these elements are vital for a choice to be correct. You will notice that many choices will correct an error, but will incorrectly change the meaning of the text. Or, they may keep the meaning the same and fix an error, but incorrectly introduce an informal tone to an otherwise formal passage. Keep in mind, too, that while conciseness is a goal, the shortest answer choice will not always be the correct one, unless it accomplishes all three of the goals (correct, concise, *and* relevant).

Now that you are familiar with the Kaplan Method for Revising/Editing Text, it's time to practice what you've learned with some test-like questions.

Practice

REVISING/EDITING Part A

DIRECTIONS: Answer the following questions, recognizing and correcting errors so that the sentences or paragraphs are grammatically correct. Re-read relevant parts of the text before choosing the best answer for each question.

---

1. Read this sentence.

> My science fair project which took weeks for me to complete, included information about how volcanoes are formed, how scientists predict eruptions, and how lava and magma differ.

Which edit should be made to correct the sentence?

(A) Insert a comma after *project*.
B. Delete the comma after *complete*.
C. Delete the comma after *formed*.
D. Insert a comma after *lava*.

2. Read this paragraph.

> (1) Given that they often spend a lot of time engaged in solitary pursuits, house cats have gained a reputation for being aloof. (2) Although they are capable of being sociable and affectionate with other felines and humans, adult cats are not known for voluntarily living in groups. (3) In fact, they are notorious for specific behaviors: they form dominance hierarchies and refuse to accept new cats. (4) Also, adult cats, protect their territory by chasing away any being perceived as a threat and is therefore considered nonsocial.

Which pair of revisions need to be made in the paragraph?

E. Sentence 1: Delete the comma after *pursuits*, AND change *have* to **has**.

F. Sentence 2: Delete the comma after *humans*, AND change *are* to **is**.

G. Sentence 3: Delete the colon after *behaviors*, AND change *refuse* to **refuses**.

H. Sentence 4: Delete the comma after *cats*, AND change *is* to **are**.

3. Read this sentence.

> After graduating from high school, Kaylee's plan to attend college in Vermont and to study American literature.

How should the sentence be revised?

A. After graduating from high school, Kaylee's plan <u>is</u> to attend college in Vermont and to study American literature.

B. After graduating from high school, Kaylee's plan will be to attend college in Vermont and to study American literature.

C. After graduating from high school, Kaylee plans to attend college in Vermont and to study American literature.

D. After graduating from high school, Kaylee's plans will be to attend college in Vermont and to study American literature.

4. Read this paragraph.

> Llamas make excellent <u>pets</u>, <u>they</u> are very friendly and are well-liked by both people and other animals. In various parts of the <u>world</u>, <u>people</u> have herded llamas in flocks. In South <u>America</u>, <u>llamas</u> helped the Andean civilization thrive in the high mountains. Besides providing <u>wool</u>, <u>llamas</u> offer a mode of transportation.

Which revision corrects the error in sentence structure in the paragraph?

E. pets. They

F. world. People

G. America. Llamas

H. wool. Llamas

REVISING/EDITING Part B

DIRECTIONS: Read the passage and answer the questions following it, improving the writing quality and correcting grammatical errors. Re-read relevant parts of the text before choosing the best answer for each question.

The Industrial Revolution

(1) The first Industrial Revolution, which occurred in Great Britain in the latter half of the eighteenth century, represented a sudden acceleration of technological and economic development that would permeate all levels of British society. (2) In particular, manufacturing and machinery were things that supplanted the traditional agrarian economy and led to one based on machines and manufacturing. (3) Very much an urban movement, the revolution gave rise to a new system of social class. (4) This was based primarily upon the relationship of the industrial capitalist to the factory worker. (5) These changes can be attributed to a number of favorable societal circumstances, including an increasing population which would provide both a larger workforce and expanding markets, a strong middle class, and stability in both the political environment and the monetary system.

(6) In the United States, the Industrial Revolution had a similar effect, well exemplified by the female factory workers in Lowell, Massachusetts. (7) Lowell had long been a textile manufacturing hub. (8) After the industrialization of textile production in 1815, the hand-spun textiles with which many families had supplemented their incomes could not compete with cheaper, factory-spun cloth. (9) The factories created a new role for the farm daughter as a factory worker. (10) The family she left behind would profit from a share of her wages, while she gained access to money—whether to save or to spend on the consumer goods created by the new industrial society.

(11) Millwork was often a deliberate step toward personal advancement for women from a limited, but not destitute, farm background. (12) The women, whose general ages ranged from 14 to 35 years, lived in company-owned, strictly controlled boarding houses. (13) These all-female establishments fostered strong friendships, as well as a cohesive community of women of similar age and socioeconomic backgrounds living and working together twenty-four hours a day. (14) Many of the men who constructed the mills were Irish immigrants fleeing from the potato famine.

(15) In America, as in England, many previously rural workers moved to the cities. (16) In some cases, this led to improvements in their lives, with urban transportation and increased opportunities. (17) However, the rush to the cities also led to overcrowding, poor living conditions, health issues, and child labor. (18) Thus the Industrial Revolution, which changed the basis of America's economy, brought both improvements and problems.

5. Which revision of sentence 2 uses the most precise language?

    A. Specifically, the traditional agrarian economy was supplanted by one based on manufacturing and machinery.

    B. In particular, things that changed a traditional economy into a different kind were manufacturing and machinery.

    C. Especially important were changes in manufacturing and machinery.

    D. They supplanted the traditional agrarian economy.

6. What is the best way to combine sentences 3 and 4 to clarify the relationship between ideas?

    E. Very much an urban movement, the revolution gave rise to a new system of society based primarily upon the relationship of the industrial capitalist to the factory worker.

    F. Very much an urban movement, the revolution gave rise to a new system of social class, and that class was based primarily upon the relationship of the industrial capitalist to the factory worker.

    G. Very much an urban movement, a new system of social class was given rise to primarily based on the relationship of the industrial capitalist to the factory worker.

    H. Very much an urban movement, the revolution gave rise to a new system of social class based primarily upon the relationship of the industrial capitalist to the factory worker.

7. Which sentence would best follow and support sentence 8?

    A. The factory-made cloth was cheaper to buy.

    B. Men could still work the farm, but women found their traditional cloth-making work devalued.

    C. Factory-spun cloth could also be made faster.

    D. The textiles were just as well spun as was homemade cloth.

8. Which transition should be added to the beginning of sentence 11?

    E. On the other hand

    F. Nevertheless

    G. Unfortunately

    H. Furthermore

9. Which sentence is irrelevant to the argument made in the passage and should be deleted?

    A. sentence 13

    B. sentence 14

    C. sentence 15

    D. sentence 16

245-253

Sentence Structure

Fragments and Run-Ons

A complete sentence must have both a subject and a verb and express a complete thought. If any one of these elements is missing, the sentence is a **fragment**. You can recognize a fragment because the sentence will not make sense as written. There are some examples in the table below.

Missing Element	Example	Corrected Sentence
Subject	*Ran a marathon.*	*Lola ran a marathon.*
Verb	*Lola a marathon.*	
Complete thought	*While Lola ran a marathon.*	*While Lola ran a marathon, her friends cheered for her.*

The fragment "While Lola ran a marathon" is an example of a dependent clause: it has a subject (Lola) and a verb (ran), but it does not express a complete thought because it starts with a subordinating conjunction (while). Notice what the word "while" does to the meaning: While Lola ran a marathon, what happened? To fix this type of fragment, eliminate the subordinating conjunction or join the dependent clause to an independent clause using a comma. Subordinating conjunctions are words and phrases such as *since*, *because*, *therefore*, *unless*, *although*, and *due to*.

Unlike a dependent clause, an independent clause can stand on its own as a complete sentence. If a sentence has more than one independent clause, however, those clauses must be properly joined. If they are not, the sentence is a **run-on**: *Lucas enjoys hiking, he climbs a new mountain every summer.* There are several ways to correct a run-on, as shown in the table below.

To Correct a Run-on	Example
Use a period	*Lucas enjoys hiking. He climbs a new mountain every summer.*
Use a semicolon	*Lucas enjoys hiking; he climbs a new mountain every summer.*
Use a colon	*Lucas enjoys hiking: he climbs a new mountain every summer.*
Make one clause dependent	*Since Lucas enjoys hiking, he climbs a new mountain every summer.*
Add a FANBOYS conjunction: for, and, nor, but, or, yet, so	*Lucas enjoys hiking, so he climbs a new mountain every summer.*
Use a dash	*Lucas enjoys hiking—he climbs a new mountain every summer.*

Semicolons

Semicolons can be confusing for some students. They are used in two specific ways:

Use semicolons to . . .	Example
Join two independent clauses that are not connected by a comma and FANBOYS conjunction, just as you would use a period	*Gaby knew that her term paper would take at least four hours to write; she got started in study hall and then finished it at home.*
Separate sublists within a longer list when those sublists contain commas	*The team needed to bring uniforms, helmets, and gloves; oranges, almonds, and water; and hockey sticks, pucks, and skates.*

To answer questions with fragment and run-on errors, familiarize yourself with the ways in which they are tested:

- Fragments
  - If a sentence is missing a subject, a verb, or a complete thought, it is a fragment.
  - Correct the fragment by adding the missing element.

- Run-ons
  - If a sentence includes two independent clauses, they must be properly joined.
  - Employ one of the following options to properly punctuate independent clauses:
    - o Use a period
    - o Insert a semicolon or colon
    - o Make one clause dependent by using a subordinating conjunction (since, because, therefore, unless, although, due to, etc.)
    - o Use a comma and a FANBOYS conjunction (for, and, nor, but, or, yet, so)
    - o Use a dash

Practice

> **DIRECTIONS:** Follow the instructions for each sentence to correct the grammatical error.

A. **Correct the fragment by adding a subject:** Brought snacks to the weekend study session.

B. **Correct the fragment by completing the thought:** After getting to the stadium.

C. **Correct the run-on sentence with the proper punctuation:** The new arts center just opened it has a crafts room for children under thirteen.

D. **Correct the run-on sentence with the proper punctuation:** Herodotus is known as one of the first historians he is even called "The Father of History."

E. **Make one clause dependent to correct the run-on sentence:** Herodotus is sometimes accused of making up stories for his histories, he claimed he simply recorded what he had been told.

DIRECTIONS: Answer the following questions, recognizing and correcting errors so that the sentences or paragraphs are grammatically correct. Re-read relevant parts of the text before choosing the best answer for each question.

1. Read this paragraph.

> (1) Before 1972, colleges could give greater support to men's sports teams; today, women's and men's teams must receive equal funding. (2) Title IX of the Education Amendments prohibits gender discrimination at colleges and other federally funded institutions. (3) Resulting in more money in athletic departments allocated for women's sports. (4) This has led to more interest in these sports, more college scholarships, better competition, and improvements in the quality of athletics for women.

Which sentence contains an error in its construction and should be revised?

A. sentence 1
B. sentence 2
C. sentence 3
D. sentence 4

2. Read this sentence.

> White roses represent unity, yellow roses show friendship, and red roses signify love however, many people believe red roses are the most cherished within the genus Rosa.

Which edit should be made to correct this sentence?

E. Delete the comma after *unity*.
F. Insert a semicolon after *love*.
G. Delete the comma after *however*.
H. Insert a semicolon after *believe*.

Modifier Placement

A **modifier** is a word or phrase that describes, clarifies, or provides additional information about another part of the sentence. Modifier questions require you to identify the part of a sentence being described and use the appropriate modifier in the proper place.

In order to be grammatically correct, the modifier must be placed as close to the word it describes as possible. Use context clues in the passage to identify the correct placement of a modifier; a misplaced modifier can cause confusion and is always incorrect on Test Day.

Note that a common way the SHSAT tests modifiers is with modifying phrases at the beginning of a sentence. Just like any other modifier, the phrase grammatically modifies whatever is right next to it in the sentence. For example, consider the sentence, "While walking to the bus stop, the rain drenched Gina." The initial phrase, "While walking to the bus stop," grammatically modifies "the rain," but this creates a sentence that doesn't make sense; the rain can't walk to the bus stop. The writer meant that Gina was walking to the bus stop, so the sentence should read, "While walking to the bus stop, Gina was drenched by the rain." Here are some additional examples.

Modifier/Modifying Phrase	Incorrect	Correct
nearly	Andre **nearly** watched the play for four hours.	Andre watched the play for **nearly** four hours.
in individual containers	The art teacher handed out paints to the students **in individual containers**.	The art teacher handed out paints **in individual containers** to the students.
A scholar athlete	**A scholar athlete**, maintaining high grades in addition to playing soccer was expected of Maya.	**A scholar athlete**, Maya was expected to maintain high grades in addition to playing soccer.

If a question includes a modifier, determine whether the modifier is placed correctly.

- Is it as near as possible to the word it logically modifies?
- If it is not in the correct place, where should it be moved?

Practice

DIRECTIONS: Edit each sentence to correct the modifier placement issue.

    A. Wearing a brown collar, Cecilia walked the dog.

    B. The dealer sold the Ford to the buyer with the hatchback.

    C. The server placed rolls on the warm table.

    D. Looking toward the west, a breeze stirred the leaves on the trees as I watched.

    E. I borrowed a blender from a neighbor that turned out to be broken.

DIRECTIONS: Answer the following questions, recognizing and correcting errors so that the sentences or paragraphs are grammatically correct. Re-read relevant parts of the text before choosing the best answer for each question.

3. Read this sentence.

> To raise money for uniforms, a car wash will be held by members of the volleyball team.

How should the sentence be revised?

A. Members of the volleyball team, on Saturday to raise money for uniforms, will hold a car wash.

B. To raise money for uniforms, on Saturday a car wash will be held by members of the volleyball team.

C. On Saturday to raise money for uniforms, members of the volleyball team will hold a car wash.

D. To raise money for uniforms, members of the volleyball team will hold a car wash on Saturday.

4. Read this paragraph.

> (1) Most gems are crystallized minerals, but amber, coral, and pearls come from organic material. (2) Amber's buoyancy suggests organic origins; unlike most gemstones, this ancient fossilized resin floats in water. (3) Coral is a discarded limestone skeleton found in the sea. (4) Taking several years to form, oysters create white, black, or pink pearls.

Which sentence contains an error in its construction and should be revised?

E. sentence 1

F. sentence 2

G. sentence 3

H. sentence 4

Practice Set

For test-like practice, give yourself 23 minutes (an average of 1 minute per stand-alone question and 1.5 minutes per passage-based question) to complete this question set. While many of the questions pertain to Sentence Structure, some touch on other English Language Arts concepts to ensure that your practice is test-like, with a variety of question types. After you're done, be sure to study the explanations, even for questions you answered correctly. They can be found at the end of this chapter.

REVISING/EDITING Part A

DIRECTIONS: Answer the following questions, recognizing and correcting errors so that the sentences or paragraphs are grammatically correct. Re-read relevant parts of the text before choosing the best answer for each question.

---

1. Read this sentence.

> The successful fundraising campaign for the school's field trip continued for a week teachers counted the money every morning with growing amazement.

Which edit should be made to correct this sentence?

A. Insert a comma after *successful*.

B. Insert a comma after *week*.

C. Insert a semicolon after *week*.

D. Insert a semicolon after *money*.

2. Read this sentence.

> The student council officers agreed to meet in two weeks in the schools library to discuss a number of issues affecting the community.

Which edit should be made to correct the sentence?

E. Change *officers* to *officers'*.

F. Change *weeks* to *weeks'*.

G. Change *weeks* to *week's*.

H. Change *schools* to *school's*.

3. Read this sentence.

> Winter weather provides us with the opportunity to do so many outdoor activities, we can ski down mountains, skate on ice, make snowmen, and glide downhill on a snowboard.

Which revision corrects the error in sentence structure in the sentence?

A. activities; we can

B. mountains; skate on

C. ice; make snowmen

D. snowmen; and glide

4. Read this sentence.

> The professor, after distributing samples of igneous lava explained that this type of rock is initially liquid magma and is formed under intense heat and pressure deep within the earth.

Which edit should be made to correct this sentence?

E. Insert a comma after *lava*.

F. Insert a dash after *explained*.

G. Insert a comma after *intense*.

H. Insert a comma after *deep*.

5. Read this paragraph.

> My favorite restaurant has <u>servers who</u> sing as they serve the <u>food. Because</u> customers enjoy the entertainment that comes with their <u>meals these</u> servers earn tips that are much higher <u>than those</u> of servers at other restaurants.

Which revision corrects the error in sentence structure in the paragraph?

A. servers, who

B. food, because

C. meals, these

D. than, those

6. Read this sentence.

> The electric fan was an ingenious invention for keeping people cool during the summer it was popular only briefly, however, until the air conditioner was invented.

Which edit should be made to correct this sentence?

E. Change the comma after *briefly* to a semicolon.

F. Insert a comma after *invention*.

G. Delete the comma after *briefly*.

H. Insert a semicolon after *summer*.

7. Read this sentence.

> Miss Adams, our swim team coach chose Sarah to swim the final lap of the three-person relay race at last week's competition in Brooklyn.

Which edit should be made to correct this sentence?

A. Delete the comma after *Miss Adams*.

B. Insert a comma after *coach*.

C. Insert a comma after *lap*.

D. Insert a comma after *competition*.

8. Read this sentence.

> My classmate Jacob said that yesterday's basketball practice involved several sets of long intense drills.

Which edit should be made to correct this sentence?

E. Insert a comma after *classmate*.

F. Insert a comma after *said*.

G. Insert a comma after *basketball*.

H. Insert a comma after *long*.

9. Read this sentence.

> The Yankees is my favorite team because it always has amazing players and has an impressive history.

How should the sentence be revised?

A. The Yankees are my favorite team because they always have amazing players and have an impressive history.

B. The Yankees are my favorite team because it always has amazing players and have an impressive history.

C. The Yankees are my favorite team because they always have amazing players and has an impressive history.

D. The Yankees is my favorite team because they always has amazing players and have had an impressive history.

10. Read this sentence.

> The special effects used in todays movies would have been unimaginable as recently as ten years ago.

How should the sentence be revised?

E. The special effect's used in todays movies would have been unimaginable as recently as ten years ago.

F. The special effects used in today's movies would have been unimaginable as recently as ten years ago.

G. The special effects used in todays movie's would have been unimaginable as recently as ten years ago.

H. The special effects used in todays movies would have been unimaginable as recently as ten year's ago.

11. Read this sentence.

> The amount of water used by Americans can be reduced by turning off faucets when not in use, decreasing the time spent in showers and running washing machines less frequently.

Which edit should be made to correct the sentence?

A. Insert a comma after *Americans*.

B. Delete the comma after *use*.

C. Insert a comma after *showers*.

D. Insert a comma after *machines*.

12. Read this sentence.

> Our <u>principal who</u> met with <u>students at</u> the start of the school year, announced that the field trips this <u>year would</u> be more enjoyable <u>than those</u> we took last year.

Which revision corrects the error in sentence structure?

E. principal, who

F. students, at

G. year, would

H. than, those

13. Read this paragraph.

> (1) Al Hirschfeld, whose caricatures were often featured in the *New York Times*, became famous for incorporating "Nina," his daughter's name, into all of his drawings. (2) In the 1920s, he began drawing political cartoons for newspapers and magazines, which captured readers' attention. (3) When he drew Broadway performers and other celebrities, he conveyed his interest in people and their expressive faces. (4) Famous museums now display some of the artistic creations that Hirschfeld produced over the course of at least 65 years.

Which sentence contains an error in its construction and should be revised?

A. sentence 1

B. sentence 2

C. sentence 3

D. sentence 4

14. Read this paragraph.

> Even though its structure and alphabet are not similar to those of Romance <u>languages, Russian</u> has many parallels to <u>French the</u> Russian alphabet used to have various versions of Cyrillic script since about the tenth century. Cyrillic is a modified Greek <u>alphabet, which</u> has a few letters resembling those in the Latin <u>alphabet. Currently,</u> approximately 300 million people throughout the world speak Russian.

Which revision corrects the sentence structure error in the paragraph?

E. languages. Russian

F. French. The

G. alphabet. Which

H. alphabet; currently

> ## REVISING/EDITING Part B
>
> **DIRECTIONS:** Read the passage and answer the questions following it, improving the writing quality and correcting grammatical errors. Re-read relevant parts of the text before choosing the best answer for each question.

Archerfish

(1) Few fish find their food outside of the water. (2) Even fewer find their food several feet above the surface. (3) And only one fish hits its food with a concentrated stream of water, thereby knocking its prey into the water. (4) That fish is called the archerfish. (5) These fish are generally small, from five to ten centimeters, they are capable of growing as large as 40 centimeters.

(6) The archerfish patrols the brackish waters of Southeast Asia and Australia and preys on insects such as moths, beetles, and grasshoppers that stray too close to the surface. (7) Lurking just below the surface, the archerfish uses its tongue to send a stream of water up into the air. (8) Elder archerfish have been documented hitting insects as far as six feet away.

(9) The fact that archerfish can shoot a stream of water is impressive, but the accuracy of their shots is astounding. (10) Sending out an accurate shot means that the fish must compensate for both gravity and the refraction of light in water. (11) As you know, gravity is a constant, both underwater and on land; light, however, changes its wavelength as it enters the water. (12) An archerfish looking up at insects on a branch will not see them where they actually are. (13) Archerfish either compensate for the refraction or shoot from a position directly below an insect, thereby eliminating the angle of refraction altogether.

(14) Interestingly, accurate aiming is not instinctual in the archerfish. (15) This is evidenced by the fact that young fish frequently miss the target. (16) To make it better, young fish hunt in small clumps to up the odds that at least one archerfish will be able to do a good job. (17) Archerfish hunting in schools are often far more successful than those that attempt lone pursuits. (18) Accuracy comes with experience, and in one study, accuracy was shown to be enhanced by watching older archerfish performing. (19) Archerfish have also been known to actually jump out of the water and catch prey with their mouths if the prey is within reach of how far the fish can jump to catch it. (20) The mantis shrimp is another animal which hunts in a strange way, using its powerful claws to smash its prey.

15. How should sentence 5 be revised?

  A. These fish are generally small, from five to ten centimeters, they is capable of growing as large as 40 centimeters.

  B. These fish are generally tiny, from five to ten centimeters, they are capable of growing as large as 40 centimeters.

  C. These fish are generally small, from five to ten centimeters, but they are capable of growing as large as 40 centimeters.

  D. Fish are generally small, from five to ten centimeters, they are capable of growing as large as 40 centimeters.

16. Which revision of sentence 11 best maintains the style established in the passage?

   E. As you may know, gravity is a constant, both underwater and on land; light, however, changes its wavelength as it enters the water.

   F. Gravity is a constant, both underwater and on land; light, however, changes its wavelength as it enters the water.

   G. It is known that gravity is a constant, both underwater and on land; light, however, changes its wavelength as it enters the water.

   H. Gravity is a constant, both underwater and on land; you may know that light, however, changes its wavelength as it enters the water.

17. Which transition should be added to the beginning of sentence 12?

   A. Moreover

   B. Thus

   C. However

   D. Nevertheless

18. What is the best way to combine sentences 14 and 15 to clarify the relationship between the ideas?

   E. Interestingly, accurate aiming is not instinctual in the archerfish; as evidenced by young fish that frequently miss the target.

   F. Interestingly, accurate aiming is not instinctual in the archerfish but it is evidenced by young fish that frequently miss the target.

   G. Interestingly, accurate aiming is not instinctual in the archerfish, as evidenced by young fish that frequently miss the target.

   H. Interestingly, accurate aiming is not instinctual in the archerfish, young fish frequently miss the target.

19. Which revision of sentence 16 uses the most precise language?

   A. To make it better, young fish hunt in small groups to increase the odds that at least one archerfish will be able to do a good job.

   B. To make it better, young fish hunt in small groups to increase the odds that at least one archerfish will be able to catch prey.

   C. To compensate for this, young fish hunt in small clumps to up the odds that at least one archerfish will be able to do a good job.

   D. To compensate for this, young fish hunt in small groups to increase the odds that at least one archerfish will be able to catch prey.

20. Which sentence presents information that shifts away from the main topic of the fourth paragraph and should be removed?

   E. sentence 17

   F. sentence 18

   G. sentence 19

   H. sentence 20

Answers and Explanations

The Kaplan Method for Revising/Editing Text

1.   A

Category: Sentence Structure

Getting to the Answer: The question asks you to fix an error, and the choices reveal that the issue is either a missing comma or an unnecessary comma. Read the sentence, looking for the error. The phrase "which took weeks for me to complete" is not essential to the sentence and must be set apart with a comma before and after it, so **(A)** is correct. All of the commas already included are necessary, so **(B)** and **(C)** are incorrect. **(D)** is incorrect because if there are only two items (rather than three or more) in a list—such as "lava" and "magma"—a comma is not needed.

2.   H

Category: Punctuation and Usage

Getting to the Answer: The question states that there is an error in the paragraph, and the answer choices include both punctuation and verb corrections. Read through the paragraph, looking for unnecessary punctuation as well as incorrect verb usage. In sentence 4, the comma after "cats" is unnecessary. Also, the verb "is" is singular, but "cats" is plural. **(H)** is correct because it fixes both errors. Sentences 1, 2, and 3 are grammatically correct, so **(E)**, **(F)**, and **(G)** should be eliminated because they introduce new grammatical errors.

3.   C

Category: Sentence Structure

Getting to the Answer: The question states that the sentence should be revised. When a sentence has an introductory phrase, make sure it is followed by what the phrase logically describes. The phrase "after graduating from high school" is referring to "Kaylee," not "Kaylee's plan." **(C)** corrects the error by changing the possessive form "Kaylee's" to the subject "Kaylee." **(A)**, **(B)**, and **(D)** are all incorrect because the introductory phrase is still incorrectly followed by "Kaylee's plan."

4.   E

Category: Sentence Structure

Getting to the Answer: The question indicates that the paragraph includes a sentence structure error. All of the answer choices change commas to periods, which is one

way to correct a run-on sentence. Check each sentence systematically to locate the run-on. "Llamas make excellent pets" and "they are very friendly and are well-liked by both people and other animals" are two independent clauses that must be properly combined. Using only a comma is grammatically incorrect. **(E)** fixes the issue by separating the clauses into two sentences. **(F)**, **(G)**, and **(H)** are incorrect because they create sentence fragments.

5.   A

Category: Knowledge of Language

Getting to the Answer: (A) retains all the information in a concise and clear structure, replacing the vague word "things" with specific reference to machinery and manufacturing. **(B)** retains the word "things" and is awkwardly structured. Though **(C)** is the most concise sentence, it deletes a great deal of the information that provides context about the economy, making it less precise. "They," in **(D)**, is imprecise because it is unclear to what "they" refers.

6.   H

Category: Organization

Getting to the Answer: When combining sentences, make sure to retain the meaning of each one and join them in a logical way. **(H)** does this best, deleting the subject and verb from sentence 4 and adding it by simply expanding sentence 3. **(E)** changes the meaning from "new social class" to "society," which are not necessarily the same ideas. **(F)** adds the redundant words "and that class," while **(G)** turns the sentence into the passive voice.

7.   B

Category: Topic Development

Getting to the Answer: Any additional sentence should add to the topic and fit in well with the previous and following sentences. **(B)**, the correct choice, expands on the previous sentence, explaining a further result of industrialization, and it also introduces the next sentence well. **(A)** essentially repeats what the previous sentence said and adds nothing new. **(C)** and **(D)** are about textiles, but the topic is industrialization and the female factory worker.

8.   H

Category: Organization

Getting to the Answer: In context, sentence 11 discusses another positive result of the Industrial Revolution, so the transition should indicate a continuation the previous idea, as **(H)** does. **(E)** and **(F)** are contrast words, and **(G)** does not reflect the generally positive tone of the third paragraph.

9.   B

Category: Topic Development

Getting to the Answer: When determining which sentence to delete, find the one that is out of place with the topic, is unnecessary to the argument, or interrupts the flow of ideas. Sentence 14, **(B)**, should be deleted. The paragraph is about female mill workers; this has nothing to do with male construction workers. All of the other sentences are on topic.

Fragments and Run-Ons

Note: These are not the only ways to correct the sentences; your answers may differ.

A.   **My friend** brought snacks to the weekend study session.

B.   After getting to the stadium, **we went looking for our seats**.

C.   The new arts center just opened. **It** has a crafts room for children under thirteen.

D.   Herodotus is known as one of the first historians; he is even called "The Father of History."

E.   **Although** Herodotus is sometimes accused of making up stories for his histories, he claimed he simply recorded what he had been told.

1.   C

Category: Sentence Structure

Getting to the Answer: A complete sentence should have a subject and a verb and express a complete thought. Sentence 3 lacks a verb, so the answer is **(C)**. **(A)**, **(B)**, and **(D)** are complete sentences.

2.   F

Category: Sentence Structure

Getting to the Answer: The question states that there is an error, so look for a grammar issue as you read the sentence. Two independent clauses need to be properly joined with a conjunction or a semicolon; otherwise, the sentence is a run-on. In this sentence, the first independent clause ends with the word "love," so placing a semicolon after "love" will correct the run-on; **(F)** is correct. **(E)** and **(G)** are incorrect because both commas are necessary; the comma after "unity" separates items in a list and the comma that follows "however" separates the transition word from the rest of the independent clause. **(H)** is incorrect because the first independent clause ends with the word "love," not "believe," so placing a semicolon after "believe" would not correct the sentence.

Modifier Placement

Note: These are not the only ways to correct the sentences; your answers may differ.

A.   Cecilia walked the dog wearing a brown collar.

B.   The dealer sold the Ford with the hatchback to the buyer.

C.   The server placed warm rolls on the table.

D.   Looking toward the west, I watched as a breeze stirred the leaves on the trees.

E.   I borrowed a blender that turned out to be broken from a neighbor.

3.   D

Category: Sentence Structure

Getting to the Answer: The question indicates that a revision is necessary. When a sentence has an introductory phrase, make sure it is followed by what the phrase modifies. As written, the phrase "To raise money for uniforms" describes "a car wash," which is not logical. **(D)** correctly places "members of the volleyball team" after the introductory phrase. **(A)** and **(B)** are incorrect because they do not fix the modifier placement error. **(C)** is incorrect because while it fixes the modifier issue, the phrase "on Saturday to raise money for uniforms" does not make sense in the middle of the sentence.

4.   H

Category: Sentence Structure

Getting to the Answer: Modifiers should be close to the words they modify. In the last sentence, "Taking several years to form" is followed by "oysters," which does not make sense; it is the pearls that are formed over time. **(H)** is correct. **(E)**, **(F)**, and **(G)** do not contain sentence construction errors.

Practice Set

1. C

Category: Sentence Structure

Getting to the Answer: Independent clauses must be joined by an appropriate conjunction or a semicolon; otherwise, the sentence is a run-on. As written, "the successful fundraising campaign for the school's field trip continued for a week" and "the teachers counted money every morning with growing amazement" are two independent clauses improperly joined. **(C)** correctly places a semicolon between them. **(B)** only inserts a comma after "week," which results in a run-on sentence. No comma is needed after "successful" because it modifies "fundraising campaign," so **(A)** is incorrect. **(D)** is incorrect because a complete idea must follow a semicolon, and "every morning with growing amazement" is not a complete idea.

2. H

Category: Sentence Structure

Getting to the Answer: The answer choices all have to do with adding an apostrophe to show ownership, so be on the lookout for nouns that should be made possessive. **(H)** is correct; in this sentence, "schools library" should be changed to the possessive form, "school's library," because the library belongs to the school. **(E)** is incorrect because a possessive word cannot come before the verb "agreed." **(F)** and **(G)** incorrectly turn the plural "weeks" into possessive forms when no ownership follows.

3. A

Category: Sentence Structure

Getting to the Answer: Notice that all of the answer choices have semicolons in them. This means that you need to locate two independent clauses in the text that need to be properly joined with a semicolon. Remember that if independent clauses are joined only with a comma, the sentence is a run-on. **(A)** correctly replaces the comma after "activities" with a semicolon. **(B)**, **(C)**, and **(D)** are incorrect because items in a list should be separated with commas rather than with semicolons.

4. E

Category: Sentence Structure

Getting to the Answer: If a phrase within a sentence is not essential to the sentence structure, it should be set off with commas. The phrase "after distributing samples of igneous lava" has a comma at its beginning, and it needs a comma at the end too. **(E)** is correct since it provides the necessary comma after "lava." **(F)** incorrectly adds a dash after the verb "explained" when the words "explained that" should not be separated by a dash. **(G)** inserts a comma separating the adjective "intense" from "heat," the noun it's modifying, which is incorrect. Similarly, **(H)** incorrectly inserts a comma between "pressure" and its modifier "deep."

5. C

Category: Sentence Structure

Getting to the Answer: Evaluate each underlined section as you read the paragraph. **(A)** is incorrect because inserting a comma after servers would make "who sing as they serve the food" nonessential information, but removing that phrase deletes information that is essential to the meaning of the sentence. **(B)** is incorrect because the two sentences are complete ideas, so they cannot be connected with a comma. This choice creates a run-on. **(C)** is correct. "Because customers enjoy the entertainment that comes with their meals" is a dependent clause describing the reason "the servers earn tips . . ." and should be separated from the independent clause with a comma. **(D)** is incorrect because it interrupts the comparison between the two "tips" with a comma.

6. H

Category: Sentence Structure

Getting to the Answer: Two independent clauses within a sentence need to be properly joined with a conjunction or a semicolon; otherwise, the sentence is a run-on. In this sentence, the first independent clause ends with the word "summer," so a semicolon should be placed after "summer." **(H)** is correct. **(E)** incorrectly places the semicolon in the middle of the second clause. **(F)** is incorrect since a comma after "invention" separates this noun from its modifying phrase "for keeping people cool . . ." **(G)** removes a necessary comma and does not fix the run-on.

7.   B

Category: Punctuation

Getting to the Answer: If a phrase within a sentence is not essential to the sentence's structure, it should be set off with commas. The phrase "our swim team coach" is nonessential information, so it needs to start and end with a comma. **(B)** is correct and **(A)** is incorrect. **(C)** and **(D)** incorrectly insert commas between nouns and their modifying phrases.

8.   H

Category: Punctuation

Getting to the Answer: When a sentence has multiple adjectives to describe a noun, check to see if a comma is needed between the adjectives. In this sentence, the "drills" are both "long" and "intense," so a comma is needed between the two adjectives; **(H)** is correct. **(E)** is incorrect because a comma after "classmate" makes "Jacob" nonessential information; also, this would require a comma following "Jacob" as well. **(F)** incorrectly places a comma between a subject and verb, and **(G)** incorrectly places a comma between an adjective and the noun it is modifying.

9.   A

Category: Usage

Getting to the Answer: This sentence has a subject-verb agreement error because the subject is "Yankees" and not "team." **(A)** is correct because "Yankees" is plural and requires the plural words "they" and "have." **(B)**, **(C)**, **(D)**, all fix part of the sentence but leave one or more agreement errors, making these choices incorrect.

10.   F

Category: Punctuation

Getting to the Answer: The answer choices all add an apostrophe somewhere in the sentence, so you just need to figure out which word actually needs an apostrophe. Apostrophes are often used to show possession, or ownership. In this sentence, "todays movies" should be changed to the possessive form "today's movies," indicating that the "movies" belong to "today." **(F)** is correct. **(E)** and **(G)** are incorrect; since "effects" and "movies" are each followed by verbs, they are not possessive. **(H)** makes "years" possessive, but that is incorrect since "ago" cannot be possessed.

11.   C

Category: Punctuation

Getting to the Answer: When a sentence has a list of at least three items, check that commas follow each item before the conjunction "and." **(C)** is correct; since there is a list of three things people can do to reduce the amount of water they use, a comma is needed after "showers." **(A)** is incorrect because the noun "Americans" should not be separated from its verb "can." **(B)** incorrectly removes a comma after "use," which is needed to separate the items in the list. **(D)** is incorrect because a comma after "machines" separates the modifier "less frequently" from "running," the word it modifies.

12.   E

Category: Sentence Structure

Getting to the Answer: When a sentence has a comma that can't be changed, check to see if the comma is a clue. In this sentence, the comma following "year" can't be changed; it's not in a list, and not followed by a conjunction, so it must be marking nonessential information. "Our principal" is the subject of the sentence, and the nonessential information is the descriptive phrase "who met with the students at the start of the school year." **(E)** correctly marks the beginning of the nonessential phrase with a comma. **(F)** incorrectly separates the noun "students" from its modifying phrase "at the start of the school year." **(G)** incorrectly marks "announced that the field trips this year" as nonessential, but that phrase contains "announced," the main verb, and so it is essential to the meaning of the sentence. **(H)** incorrectly makes "those we took last year" nonessential, which alters the meaning of the sentence.

13.   B

Category: Sentence Structure

Getting to the Answer: **(B)** is correct because modifiers should be close to the words they modify and clearly refer to only one idea. In the second sentence, either the "political cartoons," or "newspapers and magazines" could be the things that "captured readers' attention," which is unclear. **(A)**, **(C)**, and **(D)** do not have issues.

14. F

Category: Sentence Structure

Getting to the Answer: Look at the answer choices to see which one fixes the sentence structure error. **(F)** correctly fixes the run-on in the first sentence. **(E)** and **(G)** create run-on sentences. **(H)** creates a fragment error.

15. C

Category: Sentence Structure

Getting to the Answer: Sentence 5 is a run-on, combining two independent clauses ("They . . . 10 centimeters" and "they . . . 40 centimeters") with just a comma. **(C)** fixes the error by adding the coordinating conjunction "but" after the comma. None of the incorrect choices repair the run-on. **(A)** incorrectly replaces "are" with "is." **(B)** only replaces "small" with "tiny;" this does not repair the run-on. **(D)** replaces "they" with "fish," changing the meaning of the sentence.

16. F

Category: Knowledge of Language

Getting to the Answer: The passage's style is formal, and the author does not use the second person, so the correct answer must eliminate "you." **(F)** corrects the use of "you" while maintaining the passage's formal style. **(E)** and **(H)** both use the second person and are incorrect. **(G)** fixes the original error, but the use of "it is known" is vague and does not fit the author's direct, factual tone in the rest of the passage.

17. B

Category: Organization

Getting to the Answer: The transition needs to connect sentences 12 and 13. Sentence 12 discusses how light changes as it enters the water. Sentence 13 explains the outcome of this effect. **(B)** correctly adds a transition introducing a result of an action. The transition in **(A)** would be used to introduce additional information, which is incorrect. The transitions in **(C)** and **(D)** would introduce a contrast in thought, which is also incorrect in context.

18. G

Category: Organization

Getting to the Answer: Sentence 14 discusses how aiming is not instinctual for archerfish, and sentence 15 provides an example supporting this fact. **(G)** correctly joins the two sentences. **(E)** incorrectly joins an independent clause and a dependent clause with a semicolon. **(F)** joins the two sentences with the coordinating conjunction "but," which alters the intended meaning. **(H)** combines the two clauses in a way that creates a fragment.

19. D

Category: Knowledge of Language

Getting to the Answer: Sentence 16 uses vague and imprecise language with the use of "it" and "a good job." **(D)** corrects both of these errors. **(A)**, **(B)**, and **(C)** correct only one of the errors, and so these choices are all incorrect.

20. H

Category: Topic Development

Getting to the Answer: Read each of the choices in context to find one which is not on the same topic as the entire passage. **(H)** is correct; sentence 20 focuses on the mantis shrimp, which is off-topic and should be deleted. **(E)**, **(F)**, and **(G)** are all relevant to the passage's topic of archerfish.

CHAPTER 5

Punctuation & Usage

CHAPTER OBJECTIVES

By the end of this chapter, you will be able to:

- Identify and correct inappropriate uses of commas, dashes, semicolons, apostrophes, and colons
- Use punctuation to set off simple parenthetical elements
- Identify and correct verb agreement issues
- Identify and correct pronoun agreement issues
- Identify and correct modifier agreement issues

Punctuation & Usage

Punctuation

The SHSAT requires you to identify inappropriate commas, semicolons, colons, dashes, and apostrophes when they are used to indicate breaks in thought within a sentence. When you identify a Punctuation question, check to make sure the punctuation is used correctly in context.

Use commas to . . .	Example
Separate independent clauses connected by a FANBOYS conjunction (*for, and, nor, but, or, yet, so*)	*Jess finished her homework earlier than expected, so she started a project that was due the following week.*
Separate an introductory or modifying phrase from the rest of the sentence	*Knowing that soccer practice would be especially strenuous, Tia spent extra time stretching beforehand.*
Set off three or more items in a series or list	*Jeremiah packed a sleeping bag, a raincoat, and a lantern for his upcoming camping trip.*
Separate nonessential information from the rest of the sentence	*Professor Mann, who is the head of the English department, is known for the extensive assignments in his courses.*
Separate a dependent and an independent clause	*When it started to thunder, the lifeguards quickly ushered swimmers out of the pool.*
Separate coordinate adjectives	*Yogurt is a tasty, nutritious snack that is a good source of probiotics.*

SHSAT EXPERT TIP

When deciding if you need a comma between two adjectives, make sure you can (1) replace the comma with the word "and" as well as (2) reverse the order of the adjectives without altering the meaning of the sentence. For example, "the large, heavy box" can be rewritten as "the large and heavy box" as well as "the heavy, large box," so it does require a comma.

Use dashes to . . .	Example
Indicate a hesitation or a break in thought	*Going to a history museum is a good way to begin researching prehistoric creatures—on second thought, researching on the computer would likely be much more efficient.*
Set off explanatory elements within a sentence	*Rockwell's Space Transportation Systems Division handled all facets—design, development, and testing—of the reusable orbiter.*

Parenthetical elements may appear at the beginning, in the middle, or at the end of a sentence. A phrase such as "the capital of France" is considered parenthetical if the rest of the sentence is grammatically correct when it is removed. A parenthetical phrase must be properly punctuated with parentheses, commas, or dashes for the sentence to be grammatically correct. Do not mix and match; a parenthetical element must begin and end with the same type of punctuation.

Parenthetical Element Placement	Parentheses	Comma(s)	Dash(es)
Beginning	*N/A*	*The capital of France, Paris is a popular tourist destination.*	*N/A*
Middle	*Paris (the capital of France) is a popular tourist destination.*	*Paris, the capital of France, is a popular tourist destination.*	*Paris—the capital of France—is a popular tourist destination.*
End	*A popular tourist destination is Paris (the capital of France).*	*A popular tourist destination is Paris, the capital of France.*	*A popular tourist destination is Paris—the capital of France.*

As Chapter 4 discussed, semicolons are used in two specific ways:

- A semicolon may join two independent clauses that are not connected by a FANBOYS conjunction (also called a coordinating conjunction), just as you would use a period.
- Semicolons may be used to separate items in a list if those items already include commas.

Use semicolons to . . .	Example
Join two independent clauses that are not connected by a FANBOYS conjunction	*Ramon looked at each option carefully; after a few minutes of deliberation, he selected the well-worn book on the bottom shelf.*
Separate items in a series or list if those items already include commas	*The recipe required pans, pots, and spoons; herbs, spices, and salt; and onions, carrots, and celery.*

Use colons to . . .	Example
Introduce and/or emphasize a short phrase, quotation, explanation, example, or list	*Sanjay had two important projects to complete: a science experiment and an expository essay.*

Use an apostrophe to . . .	Example
Indicate the possessive form of a single noun	*My oldest **sister's** soccer game is on Saturday.*
Indicate the possessive form of a plural noun	*My two older **sisters'** soccer games are on Saturday.*
Indicate a contraction (e.g., *don't*, *can't*)	***They've** won every soccer match this season.*

Note that plural nouns are formed without an apostrophe.

Incorrect	Correct
Stingray's *are cartilaginous fish related to* ***shark's***.	***Stingrays*** *are cartilaginous fish related to* ***sharks***.
There are many ***carnival's*** *in this area every summer.*	*There are many* ***carnivals*** *in this area every summer.*

To check whether *it's* is appropriate, replace it in the sentence with *it is* or *it has*. If the sentence no longer makes sense, *it's* is incorrect. The following sentence is correct:

The tree frog blends perfectly into its surroundings. When it holds still, it's nearly invisible.

Note that *its'* and *its's* are never correct.

Knowing when punctuation should not be used is equally important. If an underlined portion includes punctuation, take time to consider if it should be included at all.

Do NOT use punctuation to . . .	Incorrect	Correct
Separate a subject from its verb	*The diligent student council, meets every week.*	*The diligent student council meets every week.*
Separate a verb from its object or a preposition from its object	*The diligent student council meets, every week.*	*The diligent student council meets every week.*
Set off elements that are essential to a sentence's meaning	*The, diligent student, council meets every week.*	*The diligent student council meets every week.*
Separate adjectives that work together to modify a noun	*The diligent, student council meets every week.*	*The diligent student council meets every week.*

If the question indicates that there is a punctuation error, evaluate the punctuation marks throughout the text, asking yourself:

- Is the punctuation used correctly?
  The punctuation needs to be the correct type (comma, dash, or colon) and in the correct location.

- Is the punctuation necessary?
  If you cannot identify a reason why the punctuation is included, the punctuation should be removed.

Practice

DIRECTIONS: Edit each sentence to correct the punctuation issue.

A. For my birthday, I asked for my favorite dinner chicken and roasted vegetables.

B. The story of Emperor Nero playing the fiddle while Rome burned has been debunked by historians but the saying based on it remains popular.

C. Koalas' fingerprints are nearly indistinguishable from human fingerprints which has occasionally led to mistakes at crime scenes.

D. Invented by Sir John Harrington in 1596 the flush toilet actually precedes modern indoor plumbing.

E. Toni Morrison born Chloe Wofford was one of America's most celebrated writers.

DIRECTIONS: Read and answer the following questions, recognizing and correcting errors so that the sentences or paragraphs are grammatically correct. Re-read relevant parts of the text before choosing the best answer for each question.

1. Read this sentence.

> Unable to decide between a career in law and one in medicine Jemma combined her two interests and studied forensic medicine.

Which edit should be made to correct this sentence?

A. Insert a comma after *law*.

B. Insert a comma after *medicine*.

C. Insert a comma after *interests*.

D. Insert a comma after *forensic*.

2. Read this paragraph.

---

(1) Often, the winner of an election is the candidate who best masters the art of the political advertisement. (2) Most voters have a stake in the issues of the day but cannot make sense of the rules and rhetoric of the real processes of government. (3) The thirty-second commercial on prime-time television—making sense out of technical political jargon plays a crucial part in the political process. (4) Those who wish to speak for an electorate must make their case to that electorate, and the political advertisement is the most direct and effective way to achieve that goal.

Which sentence contains an error in its construction and should be revised?

 E.   sentence 1

 F.   sentence 2

 G.   sentence 3

 H.   sentence 4

3. Read this paragraph.

---

(1) Bicycling is a mainstream form of transportation in Japanese cities. (2) Nearly every type of person uses a bicycle, blue-collar workers, office workers in suits, parents toting babies, and students. (3) In the United States, however, bicycling is more often seen as a recreational activity or form of exercise than as a means of transportation. (4) An exception is that American children often rely on bikes, given their more limited transportation options.

Which sentence contains an error in its construction and should be revised?

 A.   sentence 1

 B.   sentence 2

 C.   sentence 3

 D.   sentence 4

4. Read this sentence.

> Although the statue was intended, in ancient times, to tower above the landscape, it's presence is now dominated by the enormous skyscrapers that came with the city's modernization.

Which edit should be made to correct the sentence?

E. Change *it's* to **its**.

F. Insert a comma after ***presence***.

G. Insert a comma after ***skyscrapers***.

H. Change *city's* to **cities**.

Usage

Verb Tense

Verb tense indicates when an action or state of being takes place: in the past, present, or future. The tense of the verb must fit the context of the passage. Each tense can express three different types of action.

Type of Action	Past	Present	Future
Single action occurring only once	Connor **planted** vegetables in the community garden.	Connor **plants** vegetables in the community garden.	Connor **will plant** vegetables in the community garden.
Action that is ongoing at some point in time	Connor **was planting** vegetables in the community garden this morning before noon.	Connor **is planting** vegetables in the community garden this morning before noon.	Connor **will be planting** vegetables in the community garden this morning before noon.
Action that is completed before some other action	Connor **had planted** vegetables in the community garden every year until he gave his job to Jasmine.	Connor **has planted** vegetables in the community garden since it started five years ago.	Connor **will have planted** vegetables in the community garden by the time the growing season starts.

Subject-Verb Agreement

A verb must agree with its subject in person and number:

- Person (first, second, or third)
  - First: *I **ask** a question.*
  - Second: *You **ask** a question.*
  - Third: *She **asks** a question.*

- Number (singular or plural)
  - Singular: *The apple **tastes** delicious.*
  - Plural: *Apples **taste** delicious.*

The noun closest to the verb is not always the subject. For example, in the sentence, "The chair with the lion feet is an antique," the singular verb, *is*, is closest to the plural noun *feet*. However, the verb's actual subject is the singular noun *chair*, so the sentence is correct as written.

When a sentence includes two nouns, only the conjunction *and* forms a compound subject requiring a plural verb form:

- Plural: *Saliyah and Taylor **are** in the running club.*
- Singular: *Either Saliyah or Taylor **is** in the running club.*
- Singular: *Neither Saliyah nor Taylor **is** in the running club.*

Collective nouns are nouns that name entities with more than one member, such as *group*, *team*, and *family*. Even though these nouns represent more than one person, they are grammatically singular and require singular verb forms:

- *The collection of paintings **is** one of the most popular art exhibits in recent years.*
- *The team **looks** promising this year.*

Parallelism

Verbs in a list, a compound, or a comparison must be parallel in form.

Feature	Example	Parallel Form
A list	Chloe **formulated** a question, **conducted** background research, and **constructed** a hypothesis before starting the experiment.	3 simple past verb phrases
A compound	**Hunting** and **fishing** were essential to the survival of Midwestern Native American tribes such as the Omaha.	2 *-ing* verb forms
A comparison	Garrett enjoys **sculpting** as much as **painting**.	2 *-ing* verb forms

Note that parallelism may be tested using other parts of speech besides verbs. In general, any items in a list, compound, or comparison must be in parallel form. For example, if a list starts with a noun, the other items in the list must also be nouns; if it starts with an adjective, the other items must be adjectives.

Incorrect	Correct
Naomi likes **oatmeal and drinking tea** on chilly weekend afternoons.	Naomi likes **oatmeal and tea** on chilly weekend afternoons. *or* Naomi likes **eating oatmeal and drinking tea** on chilly weekend afternoons.
Which of the dogs is the **most docile and better behaved**?	Which of the dogs is the **most docile and best behaved**? or Which of the dogs is the **more docile and better behaved**?

How to Answer Verb Questions

When answering questions that ask about verb errors, check that the verb:

- Reflects the correct tense (Does it fit the context?)
- Agrees with the subject in person and number
- Is parallel in form with other verbs in a series, list, or compound (if there is one in the sentence)

Practice

DIRECTIONS: Edit each sentence to correct the verb issue.

   A.   Angel audition for the school play next week.

   B.   The song with the upbeat rhythm and catchy lyrics were wildly popular.

   C.   Either the governor or the lieutenant governor usually present the award.

   D.   By the time the last runner completed the marathon, the winner has crossed the finish line hours ago.

   E.   Few people know that Stephen Hawking both revolutionized physics and co-written children's books with his daughter.

DIRECTIONS: Read and answer the following questions, recognizing and correcting errors so that the sentences or paragraphs are grammatically correct. Re-read relevant parts of the text before choosing the best answer for each question.

5.   Read this sentence.

> The most successful scientists, spanning fields from physics to geology, sees beyond the facts and speculate about the general principles that provide a foundation for new ideas.

Which edit should be made to correct this sentence?

   A.   Change *fields* to **field**.

   B.   Change *sees* to **see**.

   C.   Change *speculate* to **speculates**.

   D.   Change *provide* to **provides**.

6.   Read this sentence.

> In the Middle Ages, when women are generally not allowed to venture outside the domestic realm, Christine de Pisan became an acclaimed poet and is considered the first woman in France to have earned renown as a writer.

Which edit should be made to correct this sentence?

   E.   Change *are* to **were**.

   F.   Change *became* to **becomes**.

   G.   Change *considered* to **considering**.

   H.   Change *earned* to **earn**.

Pronoun Forms

A pronoun is a word that takes the place of a noun. Pronouns can take three different forms, each of which is based on the grammatical role it plays in the sentence.

Form	Pronouns	Example
Subjective: The pronoun is used as the subject.	I, you, she, he, it, we, they, who	*Rivka is the student **who** will lead the presentation.*
Objective: The pronoun is used as the object of a verb or a preposition.	me, you, her, him, it, us, them, whom	*With **whom** will Rivka present the scientific findings?*
Possessive: The pronoun expresses ownership.	my, mine, your, yours, his, her, hers, its, our, ours, their, theirs, whose	*Rivka will likely choose a partner **whose** work is excellent.*

Note that a pronoun in subjective form can, logically, be the subject in a complete sentence. Pronouns that are in objective form cannot.

Pronoun-Antecedent Agreement

A pronoun's antecedent is the noun it logically represents in a sentence. If the noun is singular, the pronoun must be singular; if the noun is plural, the pronoun must be plural.

Antecedent	Incorrect	Correct
selection	*The selection of books was placed in **their** designated location.*	*The selection of books was placed in **its** designated location.*
Addison	*Addison fed the giraffes all of the lettuce **they** had purchased.*	*Addison fed the giraffes all of the lettuce **she** had purchased.*
sapling	*The sapling, along with dozens of flowers, was relocated to where **they** would thrive.*	*The sapling, along with dozens of flowers, was relocated to where **it** would thrive.*
students	*If students are confused, she should ask for clarification.*	*If students are confused, **they** should ask for clarification.*

SHSAT EXPERT NOTE

When there are two pronouns or a noun and a pronoun in a compound structure, drop the other noun or pronoun to confirm which case to use. For example: "Leo and me walked into town." Would you say, "Me walked into town"? No, you would say, "I walked into town." Therefore, the original sentence should read, "Leo and I walked into town."

Possessive Nouns and Pronouns

Possessive nouns and pronouns indicate that something that belongs to someone or something. In general, possessive nouns are written with an apostrophe, while possessive pronouns are not.

To spot errors in possessive noun or pronoun construction, look for . . .	Incorrect	Correct
Two nouns in a row	The **professors lectures** were both informative and entertaining.	The **professor's lectures** were both informative and entertaining.
Pronouns with apostrophes	The book is her's.	The book is **hers**.
Words that sound alike	The three friends decided to ride **there** bicycles to the park over **they're** where **their** going to enjoy a picnic lunch.	The three friends decided to ride **their** bicycles to the park over **there** where **they're** going to enjoy a picnic lunch.

How to Answer Pronoun Questions

If a question includes a pronoun, find the logical antecedent, which is the word(s) to which the pronoun is referring. If there is no clear antecedent, the pronoun is ambiguous and this error must be corrected. Be sure to check that the pronoun:

- Uses the correct form
  - If the pronoun is the subject of the sentence, use a subjective pronoun such as *I, you, she, he, it, we, they,* or *who.*
  - If the pronoun is an object within the sentence, use an objective pronoun such as *me, you, her, him, it, us, they,* or *whom.*
  - If the pronoun indicates possession, use a possessive pronoun such as *my, mine, your, yours, his, her, hers, its, our, ours, their, theirs,* or *whose.*

- Agrees with its antecedent
  - A singular antecedent requires a singular pronoun; a plural antecedent requires a plural pronoun.

Practice

DIRECTIONS: Edit each sentence to correct the pronoun issue.

A. Although the teacher gave the student detention after school, she was not angry.

B. My uncle likes to go bowling with my sister and I.

C. The box of nails has been moved from their usual place in the shed.

D. My favorite singer, who I have wanted to see in person for years, will give a concert a week after my birthday.

E. The cathedral of Notre Dame, with vast vaulted ceilings and intricate carvings, never fails to amaze their visitors.

DIRECTIONS: Read and answer the following questions, recognizing and correcting errors so that the sentences or paragraphs are grammatically correct. Re-read relevant parts of the text before choosing the best answer for each question.

7. Read this paragraph.

(1) Sandstone, limestone, and shale are three common types of water-made rocks, and it all can play a role in fossil creation. (2) Shale is composed of mud, often distinct layers that have dried together, and it is usually formed by erosion from landmasses. (3) By contrast, sandstone and limestone often come from the ocean bottom. (4) Sandstone is made up of grains of sand that, with the help of water, have adhered to one another over time, often trapping and fossilizing simple sea creatures and plants in the process.

Which sentence contains an error in its construction and should be revised?

A. sentence 1

B. sentence 2

C. sentence 3

D. sentence 4

8. Read this sentence.

> A wolf spider, with its large fuzzy body and hairy legs, is known for their agile hunting skills and excellent eyesight.

Which edit should be made to correct this sentence?

E. Change *spider* to **spiders**.

F. Change *its* to **their**.

G. Change *their* to **its**.

H. Change *skills* to **skill**.

Adjectives and Adverbs

Use adjectives only to modify nouns and pronouns. Use adverbs to modify everything else.

- **Adjectives** are single-word modifiers that describe nouns and pronouns: *Ian conducted an **efficient** lab experiment.*
- **Adverbs** are single-word modifiers that describe verbs, adjectives, or other adverbs: *Ian **efficiently** conducted a lab experiment.*

Note that nouns can sometimes be used as adjectives. For example, in the phrase "the fashion company's autumn line," the word "fashion" functions as an adjective modifying "company," and the word "autumn" functions as an adjective modifying "line."

Comparative/Superlative

When comparing similar things, use adjectives that match the number of items being compared. When comparing two items or people, use the **comparative** form of the adjective. When comparing three or more items or people, use the **superlative** form.

Comparative (two items)	Superlative (three or more items)
better, more, newer, older, shorter, taller, worse, younger	best, most, newest, oldest, shortest, tallest, worst, youngest

If the question includes a modifier, determine whether the modifier:

- Agrees with the word or words it is describing
  - Does the sentence require an adjective or an adverb?
  - Does the noun or pronoun show proper possession?

If the question includes an apostrophe, make sure it correctly indicates either possession or a contraction. If an apostrophe is missing, select the answer choice that places it in the correct location.

Practice

DIRECTIONS: Edit each sentence to correct the modifier agreement issue.

A.   Computers have grown exponential more efficient since their invention.

B.   Estella chose to take the route with the most attractively scenery.

C.   The leaf-tailed gecko's amazing natural camouflage enables it to blend perfectly into it's surroundings.

D.   Between basketball and baseball, basketball is the most popular sport in the United States.

E.   From Edgar Allan Poe to contemporary comedians, the infamous Spanish Inquisition has provided material for many artists.

DIRECTIONS: Read and answer the following questions, recognizing and correcting errors so that the sentences or paragraphs are grammatically correct. Re-read relevant parts of the text before choosing the best answer for each question.

9.   Read this sentence.

> Between Hugo and Kai, Hugo is the best sprinter; however, Kai is better at the long jump.

Which edit should be made to correct this sentence?

A.   Change *best* to **better**.

B.   Change *sprinter* to **at sprinting**.

C.   Change *better* to **best**.

D.   Change *long jump* to **long jumping**.

10.   Read this paragraph.

> (1) Translating any work is a much more complex process than simply exchanging one word for another, and the effect of a superbly translated play on an audience can be profound. (2) The script for a play is not a work to be appreciated on its own, but rather a map used to create such a work. (3) Since the audience for a play will rarely view the script itself, all of the plot points, emotions, subtleties—all of the meaning—must be transmitted simply through spoken dialogue. (4) Granted, when translating between close related languages, a near word-for-word process can sometimes be sufficient.

Which sentence should be revised to correct a word choice issue?

E.   sentence 1

F.   sentence 2

G.   sentence 3

H.   sentence 4

Punctation & Usage

Sometimes you will be asked to fix both punctuation and usage issues within a single question. In those cases, knowing how to fix one of the two errors will help you narrow down the answer choices.

If the question asks you to fix both a punctuation error and a usage error:

- Focus on one error at a time.
- Reread the text with the proposed changes and select the option that creates the most correct, concise, and relevant text.

Practice

> **DIRECTIONS:** Edit each sentence to correct both one punctuation error and one usage error.

A. Thorny dragons a type of Australian lizard, is covered entirely with spines shaped like upside-down cones.

B. The Pentagon building, located in Washington, D.C.; is known for it's unique five-sided shape, which was designed by American architect George Bergstrom.

C. The menu offered three type of soups chicken noodle, minestrone, and split pea.

D. The math team newly formed this year—were astounded when they came in first place.

E. The valuable, Victorian chairs with authentic upholstery was sold for an astronomical price.

> **DIRECTIONS:** Read and answer the following questions. You will be asked to recognize and correct errors so that the sentences or short paragraphs are grammatically correct. You may write in your book to take notes. You should re-read relevant parts of the sentences or paragraphs before choosing the best answer for each question.

11. Read this paragraph.

> (1) Kira spent every day after school last week practicing for the upcoming speech and debate tournament. (2) On Monday and Tuesday, she rewrote sections of her ten-minute original oratory speech to clarify her main points. (3) On Wednesday, she performs her speech in front of her friends, and team members to simulate the way she will deliver her speech in front of people. (4) On Thursday and Friday, she recited it out loud over and over, making sure she had every word memorized.

How should the paragraph be revised?

A. Sentence 1: Change *spent* to **had spent**, AND insert a comma after *upcoming*.

B. Sentence 2: Change *rewrote* to **rewrites**, AND insert a comma after *speech*.

C. Sentence 3: Change *performs* to **performed**, AND delete the comma after *friends*.

D. Sentence 4: Change *recited* to **recites**, AND delete the comma after *over*.

12. Read this paragraph.

---

(1) Okapis, which are also called forest giraffes, are native to central Africa. (2) The common ancestor of giraffes and okapis, the *Canthumeryx*, lived about 16 million years ago. (3) Animals that are now known as giraffes evolved to be quite tall and lanky, with necks that can reach leaves that grow high up on trees. (4) Okapis did not grow longer necks, but develops stripes similar to zebras to provide camouflage from predators.

Which revisions correct the errors in the paragraph?

E. Sentence 1: Delete the comma after giraffes, AND change *are* to **is**.

F. Sentence 2: Delete the comma after okapis, AND change *lived* to **lives**.

G. Sentence 3: Delete the comma after lanky, AND change *grow* to **grows**.

H. Sentence 4: Delete the comma after necks, AND change *develops* to **developed**.

Practice Set

For test-like practice, give yourself 23 minutes (an average of 1 minute per stand-alone question and 1.5 minutes per passage-based question) to complete this question set. While many of the questions pertain to Punctuation and Usage, some touch on other English Language Arts concepts to ensure that your practice is test-like, with a variety of question types. After you're done, be sure to study the explanations, even for questions you answered correctly. They can be found at the end of this chapter.

REVISING/EDITING Part A

DIRECTIONS: Answer the following questions, recognizing and correcting errors so that the sentences or paragraphs are grammatically correct. Re-read relevant parts of the text before choosing the best answer for each question.

---

1. Read this sentence.

> The newly constructed athletic complex features a myriad of amenities multi-purpose gymnasiums, an elevated jogging track, squash courts, and exercise studios.

Which edit should be made to correct the sentence?

- A. Insert a colon after *newly constructed*.
- B. Insert a colon after *complex*.
- C. Insert a colon after *amenities*.
- D. Insert a colon after *multi-purpose*.

2. Read this sentence.

> Violet Palmer—professional basketball referee and one of the first women to officiate a National Basketball Association (NBA) game started her journey to forging her name in basketball's history in a typical way: she played the sport.

Which edit should be made to correct the sentence?

- E. Insert a dash after *referee*.
- F. Insert a dash after *and*.
- G. Insert a dash after *game*.
- H. Insert a dash after *journey*.

3. Read this paragraph.

> (1) The industries showing the most rapid growth are service and technology. (2) High-tech industries include computers, pharmaceuticals, and aerospace. (3) By the mid-1980s, three-quarters of workers in the United States had jobs in the service industry. (4) Service employees, who provide information or perform tasks for a customer, works in fields such as medicine, food service, and law.

Which sentence contains an error in its construction and should be revised?

A. sentence 1

B. sentence 2

C. sentence 3

D. sentence 4

4. Read this paragraph.

> (1) Abraham Lincoln distinguished himself as a remarkable orator and was admired more for the Gettysburg Address and his two inaugural speeches. (2) His humble, patient, serious, and persuasive personality helped him gain attention. (3) When Lincoln ran for Senate reelection, he challenged Stephen A. Douglas to a discussion of issues; these became the Lincoln-Douglas debates. (4) Although Lincoln lost that election, he received countless invitations to speak all over the country.

Which sentence contains an error in its construction and should be revised?

E. sentence 1

F. sentence 2

G. sentence 3

H. sentence 4

5. Read this paragraph.

> (1) The Liberty Bell, an enormous instrument that was eventually rang during the American Revolution, received its first small crack as it was being tested. (2) When the Declaration of Independence had its first public proclamation, the people of Philadelphia heard this bell ring out. (3) The Liberty Bell's crack grew much larger when it was rung on Washington's birthday in 1846, and the bell was rendered useless. (4) At its home in Independence Hall, the bell receives a tap each year on the Fourth of July.

Which sentence contains an error in its construction and should be revised?

A. sentence 1

B. sentence 2

C. sentence 3

D. sentence 4

6. Read this paragraph.

> (1) Many adult readers of the Harry Potter series have celebrated its many plots for the depth and intrigue that they provide for readers of all ages. (2) J. K. Rowling's bestselling books have won a large number of awards for their clever use of mystery and suspense. (3) Adult readers appreciate the sophisticated portrayal of universal themes and magical adventures that transport them to a different world. (4) The books' mature heroes, creativity, and humor has made readers eager to know more about Harry Potter.

Which sentence contains an error in its construction and should be revised?

E. sentence 1

F. sentence 2

G. sentence 3

H. sentence 4

7. Read this paragraph.

    > (1) Studies show that people who participate in competitive sports when they are in college tend toward remaining physically active throughout their lives. (2) Research shows that regular physical exercise keeps the brain strong, regardless of one's age. (3) Competitive sports offer additional cognitive challenges, but any type of workout leads to the resilience of the brain later in life. (4) Complex physical activities might require more communication between various parts of the brain, which could lead to brain preservation.

    Which sentence contains an error in its construction and should be revised?

    A. sentence 1
    B. sentence 2
    C. sentence 3
    D. sentence 4

8. Read this paragraph.

    > (1) The winners of the "Best of Breed" cup and the "Best in Show" trophy are selected by a panel of breeders from the American Kennel Club. (2) Since 1884, this organization has promoted responsible dog ownership and has protected the rights of dog owners. (3) Each year, it hosts tens of thousands of events, including dog shows. (4) The American Kennel Club even reunites lost pets with their owners and offers scholarships to the brighter veterinary students.

    Which sentence contains an error in its construction and should be revised?

    E. sentence 1
    F. sentence 2
    G. sentence 3
    H. sentence 4

9. Read this paragraph.

> (1) Lacking sacred scriptures or codified dogma, Shinto is regarded as a legacy of traditional religious practices and basic values. (2) Although it has incorporated external influences from Confucianism, Taoism, and Buddhism, Shinto has stayed true to its own tradition. (3) Some shrines and works of art have officially became national treasures in Japan. (4) Many Japanese people observe ancient Shinto practices in modern social life.

Which sentence contains an error in its construction and should be revised?

A. sentence 1

B. sentence 2

C. sentence 3

D. sentence 4

10. Read this paragraph.

> (1) As a playwright, Harold Pinter is renowned for his mundane settings, his everyday yet poetic dialogue, and his aggressive, often mean-spirited characters. (2) He is one of the most important English playwrights of the twentieth century and has presented themes like reality and human interaction. (3) His talent for accurately replicating ordinary speech through his plays might surprise the audience members, who may not associate the dialogue to the unexpected events occurring onstage. (4) In his dramas, Pinter demonstrates non-traditional styles and often uses a series of plays to explore a problem.

Which sentence contains an error in its construction and should be revised?

E. sentence 1

F. sentence 2

G. sentence 3

H. sentence 4

11. Read this paragraph.

> (1) Homeschooling programs, nearly unheard of twenty years ago, are now available through many public school systems. (2) Children of all ages enjoys the unlimited opportunities and a variety of tailored options. (3) Many homeschool families choose an eclectic approach, which may combine the use of traditional textbooks, hands-on learning, online courses, and projects designed around a student's academic interests. (4) High-school students receive a transcript, which most universities accept.

Which sentence contains an error in its construction and should be revised?

A. sentence 1

B. sentence 2

C. sentence 3

D. sentence 4

12. Read this paragraph.

> (1) Attention span plays a role in many children's and teenagers' academic success. (2) Some students are unable to study for long, uninterrupted periods of time, but this does not mean they are incapable of getting good grades. (3) When families recognize a child's difficulty, they can view it of a treatable condition and attempt to adjust the study habits. (4) Countless resources offer academic advice about successfully addressing attention issues.

Which sentence contains an error in its construction and should be revised?

E. sentence 1

F. sentence 2

G. sentence 3

H. sentence 4

13. Read this paragraph.

> (1) The extensive study of atoms' movements have led scientists to theories of quantum mechanics, which hold that it is impossible to determine exactly how subatomic particles move. (2) Quantum mechanics represents a branch of physics that makes observations about atoms and the structure and behavior of matter. (3) For example, it explains the processes by which atoms form into molecules. (4) By applying quantum mechanics, scientists have developed CDs, barcode readers, and nuclear energy.

Which sentence contains an error in its construction and should be revised?

A. sentence 1

B. sentence 2

C. sentence 3

D. sentence 4

14. Read this paragraph.

> (1) A high school's guidance counselor or college counselor can offer students many resources and a great deal of support. (2) Seniors which need help with their college applications, can find immediate assistance from the guidance department. (3) For example, the department might provide access to reference books and online accounts that have detailed application requirements for each college. (4) Although the process might seem intimidating at first, college preparation can be very manageable with the right assistance.

How should the paragraph be revised?

E. Sentence 1: Change *or* to **and**, AND insert a comma after *resources*.

F. Sentence 2: Change *which* to **who**, AND delete the comma after *applications*.

G. Sentence 3: Change *For example* to **However**, AND insert a comma after *accounts*.

H. Sentence 4: Change *Although* to **Nonetheless**, AND delete the comma after *first*.

REVISING/EDITING Part B

DIRECTIONS: Read the passage and answer the questions following it, improving the writing quality and correcting grammatical errors. Re-read relevant parts of the text before choosing the best answer for each question.

Jean Piaget

(1) The study of mollusks and the formulation of a theory of the way children think may not seem like rungs of the same career ladder, but that's exactly what they were for Jean Piaget. (2) Piaget was born in Switzerland in 1896. (3) He studied at the University of Neuchatel. (4) He eventually received a doctorate in the natural sciences. (5) While observing the mollusks living in the region's many lakes, Piaget saw biological changes occurring in the creatures that could only be attributed to its environment.

(6) In 1918, Piaget moved to Zurich and switched his focus from natural science to psychology. (7) Eventually, he concluded that a person's mental development, like his or her physical growth, could be profoundly affected by the environment in which it took place. (8) He continued his studies at the Sorbonne in Paris. (9) Where he began focusing on the cognitive development of children. (10) B.F. Skinner and Albert Bandura also studied child development. (11) There, Piaget applied his knowledge of the environment's effect on biological change.

(12) Piaget's theory of cognitive development posited four stages. (13) He called the first phase, from birth to 24 months of age, the sensorimotor. (14) In this stage, babies and very young children are driven primarily by basic actions such as sucking and looking at the world around them. (15) They also begin to realize that their actions, such as crying, can produce results, such as being fed or comforted.

(16) The second stage is from 24 months to 7 years. (17) This is the preoperational stage in which children are learning to use symbols such as pictures and words. (18) From 7 to 12 years is the concrete operational stage, when thinking becomes more logical and organized.

(19) Finally, from adolescence through adulthood is the formal operational stage, characterized by the ability to think abstractly and by the capability of hypothetical and theoretical reasoning. (20) Although it may seem that humans go through these stages instinctively and without deliberative input, Piaget believed that children are active participants in each stage, as they observe, learn, experiment, and change throughout their development. (21) Piaget died in 1980, after writing more than 50 books and receiving honorary degrees from 31 universities.

15. What is the best way to combine sentences 2 through 4 to clarify the relationship between ideas?

   A. Born in Switzerland in 1896, Piaget studied at the University of Neuchatel, where he eventually received a doctorate in the natural sciences.

   B. Piaget was born in Switzerland in 1896 and studied at the University of Neuchatel and eventually received a doctorate in the natural sciences.

   C. Piaget was born in Switzerland in 1896; studied at the University of Neuchatel; eventually received a doctorate in the natural sciences.

   D. In 1896, Piaget was born in Switzerland, where he studied at the University of Neuchatel, eventually having received a doctorate in the natural sciences.

16. Which edit should be made to correct sentence 5?

    E. Change *saw* to **seen**.

    F. Change *biological changes occurring* to **the occurrence of biological changes**.

    G. Change *that* to **who**.

    H. Change *its* to **their**.

17. What is the best way to combine sentences 8 and 9 to clarify the relationship between ideas?

    A. He continued his studies at the Sorbonne in Paris; where he began focusing on the cognitive development of children.

    B. He continued his studies at the Sorbonne in Paris, where he began focusing on the cognitive development of children.

    C. He continued his studies at the Sorbonne in Paris and he began focusing on the cognitive development of children.

    D. He continued his studies at the Sorbonne in Paris. He began focusing on the cognitive development of children.

18. Where should sentence 11 be moved in order to improve the organization of the second paragraph (sentences 6–11)?

    E. to the beginning of the paragraph (before sentence 6)

    F. between sentences 6 and 7

    G. between sentences 7 and 8

    H. between sentences 9 and 10

19. Which sentence presents information that shifts away from the main topic of the second paragraph (sentences 6–11) and should be removed?

    A. sentence 7

    B. sentence 8

    C. sentence 9

    D. sentence 10

20. Which concluding sentence would best follow sentence 21 and support the argument presented in the passage?

    E. He also chaired many professional committees in several countries.

    F. He believed that growth was, in part, an adaptation to the environment.

    G. Alfred Binet also studied the cognitive development of children.

    H. His works, however, continue to form the core of many psychology courses around the world.

Answers and Explanations

Punctuation

Note: These are not the only ways to correct the sentences; your answers may differ.

A. For my birthday, I asked for my favorite dinner: chicken and roasted vegetables.

B. The story of Emperor Nero playing the fiddle while Rome burned has been debunked by historians, but the saying based on it remains popular.

C. Koalas' fingerprints are nearly indistinguishable from human fingerprints—which has occasionally led to mistakes at crime scenes.

D. Invented by Sir John Harrington in 1596, the flush toilet actually precedes modern indoor plumbing.

E. Toni Morrison—born Chloe Wofford—was one of America's most celebrated writers.

1. B

Category: Punctuation

Getting to the Answer: The question indicates that an edit is required to make the sentence grammatically correct. A comma is needed to properly combine an independent clause with a dependent clause. Inserting a comma after the last word in the independent clause, "medicine," **(B)**, is correct. **(A)**, **(C)**, and **(D)** do not address the error and place unnecessary commas within the sentence.

2. G

Category: Punctuation

Getting to the Answer: The question says that one of the sentences contains an error. Read each one, looking for a grammar issue. Sentence 3 is missing a necessary dash, so **(G)** is correct. The phrase "making sense out of technical political jargon" is a nonessential clause that must be set off from the rest of the sentence with either a pair of commas or a pair of dashes. Inserting a dash after "jargon" would fix the error.

3. B

Category: Punctuation

Getting to the Answer: Read each sentence, looking for a grammatical error. A colon is used to introduce a list, so sentence 2 should use a colon instead of a comma after "bicycle"; **(B)** is correct. **(A)**, **(C)**, and **(D)** do not contain an error.

4. E

Category: Punctuation

Getting to the Answer: The question states that the sentence contains an error. The word "it's" means "it is," but the sentence requires the possessive "its"; **(E)** is correct. The other choices do not address this punctuation error and create new issues. **(F)** and **(G)** add unnecessary commas. **(H)** incorrectly changes the singular possessive "city's" to the plural noun "cities."

Verbs

Note: These are not the only ways to correct the sentences; your answers may differ.

A. Angel **will** audition for the school play next week.

B. The song with the upbeat rhythm and catchy lyrics **was** wildly popular.

C. Either the governor or the lieutenant governor usually **presents** the award.

D. By the time the last runner completed the marathon, the winner **had** crossed the finish line hours ago.

E. Few people know that Stephen Hawking both revolutionized physics and **co-wrote** children's books with his daughter.

5. B

Category: Usage

Getting to the Answer: The question states that the sentence contains an error. In this sentence, the singular verb "sees" does not match the plural subject "scientists." **(B)** fixes the error. The other answer choices do not fix the issue and introduce new errors. **(A)** incorrectly changes a plural noun to a singular noun, and **(C)** and **(D)** create subject-verb agreement issues.

6. E

Category: Usage

Getting to the Answer: The question indicates that there is an error that needs to be fixed. Read the sentence before checking each option to see which one fixes the issue. The Middle Ages happened in the past, so the present tense "are" does not make sense in context. **(E)** fixes the issue by changing it to the past tense "were." **(F)** changes the correct past tense to the incorrect present tense, **(G)** changes the meaning of the sentence, and **(H)** creates an incorrect verb form.

Pronouns

A. Although the teacher gave the student detention after school, **the student** was not angry.

B. My uncle likes to go bowling with my sister and **me**.

C. The box of nails has been moved from **its** usual place in the shed.

D. My favorite singer, **whom** I have wanted to see in person for years, will give a concert a week after my birthday.

E. The cathedral of Notre Dame, with vast vaulted ceilings and intricate carvings, never fails to amaze **its** visitors.

7. A

Category: Usage

Getting to the Answer: The question indicates that one of the sentences in the paragraph contains an error. A pronoun must agree with its antecedent in person and number. In sentence 1, the singular pronoun "it" does not match the plural antecedent "Sandstone, limestone, and shale." **(A)** identifies the error. Sentences 2, 3, and 4 are written correctly and do not contain pronoun errors.

8. G

Category: Usage

Getting to the Answer: The question indicates that there is an error that needs to be fixed. The sentence discusses a single spider, so the plural possessive pronoun "their" is incorrect. **(G)** fixes the issue by changing the pronoun to the singular possessive pronoun "its." **(E)** changes the correct singular noun "spider" to an incorrect plural noun and **(F)** changes the correct singular possessive pronoun to an incorrect plural possessive pronoun. **(H)** does not introduce a new error, but it does not fix the original issue.

Modifier Agreement

A. Computers have grown **exponentially** more efficient since their invention.

B. Estella chose to take the route with the most **attractive** scenery.

C. The leaf-tailed gecko's amazing natural camouflage enables it to blend perfectly into **its** surroundings.

D. Between basketball and baseball, basketball is the **more** popular sport in the United States.

E. The infamous Spanish Inquisition has provided material for many artists, **from Edgar Allan Poe to contemporary comedians**.

9. A

Category: Usage

Getting to the Answer: The sentence contains an error, so read carefully to pinpoint the issue. Two people are being compared, so the comparative "better" is needed since the superlative "best" is used for three or more items, not two. **(A)** is correct. **(B)** and **(D)** do not create new errors, but they do not fix the original problem. **(C)** creates a new issue by changing the correct comparative "better" to the incorrect superlative "best."

10. H

Category: Usage

Getting to the Answer: Check each sentence systematically to find the error the question is prompting you to locate. In sentence 4, the word "related" is an adjective, so it needs to be described by the adverb "closely" rather than the adjective "close." Adjectives can only be used to describe nouns and pronouns, whereas adverbs are used to describe everything else, including adjectives. **(H)** is correct. Sentences 1, 2, and 3 are written correctly, so you can eliminate **(E)**, **(F)**, and **(G)**.

Punctuation & Usage

A. Thorny dragons**,** a type of Australian lizard**,** **are** covered entirely with spines shaped like upside-down cones.

B. The Pentagon building, located in Washington, D.C.**,** is known for **its** unique five-sided shape, which was designed by American architect George Bergstrom.

C. The menu offered three type**s** of soups**:** chicken noodle, minestrone, and split pea.

D. The math team—newly formed this year—**was** astounded when they came in first place.

E. The valuable, Victorian chairs with authentic upholstery **were** sold for an astronomical price.

11. C
Category: Punctuation & Usage

Getting to the Answer: The paragraph contains two errors, so concentrating on one at a time will help narrow down the answer choices. In sentence 3, the comma after "friends" is unnecessary because "friends and team members" is a compound phrase that should not be interrupted with any punctuation. Only **(C)** fixes that issue. Alternatively, if you spot the verb error in sentence 3, **(C)** is also the only option that changes the incorrect present tense "performs" to the past tense "performed" to reflect the fact that Kira completed the action last week. Sentences 1, 2, and 3 are correct as written, so you can eliminate **(A)**, **(B)**, and **(C)**.

12. H
Category: Punctuation & Usage

Getting to the Answer: The question indicates that a revision is necessary, and the answer choices show that there are two errors. In sentence 4, the comma after "necks" incorrectly separates the two parts of the sentence, both of which are essential to the sentence's meaning. **(H)** is correct. In addition, the present tense "develops" should be changed to the past tense "developed" to reflect that this action happened in the past. You can eliminate **(E)**, **(F)**, and **(G)** because sentences 1, 2, and 3 are correct as written.

Practice Set

1. C
Category: Punctuation

Getting to the Answer: A colon is used to introduce an explanation, example, or list. Inserting a colon after "amenities," **(C)**, properly introduces the list that follows. **(A)**, **(B)**, and **(D)** do not address the error and place unnecessary colons within the sentence.

2. G
Category: Punctuation

Getting to the Answer: A dash is used either to indicate a break in thought or to separate a nonessential phrase from the rest of the sentence. The phrase "professional basketball referee and one of the first women to officiate a National Basketball Association (NBA) game" is a nonessential clause that must be properly set off with either two commas or two dashes. Inserting a dash after "game," **(G)**, properly punctuates the nonessential phrase. **(E)**, **(F)**, and **(H)** do not address the error and place unnecessary dashes within the sentence.

3. D
Category: Usage

Getting to the Answer: In sentence 4, the subject "employees" is plural, so a plural verb is needed to match. Keep in mind that a verb might not always appear close to its subject due to intervening phrases. The sentence could be revised to read, "work in fields." The correct answer is **(D)**. In **(A)**, **(B)**, and **(C)**, the sentences do not have errors.

4. E
Category: Usage

Getting to the Answer: Check to see that sentences have proper comparatives and superlatives. In sentence 1, the word "most" should replace "more," since Lincoln gave many speeches. The word "more" would compare only two things. The sentences in **(F)**, **(G)**, and **(H)** do not include errors, so **(E)** is correct.

5.   A

Category: Usage

Getting to the Answer: Be sure to use the past participle and not the simple past tense. In sentence 1, the correct past participle would be "that was eventually rung." **(A)** is correct. **(B)**, **(C)**, and **(D)** have grammatically correct sentences.

6.   H

Category: Usage

Getting to the Answer: The last sentence presents a compound subject that is plural: "mature heroes, creativity, and humor." A verb needs to agree with its subject in number, so "has made" would need to be in the plural form, "have made." **(H)** is correct; the sentences in **(E)**, **(F)**, and **(G)** do not have errors.

7.   A

Category: Usage

Getting to the Answer: The first sentence awkwardly combines the simple present tense of a verb with the progressive tense of a verb using "toward." This could be revised to read, "are likely to remain." **(A)** is correct. **(B)**, **(C)**, and **(D)** do not have errors.

8.   H

Category: Usage

Getting to the Answer: Check to see that sentences have proper comparatives and superlatives. In sentence 4, the word "brightest" should replace "brighter," since many veterinary students would apply for the scholarships. The word "brighter" would compare only two things. The sentences in **(E)**, **(F)**, and **(G)** do not include errors, so the correct answer is **(H)**.

9.   C

Category: Usage

Getting to the Answer: The verb "became" should not be used in combination with "have." In sentence 3, the correct verb phrase would be "have officially become." **(A)**, **(B)**, and **(D)** do not have errors, so **(C)** is correct.

10.   G

Category: Usage

Getting to the Answer: Check to see that idioms are paired with the correct prepositions. In Sentence 3, "associate the dialogue to" should be replaced with "associated the dialogue with." **(E)**, **(F)**, and **(H)** do not have errors, so **(G)** is correct.

11.   B

Category: Usage

Getting to the Answer: In sentence 2, the subject "children" is plural, so a plural verb is needed. The revision could include "children of all ages enjoy." **(B)** is correct; the sentences in **(A)**, **(C)**, and **(D)** do not have errors.

12.   G

Category: Usage

Getting to the Answer: Check to see that idioms are matched with the correct prepositions. In sentence 3, "view it of a treatable condition" should be changed to "view it as a treatable condition." **(G)** is correct. **(E)**, **(F)**, and **(H)** do not have errors.

13.   A

Category: Usage

Getting to the Answer: A verb needs to agree with its subject in number, and the verb might not always appear close to its subject. In the first sentence, the subject "study" is singular, so the revision should include the verb phrase "has led." **(A)** is correct; **(B)**, **(C)**, and **(D)** have grammatically correct sentences.

14.   F

Category: Usage and Punctuation

Getting to the Answer: Use the relative pronouns "who" or "whom" to refer to people; use "that" or "which" to refer to any other kind of noun. Sentence 2 should begin with "Seniors who," so **(F)** is correct. Furthermore, the comma after "applications" is incorrect. **(E)**, **(G)**, and **(H)** introduce new errors.

15. A

Category: Organization

Getting to the Answer: (A) combines the three sentences clearly and concisely. **(B)** simply strings the three ideas together without relating them. **(C)** misuses the semicolon, since the second and third clauses are not independent. **(D)** is awkwardly worded and introduces an inconsistent verb tense.

16. H

Category: Usage

Getting to the Answer: Pronouns must agree in number with their antecedent nouns. Here, the "environment" under discussion is that of the "creatures"; since the noun "creatures" is plural, the appropriate possessive pronoun is "their," so **(H)** is correct. **(E)** introduces an incorrect verb tense. **(F)** is unnecessarily wordy. **(G)** uses the relative pronoun "who" in reference to "changes"; "who" should only be used when referring to people.

17. B

Category: Organization

Getting to the Answer: As written, sentence 9 is a fragment. Since it continues the idea of sentence 8, connecting the two sentences with a comma is the most logical way to fix the error, so **(B)** is correct. **(A)** misuses a semicolon. **(C)** is grammatically incorrect; a comma is needed before the coordinating conjunction "and." **(D)** does not connect the two ideas.

18. F

Category: Organization

Getting to the Answer: "There" at the beginning of sentence 11 indicates that this sentence would follow one that references a location. **(F)** forms a logical connection between Piaget's switch to the study of psychology and his eventual conclusion that environment impacts mental development, so **(F)** is correct. **(E)**, **(G)**, and **(H)** are illogical, as they do not place "There" near a location.

19. D

Category: Topic Development

Getting to the Answer: Every paragraph in a unified passage should stay on topic. The topic in this passage is Jean Piaget, so other psychologists—Skinner and Bandura—are off-topic and jarring. Remove sentence 10, **(D)**, to keep the focus on Piaget.

20. H

Category: Topic Development

Getting to the Answer: The final sentence in a passage should not introduce a topic not already mentioned. **(H)** is the logical sentence to end the passage since it concerns the use of Piaget's studies after his death. **(E)** would best be placed somewhere in paragraph 2. **(F)** is a rewording of some of the information in paragraph 1. **(G)** would incorrectly introduce topics not covered in the passage.

CHAPTER 6

Knowledge of Language

CHAPTER OBJECTIVES

By the end of this chapter, you will be able to:

- Revise redundant or wordy writing
- Identify and correct expressions that deviate from idiomatic English
- Identify the wording that accomplishes the appropriate purpose

Knowledge of Language

Well-written text is concise, precise, and consistent in tone. The SHSAT rewards your ability to identify and correct these Knowledge of Language issues.

Conciseness

A concise sentence does not include any unnecessary words. Phrasing that is wordy is considered stylistically incorrect on the SHSAT and needs to be revised. All words must contribute to the meaning of the sentence; otherwise, they should be eliminated or replaced with more concise wording.

A redundant sentence says something twice: "The new policy directly contributed to a crisis situation." A crisis is a type of situation, so there is no need to include both "crisis" and "situation." The sentence should be rephrased as "The new policy directly contributed to a crisis."

Wordy/Redundant Sentence	Concise Sentence
The superb musical score **added enhancement to the experience of** the play's development.	The superb musical score **enhanced** the play's development.
I **did not anticipate** the **surprising, unexpected** plot twist.	I **did not anticipate** the plot twist.
The students **increased some of their knowledge of** Tuscan architecture.	The students **learned about** Tuscan architecture.

Choose the most concise grammatically correct option that conveys the writer's intended meaning. When answering questions about conciseness:

- Identify the answer choice that creates the shortest sentence. (Note that this will not always be the correct answer, but it is an efficient place to start.)
- Identify words and phrases that have the same meaning (e.g., *thoughtful* and *mindful* or *end result* and *final outcome*). Find a choice that deletes one of the redundant expressions.

Practice

DIRECTIONS: Eliminate word(s) to make the sentences more concise without changing the writer's intended meaning.

    A. It is important to carefully consider and think about what kind of college you wish to attend.

    B. Often, a house cat will typically sleep for up to 16 hours per day.

    C. The whole team felt a sense of excited anticipation in the seconds before the whistle blew.

    D. My sister and I couldn't come to an agreement with each other about what movie we wanted to watch that afternoon.

    E. Noctilucent clouds appear approximately 82 kilometers above Earth's surface. This is an altitude which is seven times higher than commercial airlines fly.

DIRECTIONS: Read and answer the following questions, recognizing and correcting errors so that the sentences or paragraphs are grammatically correct. Re-read relevant parts of the text before choosing the best answer for each question.

1. Read this sentence.

> My sister and I spent nearly all of Saturday evening playing tennis at the park, but we had to stop when it became too difficult and challenging to see the ball.

Which edit should be made to correct this sentence?

    A. Delete *nearly*.

    B. Delete *we*.

    C. Delete *and challenging*.

    D. Delete *to see the ball*.

2. Read this paragraph.

> (1) Although Jane Austen's novels are most often admired for their eloquence and imagery, they are also highly esteemed for their subtle yet shrewd observations of nineteenth-century English society and the people living in it. (2) Austen drew from her experiences with family and acquaintances in various situations to create the characters and settings in her novels. (3) In the novel *Sense and Sensibility*, she demonstrated her sophisticated literary technique even when portraying ordinary events. (4) Consequently, Austen is respected and often beloved by people worldwide.

How should the paragraph be revised?

E. Sentence 1: Change *society and the people living in it* to **society**.

F. Sentence 2: Change *family and acquaintances* to **family**.

G. Sentence 3: Change *even when* to **when**.

H. Sentence 4: Change *respected and often beloved* to **respected**.

Precision

Some questions test your knowledge of the correct word to use in context. You must identify which word(s) best convey the writer's intended meaning.

Incorrect	Correct
The **initial** reason the students gather in the auditorium is that it is the only location large enough for all of them.	The **primary** reason the students gather in the auditorium is that it is the only location large enough for all of them.
It is common for children to **perform** the actions of their parents.	It is common for children to **mimic** the actions of their parents.
Zeke apologized for **attending** when he interrupted the private meeting.	Zeke apologized for **intruding** when he interrupted the private meeting.

A pronoun is ambiguous if its antecedent (the noun to which it refers) is either missing or unclear. When you see a pronoun, make sure you can identify the noun to which it refers and check whether the pronoun clearly refers to that noun.

Ambiguous Pronoun Use	Clear Pronoun Use
Anthony walked with Cody to the ice cream shop, and **he** bought a banana split.	Anthony walked with Cody to the ice cream shop, and **Cody** bought a banana split.

Read the surrounding text to identify the writer's intended meaning. Then evaluate the answer choices. Eliminate the answer choices that:

- Create grammatical errors
- Do not make sense in context
- Do not convey the writer's intended meaning

If one or more of the words among the answer choices are unfamiliar, process of elimination can help you get to the correct answer. If you recognize any of the options, decide whether to keep or eliminate them. For the words that remain, use roots, prefixes and suffixes, and word charge to make your decision. If all else fails, trust your instincts and guess; never leave a question blank.

Practice

> **DIRECTIONS:** Rewrite each sentence to more precisely reflect the writer's intended meaning.

A. The audience laughed as the person in front of them who was hired to tell jokes performed on stage.

B. The teacher offered to help Graciela organize her papers, which were stuffed in all sorts of ways in her backpack.

C. The cross-country road trip seemed like it would go on forever because it took two days longer than expected due to road construction.

D. Eitan is the type of person who is up for anything when it comes to food, willing to try everything from frog legs to wasp crackers.

E. The cow with a personality that many people found difficult to work with refused to leave the barn even though the farmer repeatedly tried to convince it to go outside.

> **DIRECTIONS:** Read and answer the following questions, recognizing and correcting errors so that the sentences or paragraphs are grammatically correct. Re-read relevant parts of the text before choosing the best answer for each question.

3. Read this sentence.

> Cameron made his math grade not as low as it had recently decreased by his completing of all available extra-credit projects.

Which revision uses the most precise language?

A. Cameron made his math grade better by asking for, completing, all available extra-credit projects.

B. Cameron worked on his math grade by his doing of all available extra-credit projects.

C. Cameron improved his math grade by completing all available extra-credit projects.

D. Cameron boosted his grade in math by working on and handing in all available extra-credit projects.

4. Read this sentence.

> The union agreed to concessions that included increasing wages, extending benefits, and giving them more vacation time.

How should the sentence be revised?

E. Increasing wages, extending benefits, and giving them more vacation time were concessions to which the union agreed.

F. The union agreed to concessions that included increasing wages, extending benefits, and giving full-time workers more vacation time.

G. The union agreed to three concessions: increasing wages, extending benefits, and giving them more vacation time.

H. The three concessions the union agreed to were increasing wages, extending benefits, and giving them more vacation time.

Style

A writer's style is the way in which the writer demonstrates a general attitude about a particular topic or idea. Writers select specific words to best convey their intended messages. Oftentimes, the tone of SHSAT Revising/Editing text is more formal than casual, so you'll need to eliminate answer choices that use informal words and phrases. In particular, vague phrases such as "a lot of things" and "stay on top of" do not usually match the style of the surrounding text and would not be featured in a correct answer choice.

Read the entire text to identify the writer's general style. Then evaluate the answer choices. Eliminate the answer choices that:

- Do not match the surrounding style
- Create grammatical errors
- Do not make sense in context
- Do not convey the writer's intended meaning

Process of elimination can help you identify the correct answer, so work through the options systematically. Cross out the choices that do not match the surrounding text and then select the most clear, concise, and relevant option.

Practice

> **DIRECTIONS:** Select the word or phrase that best matches the general style of each sentence.

A. The dreary weather darkened the skies, dampened spirits, and spread <u>sad feelings/gloom</u> throughout the city.

B. The <u>jubilant/happy</u> contestant shrieked with delight when the host revealed what she had won.

C. The final episode of the sitcom was easily the funniest of the entire series; each character <u>gave a hilarious performance/told a lot of jokes</u> that made even casual fans laugh.

D. The baseball team rode home in silence after a devastating loss at the <u>merciless/mean</u> hands of their biggest rivals.

E. The runner breathed deeply, heart racing and palms sweating, <u>waiting with apprehension/feeling really scared while waiting</u> for the start of the race.

> **DIRECTIONS:** Read and answer the following questions, recognizing and correcting errors so that the sentences or paragraphs are grammatically correct. Re-read relevant parts of the text before choosing the best answer for each question.

5. Read this paragraph.

> (1) Before tourism became a mainstay of the economy, the value of land in Mexico was defined by how well its soil could produce crops. (2) To many Americans, tropical tourist-oriented beach towns such as Acapulco and Puerto Vallarta characterize Mexico. (3) These may be the common types of destinations for foreign travelers, but they are certainly not representative of the entire country. (4) For better or worse, these cities, and others like them, are set up to be fun for lots of vacationers.

How should the paragraph be revised?

A. Sentence 1: Change *soil could produce crops* to **dirt could make plants grow**.

B. Sentence 2: Change *tropical tourist-oriented beach towns* to **hot, sunny vacation spots**.

C. Sentence 3: Change *destinations for foreign travelers* to **spots for people who are on vacation**.

D. Sentence 4: Change *fun for lots of vacationers* to **attractive to tourists**.

6. Read this paragraph.

> (1) Before 1793, when Eli Whitney invented the cotton gin, the method used to separate seeds from cotton fiber was enormously labor-intensive. (2) The new gadget had a rotating drum with wire spikes that took the fibers people actually wanted and tossed out seeds, which were basically garbage. (3) Hodgen Holmes improved upon Whitney's cotton gin by removing the spikes and installing a circular saw that further streamlined the process. (4) Today's cotton gins make use of the same simple yet effective principles.

Which revision of sentence 2 best maintains the formal style established in the paragraph?

E. The cotton gin consisted of a rotating drum with wire spikes that efficiently caught the desired fibers and left behind the unwanted seeds.

F. The new machine had a rotating drum with wire spikes that took the fibers people actually wanted and tossed out seeds, which weren't useful anyway.

G. The cotton gin had a rotating drum with wire spikes that caught the cotton fibers and left the unwanted seeds out of things.

H. The new machine had a rotating drum with wire spikes that took the fibers that were worth some money and tossed out seeds, which couldn't be sold for any sort of profit.

Practice Set

For test-like practice, give yourself 27 minutes (an average of 1 minute per stand-alone question and 1.5 minutes per passage-based question) to complete this question set. While many of the questions pertain to Knowledge of Language, some touch on other English Language Arts concepts to ensure that your practice is test-like, with a variety of question types. After you're done, be sure to study the explanations, even for questions you answered correctly. They can be found at the end of this chapter.

REVISING/EDITING Part A

DIRECTIONS: Answer the following questions, recognizing and correcting errors so that the sentences or paragraphs are grammatically correct. Re-read relevant parts of the text before choosing the best answer for each question.

---

1. Read this paragraph.

> (1) Babe Ruth started his career as a pitcher for the Boston Red Sox and then joined the New York Yankees. (2) In baseball's early days, hitting 20 home runs in a season was considered extraordinary, but that was drastically changed by Babe Ruth when he hit 54 home runs in 1920. (3) When he retired in 1935, he had made a total of 714 home runs. (4) Two movies about Babe Ruth feature his accomplishments, which include becoming the first player to hit three home runs in one game.

Which sentence contains an error in its construction and should be revised?

A. sentence 1

B. sentence 2

C. sentence 3

D. sentence 4

2. Read this paragraph.

> (1) The Northern Lights can awe many local residents, since they rarely appear in southern regions. (2) These shimmering lights occur most often near Earth's north and south magnetic poles. (3) When the mysterious presentations occur far away from the poles, they light up the sky more frequently during periods of solar activity such as sunspots. (4) It is important to note that the Northern Lights can display not only rays of intense colors but also shimmering arcs and bright curtains.

Which sentence contains an error in its construction and should be revised?

E. sentence 1

F. sentence 2

G. sentence 3

H. sentence 4

3. Read this paragraph.

> Recent fossil evidence suggests that carnivorous dinosaurs were accomplished swimmers. The *Baptornis* looked like a <u>diving bird whose small wings</u> could have helped it steer underwater. It probably <u>had webbed feet and</u> a torpedo-shaped body that would <u>have allowed it to</u> dive. If this dinosaur was indeed a <u>swimmer; it must</u> have used its small, sharp teeth to locate fish in central North America's shallow seas.

Which revision corrects the error in sentence structure in the paragraph?

A. diving bird; whose small wings

B. had webbed feet, and

C. have allowed it to,

D. a swimmer, it must

4. Read this paragraph.

> (1) Although eventually embraced by mainstream media, the term *blogging,* which refers to online journaling, was initially utilized only by cutting-edge Internet users. (2) The term *blog* is short for "web log," and anyone can create or share a blog. (3) When people go online, their searches might lead them to blogs that offer various types of instructions or the latest entertaining anecdotes. (4) Blogs can stay up-to-date because the Internet is so flexible, unlike a book, which need to be reprinted to correct mistakes, a web page can be corrected and relaunched in a matter of minutes.

Which sentence contains an error in its construction and should be revised?

E. sentence 1

F. sentence 2

G. sentence 3

H. sentence 4

5. Read this paragraph.

> (1) Recent experiments seem to indicate that the most effective defense against skin cancer is using sunscreen properly and consistently. (2) Today, 80 percent of Americans buy or purchase sunscreen, but they might need reminders to reapply it every two hours. (3) Melanoma and other types of skin cancer remain a problem, but careful sunscreen application minimizes the risk of skin damage. (4) In addition, people might consider switching to a more natural sunscreen, which is safer for human and marine life.

Which sentence contains an error in its construction and should be revised?

A. sentence 1

B. sentence 2

C. sentence 3

D. sentence 4

6. Read this paragraph.

> (1) According to Howard Gardner, there are people that learn best when they hear information, but most learners benefit from having visual displays. (2) College students have adapted to traditional types of instruction, yet even auditory learners tend to have multiple learning styles. (3) University professors are, therefore, frequently encouraged to utilize multimedia materials in their class presentations. (4) With new advances each day, educational technology offers students and educators a wealth of options.

Which sentence contains an error in its construction and should be revised?

E. sentence 1

F. sentence 2

G. sentence 3

H. sentence 4

REVISING/EDITING Part B

DIRECTIONS: Read each passage and answer the questions following it, improving the writing quality and correcting grammatical errors. Re-read relevant parts of the text before choosing the best answer for each question.

Noctilucent Clouds

(1) We generally agree that a change in atmospheric phenomena may signal pending changes to Earth's climate. (2) When NASA began to document increased sightings of noctilucent clouds in the latter half of the twentieth century, the agency instituted plans for a study to determine the cause and to learn what effect, if any, this may have on future weather patterns.

(3) This is because NLCs (as they are known in the scientific community) generally occur north of 50° latitude, above the polar region. (4) Noctilucent, or night-shining, clouds are virtually unknown to most people, even those who stargaze on a regular basis. (5) These clouds, however, are becoming increasingly visible in areas farther south. (6) In 1999, a dramatic display of NLCs appeared over Colorado and Utah, nearly 10° below the latitudes where scientists have come to expect them. (7) Seeing these things in Europe has also happened more and more in the past 50 years, for reasons that remain unsure.

(8) Ordinary clouds occur approximately 10 kilometers from Earth's surface. (9) Noctilucent clouds are found at about 82 kilometers. (10) This is more than seven times higher than commercial airlines fly. (11) Cirrus clouds are about six kilometers high. (12) Although most scientists believe NLCs are formed of ice crystals, some are convinced that they are composed of cosmic or volcanic dust. (13) This theory is most likely attributable to the fact that the first NLC sightings were documented following a large volcanic explosion in Indonesia.

(14) What might be the connection between NLCs and changing weather patterns? (15) Atmospheric scientist Gary Thomas has studied the fact that early NCL sightings came about at the same time that the Indonesian volcano Krakatoa first erupted in 1883, sending a great deal of polluting ash into the air, and also during the early part of the Industrial Revolution, which resulted in air and water pollution. (16) Other scientists speculate that an increase in greenhouse gasses makes the atmosphere cooler, which gives rise to more and wider-spread NCLs.

7. Which revision of sentence 1 best maintains the style established in the passage?

   A. I generally agree with NASA that a change in atmospheric phenomena may signal pending changes to Earth's climate.

   B. Scientists generally agree that a change in atmospheric phenomena may signal pending changes to Earth's climate.

   C. Scientists define noctilucent clouds as ice crystals that are only visible during astronomical twilight.

   D. Noctilucent clouds are ice crystals that are only visible during astronomical twilight.

8. Which transition phrase should be added to the beginning of sentence 2?

   E. Consequently, NASA began to document increased sightings of noctilucent clouds

   F. Usually, NASA document increased sightings of noctilucent clouds

   G. That is, NASA documented increased sightings of noctilucent clouds

   H. In this case, NASA began to document increased sightings of noctilucent clouds

9. Where should sentence 4 be moved in order to improve the organization of the second paragraph (sentences 3–7)?

   A. to the beginning of the paragraph (before sentence 3)

   B. between sentences 5 and 6

   C. between sentences 6 and 7

   D. to the end of the paragraph (after sentence 7)

10. Which revision of sentence 7 best maintains the formal style established in the passage?

    E. Over the past 50 years, for reasons that remain unsure, seeing these things in Europe has also become more frequent.

    F. Sightings of these things in Europe has also become more frequent in the past 50 years, for reasons that remain unclear.

    G. Sightings in Europe have also become more frequent in the past 50 years.

    H. Sightings in Europe have also become more frequent in the past 50 years, for reasons that remain unclear.

11. What is the best way to combine sentences 8, 9, and 10?

    A. Ordinary clouds occur approximately 10 kilometers from Earth's surface, noctilucent clouds are found at about 82 kilometers, and this is more than seven times higher than commercial airlines fly.

    B. Ordinary clouds occur approximately 10 kilometers from Earth's surface; while noctilucent clouds, being found at about 82 kilometers, which is more than seven times higher than commercial airlines fly.

    C. Ordinary clouds occur approximately 10 kilometers from Earth's surface, but noctilucent clouds are found at about 82 kilometers, which is more than seven times higher than commercial airlines fly.

    D. Ordinary clouds occur approximately 10 kilometers from Earth's surface, so noctilucent clouds are found at about 82 kilometers, which is more than seven times higher than commercial airlines fly.

12. Which sentence presents information that shifts away from the main topic of the third paragraph (sentences 8–13) and should be removed?

    E. sentence 10

    F. sentence 11

    G. sentence 12

    H. sentence 13

13. Which concluding sentence should be added after sentence 16 to support the topic presented in the final paragraph (sentences 14–16)?

    A. If changing weather and climate patterns on Earth stop, fewer NLCs will be seen by the scientists who study them.

    B. Scientists do not have any theories about the relationship between the more NLCs and changing weather and climate patterns on Earth.

    C. Though many scientists think that there is a connection between the increased appearance of NLCs and changing weather and climate patterns, this possible connection remains very controversial.

    D. In the next ten years, NLCs may become more common south of 50° latitude, suggesting changing weather and climate patterns.

Icebreakers

(1) Scientists working in the Arctic and Antarctic have been investigating the effects of climate change. (2) However, research on climate change could not be accomplished without the aid of a tough and reliable icebreaker, a tool which has only been around for slightly more than a hundred years.

(3) Before that, when people needed to sail in ice-clogged waters, they adapted their traditional ship designs. (4) The indigenous Arctic people, who have been faced with ice for millennia, used their lightweight kayaks to skim over the ice rather than break through it. (5) In the eleventh century, Russians who lived by Arctic shores built *kochi*, traditional sailing ships with skin-reinforced areas at the water line. (6) The winter of 1880–1881 also froze the Elbe river in Germany. (7) Steam-powered ships, with their vastly increased propelling strength, ushered in the age of icebreaker shipbuilding. (8) City Iceboat No. 1, constructed in 1837, had wood paddles reinforced with iron and was powered by two 250-horsepower steam engines. (9) Over time, ship ice-breaking capability continued to improve.

(10) The ice is instead crushed under the weight of the ship's bow, which is pushed through by powerful engines. (11) Though most people think that modern icebreakers literally break through the ice, in reality, icebreakers do not "push" the thick expanses of ice. (12) The ship then reverses, powers ahead, and runs up onto the ice again. (13) It clears a path for itself.

(14) This process is time-consuming because it can be up to 16 feet thick. (15) Rather, their ability to break through thick ice is due to several unique design features: the bow, the hull, and the propulsion system. (16) It must perform well in open water, too. (17) For example, the bow of an icebreaker does not go straight down, but rather slopes at a 30-degree angle.

(18) Aside from their role in helping scientists study climate change, icebreakers have other uses. (19) They are used to do helpful things about snow, ice, frozen ground, and other materials in cold places.

14. Which sentence presents information that shifts away from the main topic of the second paragraph (sentences 3–9)?

    E.   sentence 4

    F.   sentence 5

    G.   sentence 6

    H.   sentence 7

15. Where should sentence 10 be moved to improve the organization of the third paragraph (sentences 10–13)?

    A.   between sentences 11 and 12

    B.   between sentences 12 and 13

    C.   it does not need to be moved

    D.   to the end of the paragraph (after sentence 13)

16. What is the best way to combine sentences 12 and 13?

    E. The ship then reverses, powers ahead, and runs up onto the ice again, by which the vessel clears a path for itself.

    F. The ship then reverses, powers ahead, and runs up onto the ice again, because the vessel clears a path for itself.

    G. The ship then reverses, powers ahead, and runs up onto the ice again, and the vessel, clearing a path for itself.

    H. The ship then reverses, powers ahead, and runs up onto the ice again so that the vessel clears a path for itself.

17. Which revision of sentence 14 best supports the passage?

    A. This process is lengthy because it can be up to 16 feet thick.

    B. This process is time-consuming and lengthy because the ice can be up to 16 feet thick.

    C. This process is time-consuming because the ice can be up to 16 feet thick.

    D. This process is time-consuming because it can be up to 16 feet high.

18. Which sentence would best come before and support sentence 15?

    E. Icebreakers do not have an immense weight that breaks the ice.

    F. It's cold on an icebreaker.

    G. Icebreakers may lead to decreased global warming.

    H. Icebreakers are also used by the army.

19. Which sentence presents information that shifts away from the main topic of the third paragraph (sentences 14–17) and should be removed?

    A. sentence 14

    B. sentence 15

    C. sentence 16

    D. sentence 17

20. Which revision of sentence 19 best maintains the formal style established in the passage?

    E. They are used to conduct fundamental research about snow, ice, frozen ground, and other materials in cold places.

    F. They are used to conduct fundamental research to understand stuff about snow, ice, frozen ground, and other such materials in cold regions.

    G. They are used to conduct fundamental research to understand snow, ice, frozen ground, and other such cold things.

    H. They are used to conduct fundamental research to understand the nature and characteristics of snow, ice, frozen ground, and other materials in places such as Antarctica, the Arctic circle, and other cold areas.

Answers and Explanations

Conciseness

A. It is important to carefully consider ~~and think about~~ what kind of college you wish to attend.

B. ~~Often, a~~ **A** house cat will typically sleep for up to 16 hours per day.

C. The whole team felt ~~a sense of~~ **excited** ~~anticipation~~ in the seconds before the whistle blew.

D. My sister and I couldn't ~~come to an~~ **agreement** ~~with each other~~ about what movie we wanted to watch that afternoon.

E. Noctilucent clouds appear approximately 82 kilometers above Earth's surface. ~~This is an altitude,~~ which is seven times higher than commercial airlines fly.

1. C

Category: Knowledge of Language

Getting to the Answer: The question indicates that there is an error that needs to be corrected. The phrase "difficult and challenging" is redundant because "difficult" and "challenging" have the same meaning in this sentence, so **(C)** is correct. **(A)** and **(D)** are incorrect because they alter the meaning of the sentence. **(B)** is incorrect because it introduces an error; removing "we" makes the second clause dependent, so the comma in front of "but" would need to be deleted as well to make the sentence grammatically correct.

2. E

Category: Knowledge of Language

Getting to the Answer: Check each sentence systematically to locate the error since the question indicates that a revision is necessary. In sentence 1, the phrase "and the people living in it" is unnecessary because the word "society" directly refers to a group of people living in a community; **(E)** is correct. **(F)**, **(G)**, and **(H)** are incorrect because editing the phrases in sentences 2, 3, and 4 would alter the writer's intended meaning.

Precision

Note: These are not the only ways to correct the sentences; your answers may differ.

A. The audience laughed as the ~~person in front of them who was hired to tell jokes~~ **comedian** performed on stage.

B. The teacher offered to help Graciela organize her papers, which were **haphazardly** stuffed ~~in all sorts of ways~~ in her backpack.

C. The cross-country road trip seemed **interminable** ~~like it would go on forever~~ because it took two days longer than expected due to road construction.

D. Eitan is **an adventurous eater** ~~the type of person who is up for anything when it comes to food~~, willing to try everything from frog legs to wasp crackers.

E. The **stubborn** cow ~~with a personality that many people found difficult to work with~~ refused to leave the barn even though the farmer repeatedly tried to convince it to go outside.

3. C

Category: Knowledge of Language

Getting to the Answer: The question is asking for the most precise language. **(C)** is correct because "improved his math grade" and "by completing" replace the unnecessarily complicated phrases "made his math grade not as low as it had recently decreased" and "by his completing of." **(A)**, **(B)**, and **(D)** change the original wording, but they do not provide the most straightforward, precise language.

4. F

Category: Knowledge of Language

Getting to the Answer: The question indicates that there is a grammar issue that needs to be fixed. The pronoun "them" is ambiguous because it does not specify which group of people received more vacation time. **(F)** fixes the error by changing the ambiguous pronoun to a specific noun, "full-time workers." **(E)**, **(G)**, and **(H)** do not fix the pronoun ambiguity issue.

Style

A. The dreary weather darkened the skies, dampened spirits, and spread **gloom** throughout the city.

B. The **jubilant** contestant shrieked with delight when the host revealed what she had won.

C. The final episode of the sitcom was easily the funniest of the entire series; each character **gave a hilarious performance** that made even casual fans laugh.

D. The baseball team rode home in silence after a devastating loss at the **merciless** hands of their biggest rivals.

E. The runner breathed deeply, heart racing and palms sweating, **waiting with apprehension** for the start of the race.

5. D

Category: Knowledge of Language

Getting to the Answer: The paragraph uses descriptive vocabulary to discuss the way foreign travelers often view and experience Mexico. In sentence 4, the phrase "fun for lots of vacationers" is too informal to match the style of the rest of the paragraph and should be changed; **(D)** is correct. **(A)**, **(B)**, and **(C)** are incorrect because they offer informal phrases that would be out of place in this paragraph.

6. E

Category: Knowledge of Language

Getting to the Answer: The paragraph has a straightforward, scholarly style that is not reflected in sentence 2. Look for the choice that uses higher-level, formal vocabulary while explaining the cotton gin like a textbook would. **(E)** is both formal and informative, so it is correct. **(F)**, **(G)**, and **(H)** are incorrect because they contain phrases such as "tossed out," "out of things," and "any sort of," which do not match the tone of the surrounding text.

Practice Set

1. B

Category: Knowledge of Language

Getting to the Answer: Sentence 2 makes an ambiguous reference to something that *was drastically changed*. The sentence should instead include a specific subject, such as *that record*. **(B)** is correct. All the other sentences are free of errors.

2. E

Category: Knowledge of Language

Getting to the Answer: In sentence 1, the pronoun "they" is ambiguous, since it could refer to either of the sentence's plural nouns: "Northern Lights" or "residents." **(E)** is correct. In **(F)**, **(G)**, and **(H)**, there are no errors.

3. D

Category: Punctuation

Getting to the Answer: All the answers deal with commas or semicolons. In **(D)**, changing the semicolon to a comma corrects a sentence fragment. All the other sentences use correct punctuation, so **(A)**, **(B)**, and **(C)** create new errors.

4. H

Category: Usage

Getting to the Answer: **(H)** is correct because sentence 4 has a subject-verb agreement error between "book" and "need." **(E)**, **(F)**, and **(G)** do not have errors.

5. B

Category: Knowledge of Language

Getting to the Answer: Using two words with the same meaning in one sentence is redundant. **(B)** is correct; "buy" and "purchase" mean the same thing. **(A)**, **(C)**, and **(D)** do not have any issues.

6. E

Category: Knowledge of Language

Getting to the Answer: Sentences use the relative pronouns "who" or "whom" to refer to people and "that" or "which" to refer to any other kind of noun. **(E)** is correct because "that learn" incorrectly follows "people." **(F)**, **(G)**, and **(H)** do not have errors.

7. B

Category: Knowledge of Language

Getting to the Answer: As it is written, the use of "we" does not fit the rest of the passage, which uses the third person. **(B)** correctly fixes the point-of-view error. **(A)** switches into the first person singular. **(C)** and **(D)** fix the point-of-view error, but they both change the author's meaning.

8. E

Category: Organization

Getting to the Answer: Transitions show connections between ideas in the passage. The correct answer will show how sentences 1 and 2 relate to each other. **(E)** correctly shows a cause-and-effect relationship. **(F)** shows a generalization relationship. **(G)** introduces a restatement of the last idea. **(H)** introduces an example of the last statement.

9. A

Category: Organization

Getting to the Answer: Sentence 3 starts with "This is," showing that it offers an explanation for something in the passage. Its explanation describes what sentence 4 discusses, so sentence 4 needs to come before sentence 3. **(A)** has this correct placement. **(B), (C)** and **(D)** all offer placements that do not make sense.

10. H

Category: Knowledge of Language

Getting to the Answer: Sentence 7 uses vague and imprecise language and needs to be corrected. **(H)** correctly uses precise and specific language. **(E)** and **(F)** do not fix the vagueness of the original sentence. **(G)** fixes the vague language, but it also changes the meaning of the sentence by removing the idea that scientists do not know why there has been an increase in sightings.

11. C

Category: Topic Development

Getting to the Answer: When combining sentences, the relationship between ideas must be maintained. **(C)** combines the sentences correctly using "but" to indicate the contrast between the first two clauses and

"which" to make the third clause subordinate. **(A)** merely strings the sentences together without relating their ideas. **(B)** misuses the semicolon splice, since the second clause is not independent. In **(D)**, the transition word "so" indicates an incorrect cause-and-effect relationship between the first and second clauses.

12. F

Category: Topic Development

Getting to the Answer: The focus of the passage is on what NLCs are and how they might affect Earth's weather. **(F)** is correct; sentence 11 shifts the focus to cirrus clouds and should be removed. All other sentences are in line with the focus of the passage.

13. C

Category: Topic Development

Getting to the Answer: The final paragraph talks about two theories on why sightings of NLCs occur. **(C)** correctly continues this topic. **(A)** and **(D)** both change the focus away from the main topic. **(B)** contradicts the rest of the passage, making it illogical.

14. G

Category: Topic Development

Getting to the Answer: This paragraph is about the history of icebreaking ships. **(G)** correctly removes sentence 6; the fact that the Elbe froze is not relevant to the topic. All of the other sentences are focused on the topic of the history of icebreakers.

15. A

Category: Organization

Getting to the Answer: The word "instead" suggests that sentence 10 presents an idea in contrast to a previous statement. **(A)** correctly places the sentence after sentence 11, providing a contrast between the idea of how "most people think that modern icebreakers" work and the description introduced in sentence 10.

16. H

Category: Knowledge of Language

Getting to the Answer: The use of "it" and "itself" is unclear in sentence 13. **(H)** clarifies the ambiguous pronouns. **(E)** contains an illogical antecedent for the word "which." **(F)** creates an illogical cause-and-effect relationship between the clauses. **(G)** leaves the meaning of the second clause incomplete.

17. C

Category: Knowledge of Language

Getting to the Answer: In context, the meaning of the pronoun "it" is unclear. **(C)** eliminates the ambiguity by specifying that "it" is "the ice." **(A)** and **(D)** do not addresses the error. Although **(B)** fixes the error, it creates a redundancy between "time-consuming" and "lengthy."

18. E

Category: Topic Development

Getting to the Answer: Use context clues to determine the proper placement of new information. Since sentence 15 begins with "Rather," the sentence that comes before it should provide a contrast to the idea that design features are what allow icebreakers to do their job. **(E)** correctly provides this contrast. **(F)** is Out of Scope and also uses a pronoun without a clear antecedent. **(G)** and **(H)** shift the focus of the paragraph to topics discussed in other paragraphs.

19. C

Category: Topic Development

Getting to the Answer: The topic of the paragraph is icebreaking, so the correct answer is the sentence that does not focus on this topic. **(C)** correctly identifies the shift in sentence 16 from icebreaking to running on open water. **(A)**, **(B)**, and **(D)** all support the topic of the paragraph and should not be removed.

20. H

Category: Knowledge of Language

Getting to the Answer: Sentence 19 uses vague and imprecise language in the statement "helpful things." **(H)** correctly uses precise and specific language. **(E)** uses the vague "other materials in cold places." **(F)** incorrectly uses "other such materials in cold regions." **(G)** is imprecise because of "other such cold things."

CHAPTER 7

Organization & Topic Development

CHAPTER OBJECTIVES

By the end of this chapter, you will be able to:

- Determine the need for transition words or phrases to establish logical relationships within and between paragraphs
- Determine the most logical place for a sentence in a paragraph or passage
- Determine the relevance of a sentence within a passage
- Provide an introduction or conclusion to a paragraph or passage
- Provide supporting text for a paragraph or passage

Organization & Topic Development

Organization

Organization questions require you to read specific text and assess the logic and coherence, or how well it can be understood. These questions differ in scope; you might be asked to organize the writing at the level of a sentence, a paragraph, or even an entire passage.

Writers use transitions to show relationships such as contrast, cause and effect, continuation, emphasis, and chronology (order of events). Knowing which words indicate which type of transition will help you choose the correct answer on Test Day.

Contrast Transitions	Cause-and-Effect Transitions	Continuation Transitions	Emphasis Transitions	Chronology Transitions
although, but, despite, even though, however, in contrast, nonetheless, on the other hand, rather than, though, unlike, while, yet	as a result, because, consequently, since, so, therefore, thus	also, furthermore, in addition, moreover	certainly, in fact, indeed, that is	before, after, first (second, etc.), then, finally

Questions may ask you to combine sentences to clarify the relationship between the ideas. The question may be a standalone question or accompany a passage. Your goal is to ensure that information and ideas are logically conveyed using correct grammar.

Some Organization questions task you with moving a sentence to improve the organization of a paragraph within the passage. To answer these questions effectively, evaluate each answer choice by looking for keywords that indicate where the sentence should be placed. If the sentence you are moving starts with "For example," you need to place the sentence after a statement that it would best support. If the sentence includes a chronological transition such as "next" or "after that," it must be placed in the most logical spot within a sequence of events the writer is discussing.

Other questions will ask you to check and potentially fix the placement of a sentence within a paragraph (or a paragraph within a passage, though this is rare). Others will ask you for the best place to insert a new sentence. Your approach in both cases should be the same.

Transitions

If a question asks about a transition word, phrase, or sentence, determine the writer's intended meaning and select the transition that best conveys this information.

Combining Sentences

Process of elimination is an important strategy for combining sentences. Eliminate any option that creates a comparison or relationship the writer did not intend. For example, if a writer presents two related ideas that convey similar information, you can cross out choices that use contrast transitions such as "but," "however," or "although."

Moving Sentences

Look for specific clues that indicate the best organization. Common clues include:

- **Chronology:** If the information is presented in order by the time when it occurred, place the sentence within the correct time frame.

- **Explanation of a term or phrase:** If the passage features a term, the writer will explain what it is before using the term in other contexts.

- **Introduction of a person:** If the passage introduces someone, such as Grace Hopper, the writer will first refer to the person by first and last name before referring to the person by either first name (Grace) or last name (Hopper) only.

- **Examples:** A general statement is often followed by support in the form of examples.

- **Logic:** Transition words such as "however," "also," "furthermore," and "therefore" may signal the logic of the paragraph. For example, the word "therefore" indicates that a conclusion is being drawn from evidence that should logically come before it.

Practice

> **DIRECTIONS:** Select the transition that most accurately reflects the writer's intended meaning.

- **A.** The train was delayed; (<u>therefore/in addition</u>), we arrived at our destination two hours late.

- **B.** (<u>Since/Although</u>) the critics agreed that the movie was terrible, I went to see it anyway.

- **C.** We need to finish our project (<u>consequently/before</u>) we leave this afternoon.

- **D.** The hiking trail was difficult to navigate; (<u>finally/indeed</u>), state park guidelines recommend that only experienced hikers attempt the climb.

- **E.** The morphology of the amoeba is more complex than you might expect; (<u>furthermore/in contrast</u>), the mechanism underlying amoeboid motion is still not fully understood.

DIRECTIONS: Read the text below and answer the questions following it, improving the writing quality and correcting grammatical errors. Re-read relevant parts of the text before choosing the best answer for each question.

The Vinland Map

(1) One of the most notorious pieces in the Yale University Library is the Vinland map. (2) Valued at $1 million when it was donated in the 1950s, the map and its authenticity has been hotly debated for years. (3) It is alleged to be a fifteenth-century artifact of the Vikings' first voyage to North America. (4) Chemical analyses of its ink indicate that it could be a modern forgery on previously blank fifteenth-century parchment. (5) Many experts are convinced that the map is a reproduction, controversy remains.

(6) The Vinland map is not the only one for which authentication is difficult. (7) There are several benchmarks that experts use to make that decision. (8) In 1972, a team of specialists identified titanium dioxide in the ink. (9) That component in ink has been used in certain pigments only since the 1920s, providing support that the Vinland map is a fake. (10) Early paper was handmade from the pulp of rags mixed with liquid, then spread out to dry. (11) The result was paper that was usually of uneven thickness. (12) Even when machine-made paper became available, and thickness was more regular, paper quality varied. (13) Authentic maps were most often produced on high quality, low acidity paper. (14) Experts have found that color, printing techniques, text, and stitching can provide useful clues about the date and authenticity of a map, too. (15) Paper can also provide essential clues that help experts determine if a map is genuine.

(16) Fake maps have value since it takes time and effort to make them. (17) Some reproductions are products of highly-skilled artistic talent achieved only after years of honing one's craft. (18) For the Vinland map—and others shown to be superb but fake—a question remains: if these maps do not have the same value as true artifacts, will they retain historical worth as great forgeries of modern times?

1. What is the best way to combine sentences 3 and 4?

   A. It is alleged to be a fifteenth-century artifact of the Vikings' first voyage to North America, and chemical analyses of its ink indicate that it could be a modern forgery on previously blank fifteenth-century parchment.

   B. While it is alleged to be a fifteenth-century artifact of the Vikings' first voyage to North America, chemical analyses of its ink indicate that it could be a modern forgery on previously blank fifteenth-century parchment.

   C. Because it is alleged to be a fifteenth-century artifact of the Vikings' first voyage to North America, chemical analyses of its ink indicate that it could be a modern forgery on previously blank fifteenth-century parchment.

   D. Chemical analyses of the ink in the Vinland map, which is alleged to be a fifteenth-century artifact of the Vikings' first voyage to North America, indicate that it could be a modern forgery on previously blank fifteenth-century parchment.

2. Which transition should be added to the beginning of sentence 5?

    E.   Although

    F.   Because

    G.   Since

    H.   Given that

3. Where should sentence 15 be moved to improve the organization of the second paragraph (sentences 6–15)?

    A.   to the beginning of the paragraph (before sentence 6)

    B.   between sentences 7 and 8

    C.   between sentences 9 and 10

    D.   between sentences 13 and 14

4. Which revision of sentence 16 provides the best transition to the argument in the third paragraph (sentences 16–18)?

    E.   Fake maps may have anywhere from a little to a lot of value.

    F.   The amount of skill required to make fake maps is directly proportional to their value.

    G.   It is worth considering how much value fake maps may have.

    H.   Experts often believe that fake maps do not have any value because it is illegal to create forgeries.

Topic Development

Topic Development questions test your ability to determine why a passage is written and whether particular information helps accomplish that purpose.

Some Topic Development questions task you with adding or replacing sentences to better support the information in the passage. To answer these questions effectively, determine the writer's intended purpose, eliminate answer choices that do not reflect this purpose, and choose the most correct and relevant option.

SHSAT EXPERT NOTE

While conciseness is important, it should not be a primary goal when answering Topic Development questions. Instead, focus on picking answer choices that make the most sense logically, given your understanding of the writer's tone and purpose.

When asked to delete information, determine which sentence does not specifically relate to the development of the passage. The passage should flow smoothly and logically when the irrelevant sentence is removed.

Take the time to determine the writer's intended purpose before selecting an answer. Correct answers will include information that the writer would agree is both relevant and in keeping with the general style and tone of the passage as a whole.

Practice

DIRECTIONS: Underline a single phrase within each sentence that best conveys the main idea.

A. The plane ride was long because we had two long layovers, one in Dallas and one in Los Angeles.

B. After walking up and down each aisle at least three times, I chose a perfect present for my sister.

C. My dog, Bailey, is stubborn; no matter what I do, Bailey will not sit, shake, or roll over even though she knows how.

D. Before the library opened for the day, I helped the librarian organize various books and toys as well as several games because we wanted story hour to go well.

E. I was very hungry, so I helped myself to soup, salad, chicken, rice, and green beans.

DIRECTIONS: Read the text below and answer the questions following it, improving the writing quality and correcting grammatical errors. Re-read relevant parts of the text before choosing the best answer for each question.

Irrigation

(1) Irrigation is a process in which plants are watered by controlled release of river or lake water, especially in areas with insufficient rainfall or during particularly dry seasons. (2) The need for irrigation is a major reason why early settlements formed near rivers; rivers were their source of water not only for drinking and cooking, but also for watering crops.

(3) The ancient Egyptians controlled water coming from the annual flooding of the Nile River to inundate the planting land. (4) Ancient Persians used a system of sloping wells and tunnels to direct water to their barley fields. (5) The Dujiangyan Irrigation System, built in 256 B.C.E. in the Sichuan region of China, irrigated an enormous area of farmland. (6) Even today, it provides water for over 5,300 square kilometers of agricultural land. (7) In North America, the Hohokam people, a native culture living in what is now central Arizona, constructed canals to irrigate their crops of cotton, tobacco, and maize, among other crops. (8) The Hohokam are also known for their establishment of trading posts. (9) Modern irrigation systems, using powerful diesel and electric engines, have enormously increased the amount of both groundwater and either river or lake water that can be directed toward crops. (10) However, such irrigation can have the negative effect of depleting water faster than it can be replenished.

(11) The reasons for the influence of irrigation are twofold. (12) The development of irrigation allowed for extremely efficient agricultural production, creating the surplus of food resources, which must serve as the foundation for any civilization. (13) Furthermore, constructing the elaborate system of canals and drainage networks is a task of tremendous complexity. (14) The tough work that made irrigation possible was worth the effort because it led to important things.

1. Which sentence should follow sentence 2 to best state the main claim in the passage?

   A. Irrigation is definitely something people had to figure out if they wanted plants to grow.

   B. The first irrigation processes in Australia were centered around the Murray-Darling system, located in the southwest portion of the continent.

   C. If ancient people didn't find a way to get water, they weren't going to have an easy time making a city that could survive.

   D. There is considerable evidence that irrigation may have played a pivotal role in the foundation of the earliest civilizations, such as that of Sumer in the Tigris-Euphrates valley.

2. Which sentence presents information that shifts away from the main topic of the second paragraph (sentences 3–10) and should be removed?

   E. sentence 6

   F. sentence 7

   G. sentence 8

   H. sentence 9

3. Which sentence would best follow and support sentence 10?

   A. There are other irrigation problems, but irrigation has a long history.

   B. Despite some negative results of irrigation, it has been and remains crucial to the development of communities.

   C. There are several reasons why irrigation is important.

   D. Ancient civilizations took the bad and the good of irrigation in stride.

4. Which concluding sentence should replace sentence 14 to best support the topic presented in the passage?

   E. The really important science that made irrigation an actual option for people led to important cities being built.

   F. The centers of commerce, administration, and science that accomplished the task eventually blossomed into the cities that served as the cornerstones of many ancient civilizations.

   G. Irrigation was great in two ways: the building of it and the stuff that happened as a result.

   H. Between 550 and 200 B.C.E., there were noteworthy improvements in not only the irrigation-related features but also the extensive canal systems throughout Mexico.

Practice Set

For test-like practice, give yourself 26 minutes (an average of 1 minute per stand-alone question and 1.5 minutes per passage-based question) to complete this question set. While many of the questions pertain to Organization and Topic Development, some touch on other English Language Arts concepts to ensure that your practice is test-like, with a variety of question types. After you're done, be sure to study the explanations, even for questions you answered correctly. They can be found at the end of this chapter.

REVISING/EDITING Part A

DIRECTIONS: Answer the following questions, recognizing and correcting errors so that the sentences or paragraphs are grammatically correct. Re-read relevant parts of the text before choosing the best answer for each question.

---

1. Read this paragraph.

> Samuel Barber composed numerous symphonies, operas, and <u>quartets,</u> <u>all</u> of which express personal emotion. Encouraged by his musical family, he took <u>piano and vocal</u> lessons and began composing the first piece of his musical career at age seven. Although the orchestral arrangement is more <u>famous Samuel</u> Barber's *Adagio* was originally written for string quartet. For an <u>American,</u> <u>Barber</u> had impressive command of operatic tradition, which helped him earn two Pulitzer Prizes.

Which revision corrects the error in sentence structure in the paragraph?

A. quartets; all

B. piano, vocal

C. famous, Samuel

D. American. Barber

2. Read this paragraph.

> (1) Technology has greatly improved bicycles over the years; in 1868, the first known bike race featured bicycles that each weighed 160 pounds. (2) Today, racing bicycles weigh under twenty pounds. (3) These lighter bikes, often without brakes and gears are used by professional cyclists for time trials. (4) These bicycles also have specialized racing tires with an inner tube made of thin rubber and an outer tire cover made of cotton or silk.

Which sentence contains an error in its construction and should be revised?

E. sentence 1

F. sentence 2

G. sentence 3

H. sentence 4

3. Read this paragraph.

> (1) Rosalind Franklin used the technique of X-ray crystallography to depict the structure of DNA by mapping the basic structure of the tiny molecules. (2) Because she has been celebrated by today's genetic researchers, Franklin was never recognized during her lifetime for her groundbreaking work. (3) Her valuable photos of a hydrated form of DNA greatly helped Watson and Crick portray the full structure of DNA. (4) As a result, these men received the Nobel Prize for their work.

Which sentence contains an error in its construction and should be revised?

A. sentence 1

B. sentence 2

C. sentence 3

D. sentence 4

4. Read this paragraph.

> (1) Homeopathic remedies, though less widely prescribed than more traditional medications, are of interest to many consumers. (2) This alternative system of natural treatment began in the nineteenth century. (3) According to homeopathic theory, a disease can be treated with remedies having effects that mimic the ailment. (4) Patients may have chosen to use a homeopathic remedy to avoid the side effects of conventional medicines, get relief when these medicines failed or reduce the cost of treatment.

How should the paragraph be revised?

E. Sentence 1: Change *prescribed* to **prescribe**, AND delete the comma after *are*.

F. Sentence 2: Change *began* to **had begun**, AND insert a comma after *treatment*.

G. Sentence 3: Change *can be* to **will be**, AND insert a comma after *remedies*.

H. Sentence 4: Change *have chosen* to **choose**, AND insert a comma after *failed*.

5. Read this paragraph.

> The island continent of Australia consists of plateaus, ranges, plains, and coasts, which attract tourists and other people seeking adventure. Most Australians live in the warm and sunny coastal cities, including Sydney. Over the years, immigrants have arrived from places such as Europe and the United States for the gold rushes, many other reasons.

Which revision corrects the error in sentence structure in the paragraph?

A. island and continent

B. coast. Which

C. warm, sunny

D. rushes, among

6. Read this paragraph.

> (1) Dolores Huerta, one of the founders of the United Farm Workers union, has been a tireless advocate for California's field workers. (2) The combined efforts of the United Farm Workers union also included the work of Cesar Chavez, who organized the Chicano migrant farmers in California. (3) Both worked hard to help farmworkers. (4) After persevering through confrontations, strikes, and pickets, farmworkers eventually received improved working conditions.

Which sentence contains an error in its construction and should be revised?

E. sentence 1

F. sentence 2

G. sentence 3

H. sentence 4

7. Read these sentences.

> (1) The restaurant has had good business over the past two years.
> (2) An increase in business has allowed the restaurant to expand.

What is the best way to combine the sentences to clarify the relationship between the ideas?

A. Despite having good business over the past two years, the restaurant has been able to expand.

B. The restaurant expanded, increasing the restaurant's business over the past two years.

C. Because it has had good business over the past two years, the restaurant expanded.

D. For two years, the restaurant has had good business, expanding its business.

8. Read this paragraph.

> (1) To dissect vital communications, the cryptologist, a specialist in the technology of deciphering messages, typically employs a host of complex mathematical formulas. (2) For example, the specialist unlocks codes and ciphers, which are devices that secretly send information. (3) Machines create complex messages consisting of letters, words, numbers, or symbols. (4) During wartime, international groups have attempted to monitor and solve systems even though having the opponent's information could provide a major advantage.

Which sentence contains an error in its construction and should be revised?

E. sentence 1

F. sentence 2

G. sentence 3

H. sentence 4

REVISING/EDITING Part B

DIRECTIONS: Read each passage and answer the questions following it, improving the writing quality and correcting grammatical errors. Re-read relevant parts of the text before choosing the best answer for each question.

Music Education

(1) A few years ago, after much debate and countless budget meetings, my high school decided to eliminate all music programs. (2) My friends and I disagreed with the decision, so we developed a pamphlet that discussed our opinions, complete with persuasive anecdotes and compelling arguments, such as the way music and math work together and how some of the most intelligent and interesting people, like Albert Einstein, played musical instruments. (3) We handed out pamphlets to a lot of students, and many of them approached us after reading the material and said that we changed the way they thought about music. (4) Those comments made us feel that we were really effecting our school atmosphere. (5) We hoped our actions would make the school change its policy and reinstate music programs in the curriculum.

(6) We hoped in vain. (7) There will be no chorus, band, or string classes, let alone private lessons or music theory. (8) The school board said that it was because music wasn't an important skill to develop in comparison to math, English, and science. (9) I understand the need to focus on core academics, but experts have shown that the development of musical ability can improve many aspects of a person's life. (10) I strongly disagree with my school's decision. (11) Music teaches you to listen for patterns and ideas that aren't in words. (12) Learning how to read and perform music is like learning a second language—it is the same because it's another way to express yourself.

(13) Furthermore, learning how to play an instrument fosters important skill development. (14) In particular, discipline, concentration, and practice are skills that are equally important for school. (15) In fact, studies show that students should practice their instruments no more than two hours each day. (16) People should be informed about the importance of music education, and students must work to provide this information.

9. Which revision of sentence 4 best maintains the style established in the passage?

   A. Those comments made them feel that we were really effecting our school atmosphere.

   B. Those comments made them feel that we were really affecting our school atmosphere.

   C. Those comments made us feel that we were really affecting our school atmosphere.

   D. Those comments made us feel that we were really affecting our school and academic atmosphere.

10. Which transitional phrase should be added to the beginning of sentence 6?

   E. Thus

   F. However

   G. Hence

   H. Therefore

11. Which sentence can best follow sentence 6 and support the second paragraph?

    A. We were too optimistic.

    B. Our pamphlet was very effective.

    C. The school continued their policies.

    D. The school continued its policy.

12. Where should sentence 10 be moved to improve the organization of the second paragraph (sentences 3–12)?

    E. between sentences 7 and 8

    F. between sentences 8 and 9

    G. between sentences 11 and 12

    H. to the end of the paragraph (after sentence 12)

13. Which revision of sentence 12 best maintains the style established in the passage?

    A. Learning how to read music and perform it is like learning a second language—because it's another way to express yourself.

    B. Learning how to read and perform music is like learning a second language—it is the same way to express yourself.

    C. Learning how to read and perform music is like learning a second language—music is the same because it's another way to express yourself.

    D. Learning how to read and perform music is like learning a second language—it's another way to express yourself.

14. Which sentence presents information that shifts away from the main topic of the third paragraph (sentences 13–16) and should be removed?

    E. sentence 13

    F. sentence 14

    G. sentence 15

    H. sentence 16

Nizhny Novgorod

(1) The Russian city of Nizhny Novgorod has long been an important city in the Volga Vyatka economic region of the country. (2) Substantially contributing to the gross national product. (3) Founded in 1221, it stands at the meeting of two great rivers, the Volga and the Oka. (4) Its history was one of invasion and battle until 1612, when the Russian Romanov dynasty was established. (5) Nizhny Novgorod became a cultural center, with museums, art galleries, concert halls, and theaters.

(6) Perhaps its most famous museum is the Nizhny Novgorod State Art Museum, founded in 1896. (7) In that same year, it was part of a grand exhibition of art and industry. (8) It featured industrial exhibits including the first Russian car, a radio receiver, oil products, and other examples of new Russian technology. (9) The exhibit showcased two conflicting visions of Russian art, one of which was avant-garde. (10) It was the art, however, which generated a storm of controversy in Russian newspapers. (11) There were numerous examples of various avant-garde art movements. (12) These included Cubo-Futurism, Neo-primitivism, Suprematism, and others. (13) The other art form was more academic, and according to some critics, very superficial. (14) Of the critics raising their voices on the matter, it is Maxim Gorky who is most remembered. (15) Gorky was a distinguished Russian author and activist. (16) The fact that he was quite young at the time, Gorky's opinions on the exhibit would prove to be remarkably in keeping with his political beliefs later in life.

(17) As Gorky saw it, the majority of the art on display had been generated by an economy of exploitation that only rewarded artists who created works inaccessible to the general population, such as those in the avant-garde styles. (18) Gorky took the side of those deriding the artwork as aimed only at the elite, and stated, "It is not artists, but the public who need art, and therefore the public should be given such paintings as it can understand." (19) This was an early manifestation of his later political activism as a supporter of the new Marxist-Socialist movement. (20) Nizhny Novgorod was renamed Gorky from 1932–1990.

15. What is the best way to combine sentences 1 and 2?

   A. The Russian city of Nizhny Novgorod has long been an important city in the Volga Vyatka economic region of the country; substantially contributing to the gross national product.

   B. The Russian city of Nizhny Novgorod has long been an important city in the Volga Vyatka economic region of the country, however, substantially contributing to the gross national product.

   C. The Russian city of Nizhny Novgorod has long been an important city in the Volga Vyatka economic region of the country, substantially contributing to the gross national product.

   D. The Russian city of Nizhny Novgorod, has long been an important city in the Volga Vyatka economic region of the country, whereas it substantially contributes to the gross national product.

16. What is the best way to combine sentences 7 and 8 to clarify the relationship between ideas?

    E. In that same year, it was part of a grand exhibition of art and industry, it featured industrial exhibits including the first Russian car, a radio receiver, oil products, and other examples of new Russian technology.

    F. In that same year, it was part of a grand exhibition of art and industry featuring industrial exhibits including the first Russian car, a radio receiver, oil products, and other examples of new Russian technology.

    G. In that same year, it was part of a grand exhibition of art and industry; featuring industrial exhibits including the first Russian car, a radio receiver, oil products, and other examples of new Russian technology.

    H. In that same year, it was part of a grand exhibition of art and industry, which featured industrial exhibits including the first Russian car, a radio receiver, oil products, and other examples of new Russian technology.

17. Where should sentence 10 be moved to improve the organization of the second paragraph (sentences 6–16)?

    A. to the beginning of the paragraph (before sentence 6)
    B. between sentences 6 and 7
    C. between sentences 8 and 9
    D. between sentences 12 and 13

18. What is the best way to combine sentences 11 and 12 to clarify the relationship between ideas?

    E. There were numerous examples of various avant-garde art movements, includes Cubo-Futurism, Neo-primitivism, Suprematism, and others.

    F. There were numerous examples of various avant-garde art movements; some of the examples of avant-garde art movements included Cubo-Futurism, Neo-primitivism, Suprematism, and others.

    G. There were numerous examples of various avant-garde art movements not excepting Cubo-Futurism, Neo-primitivism, Suprematism, and others.

    H. There were numerous examples of various avant-garde art movements, including Cubo-Futurism, Neo-primitivism, Suprematism, and others.

19. Which transition phrase should be added to the beginning of sentence 16?

    A. In fact
    B. Despite
    C. All in all
    D. In essence

20. Which sentence presents information that shifts away from the man topic of the third paragraph (sentences 17–20) and should be removed?

    E. sentence 17
    F. sentence 18
    G. sentence 19
    H. sentence 20

Answers and Explanations

Organization

A. The train was delayed; **therefore**, we arrived at our destination two hours late.

B. **Although** the critics agreed that the movie was terrible, I went to see it anyway.

C. We need to finish our project **before** we leave this afternoon.

D. The hiking trail was difficult to navigate; **indeed**, state park guidelines recommend that only experienced hikers attempt the climb.

E. The morphology of the amoeba is more complex than you might expect; **furthermore**, the mechanism underlying amoeboid motion is still not fully understood.

1. B
Category: Organization

Getting to the Answer: The question asks you to combine two sentences, so the first step is to determine the relationship between them. Sentence 3 states that the map is thought to be from the fifteenth century, and sentence 4 states that ink indicates that it may be a forgery, or a copy, rather than a document that was actually created hundreds of years ago. The two sentences offer contrasting, or opposite, ideas, so using a contrast transition to combine them would work well. **(B)** is correct because the contrast transition "While" logically conveys the writer's intended meaning. **(A)**, **(C)**, and **(D)** are incorrect because the transitions "and," "Because," and "which" do not show a necessary contrast.

2. E
Category: Organization

Getting to the Answer: The question asks which transition should be added, so read sentence 5 to determine the best word or phrase to use. The first part of the sentence says that many experts think the map is fake. However, the final phrase says, "controversy remains," which indicates that some people may not agree with the experts who think the map is a forgery. The two opposing ideas are best conveyed using the contrast keyword "Although," so **(E)** is correct. **(F)**, **(G)**, and **(H)** are incorrect because they use continuation keywords, which do not make sense in context.

3. C
Category: Organization

Getting to the Answer: The question indicates that sentence 15 needs to be moved, so you need to look for specific clues that indicate the best place to relocate it. Sentence 15 states that paper can help experts determine if a map is authentic. Sentences 10, 11, and 12 also discuss paper, so sentence 15 should be placed near them. **(C)** provides a perfect spot, with sentence 15 introducing the concept of using paper as part of expert analysis. **(A)**, **(B)**, and **(D)** are incorrect because they place sentence 15 apart from sentences 10–12, which is not logical.

4. G
Category: Organization

Getting to the Answer: The best transition for the beginning of a paragraph is a topic sentence that introduces the main idea of the paragraph and maintains the established tone. The third paragraph is written in an informative tone; it discusses how forged maps take great skill to create and do have value, although perhaps not as much as authentic maps. **(G)** is correct because it matches both the tone and the main idea. **(E)** is too informal to match the writer's tone. **(F)** and **(H)** include ideas that are not mentioned; the writer does not say that skill and value are proportional or that experts think that fake maps do not have value.

Topic Development

A. **The plane ride was long** because we had two long layovers, one in Dallas and one in Los Angeles.

B. After walking up and down each aisle at least three times, **I chose a perfect present for my sister**.

C. **My dog, Bailey, is stubborn**; no matter what I do, Bailey will not sit, shake, or roll over even though she knows how.

D. Before the library opened for the day, I helped the librarian organize various books and toys as well as several games because **we wanted story hour to go well**.

E. **I was very hungry**, so I helped myself to soup, salad, chicken, rice, and green beans.

1. D

Category: Topic Development

Getting to the Answer: A sentence placed after sentence 2 should logically fit between sentence 2 and the next paragraph. Sentence 2 discusses the reason why early settlements formed near rivers, and paragraph 2 provides examples of civilizations that used irrigation. **(D)** provides a logical transition between the importance of irrigation and examples of its use. **(A)** and **(C)** do not match the informational tone of the passage, and **(B)** provides a specific example of early irrigation processes, which would fit better in paragraph 2 than in paragraph 1.

2. G

Category: Topic Development

Getting to the Answer: The entire passage is about irrigation, so anything other than that topic is irrelevant. Though reference to the Hohokam tribe is relevant, the fact that they established trading posts is not, so sentence 8, **(G)**, should be deleted. All other sentences fit with the topic of the passage.

3. B

Category: Topic Development

Getting to the Answer: A sentence placed after sentence 10 should be a transition between paragraphs 2 and 3. Paragraph 1 introduces irrigation. Paragraph 2 describes irrigation methods, ending with a mention of one downside of irrigation, and paragraph 3 explains the reasons for the importance of irrigation; therefore, a transition sentence must bridge these ideas. **(B)** does this, alluding to the last sentence of paragraph 2 and introducing the topic of paragraph 3. **(A)** focuses on the problems of irrigation, which are irrelevant to paragraph 3. **(C)** is redundant, and **(D)** is off topic.

4. F

Category: Topic Development

Getting to the Answer: The passage discusses how irrigation benefited ancient civilizations in a variety of ways, which **(F)** reflects. **(E)** and **(G)** do not match the tone of the passage. **(H)** is appropriate in tone but outside the scope of the passage.

Practice Set

1. C

Category: Punctuation

Getting to the Answer: **(C)** is correct. In the third sentence, the introductory modifying phrase "Although the orchestral arrangement is more famous" must be followed by a comma. **(A)** incorrectly precedes a dependent clause with a semicolon, **(B)** removes the connector "and" that is required to describe the two types of lessons, and **(D)** removes the comma that is necessary following an introductory modifying phrase.

2. G

Category: Punctuation

Getting to the Answer: When nonessential information is in a sentence, it needs to be offset with a pair of commas. **(G)** is correct; sentence 3 needs a comma between "gears" and "are." The other sentences are correct as written.

3. B

Category: Organization

Getting to the Answer: The transition "Because" in Sentence 2 should be "Although" or another contrast keyword because this sentence has contrasting ideas. Franklin did not get credit when she was alive but is now being celebrated by scientists in her field. **(B)** is correct. The sentences in **(A)**, **(C)**, and **(D)** do not contain any errors.

4. H

Category: Usage

Getting to the Answer: Each answer contains a verb tense change and change in punctuation. Look at each sentence to see which one contains these errors. **(H)** is correct because after describing actions in the past in sentences 1 ("prescribed") and 2 ("began"), sentence 3 properly changes tense to discuss actions that are happening now ("can," "mimic"). Sentence 4 should therefore continue in present tense. Sentence 4 also provides a list of three reasons patients may choose homeopathic remedies, and a comma is needed after each reason. **(E)**, **(F)**, and **(G)** do not have any errors.

5. D

Category: Sentence Structure

Getting to the Answer: The last sentence ends with "many other reasons," which does not make sense. **(D)** correctly fixes this by changing "many" to "among." The other underlined portions contain no errors.

6. G

Category: Knowledge of Language.

Getting to the Answer: Sentence 3 is unclear because it is impossible to know what the pronoun "both" is referring to in the sentence. It could be referring to Huerta and Chavez, the United Farm Workers, or Chicano migrant farmers. **(G)** is correct. The other sentences do not contain errors.

7. C

Category: Organization

Getting to the Answer: The correct sentence will show a cause-and-effect relationship of the good business leading to the expansion of the restaurant. **(C)** is correct. **(A)** suggests that it is a surprise that good business would cause expansion. **(B)** reverses the relationship, changing the meaning of the second sentence. **(D)** also changes the meaning of the second sentence. The restaurant itself expanded, not just its business.

8. H

Category: Organization

Getting to the Answer: The second part of sentence 4 provides the reason "international groups have attempted to monitor and solve systems" and requires a cause-and-effect transition such as "because" rather than the contrast transition "even though." **(H)** is correct. **(E)**, **(F)**, and **(G)** do not have errors.

9. C

Category: Knowledge of Language

Getting to the Answer: Although they sound the same, the noun "effect" and the verb "affect" are spelled differently. This sentence requires the verb "affecting," so **(C)** is correct. For the incorrect choices, **(A)** does not correct the initial error. **(B)** changes the meaning of the original sentence; the narrator and the narrator's friends are the subjects of "feeling," so the correct pronoun is "us." **(D)** is

redundant; "school" and "academic" mean the same thing in context, so only one of those words should be used.

10. F

Category: Organization

Getting to the Answer: Sentence 6 introduces a contradiction between sentence 5 and the second paragraph. A contrast transition word that shows this contradiction is needed at the beginning of the paragraph. **(F)** is correct; "However" shows that the outcome in the second paragraph is the opposite of what they hoped for in sentence 5. **(E)**, **(G)**, and **(H)** all are conclusion transitions that suggest an expected result.

11. D

Category: Topic Development

Getting to the Answer: When asked to add new information, consider how the sentences before and after the new sentence are related. Sentence 7 does not clearly follow from sentence 6. **(D)** is correct; adding information that the school's policy continued makes it clear why the students' hopes were in vain. **(A)** simply repeats the content of sentence 6 and does not add any clarifying information. **(B)** is illogical; the students' hopes would not have been in vain had their pamphlet resulted in a change in policy. **(C)** uses a plural pronoun to refer to the singular noun "school."

12. F

Category: Organization

Getting to the Answer: Sentence 10 reads "I disagree," so it should logically come after a statement the author opposes. The most logical place for this sentence is after the one that states the school's position on the importance of music education, sentence 8. **(F)** is correct. None of the other choices creates a logical flow of ideas in the paragraph.

13. D

Category: Knowledge of Language

Getting to the Answer: This sentence doesn't include a grammatical error, but it lacks conciseness. **(D)** is more concise while retaining the sentence's meaning and is the correct answer. **(A)** introduces a punctuation error; the dash is no longer needed. **(B)** changes the meaning of the sentence. **(C)** is even wordier than the original.

14. G

Category: Topic Development

Getting to the Answer: The final paragraph focuses on the skills that playing an instrument helps develop. **(G)** correctly removes information about the number of hours students should practice their instruments, which is not relevant to the topic. The other three sentences discuss skill development and should be retained.

15. C

Category: Organization

Getting to the Answer: As the two sentences are written, the second is not a complete idea and therefore cannot stand on its own. **(C)** is correct because it makes sentence 2 a dependent clause. **(A)** joins the two with a semicolon, which is incorrect when joining a sentence and a dependent clause. **(B)** incorrectly introduces the contrast word "however"; the information supports the first idea. **(D)** adds an unnecessary logic keyword, "whereas."

16. H

Category: Sentence Structure

Getting to the Answer: Sentence 7 states that the museum was part of an art and industry exhibition, and sentence 8 describes the industrial exhibits. However, the pronoun "it" refers to the museum, not the exhibition. **(H)** removes the ambiguous pronoun, clearly makes the descriptive phrase a dependent clause, and is correct. **(E)** incorrectly connects two complete ideas with a comma, and does not clarify the pronoun. **(F)** needs a comma after "industry" to introduce the explanatory information. **(G)** incorrectly connects an independent and dependent clause with a semicolon.

17. C

Category: Organization

Getting to the Answer: The word "however" in sentence 10 is a clue that this sentence is introducing a contrasting idea. "Art," one of the two types of exhibits, is contrasted in sentence 10 with "industrial exhibits" in sentence 8. **(C)** is the correct placement.

18. H

Category: Organization

Getting to the Answer: Sentence 12 gives examples to support sentence 11, thus it makes sense to combine them. **(H)** is correct. It does this in the most concise and clear way, making sentence 12 a dependent clause and adding it to sentence 11 with a comma. **(E)** uses the word "includes" when the proper usage is "including." **(F)** properly joins two complete sentences with a semicolon but makes the resulting sentence wordy and redundant. The phrase "not excepting" in **(G)** means "including" but is an awkward way to express this idea.

19. B

Category: Organization

Getting to the Answer: The introductory modifying phrase describes "Gorky's opinions" and contrasts these with "his political beliefs later in life." **(B)** is correct. The incorrect choices are transitions showing conclusions, not contrast.

20. H

Category: Topic Development

Getting to the Answer: All sentences in a paragraph should be on the same topic, though perhaps from different angles. A sentence that brings in new information irrelevant to the paragraph is out of place and should be deleted. The topic of this paragraph is Gorky's criticism of the art exhibit, so sentence 20, which introduces extraneous information about the city's name change, is irrelevant and a poor concluding sentence. **(H)** is correct. All the other sentences are relevant to paragraph 3.

CHAPTER 8

The Kaplan Method for Reading Comprehension

CHAPTER OBJECTIVES

By the end of this chapter, you will be able to:

- Read SHSAT Reading passages strategically
- Apply the Method for Reading Comprehension efficiently and effectively to SHSAT Reading questions

The Kaplan Method for Reading Comprehension

The SHSAT includes six reading passages with 6–10 questions each for a total of 46–48 questions. On Test Day, you want to use no more than five minutes actively reading each passage and one minute answering each question.

Kaplan has a method for all of the question types on the SHSAT because it is in your best interest to approach both the test as a whole and the individual sections systematically. When you first start practicing with the method, you'll likely find yourself spending more than five minutes on each passage. As you continue practicing, pay attention to your timing. The best way to cut down your time is to get used to utilizing the Kaplan Method. If you approach every passage the same way, you will work your way through the Reading Comprehension passages and questions efficiently.

The Kaplan Method for Reading Comprehension has three steps:

Step 1: Read actively

Step 2: Examine the question stem

Step 3: Predict and answer

You may notice that the first two steps of the Kaplan Method for Reading Comprehension are flipped, compared to the Kaplan Method for Revising/Editing Text. While you should examine the question first in Revising/Editing questions, you need to actively read the whole passage when it comes to Reading Comprehension. This is because the Reading Comprehension section tests your knowledge of the passage as a whole, as well as specific elements of it; so, you need to have a solid understanding of the entire passage in order to best answer all of the questions that accompany it.

Step 1: Read Actively

Active reading means that as you read the passage, you are asking questions and taking notes. You should ask questions such as:

- What do the **keywords** indicate?
- What is a good **summary** of each paragraph?
- What **specific information** is provided in the passage?
- What **inferences** can be made based on the information the author provides?
- What is the **main idea** of the passage?

Keywords

Use the keywords in the paragraph to answer the accompanying questions.

> Some literary experts would say that writing in verse form cannot qualify as poetry unless it awakens the senses on a nonverbal level or elevates the emotions. However, the question of whether a verse fulfills these criteria may depend on the reader. Many haikus, for example, may awaken the senses on a nonverbal level in some readers but not in others. Thus, their classification as poems, according to experts, may depend on what the haiku means to readers, rather than on what they say.

A. What does the word "However" indicate about the second sentence?

B. What do the words "for example" indicate about the third sentence?

C. What does the word "Thus" indicate about the fourth sentence?

> ## SHSAT EXPERT NOTE
>
> Mark up the passage as you read!
>
> The first sentence or two of a paragraph will usually express the topic of the paragraph.

Summarizing

Actively read the following paragraph. Then answer the accompanying questions that ask about summarizing the paragraph.

> The four brightest moons of Jupiter were the first objects in the solar system discovered with the use of the telescope, and they played an important role in Galileo's famous argument supporting the Copernican model of the solar system. For several hundred years after the moons' discovery by Galileo in 1610, scientific understanding of these moons increased slowly but regularly. However, the spectacular close-up photographs sent back by the 1979 Voyager missions forever changed scientists' impressions of these bodies.

D. Why wouldn't "the early history of astronomy" be a good summary for this paragraph?

E. Why wouldn't "discoveries of the Voyager missions" be a good summary?

F. If you had to summarize this paragraph in just a few words, what would they be?

Specific Information

Use the details in the passage to answer the accompanying questions.

> A human body can survive without water for several days and without food for as many as several weeks. If breathing stops for as little as 3–6 minutes, however, death is likely to occur. All animals require a constant supply of oxygen to the body tissues, especially to the heart and brain. In the human body, the respiratory system performs this function by delivering air, containing oxygen, to the blood.
>
> But respiration in large animals possessing lungs involves more than just breathing. It is a complex process that delivers oxygen to internal tissues while eliminating carbon dioxide waste produced by cells. More specifically, respiration involves two processes known as bulk flow and diffusion. Oxygen and carbon dioxide are moved in bulk through the respiratory and circulatory systems; gaseous diffusion occurs at different points across thin tissue membranes.

G. What bodily function mentioned is the most critical to human survival? Least critical?

H. What need is shared by all animals?

I. What two processes are involved in respiration in large animals?

J. Where does gaseous diffusion occur?

Inference

Read the following paragraph. Then answer the accompanying questions that ask about making inferences.

Between the ages of 1 and 17, the average person learns the meaning of about 14 words per day. Dictionaries and traditional classroom vocabulary lessons account for only part of this spectacular growth. Far more influential is individuals' verbal interaction with people whose vocabularies are larger than their own. Conversation offers several benefits that make vocabulary learning interesting: it supplies visual information, offers frequent repetition of new words, and gives students the chance to ask questions.

K. The author would most likely recommend which method of increasing a student's vocabulary: classroom lessons or conversation?

L. How would the author most likely describe traditional classroom vocabulary lessons?

SHSAT EXPERT NOTE

Be an active reader:

- Look for the main idea.
- Identify the paragraph topics.

Move efficiently, and take short, straightforward notes. You don't want to take valuable time writing too much; you can always return to part of a passage if you need to refresh your memory about the smaller details.

Step 2: Examine the Question Stem

A set of 6 to 10 questions will follow the passage. The first thing you'll need to do with each question is to determine exactly what is being asked before you can answer the question. Basically, you need to make the question make sense to you.

Step 3: Predict and Answer

This means you should:

- Predict, or **prephrase**, an answer before looking at the answer choices, also known as "predict before you peek"
- Select the best match

Predicting or prephrasing before you peek helps you:

- Know precisely what you are looking for in the answer choices
- Avoid weighing each answer choice equally, which saves time
- Eliminate the possibility of falling into wrong answer traps

Practice

Read Actively

Actively reading the passage includes taking notes to create a Roadmap of a passage, which should include the main idea of the passage and the topic of each paragraph.

The Evolution of Ancient Greek Poetry

1 The poems of the earliest Greeks, like those found in other ancient societies, consisted of magical charms, mysterious predictions, prayers, and traditional songs of work and war. We can infer that these poems were intended to be sung or recited, rather than written down, if only because they were created before the Greeks began to use writing for literary purposes. Unfortunately, little is known about these ancient Greek poems because all that remain are fragments mentioned by later Greek writers. Homer, for example, quoted an ancient work song for harvesters, and Simonides adapted the ancient poetry of ritual lamentation—songs of mourning for the dead—in his writing.

    A. What words are mentioned repeatedly throughout paragraph 1?

    B. What do the words "for example" tell us about the last sentence of paragraph 1?

    C. What is the topic of paragraph 1?

2 Although little is preserved of these earliest forms of Greek poetic expression, scholars have been able to ascertain some information. The different forms of early Greek poetry all had something in common: they described the way of life of a culture. This poetry expressed ideas and feelings that were shared by everyone in a community— their folktales, their memories of historical events, and their religion. What remains of these poems suggests that the works were of collective significance, with little emphasis on the individual achievements of particular characters. Greek poets didn't spend time developing imagined narrative stories. This style of retelling the everyday events and beliefs of everyday people was referred to as "folk poetry," and it stands in stark contrast to the style of expression that came later.

    D. What is similar in paragraph 1 and paragraph 2?

    E. How does paragraph 2 differ from paragraph 1?

    F. What is the topic of paragraph 2?

3 In the "age of heroes," the content and purpose of Greek poetry shifted dramatically. By this later period, Greek communities had become more stratified into separate classes, including those who ruled and those who were ruled. In contrast to the way people lived before, now those living in the same community had different, even opposing, interests. As such, they shared fewer daily experiences and probably shared fewer ideas and even emotions. The poetry of the Greek people reflected this shift. Whereas the earliest Greek literature conveyed larger themes related to the whole culture, now the particular outlook of the warlike upper classes predominated.

    G. What phrase at the beginning of paragraph 3 indicates a change in the passage's focus?

    H. How is the content of paragraph 3 different from that of paragraph 2?

    I. How is later Greek poetry different from earlier Greek poetry?

    J. What is the topic of paragraph 3?

4 One need only study Homer's *Iliad* and *Odyssey*, which are recorded examples of the epic poetry that was sung in the Heroic Age, to understand the influence that the upper class had on poetry. Poetic content in this time period told stories of the lives of great individuals, including warriors and kings, and it lost much of its religious character. Thus, the poetry of the Heroic Age could no longer be called folk poetry because poets were assigned a new task: to celebrate the accomplishments of outstanding characters, whether real or imaginary, rather than to catalog and preserve the activity and history of the community as a whole. This focus is indeed the reason why the Heroic Age is so named.

    K. How is the focus of paragraph 4 different from the focus of paragraph 3?

    L. What is the topic of paragraph 4?

    M. What is the main idea of the passage?

Answer the questions below. Understanding these question stems on their own, and predicting an answer now, will help you to quickly and easily answer the full questions later on.

Examine the Question Stem and Predict

1. Which statement best describes the central idea of the passage?

    A. Where will you look for the answer to this question?

    B. Predict the answer to the question stem.

2. Read this sentence from paragraph 2.

> **The different forms of early Greek poetry all had something in common: they described the way of life of a culture.**

The sentence contributes to the development of ideas in the excerpt by

    C. What specific text is helpful?

    D. Predict the answer to the question stem.

3. Read this sentence from paragraph 4.

> **Thus, the poetry of the Heroic Age could no longer be called folk poetry because poets were assigned a new task: to celebrate the accomplishments of outstanding characters, whether real or imaginary, rather than to catalog and preserve the activity and history of the community as a whole.**

The phrase "folk poetry" most clearly conveys that poetry created before the Heroic Age primarily focused on the

    E. What aspect of folk poetry is the question asking about?

    F. Predict the answer to the question stem.

4. Which sentence best explains the subject matter that Heroic Age poetry primarily celebrated?

    G. What aspect of this poetry is the question asking about?

    H. What specific text from the passage is helpful in answering this question?

    I. Predict the answer to the question stem.

5. Compared to communities in an earlier period, Greek communities during the Heroic Age most likely

    J. What important elements in the question stem tell you where to direct your research?

    K. What can you infer about how Greek communities changed between these periods?

    L. Predict the answer to the question stem.

Now that you've practiced examining the question stems and predicting the answers, answer the full version of these questions below. Select the choice that best matches your prediction.

1. Which statement best describes the central idea of the passage?

    A. The role of early Greek poetry changed over time.

    B. Greek communities became separated into classes.

    C. Early Greek poetry is more admired than later Greek poetry.

    D. The *Iliad* and the *Odyssey* were written by the upper class.

2. Read this sentence from paragraph 2.

> **The different forms of early Greek poetry all had something in common: they described the way of life of a culture.**

The sentence contributes to the development of ideas in the excerpt by

    E. revealing how royalty such as kings and queens became known throughout Greece.

    F. identifying the fame and prestige early Greek poets sought.

    G. suggesting that early Greek poetry expressed commonly held beliefs.

    H. demonstrating the importance of celebrating the lives of warriors.

3. Read this sentence from paragraph 4.

> Thus, the poetry of the Heroic Age could no longer be called folk poetry because poets were assigned a new task: to celebrate the accomplishments of outstanding characters, whether real or imaginary, rather than to catalog and preserve the activity and history of the community as a whole.

The phrase "folk poetry" most clearly conveys that poetry created before the Heroic Age primarily focused on the

A. adventures of warriors.

B. viewpoint of a ruling class.

C. problems of a new lower class.

D. concerns of a whole culture.

4. Which sentence best explains the subject matter that Heroic Age poetry primarily celebrated?

E. "Unfortunately, little is known about these ancient Greek poems because all that remains are fragments mentioned by later Greek writers." (paragraph 1)

F. "This poetry expressed ideas and feelings that were shared by everyone in a community— their folktales, their memories of historical events, and their religion." (paragraph 2)

G. "Poetic content in this time period told stories of the lives of great individuals, including warriors and kings, and it lost much of its religious character." (paragraph 3)

H. "This focus is indeed the reason why the Heroic Age is so named." (paragraph 4)

5. Compared to communities in an earlier period, Greek communities during the Heroic Age most likely

A. were less prosperous.

B. were less unified.

C. were better organized.

D. were more peaceful.

Practice Set

For test-like practice, give yourself 40 minutes (an average of 5 minutes per passage and 1 minute per question) to complete this question set. After you're done, be sure to study the explanations, even for questions you answered correctly. They can be found at the end of this chapter.

DIRECTIONS: Read the passages and answer the corresponding questions. Re-read relevant parts of the text before choosing the best answer for each question. Base your answers only on the content within each passage.

Bogart's Extraordinary Career

1 Although Humphrey Bogart became one of the greatest Hollywood stars to ever live, his early acting career was far from promising. In fact, when one considers Bogart's troubled youth and the intentions of his parents that he study medicine, it is perhaps surprising that he ever made it onto the screen at all. Even when he did enter show business, it was years before he found his acting niche. Eventually Bogart found his place in Hollywood, developed a signature style that attracted legions of fans, and attained the status of an icon. His fame has endured to this day.

2 Born in New York City in 1899 as the son of a prominent surgeon, young Humphrey was eagerly placed on the academic track to medical school by his parents. He attended the prestigious Phillips Academy in Andover, Massachusetts to prepare himself for medical studies at Yale University. Bogart, however, was not inclined toward academics; he was often described during his adolescent years as rather belligerent and a frequent instigator of trouble. Indeed, soon after he had arrived at Andover, he ran into disciplinary problems and was eventually expelled.

3 After this expulsion, Bogart volunteered for the Navy, which, in hindsight, seemed a better fit than medical school. In fact, Bogart was described as a model soldier. It was 1918, and with World War I in full swing, Bogart had ample opportunity to see action. It may have been in the service when he received a providential injury to his mouth that partially paralyzed his upper lip. Although accounts of the event differ (at times it has been suggested the injury arose in childhood or possibly in a bar brawl), this injury was significant in that it was responsible for Bogart's distinctive snarl that became the cornerstone of his acting style.

4 After his honorable discharge from the Navy in 1920, Bogart next turned his attention to a number of working class pursuits, and then, interestingly, to the theater. The transition is a remarkable one given that Bogart had shown no inclination toward acting in his youth. However, a random connection with an old family friend who had show-business contacts introduced Bogart to show business. He began first as a staffer in a New York theater office, but he eventually became stage manager and finally worked himself into some minor stage roles. His inexperience showed however, and he struggled with poor reviews and the inability to find any substantive parts.

5 In the early 1930s, Bogart set out for Hollywood hoping to jump start his career and quickly signed a contract with Fox Pictures. Unfortunately, even under contract, Bogart appeared in only three films—all of them bit roles. Frustrated, he returned to the Broadway stage, where he finally caught his break with a remarkable performance as Duke Mantee in the play *The Petrified Forest*. The production was a hit, and Bogart's performance as the quintessential tough guy was critically acclaimed. Reprising the role for its screen adaptation, Bogart earned accolades and signed for a long-term contract with Warner Brothers. Bogart, back out in Hollywood, would go on to make 28 films often as a gangster or other tough guy.

6 Whether it was as gumshoe Sam Spade in *The Maltese Falcon* or as café owner Rick Blaine in *Casablanca*, Bogart consistently created rich and complex screen images infused with a hangdog expression, perennial five o'clock shadow, dangling cigarette, and world-weary attitude. The lip injury-induced snarl fit in well with this persona, but Bogart's great appeal went far beyond these elements. Bogart played the tough guy who managed to seem somehow tender. Both cynical and sentimental, Bogart walked a line that appealed to legions of both male and female fans alike and his performances came to personify male elegance on the screen. It is unlikely that his illustrious career will ever be forgotten.

1. Which statement best describes the central idea of the passage?

    A. Humphrey Bogart found success at an early age as an actor.

    B. Humphrey Bogart's early life experiences shaped his portrayal of tough-guy characters on the screen.

    C. Humphrey Bogart ignored his studies and his father's wishes to follow his dreams of acting.

    D. Humphrey Bogart's tremendous fame as an actor arose almost accidentally after his rather unsuccessful early life.

2. Which sentence from the excerpt best explains why Bogart never went to medical school?

    E. "He attended the prestigious Phillips Academy in Andover, Massachusetts to prepare himself for medical studies at Yale University." (paragraph 2)

    F. "Indeed, soon after he had arrived at Andover, he ran into disciplinary problems and was eventually expelled." (paragraph 2)

    G. "It was 1918, and with World War I in full swing, Bogart had ample opportunity to see action." (paragraph 3)

    H. "After his honorable discharge from the Navy in 1920, Bogart next turned his attention to a number of working class pursuits, and then, interestingly, to the theater." (paragraph 4)

3. The reason that Bogart's early performances were not well received is best illustrated by the

    A. way he caught his break by finally making it onto the Broadway stage.

    B. long-term contract with Warner Brothers that trapped him in bit roles.

    C. poor reviews he received for his inexperienced acting on the Broadway stage.

    D. way he was able to sign a lucrative contract with Fox Pictures.

4. With which statement would the author of this excerpt most likely agree?

    E. The only way to achieve your dream is to continually work toward it through good times and bad times alike.

    F. A capacity for greatness is not always apparent in a person's formative years.

    G. Your experiences and hardships in life influence the way you go about doing your job.

    H. Only those born with clear talent and skill can make it to the peak of their chosen field.

From Discovery to Fallout: the Implications of Radioactivity

1   In 1895, Wilhelm Conrad Röntgen first identified electromagnetic radiation occurring in the wavelength band now known as X-rays. It was a new kind of light with penetrating properties that were not only remarkable in that they could "see" through skin, but seemed clearly applicable to various fields of technology. Scientists, energized by the discovery, quickly sought to understand the properties and potential uses of these rays. Although no one at the time had any reason to suspect the potential for great danger, over the decades it became clear that radiation had tremendous potential to benefit humanity as well as a disturbing power to harm it.

2   Scientific knowledge of radiation expanded quickly over the next few years with a host of subsequent discoveries. In 1896, French physicist Antoine Henri Becquerel accidentally discovered that unexposed photographic plates left in a darkened drawer with uranium crystals became partially developed. Becquerel recognized that an invisible source of energy must have been emitted from the uranium in order to cause this phenomenon. Becquerel's discovery marked the beginning of scientific work with radioactivity, a different, yet closely related property to the idea of radiation.

3   Radioactivity is the name given to the decay or rearrangement of an atom's nucleus. The mysterious energy emanating from Becquerel's uranium crystals existed at the atomic level. Atoms of all elements have heavy positively charged cores, or nuclei, made up of protons and neutrons. The bulk of an atom's mass lies in this nucleus. Some atoms are so big that their nuclei are unstable and cannot remain cohesive. Decay will happen naturally and spontaneously to such unstable nuclei. In many cases, the breaking up is accompanied by the release of a particle, and that particle release is what we now know as radiation. High energy electromagnetic radiation (such as Röntgen's X-rays) is one kind of radiation. Different kinds of radiation differ in their ability to penetrate materials and to cause damage.

4   One of the most important findings that built upon this original research was that radioactive decay occurred at a specific rate, and further, that the rate of decay was predictable and measurable. The husband and wife team of Pierre and Marie Curie and other pioneers measured rate of decay using the term "half-life" to describe the relationship between time and the amount of decay of radioactive material. The Curies discovered that a uranium ore termed "pitchblende" had more than 300 times the radioactive energy than a sample of the same amount of pure uranium. They reasoned that other radioactive elements present in pitchblende were responsible for this discrepancy, and through this knowledge, they were eventually able to isolate the previously undiscovered elements of radium and polonium. The studies of such elements were challenging in that, given the extremely short half-life of even the longest-lived polonium isotope, the raw material rapidly disappeared even while they were performing calculations with it. This concept of half-life was broadly applicable to many fields and was used by later scientists to develop techniques for determining the age of samples through a method called radiocarbon dating, making it invaluable in the fields of anthropology and archaeology.

5   From this early work with radiation, modern nuclear science was also born. Scientists discovered that when an atom of radioactive material was split into lighter atoms, a sudden, powerful release of energy would result. This laid open the path to harnessing nuclear energy as a source of power, as well as to the development of nuclear weapons, with the power to destroy civilization as we know it.

6 It is clear that the discovery of radioactivity and the subsequent development of nuclear science have proven to be both beneficial and troubling for humanity. Many of the early scientists that worked with radiation made great sacrifices in the name of the expansion of knowledge, including Marie Curie and Antoine Henri Becquerel, who died from conditions related to their exposure to radiation. Yet their discoveries led to more precise models of the atom and more accurate information about the nature of matter as well as many positive practical applications, including diagnostic medicine and even the use of radioactive isotopes for treating cancer. Ironically, human knowledge of nuclear properties has the potential to both protect us and annihilate us. It is hard to imagine too many fields of knowledge that have this same range of awesome power.

5. Which statement best describes the central idea of the passage?

   A. The discovery of radioactivity resulted from the hard work of the Curies in establishing the field of nuclear science.

   B. The discovery of radioactivity has been very harmful to the human race over the last several decades.

   C. The discovery of radioactivity has had significant consequences for humanity.

   D. The discovery of radioactivity is the story of the life and work of Antoine Henri Becquerel.

6. Which sentence from the excerpt best explains why radiation possesses a power that is "disturbing" (paragraph 1)?

   E. "In 1896, French physicist Antoine Henri Becquerel accidentally discovered that unexposed photographic plates left in a darkened drawer with uranium crystals became partially developed." (paragraph 2)

   F. "The husband and wife team of Pierre and Marie Curie and other pioneers measured rate of decay using the term 'half-life' to describe the relationship between time and the amount of decay of radioactive material." (paragraph 4)

   G. "Scientists discovered that when an atom of radioactive material was split into lighter atoms, a sudden, powerful release of energy would result." (paragraph 5)

   H. "Yet their discoveries led to more precise models of the atom and more accurate information about the nature of matter as well as many positive practical applications, including diagnostic medicine and even the use of radioactive isotopes for treating cancer." (paragraph 6)

7. How does paragraph 4 fit into the overall structure of the excerpt?

   A. It provides a specific example of early research into radioactivity and the implications of that research.

   B. It contrasts the methodical research of early pioneers in the field with the guesswork of the Curies.

   C. It elaborates on the physical properties of radioactivity and how it is generated.

   D. It introduces the dangerous effects of radiation on the human body by showing how the Curies were poisoned by radiation.

8. What is the purpose of the mention of diagnostic medicine (paragraph 6)?

    E.   to give an example of a potential benefit of nuclear science that may be possible after much more research

    F.   to illustrate how nuclear science can currently offer at least a few positive developments for humanity

    G.   to refute the notion that the discovery of radioactivity has proven to be a mixed blessing

    H.   to explain why the discovery of radioactivity has only ever been beneficial for humanity

The Cane Toad Debacle

1   In a notorious case of ecological mismanagement on the grandest of scales, the cane toad (*Rhinella marina*) was introduced to Australia by the sugarcane industry in order to deal with a beetle infestation—a decision with implications that have continued to rock Australia to this day. The sugarcane industry could hardly have picked a worse creature for their purposes. The cane toad is a prolific breeder with a dangerous skin toxin and an extremely hardy and highly adaptive lifestyle. Since its introduction in 1935, Australia has suffered depletion of native species, poisoning of pets and humans, loss of native plant life, and a host of other ills, as well as the embarrassment of knowing that the cane toad failed to properly control the beetle, for which purpose it had been brought to the continent.

2   How this all came to be is a study in human naïveté as well as the astonishing hardiness of a truly fascinating invasive creature. A native of the Americas, this very large, brightly colored amphibian was known to be a predator of the cane beetle (*Dermolepida albohirtum*), an insect that had been devouring sugarcane crops and tormenting farmers in Australia since the early 1900s. The beetle had become such a significant economic threat that it must have seemed like an excellent idea to introduce an effective biological control, in the form of an enormous toad expected to feast on and eradicate the beetle. In hindsight, this was probably a misguided hope from the start, given that the cane toad had already been introduced elsewhere around the globe and had failed to control similar populations, but the introduction moved forward anyway.

3   In 1935, the Bureau of Sugar Experiment Stations brought a breeding sample of 100 cane toads from Hawaii to the Australian continent. The breeding was successful, and in just a few months, some 2,400 toads were released into the Gordonvale area of Queensland. No impact studies were done prior to this release to assess the toads' potential effect on the natural environment, nor were any tests first conducted to see if the toads would even eat the beetle, in a lab or in the wild. From the outset, some scientists were concerned about the implications of this untested release. For instance, Walter Froggatt, a prominent entomologist, feared that the toad had the potential to become a significant pest and he successfully pressured the government to implement a ban on any further release of toads. However, the government lifted this ban almost as soon as it had declared it, and additional releases of the cane toad soon took place in 1936.

4   One thing the cane toads did immediately and extremely well was to multiply. A female cane toad can lay up to 30,000 eggs in a season, requiring only a small pool of water of almost any description for this purpose. The eggs hatch in two to three days, staying in a tadpole stage for four to eight weeks, then growing quickly to reach full maturity typically within one year. Thus, it wasn't long before Australia could observe the real-time, real-life cane toad experiment unfolding in the cane fields of North Queensland. Some of the newly bred toads descended as planned upon the sugarcane crops and began to eat cane beetles. However, most of the toads lost soon interest in that habitat. For one thing, the mature cane beetles could fly away from their predators, forcing these slow, fat toads to work very hard for their food. In addition, the fields were hot and dry and provided little sleeping shelter for the newcomers, who generally preferred wet shade.

5   Yet these adverse conditions were not severe enough to kill off the toads; instead, the adaptable toads began to look elsewhere for food and shelter. The nearby towns, full of lush gardens and well-watered lawns, were extremely inviting, and soon the toads had overrun entire residential areas. Unfortunately, the toads' close proximity to humans led to a whole host of ills. The cane toad is extremely toxic to anything that eats or even touches it. It thus became a threat to Australia's domesticated animals, as well as to any person who got too close. Further, these toads can eat a variety of small native species (besides the beetle), including the food of other native species. They have even interfered with beekeeping by eating a large number of honeybees. Omnivorous and not picky, the cane toad can eat almost anything that fits into its enormous mouth. And, sadly, Australian fauna was able to provide few native predators that could control the toad, given its extremely toxic nature.

6 Although it has now been over 80 years since the toad was introduced, the problems have not abated. In fact, they have increased. The cane toad expanded its range in an alarming way over the years and has continued to colonize more and more of Australia at the rate of 40–60 km per year. Now, easily numbering into the hundreds of millions—an exact figure has been impossible to calculate—the cane toad has spread out of Queensland to the south and west into New South Wales. In an absurd footnote to history, just five years short years after the fateful decision to release these invasive toads, an effective insecticide spray became available, which easily exterminated the cane beetles. Yet scientists, as well as the Australian government, continue to grapple with the cane toad problem.

9. Which statement best describes the central idea of the passage?

   A. The cane toad was introduced to Australia by sugarcane farmers to control a beetle infestation.

   B. The cane toad possesses physical and behavioral characteristics that facilitated its rapid population expansion.

   C. The cane toads preferred residential areas to the unfriendly environment of the sugarcane fields.

   D. The cane toads proved to be a disaster after being introduced to Australia by sugarcane farmers.

10. In paragraph 2, how do the words "devouring" and "tormenting" contribute to the development of the excerpt?

   E. They illustrate how effective the cane toad is as a predator.

   F. They emphasize the pressure to introduce the cane toad.

   G. They highlight the impact the cane toad has on Australia.

   H. They indicate how little most Australians appreciated the danger of introducing the cane toad.

11. Which sentence from the excerpt best explains why the cane toads began to migrate away from the sugarcane fields?

   A. "No impact studies were done prior to this release to assess the toad's potential effect on the natural environment, nor were any tests first conducted to see if the toads would even eat the beetle, in a lab or in the wild." (paragraph 3)

   B. "A female cane toad can lay up to 30,000 eggs in a season, requiring only a small pool of water of almost any description for this purpose." (paragraph 4)

   C. "In addition, the fields were hot and dry and provided little sleeping shelter for the newcomers, who generally preferred wet shade." (paragraph 4)

   D. "The cane toad expanded its range in an alarming way over the years and has continued to colonize more and more of Australia at the rate of 40–60 km per year." (paragraph 6)

12. Which sentence from the excerpt best illustrates the incredible size of the cane toad population?

   E. "The breeding was successful and in just a few months, some 2,400 toads were released into the Gordonvale area of Queensland." (paragraph 3)

   F. "The eggs hatch in two to three days, staying in a tadpole stage for four to eight weeks, then growing quickly to reach full maturity typically within one year." (paragraph 4)

   G. "Yet these adverse conditions were not severe enough to kill off the toads; instead, the adaptable toads began to look elsewhere for food and shelter." (paragraph 5)

   H. "Now, easily numbering into the hundreds of millions—an exact figure has been impossible to calculate—the cane toad has spread out of Queensland to the south and west into New South Wales." (paragraph 6)

13. How does the author's use of specific numbers in paragraph 6 contribute to the development of ideas in the passage?

   A. It shows how the cane toad failed to solve the cane beetle problem.

   B. It emphasizes the scale of the damage caused by the cane toad.

   C. It conveys how little is understood about the cane toad even today.

   D. It illustrates the dangers that cane toads pose to people and pets.

14. With which statement would the author of this excerpt most likely agree?

   E. Actions have consequences that can be expected beforehand.

   F. All animal life is precious and must be protected.

   G. Solving one problem can cause another, even worse problem.

   H. Human knowledge and understanding are not perfect.

The Bebop Revolution

1 For a jazz musician in the early 1940s, the most interesting place to spend the hours between midnight and dawn would have been at a small Harlem nightclub called *Minton's*. There almost every important jazz musician of the time plied his or her craft while the nightclub served as ground zero for an astounding revolution of the genre: the birth of bebop.

2 It was at *Minton's* that Charlie Parker, Dizzy Gillespie, Kenny Clarke, and Thelonious Monk gathered for impromptu jam sessions, informal performances featuring lengthy group and solo improvisations. The new style of jazz grew organically from these sessions, with the audience listening in awe, mesmerized by this new, true, sound. The musicians who pioneered bebop shared two common elements: a vision of the genre's new possibilities and astonishing improvisational skill—the ability to play or compose a musical line on the spur of the moment. It was not every musician who was capable, but those who caught on and were able to perform in this style made bebop unlike anything that had come before.

3 Bebop was often blindingly fast, incorporating tricky, irregular rhythms and discordant sounds that jazz audiences had never heard before. Earlier jazz, like practically all of Western music up to that time, used an 8-note scale. Bebop, in contrast, was based on a 12-note scale, with an innovative approach to harmonic structure that opened up vast new opportunities for musicians. Unlike swing, the enormously popular style of jazz that was played for entertainment in the 1930s, bebop was considered art music. It was played for listening, and the performers considered themselves artists, not entertainers. Unfortunately, as records were made of vinyl, the war effort of the 1940s meant that the petroleum needed to create vinyl had to be conserved. The creative ferment that first produced bebop was thus largely undocumented.

4 Like any true revolution, the birth of bebop was multifaceted and contextualized and related to larger social issues—in this case, World War II and segregation—beyond those within the art form. Bebop, like jazz itself, is considered an African American invention and developed in part as a reaction to what was perceived by many as the commercialization of jazz with mass-produced, orchestrated bands. Swing bands were large and harder to promote during the war. Unlike the expansive, planned sounds of big band swing, bebop was fundamentally small and engaged, with an emphasis on improv and a re-emphasis on blues. And, as with other revolutions, the bebop movement encountered heavy resistance. Opposition came from older jazz musicians initially, but also from a general public alienated by the music's complexity and sophistication, once it spilled out beyond the intimate borders of *Minton's* club in Harlem.

5 However, bebop changed the face of jazz, if for no other reason than it marked the first time that both jazz musicians and their audience became aware that jazz was an art form. For the first time, technical and aesthetic elements were the most important aspect of the genre, and creative enterprise took priority over the marketplace. Bebop made all subsequent modernizations of jazz possible and influenced future generations. Today there is a resurgence of respect for the genre found in neo bop stylings, and its influence can even be seen in today's rap music.

15. Which statement best describes the central idea of the passage?

A. The development of bebop was made possible thanks to Charlie Parker's contribution to jazz.

B. The development of bebop was caused by informal jam sessions during the 1940s.

C. The development of bebop marks the culmination of the history of jazz music in the United States.

D. The development of bebop marks the birth of the modern jazz movement.

16. The reason bebop music was different from the swing music of the 1930s is best illustrated through the

    E. mainstream success that bebop music enjoyed.

    F. use of an 8-note scale in bebop music.

    G. description of bebop music featuring discordant sounds.

    H. better dance tempos of bebop music.

17. Which of the following best describes one of the ways in which early jazz was distinct from bebop music?

    A. "For a jazz musician in the early 1940s, the most interesting place to spend the hours between midnight and dawn would have been at a small Harlem nightclub called Minton's." (paragraph 1)

    B. "Earlier jazz, like practically all of Western music up to that time, used an 8-note scale." (paragraph 3)

    C. "It was played for listening, and the performers considered themselves artists, not entertainers." (paragraph 3)

    D. "Bebop, like jazz itself, is considered an African American invention and developed in part as a reaction to what was perceived by many as the commercialization of jazz with mass-produced, orchestrated bands." (paragraph 4)

18. How did the advent of World War II influence the bebop movement?

    E. It fractured the genre and produced neo bop.

    F. It spurred an increased focus on bebop's blues element.

    G. It accounted for why early bebop is lost to time.

    H. It led to a decline in bebop's popularity as large, orchestrated bands became difficult to promote.

19. Which sentence best explains the bebop movement's unpopularity with the general public?

    A. "The musicians who pioneered bebop shared two common elements: a vision of the genre's new possibilities and astonishing improvisational skill[.]" (paragraph 2)

    B. "Bebop, in contrast, was based on a 12-note scale, with an innovative approach to harmonic structure that opened up vast new opportunities for musicians." (paragraph 3)

    C. "Unlike swing, the enormously popular style of jazz that was played for entertainment in the 1930s, bebop was considered art music." (paragraph 3)

    D. "Unlike the expansive, planned sounds of big band swing, bebop was fundamentally small, engaged, with an emphasis on improv and a re-emphasis on blues." (paragraph 4)

20. With which statement would the author of this excerpt most likely agree?

    E. Art should be produced with a mass audience in mind.

    F. Improvisation is the greatest of all musical skills.

    G. Technically sophisticated music may not appeal to a mass audience.

    H. Art made for the sake of art is pointless self-indulgence.

Answers and Explanations

Keywords

A. "However" indicates a contrast, or change in direction.

B. The words "for example" indicate that the author is providing an instance that will demonstrate something that was discussed in the preceding sentence.

C. "Thus" indicates a conclusion.

Summarizing

D. The paragraph focuses on four of Jupiter's moons, so "the early history of astronomy" isn't specific enough to be a good summary.

E. Only one sentence mentions the Voyager missions, so "discoveries of the Voyager missions" isn't broad enough to be a good summary.

F. Jupiter's four brightest moons

Specific Information

G. Breathing is the most critical. ("If breathing stops for as little as 3–6 minutes, however, death is likely.") Eating is the least critical. ("A human body can survive . . . without food for as many as several weeks.")

H. Oxygen is a need shared by all animals. ("All animals require a constant supply of oxygen to the body tissues.")

I. The two processes are bulk flow and diffusion.

J. Gaseous diffusion occurs across tissue membranes.

Inference

K. The author would recommend conversation with people with larger vocabularies to increase a student's vocabulary. ("Far more influential" and "offers several benefits that make vocabulary learning interesting.")

L. The author would describe traditional classroom vocabulary lessons as not as influential as conversations with people with larger vocabularies. In addition, traditional classroom vocabulary lessons do not offer benefits that make vocabulary learning interesting.

Read Actively

A. Words repeated in paragraph 1 include "poetry" and "Greek."

B. The phrase "for example" tells you that this sentence provides an example of something that has already been mentioned.

C. Early Greek poetry characteristics

D. Both paragraph 1 and paragraph 2 are about early Greek poetry.

E. Paragraph 2 elaborates on the topic of paragraph 1, focusing on a single common element of all early Greek poetry.

F. Early Greek poetry focused on community.

G. The phrase "shifted dramatically" indicates a change of direction in the passage.

H. Paragraph 2 discusses a common theme in early Greek poetry, while paragraph 3 introduces later Greek poetry.

I. Early Greek poetry focused on the community. Later poetry focused on individuals.

J. Poetry changed as society changed, and there was more focus on individuals.

K. Paragraph 3 describes the purpose of later Greek poetry. Paragraph 4 describes the changed role of the poets who composed it.

L. Heroic Age poetry was influenced by upper class and individualism.

M. While early Greek poetry focused on the community as a whole, later Greek poetry was crafted by and about individuals.

Examine the Question Stem and Predict

1. **A.** Look for the answer in the Roadmap notes.

   B. Early Greek poetry focused on community; later poetry focused on individuals.

2. **C.** The next sentence in the paragraph, which elaborates on some examples of the ideals that Greek communities shared ("their folktales, their memories of historical events, and their religion").

   D. The sentence is introducing the idea that early Greek poetry represented shared culture, and the next sentence provides some examples.

3. **E.** The phrase "primarily focused on" means that the question is asking about the general subject of this type of poetry.

   F. Folk poetry's general subject was the whole community.

4. **G.** The phrase "primarily celebrated" means that the question is asking about the purpose of this type of poetry.

   H. Paragraph 4 states that the focus of Greek poetry had shifted to influential individuals. ("Poetic content in this time period told stories of the lives of great individuals, including warriors and kings . . .")

   I. Later Greek poetry celebrated extraordinary individuals.

5. **J.** Paragraph 2 states that early Greek poetry expressed ideas and feelings that everyone shared, while paragraph 3 states that people living in the same community began to have different interests.

   K. Later Greek communities became divided into different classes, so they were less unified than earlier ones.

   L. Greek communities during the Heroic Age were more diverse than during earlier periods.

Passage Analysis: The purpose of the passage is to contrast the characteristics of two periods of Greek poetry. The main idea of the passage is that, although the earliest Greek poetry focused on the community as a whole, later Greek poetry of the Heroic Age celebrated individuals. Paragraph 1 describes general characteristics of the earliest Greek poetry. Paragraph 2 explains that the earliest Greek poetry focused on the community. Paragraph 3 explains that, after Greek society became separated into classes, poetry of the Heroic Age came to focus on accomplishments of individuals. Paragraph 4 explains that Heroic Age poets wrote epic poems focused on the upper class.

1. **A**

Category: Global

Getting to the Answer: Global questions such as this one ask you for the main idea. Remember, the scope of the correct answer will incorporate everything discussed in the passage, but no more. In this case, the main idea involves the change in Greek poetry from the earliest poets focused on the community to the Heroic Age poets focused on individuals. In other words, the passage is about how the role of early Greek poets changed. **(A)** is correct. The author does not discuss how Greek communities became separated into classes or the superiority of early Greek poetry, making **(B)** and **(C)** Out of Scope. **(D)** is incorrect because it only mentions examples, which are not the focus of the entire passage; also, the poems focused on the upper class, but the upper class did not necessarily write them.

2. G

Category: Function

Getting to the Answer: You know from the paragraph topic in your Roadmap that the earliest poets focused on the community, so look for the choice that is consistent with that focus. **(G)** is correct. **(E)** and **(H)** are both Distortions; celebrating kings and warriors is characteristic of later Heroic Age poetry, not early poetry. **(F)** is Out of Scope since the author never suggests that poets sought fame for themselves.

3. D

Category: Inference

Getting to the Answer: Go back to the passage and study the context in which this phrase is used. Paragraph 4 says that poetry that celebrates individuals of the upper class can no longer be called "folk poetry." You can infer from "no longer" that earlier Greek poetry must have been folk poetry. Because the key difference discussed in the passage is that earlier poetry was concerned with the community as a whole, you can infer that this must be a characteristic of folk poetry. **(D)** reflects this best. Paragraph 4 says that folk poetry is not about warriors and the ruling class, making **(A)** and **(B)** incorrect. **(C)** is Out of Scope; the problems of the lower class are never discussed.

4. G

Category: Detail

Getting to the Answer: Use your Roadmap to find the answer. Paragraph 3 explains that Heroic Age poetry focused on individuals. **(G)** is correct. **(E)** and **(H)** are incorrect because they do not provide specific details about the focus of Heroic Age poetry. **(F)** is incorrect because community life was a subject of earlier poetry.

5. B

Category: Inference

Getting to the Answer: What does the passage tell you about changes in Greek communities between the two periods? Paragraph 3, which provides the transition from the early period into the Heroic Age, tells you that "Greek communities had become separated into classes." If the communities were separated, the inference is that they were less unified; **(B)** reflects this. The passage does not compare the communities in terms of prosperity, organization, or peace, making **(A)**, **(C)**, and **(D)** Out of Scope.

Practice Set

Passage Analysis: The passage describes the early stages of Humphrey Bogart's career and his eventual, if unlikely, rise to fame. Paragraph 1 sets forth the idea that Bogart achieved great fame despite a troubled youth. Paragraph 2 describes Bogart's academic troubles. Paragraph 3 goes into Bogart's naval service and also explains how he got his characteristic facial feature, his snarl. Paragraph 4 describes his early, unsuccessful efforts in theater and acting. Paragraph 5 describes his ultimate success both on Broadway and in film after his initial Hollywood bust. Paragraph 6 sums up Bogart's public image and career.

1. D

Category: Global

Getting to the Answer: First, in order to find the best summary of the passage, make sure to identify a common theme running through every paragraph. In this case, every paragraph, in one way or another, focuses on how Bogart's eventual fame came from rather unlikely beginnings, which matches **(D)**. **(A)** is a Distortion; while Bogart eventually succeeded as an actor, this happened later in his life, after multiple challenges. **(B)** is Out of Scope; the passage does explore a direct connection between Bogart's early life and his various screen portrayals, but this does not describe the passage as a whole. **(C)** is a Distortion; the passage never suggests that Bogart ignored his studies or that he defied his father's wishes.

2. F

Category: Detail

Getting to the Answer: The author describes Bogart as a troublemaker and states that he was expelled from Andover. He also describes Bogart as being "not inclined toward academics" (paragraph 2). All this information supports the fact that Bogart did not pursue medical school. Thus, **(F)** is correct. **(E)** is a Misused Detail; the preparation that Bogart did do for a career in medicine does not explain why he abandoned that career. **(G)** and **(H)** are Misused Details; Bogart had already abandoned the track towards medical school at this point, as paragraph 3 notes that the Navy "seemed a better fit than medical school" for him.

3. C

Category: Detail

Getting to the Answer: Because the entire passage, with the exception of paragraphs 2 and 3, describes Bogart's acting career, use the answer choices to direct your research of the passage's content. Be wary of answer choices that use wordings directly from the text but in fact misrepresent the information provided. Also note the chronological structure of the passage as it relates to Bogart's life. Paragraph 3 mentions that Bogart "struggled with poor reviews" in his early theater work; this matches **(C)**. **(A)** is a Misused Detail; while Bogart did catch his big break on the Broadway stage, this came later in his career after less successful theater and movie bit roles. **(B)** and **(D)** are Distortions; while they describe events that happened to Bogart, they distort the studios involved. **(B)** involved Fox Pictures, not Warner Brothers. **(D)** was the reverse.

4. F

Category: Inference

Getting to the Answer: When considering which statement an author would agree with, think about the purpose of the passage as a whole. In this case, the passage dealt with Bogart's unlikely rise to stardom. Thus, **(F)** is correct. **(E)** is incorrect because Bogart is not described as having had a dream or ambition to act. **(G)** is Out of Scope; although the scar on his lip influenced Bogart's image, nothing is made clear about how much his life experiences influenced his acting. **(H)** is incorrect because Bogart is described as having had a slow, unlikely rise to stardom. His early acting career met with poor reviews from critics.

Passage Analysis: The main focus of the passage is the discovery of radioactivity as well as the development and application of nuclear science. The focus of paragraph 1 is the discovery of radiation, including the positive and negative impacts of this discovery. Paragraph 2 discusses the research field's earliest years, as well as Becquerel's discovery of radioactivity. Paragraph 3 elaborates on how radioactivity occurs. Paragraph 4 deals with the work the Curies did with radioactive decay. Paragraph 5 transitions into modern nuclear science. Paragraph 6 is about the positive and negative consequences of nuclear science.

5. C

Category: Global

Getting to the Answer: In this passage, the idea that recurs throughout is the discovery of radioactivity and the subsequent development of nuclear science, and that these discoveries and developments have had a significant impact on the world. Look for an answer choice that agrees with this focus. **(C)** best fits that prediction. **(A)** is a Misused Detail; the work of the Curies is discussed only in paragraph 4. **(B)** is Extreme; the passage does assert that nuclear science has negative applications, but the overall tone of the passage is mixed and does not support this statement. **(D)** is a Misused Detail; although Becquerel's discovery of radioactivity is discussed in the passage, the passage does not focus on his life and work.

6. G

Category: Detail

Getting to the Answer: Look for the answer choice that best matches the context of a "disturbing" power. Paragraph 5 discusses how nuclear science led to the development of nuclear weapons, which have the "power to destroy civilization." This results from the ability to split the atom. Thus, **(G)** is correct. The remaining answer choices are all Misused Details. **(E)** and **(F)** are incorrect because they describe research into radiation in neutral terms. **(H)** presents a beneficial product of nuclear science, diagnostic medicine, rather than a "disturbing" one.

7. A

Category: Global

Getting to the Answer: Paragraph 4 deals with the research of the Curies into radioactivity, as well as their discovery of the half-life concept. Pick the answer choice that best fits that summary; **(A)** is correct. **(B)** is Opposite; the early research into radioactivity was largely guesswork and happy accidents, while the Curies methodically investigated the field. **(C)** is a Misused Detail; the physical properties of radioactivity are described in paragraph 3, not paragraph 4. **(D)** is a Misused Detail; the death of the Curies from radiation poisoning is not mentioned until paragraph 6.

8. F

Category: Function

Getting to the Answer: Paragraph 6 contrasts the costs and benefits of radioactivity, noting that nuclear science can "both protect us and annihilate us." Diagnostic medicine is used as an example of the former. Thus, **(F)** is correct. **(E)** misrepresents diagnostic medicine based on nuclear science as something not yet in use, while in paragraph 6 it is described as an existing tool. **(G)** is Extreme; while the author is contrasting the costs of radioactivity with its benefits, the author is not refuting all its negatives. Instead, the author is presenting the reality as a mixed bag. **(H)** is likewise Extreme; diagnostic medicine is mentioned as a positive, but it comes after the death of the Curies from radiation poisoning is discussed.

Passage Analysis: The passage's purpose is to describe the consequences of introducing cane toads into Australia. Paragraph 1 summarizes the dangers of and ills caused by the cane toad. Paragraph 2 explains why the cane toad was introduced to Australia. Paragraph 3 deals with the release of the toads into the wild. Paragraph 4 describes their breeding and behavior. Paragraph 5 elaborates on the invasive nature of the species. Paragraph 6 describes the state of the cane toad in Australia today.

9. D

Category: Global

Getting to the Answer: Because you are looking for a statement that summarizes the entire passage, the correct answer must capture the focus of all six paragraphs. In this case, every paragraph of the passage focuses on the introduction of the cane toad into Australia and the resulting, disastrous consequences, so look for an answer choice that best represents this overall focus. That answer is **(D)**. **(A)** is a Misused Detail; the passage states that the farmers brought the toads to Australia to eradicate the cane beetle, but this fact is not the focus of the passage. **(B)** and **(C)** are also Misused Details; the passage only briefly mentions cane toad habits, falling far short of focusing the entire passage on those habits, and while the passage mentions the reasons why the toads moved away from the sugarcane fields, this is not the focus.

10. F

Category: Function

Getting to the Answer: Understanding context is vital when answering a Function question. In this case, "devouring" and "tormenting" refer to the cane beetle and the negative impact they had on Australian sugarcane farmers. This establishes why the cane toad was introduced; thus, **(F)** is correct. **(E)**, **(G)**, and **(H)** are incorrect because all of these answer choices incorrectly presume that "devouring" and "tormenting" refer to the cane toad, rather than the cane beetle.

11. C

Category: Detail

Getting to the Answer: First, use your Roadmap to identify the place in the passage to which this question stem refers, as you may not immediately remember from your first reading all of the reasons given for the toad migration. Paragraph 4 gives two major reasons that the toads left the fields: the beetles could fly and there was not enough damp shade. Look for an answer choice that takes into account at least one of these reasons. The answer is **(C)**. **(A)** is a Distortion; the passage never suggests that no beetles were eaten. **(B)** is Out of Scope; the passage never mentions the females needing more water for reproduction than was available in the wild. **(D)** is a Distortion; the explosive reproductive force of the cane toads does not tie into them migrating away from the cane fields.

12. H

Category: Detail

Getting to the Answer: The main idea of this passage revolves around the idea of the cane toad being an invasive species that is spreading uncontrollably throughout Australia. Ideally, you want to describe both their sheer numbers and their geographic extent. **(H)** is the best fit as it does both. **(E)** is a Misused Detail; the introduction of the cane toads to Australia does not tell us what they are like today. **(F)** is also a Misused Detail; the quick maturation of cane toads does not tell us how many cane toads there are or how far they have spread. **(G)** is another Misused Detail because it touches on how the toads first began to spread out of the sugarcane fields but provides no numerical or geographical context to that spread.

13. B

Category: Function

Getting to the Answer: Remember, a Function question is essentially asking what job a cited feature is doing in the text. In paragraph 6, the concrete numbers offered for the cane toad population and their rate of expansion in Australia help ground the main idea. Cane toads are an invasive species, but paragraph 6 conveys just how invasive and how far they have spread. This job of the cited feature is best described by **(B)**. **(A)** is a Misused Detail; that the cane toad failed in their original purpose is irrelevant to their present-day expansion. **(C)** is incorrect because it is at odds with the rundown of facts concerning the cane toad offered throughout the passage. **(D)** is a Misused Detail; the dangers presented by the cane toad do not closely tie in with their population and spread. Also, **(D)** does not touch on the effect the cane toads have on wildlife in Australia, a major point discussed throughout the passage. It only discusses their effect on people and pets.

14. H

Category: Inference

Getting to the Answer: For this sort of Inference question, consider both the main idea and the author's overall approach to it. Here, the main idea concerns the unwise introduction of the cane toad to Australia and the environmental ramifications that continue to this day. What was their tone? Paragraph 3 refers to the cane toads as a "misguided" hope for sugarcane farmers. Paragraph 4 discusses how little study was done ahead of time. The passage ends with the cane toads revealed as unnecessary thanks to a subsequently developed insecticide. Pick the answer choice that best matches that topic and the tonal treatment of it. **(H)** best captures it. **(E)** is incorrect because few foresaw the impact of the cane toads ahead of time. **(F)** is incorrect because the passage does not contain a defense of the cane toad as an animal deserving of protection. **(G)** is tempting but incorrect, as the cane toads are not described as solving the sugar beetle problem.

Passage Analysis: The main focus of this passage is on bebop jazz, its characteristics, and its history. Paragraph 1 introduces bebop's origin. Paragraph 2 describes bebop's development. Paragraph 3 compares bebop to previous jazz movements. Paragraph 4 describes its historical context and criticism. Paragraph 5 describes bebop's legacy.

15. D

Category: Global

Getting to the Answer: Global questions test your comprehension of the passage as a logical whole. In order to correctly answer Global questions, you must be able to correctly synthesize information from each paragraph. In this case, each paragraph in the passage discusses bebop jazz, its characteristics, and its development. The correct answer is **(D)**. **(A)** is a Misused Detail; Charlie Parker is mentioned more than once for his contribution to bebop jazz, but this is not the primary focus of the passage. **(B)** is a Misused Detail; these sessions, while important to the development of bebop jazz, are not the main focus of the passage. **(C)** is also a Misused Detail; the passage is concerned with bebop jazz, not jazz in general.

16. G

Category: Detail

Getting to the Answer: Research the part of the passage that the question is referring to, and form your prediction based on this reexamination of the text. In this case, the question refers to the comparison between bebop and swing jazz addressed in paragraphs 3 and 4. After researching these paragraphs, you should note that the fast speed and discordant sounds of bebop jazz were the elements that jazz audiences had never heard before. The correct answer is **(G)**. **(E)** is Opposite; the passage states that swing jazz was more popular than bebop jazz. **(F)** is also Opposite; the passage states that swing jazz was played on an 8-note scale, whereas bebop was played on a 12-note scale. **(H)** is a Distortion; the passage never states that swing was better dance music because of its tempos.

17. B

Category: Detail

Getting to the Answer: Paragraph 3 of the passage directly states that "Bebop, in contrast, was based on a 12-note scale[.]" According to this information, the 12-note scale created new opportunities not possible with the 8-note scale of other music. The answer is **(B)**. **(A)** is a Distortion; the clubs of the 1940s gave rise to bebop, but that was not the only type of jazz played there. **(C)** is Opposite; it refers to bebop, not earlier jazz styles. **(D)** is incorrect because it describes similarities between early jazz and bebop, not ways in which they are distinct.

18. G

Category: Detail

Getting to the Answer: The passage states in paragraph 4 that bebop went largely undocumented, partly because it was unpopular, and partly because of a shortage of vinyl used to make records. The vinyl shortage was due to wartime rationing of petroleum, from which vinyl is made. Thus, **(G)** is correct. **(E)** is a Misused Detail; while bebop eventually inspired neo bop, it was not because of the advent of World War II. **(F)** is also a Misused Detail; bebop's renewed focus on a blues element compared to other forms of jazz was not due to World War II. **(H)** is Opposite; swing bands were large and orchestrated, while bebop bands were smaller and more intimate.

19. C

Category: Detail

Getting to the Answer: Paragraph 4 discusses the resistance encountered by the bebop jazz movement. The passage states that older musicians resisted bebop, the general public disliked its complexity, and, because of the rationing of petroleum, it was poorly documented. **(C)** contains one of these elements, so it is the correct answer. **(A)** and **(B)** are Misused Details; while the passage discusses how improvisation and artistic potential attracted musicians to bebop, these do not explain its public unpopularity. While tempting, **(D)** is also a Misused Detail. The small-scale, blues-inspired nature of bebop does not necessarily explain its unpopularity in the same way as calling it "art music" like in **(C)**.

20. G

Category: Inference

Getting to the Answer: The passage discusses the origin of bebop and its influence on jazz, especially as it relates to bebop being more artistic in nature than most music. If you are not sure how that main idea leads to an obvious answer choice, then eliminate your options as you go. **(E)** is incorrect because bebop is described as not being made with a mass audience in mind. It was unpopular with the masses and, moreover, was created as a reaction against the commercialization of swing jazz. **(F)** is Extreme; in paragraph 2, the author describes the ability to improvise as a difficult prerequisite to being able to play bebop but not as a skill that trumps all others. **(H)** is incorrect because it does not match the tone of the passage. While bebop is described as art music, it is not discussed in a negative way. In fact, the passage is generally supportive of bebop and its merits. Thus, **(G)** remains as an answer choice. Bebop is described as requiring certain skills to play, and bebop itself never gained the mass popularity of other forms of jazz because it was not made with dancing in mind. It was mainly popular in jazz clubs, places that would attract a particular kind of audience already knowledgeable about jazz. Thus, **(G)** is correct.

CHAPTER 9

SHSAT Reading Question Types

CHAPTER OBJECTIVES

By the end of this chapter, you will be able to:

- Distinguish among five SHSAT Reading question types
- Apply strategies to answer Reading questions correctly

SHSAT Reading Question Types

As you already know, you get points from answering the questions, not simply reading the passages. In order to increase your chances of getting the most points, you should approach Reading questions strategically; part of this is understanding the various types of questions you'll encounter on Test Day.

There are five basic question types in the Reading section: Global, Detail, Function, Inference, and Infographic. Each question type will include choices that fall into classic wrong answer trap categories.

Wrong Answer Trap	Description
Distortion	The choice slightly alters details from a passage so that they are no longer correct.
Extreme	The choice takes a stronger position (often more positive or more negative) than the passage takes.
Misused Detail	The choice is a true statement from the passage, but it doesn't answer the question.
Opposite	The choice contradicts information in the passage.
Out of Scope	The choice includes information that is not in the passage.

Depending on the question type, some wrong answer traps are more common than others. Knowing how to tackle each question type as well as which wrong answer traps to avoid are key components for Test Day success.

Global Questions

Global questions either ask you to choose a correct summary of the passage as a whole or to identify key information and ideas within the passage. You can recognize Global questions because they will often use phrases like "the central idea" or "overall tone/theme/plot."

To answer Global questions successfully:

- Identify the central idea or theme of the passage
- Use your Roadmap as a brief summary (do not re-read the entire passage)

Avoid these common wrong answer traps when answering Global questions:

- Out of Scope
- Misused Detail
- Extreme

SHSAT EXPERT NOTE

A key strategy for Global questions is to look for a choice that summarizes the entire passage—not just a detail that's mentioned once or discussed in a single paragraph. The information should be present throughout the whole passage.

Detail Questions

Detail questions ask you to track down a piece of information directly stated in the passage. Remember that you will not (and should not!) remember every detail from your reading of the passage. Your Roadmap can help you find the *location* of the detail in question; then, you should research the passage text to find the answer. You can recognize Detail questions because they will often use wording like "According to the passage/author/paragraph," or "The author states."

To answer Detail questions successfully:

- Use line references or specific phrasing in the question to find the relevant section of the passage
- Quickly skim through the relevant section to find specific evidence for your prediction; you should be able to put your finger on the exact information required to answer the question
- Rephrase the evidence in the passage in your own words to make a prediction and find a match among the answer choices

Avoid these major wrong answer traps when answering Detail questions:

- Misused Detail
- Distortion

Function Questions

Function questions ask about the purpose of a particular part of the passage. They can ask about the purpose of any of the following: a word, a sentence, a paragraph, a detail, a quote, or punctuation.

To answer Function questions successfully:

- Focus on the author's reason for including the cited feature
- Read around the cited text and take note of any transition words to get context and understand the author's reasoning

Avoid these major wrong answer traps when answering Function questions:

- Distortion
- Out of Scope

Inference Questions

An Inference question, like a Detail question, asks you to find relevant information in the passage. These questions will use phrases such as "most likely" or "suggests," and they may ask with what the author would most likely agree. Once you've located the relevant details, you need to go one step further: to figure out the underlying point of a particular phrase or example.

To answer Inference questions successfully:

- Look for clues that show how the author connects relevant details within the passage
- Consider how the author's point of view limits the range of what could be true

Avoid these major wrong answer traps when answering Inference questions:

- Out of Scope
- Extreme
- Misused Detail

Infographic Questions

An SHSAT Reading passage may be accompanied by up to two infographics, which are graphs, tables, or images that represent information related to the passage. For example, if a passage discusses the development of trade between two continents, a map of the trade routes or a bar graph showing the number of goods transported each year may accompany the passage.

Infographic questions ask you how the information in the graph, table, or image supports ideas presented in the passage. To answer Infographic questions successfully:

- Evaluate the information in the question stem (e.g., "topic," "central idea," "paragraph 7")
- Identify units, labels, and titles in the infographic
- Circle the parts of the infographic that relate to the question

Avoid these major wrong answer traps when answering Infographic questions:

- Out of Scope
- Distortion

Practice

Read Actively

Actively read the following passage, taking notes to create a Roadmap. Be sure to write down the topic of each paragraph and the main idea of the passage.

Industrial Progress

1   Is industrial progress a mixed blessing? A hundred years ago, this question was seldom asked. Science and industry were flooding the world with products that made life easier. Inventions such as dishwashers and electric washing machines automated many of the tasks that used to take hours to perform by hand. Industrialization was a major driving factor behind the increased educational opportunities, disposable income, and time for leisure activities that characterized the twentieth century. In the face of such technological convenience, few gave thought to how these miraculous machines and the companies that made them affected the natural world.

2   Today, however, we know that many industrial processes create pollution that can destroy our environment. Industries produce toxic waste, discharging harmful chemicals directly into lakes, rivers, and the air. One of the most noticeable results of this growing contamination is acid rain.

3   Acid rain is caused by industrial processes that release compounds of nitrogen and sulfur. When these pollutants combine with clean air, the results are nitric and sulfuric acids. Air, clouds, and rain containing acids can have terrible effects on human, animal and plant life. Acid droplets in the air can be inhaled, causing illness. When these acid droplets fall from clouds as rain, they can accumulate and kill plant life if natural chemical processes in soils do not deactivate the acids. In some parts of the Northeast and Midwest, 10 percent of all lakes show dangerous acid levels. In eastern mountains, large forest tracts have been lost at elevations where trees are regularly bathed in acidic clouds. This loss of vegetation creates a trickle-down effect, impacting countless species of animals that depend on these forests for food or shelter.

4   The main components of acid rain are oxides of nitrogen and sulfur dioxide, exhausted from oil- and coal-burning power plants. To reduce acid rain, emissions from these plants, particularly sulfur dioxide, must be restrained. One way is to install machines that remove sulfur dioxide from a plant's exhausts. Another is to build new industrial plants, modeled on experimental designs that produce less sulfur dioxide. Since acid rain poses such an immense risk to human, animal, and plant health, finding ways to reduce its impact is an important and ongoing area of research for industrialists.

5   Happily, it seems that many companies today are becoming increasingly aware of their impact on the environment. Tech behemoths such as Google and Facebook rely more and more on renewable energy sources to power their data centers and actively look for ways to reduce their carbon footprint. Car companies are re-evaluating their manufacturing processes and looking for ways to do more with less. Even the average citizen is probably more environmentally conscious than a citizen from a century ago. Practices such as composting and recycling are gaining ground in the public consciousness, and being concerned with the state of the environment is no longer considered a radical, countercultural view.

6   A century ago, industrial progress was viewed as a battle against nature; for humanity to make progress, nature must recede. Contemporary opinion holds that humanity and nature must cooperate, or both will be destroyed.

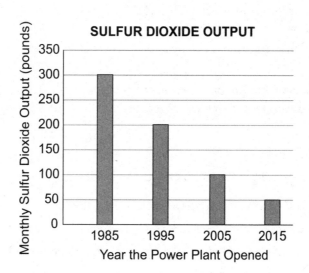

A.   ¶ 1 Topic
B.   ¶ 2 Topic
C.   ¶ 3 Topic
D.   ¶ 4 Topic
E.   ¶ 5 Topic
F.   ¶ 6 Topic
G.   Passage Main Idea

Global

1.   Which statement best describes the central idea of the passage?

   A.   The drawbacks of industrial progress far outweigh the economic and social benefits.

   B.   People are now working to limit acid rain, as well as other types of pollution, to protect the environment.

   C.   Industrial leaders have been irresponsible and should be held accountable for their poor environmental practices.

   D.   To understand current environmental conditions, a comparison between industry in the nineteenth century and industry today is necessary.

Detail

2.   Which sentence from the passage demonstrates a harmful effect of acid rain?

   E.   "In the face of such technological convenience, few gave thought to how these miraculous machines and the companies that made them affected the natural world." (paragraph 1)

   F.   "In eastern mountains, large forest tracts have been lost at elevations where trees are regularly bathed in acidic clouds." (paragraph 3)

   G.   "To reduce acid rain, emissions from these plants, particularly sulfur dioxide, must be restrained." (paragraph 4)

   H.   "A century ago, industrial progress was viewed as a battle against nature; for humanity to make progress, nature must recede." (paragraph 6)

Function

3.   The question at the beginning of the passage contributes to the development of ideas by

   A.   outlining why acid rain is so harmful to humans and plants.

   B.   explaining the causes of acid rain as well as potential methods for its reduction.

   C.   pointing out that the effect of industrial progress on the environment is a puzzling phenomenon.

   D.   introducing a discussion about the benefits and detriments of industrial progress.

Inference

4. What is the most likely purpose of the "experimental designs" mentioned in paragraph 4?

   E. to increase sulfur dioxide output

   F. to reduce the pollution-driven deforestation

   G. to deactivate sulfuric acid that falls in rain

   H. to neutralize the acidity of contaminated lakes

Infographic

5. How does the bar graph support the ideas in paragraph 4?

   A. It indicates how machines that remove sulfur dioxide are effective in plants built in the 1980s and 1990s.

   B. It reveals that dangerous acid levels in Northeast and Midwest lakes have decreased over time.

   C. It provides evidence that more recently built power plants emit less sulfur dioxide than older power plants.

   D. It shows how improvements in ecosystems have positively affected the amount of sulfur dioxide emitted each month.

Practice Set

For test-like practice, give yourself 46 minutes (an average of 5 minutes per passage and 1 minute per question) to complete this question set. After you're done, be sure to study the explanations, even for questions you answered correctly. They can be found at the end of this chapter.

DIRECTIONS: Read the passages and answer the corresponding questions. Re-read relevant parts of the text before choosing the best answer for each question. Base your answers only on the content within each passage.

Tracing the Path to the Great Stock Market Crash of 1929

1   On October 29, 1929, the stock market crashed. The sheer scale of the crash resulted in the worst financial panic in American history, and the ensuing economic meltdown was so severe that it became known as the Great Depression. Economists to this day study what went wrong in order to keep history from repeating itself.

2   The roots of the crash can be traced all the way back to the period leading up to the United States' entry into World War I. Before America entered the war, it began to pull out of an economic recession as Europeans bought American goods to supply their war effort. America's initial neutrality placed it in a strong position to meet these needs, while its subsequent entry into the war produced further financial benefit when the federal government initiated unprecedented spending in order to mobilize for the war. Further, many everyday Americans joined the effort by buying war bonds, which first introduced many to the idea of investment. The success of the war led to financial power for the nation as well as to greater wealth in the hands of everyday Americans.

3   These economic factors took place at a time when the good life began to feel particularly good. It was a booming time for technology. Products like vacuum cleaners and automobiles were relatively cheap. Hordes of regular people were noticing the strong economy and seeking a share of it. Many people had a bit of extra money, if not financial prowess, creating a desire to invest, just as they had invested in war bonds. Thus, many Americans, not just the rich, began to play the stock market.

4   And the stock market was booming. People believed they could make a tremendous fortune by getting in, even though they did not have enough capital to invest. A financial process known as "buying on the margin" made their investments possible. The laws of the day required only a percent, or a "margin," of an investment to be paid immediately, with the rest payable over time. The broker loaned the rest, and a "buy now pay later" mentality thrived. By the late 1920s, three million Americans were investors in the stock market. Economists worried about how much investing was being done by those who could not afford the losses if the market crashed, but government policy called for nonintervention. So, in a market that was neither fair nor democratic, savvy investors manipulated conditions to benefit themselves while amateur investors remained oblivious.

5   Because all markets are cyclical in nature, even the strongest bull market will eventually fail. It was just a matter of time before the bubble burst, creating fallout for an unprecedented number of people. By 1929, many investors began to get nervous and started to unload their stocks. When the pressure of everyone trying to sell at once became too much, a panic ensued and the market began a downward spiral from which there was no easy recovery.

6   The lessons of 1929 have taught investors that the stock market is no game. Laws have been passed that significantly reduce margin investing. In addition, many safeguards have been implemented to stem financial panic when the market starts to decline. Although the economy will always have high and low points, by moderating behavior, the raw panic that allowed the crash can be prevented.

Conditions in 1920s that Led to Stock Market Crash

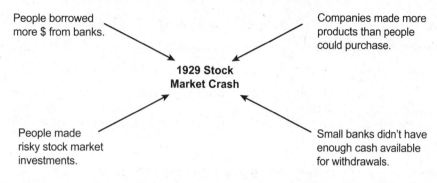

New York Stock Exchange Shares Sold

1. Which statement best describes the central idea of the passage?

   A. The great stock market crash of 1929 resulted in unwise, panicked decisions by investors.

   B. The great stock market crash of 1929 stemmed from excessive government regulation.

   C. The great stock market crash of 1929 was unable to be stopped by economists of that era.

   D. The great stock market crash of 1929 holds many valuable lessons for the present day.

2. How does the 1929 Stock Market Crash diagram provide additional support for the topic presented in the passage?

   E. It emphasizes that the stock market crash was solely due to the lack of cash held in small banks.

   F. It reveals that margin investing was the primary cause of the stock market crash.

   G. It illustrates how the government, banks, investors, and companies reacted to the Great Depression.

   H. It shows that multiple factors, such as risky investments and overproduction, contributed to the stock market crash.

3. How does the line graph support the ideas in paragraph 4?

   A. It indicates that a surprising number of rich people bought shares on the stock market in the 1920s until the stock market crash in 1929.

   B. It illustrates that the stock market crash of 1929 was part of a cycle of strong and weak markets.

   C. It cautions Americans against margin investing in the stock market in the future.

   D. It shows the dramatic upward trend in market activity in the 1920s when many more Americans purchased stock market shares.

4. What is the most likely reason the author mentions vacuum cleaners and automobiles (paragraph 3)?

    E. to give examples of new devices that were being invented during the 1920s

    F. to illustrate the types of things that were not available to Americans with lower incomes

    G. to describe the types of companies that were making money during the 1920s

    H. to demonstrate how many Americans could afford new items in the 1920s

5. The reason more Americans were able to invest in the stock market during the 1920s is best illustrated through the

    A. ability to buy large quantities of stock at only a fraction of the purchase price.

    B. description of the booming economy of the United States in that decade.

    C. encouragement that the United States government provided to spur more investment.

    D. restrictions in place that prevented margin investing.

6. In paragraph 4, how do the words "savvy" and "oblivious" contribute to the meaning of the excerpt?

    E. They illustrate how amateur investors ignored the market's cyclical nature.

    F. They highlight the lack of awareness about how U.S. tariff policies affected the stock market.

    G. They convey how little everyone appreciated the government oversight of the economy.

    H. They emphasize the vulnerability of inexperienced investors in the 1920s.

7. How does paragraph 5 fit into the overall structure of the excerpt?

    A. It underscores how financial regulation can prevent panic at the stock market as well as avert market declines entirely.

    B. It contrasts the booming economy of the 1920s with the Great Depression of the 1930s.

    C. It highlights the changes that have been made to financial regulations to prevent another similar panic.

    D. It provides a transition from a discussion of the crash's causes to a discussion of the crash's legacy.

8. The line graph at the end of the passage contributes to the development of ideas by

    E. highlighting the financial regulations that might have averted the 1929 stock market crash.

    F. illustrating the effect of three million Americans trying to play the stock market.

    G. summarizing the four primary causes of the 1929 stock market crash.

    H. conveying the specific ways in which the stock market crash would impact Americans.

Akira Kurosawa

1   What do samurai[1], cowboys, shoguns[2], gangsters, peasants, and William Shakespeare all have in common? These are just some of the varied influences on the work of Akira Kurosawa (1910–1998), a Japanese film director considered by movie critic Leonard Maltin to be "one of the undisputed giants of cinema." Over his career, Kurosawa's unique blend of Western themes and Eastern settings has made him arguably the most important Japanese filmmaker in history.

2   Kurosawa's style reflects his own experiences. As a young man, he studied Western art and literature and decided to be a painter. However, World War II led Kurosawa to film; he acted as an assistant director of wartime propaganda films in Tokyo. After Japan's surrender in 1945, he took the lessons he learned in Tokyo and began making his own films—works that took the values and traditions of the West and reinterpreted them with a Japanese sensibility and distinctly Japanese settings and characters.

3   The most famous example of Kurosawa's style is his 1954 film *Seven Samurai*. Although the setting is medieval Japan, with peasants and samurai, its story is influenced by Western films: a group of villagers, terrorized by local bandits, turns to a down-on-his luck, yet good-hearted, samurai for their protection. Like the movie cowboy, the samurai is a lonely hero, sure of his morals and battling clear forces of evil. This contrasts with the traditional Japanese version of a samurai as a noble, often distant, symbol of Japan's imperial heritage. To Kurosawa, the samurai was a distinctly human character, with a conscience and the willful action to correct the wrongs around him.

4   Although Kurosawa's films enjoyed—and still enjoy—a lofty reputation in the West, Japanese audiences have regarded his work with suspicion. By using Western ideals and themes—even reinterpreting Western authors such as William Shakespeare and Fyodor Dostoyevsky (his favorite author)—Kurosawa is regarded by many critics and moviegoers in his home country as not being particularly Japanese. They see him using Japanese culture as mere "window dressing" to what were essentially foreign stories. Ironically, it was Kurosawa's success that opened the door for other, "more Japanese" directors, such as Yasujiro Ozu and Kenji Mizoguchi, to gain a wider audience. Kurosawa's films have also been called elitist because they emphasize the struggles and triumphs of imposing and sometimes inaccessible hero figures, not the common man.

5   Regardless of this criticism, Kurosawa's effect on Western filmmaking is beyond dispute. He was a consummate craftsman, familiar with all aspects of the film-making process. Unlike most directors of his day, he both directed and edited all of his films. He once said that he found editing to be the most creatively satisfying aspect of filmmaking, even going so far as to claim that he shot new footage simply to give himself something to edit. Kurosawa always thought carefully about the soundtrack of both the movie as a whole and what was playing in each particular scene. He viewed music as "counterpoint," a way to add an ironic commentary on the action, not something that should parallel the mood of that particular scene. This was also in striking opposition to the practices of his day. Perhaps most importantly, Kurosawa often worked with his screenwriters to produce the highest quality script possible. To him, a well-written script was paramount; he did not think a quality movie could exist without a quality script. Finally, Kurosawa inspired an unusual amount of loyalty in the people he worked with. Indeed, the *Kurosawa-gumi* (Kurosawa group) was well-known in the Japanese film world for its exceptionally high caliber productions.

[1] samurai: noble warriors of medieval Japan, similar to European knights
[2] shoguns: military dictators of Japan from 1603 to 1868

6 Perhaps Kurosawa's most distinctive technical device was his frequent use of "the wipe." In this editing technique, a line appears to move across the screen, "wiping" away the old image and replacing it with a new one. This type of scene transition was common in the silent films of earlier generations but relatively rare in the films of Kurosawa's time. Kurosawa employed it so often (sometimes up to 12 times in a single film) that it came to be regarded as one of his signatures.

7 Ironically, his films have influenced the very same American movie genres that Kurosawa admired so much. *Seven Samurai* became the basis for the American Western epic *The Magnificent Seven*. *Yojimbo*, another story of a samurai for hire, strongly influenced the film *A Fistful of Dollars*. Other genres benefited from Kurosawa's work as well; *Rashomon*, a crime story told from different points of view, has influenced almost every crime movie since. Finally, *The Hidden Fortress*, about two peasants escorting a princess during a war, became George Lucas's expressed basis for the science fiction masterpiece *Star Wars*.

8 Although Akira Kurosawa did not become a "household name" in the same way that Orson Welles and Alfred Hitchcock were, his contributions to cinematic history are no less worthy of recognition than those of these two giants.

9. Which statement best describes the central idea of the passage?

   A. The American Western film genre gained popularity in Japan through the work of Akira Kurosawa.

   B. Akira Kurosawa's contributions to filmmaking make him the most important director in history.

   C. Kurosawa's work compares favorably to that of other Japanese directors such as Ozu and Mizoguchi.

   D. Kurosawa's controversial style is one of the most important and influential in filmmaking.

10. Kurosawa's experience making wartime propaganda films during World War II influenced his later films by

    E. enabling him to effectively use Japanese locations and characters to convey Western ideas.

    F. providing him with the technical training necessary for his later innovations in filmmaking.

    G. introducing him to many film technicians who would later become his expert Kurosawa-gumi.

    H. motivating him to create *Seven Samurai* as an example of Western ideals portrayed in a Japanese setting.

11. Which sentence best supports the idea that Japanese audiences have regarded Kurosawa's work with "suspicion"?

    A. "However, World War II led Kurosawa to film; he acted as an assistant director of wartime propaganda films in Tokyo." (paragraph 2)

    B. "This contrasts with the traditional Japanese version of a samurai as a noble, often distant, symbol of Japan's imperial heritage." (paragraph 3)

    C. "They see him using Japanese culture as mere "window dressing" to what were essentially foreign stories." (paragraph 4)

    D. "Kurosawa's films have also been called elitist because they emphasize the struggles and triumphs of imposing and sometimes inaccessible hero figures, not the common man." (paragraph 4)

12. How did Kurosawa's approach to filmmaking differ from that of the other directors of his time?

    E. He incorporated foreign themes, morals, and images into local settings, characters, and situations.

    F. He edited his own work, used music to contrast mood, and insisted on expert writing and production skills.

    G. He was highly regarded by foreign audiences at the same time he was sharply criticized by his own audiences.

    H. He would only work with the Kurosawa-gumi, a group of expert film technicians he had trained over the years.

13. The word "Ironically" in paragraph 7 affects the tone of the paragraph because it

    A. indicates that Lucas was more successful with *Star Wars* than Kurosawa was with *The Hidden Fortress*.

    B. emphasizes the wide variety of film genres that were influenced by different Kurosawa films.

    C. conveys how Westerns, crime stories, and science fiction have all benefited from Japanese directors.

    D. highlights the fact that Kurosawa would come to influence the same types of films that gave him inspiration.

14. Read this sentence from paragraph 7.

> **Although Akira Kurosawa is not a "household name" in the same way that Orson Welles and Alfred Hitchcock are, his contributions to cinematic history are no less worthy of recognition than those of these two giants.**

The author's use of the phrase "household name" contributes to the ideas in the passage by

    E. comparing Kurosawa's films favorably to those of Welles and Hitchcock.

    F. predicting Kurosawa's eventual recognition as a giant in cinematic history.

    G. recognizing Kurosawa's innovative influence in modern filmmaking.

    H. contrasting Kurosawa's obscurity with the importance of his films.

John Ford

1   The collected works of John Ford, one of the most celebrated American film directors of the twentieth century, are difficult to categorize. He set films in a variety of countries, including Ireland—the setting for his 1952 Oscar-winning film, *The Quiet Man*. Yet repeatedly throughout his career, Ford turned his attention to the Western genre. From the 1939 classic film *Stagecoach*—which fellow director Orson Welles claimed to have watched more than 40 times—to nostalgic cowboy dramas like *Cheyenne Autumn*, which closed out his career in the mid-1960s, Ford repeatedly tapped into the American fascination with renegades of the Old West.

2   Born in 1895 as Sean Aloysius O'Fearna, Ford began directing in 1917 after serving as an apprentice to his brother Francis, a director of silent movies. Shortly after taking this apprenticeship, Sean began acting in his brother's projects, and it was with this spirit of drama that he adopted the name of the famed British dramatist John Ford. Ford's earliest works, mostly short films, are still considered noteworthy today, but it was not until the release of the Western *The Iron Horse* in 1924 that critics began to recognize a "Fordian" style.

3   *The Iron Horse* described the creation of the First Transcontinental Railroad and was an extremely ambitious project for its time. Shot on site in remote locations in the rugged Sierra Nevada mountains, it presented unique logistical challenges. During the course of filming, the production crew constructed two new towns and employed 5,000 extras, 13,00 buffalo, 2,000 horses, and 10,000 cattle. Ford was also in constant conflict with his crew member and brother Eddie, which contributed to the overall tense atmosphere on set. On top of everything else, Ford was not provided with a complete script. Instead, he was given only a brief outline of the film's intended contents, which forced him to shoot scenes piecemeal and stitch them together later. Because of all of these factors, production soon fell behind schedule. Fox executives constantly sent Ford telegrams demanding results, which Ford either tore up or gave to stunt gunman Edward Jones to use for target practice. Luckily, everything came together in the end. The film cost $280,000 but grossed over $2,000,000, making it one of the most commercially successful pictures of the 1920s.

4   After a particularly successful and prolific period of filmmaking in the 1930s, the decade in which Ford commanded the American film scene as a director of Westerns, he was sent to the Pacific for the Second World War as head of the newly formed Navy Field Photographic Unit. This stint in the military led to his direction of several war films—including the acclaimed 1942 documentary The Battle of Midway—but, upon his return to Hollywood, Ford again focused on the Western. The result was one of Ford's most famous works, the 1946 film *My Darling Clementine*, which told the story of the town of Tombstone, Arizona, and the infamous 1890s gunslinger Wyatt Earp.

5   Working with Ford could be challenging. On the one hand, he did form close relationships with his production crew and loyally used the same actors many times throughout his career. However, he was a temperamental man with a wide variety of strange and bewildering habits. One of his most well-known was his custom of chewing on the corners of handkerchiefs while shooting. Each day, his wife delivered him fresh handkerchiefs and removed the old ones, which had been torn to shreds. Ford was also intensely focused and actively discouraged idle banter on the set. He was especially sensitive to profane language, particularly if it was used in front of a woman. Although he did not drink while working, after each completed movie he would wrap himself up in a bedsheet and go on a drinking binge that lasted several days.

6   Film scholars, explaining a reason for Ford's success as a director of Westerns, labeled Ford's directorial style as "measured simplicity." Ford's cameras are almost always placed at the viewer's eye level, and there is often little camera movement. In fact, one of Ford's former assistant directors recalled suggesting that an

opening shot of John Wayne's character be taken from an overhead bridge. Ford quickly dismissed this idea, asking, "Do you stand on a stepladder when you meet someone?" Such simplicity of direction and editing makes Ford's Westerns particularly accessible to both the casual viewer and the more demanding critic who can marvel at his cinematic efficiency.

15. Which statement best describes the central idea of the passage?

    A. The Western film genre captivated the American public.

    B. John Ford focused his career on Western films.

    C. John Ford returned to Westerns following World War II.

    D. The Western film genre captured John Ford's fascination as a director.

16. What is the most likely reason the author mentions that Orson Welles watched *Stagecoach* "more than 40 times" (paragraph 1)?

    E. to establish John Ford's tendency to incorporate the suggestions of other directors into his work

    F. to convey the immense box office success of John Ford's *Stagecoach*

    G. to illustrate Orson Welles's criticism of John Ford's approach to the Western genre

    H. to show the respect others in the industry had for John Ford's work

17. What film best indicated the establishment of Ford's style?

    A. *Stagecoach*

    B. *The Battle of Midway*

    C. *The Iron Horse*

    D. *The Quiet Man*

18. Based on the passage, how did John Ford contribute to the American effort in World War II?

    E. as a celebrity entertainer for the troops

    F. as a soldier in the Battle of Midway

    G. as a naval officer in the Battle of Midway

    H. as a naval photographer

19. What is the most likely reason the author mentions Ford's efficiency (paragraph 6)?

    A. to show his refusal to waste money shooting from stepladders

    B. to establish his extravagant yet successful directing style

    C. to illustrate his insistence that his films come in under budget

    D. to convey his ability to entertain with a simple filmmaking style

20. The author mentions the film *The Quiet Man* to indicate that Ford most likely

    E. was quite reserved as a person.

    F. made films other than Westerns.

    G. preferred to keep his film subjects varied.

    H. was interested in the lives of the Irish.

The Hudson River School

1   The first truly American art movement, the Hudson River School was formed by a group of landscape painters who emerged in the early nineteenth century. The first works in this style were created by Thomas Cole, Thomas Doughty, and Asher Durand, a trio of painters who worked during the 1820s in the Hudson River Valley and surrounding locations. Today, scholars believe that the Hudson River School embodies the three dominant trends of nineteenth-century America: discovery, exploration, and settlement.

2   Cole is generally acknowledged to be the founder of the school. When sailing up the Hudson River in a steamship, Cole was struck by the brilliant autumn colors of the surrounding landscape. Awed by the beauty of the Hudson valley, he hiked into the Catskill mountains and painted the crags, lakes, and rivers he found there. In addition to his landscape paintings, Cole also painted a series of works called *The Course of Empire*. This series of five paintings shows pristine wilderness being transformed into a city and then eventually returning back to wilderness. The supremacy of nature and the "corrupting" influence of human-kind were recurring themes in both his work and the work of the Hudson River School as a whole.

3   Heavily influenced by European Romanticism, these painters set out to convey the remoteness and splendor of the American wilderness. The Romantic movement stressed the primacy of emotion over reason, was skeptical of increasing industrialism, and sought a return to the noble simplicity of nature. Another major feature of this movement was the idea of "the sublime." Although the precise meaning of this term is debated, it usually refers to scenes of unspeakable grandeur or any artistic experience that brings us "outside ourselves." Many Romantic poets, particularly Wordsworth and Coleridge, found examples of the sublime in the unspoiled beauty of nature and contrasted the purity of ancient cultures with the perceived excesses of their day. The Hudson River School painters profited from this general air of nostalgia because they effec-tively represented the American continent the way it used to be.

4   The Hudson River School painters attempted to record what they saw as accurately as possible. Unlike European painters, who brought to their canvases the styles and techniques of centuries, the Hudson River School painters sought neither to embellish nor to idealize their scenes, portraying nature with objectivity and attention to detail. Although many of the artists studied in Europe, their paintings show a desire to be free of European artistic rules.

5   This desire to shake off the old European traditions was paralleled in the historical events of the era and the general feeling of Americans in the nineteenth century. The War of 1812 had given the United States a new sense of pride in its identity, and as the nation continued to grow, there was a desire to compete with Europe on both economic and cultural grounds. The vast panoramas of the Hudson River School fit perfectly by providing a new movement in art that was unmistakably American in origin. The strongly nationalistic tone of their paintings caught the spirit of the times, and within a generation, the movement had mushroomed to include landscape painters from all over the United States. Canvases celebrating such typically American scenes as Niagara Falls, Boston Harbor, and the expansion of the railroad into rural Pennsylvania were greeted with enormous popular acclaim.

6   In addition to their paintings, many members of the school contributed to American cultural identity in other important ways. The so-called "second generation" Hudson River School (1855–1875) included such artists as Frederic Edwin Church, John Frederick Kensett, and Sanford Robinson Gifford. Several of these men were instrumental in establishing the New York Metropolitan Museum of Art, one of the largest and most popular art museums in the world today. This gave America an art institution comparable to the great European collections of the Louvre or the British Museum.

7   The Hudson River School arrived at a time when writers in the United States were turning their attention to the wilderness as a unique aspect of their nationality. The view that the American character was formed by the frontier experience was widely held, and many writers were concerned about the future of a country that was becoming increasingly urbanized. Several of the paintings from the Hudson River School helped galvanize lawmakers to designate areas of wilderness as national parks and establish smaller parks in cities. As such, it is hard to overestimate the formative influence that this school had on the young United States. Many of our images of classic Americana trace back to paintings from this era, and for most, the words "American wilderness" call forth images in the style of this school. The work of Cole and his contemporaries has been forever embedded in the public consciousness of Americans and will likely remain so for generations to come.

21. Which statement best describes the central idea of the passage?

   A.   The Hudson River School responded to increasing urbanization.

   B.   The Hudson River School gained lasting popularity with the American public.

   C.   The Hudson River School influenced a generation of European painters.

   D.   The Hudson River School romanticized the American wilderness and rejected all industrialization.

22. Based on the passage, what were the Hudson River School painters primarily famous for painting?

   E.   the War of 1812

   F.   the Hudson River Valley and its surrounding locations

   G.   themes of European Romanticism

   H.   landscapes throughout the United States

23. Which evidence supports the description of Thomas Cole as the founder of the Hudson River School?

   A.   the details about the influence of "the sublime" on Cole

   B.   the details about Cole's series, *The Course of Empire*

   C.   the details about the influence European styles had on Cole

   D.   the details about Cole hiking in the Catskill mountains

24. With which statement about the popularity of Hudson River School paintings would the author of this excerpt most likely agree?

   E.   They conformed to the accepted rules of painting.

   F.   They appealed to widespread nationalistic sentiments.

   G.   They were fine imitations of European paintings.

   H.   They primarily portrayed the dangers of urban development.

25. The phrase "fit perfectly" in paragraph 5 conveys the idea that

    A. the paintings depicted famous battle scenes.

    B. the paintings were very successful commercially.

    C. the paintings reflected a new pride in the United States.

    D. the paintings were favorably received in Europe.

26. With which statement would the author of this excerpt most likely agree?

    E. Hudson River School paintings should sell for millions.

    F. Modern cultures lack the purity of ancient cultures.

    G. Americans were bloated with pride after the War of 1812.

    H. Artists can change the world with their work.

Answers and Explanations

Read Actively

A.   ¶1 Topic: Industrialization effects

B.   ¶2 Topic: Industrial pollution and acid rain

C.   ¶3 Topic: Why acid rain is so harmful

D.   ¶4 Topic: Methods for reducing acid rain

E.   ¶5 Topic: Companies and citizens working to reduce pollution

F.   ¶6 Topic: Industry and nature must find a healthy balance

G.   Passage Main Idea: Acid rain is harmful to the environment, but companies and citizens are reducing environmentally harmful effects.

Global

1.   B

Category: Global

Getting to the Answer: If you have already identified the main idea on your own, you will have a much easier time finding the correct answer choice. Remember, the correct choice will match both the tone and the scope of the passage. **(B)** does this best. **(A)** is a Misused Detail; the passage mentions economic and social benefits, but the author does not take a position about whether they are worth the environmental cost. Since the author is not openly critical of anyone, **(C)** doesn't match the tone of the passage either. **(D)** is Out of Scope since the nineteenth century (1800–1899) is never discussed.

Detail

2.   F

Category: Detail

Getting to the Answer: Use your Roadmap to find your way back to the paragraph that discusses the effect of acid rain. Paragraph 3 discusses why acid rain is so harmful, which matches **(F)**. **(E)**, **(G)**, and **(H)** are incorrect because they are from paragraphs 1, 4, and 6, which do not directly discuss the effects of acid rain.

Function

3.   D

Category: Function

Getting to the Answer: The question at the beginning of the passage includes the phrase "mixed blessing," which indicates that industrial progress has created both good and bad results. **(D)** is correct. **(A)** describes the function of paragraph 3, and **(B)** describes the function of paragraph 4, so they are incorrect. **(C)** is a Distortion; the author is not puzzled or confused by the effects of industrial progress.

Inference

4.   F

Category: Inference

Getting to the Answer: The purpose of the experimental designs is to reduce pollution. One of the effects of pollution described in paragraph 3 is the loss of forests. You can infer, therefore, that by reducing pollution, the experimental designs would reduce pollution-driven deforestation; **(F)** is correct. **(E)** is Opposite because the experimental designs would reduce the sulfur dioxide that causes pollution, not increase it. **(G)** and **(H)** are both Distortions; the passage does not claim that the experimental designs would deactivate the acid that falls as rain or clean up the existing pollution.

Infographic

5.   C

Category: Infographic

Getting to the Answer: Paragraph 4 discusses methods for reducing acid rain, which include building "new industrial plants, modeled on experimental designs that produce less sulfur dioxide" The graph shows how power plants that were opened more recently have lower monthly sulfur dioxide output. **(C)** correctly explains the relationship between the passage and the infographic. **(A)** is incorrect because, while paragraph 4 mentions machines that remove sulfur dioxide from a plant's exhausts, the plants built in 1985 and 1995 have higher emissions than the more recently built plants. **(B)** and **(D)** are incorrect because they are not mentioned in paragraph 4 and are not supported by the graph.

Practice Set

Passage Analysis: The main focus of the passage is the stock market crash of 1929 and the lessons learned from it. Paragraph 1 introduces the crash of 1929 and previews its effects. Paragraph 2 describes how war bonds sparked public interest in investment. Paragraph 3 deals with the economic and technological optimism of the 1920s. Paragraph 4 describes how the stock market bubble formed. Paragraph 5 discusses how the crash actually happened. Paragraph 6 discusses steps taken by the government to try to prevent future crashes. The infographics summarize the crash's causes, as well as illustrate the scale of the bubble.

1.   D

Category: Global

Getting to the Answer: Global questions ask you to summarize the main idea that runs throughout the passage. In this case, the passage discusses the stock market crash of 1929 and the lessons learned from it. The correct answer will best summarize this focus; **(D)** is a great match for your prediction. **(A)** is a Misused Detail; although the passage does discuss panic in investment, the wider scope of the passage discusses the stock market bubble. **(B)** is Opposite; the passage mentions that there was too little government regulation ahead of the crash. **(C)** is Extreme; economists were able to voice concerns, but these were not taken seriously by policymakers.

2.   H

Category: Infographic

Getting to the Answer: The main idea of the passage is the causes of the stock market crash of 1929 and the lessons learned so that people can avoid a similar crash in the future. The diagram shows some causes of the stock market crash explained in the text, along with some that are not explained. Predict that the correct answer will focus on the multiple causes of the stock market crash; the best match is **(H)**. The diagram does not emphasize one cause over another, so **(E)** and **(F)**

are incorrect. **(G)** is a Distortion because both the diagram and the passage focus on the 1929 stock market crash that then led to the Great Depression, not the aftermath.

3.   D

Category: Infographic

Getting to the Answer: Paragraph 4 describes how many more Americans became able to invest in the stock market in the 1920s—an opportunity made possible by margin investing. The line graph shows that the number of shares sold rose sharply until 1929. Predict that the correct choice will link the increasing number of Americans investing with the increasing number of shares sold; the best match is **(D)**. **(A)** is incorrect because paragraph 4 directly contradicts this choice when it states that "not just the rich" played the stock market. Your Roadmap is the best way to spot Misused Details, such as those evident in **(B)** and **(C)**. The cyclical nature of the stock market is not mentioned until paragraph 5, so **(B)** is incorrect. Discussion of the lessons learned from margin investing does not take place until later in the passage, so **(C)** is incorrect.

4.   H

Category: Inference

Getting to the Answer: Vacuum cleaners and automobiles are mentioned in paragraph 3 to demonstrate how mass production made prices lower and products available to more Americans. Therefore, **(H)** is correct. **(E)** and **(G)** are Out of Scope; the passage does not mention inventions of the 1920s nor the types of companies that made money during the 1920s. **(F)** is Opposite; the passage indicates that such things were available to more Americans than ever before.

5.   A

Category: Detail

Getting to the Answer: Paragraph 2 discusses the new financial power of Americans during the 1920s. It states, "The laws of the day required only a percent, or a 'margin,' of an investment to be paid immediately, with the rest payable over time." From this information, you can see that investors did not need to have the money all at once to buy stock. **(A)** matches this prediction. **(B)** is a Misused Detail; although the passage does state that the economy was booming, this detail is used to illustrate that most Americans had money to spare, not that they were all investing in the stock market. **(C)** is a Distortion; the passage states that the government did not interfere in business affairs, so it is unlikely that the government would have encouraged investment. **(D)** is Opposite; the passage states that the laws allowed, rather than prevented, margin investing.

6. H

Category: Function

Getting to the Answer: To answer Function questions, remember to focus on the author's reason for including the cited feature as well as the specific context of the cited feature in the passage. In this case, the words "savvy" and "oblivious" help contrast experienced investors with amateurs, especially in the context of the dangers posed by the stock market. Thus, **(H)** is correct. **(E)** is a Distortion; amateur investors could not ignore the market's cyclical nature if they were described as oblivious, a term which conveys a lack of awareness. **(F)** is Out of Scope; tariff policies are not mentioned in the excerpt. **(G)** is a Distortion; before the 1929 stock market crash, the government had little to no oversight of the economy.

7. D

Category: Global

Getting to the Answer: Your Roadmap should include a brief summary of each paragraph. In this case, paragraph 5 covers the 1929 crash itself, bridging paragraph 4's lead-up to the crash with paragraph 6's long-term aftermath and response. Thus, **(D)** is correct. **(A)** is a Distortion; paragraph 6 mentions regulations "to stem" financial panics "when the market starts to decline." In other words, **(A)** is half-right, half-wrong; although financial regulation may prevent panic at the stock market, there is no suggestion in the passage that such regulation can avert all market declines. **(B)** is Out of Scope; while the stock market crash of 1929 is mentioned in paragraph 5, the resulting Great Depression is not explored. **(C)** is a Misused Detail; the regulatory changes are mentioned in paragraph 6, not paragraph 5.

8. F

Category: Infographic

Getting to the Answer: Infographics present a dense amount of information in a quick, easily digestible format. In the case of the line graph, it depicts the increase and spike in stock purchases, followed by a sharp decline at the exact time the Great Depression began (1929); this shows how the stock market purchases directly impacted the crash. Thus, **(F)** is correct. **(E)** is Out of Scope; financial regulations are not mentioned in the line graph. **(G)** is incorrect because it describes the diagram, not the line graph. **(H)** is Out of Scope; the line graph does not include specific information about the effects on Americans.

Passage Analysis: This passage describes the films of director Akira Kurosawa and their importance. Paragraph 1 establishes the high stature of Kurosawa. Paragraph 2 details some of Kurosawa's experiences and the impact they had on his filmmaking. Paragraph 3 talks about *Seven Samurai*, Kurosawa's most important film. Paragraph 4 contrasts the West's high regard for Kurosawa with the criticisms he has received in Japan. Paragraph 5 provides details of how Kurosawa's films were distinctive. Paragraph 6 describes "the wipe," Kurosawa's signature device. Paragraph 7 explains Kurosawa's influence on various genres of film, and finally, paragraph 8 sums up the author's view of Kurosawa as one of the "greats" in the history of film.

9. D

Category: Global

Getting to the Answer: To answer Global questions, use your Roadmap or paragraph notes to locate the main idea of the passage. Here, the main idea is Kurosawa—his unique style, its controversy, and his influence on films. **(D)** is correct. **(A)** is Out of Scope; the popularity of American Westerns in Japan is never discussed in the passage. **(B)** is Extreme; Kurosawa is referred to as the most important Japanese filmmaker in cinema history, not the most important filmmaker of any nationality. **(C)** is a detail from the passage, not the main idea. Since Kurosawa is considered "the most important Japanese filmmaker in history," and Ozu and Mizoguchi are not, it likely that Kurosawa's work compares favorably to that of the other directors. However, this comparison is not the main idea of the passage.

10. E

Category: Detail

Getting to the Answer: When reading, note where important details are located in the passage and understand how they fit into the structure of the text. In this case, paragraph 2 discusses Kurosawa's work on Japanese propaganda films. The last sentence states, "He took the lessons he learned in Tokyo and began making . . . works that took the values and traditions of the West and reinterpreted them with a Japanese sensibility and distinctly Japanese settings and characters." **(E)** matches this information, and is correct. **(F)** is Out of Scope; Kurosawa's technical training is never discussed. **(G)** is a Misused Detail; the Kurosawa-gumi were his team of expert technicians, but this group is never connected with Kurosawa's work in propaganda films. **(H)** is a Distortion; *Seven Samurai* is an example of Kurosawa blending Western ideals with a Japanese setting, but this film is not mentioned as motivated by his work in propaganda films.

11. C

Category: Detail

Getting to the Answer: Understand the general ideas of the passage, but don't try to memorize every word. Instead, use your Roadmap to guide you to specific details. Paragraph 4 explains the Japanese suspicion towards Kurosawa—that his films are not really Japanese and are overly influenced by the West. **(C)** is the support for this idea and the correct answer. **(A)** may seem to be a good reason to be "suspicious" of a person, but the passage does not connect Kurosawa's work in propaganda films with the feelings of Japanese audiences. **(B)** is a Misused Detail. The contrast mentioned in the choice is not the reason the Japanese audiences were "suspicious" of Kurosawa. **(D)** is also a Misused Detail. This sentence provides a second criticism of Kurosawa, but not the reason the audiences were "suspicious."

12. F

Category: Detail

Getting to the Answer: Look for context clues in the question to determine the answer's location in the passage. Here, the differences between Kurosawa's work and that of other directors are discussed in paragraph 5. **(F)** summarizes the points listed there, and is correct. **(E)** and **(G)** are Misused Details. These two points are made in the passage but are not presented as

ways Kurosawa was different from other directors. **(H)** is a Distortion. Paragraph 5 does state that Kurosawa-gumi were loyal to Kurosawa, but not that they were the only people with whom he would work.

13. D

Category: Function

Getting to the Answer: Irony is when something happens that is contrary to normal expectations. The first sentence of paragraph 7 describes what happened: Kurosawa's "films have influenced the very same American movie genres that Kurosawa admired so much." Because Kurosawa was influenced by Westerns at first, it is ironic that his films ended up influencing later Westerns. **(D)** reflects that irony and is the correct answer. **(A)** is a Distortion; the passage never states that George Lucas was more successful than Kurosawa. **(B)** is a Misused Detail; although this information is stated in the passage, "ironically" does not relate to the variety of film genres Kurosawa influenced. **(C)** is also a Distortion; these genres have benefited from Kurosawa, not Japanese directors in general.

14. H

Category: Function

Getting to the Answer: When a question asks how a part of the passage "contributes to the ideas in the passage," start by recalling the main idea. In this passage, the main idea was Kurosawa's importance as an innovator in filmmaking. Now consider the phrase "household name"—a name so well-known, everyone in a "household" would be familiar with it—and think about how this idea relates to Kurosawa. The author's use of the contrast keyword "although" indicates that many people who might know Welles or Hitchcock may not know Kurosawa, and the author believes Kurosawa's achievements are "no less worthy of recognition." The author is contrasting the fact that Kurosawa is not well-known with his important achievements. **(H)** is correct. **(E)** distorts the information in the text. The sentence is comparing Kurosawa's lack of recognition with the wide, "household" recognition of Welles and Hitchcock. The sentence is not comparing their films. **(F)** is Out of Scope. Although the author believes Kurosawa is worthy of this recognition, no prediction is made in the passage. **(G)** is a Misused Detail. The author does make this statement, but does not convey this idea through the use of the phrase "household name."

Passage Analysis: This passage gives an overview of the career of John Ford, a celebrated director of Westerns. Paragraph 1 describes how Ford directed Westerns throughout his career. Paragraph 2 describes Ford's early history and his entrance into film. Paragraph 3 describes how a film of his, *The Iron Horse*, encapsulated Ford's style. Paragraph 4 advances the chronology of Ford's career through the 1930s, the Second World War, and back to Westerns in the 1940s. Paragraph 5 describes the challenges of working with Ford. Paragraph 6 describes the simplistic style of directing Ford used in his successful career.

15. B
Category: Global

Getting to the Answer: When asked to find the primary purpose of an entire passage, make sure to identify a common theme that runs through every paragraph. In this case, every paragraph of the passage—from the words in paragraph 1 ("Ford turned his attention to the Western") to paragraph 3, which focuses on Ford's particular style of Western—describes Ford's career as a director of Westerns. Look for the answer choice that best captures this focus. **(B)** is correct. **(A)** is Out of Scope; the passage mentions such captivation but does not focus on the American public. **(C)** is a Misused Detail; the passage states that Ford refocused on the Western following World War II but that was not the main idea of the passage as a whole. **(D)** is Out of Scope; the passage never explains why Ford was fascinated with Westerns.

16. H
Category: Inference

Getting to the Answer: When presented with an Inference question that requires you to identify the reasons behind a particular decision made by the author, be sure to examine the context of the referenced words. Orson Welles's watching *Stagecoach* "more than 40 times" serves to establish Ford's significance as a director and the respect he received from others in the industry. Look for an answer choice that best represents this; **(H)** does exactly that. **(E)** is Out of Scope; the passage never suggests that Ford incorporated the suggestions of other directors. **(F)** is Out of Scope; the passage never states whether *Stagecoach* was a success at the box office. **(G)** is Opposite; the line referenced by the question is used to demonstrate Welles's respect for Ford as a director.

17. C
Category: Detail

Getting to the Answer: It is especially important with Detail questions to read the wording of the question stem very carefully. Your Roadmap should direct you to the end of paragraph 2, about Ford's early entrance into film. The last sentence of this paragraph mentions the emergence of a specific "Fordian" style in 1924 with the film *The Iron Horse*. Thus, **(C)** is correct. The other answers are Misused Details. **(A)** is incorrect because *Stagecoach* was merely a classic of his already-developed style. **(B)** is incorrect because Ford's documentary about Midway was not a fictional work like his peacetime career. **(D)** is incorrect because *The Quiet Man* was a 1952 film, made well into his career.

18. H
Category: Detail

Getting to the Answer: Your Roadmap will direct you to paragraph 4, which mentions Ford's involvement in the war. The author describes Ford's contribution to the war effort as "head of the newly formed Navy Field Photographic Unit," information that implies that Ford was a war photographer. **(H)** is a good match: the fact that Ford was a naval photographer is a reasonable conclusion that can be drawn from the text. **(E)** is a Distortion; although Ford was a celebrity, the passage never suggests Ford was an "entertainer" for the troops. **(F)** is a Distortion; the passage mentions Ford's documentary about Midway but never suggests he participated as a soldier in that battle. **(G)** is Out of Scope; the passage describes Ford as "head" of a particular naval unit but never states that he was an officer.

19. D
Category: Inference

Getting to the Answer: Inference questions ask you to find relevant details in the passage and then figure out an underlying point. In this case, the word "efficiency" is the relevant detail. The author describes Ford's career as prolific and his simple style as successful; **(D)** is correct. **(A)** is a Misused Detail; the passage never suggests Ford did not want to use a stepladder in his shooting in order to save money. **(B)** is Opposite; the passage describes Ford's style as simple, not extravagant. **(C)** is Out of Scope; the passage never describes Ford focusing on budgeting for his films.

20. F

Category: Function

Getting to the Answer: Scan the passage for *The Quiet Man* to guide your research. This will lead you to paragraph 1. With Function questions, it is always important to read around the cited text to get context. In this case, the author's reasoning was that *The Quiet Man* serves as an example of films other than Westerns that Ford created. This matches **(F)**. **(E)** is Out of Scope; the passage never suggests that the title of this film was in any way autobiographical. **(G)** is Opposite; even though *The Quiet Man* was not a Western, the passage describes Ford as particularly focused on Westerns, not a variety of subjects. **(H)** is Out of Scope; the passage never describes Ford's interest in Irish life.

Passage Analysis: Paragraph 1 discusses the emergence of the Hudson River School and identifies it as the first truly American art movement. Paragraph 2 describes the founding influence of Thomas Cole on the Hudson River School. Paragraph 3 considers the impact of European Romanticism and "the sublime." Paragraph 4 examines the differences between European and American landscape painters. Paragraph 5 describes the nationalistic motivations and subject matter of the Hudson River School. Paragraph 6 details the influence of the Hudson River School members on American cultural identity. Finally, paragraph 7 summarizes the historical context of the Hudson River School and its impact on America. Overall, the author's purpose is to inform the reader about the Hudson River School. The main idea is that the Hudson River School, influenced by nationalism in both subject and style, was the first truly American art movement.

21. B

Category: Global

Getting to the Answer: The answer to a Global question must match the passage's overall topic and tone. Therefore, **(B)** is correct. **(A)** is a Misused Detail; urbanization is mentioned in paragraph 7 alone. It is not a theme that pervades the entire passage. **(C)** is incorrect because it reverses the details in the passage; the European painters actually influenced the Americans. **(D)** is Extreme; while the members of the Hudson River School were concerned about some effects of industrialization, the passage does not say they rejected all of it. In fact, paragraph 5 mentions a painting celebrating a new railway.

22. H

Category: Detail

Getting to the Answer: Pay careful attention to the wording of this question. Which choice describes the works of the Hudson River School as a whole? The very first sentence of the passage tells you that the members of the Hudson River School were "landscape painters," which matches **(H)**. **(E)** and **(G)** are both Distortions; while the passage mentions the War of 1812 and European Romanticism, neither are described as subjects of paintings. **(F)** is a Misused Detail. While the Hudson River Valley and its surroundings inspired the first artists of the Hudson River School, paragraph 5 states that the movement expanded to include painters who depicted landscapes throughout the rest of the United States.

23. D

Category: Detail

Getting to the Answer: Detail questions ask you to track down a piece of information that is directly stated in the passage. **(D)** is correct because it describes how Cole explored the Catskill mountains just before he made his first paintings of the Hudson River Valley. **(A)** is a Misused Detail; while the Hudson River School painted "sublime" scenes, the sublime scenes are not connected to the actual founding of the school. **(B)** is also a Misused Detail; *The Course of Empire* series was painted after the school was founded. **(C)** is a Distortion; American Romantics actively sought to differentiate themselves from their European counterparts.

24. F

Category: Inference

Getting to the Answer: Even though this Inference question does not ask about the main idea directly, anything the author is likely to agree with will never stray far from the main idea. A central part of the main idea is America's growing nationalism; **(F)** is correct because it draws a connection between this nationalism and why the paintings were widely popular in America. **(E)** and **(G)** are incorrect because these painters sought "to be free of European artistic rules," as noted in paragraph 4, so this would not be a reason for their popularity. **(H)** is Extreme; the painters were skeptical about industrialization and urban development, but they did not seek to portray the dangers as their primary goal, and this was not the reason their paintings were popular.

25. C

Category: Function

Getting to the Answer: The cited phrase is used in the discussion of America's growing national pride after the War of 1812. Therefore, **(C)** is correct. **(A)** is a Distortion; the War of 1812 is mentioned, but the passage never says that these artists painted battle scenes. **(B)** and **(D)** are Out of Scope; these ideas are never mentioned in the passage.

26. H

Category: Inference

Getting to the Answer: Broadly phrased Inference questions test your understanding of the underlying ideas of the passage. The passage discusses the long-term impact of the Hudson River School on American society, including the founding of the New York Metropolitan Museum of Art and the way the paintings inspired lawmakers to set aside land for the national park system. **(H)** is correct. **(E)** is Out of Scope; the passage does not discuss how much these paintings sell for. Even though inferences are not directly stated in the passage, they will not deviate from information and ideas stated in the passage. **(F)** is a Misused Detail; paragraph 3 states that Romantic poets saw ancient cultures as purer than modern ones, but the author does not elaborate on this point or take a strong position regarding it. **(G)** is Extreme; while American nationalism grew after the War of 1812, the passage describes this growth in neutral terms, and "bloated" is too negative of a descriptor.

CHAPTER 10

SHSAT Science Passages & Elimination Strategies

CHAPTER OBJECTIVES

By the end of this chapter, you will be able to:

- Identify key information and ideas within a science passage
- Identify the five SHSAT Reading wrong answer traps

SHSAT Science Passages

You can expect to see at least one passage in the Reading section that deals with a scientific or technical topic. An important thing to remember is that you do not have to understand every word in the passage (such as specific terminology) in order to be able to answer the questions. For example, in the following passage, you don't need to stress about scientific phrases like "mathematical model" and "light densities." Additionally, keep in mind that you are *not* being tested on any outside science knowledge, so do not answer the questions based on anything other than the information contained in the passage.

A surefire way to keep your focus on the information in the passage is to follow the Kaplan Method. Practice the steps of the method as you read the following passage.

Practice

Read Actively

Actively reading the passage includes taking notes to create a Roadmap of a passage, which should include the main idea of the passage and the topic of each paragraph.

Green Sea Turtle Migration

1 Green sea turtles, shelled reptiles that plowed the oceans eons before mammals evolved, are known for their prodigious migrations. One group of green sea turtles makes a regular journey from feeding grounds near the Brazilian coast to breeding beaches on Ascension Island, a barren, relatively predator-free island in the central equatorial Atlantic. Notoriously slow on land, these turtles cover a distance of more than 2,000 kilometers in as little as two weeks. But how is this navigation of deep, featureless ocean accomplished? Scientists have several different hypotheses.

    A.   What is the passage about?

    B.   What is the topic of paragraph 1?

2 Green turtles appear to have an excellent sense of smell, so the turtles may orient themselves by detecting traces of substances released from Ascension Island itself. Because Ascension Island lies in the midst of a major westward-flowing ocean current, scientists believe that chemical substances picked up from the islands would tend to flow westward toward the feeding grounds of the turtle. As a result, these substances may provide a scented chemical trail that the turtles are able to follow. A mathematical model has been used to show that a concentration of substances delivered from Ascension to the turtles' feeding grounds, though diluted, may be sufficient to be sensed by the turtles. However, it is likely that other factors help the turtles orient themselves.

    C.   What does the first sentence indicate?

    D.   What is the topic of paragraph 2?

3 In addition to possessing a strong sense of smell, the turtles also have keen eyesight. This may help direct the turtles from their feeding grounds into the path of this chemical trail. It is an established fact that turtles are capable of distinguishing between different light densities. Turtles recognize at least four colors and are especially attuned to the color red because it often appears in their shell coloration. Researchers believe that these turtles swim east toward the rising sun at the beginning of their migration, changing course toward Ascension's beaches as soon as their route intersects with the scented path.

    E.   What new topic is discussed in detail here?

    F.   What is the topic of paragraph 3?

4 Finally, turtles may also have the ability to orient themselves using Earth's magnetic field. Since this sense is deeper than either sight or smell, it may serve as an additional guide during cloudy days or times when the turtle has difficulty picking up the scent trail. Experimental results have shown that turtle hatchlings have the ability to use magnetic fields to determine the direction in which they are swimming. Furthermore, since turtles are known to return to the exact beach from which they hatched, they may "imprint" the magnetic field of this particular beach at a very young age.

    G.   How is the focus of paragraph 4 different from the focus of paragraph 3?

    H.   What is the topic of paragraph 4?

5 Green sea turtles are an endangered species, and their numbers are steadily decreasing throughout the world. Understanding how they accomplish their migrations will allow scientists to make intelligent recommendations to policy makers and help ensure the survival of this magnificent animal. For example, since the turtles use light to navigate, they are especially vulnerable to light pollution from coastal developments. Similarly, their acute sense of smell means that an excessive amount of foreign materials in the water may disorient them. Human decisions in the coming years will determine whether the seas will continue to be inhabited by the green sea turtle or if its celebrated migrations will be only a memory.

    I.   What is the topic of paragraph 5?

    J.   What is the main idea of the passage?

Now, use your Roadmap and your researching skills to answer the following questions.

1.   Which statement best describes the central idea of the passage?

    A.   Green sea turtles are an endangered species that cannot survive if their natural habitat continues to be polluted.

    B.   The green turtle's outstanding eyesight and sense of smell have evolved over many eons.

    C.   The tropical weather in the central equatorial Atlantic is an integral part of the 2,000-kilometer ocean migration.

    D.   The migratory behavior of green sea turtles is made possible by a variety of factors.

2. What is the most likely reason green sea turtles breed on Ascension Island?

   E. There is an abundance of food there.

   F. It has a cooler climate than Brazil.

   G. The turtles have fewer natural enemies there.

   H. Its beaches are cleaner than Brazil's beaches.

3. The phrase "several different hypotheses" conveys the idea that

   A. scientists have not fully tracked the migration patterns of green sea turtles.

   B. green sea turtles use their sense of smell to compensate for their poor eyesight.

   C. knowledge about green sea turtles is limited by a lack of scientific evidence.

   D. there is more than one way to explain how green sea turtles navigate toward their breeding grounds.

4. What is one way turtles find the trail of chemical substances that are released from Ascension Island?

   E. the position of the rising sun

   F. an instinctive sense of direction

   G. the path of underwater ocean currents

   H. a mathematical model

5. Turtles are especially sensitive to the color red most likely because

   A. it helps them identify other turtles.

   B. it is the most intense of the primary colors.

   C. it matches the colors of the rising sun.

   D. it seems more attractive than other colors.

SHSAT Reading Elimination Strategies

Elimination Strategies

One key strategy for determining the correct answer choice is to eliminate the incorrect choices. This can be especially helpful if you encounter a passage or question that you're not confident about. As Chapter 9 discussed, wrong choices most often fall into specific categories. Once you know the categories, elimination is much easier!

Wrong Answer Trap	Description
Distortion	The answer slightly alters details from a passage so they are no longer correct.
Extreme	The answer takes a stronger position (often more positive or more negative) than the passage takes.
Misused Detail	The answer is a true statement from the passage, but it doesn't answer the question.
Opposite	The answer contradicts information in the passage.
Out of Scope	The answer includes information that is not in the passage.

Global questions ask you to summarize the main idea of the passage. The correct answer choice should correspond to what you have written in your Roadmap. Out of Scope, Misused Detail, and Extreme are the most common wrong answer traps for Global questions.

Detail questions ask you to research information that is directly stated in the passage. There are two common types of wrong answer choices for Detail questions: Misused Detail and Distortion.

Function questions ask about the purpose of a particular part of the passage. They can ask about the purpose of a word, sentence, paragraph, detail, or even punctuation. Distortion and Out of Scope wrong answer traps are the most common incorrect answers that accompany Function questions.

Inference questions ask you to figure out the underlying point of a particular phrase or example. The three common types of wrong answer choices for Inference questions are Out of Scope, Extreme, and Misused Detail.

Infographic questions ask you how the information in the graph, table, or image supports ideas presented in the passage. Out of Scope and Distortion are the most common wrong answer traps that accompany Infographic questions.

Practice

Read Actively

Actively read the following passage, taking notes to create a Roadmap. Be sure to write down the topic of each paragraph and the main idea of the passage.

Bird Courtship Behavior

1 Since there are thousands of species of birds in the natural world and many of these species tend to congregate in the same habitats, nearly every species has its own special courtship procedures and "identification checks." Identification checks allow birds to ensure that they are mating with members of their own species. Identification checks are important because if members of different species mate, the offspring are usually sterile or badly adapted to their surroundings. Once the species of a potential partner is confirmed, courtship rituals enable birds to assess the quality of their mates.

2 For many bird species, plumage plays a key role in both identification and courtship. During breeding season, male birds acquire distinctive plumage that they use to attract females, and the females respond only to males with the correct markings. The most striking example of such plumage is the magnificently colored head, chest, and tail feathers of the male bird of paradise. When attempting to attract a mate, the male perches on a branch and then gradually leans forward until he is hanging upside down, covered with his own brilliant feathers. A female bird of paradise will watch the display and then respond. Scientists refer to the bird displaying the plumage as the "actor," while the bird that observes is the "reactor." Although the male is the actor and the female is the reactor in the case of birds of paradise, the females of some species are more brightly colored than the males, and the courtship roles are reversed. Distinctive behavioral changes can also be important aspects of courtship and breeding activity.

3 Aggressiveness among males, and sometimes among females, is quite common. Some birds, such as whooping cranes and trumpeter swans, perform wonderfully elaborate courtship dances in which both sexes are enthusiastic participants. The purpose of the dance is to establish and maintain a "pair bond" that will last between the male and female through the period of the reproductive season, or at least until the nesting has been completed. Each species has its own set of inherited courtship behaviors, which also helps prevent mating between birds of different species.

4 Bird calls are another key part of identification between individuals in a given species. When a female migrates to her breeding region in the spring, she often encounters numerous birds of different species. The males of her species identify themselves by their singing and communicate to her that they are in breeding condition. This information allows the female to predict the response of a male to her approach. Later, after mating has taken place, the note patterns of a particular male's song enable the nesting female to continue to identify her partner.

5 Nature lovers do not need to travel to exotic lands to see these fascinating rituals take place. The northern cardinal, a common sight in the eastern and midwestern United States, is an excellent example of a territorial bird. Males perch on tall trees and sing high-pitched, piercing notes to announce that the surrounding area is their territory. They are so aggressive about defending it that they will sometimes mistake their reflection in a window or car as an invading male and attempt to fight it. During courtship, males will feed females, placing the food directly into her beak. Cardinals usually mate for life, and pairs will often sing to each other at dusk. Once the chicks have hatched, they are fed and cared for by the male cardinal, who listens carefully for their unique fledgling call.

6 The American goldfinch is another common bird with spectacular courtship behaviors. When a male is ready to mate, he will actually chase the prospective female. The female attempts to outmaneuver him by flying in zig-zag patterns, and the male signals his fitness and worthiness as a mate by matching her move for move. Once the two birds are pair-bonded, the male will establish his territory by flying from tree to tree, singing a unique warbling song as he goes. He will circle the perimeter twice: once in a low, flat flight and again in "daredevil" display involving abrupt drops to the ground and loops. As with the cardinal, the male shoulders the responsibility of caring for the chicks once they have hatched. These displays and rituals illustrate how complex behavior can emerge from the most primitive of biological needs—reproduction.

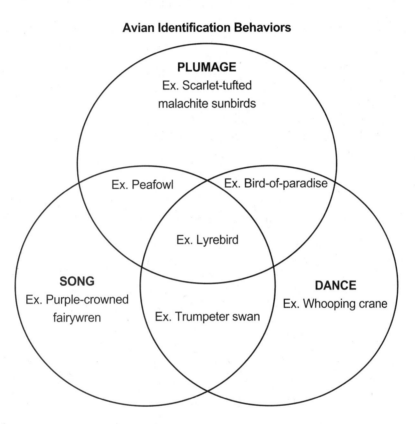

Avian Identification Behaviors

A. ¶ 1 Topic

B. ¶ 2 Topic

C. ¶ 3 Topic

D. ¶ 4 Topic

E. ¶ 5 Topic

F. ¶ 6 Topic

G. What is the main idea of the passage?

Now, use your Roadmap and your researching skills to answer the following questions.

Global

1. Which statement best describes the central idea of the passage?

   A. Birds create nests in a variety of ways, depending on their species and general habitat.

   B. The mating activities of birds involve several different types of behaviors and approaches.

   C. Bird calls provide important migratory directions in addition to playing a key role in courtship.

   D. A "pair bond" generally lasts at least as long as it takes the two birds to create a nest, if not longer.

Detail

2. Which sentence best demonstrates the function of male bird calls?

   E. "Identification checks allow birds to ensure that they are mating with members of their own species." (paragraph 1)

   F. "During breeding season, male birds acquire distinctive plumage that they use to attract females, and the females respond only to males with the correct markings." (paragraph 2)

   G. "Aggressiveness among males, and sometimes among females, is quite common." (paragraph 3)

   H. "The males of her species identify themselves by their singing and communicate to her that they are in breeding condition." (paragraph 4)

Function

3. Read this sentence from paragraph 3.

   > Some birds, such as whooping cranes and trumpeter swans, perform wonderfully elaborate courtship dances in which both sexes are enthusiastic participants.

   The sentence contributes to the development of ideas in the passage by

   A. suggesting that some bird species seldom participate in courtship procedures.

   B. explaining how whooping cranes and trumpeter swans acquire distinctive breeding plumage.

   C. providing an example of species that behave in an unusual way during courtship.

   D. demonstrating a reversal of the typical male and female courtship roles.

Inference

4. In bird species for which sounds are a crucial form of identification check, the female bird most likely

    E. is unable to sing.

    F. is not aggressive.

    G. chooses the mate.

    H. must be in breeding condition.

Infographic

5. How does the Venn diagram contribute to the development of the topic of the passage?

    A. It emphasizes that the males of some avian species can use a variety of behaviors to attract a mate.

    B. It shows that birds are more likely to use a single courtship behavior, rather than multiple techniques.

    C. It indicates that some species of birds may use more than one "identification check" behavior.

    D. It tells how male birds-of-paradise both develop distinctive plumage and perform a dance to attract females.

Practice Set

For test-like practice, give yourself 45 minutes (an average of 5 minutes per passage and 1 minute per question) to complete this question set. After you're done, be sure to study the explanations, even for questions you answered correctly. They can be found at the end of this chapter.

DIRECTIONS: Read the passages and answer the corresponding questions. Re-read relevant parts of the text before choosing the best answer for each question. Base your answers only on the content within each passage.

The Animals of the Galápagos Islands

1   The Galápagos Islands, located 600 miles off the Pacific coast of Ecuador, are a chain of volcanic islands whose unique geological past has contributed to the diversity of their animal life. They caught the attention of the Western world when famed naturalist Charles Darwin visited the 13 islands during a voyage in the 1830s. This small, isolated archipelago[1], administered as a province of Ecuador, is home to a number of unique species of plant and animal life. Many of these species are so rare that they can be found only in the Galápagos. In fact, Darwin's revolutionary theory of evolution owes much to the time he spent documenting and making sketches of the native fauna, many of which had been isolated for generations.

2   One of the most fascinating of these species is the cormorant, a bird whose rather ordinary-looking brown feathers might not cause one to immediately place it in the same category as some of the islands' more spectacular creatures. Yet the cormorants that live on these volcanic islands are unlike any other species of cormorant in the world because they have lost the ability to fly.

3   The Galápagos Islands' flightless cormorant species is distinguished by an abnormally small breastbone that supports two scruffy, stunted wings. These undersized wings are so disproportionate to the rest of the cormorant's body that the bird appears almost comical. These flightless cormorants, though somewhat less than impressive, do have some advantages over their flying relatives. Instead of strong wings, the flightless cormorant has heavier and more powerful legs that it uses to propel its sleek body quickly through the water after various prey. In addition, although the common cormorant must hold out its sizeable wings to dry in the sun upon emerging from an underwater hunting session, the flightless cormorant need not wait so long to dry out.

4   Most naturalists attribute these significant differences to the isolated environment of the Galápagos. Like many of the islands' creatures, the flightless cormorant has no known natural predators. Despite this evolutionary advantage, these birds are among the rarest of the Galápagos seabirds, with a population size of only about 800 pairs. Scientists, however, do not consider the flightless cormorant an endangered species, partly because of the female's ability to breed as many as three times a year and the independent nature of newly born chicks. For these reasons, the flightless cormorant population has been able to recover relatively quickly from the various environmental disasters that have struck the Galápagos over the years—a resiliency that bodes well for the survival of these distinctive birds far into the future.

5   Another species endemic to the Galápagos is the waved albatross. It is in many ways the opposite of the flightless cormorant. Although most birds weigh a mere eight to nine pounds, their wingspan is gigantic, sometimes up to 9 feet across. They are built to soar above the water, sometimes going out as far as 60 miles from the shore in search of food. To save energy on long flights, they angle their wings into the wind and

[1]archipelago: chain of islands

use it to gain "free" altitude. They then glide down in the direction that they want to go before catching the next updraft. This type of flight, known as "dynamic soaring," allows some species of albatross to reach speeds of almost 70 miles per hour. While the adults make their trips out into the ocean to feed, they "park" their chicks at home. After foraging in the open seas, adults sometimes regurgitate up to 4 pounds of predigested food to feed their chicks. Scientists estimate that there are about 30,000 waved albatrosses. Although this number may appear large, especially when compared to the flightless cormorant, the albatross is much more vulnerable because it breeds more slowly and is often inadvertently killed by commercial fishing line.

6   Another marvelous bird species of the Galápagos is the blue-footed booby. Although this bird is not unique to the Galápagos, about one-half of breeding pairs make their home in the islands. Their courtship ritual is quite remarkable. The male will strut in front of the female and dance to display his blue feet. He then presents his nesting material for her approval. Finally, he finishes off with one more display of his feet. The booby is a fish eater and can dive up to 82 feet in search of sardines, anchovies, mackerel, and flying fish.

7   The namesake of the islands, the Galápagos, or giant, tortoise has a multifaceted relationship with the native birds. Several species of finch and mockingbird will hop in front of a tortoise, indicating that they are ready to feed. In response, the tortoise extends its limbs and neck, allowing the birds access to areas of his body that would normally be hidden. The birds benefit from a free meal of ticks, fleas, and other parasites, and the tortoise finds relief. Perversely, some tortoises have been observed to exploit this usual exchange of services. When the birds are ready to feed, the tortoise extends his limbs as usual. However, when he observes the birds underneath him, he quickly withdraws back into his shell and crushes them with his massive weight. The tortoise then eats the birds, presumably as an extra source of protein.

8   The Galápagos Islands are home to so many special creatures. In recent years, however, the human population on the island has exploded. Native species are feeling increasing pressure from humans and human-reared animals such as domestic cats and goats. The Galápagos Islands form part of our common world heritage. We must work together to preserve them so that future generations can appreciate its wonders.

1.   Which statement best describes the central idea of the passage?

   A.   Many species of seabirds have evolved into unique varieties found only in the Galápagos Islands because the islands are so far from the nearest land.

   B.   The isolation of the Galápagos Islands allowed many unique species to evolve and made the islands central to Darwin's research.

   C.   Because of their location, importance to Darwin's theory of evolution, and wide variety of unique species, the Galápagos Islands should be safeguarded.

   D.   The rapid growth of the human population in the Galápagos Islands puts many native species at increased risk and must be carefully monitored.

2. Which sentence best supports the idea that "Darwin's revolutionary theory of evolution owes much to the time he spent documenting and making sketches of the native fauna" of the Galápagos Islands? (paragraph 1)

    E. "Yet the cormorants that live on these volcanic islands are unlike any other species of cormorant in the world because they have lost the ability to fly." (paragraph 2)

    F. "The Galápagos Islands' flightless cormorant species is distinguished by an abnormally small breastbone that supports two scruffy, stunted wings." (paragraph 3)

    G. "Most naturalists attribute these significant differences to the isolated environment of the Galápagos." (paragraph 3)

    H. "The namesake of the islands, the Galápagos, or giant, tortoise, has a multifaceted relationship with the native birds." (paragraph 7)

3. The phrase "evolutionary advantage" in paragraph 4 conveys the idea that the flightless cormorant

    A. should be found in larger numbers than they are currently.

    B. is able to produce new chicks three times in each year.

    C. is able to swim faster than the common cormorant.

    D. is not preyed upon in its native environment.

4. How do the details in paragraph 6 about the blue-footed booby convey a central idea of the passage?

    E. by describing the unique characteristics of an interesting bird that is found in locations other than the Galápagos Islands

    F. by detailing the many interesting behaviors of a bird species that is only found in the Galápagos Islands

    G. by illustrating how the expanding human population threatens the survival of this and other species of the Galápagos Islands

    H. by confirming that there are sufficient individuals to guarantee the survival of a species in spite of environmental pressures

5. Which sentence from the passage best supports the idea that "the Galápagos, or giant, tortoise, has a multifaceted relationship with the native birds" (paragraph 7)?

    A. "Several species of finch and mockingbird will hop in front of a tortoise, indicating that they are ready to feed."

    B. "In response, the tortoise extends its limbs and neck, allowing the birds access to areas of his body that would normally be hidden."

    C. "The birds benefit from a free meal of ticks, fleas, and other parasites, and the tortoise finds relief."

    D. "Perversely, some tortoises have been observed to exploit this usual exchange of services."

6. The author of the passage develops the idea that the Galápagos Islands should be preserved mainly by

    E. revealing the survival statistics of two types of seabirds.

    F. explaining how the islands' location contributed to Darwin's theory.

    G. detailing how quickly the human population is growing.

    H. describing a number of animals that are not found in any other location.

Ska

1   Many modern forms of music can trace their lineage to earlier, often forgotten, styles. Rock and roll, for example, owes much of its power to the blues sounds of the Mississippi Delta. Likewise, jazz can be directly traced to the jaunty rhythms of ragtime and early Tin Pan Alley. The most representative sound of Jamaica, reggae, also has a somewhat obscure grandparent: ska. Though often overshadowed by other genres of music, ska has had an influence far greater than the confines of its small Caribbean birthplace.

2   Ska developed in the 1950s as urban dance music for young Jamaicans. The years immediately following World War II saw the youth of Jamaica buying radios in increasing numbers. Using this new technology, they were able to tune into the radio stations of the southeastern United States and absorb the exciting new sounds of the era. Artists such as Fats Domino and Louis Jordan were particularly admired. Large numbers of military personnel stationed in Jamaica also magnified the influence of American culture. Thus, although many Jamaicans believe that ska is indigenous to their island, it is in fact a derivative style like rock or jazz. Ska has elements of rhythm and blues, a predecessor of rock and roll, as well as American boogie-woogie jazz and several Caribbean rhythms, most notably the mambo from Cuba and the mento from Jamaica. The blending together of such disparate elements created ska's distinctive sound: a walking bass line; an emphasis on the upbeats of each measure; and a pulsating, multilayered rhythm driven by horns, saxophones, trumpets, trombones, pianos, and guitars. The accented upbeats may be the most distinctive feature of this musical style.

3   Because of the layered nature of the music, ska was primarily an instrumental genre, and groups such as Toots and the Maytals and the Skatalites gained prominence. Most ska bands backed a select number of vocalists, most important among them Derrick Morgan, Prince Buster, and Desmond Dekker. Ska lyrics, like its music, drew much from outside influences but with a distinctive native flair; besides perennially popular themes of love and heartbreak, many songs took on political issues such as poverty, police brutality, and Jamaica's growing cry for independence from Great Britain. When Jamaica finally gained independence in 1962, ska achieved its high point as it celebrated the country's new autonomy.

4   In the subsequent decades, ska evolved into different styles, including rocksteady and reggae. The connections between these styles and ska were immediately apparent. Reggae, for example, the sound most closely associated with Jamaica today, is actually just an extremely slow version of ska, with varying instruments and lyrical themes. This similarity helped ska groups like Toots and the Maytals easily adapt to changing tastes. Even Bob Marley, reggae's most famous artist, began his career as a ska performer.

5   The genre also influenced many musicians outside of Jamaica. In 1964, the Beatles recorded "I Call Your Name," which included a brief instrumental ska interlude. In the 1970s, other British rock bands such as The Clash, The Specials, Madness, and The Police further developed and adapted ska, using their own styles of punk and new wave. In the 1990s, American groups like No Doubt, Sublime, and The Mighty Mighty Bosstones also made use of ska rhythms in their own way, though they did not necessarily bill their music as ska. Throughout the decades, "pure" ska has also experienced many different revivals, the most important of these perhaps occurring in the mid-1990s. Usually, but not always, these revivals are motivated by the prevailing political climate at the time.

6   Although largely masked by the din of mainstream music, ska has played a prominent—if quiet—role in the development of popular music worldwide.

7. Which statement best describes the central idea of this passage?

   A. Jamaican music has been influenced by American rhythm and blues, boogie-woogie jazz, the Cuban mambo, and ska.

   B. Ska music has both developed from existing styles and contributed to the development of later styles.

   C. Ska music is usually performed as instrumental music, although some singers used ska to protest social problems.

   D. Musical artists in Jamaica, America, Britain, and Europe have adapted and included ska rhythms in their musical works.

8. The phrase "Jamaica's growing cry for independence" in paragraph 3 conveys the idea that ska

   E. expressed the political views of vocalists Derrick Morgan, Prince Buster, and Desmond Dekker.

   F. included the Jamaicans' desire for freedom as one of its themes.

   G. influenced Great Britain's decision to grant Jamaica independence.

   H. became even more popular after Jamaica gained its independence.

9. Read this sentence from paragraph 4.

   > **The connections between these styles and ska were immediately apparent.**

   How does the sentence contribute to the structure and development of ideas in the passage?

   A. It signals a shift from a neutral viewpoint in paragraph 3 to the presentation of an argument.

   B. It provides a contrast transition from the opinion presented in paragraph 3.

   C. It presents a viewpoint that paragraph 4 will later argue against.

   D. It introduces the support for a claim presented in paragraph 4.

10. Read these sentences from paragraph 5.

    > **Throughout the decades, "pure" ska has also experienced many different revivals, the most important of these perhaps occurring in the mid-1990s. Usually, but not always, these revivals are motivated by the prevailing political climate at the time.**

    The use of quotation marks around the word "pure" is most likely intended to emphasize that ska

    E. should be distinguished from the many musical styles that it later influenced around the world.

    F. was appreciated as its own musical style with the power to inspire its listeners long after its emergence.

    G. contributed to the development of a distinctive style of Jamaican political music as well as popular music.

    H. owes a debt of gratitude to Jamaican politics for ska's continued popularity and many revivals in the 1990s.

11. Read this sentence from paragraph 7.

> **Although largely masked by the din of mainstream music, ska has played a prominent—if quiet—role in the development of popular music worldwide.**

Which sentence from paragraph 5 provides support for this statement?

A. "The genre also influenced many musicians outside of Jamaica."

B. "In 1964, the Beatles recorded 'I Call Your Name,' which included a brief instrumental ska interlude."

C. "In the 1990s, American groups like No Doubt, Sublime, and The Mighty Mighty Bosstones also made use of ska rhythms in their own way, though they did not necessarily bill their music as ska."

D. "Throughout the decades, 'pure' ska has also experienced many different revivals, the most important of these perhaps occurring in the mid-1990s."

12. How does the author's use of chronological structure contribute to the development of ideas in the passage?

E. It illustrates how quickly ska became important, and how quickly other musical styles incorporated ska.

F. It explains why ska developed in the 1950s and why it became a largely instrumental form of music.

G. It emphasizes the key reasons ska developed and changed over the years, and how it was adapted into other music.

H. It highlights how ska was influenced by other musical styles and later became an influence on other styles.

James Polk

1   For much of his life, James Knox Polk followed in the footsteps of Andrew Jackson[1]. Like the fiery Jackson, Polk was born in North Carolina and moved to Tennessee to begin a political career. In fact, "Young Hickory's" policies were very similar to Jackson's: both men favored lower taxes, championed the frontiersmen, farmers, and workers, and opposed the controversial Bank of the United States. Polk, however, did not share Jackson's rather fierce temperament but was instead known for remaining soft-spoken even as he worked energetically toward his goals. Although history will likely always remember the frontier persona of Andrew Jackson, it was Polk who did much more to shape the course of American history.

2   Polk was born in Mecklenburg, North Carolina, in 1795, as the oldest of 10 children. From an early age, Polk suffered ill health that would turn out to be a lifelong affliction. Despite his physical shortcomings, he was an able student and graduated from the University of North Carolina with honors in 1818. Two years later, Polk was admitted to the bar, and in 1823, he was elected to the Tennessee House of Representatives. From there, he was elected to the U.S. House of Representatives in 1825, serving until 1839. Polk was also Speaker of the House from 1835 to 1839, a post that catapulted him into a position of political prominence.

3   After he left Congress to serve as governor of Tennessee in 1839, it became clear that Polk's political aspirations were high indeed. During the 1844 presidential campaign, the leading Democratic candidate was ex-President Martin Van Buren, and the Whig candidate was Henry Clay. Both men, as part of their platforms, opposed policies to expand American territory, and neither intended to annex the independent state of Texas or the Oregon Territory. Polk, spurred on by Jackson's advice, recognized that neither candidate had correctly surmised the feelings of the people, so he publicly announced that, as president, he would do his utmost to acquire Texas and Oregon. Polk was the first political "dark horse" in American politics, coming out of nowhere to win the Democratic nomination and the election.

4   Today, historians consider Polk to be the greatest United States president before the Civil War. He had a tremendous work ethic, often spending more than ten hours a day at his desk. In his own words, "No President who performs his duty faithfully and conscientiously can have any leisure. I prefer to supervise the whole operations of the government myself rather than entrust the public business to subordinates, and this makes my duties very great." His hands-on approach paid dividends; he fulfilled every major domestic and foreign policy promise that he set during his campaign. Although he served but one term, his depth of achievement is remarkable.

5   As the eleventh president of the United States, Polk is primarily remembered for his tireless work to expand the borders of the nation. Since the 18th century, America and Britain had disputed the boundaries of Britain's Oregon territory. Both sides saw it as rightfully theirs. The British claimed that the explorations of James Cook and George Vancouver had established the region as a British possession. Americans cited the land expedition of Lewis and Clark and the discovery of the Columbia River by Robert Gray as their precedent. Although the status of the territory had long been disputed, both sides relied on negotiation, due to the expense of fighting a war in such a remote location. However, under Polk, war began to look like a possibility. The slogan "54-40 or Fight" was adopted as a rallying cry for those Americans who sought the annexation of the complete British territory. Since both Britain and the United States recognized the crucial geographical significance of this region, negotiations were heated. Finally, Polk reached an agreement with England in 1846 that divided the Oregon Territory along the 49th parallel, carving out the present-day states of Washington and Oregon.

[1]Seventh U.S. President from 1829 to 1837 and War of 1812 hero, often referred to as "Old Hickory"

6   Polk also quickly annexed Texas in 1845. This action provoked war with Mexico and allowed the United States to acquire California and the New Mexico territory. With the treaty of Guadalupe Hidalgo in 1848, the Mexican-American war officially ended, and the borders of the modern continental United States were essentially established.

7   While these triumphs were somewhat diminished by controversy from abolitionists who opposed the spread of slavery into new territories, under Polk's leadership the dream of "manifest destiny" became a reality and the United States fully extended its borders from the Atlantic to the Pacific.

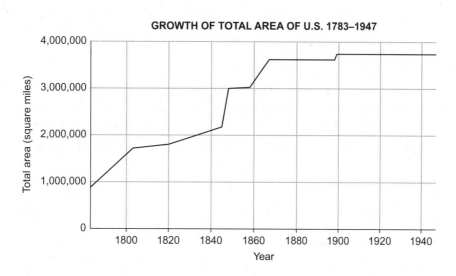

GROWTH OF TOTAL AREA OF U.S. 1783–1947

13.   Which statement best describes the central idea of the passage?

    A.   The presidency of James Polk had a greater impact on American history than did the presidency of his mentor, Andrew Jackson.

    B.   Polk's decisions as president led to the Mexican-American War, although the United States' victory allowed the annexation of several states.

    C.   His strong work ethic and sense of personal responsibility were primarily responsible for James Polk's many achievements as president.

    D.   The boundaries of the modern continental United States were largely established under the successful presidency of James Polk.

14.   The words "fiery," "fierce," and "frontier persona" in paragraph 1 affect the tone of the paragraph because they

    E.   describe the intense style that will lead Polk to his many successes.

    F.   illustrate why Jackson criticized Polk's soft-spoken approach.

    G.   convey why Jackson was able to have Polk follow his suggestions.

    H.   emphasize the different personalities of Jackson and Polk.

15.   The phrase "catapulted him into a position of political prominence" in paragraph 2 conveys the idea that

    A.   Polk quickly gained political power from this new role.

    B.   Polk rapidly took control of the Democratic Party.

    C.   Polk suddenly became known throughout the country.

    D.   Polk became the leading Democratic candidate for president.

16. How did Polk win the 1844 presidential election?

    E. He worked long hours, often spending over ten hours a day at his desk, and assured the voters that he would continue to do so as president.

    F. He sharply criticized his opponents, ex-President Martin van Buren and Henry Clay, and won most of the presidential debates.

    G. He determined that the voters wanted to add territory to the United States and promised that he would obtain Oregon and Texas.

    H. He relied on the support of former president Andrew Jackson and received the nomination of the Democratic Party after Jackson's presidency.

17. Read these sentences from paragraph 4.

> **In his own words, "No President who performs his duty faithfully and conscientiously can have any leisure. I prefer to supervise the whole operations of the government myself rather than entrust the public business to subordinates, and this makes my duties very great."**

The sentences contribute to the development of ideas in the passage by showing that Polk

    A. was willing to spend his time on tasks that others could have completed for him.

    B. would not pursue any recreational activities during his term as president.

    C. would work diligently to achieve the many accomplishments of his presidency.

    D. considered his position as president to be an important and serious job.

18. Which sentence gives the best summary of the dispute over the Oregon Territory? (paragraph 5)

    E. Polk successfully annexed the territory following a war with Britain that was difficult and expensive due to the remote location of the fighting.

    F. British and American expeditions had independently claimed the region, negotiations ensued, and on the threshold of war, Polk successfully negotiated a compromise.

    G. Americans rallied for annexation of the complete territory, Polk promised to acquire it, and despite heated negotiations with Britain, Polk succeeded.

    H. After President Polk conducted heated negotiations, Britain agreed to surrender the territory to the United States because the territory was adjacent to the American border.

19. How does the graph contribute to the development of a central idea of the passage?

    A. It illustrates that the United States almost quadrupled in area between 1783 and 1947, thus fulfilling Polk's dream of "manifest destiny."

    B. It emphasizes that the United States had acquired most of its present land area after 1870.

    C. It proves that during Polk's presidency, the United States acquired more land than during Jackson's presidency.

    D. It shows the dramatic increase in the rate at which the United States acquired land during Polk's presidency, affecting the course of American history.

Jupiter

1 As the fifth planet from the Sun and by far the most massive in our solar system, Jupiter has fascinated scientists for centuries. Since it is clearly visible to the naked eye, it has been known since ancient times. Cultures such as the Babylonian, Chinese, and Indian studied its orbit and used it in their astronomical reckonings. Since it was so bright and prominent in the night sky, the Romans called it "the star of Jupiter" to honor the chief god of their pantheon, and this is the name we still use today.

2 In 1610, the Italian astronomer Galileo used his telescope to study Jupiter. In addition to seeing the clearest images possible at that time, he also spotted four large moons in orbit around this enormous planet. It was these moons, now known as the Galilean moons, that provided important evidence for Galileo's outspoken support of Copernicus's heliocentric theory of planetary movement. These moons seemed to revolve around a planet other than Earth; up until that time, the dominant theory was that Earth was the center of the universe and the Sun and the planets moved around it. Many more moons have been discovered since Galileo's time. In fact, scientists now believe that Jupiter may have up to 79 distinct moons, but the four Galilean moons are by far the most massive.

3 In addition to galvanizing scientists to rethink the structure of the cosmos, Jupiter's moons also provided some of the first evidence we have of water outside of Earth in our solar system. The smallest of the Galilean moons, Europa, may contain an ocean hidden underneath a thick layer of ice. If it does, it is one of the likeliest candidates for extraterrestrial life in our solar system. Scientists theorize that Europa's hidden ocean could contain an environment similar to that of the hydrothermal vents in the deep oceans of Earth. Large bacterial colonies could be below the ice, just as they are found clustered around these vents on Earth.

4 The first close look at Jupiter came in 1973, when the unmanned NASA probe Pioneer 10 completed a successful flyby and collected important data regarding the planet's chemical composition and interior structure. Designated as one of the gas planets—along with Saturn, Uranus, and Neptune—Jupiter is composed of about 90 percent hydrogen and 10 percent helium and has no solid surface, only varying densities of gas. In fact, very little is known about the interior of Jupiter. What is visible when looking at a gas planet like Jupiter is really only the tops of clouds making up the outermost atmosphere, and probes have been able to penetrate only about 90 miles below this layer. Scientists, however, believe it is likely, largely due to the traces of water and minerals that have been collected from Jupiter's atmosphere, that the planet has a core of rocky material amounting to a mass perhaps as much as 15 times that of Earth.

5 Like other gaseous planets, Jupiter has high-velocity winds that blow in wide bands of latitude, each moving in an alternate direction. Slight chemical and temperature differences between these bands, and the result-ing chemical reactions, are probably responsible for the array of vibrant colors that dominate the planet's appearance. Measurements taken by a number of probes indicate that the powerful winds moving these bands can reach speeds exceeding 400 miles per hour.

6 One of Jupiter's most famous features is its Great Red Spot, a swirling storm that has been observed since at least 1830 and is large enough to engulf Earth in its entirety. Scientists are unsure why the spot is red, but infrared readings indicate that the spot is colder than any of the other clouds in the atmosphere. The storm's incredible longevity is partially explained by the fact that there is little to no friction between it and the planet's gaseous surface; it can continue to glide around the atmosphere indefinitely since nothing can slow it down.

7 Yet perhaps the most fascinating characteristic of this planet is the rotational speed of the entire globe of gas itself. While Earth takes 24 hours to make a full revolution, Jupiter completes a full revolution in less than half that time, an amazingly short period of time for a planet with a diameter roughly 11 times that of our own planet. How Jupiter is able to rotate so quickly is just one of the many mysteries that scientists continue to explore in their efforts to understand our largest neighbor.

8 The next scheduled mission to Jupiter is the European Agency's Jupiter Ice Moon Explorer, with a prospective launch date of June 2022. As the name suggests, the objective is to study the Galilean moons, particularly Europa, and determine if they do indeed have the ability to support life. Scientists and space enthusiasts will have a while to wait, however, as the probes will not arrive at Jupiter until approximately October 2029.

20. Which statement best describes the central idea of the passage?

   E. Jupiter, the gas giant planet closest to Earth, has a specific chemical composition that influences unique principal characteristics.

   F. The discovery of Jupiter led to the popular acceptance of Copernicus's heliocentric theory.

   G. Recent unmanned probes have gathered some information about Jupiter, but many questions remain.

   H. The study of Jupiter over the centuries has revealed many interesting characteristics, yet many mysteries remain.

21. According to paragraph 2, Copernicus's "heliocentric theory of planetary movement" included the idea that

   A. multiple moons orbit the planet Jupiter.

   B. the Sun and the planets revolve around Earth.

   C. planets do not necessarily revolve around Earth.

   D. Jupiter orbits the Galilean moons.

22. Which evidence from the passage is most relevant to the claim in paragraph 3 that Jupiter galvanized "scientists to rethink the structure of the cosmos?"

   E. Galileo's observation of Jupiter's largest moons

   F. the likely presence of water on Europa

   G. the large number of moons circling Jupiter

   H. Jupiter's gaseous composition

23. How does paragraph 3 fit into the overall structure of the passage and contribute to the development of ideas?

   A. It introduces a key characteristic of Jupiter that the remainder of the passage continues to discuss.

   B. It introduces the first finding from the 1973 Pioneer 10 probe discussed in the following paragraph.

   C. It reveals the reason scientists have been able to determine the first presence of extraterrestrial life in the solar system.

   D. It reveals the evidence for one of the most important questions the probe in paragraph 8 will attempt to answer.

24. Which statement from the passage provides the best support for the claim made in paragraph 6 that "the storm's incredible longevity is partially explained by the fact that there is little to no friction between it and the planet's gaseous surface"?

    E. "The smallest of the Galilean moons, Europa, may contain an ocean hidden underneath a thick layer of ice." (paragraph 3)

    F. "Designated as one of the gas planets—along with Saturn, Uranus, and Neptune—Jupiter is composed of about 90 percent hydrogen and 10 percent helium and has no solid surface, only varying densities of gas." (paragraph 4)

    G. "Like other gaseous planets, Jupiter has high-velocity winds that blow in wide bands of latitude, each moving in an alternate direction." (paragraph 5)

    H. "While Earth takes 24 hours to make a full revolution, Jupiter completes a full revolution in less than half that time, an amazingly short period of time for a planet with a diameter roughly 11 times that of our own planet." (paragraph 7)

25. The author conveys a point of view on the study of the planet Jupiter mainly by

    A. comparing ancient and modern methods of observing and measuring the planet's characteristics.

    B. critiquing the studies that have been completed because many questions still remain to be answered.

    C. explaining how modern probes have shown that previously held beliefs were incorrect.

    D. providing details of significant findings and pointing out what remains to be learned.

Answers and Explanations

Read Actively

A. Green sea turtles and their migrations—specifically, one group that goes from Brazil to Ascension Island to breed.

B. Green sea turtles make great migrations in short time spans.

C. The paragraph will discuss green sea turtles' sense of smell.

D. Green turtles' strong sense of smell helps them detect a scented chemical trail.

E. The green sea turtles' eyesight

F. The turtles' eyesight helps them find the path of the chemical trail.

G. It discusses how Earth's magnetic field, rather than the turtles' eyesight, helps them migrate.

H. Earth's magnetic field is an additional guide that turtles use to find the scent trail.

I. Green sea turtles are an endangered species.

J. Excellent sense of smell, good eyesight, and Earth's magnetic field help the green sea turtle migrate long distances.

1. D

Category: Global

Getting to the Answer: The point of the passage is to describe how green sea turtles make their "prodigious migrations." This matches **(D)**. The passage doesn't discuss the importance of ocean currents or how the turtles swim, making both **(A)** and **(C)** Out of Scope. **(B)** is a Misused Detail since it does not include anything about migration.

2. G

Category: Inference

Getting to the Answer: Ascension Island is described in paragraph 1 as "relatively predator-free," which supports **(G)**. The turtles leave their feeding grounds to go to Ascension Island, making **(E)** incorrect. The passage does not compare Brazil and Ascension Island in terms of climate or cleanliness, making both **(F)** and **(H)** Out of Scope.

3. D

Category: Inference

Getting to the Answer: "Several different hypotheses" refers back to the question of how green sea turtles navigate the ocean. The passage states that the turtles use their eyesight to track the sun and their sense of smell to follow a chemical trail to Ascension Island. The phrase "several different hypotheses" suggests that green sea turtles use more than just their eyesight to navigate, which matches **(D)**. **(A)** is incorrect because the phrase "several different hypotheses" isn't referring to scientists' understanding. **(B)** is Opposite because the turtles have good eyesight. **(C)** is Out of Scope; the passage doesn't discuss the limitations of scientific evidence concerning green sea turtles.

4. E

Category: Detail

Getting to the Answer: According to paragraph 3, researchers think that the turtles swim toward the rising sun until they come across the chemical trail. Thus, the position of the sun leads turtles to the chemical trail, **(E)**. Paragraph 3 doesn't mention the turtles' sense of direction, making **(F)** incorrect. **(G)** and **(H)** are both Distortions of information provided in the passage.

5. A

Category: Inference

Getting to the Answer: Paragraph 3 states that the turtles are especially sensitive to red because it "appears in their shell coloration." This suggests that seeing red helps them to see other turtles' shells. This supports **(A)**. The passage doesn't compare the "intensity" of the primary colors or address the "attractiveness" of the color red, making **(B)** and **(D)** Out of Scope. **(C)** is incorrect because the passage doesn't make a connection between the color red and the sun.

Read Actively

A. ¶1 Topic: Identification checks help ensure healthy offspring

B. ¶2 Topic: Bright plumage is used by some birds to identify and attract mates (ex. birds of paradise)

C. ¶3 Topic: Courtship dances help to establish and maintain "pair bonds"

D. ¶4 Topic: Bird calls help with determining identity and level of interest

E. ¶5 Topic: Northern cardinal mating behaviors

F. ¶6 Topic: American goldfinch mating behaviors

G. Passage Main Idea: Plumage, courtship dances, and bird calls are important aspects of bird courtship and breeding behavior.

Global

1. **B**

Category: Global

Getting to the Answer: (B) is correct because it states the basic theme that runs through all four paragraphs: key aspects of birds' mating activities. **(A)** and **(C)** are Out of Scope; how birds make nests and migration direction are not discussed. **(D)** is a Misused Detail because pair "bonds" are only mentioned in paragraph 3.

Detail

2. **H**

Category: Detail

Getting to the Answer: (H) is correct because it explains in paragraph 4 that male birds use their calls, or songs, to identify themselves as potential mates of the same species and to give females a way of determining the male's level of interest. **(E)**, **(F)**, and **(G)** are incorrect because they are from paragraphs 1, 2, and 3, all of which do not directly discuss bird calls.

Function

3. **C**

Category: Function

Getting to the Answer: (C) is correct because whooping cranes and trumpeter swans are mentioned in

paragraph 3 as examples of birds with unique courtship procedures. **(A)** is incorrect because it is Opposite: the whooping crane and the trumpeter swan *do* participate in courtship procedures. **(B)** is Out of Scope because the whooping crane's plumage is never discussed. **(D)** is a Distortion; the passage mentions that roles are reversed in different species, but it never establishes "typical" male and female courtship roles.

Inference

4. **G**

Category: Inference

Getting to the Answer: (G) is correct because in the final paragraph, it is stated that males identify themselves by their singing and that the female interprets their singing in order to predict "the response of a male to her approach." Since the female makes the approach, it is implied that she chooses the male. **(E)** is Extreme; just because the female's singing ability is never mentioned does not mean that it doesn't exist. Aggression is not mentioned in regard to bird sounds, making **(F)** Out of Scope. The breeding condition of the females is never mentioned, making **(H)** also Out of Scope.

Infographic

5. **C**

Category: Infographic

Getting to the Answer: The main idea of the passage is key aspects of identification checks within courtship behaviors of birds. The Venn diagram shows how birds can exhibit the three behaviors discussed in the passage in combination with one another or alone. The correct answer, **(C)**, features these behaviors and shows how they overlap for seven bird species. Eliminate **(A)** as a Distortion because paragraphs 3 and 4 state that both sexes participate in these behaviors, not just males. Eliminate **(B)** as Extreme because neither the passage nor the Venn diagram say that birds are limited to these behaviors. **(D)** is a Misused Detail; the question is asking how the graphic supports the whole passage, not just paragraph 2, where birds of paradise are discussed.

Practice Set

Passage Analysis: This passage describes several animals native to the Galápagos Islands. Paragraph 1 describes the Galápagos Islands and the reason for their unique wildlife. Paragraph 2 introduces the cormorant. Paragraph 3 discusses the difference between the flightless cormorant and other cormorants. Paragraph 4 discusses the survival prospects of the cormorant. Paragraph 5 describes the waved albatross, and paragraph 6 the blue-footed booby. Paragraph 7 describes the islands' namesake, the Galápagos tortoise. Paragraph 8 discusses the impact of the growing human population and the need to protect the islands' distinctive species.

1. C

Category: Global

Getting to the Answer: When you are asked for the main idea of a passage, look for a common theme that runs through every paragraph. Here, all the paragraphs discuss different aspects of the Galápagos Islands, so find an answer choice that reflects this. **(C)** is correct. **(A)** is too broad; the passage discusses only three species of seabirds. **(B)** is a Misused Detail; although the passage does mention this fact, it is not the focus of the passage. This choice does not include any part of paragraph 8. **(D)** is another Misused Detail. This choice only reflects paragraph 8, not any of the earlier paragraphs in the text.

2. G

Category: Detail

Getting to the Answer: Go back to paragraph 1 and re-read around the sentence identified in the question to identify the context of the statement. The Galápagos Islands were important to Darwin's work because the animals there are so different; they are so different because the islands are isolated. **(G)** supports this idea with the viewpoint of "most naturalists" and is correct. The incorrect choices are all Misused Details describing features of some of the different animals but do not provide support for the reason that the Galápagos Islands were important to Darwin's work.

3. D

Category: Detail

Getting to the Answer: Whenever you are given a phrase from the passage, read a little bit before and after it until you understand the context. The pronoun "this" introducing the clue phrase "evolutionary advantage" means that the "evolutionary advantage" was defined in the previous sentence. There, it is described as "the flightless cormorant has no known natural predators," matching **(D)**, the correct answer. **(A)** is a Distortion; the author mentions that, even with this advantage, the number of birds is quite low, but never states that there "should" be more. **(B)** is a Misused Detail; this point is mentioned in the passage but is not described as an evolutionary advantage. **(C)** is another Distortion; the flightless cormorant is described as a strong swimmer, but not compared to the common cormorant. These choices are all incorrect.

4. E

Category: Function

Getting to the Answer: The question asks how a feature of the passage contributes to the main idea, so refresh your memory of the main idea—the Galápagos Islands have an important history, unique animals, and should be preserved—then determine how paragraph 6 fits into that idea. From your Roadmap or paragraph notes, paragraph 6 describes one of the species found on the Galápagos Islands, and the author notes that this is not the only place where the blue-footed booby lives, but that it is still an interesting animal. **(E)** is correct. **(F)** is a Distortion; the second sentence says that half of the blue-footed booby population is found in the Galápagos Islands. **(G)** is part of the main idea of the passage, but is not discussed in paragraph 6. **(H)** is a Misused Detail from paragraph 4. The flightless cormorant, not the blue-footed booby, has sufficient numbers and is not endangered.

5. D

Category: Detail

Getting to the Answer: When a question mentions a part of the passage, return to that section and read carefully to find the answer to that exact question asked. In this case, you need evidence that supports the idea that there are different aspects to the relationship between the tortoise and the birds. **(D)** is correct because "perverse" means "improper," and "exploit" means "to take unfair advantage of" another. After getting "relief" from the birds, the tortoise "exploits" them by crushing and eating them, so the relationship between the two species is first beneficial to both, but then later beneficial only to the tortoise. The incorrect choices, **(A)**, **(B)**, and **(C)**, are all Misused Details that only describe one aspect of the mutually beneficial relationship, not any different or "multifaceted" aspects.

6.   H

Category: Detail

Getting to the Answer: The preservation of the Galápagos Islands is part of the main idea, and most of the passage is describing the unique animals found on the islands. **(H)** is correct. The incorrect choices are all Misused Details from the text. **(E)** is mentioned in paragraphs 4 and 5 but is not connected to the author's call for preservation in paragraph 8. Similarly, **(F)** is mentioned in paragraphs 1 and 4, but not related to paragraph 8. **(G)** is from paragraph 8, but is a reason the islands are at risk, not a reason they should be saved.

Passage Analysis: This passage discusses the characteristics and influence of ska music. Paragraph 1 tells of genres that have borrowed from earlier styles and introduces ska as an example of this phenomenon. Paragraph 2 details the influences that created ska's unique sound. Paragraph 3 highlights selected ska artists and discusses the themes in ska lyrics. Paragraph 4 tells of ska's seamless evolution into reggae. Paragraph 5 discusses ska's influence outside of Jamaica, and paragraph 6 summarizes the main idea—ska has been an important influence in popular music.

7.   B

Category: Global

Getting to the Answer: The answer to a Global question should capture the idea that runs through each paragraph of the passage. Here, the correct answer should involve the development and influence of ska music, as this idea is prominent throughout the passage. **(B)** is correct. **(A)**, **(C)**, and **(D)** are all Misused Details. **(A)** focuses on all of Jamaican music, not just ska. **(C)** only addresses how ska is performed, and **(D)** captures only part of the main idea—the influence of ska—but does not take into account ska's development.

8.   F

Category: Inference

Getting to the Answer: When you are asked about the meaning of a phrase in context, re-read a little before and a little after the quoted phrase. Here, the passage says that "many songs took on political issues such as . . . Jamaica's growing cry for independence from Great Britain." **(F)** is correct. **(E)** is a Misused Detail; the vocalists of ska are mentioned, but their political views are not. **(G)** is a Distortion; ska music had Jamaican independence as a theme, but the passage never states that ska had any effect on Great Britain's decision. **(H)** is another Distortion; if ska's "high point" came with independence, then ska was most popular then and declined in importance after that time.

9.   D

Category: Function

Getting to the Answer: The question asks about the ideas in the entire passage, so review your Roadmap or paragraph notes, concentrating on paragraph 4, and note the paragraph's connections to those before and after it. Paragraph 3 ends the discussion of ska's development, paragraph 4 begins the discussion of ska's influence on other Jamaican music styles, and paragraph 5 broadens that discussion to ska's influence on music styles in other countries. Now, consider the author's use of the sentence in the question. After introducing the idea that ska influenced rocksteady and reggae, the author uses the sentence to clearly connect them and then gives examples. **(D)** is correct. The claim mentioned in the choice is "In the subsequent decades, ska evolved into different styles, including rocksteady and reggae" and the keyword phrase "for example" following the sentence indicates that more support will follow. **(A)** is incorrect because the author does not present an argument in paragraph 4. **(B)** is incorrect because paragraph 4 develops, not contrasts, the view presented in paragraph 3. **(C)** is incorrect because paragraph 4 supports, not argues against, the ideas presented.

10. F

Category: Inference

Getting to the Answer: When a question asks how or why the author used a feature of the passage, always keep the main idea in mind. Here, recall that the main idea is that ska music was first influenced by 1950s American music and then later influenced many other musical styles. Next, use either your Roadmap or your paragraph notes to determine how paragraph 5 contributed to the main idea. Paragraph 5 discusses ska's influence on many other musical styles around the world. Now consider the use of the word "pure." Up until this point in the paragraph, the author is discussing the musical styles inspired by ska, but now uses the word "pure" to shift the focus to ska itself because, decades after its development, and after influencing other music styles, ska was still popular in the mid-1990s. **(F)** is correct. **(E)** is a Misused Detail; the author does distinguish between ska and the music styles it has inspired, but the purpose of that distinction is to make the broader point about ska's longevity as its own musical style. **(G)** and **(H)** are both Distortions and are also incorrect. They both twist the idea that some of ska's revivals were motivated by the political climate, but Jamaican political music mentioned in **(G)** is never discussed. **(H)** goes too far by saying that the political climate was the only thing that caused ska's revived popularity.

11. C

Category: Detail

Getting to the Answer: Before reading the choices, carefully evaluate the sentence in the question. The sentence states that ska's influence is both "prominent" ("important") and "quiet" ("hidden"). **(C)** supports this statement by listing several groups that did not call themselves ska musicians, although their music was influenced by ska, and is the correct answer. **(A)** and **(B)** both indicate that ska influenced at least one group, but neither includes the "prominent" or "quiet" characteristics mentioned in the sentence. **(D)** only mentions ska's revivals, not its influence, and does not relate to, much less support, the statement in the question.

12. H

Category: Function

Getting to the Answer: When asked about the ideas in the entire passage, keep the main idea in mind. In this case, how ska was both influenced by earlier music styles, and how ska later influenced other styles. The author uses the chronological structure to systematically recount how this happened over time. **(H)** is correct. The incorrect choices are all Distortions of information in the passage. For **(E)**, the author discusses the importance of ska, but not how quickly (or slowly) it developed. For **(F)**, ska did develop in the 1950s and was a largely instrumental form of music, but no reasons are provided. Similarly, for **(G)**, how ska developed, changed, and was adapted into other musical styles is discussed, but no reasons are mentioned in the text.

Passage Analysis: The focus of this passage is the life and successful presidency of James K. Polk. Paragraph 1 compares Polk with his political role model, Andrew Jackson. Paragraph 2 discusses Polk's early life and the beginning of his political career. Paragraph 3 discusses the 1844 presidential campaign and Polk's election as a "dark horse" candidate. Paragraph 4 provides historians' view of Polk as the greatest pre-Civil War president. Paragraph 5 details Polk's success in acquiring the Oregon Territory, and paragraph 6 outlines the acquisition of Texas, New Mexico, and California. Paragraph 7 concludes with Polk's success in fulfilling "manifest destiny" and mentions one point of controversy.

13. D

Category: Global

Getting to the Answer: Global questions require an understanding of the passage as a whole and seeing the unifying idea that connects all of the content together. In this case, the passage discusses the life and primary success of James K. Polk's "tireless work to expand the borders of the nation," so **(D)** is correct. **(A)** is a Misused Detail; the passage does state that Polk had a greater impact on American history, but the comparison with Jackson is not the focus of the passage. **(B)** is also a Misused Detail; the passage mentions the United States provoking war with Mexico, but this is not the focus of the entire passage. **(C)** is Extreme; the passage mentions Polk's tremendous work ethic but does not describe it as the "primary" cause of his political effectiveness.

14. H

Category: Global

Getting to the Answer: The main idea of the passage is the description of the successful presidency of James Polk, but the adjectives in the question describe former president Andrew Jackson, so look back in the paragraph to find why the author described Jackson. The fourth and fifth sentences provide the answer: the author is contrasting the different approaches used by the two men. **(H)** is correct. **(E)** is Opposite, the adjectives describe Jackson, not Polk. **(F)** is Out of Scope; the passage only mentions Jackson's support of Polk, not any criticism. **(G)** is a Distortion; Polk may have followed Jackson's advice, but the passage never states he did so because of Jackson's strong personality.

15. A

Category: Inference

Getting to the Answer: The passage tells you that Polk became Speaker of the House of Representatives and was catapulted "into a position of political prominence." Not long after this, Polk became president as a "dark horse" candidate, who came "out of nowhere." So becoming Speaker may have made Polk powerful but not necessarily famous. **(A)** is correct. **(B)** is Extreme; Polk may have become more powerful, but nothing in the passage states that he took control of the Democratic Party. **(C)** is a Distortion; this choice does not fit the information that Polk was a "dark horse" candidate later in his career. **(D)** is Opposite; the passage states that Polk came "out of nowhere" to win the Democratic nomination for president and that Van Buren was initially the leading Democratic candidate.

16. G

Category: Detail

Getting to the Answer: Always use the clues in the question to look up the answer in the passage. Use your Roadmap or paragraph notes to locate the 1844 presidential election in paragraph 3, then read carefully to find out how Polk won. The fourth sentence of that paragraph describes Polk's strategy: he thought most voters wanted to acquire Texas and Oregon and promised to work hard to accomplish this. The correct answer is **(G)**. **(E)** is a Misused Detail. Polk's work ethic as president was described, but this was not the reason he won the election. **(F)** is Out of Scope; neither Polk's criticism of his opponents or any presidential debates are mentioned in the passage. **(H)** is another Misused

Detail; Jackson's advice is mentioned, and Polk did receive the nomination of the Democratic Party, but the passage does not describe these as the reason Polk won the election.

17. C

Category: Global

Getting to the Answer: The question asks how the sentence contributes to the development of ideas in the passage, so recall the main idea: Polk's presidency was one of the most successful in history. Now consider why the author included the quote in the question. The following sentence attributes Polk's success to his "hands-on approach," and this matches **(C)**, the correct answer. The incorrect answers, **(A)**, **(B)**, and **(D)** are all Misused Details; they are each an element of the quotation but do not reflect an idea that is later developed in the passage.

18. F

Category: Detail

Getting to the Answer: The question identifies the discussion of the Oregon Territory in paragraph 5. Re-read the paragraph carefully, and put the main ideas in your own words as you read. The third sentence says both Britain and the United States saw the territory "as rightfully theirs"; the next two sentences list the expeditions cited to support each country's claims. The next sentence indicates that negotiations were conducted, but war was beginning to look more likely. The last sentence indicates that Polk and Britain "divided the Oregon Territory." **(F)** matches this summary and is correct. **(E)** and **(H)** are Opposite choices, and are incorrect. The passage states that war was avoided **(E)** and that both sides "saw it as rightfully theirs" **(H)**. **(G)** is a Distortion, and also incorrect. The territory was divided between Britain and the United States.

19. D

Category: Infographic

Getting to the Answer: The passage focuses on the life and presidency of James Polk, particularly his policy regarding the expansion of U.S. borders. Line graphs are especially helpful at showing the rates at which variables increase or decrease, and this line graph shows the rate at which the United States acquired land area throughout the 1800s. Notice how steep the line is from 1845–1849, the years of Polk's presidency.

Predict that the correct answer will describe this increase; the best match is **(D)**. Though the graph does show that the United States quadrupled in area between 1783 and 1947, that fact does not help develop the ideas in the passage; eliminate **(A)**. Identify **(B)** as Opposite; the graph shows that after 1870, the United States did not acquire much more land area. Eliminate **(C)** as a Misused Detail because a comparison between Polk's presidency and Jackson's presidency is not a focus of the passage, though the two are compared in paragraph 1.

Passage Analysis: The purpose of the passage is to describe the planet Jupiter, its discovery, and the subsequent explorations of its chemical composition, interior structure, and other characteristics. Paragraph 1 describes the ancient recognition of Jupiter. Paragraph 2 describes Galileo's discovery of Jupiter's moons and its implications. Paragraph 3 discusses Europa, one of these moons. Paragraph 4 describes the first modern probe and Jupiter's gaseous structure. The next three paragraphs describe characteristics of Jupiter: winds and bands in paragraph 5, the Great Red Spot in paragraph 6, and rotational speed in paragraph 7. Paragraph 7 concludes by noting there is much more about Jupiter that is still to be learned. Paragraph 8 discusses the next scheduled probe.

20. H

Category: Global

Getting to the Answer: First, identify the main idea; in this case, the entire passage focuses on what is known about Jupiter from the hundreds of years that scientists have been studying the planet and what is still not completely understood. Look for an answer choice that takes this focus into account. Since **(H)** includes the study of Jupiter and what scientists do and do not know about the planet, this is the correct answer. **(E)**, **(F)**, and **(G)** are all Misused Details. Each is a fact from the passage, but each is also too narrow to convey the main idea.

21. C

Category: Detail

Getting to the Answer: Although you may not be able to precisely define the word "heliocentric" on your own, the passage provides the clues needed to determine its

meaning. Paragraph 2 explains that Galileo's observations supported Copernicus's theory, and Galileo observed that "these moons seemed to revolve around a planet other than Earth." **(C)** restates that idea, and is correct. **(A)** is a Misused Detail; the many moons of Jupiter are mentioned, but not in connection with Copernicus's theory. **(B)** is an Opposite choice that describes "the dominant theory" of the time that all heavenly bodies orbited Earth, not Copernicus's theory. **(D)** is another Opposite choice; the passage states that the Galilean moons orbit Jupiter.

22. E

Category: Detail

Getting to the Answer: Whenever a question provides a quotation from the passage, return to that section and read above and below the quotation to determine the context. Here, the keyword phrase "in addition to" at the start of the quotation indicates that a new point will follow, so read above the quotation for the discussion of what galvanized "scientists to rethink the structure of the cosmos." Paragraph 2 discusses Galileo's discovery of Jupiter's moons, so **(E)** is correct. **(F)**, **(G)**, and **(H)**, the incorrect choices, are all Misused Details mentioned in the passage, but none of these were the reason scientists changed their thinking on the structure of the cosmos.

23. D

Category: Global

Getting to the Answer: Since the question asks about the overall structure of the passage, review your Roadmap or paragraph notes to refresh your memory of the passage structure, then determine how paragraph 3 contributes to the structure. The entire passage describes key features of Jupiter while outlining how much is still not known about this planet. Paragraph 3 discusses Europa, one of Jupiter's moons that is especially interesting because it may be the first place extraterrestrial life is discovered. Paragraph 8 returns to this idea because of its importance. **(D)** matches this prediction, and is correct. **(A)** is incorrect because Europa is not discussed in paragraphs 4, 5, 6, or 7. **(B)** is a Distortion; the discovery of ice on Europa is not mentioned as one of the results of the Pioneer 10 probe. **(C)** is Extreme. The passage only states that extraterrestrial life on Europa may be possible, not that it has been found.

24. F

Category: Detail

Getting to the Answer: The question asks for evidence to support the quoted claim, so start by returning to paragraph 6 to put the quotation into context. Paragraph 6 discusses the Great Red Spot, a storm that has been observed on Jupiter's surface since 1830. The paragraph goes on to explain why the storm has lasted so long: there's very little friction between the storm and Jupiter's gaseous surface. **(F)** introduces Jupiter's gaseous surface and is correct. The remaining incorrect choices are all Misused Details. **(E)**, **(G)**, and **(H)** all describe other features of Jupiter, but not its gaseous surface.

25. D

Category: Function

Getting to the Answer: This question asks how the author presented a point of view in the passage, so review your Roadmap or paragraph notes. Each paragraph provides a description of an interesting characteristic of Jupiter, and the end of the passage states that there are still many questions to be answered. **(D)** is correct. **(A)** is a Distortion; ancient and modern techniques of observing Jupiter are discussed, but not compared. **(B)** is Extreme. The author mentions that previous studies left unanswered questions, but never criticized them because of this. **(C)** is a Distortion; Galileo's ancient work corrected a previously held belief. Probes are not mentioned in this context.

CHAPTER 11

SHSAT Fiction & Poetry

CHAPTER OBJECTIVES

By the end of this chapter, you will be able to:

- Identify keywords that promote active reading and relate passage text to the questions
- Draw inferences about characters' motivations and relationships
- Apply strategies to answer fiction and poetry questions correctly

SHSAT Fiction & Poetry

Literary Terms

SHSAT Reading Comprehension questions that accompany fiction and poetry passages may ask about **literary terms**. Knowing some common literary terms will help you as you tackle those passages. Two of the more prominent literary terms that you will be tested on are **tone** and **theme**.

Tone is an attitude, such as humorous, concerned, or sad, that a writer chooses to show to readers using specific words and phrases. Questions about tone will ask how a word, phrase, or sentence affects the tone of the passage.

When answering these questions, first identify the tone by locating keywords throughout the passage. If the author uses words such as "delightful," "joy," and "smiling," the tone is happy. If the author chooses words such as "terror," "distress," and "dread," the tone is fearful. Once you have pinpointed the tone, you can select the answer choice that best matches it.

The theme of a passage is the overall idea, moral, or lesson the author wants the reader to understand. For example, *The Outsiders* by S.E. Hinton is known for its theme of social class differences. The characters of two rival groups learn about both the contrasts and the similarities among social classes as the novel progresses.

An SHSAT Reading Comprehension question may ask, "How does the conversation in paragraphs 4–6 contribute to the development of the theme?" Before you look at the answer choices, ask yourself, "What does the author want me to know now that I've read the passage?" You can use your answer to find the best match.

Throughout a single passage, an author may use multiple literary devices along with tone and theme. Familiarizing yourself with these literary terms ahead of time will help you both to better understand the passage and to answer questions more efficiently and accurately. Below is a list of literary terms you may see on the SHSAT.

Term	Definition	Example
Character	A person (or animal) who takes part in a story	Jo March is the main character in the novel *Little Women* by Louisa May Alcott.
Conflict	A problem between characters or a struggle within a character	The siblings argued nearly every day about who was the better athlete.
Dialogue	A conversation between characters	"Welcome to my home," Andres said, opening the front door. "Thank you," replied Jade as she stepped inside.
Imagery	Words and phrases that provide information about what someone may see, hear, feel, touch, or taste	The cool water tasted clean and crisp as I gulped it loudly, clutching the worn green canteen in my sweating palms.
Irony	A surprising contradiction or contrast	In the short story, "The Gift of the Magi" by O. Henry, a wife sells her hair to buy her husband a chain for his beloved watch, not knowing that her husband has just sold his watch to buy decorative combs for her beautiful long hair.
Metaphor	A comparison of two things that does not use the words "like" or "as"	The singer was a beautiful sparrow on stage.

Term	Definition	Example
Moral	A lesson the author hopes readers will learn from the story	The moral of "The Tortoise and the Hare" is that you will be more successful if you work steadily than if you act quickly and carelessly.
Narrator	The speaker or character who tells the story	Jean Louise "Scout" Finch is the narrator of *To Kill a Mockingbird* by Harper Lee.
Personification	Words or phrases that give a nonhuman subject human characteristics	The flowers danced in the light breeze.
Plot	The sequence of events in a story	The plot of "Little Red Riding Hood" starts with Little Red meeting the wolf in the woods. The wolf goes to Granny's house before Little Red, Little Red sees the wolf impersonating her grandma, and the woodcutter arrives to rescue Little Red and Granny.
Point of view	A particular attitude about something	From an environmentalist's point of view, a factory that causes high levels of pollution should be closed; from the factory employees' point of view, it should remain open so they can keep their jobs.
Rhyme	The repetition of sounds at the end of words	The sun was done, but we felt like we won; we had run and spun having fun.
Setting	The time and place of a story	*Anne of Green Gables* by Lucy Maud Montgomery is set in Prince Edward Island, Canada in the early 1900s.
Simile	A comparison of two things that uses "like" or "as"	She ran as swiftly as a deer.
Stanza	A group of lines in a poem	The first stanza of "Success" by Emily Dickinson is: Success is counted sweetest By those who ne'er succeed. To comprehend a nectar Requires sorest need.
Structure	The order and format of a passage or poem	The structure of the poem "I Have Found What You Are Like" by E.E. Cummings reinforces the poet's comparison of a person to falling raindrops: —in the woods which stutter and sing
Symbol	Something that is used to represent a particular idea	A red rose is a symbol of love.
Turning point	A specific moment in a story when something begins to change	The turning point in "The Three Little Pigs" is when the wolf cannot blow down the third house, which is made of bricks instead of sticks or straw.

Directions: Match the literary term on the right to the example on the left.

1. Simile	A. Hazel Lancaster shares her experiences in the novel *The Fault in Our Stars* by John Green.
2. Conflict	B. The parking lot was a lake after the rainstorm.
3. Metaphor	C. The story about the boy who cried wolf teaches the importance of telling the truth.
4. Character	D. *A Christmas Carol* by Charles Dickens takes place in London, England in the mid-1800s.
5. Irony	E. The wind howled outside my window.
6. Moral	F. A white dove represents peace.
7. Personification	G. The lake was as smooth as glass.
8. Setting	H. The rival teams played against each other each year in the regional semifinals.
9. Symbol	I. Lola raced to get to school on time only to find out when she arrived that it was Saturday.

Directions: Use the literary terms in the word bank to complete the sentences below. Use each word only once.

Plot	Rhyme	Point of view	Turning point
Narrator	Imagery	Structure	Stanza

10. Words that _____ have similar ending sounds, such as "tree," "key," and "plea."

11. Writers use _____ to provide vivid descriptions that help readers visualize what someone may see, hear, feel, touch, or taste.

12. The _____ is the sequence of events in a story.

13. A specific moment in a story when something begins to change is the _____.

14. The order and format of a passage or poem is called its _____.

15. The _____ is the speaker or character who tells the story.

16. A _____ is a group of lines in a poem.

17. A particular attitude about something is called _____.

Applying the Kaplan Method to Fiction Passages

You will use the same Kaplan Method for fiction passages that you use for other Reading Comprehension passages on the SHSAT.

Step 1: Read actively

Step 2: Examine the question stem

Step 3: Predict and answer

However, there are some differences in what is involved with each of these steps that are particular to fiction passages.

Active reading means that as you read the passage, you are asking questions and taking notes. As you read a fiction passage, you should:

Identify the characters, evaluate how the author describes them, and determine the relationships among the characters.

- Who are the characters?
- What are the characters doing?
- What adjectives describe each character?

Assess the characters' opinions of each other and themselves.

- Do they like or dislike each other?
- Why does each character make particular decisions or take particular courses of action?

Identify the tone and themes within the passage.

- What is the overall tone of the passage?
- What are the themes (morals, lessons, or messages) the author conveys?

Summarize the plot.

- What happens in the passage?
- What are the "turning points" in the passage?

Read the following passage and answer the questions to practice applying the Kaplan Method to fiction passages.

Identify the Characters

Excerpt from *The Story of Dr. Dolittle*

by Hugh Lofting

1 All the folks, young and old, knew him well by sight. And whenever he walked down the street in his high hat everyone would say, "There goes the Doctor!—He's a clever man." And the dogs and the children would all run up and follow behind him; and even the crows that lived in the church-tower would caw and nod their heads. The house he lived in, on the edge of the town, was quite small; but his garden was very large and had a wide lawn and stone seats and weeping willows hanging over. His sister, Sarah Dolittle, was housekeeper for him; but the Doctor looked after the garden himself.

    A. Who are the characters?

    B. What are the characters doing?

    C. What adjectives describe each character?

Assess the Characters' Opinions

2 He was very fond of animals and kept many kinds of pets. Besides the goldfish in the pond at the bottom of his garden, he had rabbits in the pantry, white mice in his piano, a squirrel in the linen closet and a hedge-hog in the cellar. His sister used to grumble about all these animals and said they made the house untidy. And one day when an old lady with rheumatism came to see the Doctor, she sat on the hedgehog who was sleeping on the sofa and never came to see him anymore, but drove every Saturday all the way to Oxen-thorpe, another town ten miles off, to see a different doctor. Then his sister, Sarah Dolittle, came to him and said, "John, how can you expect sick people to come and see you when you keep all these animals in the house? That's the fourth personage these animals have driven away. We are getting poorer every day. If you go on like this, none of the best people will have you for a doctor."

    D. Do the characters like or dislike each other? What is the overall tone of the passage?

    E. Why does each character make a particular decision or take a particular course of action?

Identify the Tone and Themes

3 But he kept on getting still more pets; and of course it cost a lot to feed them. And the money he had saved up grew littler and littler. And now, when he walked down the street in his high hat, people would say to one another, "There goes John Dolittle, M.D.! There was a time when he was the best known doctor in the West Country—Look at him now—He hasn't any money and his stockings are full of holes!" But the dogs and the cats and the children still ran up and followed him through the town—the same as they had done when he was rich.

    F. What is the overall tone of the passage?

    G. What are the themes (morals, lessons, or messages) the author conveys?

Summarize

    H. What happens in the passage?

    I. What are the "turning points" in the passage?

Fiction passages, just like other SHSAT passages, will be accompanied by Global, Detail, Inference, and Function questions. The way a question stem is worded can tell you what type of question it is, and knowing this can help you get to the answer more quickly. The following are some reminders and tips about question types.

Global questions ask about the theme or central idea of the passage. Use your active reading notes to help you identify the main idea or theme of the passage. (Do not re-read the entire passage.)

Detail questions ask about specific information from the passage. They may ask about a word, a phrase, or an idea. Use line references or specific phrasing in the question to find the relevant section of the passage. Skim this section to find specific evidence; put your finger on the exact information required to answer the question.

Inference questions ask you about the underlying meaning of a particular phrase or example. These questions often use words like "imply" or "suggest." Look for clues that show the author's point of view or why the author chose to write in a certain way.

Function questions identify a feature of the passage—a line, a paragraph, an example, or an opinion—and ask you to consider either why or how the author uses the feature. Focus on the author's reason for including the cited feature. Take note of any transition words, and read around the cited text for context.

To answer fiction questions successfully, go back to the lines mentioned in the question or to the section of the passage where the idea in the question is discussed, and research the answer in the passage. Predict an answer using supporting information from the passage. Then, see which answer choice matches best with your prediction. Don't rely on your memory or answer based on outside knowledge. It's an open-book test, so use the passage!

Actively reading a fiction passage includes taking notes to create a Roadmap. Complete the Roadmap questions below about the characters, their opinions, and the tone and themes of the passage as you read the excerpt that follows.

Excerpt from "The Shinansha"
compiled by Yei Theodora Ozaki

1   The compass, with its needle always pointing to the North, is quite a common thing, and no one thinks that it is remarkable now, though when it was first invented it must have been a wonder.

2   Now long ago in China, there was a still more wonderful invention called the shinansha. This was a kind of chariot with the figure of a man on it always pointing to the South. No matter how the chariot was placed the figure always wheeled about and pointed to the South.

3   This curious instrument was invented by Kotei, one of the three Chinese Emperors of the Mythological age. Kotei was the son of the Emperor Yuhi. Before he was born his mother had a vision which foretold that her son would be a great man.

4   One summer evening she went out to walk in the meadows to seek the cool breezes which blow at the end of the day and to gaze with pleasure at the star-lit heavens above her. As she looked at the North Star, strange to relate, it shot forth vivid flashes of lightning in every direction. Soon after this her son Kotei came into the world.

5   Kotei in time grew to manhood and succeeded his father the Emperor Yuhi. His early reign was greatly troubled by the rebel Shiyu. This rebel wanted to make himself King, and many were the battles which he fought to this end. Shiyu was a wicked magician, his head was made of iron, and there was no man that could conquer him.

6 At last Kotei declared war against the rebel and led his army to battle, and the two armies met on a plain called Takuroku. The Emperor boldly attacked the enemy, but the magician brought down a dense fog upon the battlefield, and while the royal army were wandering about in confusion, trying to find their way, Shiyu retreated with his troops, laughing at having fooled the royal army.

7 No matter however strong and brave the Emperor's soldiers were, the rebel with his magic could always escape in the end.

8 Kotei returned to his Palace, and thought and pondered deeply as to how he should conquer the magician, for he was determined not to give up yet. After a long time he invented the shinansha with the figure of a man always pointing South, for there were no compasses in those days. With this instrument to show him the way he need not fear the dense fogs raised up by the magician to confound his men.

Read Actively

1. Characters

   A. Who are the characters?

   B. What are the characters doing?

   C. What adjectives describe each character?

2. Characters' Opinions

   D. Do they like or dislike each other?

   E. Why does each character make particular decisions or take particular courses of action?

3. Tone and Themes

   F. What is the overall tone of the passage?

   G. What are the themes (morals, lessons, or messages) the author conveys?

4. Summarize

   H. What happens in the passage?

   I. What are the "turning points" in the passage?

Examine the Question Stem and Predict

The following section includes just the question stems of some test-like questions that you will see later, followed by guiding questions to help you make strong predictions. Answering these guiding questions will help you build your skills before you try your hand at the full questions and answer choices.

1. Read this sentence from paragraph 1.

> The compass, with its needle always pointing to the North, is quite a common thing, and no one thinks that it is remarkable now, though when it was first invented it must have been a wonder.

    How does the sentence contribute to the development of the plot?

    A. What are the "turning points" in the passage that contributed to the plot?

    B. Predict the answer to the question stem.

2. In paragraph 3, how does the phrase "of the Mythological age" affect the tone of the excerpt?

    C. What is the overall tone of the passage?

    D. Predict the answer to the question stem.

3. Which of the following best explains why Kotei's mother thought her son would be great?

    E. What is Kotei's mother's opinion of her son?

    F. Predict the answer to the question stem.

4. The phrase "strange to relate" in paragraph 4 shows that the author

    G. What important element in the question stem tells you where to direct your research?

    H. Predict the answer to the question stem.

Match Your Prediction to the Correct Answer

Now that you've practiced examining the question stems and predicting the answers, try answering the full version of these questions below. Select the choice that best matches your prediction.

1. Read this sentence from paragraph 1.

> The compass, with its needle always pointing to the North, is quite a common thing, and no one thinks that it is remarkable now, though when it was first invented it must have been a wonder.

    How does the sentence contribute to the development of the plot?

    A. It defines what a compass is so that the reader better appreciates Kotei's invention of it.

    B. It explains the background of Kotei leading up to his birth.

    C. It suggests that the shinansha is a marvel on par with Shiyu's magical fog.

    D. It explains that "shinansha" is just a synonym for a north-pointing compass.

2. In paragraph 3, how does the phrase "of the Mythological age" affect the tone of the excerpt?

    E. It establishes the excerpt's factual tone, which matches the fact that events from recorded history are recounted.

    F. It highlights the excerpt's comedic tone, which highlights that magical events are presented as historical fact.

    G. It illustrates the excerpt's heroic tone about events that took place before China had any emperors.

    H. It establishes the excerpt's epic tone, which suggests to the reader that events are set in an era of heroes and magic.

3. Which of the following best explains why Kotei's mother thought her son would be great?

    A. "This curious instrument was invented by Kotei, one of the three Chinese Emperors of the Mythological age." (paragraph 3)

    B. "Kotei was the son of the Emperor Yuhi." (paragraph 3)

    C. "As she looked at the North Star . . . it shot forth vivid flashes of lightning in every direction." (paragraph 4)

    D. ". . . his head was made of iron, and there was no man that could conquer him." (paragraph 5)

4. The author most likely used the phrase "strange to relate" (paragraph 4) to show that

    E. the event he is about to describe is difficult to put into words.

    F. the event he is about to describe was hard for Kotei's mother to understand.

    G. the event he is about to describe is surprising and curious.

    H. the event Kotei's mother witnessed was unimportant.

Applying the Kaplan Method to Poetry Passages

Just like with fiction passages, you will use the same Kaplan Method for poetry passages, but there are a few extra things to keep in mind that specifically apply to poetry.

Step 1: Read actively

Step 2: Examine the question stem

Step 3: Predict and answer

As you read the poem, ask yourself questions and take notes. Be sure to:

Identify the topic and the narrator (when applicable).

- What is the poem about?
- Does the poem have a narrator? If yes, who (or what) is speaking?

Identify the mood.

- What feelings does the poem create in the reader?
- What words would you use to describe the mood?

Paraphrase the poet's words.

- What does the poem mean in your own words?
- What information is the poet trying to convey?

Read the following poem and answer the accompanying questions to practice applying to Kaplan Method to poetry passages.

Identify the Topic

"The Road Not Taken"

by Robert Frost

> Two roads diverged in a yellow wood,
> And sorry I could not travel both
> And be one traveler, long I stood
> And looked down one as far as I could
> 5 To where it bent in the undergrowth;
>
> Then took the other, as just as fair,
> And having perhaps the better claim,
> Because it was grassy and wanted wear;
> Though as for that the passing there
> 10 Had worn them really about the same,

A. What is the topic?

B. Does the poem have a narrator? If yes, who (or what) is speaking?

Identify the Mood

> And both that morning equally lay
> In leaves no step had trodden black.
> Oh, I kept the first for another day!
> Yet knowing how way leads on to way,
> 15 I doubted if I should ever come back.

C. What feelings does the poem create in the reader?

D. What words would you use to describe the mood?

Paraphrase

> I shall be telling this with a sigh
> Somewhere ages and ages hence:
> Two roads diverged in a wood, and I—
> I took the one less traveled by,
> 20 And that has made all the difference.

E. What does the poem mean in your own words?

F. What information is the poet trying to convey?

Poetry passages will be accompanied by Global, Detail, Inference, and Function questions. Here are some reminders and tips about the question types, and how they may look when connected to a poem.

Global questions ask about the theme or central idea of the poem. This should be something you take note of while actively reading, so use your notes and avoid re-reading the whole poem.

Detail questions ask about specific information in the poem. They may ask about a word, a phrase, or specific language the poet includes. Use line or stanza references, or specific phrasing in the question, to find the relevant section of the poem.

Inference questions ask you to support an idea that the poem conveys, or to explain the meaning of imagery in the poem. Looks for clues and make sure you can always back up your answer with evidence in the poem.

Function questions identify a feature of the poem—a line, a stanza, or imagery—and ask you to consider either why or how the poet uses the feature. Think about why the author may have included this cited feature, and make sure to read a bit before and after the cited feature to get the proper context.

To answer poetry questions successfully, read each question carefully and thoroughly. Determine exactly what the question is asking. Go back to the lines or stanza mentioned in the question to look up the answer in the poem. Find support for your answer using information from the poem before you pick your answer from among the other choices.

Read Actively

Actively reading a poetry passage includes taking notes to create a Roadmap. As you read the following poem, complete the Roadmap questions below about the topic, mood, and paraphrasing.

"Storm"
by Hilda Doolittle

> You crash over the trees,
> you crack the live branch—
> the branch is white,
> the green crushed,
> 5 each leaf is rent like split wood.
>
> You burden the trees
> with black drops,
> you swirl and crash—
> you have broken off a weighted leaf
> 10 in the wind,
> it is hurled out,
> whirls up and sinks,
> a green stone.

1. Topic

    A. What is the topic?

    B. Does the poem have a narrator? If yes, who (or what) is speaking?

2. Mood

    C. What feelings does the poem create in the reader?

    D. What words would you use to describe the mood?

3. Paraphrasing

    E. What does the poem mean in your own words?

    F. What information is the poet trying to convey?

Examine the Question Stem and Predict

Answer the questions below. Understanding these question stems on their own, and predicting an answer now, will help you to quickly and easily answer the full questions later on.

1. Lines 1–5 contribute to the development of ideas in the poem by

    A. What is the topic?

    B. What words would you use to describe the mood?

    C. Predict the answer to the question stem.

2. What impact do the words "crash," "crack," and "crushed" in lines 1–4 have on the meaning of the poem?

    D. How do these words convey the author's message?

    E. Predict the answer to the question stem.

3. Read lines 1–2 and 6–8 that begin the two stanzas.

> **You crash over the trees,**
> **you crack the live branch—**
>
> **You burden the trees**
> **with black drops,**
> **you swirl and crash—**

The purpose of the parallel structure of the two stanzas is to

    F. How does the similar structure help convey the poet's meaning?

    G. Predict the answer to the question stem.

4. Read lines 6–7.

> **You burden the trees**
> **with black drops,**

The lines help develop the theme of the poem by suggesting that the rain

    H. What does this part of the poem mean in your own words?

    I. Predict the answer to the question stem.

Match Your Prediction to the Correct Answer

Now, answer the full questions below by selecting the choice that best matches your prediction.

1. Lines 1–5 contribute to the development of ideas in the poem by

    A. depicting the dramatic way a leaf falls in a storm.

    B. mimicking the sound of a raging wind.

    C. using colors to evoke the devastation of the storm.

    D. describing the effect of a powerful storm on a tree.

2. What impact do the words "crash," "crack," and "crushed" in lines 1–4 have on the meaning of the poem?

    E. Their similar sounds unite the first and second stanzas.

    F. Their harsh sounds emphasize the fury of the storm.

    G. Their rhythmic, repeated beginnings imitate the sound of the rain.

    H. They provide a dramatic contrast to the quiet peace that follows the storm.

3.   Read lines 1–2 and 6–8 that begin the two stanzas.

> **You crash over the trees,**
> **you crack the live branch—**
> **You burden the trees**
> **with black drops,**
> **you swirl and crash—**

The purpose of the parallel structure of the two stanzas is to

A.   contrast the effects at the start of the storm with those at the end of the storm.

B.   indicate that the wind mentioned in the first stanza is less important than the rain.

C.   emphasize that the second stanza will be a continuation of the first.

D.   show that the first stanza was more important than the second.

4.   Read lines 6–7.

> **You burden the trees**
> **with black drops,**

The lines help develop the theme of the poem by suggesting that the rain

E.   is so heavy it may damage the trees.

F.   will harm the trees because it is black from pollution.

G.   is necessary for the growth of the trees.

H.   will cause widespread flooding.

Practice Set

For test-like practice, give yourself 50 minutes (an average of 5 minutes per passage and 1 minute per question) to complete this question set. After you're done, be sure to study the explanations, even for questions you answered correctly. They can be found at the end of this chapter.

DIRECTIONS: Read the passages and answer the corresponding questions. Re-read relevant parts of the text before choosing the best answer for each question. Base your answers only on the content within each passage.

Excerpt from *Three Men and a Maid*
by P. G. Wodehouse

1 Through the curtained windows of the furnished apartment which Mrs. Horace Hignett had rented for her stay in New York rays of golden sunlight peeped in like the foremost spies of some advancing army. It was a fine summer morning. The hands of the Dutch clock in the hall pointed to thirteen minutes past nine; those of the ormolu clock in the sitting-room to eleven minutes past ten; those of the carriage clock on the bookshelf to fourteen minutes to six. In other words, it was exactly eight; and Mrs. Hignett acknowledged the fact by moving her head on the pillow, opening her eyes, and sitting up in bed. She always woke at eight precisely.

2 Was this Mrs. Hignett the Mrs. Hignett, the world-famous writer on Theosophy, the author of "The Spreading Light," "What of the Morrow," and all the rest of that well-known series? I'm glad you asked me. Yes, she was. She had come over to America on a lecturing tour.

3 The year 1921, it will be remembered, was a trying one for the inhabitants of the United States. Every boat that arrived from England brought a fresh swarm of British lecturers to the country. Novelists, poets, scientists, philosophers, and plain, ordinary bores; some herd instinct seemed to affect them all simultaneously. It was like one of those great race movements of the Middle Ages. Men and women of widely differing views on religion, art, politics, and almost every other subject; on this one point the intellectuals of Great Britain were single-minded, that there was easy money to be picked up on the lecture platforms of America and that they might just as well grab it as the next person.

4 Mrs. Hignett had come over with the first batch of immigrants; for, spiritual as her writings were, there was a solid streak of business sense in this woman and she meant to get hers while the getting was good. She was half way across the Atlantic with a complete itinerary booked before 90 per cent of the poets and philosophers had finished sorting out their clean collars and getting their photographs taken for the passport.

5 She had not left England without a pang, for departure had involved sacrifices. More than anything else in the world she loved her charming home, Windles, in the county of Hampshire, for so many years the seat of the Hignett family. Windles was as the breath of life to her. Its shady walks, its silver lake, its noble elms, the old grey stone of its walls—these were bound up with her very being. She felt that she belonged to Windles, and Windles to her. Unfortunately, as a matter of cold, legal accuracy, it did not. She did but hold it in trust for her son, Eustace, until such time as he should marry and take possession of it himself. There were times when the thought of Eustace marrying and bringing a strange woman to Windles chilled Mrs. Hignett to her very marrow. Happily, her firm policy of keeping her son permanently under her eye at home and never permitting him to have speech with a female below the age of fifty had averted the peril up till now.

6 Eustace had accompanied his mother to America. It was his faint snores which she could hear in the adjoining room, as, having bathed and dressed, she went down the hall to where breakfast awaited her. She smiled tolerantly. She had never desired to convert her son to her own early rising habits, for, apart from not allowing him to call his soul his own, she was an indulgent mother. Eustace would get up at half-past nine, long after she had finished breakfast, read her mail, and started her duties for the day.

7 Breakfast was on the table in the sitting-room, a modest meal of rolls, cereal, and imitation coffee. Beside the pot containing this hell-brew was a little pile of letters. Mrs. Hignett opened them as she ate. The majority were from disciples and dealt with matters of purely theosophical interest. There was an invitation from the Butterfly Club asking her to be the guest of honour at their weekly dinner. There was a letter from her brother Mallaby—Sir Mallaby Marlowe, the eminent London lawyer—saying that his son Sam, of whom she had never approved, would be in New York shortly, passing through on his way back to England, and hoping that she would see something of him. Altogether a dull mail. Mrs. Hignett skimmed through it without interest, setting aside one or two of the letters for Eustace, who acted as her unpaid secretary, to answer later in the day.

1. In paragraph 1, how does the phrase "sunlight peeped in like the foremost spies of some advancing army" affect the tone of the excerpt?

   A. It creates the martial tone that runs through Mrs. Hignett's first-person narration.
   B. It sets the dry, humorous tone of the third-person narration.
   C. It establishes the sullen tone of Mrs. Hignett's first-person perspective.
   D. It introduces the factual tone of the third-person narration.

2. Read these sentences from paragraph 1.

> The hands of the Dutch clock in the hall pointed to thirteen minutes past nine; those of the ormolu clock in the sitting-room to eleven minutes past ten; those of the carriage clock on the bookshelf to fourteen minutes to six. In other words, it was exactly eight; and Mrs. Hignett . . . always woke at eight precisely.

How do these sentences contribute to the development of Mrs. Hignett's character?

   E. They show that Mrs. Hignett is rooming with other people working on different schedules.
   F. They show that Mrs. Hignett needs repeated reminders by multiple alarm clocks to wake up.
   G. They illustrate Mrs. Hignett's homesickness, as the clocks are still set to her native time zone.
   H. They illustrate Mrs. Hignett's willpower, as she does not need clocks to wake on schedule.

3. Read these sentences from paragraph 2.

> **Was this Mrs. Hignett the Mrs. Hignett, the world-famous writer on Theosophy, the author of "The Spreading Light," "What of the Morrow," and all the rest of that well-known series? I'm glad you asked me. Yes, she was.**

How do these sentences affect the tone of the excerpt?

A. They create a formal, ponderous impression of the lecture circuit's role in American culture.

B. They establish the informal, chatty nature of the narrator when relaying the story.

C. They suggest that the narration will be an erudite, professional overview of famous writers.

D. They introduce a serious and deep author of profound philosophical books.

4. Which of the following best explains why so many English lecturers were coming to the United States in 1921?

E. The history of the Middle Ages was a topic of interest to Americans.

F. Americans needed a great deal of education on numerous topics.

G. There were no Americans who spoke on lecture tours.

H. Americans were willing to pay money to attend lectures.

5. Read this sentence from paragraph 4.

> **She was half way across the Atlantic with a complete itinerary booked before 90 per cent of the poets and philosophers had finished sorting out their clean collars and getting their photographs taken for the passport.**

How does the sentence contribute to the development of the central idea of the excerpt?

A. It emphasizes that Mrs. Hignett acts decisively.

B. It illustrates how desperate Mrs. Hignett is for lecture circuit money.

C. It shows how Mrs. Hignett has traveled to America several times in the past.

D. It illustrates that Mrs. Hignett is willing to sabotage her rivals to secure her fame.

6. Read this sentence from paragraph 5.

> **Unfortunately, as a matter of cold, legal accuracy, it did not.**

Which statement best describes how the sentence fits into the overall structure of the excerpt?

E. It signals a shift from the perspective of Mrs. Hignett to the perspective of her son.

F. It signals a shift from the description of Mrs. Hignett's family home to the means by which she has held onto that home.

G. It provides the reason that Mrs. Hignett is traveling the lecture circuit by herself despite having living family members.

H. It provides the reason that the Hignett's family home has been lost to them.

7. How does Windles being held in a legal trust influence Mrs. Hignett's behavior?

A. She has grown to dislike her family's home because it no longer belongs to her.

B. She goes on the lecture circuit in order to make enough money to save her family's home.

C. She has tried to buy her son's affection so that he won't throw her out.

D. She closely monitors her son and steers him away from young, single women.

Excerpt from *My Ántonia*

by Willa Cather

1 As I looked about me I felt that the grass was the country, as the water is the sea. The red of the grass made all the great prairie the colour of winestains, or of certain seaweeds when they are first washed up. And there was so much motion in it; the whole country seemed, somehow, to be running.

2 I had almost forgotten that I had a grandmother, when she came out, her sunbonnet on her head, a grain-sack in her hand, and asked me if I did not want to go to the garden with her to dig potatoes for dinner.

3 The garden, curiously enough, was a quarter of a mile from the house, and the way to it led up a shallow draw past the cattle corral. Grandmother called my attention to a stout hickory cane, tipped with copper, which hung by a leather thong from her belt. This, she said, was her rattlesnake cane. I must never go to the garden without a heavy stick or a corn-knife; she had killed a good many rattlers on her way back and forth. A little girl who lived on the Black Hawk road was bitten on the ankle and had been sick all summer.

4 I can remember exactly how the country looked to me as I walked beside my grandmother along the faint wagon-tracks on that early September morning. Perhaps the glide of long railway travel was still with me, for more than anything else I felt motion in the landscape; in the fresh, easy-blowing morning wind, and in the earth itself, as if the shaggy grass were a sort of loose hide, and underneath it herds of wild buffalo were galloping, galloping. . . .

5 Alone, I should never have found the garden—except, perhaps, for the big yellow pumpkins that lay about unprotected by their withering vines—and I felt very little interest in it when I got there. I wanted to walk straight on through the red grass and over the edge of the world, which could not be very far away. The light air about me told me that the world ended here: only the ground and sun and sky were left, and if one went a little farther there would be only sun and sky, and one would float off into them, like the tawny hawks which sailed over our heads making slow shadows on the grass. While grandmother took the pitchfork we found standing in one of the rows and dug potatoes, while I picked them up out of the soft brown earth and put them into the bag, I kept looking up at the hawks that were doing what I might so easily do.

6 When grandmother was ready to go, I said I would like to stay up there in the garden awhile.

7 She peered down at me from under her sunbonnet. "Aren't you afraid of snakes?"

8 "A little," I admitted, "but I'd like to stay, anyhow."

9 "Well, if you see one, don't have anything to do with him. The big yellow and brown ones won't hurt you; they're bull-snakes and help to keep the gophers down. Don't be scared if you see anything look out of that hole in the bank over there. That's a badger hole. He's about as big as a big 'possum, and his face is striped, black and white. He takes a chicken once in a while, but I won't let the men harm him. In a new country a body feels friendly to the animals. I like to have him come out and watch me when I'm at work."

10 Grandmother swung the bag of potatoes over her shoulder and went down the path, leaning forward a little. The road followed the windings of the draw; when she came to the first bend, she waved at me and disappeared. I was left alone with this new feeling of lightness and content.

11 I sat down in the middle of the garden, where snakes could scarcely approach unseen, and leaned my back against a warm yellow pumpkin. There were some ground-cherry bushes growing along the furrows, full of fruit. I turned back the papery triangular sheaths that protected the berries and ate a few. All about me giant grasshoppers, twice as big as any I had ever seen, were doing acrobatic feats among the dried vines.

The gophers scurried up and down the ploughed ground. There in the sheltered draw-bottom the wind did not blow very hard, but I could hear it singing its humming tune up on the level, and I could see the tall grasses wave. The earth was warm under me, and warm as I crumbled it through my fingers. Queer little red bugs came out and moved in slow squadrons around me. Their backs were polished vermilion, with black spots. I kept as still as I could. Nothing happened. I did not expect anything to happen. I was something that lay under the sun and felt it, like the pumpkins, and I did not want to be anything more. I was entirely happy. Perhaps we feel like that when we die and become a part of something entire, whether it is sun and air, or goodness and knowledge. At any rate, that is happiness; to be dissolved into something complete and great. When it comes to one, it comes as naturally as sleep.

8. Read this sentence from paragraph 1.

> As I looked about me I felt that the grass was the country, as the water is the sea.

The imagery used in the sentence affects the tone of the paragraph by emphasizing a

- E. sense of fear as the narrator realizes the danger hiding in the grass.
- F. feeling of awe as the narrator ponders the vast expanse.
- G. feeling of dread as the narrator considers the surrounding desolation.
- H. sense of amazement as the narrator imagines how the grass grew so extensively.

9. Which sentence from the excerpt best supports the idea that the narrator is unfamiliar with the area where grandmother lives?

- A. "And there was so much motion in it; the whole country seemed, somehow, to be running."
- B. "I had almost forgotten that I had a grandmother, when she came out, her sunbonnet on her head, a grain-sack in her hand, and asked me if I did not want to go to the garden with her to dig potatoes for dinner."
- C. "The garden, curiously enough, was a quarter of a mile from the house, and the way to it led up a shallow draw past the cattle corral."
- D. "Alone, I should never have found the garden—except, perhaps, for the big yellow pumpkins that lay about unprotected by their withering vines—and I felt very little interest in it when I got there."

10. Read this sentence from paragraph 5.

> **The light air about me told me that the world ended here: only the ground and sun and sky were left, and if one went a little farther there would be only sun and sky, and one would float off into them, like the tawny hawks which sailed over our heads making slow shadows on the grass.**

The imagery in this sentence conveys the narrator's

E. discomfort with the situation on grandmother's homestead.

F. happiness that the day is so clear and sunny.

G. frustration that the hawks are able to fly, but the narrator cannot.

H. amazement at the vastness of the horizon.

11. How does the grandmother's description of the wildlife in paragraph 9 emphasize a theme of the excerpt?

A. It encourages the narrator in her decision to linger in the garden.

B. It encourages the narrator to return with grandmother because of the danger.

C. It frightens the narrator, who then overcomes the fear and stays in the garden.

D. It describes the precautions the narrator should take to remain safe.

12. Read this sentence from paragraph 11.

> **Nothing happened. I did not expect anything to happen.**

How does the sentence contribute to the development of the plot?

E. It explains why the narrator feels bored while sitting in the garden.

F. It shows how comfortable and content the narrator feels in the garden.

G. It illustrates the narrator's discouragement due to the difficulties described earlier.

H. It contrasts the quiet of the garden with the motion of the grass on the prairie.

13. How does the narrator's experience in paragraph 11 emphasize a theme of the excerpt?

A. It confirms the importance of grandmother's warnings.

B. It reinforces the narrator's earlier impression of the landscape in motion.

C. It illustrates the narrator's sense of harmony with all that is around her.

D. It causes the narrator to recall other beautiful memories.

14. The central idea that "that is happiness; to be dissolved into something complete and great" (paragraph 11) is conveyed mainly through the

    E. comparisons of the movement of the grass with that of the sea.

    F. repeated images of calm majesty and eternity.

    G. humorous descriptions of the grasshoppers and bugs.

    H. the cheerful wave of grandmother as she returns home.

15. Which of the following explains why the narrator says in paragraph 5, "I felt very little interest in it when I got there"?

    A. "A little girl who lived on the Black Hawk road was bitten on the ankle and had been sick all summer." (paragraph 3)

    B. "[I]f one went a little farther there would be only sun and sky, and one would float off into them" (paragraph 5)

    C. "There were some ground-cherry bushes growing along the furrows, full of fruit." (paragraph 11)

    D. "Nothing happened. I did not expect anything to happen." (paragraph 11)

16. How do grandmother's cautions in paragraph 3 contribute to a theme of the excerpt?

    E. They illustrate the many dangers on the way to the garden.

    F. They emphasize the narrator's serenity by providing a contrast.

    G. They show the importance of the narrator's obedience.

    H. They describe the daily routine on the homestead.

"Ozymandias"

by Percy Shelley

I met a traveller from an antique land
Who said: Two vast and trunkless legs of stone
Stand in the desert. Near them on the sand,
Half sunk, a shatter'd visage lies, whose frown
5 And wrinkled lip and sneer of cold command
Tell that its sculptor well those passions read
Which yet survive, stamp'd on these lifeless things,
The hand that mock'd them and the heart that fed.
And on the pedestal these words appear:
10 "My name is Ozymandias, king of kings:
Look on my works, ye Mighty, and despair!"
Nothing beside remains: round the decay
Of that colossal wreck, boundless and bare,
The lone and level sands stretch far away.

17. Read lines 10–13 from the poem.

> **"My name is Ozymandias, king of kings:**
> **Look on my works, ye Mighty, and despair!"**
> **Nothing beside remains: round the decay**
> **Of that colossal wreck, boundless and bare,**

How do the lines develop the central theme of the poem?

A. They suggest that all objects will deteriorate over time.

B. They paint a picture of the vast size and desolation of the desert.

C. They suggest that Ozymandias has continued to be a powerful and glorious figure.

D. They highlight the impermanence of power and glory.

18. How does the author's use of words like "half sunk," "shatter'd," "wrinkled," and "sneer" contribute to the meaning of the poem?

E. They evoke a sense of desolation and loss of a powerful figure.

F. They imply that the statue was marred and unpleasant to look at.

G. They suggest that the statue was of someone old and decrepit.

H. They highlight the unhappiness of the figure depicted in the statue.

19. Ozymandias most likely cautions those who see the statue to "despair" (line 11) because

A. they will never be able to match his power.

B. they will surely be defeated in war.

C. his face is sad and inspires despair.

D. he knows his reign will soon end.

20. Which detail from the poem best supports the fact that the statue lies in ruins?

   E. "[W]hose frown And wrinkled lip and sneer of cold command" (lines 4–5)

   F. "The hand that mock'd them and the heart that fed." (line 8)

   G. "And on the pedestal these words appear: 'My name is Ozymandias, king of kings:'" (lines 9–10)

   H. "Nothing beside remains: round the decay Of that colossal wreck, boundless and bare," (lines 12–13)

21. Which of the following lines from the poem best supports the idea that a skillful sculptor crafted a true likeness of Ozymandias?

   A. "Two vast and trunkless legs of stone Stand in the desert. Near them on the sand, Half sunk, a shatter'd visage lies," (lines 2–4)

   B. "Tell that its sculptor well those passions read Which yet survive, stamp'd on these lifeless things," (lines 6–7)

   C. "My name is Ozymandias, king of kings: Look on my works, ye Mighty, and despair!" (lines 10–11)

   D. "Of that colossal wreck, boundless and bare, The lone and level sands stretch far away." (lines 13–14)

22. How does the phrase "colossal wreck" (line 13) develop the theme of the poem?

   E. It symbolizes the power and might of King Ozymandias by suggesting that the statue was enormous.

   F. It contributes to the poem's irony to reveal that a significant tribute to a powerful ruler now stands in ruins.

   G. The phrase evokes a sense of the magnitude of the archeological find that the traveler stumbled upon.

   H. It is meant to stir disgust and anger over the fact that the statue has been broken.

"A Musical Instrument"

by Elizabeth Barrett Browning

What was he doing, the great god Pan,
Down in the reeds by the river?
Spreading ruin and scattering ban,
Splashing and paddling with hoofs of a goat,
5 And breaking the golden lilies afloat
With the dragon-fly on the river.

He tore out a reed, the great god Pan,
From the deep cool bed of the river:
The limpid water turbidly ran,
10 And the broken lilies a-dying lay,
And the dragon-fly had fled away,
Ere he brought it out of the river.

High on the shore sat the great god Pan
While turbidly flowed the river;
15 And hacked and hewed as a great god can,
With his hard bleak steel at the patient reed,
Till there was not a sign of the leaf indeed
To prove it fresh from the river.

He cut it short, did the great god Pan,
20 (How tall it stood in the river!)
Then drew the pith, like the heart of a man,
Steadily from the outside ring,
And notched the poor dry empty thing
In holes, as he sat by the river.

25 'This is the way,' laughed the great god Pan
(Laughed while he sat by the river),
'The only way, since gods began
To make sweet music, they could succeed.'
Then, dropping his mouth to a hole in the reed,
30 He blew in power by the river.

Sweet, sweet, sweet, O Pan!
Piercing sweet by the river!
Blinding sweet, O great god Pan!
The sun on the hill forgot to die,
35 And the lilies revived, and the dragon-fly
Came back to dream on the river.

Yet half a beast is the great god Pan,
To laugh as he sits by the river,
Making a poet out of a man:
40 The true gods sigh for the cost and pain,—
For the reed which grows nevermore again
As a reed with the reeds in the river.

23. What impact does the phrase "hard bleak steel" have on the development of ideas in the third stanza (lines 13–18) of the poem?

    A. It provides contrast for the relative fragility of the reed.

    B. It suggests that the reed is so tough that it required the strongest steel to cut.

    C. It proves that Pan's only option was to cut the reed with the steel.

    D. It symbolizes Pan's anger at the reed, which is why he cuts it so forcefully.

24. Read the fourth stanza (lines 19–24) of the poem.

> He cut it short, did the great god Pan,
> (How tall it stood in the river!)
> Then drew the pith, like the heart of a man,
> Steadily from the outside ring,
> And notched the poor dry empty thing
> In holes, as he sat by the river.

This stanza is most likely included to emphasize

    E. the river's importance to the events of the poem.

    F. Pan's skill in being able to cut and shape the reed.

    G. the narrator's sympathy toward the reed and its fate.

    H. the fact that the reed is too dry to be useful to Pan.

25. The lines in the final stanza (lines 37–42) help to develop a central idea of the poem by

    A. proving that because he laughs near the edge of the river, Pan isn't a real god after all.

    B. illustrating that Pan's actions weren't a big deal because there were other reeds in the river.

    C. revealing that all joys require at least some amount of pain.

    D. recognizing that although Pan made sweet music, it came at a lasting cost.

26. Read the second stanza (lines 7–12) from the poem.

> He tore out a reed, the great god Pan,
> From the deep cool bed of the river:
> The limpid water turbidly ran,
> And the broken lilies a-dying lay,
> And the dragon-fly had fled away,
> Ere he brought it out of the river.

How does the stanza contribute to the development of themes in the poem?

    E. It describes the results of an event that put Pan in conflict with the river environment.

    F. It explains that Pan tore out the reed because the water was not clear enough.

    G. It shows that Pan tore out the reed for the purpose of bringing destruction to the area.

    H. It suggests that there were too many plants growing in the water before Pan tore out the reed.

27. The comparison in lines 19–20 contributes to the development of ideas in the stanza by

    A. contrasting the appearance of the reed both before and after Pan has cut it down.

    B. highlighting Pan's physical prowess in being able to tear down the reed.

    C. indicating that only tall reeds are appropriate for Pan's use.

    D. claiming that only great gods are able to cut down reeds from the river.

28. How does the fifth stanza (lines 25–30) contribute to the theme of the poem?

    E. It introduces Pan's perspective on the events of the poem.

    F. It shows that Pan thinks that what he has done to the river is funny.

    G. It implies that the actions described in the poem occur at this river frequently.

    H. It illustrates a change in the narrator's perspective.

29. Which of the following best describes how lines 31–36 contribute to the development of the ideas in the poem?

    A. They provide specific examples that prove Pan was justified in cutting the reed from the river.

    B. They illustrate the positive qualities of Pan's music before the narrator introduces the lasting negative impact of Pan's actions.

    C. They show that, because Pan's music revived the lilies and brought back the dragonfly, his actions ultimately had no impact on the river's environment.

    D. They explain that Pan's music was detrimental because it pierced and blinded the creatures that lived near the river.

30. How does the repeated use of the phrase "the great god Pan" contribute to the development of ideas in the poem?

    E. It emphasizes that Pan is one of the greatest of all the gods.

    F. It is redundant and does not contribute meaningfully to the poem.

    G. It is used as a contrast with his aggressive actions.

    H. It asserts that Pan is so great that he is above all criticism.

Answers and Explanations

Literary Terms Practice

1. G

2. H

3. B

4. A

5. I

6. C

7. E

8. D

9. F

10. rhyme

11. imagery

12. plot

13. turning point

14. structure

15. narrator

16. stanza

17. point of view

Identify the Characters

A. Dr. Dolittle and his sister, Sarah Dolittle

B. Dr. Dolittle is a doctor who likes to garden. Sarah Dolittle is both his sister and his housekeeper.

C. Dr. Dolittle is clever and popular among the townspeople. His sister Sarah Dolittle is helpful.

Assess the Characters' Opinions

D. Dr. Dolittle is focused more on his fondness for animals than his feelings toward his sister. Sarah Dolittle is frustrated with her brother because his obsession with animals is affecting their way of life.

E. Dr. Dolittle is more concerned about his animals than his human patients. Sarah Dolittle is afraid that Dr. Dolittle will lose all of his clients because there are so many animals in the house.

Identify the Tone and Themes

F. The tone is mixed; while it is a little sad that Dr. Dolittle used to be the best doctor in the West and now he is looked down upon by his community, the tone is also positive: Dr. Dolittle enjoys his work with animals, and the animals give him the same love and attention that they always did.

G. The author's messages include the importance of having compassion for animals and following one's passion even when others do not agree.

Summarize

H. Dr. Dolittle was a good doctor who was loved by many, but people thought he was foolish because he chose his love for animals over his medical practice.

I. Dr. Dolittle kept on getting more pets, but he couldn't afford to feed them all. He lost customers and spent his savings because of his love for animals.

Read Actively

A. Kotei, Kotei's mother, and Shiyu

B. Kotei grows up, becomes Emperor, and fights the rebel magician Shiyu.

C. Kotei is determined; Shiyu is wicked.

D. Kotei and Shiyu are enemies.

E. Shiyu creates a dense fog so Kotei's army cannot defeat him, but Kotei uses the shinansha to navigate through the fog and is triumphant.

F. The tone is admiring; the author says that Kotei's compass was a "wonderful invention."

G. The author's message is that it's important to keep working to achieve a goal; Kotei defeated Shiyu because he was determined not to give up.

H. Emperor Kotei is faced with the rebel magician Shiyu, who wants to be king. Kotei and Shiyu go to war, but Kotei's forces are rendered helpless and confused by a magic fog that Shiyu spreads over the battlefield. It seems as if the Emperor's forces could never defeat Shiyu until Kotei develops the shinansha, which always points south and shows his soldiers the way, even in the densest magical fog.

I. In paragraph 8, Kotei invents the shinansha, which is the key to his victory.

Examine the Question Stem and Predict

1.

A. Kotei invents the shinansha, which is the key to his victory.

B. The invention of the shinansha makes Emperor Kotei appear as impressive as the magical Shiyu.

2.

C. The overall tone is admiring.

D. Knowing that this passage is considered part of the Mythological age helps convey the common folktale theme of good versus evil.

3.

E. She thought he would achieve greatness when he grew up.

F. Before he was born, Kotei's mother saw the North Star flash with lightning.

4.

G. The quote shows exactly where to look in paragraph 4.

H. The author is pointing out that the event is not an everyday occurrence; it is considered odd and surprising.

Match Your Prediction to the Correct Answer

Passage Analysis: The folktale from China describes the invention of the shinansha, a directional instrument that always points south. Paragraph 1 notes how common a compass is today, while paragraph 2 introduces an instrument invented even before the compass—the shinansha. Paragraph 3 describes Emperor Kotei, the inventor, while paragraph 4 tells of the strange event

Kotei's mother witnessed while pregnant with Kotei, which seemed to be an omen of greatness. As the passage continues, Kotei grows up, becomes Emperor, and is faced with the rebel magician Shiyu, who wants to be king. In paragraph 6, Kotei and Shiyu go to war, but Kotei's forces are rendered helpless and confused by a magic fog that Shiyu spreads over the battlefield. It seems as if the Emperor's forces could never defeat Shiyu, until, in paragraph 8, Kotei ponders how to overcome this fog and develops the shinansha, which always points south—thus, always showing his soldiers the way, even in the densest magical fog.

1. C

Category: Global

Getting to the Answer: Because a compass is a commonplace tool in the modern world, the author makes an effort to explain how wondrous it must have seemed when first invented. The author then uses the discussion of the compass as a springboard to talk about a similar invention, the mythic shinansha. This functions as a way to make Emperor Kotei appear as impressive as the Shiyu's fog magic. Thus, **(C)** is correct. Kotei does not invent the compass, which points north, but the shinansha, which points south; **(A)** is incorrect. While the excerpt goes on to talk about omens that heralded Kotei's greatness ahead of his birth, this happens in paragraphs 3 and 4, not paragraph 1; **(B)** is incorrect. A shinansha, which points south, is not a compass, which points north; **(D)** is incorrect.

2. H

Category: Function

Getting to the Answer: As with so many folktales from around the world, this one pits good against evil. The magician rebel, with his iron head and magic fog, represents evil, while the Emperor, determined and intelligent, creates the shinansha, overcoming the evil magician. This is a mythological, or epic, style of story; **(H)** is correct. As mythological events are ones that did not actually occur, **(E)** is incorrect. Although events involving magic happen in the passage, the tone throughout is not comedic; **(F)** is incorrect. The excerpt defines Kotei as one of the three Chinese Emperors of the Mythological age; **(G)** is incorrect.

3.   C

Category: Detail

Getting to the Answer: Kotei's mother was gazing at the night sky and saw "vivid flashes of lightning in every direction" (paragraph 4). This omen foreshadowed the greatness of her son; **(C)** is correct. Although **(A)** is tempting because Kotei did invent the shinansha, it is incorrect because Kotei's mother had no way of knowing that her son would create this specific invention many years later. While Kotei was the son of the Emperor, **(B)** is incorrect because that does not explain why his mother thought he would be especially great when he took the throne from his father. **(D)** is incorrect because it describes the rebel Shiyu rather than Kotei.

4.   G

Category: Inference

Getting to the Answer: Inference questions will not be stated directly in the passage, but the answer will be evident by studying the passage. Look at paragraph 4: lightning shooting out from the North Star is not an everyday occurrence. The author acknowledges uses the phrase "strange to relate" to acknowledge that it is considered odd and surprising. **(G)** is correct. Because the author managed to put the event into words, it could not have been too difficult to express; **(E)** is incorrect. The mother knew that the lightning signaled that her son would be a "great man" (paragraph 3). So, she did understand the strange omen, and there is no suggestion that the event was not significant; **(F)** and **(H)** are incorrect.

Identify the Topic

A.   The narrator is considering which one of two different paths is better to take.

B.   The poem does have a narrator, and the narrator is a person.

Identify the Mood

C.   The poem creates a feeling of uncertainty.

D.   The mood is thoughtful and cautious.

Paraphrase

E.   A person comes to a place where one road branches into two, and the person must decide which path to choose.

F.   There are times when people must choose between two options, and sometimes the better option is the hard one that most people prefer not to try.

Read Actively

A.   The topic is a raging storm and its effect on the trees.

B.   The poem's narrator is a witness who is watching the storm.

C.   The poem creates feelings of concern for the trees as well as awe of the storm.

D.   The mood is stormy and powerful.

E.   The wind roars, a branch breaks, and leaves are damaged. One leaf breaks off, is flung wildly around, and finally falls to the ground.

F.   The poet is showing how nature is unstoppable.

Examine the Question Stem and Predict

1.

  A. The topic is a raging storm and its effect on the trees.
  B. The mood is stormy and powerful.
  C. The first stanza shows that the storm "crashes" in, breaks off a branch, and tears the leaves of a tree.

2.

  D. The author uses these short, harsh words to emphasize how strong the storm is.
  E. The mood is stormy and powerful.

3.

  F. The two stanzas of the poem both describe the storm's fury.
  G. The poet's repetition of the "You . . ." structure indicates that the second stanza will continue to discuss the topic introduced in the first stanza.

4.

  H. The storm weighs the trees down with big, heavy raindrops.
  I. The raindrops are so heavy that the force of them may be bad for the trees.

Match Your Prediction to the Correct Answer

Poem Analysis: This short poem by Hilda Doolittle, who wrote under the pen name H. D., displays her powerful imagery conveyed with an economy of words. There are two stanzas, together describing a raging storm and its effect on the trees. The first stanza tells of how the wind roars and, perhaps, of how lightning breaks a branch and rends leaves. The second stanza describes how a leaf breaks off, is flung wildly around, and finally falls to the ground.

1. **D**

Category: Global

Getting to the Answer: The poem describes how a storm wreaks havoc on a tree and its leaves. The first stanza shows that the storm "crashes" in, breaks off a branch, and tears the leaves of a tree; **(D)** is correct. **(A)** is incorrect because it describes the falling leaf of the second stanza. **(B)** is incorrect because the wind is merely an aspect of the poem, not a central idea. **(C)** is incorrect because the author uses colors to describe the tree branch, not the storm, and the branch is just one aspect of the storm's effects on the tree.

2. **F**

Category: Function

Getting to the Answer: The poem describes a violent storm, and the author's use of "crash," "crack," and "crushed" almost sound like thunder. The author uses these short, harsh words to emphasize how strong the storm is; **(F)** is correct. While "crash" is repeated in the second stanza, the word doesn't appear until the end of the third line. The word is not being used to unite the stanzas; **(E)** is incorrect. **(G)** is incorrect because the author is not describing the sound of the rain, but rather the violent effects of the wind and the rain. **(H)** is incorrect because the poem does not close with a description of the calm that followed the storm.

3. **C**

Category: Function

Getting to the Answer: The two stanzas of the poem both describe the storm's fury, and the poet's repetition of the "You . . ." structure indicates that the second stanza will continue to discuss the topic introduced in the first stanza; **(C)** is correct. **(A)** is incorrect because there is no language in the poem to indicate that the storm is ending. **(B)** is incorrect because the second stanza discusses the violence of the wind, not the rain. Also, there is no comparison made between the wind and the rain. **(D)** is incorrect because the similar structure indicates the stanzas are basically similar. While parallel structure can be used to contrast two ideas, this poem does not contrast the two stanzas.

4. E

Category: Inference

Getting to the Answer: These lines are describing the heavy rain that accompanies the storm. Rain is usually helpful for trees, but in this storm, it is a "burden." The poet describes the drops as "black," a dark, heavy color that is usually a symbol for death or sadness. So, **(E)** is correct. **(F)** is incorrect because "black" is a symbolic color, evoking a very heavy rain where the sun is darkened. There is no mention of pollution turning the rain black. **(G)** is incorrect because while water is certainly needed for the growth of trees, this rain is described as a "burden." **(H)** is incorrect because there is no mention in the poem of flooding.

Practice Set

Passage Analysis: This excerpt from a story by noted British humorist P. G. Wodehouse introduces the somewhat eccentric writer and lecturer, Mrs. Horace Hignett. The first moment of the excerpt describes three clocks that all tell different times; however, Mrs. Hignett knew it was exactly 8 o'clock. From this point onwards, we are drawn into the life of this rather odd woman. Paragraph 1 introduces Mrs. Hignett, and paragraph 2 notes that she is a famous writer of Theosophy (a philosophy based on mysticism). Paragraph 3 explains that 1921 was witness to a vast influx of English lecturers to the United States, all determined to earn "easy" money on the lecturing circuit. Paragraph 4 explains that Mrs. Hignett was one of the first lecturers to come, eager to earn that "easy" money. Paragraphs 5 and 6 describe Mrs. Hignett's thoughts and actions as she began her daily tasks while her son still slept, and paragraph 7 relates her reason for leaving England and her emotions about it.

1. B

Category: Global

Getting to the Answer: The phrase "sunlight peeped in like the foremost spies of some advancing army" affects the tone of the excerpt by setting the dry, humorous tone of the third-person narration. This tone is later fully established when the narrator directly addresses the reader in paragraph 2. **(B)** is correct. While Mrs. Hignett does display a certain martial vigor in how she wakes and how she tackles both problems and opportunities, that is not the tone of voice of the excerpt; **(A)** is incorrect.

It is also never Mrs. Hignett's first-person narration. **(C)** and **(D)** are incorrect because the tone is not sullen or strictly factual, but humorous.

2. H

Category: Function

Getting to the Answer: The sentences from paragraph 1 contribute to the development of the plot by illustrating Mrs. Hignett's willpower. She does not need any of the clocks to wake on schedule, but instead wakes precisely at eight. Thus, **(H)** is correct. There is nothing to suggest that Mrs. Hignett is rooming with other people; **(E)** is incorrect. Likewise, there is no indication that Mrs. Hignett struggles to wake up and needs multiple alarms; **(F)** is incorrect. Although **(G)** is tempting because Mrs. Hignett does display homesickness later in the excerpt, **(G)** is incorrect because the three clocks are described as being set to wildly different times, not one time zone.

3. B

Category: Global

Getting to the Answer: Think about the words Wodehouse uses in the excerpt. He addresses the reader as "you" and says, "I'm glad you asked me," giving the impression that the author is having a conversation with someone he knows. He also indicates that the reader knows about Mrs. Hignett and the events of 1921, assuming that he and the reader know the same things; in other words, he implies that he and the reader are two (or more) of a kind. His tone is therefore informal and chatty; he is relating a story to a friend, as **(B)** states. **(A)**, **(C)**, and **(D)** are incorrect because they refer to an excerpt which would be formal and stilted in language, creating distance between the reader and the author.

4. H

Category: Detail

Getting to the Answer: As the excerpt states, English lecturers expect to make "easy money" (paragraph 3) on the American lecture tour. That money would have come from people paying to attend those lectures, so **(H)** is correct. The Middle Ages are mentioned in the excerpt, but only as a point of comparison; the excerpt does not state that Americans were interested in the history of the Middle Ages, so **(E)** is incorrect. It can't be inferred that Americans needed to be educated on these topics; perhaps they attended lectures because they already knew a great deal about the topics and were especially interested in them. So, eliminate **(F)**. **(G)** is likewise Extreme; there may have been many Americans who also lectured.

5.   A

Category: Global

Getting to the Answer: The sentence from paragraph 4 contributes to the development of the central idea of the excerpt by emphasizing that Mrs. Hignett acts decisively. It contrasts her with the slower pace of 90 percent of the other English people on the American lecture circuit. Thus, **(A)** is correct. There is nothing in the excerpt to suggest that Mrs. Hignett is desperate for money; **(B)** is incorrect. Likewise, there is nothing to suggest that she has visited America in the past, nor that she took steps to sabotage her rivals on the lecture circuit. Given how she wakes precisely at eight in the morning without the aid of a clock, the implication is that she is merely a determined person; **(C)** and **(D)** are incorrect.

6.   F

Category: Function

Getting to the Answer: The sentence from paragraph 5 signals a shift from the fond, loving description of Mrs. Hignett's family home to the means by which she has held onto that home. Namely, she made sure that her son never married and thus would not kick her out of the house in favor of his wife and possible children. **(F)** is correct. **(E)** is incorrect because the excerpt is always told in third-person narration, and it stays focused on Mrs. Hignett. Although **(G)** discusses Mrs. Hignett's history with her son, there is no indication or motive given for why she is traveling without him. **(H)** is incorrect because their family home has not been lost.

7.   D

Category: Detail

Getting to the Answer: Recall that in paragraph 5, Windles is described as Mrs. Hignett's long-time family home in the county of Hampshire. She is very attached to it and feels as if she belongs to it. As the paragraph states, Mrs. Hignett is holding it "in trust," and she is "chilled" to think of her son marrying and owning it with a strange woman. Consequently, Mrs. Hignett has tried to keep her son away from marriageable women, as the house would then leave her trust. Thus, **(D)** is correct. There is no suggestion that her son or anyone else had

already taken possession of it **(A)**, that she could not afford the house **(B)**, or that she needed money to keep her in the good graces of her son **(C)**.

Passage Analysis: Paragraphs 1 and 2 describe the narrator's reflections on the wilderness encountered after arriving at her grandmother's homestead. Although precise details are not provided, from the fact the narrator "had almost forgotten" she had a grandmother, and "long railway travel" is mentioned, you can infer that the narrator is unfamiliar with the place. In paragraphs 3 through 5, the narrator and grandmother walk to the garden, and the grandmother's warnings about snakes are contrasted with the narrator's impressions on the expanse of the land. In paragraphs 6 through 11, the narrator and her grandmother dig potatoes, and then the narrator chooses to stay in the garden. Despite the unfamiliarity, the narrator experiences a deep sense of happiness and unity with the surroundings.

8.   F

Category: Function

Getting to the Answer: The sentence containing the simile says just as the water makes up the sea, the grass seems to make up the entirety of the land surrounding the narrator. The paragraph continues the imagery, with the narrator comparing the waving of the grass to the waves of the sea. Consider the experience of gazing out over a large sea, and consider the overall theme of the excerpt. The paragraph introduces the narrator's calm sense of the beauty and majesty around her. **(F)** is correct. **(E)** and **(G)** are not supported by the tone of the rest of the paragraph or the excerpt, and are incorrect. Although grandmother warns the narrator of snakes later in the excerpt, the tone is informative, not one of fear, **(E)**, or dread, **(G)**. **(H)** is a Distortion of information in the excerpt. Although the author seems to experience amazement, the cause is the landscape itself, not the process by which the grass grew so extensively.

9.   D

Category: Detail

Getting to the Answer: The narrator does not know how to get to the garden, so she likely hasn't been a regular visitor. **(D)** is correct. **(A)** is the narrator's impression of the landscape. **(B)** indicates that she is deeply absorbed in observing the land around her but does not indicate that she is unfamiliar with the location. **(C)** establishes that the narrator knows where the garden is, and how to get there, so this does not indicate that she's unfamiliar with the area.

10. H

Category: Function

Getting to the Answer: Keep the overall theme of the excerpt—the narrator's sense of comfort and delight in the natural beauty around her—in mind when answering this Function question. This sentence is about how the narrator can tell that "the world ended here," meaning that the narrator could see all the way across the vast landscape. This matches **(H)**. **(E)** is incorrect because there is no evidence of discomfort in the narrative. **(F)** is incorrect because the sun is only one feature mentioned, and it is not the sole focus of the narrator. **(G)** is a Distortion of the idea in the excerpt. The narrator imagines floating off like a hawk, but is not frustrated that she cannot do so.

11. A

Category: Global

Getting to the Answer: Keep the overall theme of the excerpt—the narrator's sense of happiness and unity with the unfamiliar surroundings—in mind when answering a Global question. In the previous paragraph, the narrator admits that she is a little frightened, but wants to remain in the garden. The descriptions of the wildlife grandmother then provides are all creatures of which the narrator does not need to be frightened. **(A)** is correct. **(B)** and **(C)** are Opposite; the narrator is not encouraged to return with grandmother nor frightened by the information about the wildlife. **(D)** is a Misused Detail from the excerpt that does not pertain to paragraph 9 specifically.

12. F

Category: Global

Getting to the Answer: For Global questions, always recall the overall theme of the excerpt, then consider how the feature of the excerpt mentioned in the question supports that theme. The theme of this excerpt is the narrator's sense of peace and unity in the landscape. Since she is able to sit calmly in the garden, without expecting anything to happen, **(F)** is the correct answer. **(E)** and **(G)** are not discussed in the excerpt and

are incorrect; the narrator never expresses boredom or discouragement. **(H)** is a Misused Detail; the narrator does describe the motion of the grass, but never contrasts that motion with the quiet in the garden.

13. C

Category: Global

Getting to the Answer: Keep the overall theme of the excerpt in mind when answering Global questions. In this excerpt, the theme was the narrator's comfort and feeling of unity with the awesome landscape that surrounded her. In paragraph 11, the narrator describes her quiet experience in the garden in detail, ending with her statement that happiness is "to be dissolved into something complete and great." This matches **(C)**, the correct answer.

14. F

Category: Global

Getting to the Answer: Since the question identifies the central idea as "that is happiness; to be dissolved into something complete and great," think about what it is that the narrator considers "complete and great." Throughout the excerpt, the narrator is commenting on the expansive, majestic landscape. Some examples include: "I felt that the grass was the country, as the water is the sea" (paragraph 1); "the world ended here . . . if one went a little farther there would be only sun and sky, and one would float off into them" (paragraph 5); and "I was something that lay under the sun and felt it, like the pumpkins, and I did not want to be anything more" (paragraph 11). **(F)** is correct. **(E)** is one of the images used by the author, but this choice is too narrow to refer to the entire excerpt and is incorrect. **(G)** and **(H)** are also incorrect. These are details of the excerpt that contribute to the tone of the excerpt but, again, are too narrow to apply to the entire passage.

15. B

Category: Detail

Getting to the Answer: Go back to the excerpt to re-read paragraph 5 and answer in your mind why the narrator was not very interested in the garden. The next sentence says she wanted "to walk straight on through the red grass and over the edge of the world, which could not be very far away." She was more interested in the horizon and experiencing what would happen beyond the garden. This matches **(B)**, the correct answer. **(A)** and **(C)** are details from the passage that do not directly relate to the narrator's experience in the garden and are incorrect. **(A)** explains the danger of snakes and **(C)** describes the fruit in the garden, but neither are the reason the narrator is not interested in the garden. **(D)** summarizes the narrator's experience in the garden, but the narrator is not interested in the garden because of what lies beyond it, not because "nothing happened." This choice is also incorrect.

16. F

Category: Global

Getting to the Answer: Because this question asks about the "theme of the excerpt," it is a Global question, so keep the main idea—the narrator's experience of peace and unity with the landscape—in mind. Grandmother warns the narrator to take precautions when going to the garden, but in spite of these warnings, the narrator chooses to stay in the garden and describes feelings of calm wonder. **(F)** is correct. **(E)** describes the content of grandmother's warnings, but these dangers are not a theme of the excerpt. **(G)** is Out of Scope; the need for the narrator's obedience is not mentioned in the passage. **(H)** is incorrect because although grandmother insists that her warnings be followed whenever the narrator goes to the garden, the text does not describe this as a daily routine, or activity. More importantly, the details of daily life on the homestead are not a main theme of the excerpt.

Poem Analysis: The sonnet "Ozymandias" tells of the speaker meeting a traveler who described seeing the stark remains of what once was a great statue in an "antique" land—most likely Egypt. On the pedestal, the statue is identified as that of Ozymandias, the mightiest of kings, yet the statue is now a ruin, alone and insignificant in the sands of the desert. The contrast between a great tribute to a once-mighty king and the present ruined sculpture is a powerful literary device.

17. D

Category: Global

Getting to the Answer: This Global question asks for something that contributes to the poem's central theme. Look for an answer that speaks to the main idea expressed in the poem—that the statue of Ozymandias, the "king of kings," is now just a crumbling, fragmentary statue in the desert sands. Shelley is saying that all

things that may have once been great and mighty inevitably crumble into nothingness; match this with **(D)**. **(A)** is too broad; the poem is specifically about the statue, not about all things deteriorating. **(B)** is incorrect because the desolation of the desert is not related to the poem's central theme. **(C)** is incorrect because this is the opposite of the poem's meaning.

18. E

Category: Function

Getting to the Answer: The question asks how certain words are used to highlight the poem's meaning; thus, it is a Function question. Consider how and why the author chose these terms. They are bold, negative ideas that collectively present a picture of something impressive, even intimidating, that has now sunk. **(E)** is a good match. Whether the statue was aesthetically pleasing (ugly or beautiful) is never discussed, which eliminates **(F)**. **(G)** is incorrect; the statue's features do not suggest old age or decrepitude. **(H)** is incorrect because the author never states or suggests that Ozymandias was sad; though the word "despair" appears later in the poem, it is in another context.

19. A

Category: Inference

Getting to the Answer: The answer to an Inference question may not be found directly in the text cited, but it is implied in its meaning. This portion of the poem tells us that the sculpture was of a man named Ozymandias and that he is "king of kings." That alone suggests that he is the most powerful of all, but the statue's inscription cements that idea further by declaring that others should look at the things Ozymandias has done and understand that they will never match his power and glory, so they should "despair"; **(A)** is correct. No place in the poem hints at a war, making **(B)** incorrect. **(C)** is incorrect because it is a distortion of the idea of "despair." The term is used as described above, not to suggest a sad face. **(D)** is incorrect because it is unsupported by anything in the poem and cannot be inferred.

20. H

Category: Detail

Getting to the Answer: This Detail question asks for a line from the poem that tells the reader that the statue lies in ruins. The ruined state of the statue is mentioned in several places in the poem, including in lines 12–13 cited in the correct answer, **(H)**. Eliminate **(E)**, **(F)**, and **(G)** because these are unrelated to the state of the statue.

21. B

Category: Inference

Getting to the Answer: This Inference question asks the reader to glean meaning from the poem based on the author's statements. Where in the poem do we get the suggestion that the statue was crafted by a talented artist? Where do we learn anything about who made the statue? In lines 6–7, the author tells us about the sculptor. The poem states that the person depicted in the statue has certain particular features (a frown, a wrinkled lip, and a sneer of command) and the fact that the sculptor included them in the statue shows that this artisan was able to "read" these qualities "well." **(B)** is correct. Eliminate **(A)** and **(D)** because each suggests the setting the sculpture is found in but nothing about the artist who made it. **(C)** is incorrect because it gives a detail about the inscription but does not suggest that it took talent to craft that label.

22. F

Category: Global

Getting to the Answer: The idea of a "colossal wreck" is an interesting one. "Colossal" means huge, impressive, and significant, while "wreck" conjures ideas of devastation and destruction. This phrase is a condensed expression of the central irony of the poem: that a magnificent tribute to a great leader now stands in ruins. **(F)** is correct. **(E)** is incorrect because its suggestion that the statue was large misses the point. The size of the statue is not addressed and is not part of the author's purpose. Regarding **(G)**, while it might be true that this would be a great archaeological find, nothing in the poem addresses that, so this is incorrect. Although line 13 focuses on destruction, nothing in the poem suggests that the reader is meant to feel disgusted or angry over that; **(H)** is incorrect.

Poem Analysis: The poem is about the dual nature of making art: it has the potential to be both beautiful and destructive. In the first two stanzas, the narrator describes Pan (an ancient Greek god of wild nature) stomping through the water and pulling up a reed. In the third and fourth stanzas, Pan violently cuts and shapes the reed to make a part for his flute. He states, in the fifth stanza, that altering the reed like this is the only way to make music. The sixth stanza details how beautiful the music is, but in the seventh and final stanza, the narrator laments the destruction that was part of the process.

23. A

Category: Function

Getting to the Answer: The question asks what effect the given phrase has on the poem. The phrase "hard bleak steel" describes the texture and strength of the blade used by Pan; this contrasts with the reed, which is described as being "patient" and "a poor dry empty thing." **(A)** is correct. **(B)** is incorrect because, although the blade is described as being quite strong, there is no indication in the poem that the reed couldn't be cut with a less strong weapon. **(C)** is incorrect because, while Pan says this is the only way, there is no proof in the poem that this is true. **(D)** is incorrect because nothing in the poem indicates that Pan is angry at the reed. In fact, Pan spends much of his time laughing, indicating that it is unlikely that he is angry at all.

24. G

Category: Inference

Getting to the Answer: The question asks for the most likely reason why the fourth stanza (lines 19–24) was included in the poem. The narrator describes how much shorter the reed looks once it has been cut down by Pan and even goes so far as to say that the reed is a "poor dry empty thing." The narrator describes the pith as being "like the heart of a man" which makes Pan's actions seem that much more violent. These descriptions imply that the narrator feels sorry for the reed, so **(G)** is the correct answer. **(E)** is incorrect because although the river is mentioned in the stanza, it does not play an important part in the events that are taking place. **(F)** is incorrect because the focus of this stanza is on how Pan's actions are affecting the reed itself, not on Pan's skill in cutting it apart. **(H)** is incorrect because there is no indication that the reed being dry means that it is no longer useful to Pan. In fact, later in the poem, Pan goes on to use the reed to make his music.

25. D

Category: Global

Getting to the Answer: The question asks how the final stanza (lines 37–42) contributes to the development of ideas in the poem. The final stanza says that even though Pan was able to make sweet music through his use of the reed, there is reason for sadness in that the reed will never grow again. This matches with **(D)**. **(A)** is incorrect because the author never argues that Pan isn't really a god, simply that his actions are more beastly than a god's should be. **(B)** is incorrect because the narrator discusses the impacts of Pan's actions, implying that Pan has caused lasting damage even though there are other reeds. **(C)** is is too extreme; while pain was part of the joy of Pan's music, the poem does not indicate that this pain is necessary for all joys.

26. E

Category: Global

Getting to the Answer: The question asks how the second stanza (lines 7–12) contributes to the development of the theme in the poem. The stanza describes Pan pulling a reed out of the river. It also mentions that "the broken lilies a-dying lay" and "the dragon-fly had fled away." These details tell us that Pan has disturbed the river and its wider environment, which matches **(E)**. **(F)** is a Distortion; the stanza does mention that the water is turbid, or unclear, but there is no indication that this is the reason why Pan tore the reed out of the river. **(G)** is Extreme; Pan did ultimately cause destruction to the area, but it is not stated in the passage that Pan intended to bring destruction. **(H)** is Out of Scope; there is no discussion in this stanza of too many plants growing in the river.

27. A

Category: Function

Getting to the Answer: The question asks how the given comparison contributes to the development of ideas in the stanza. The first line mentions that when Pan cut down the reed, he "cut it short," and that before the reed was cut, it stood tall. This is a direct comparison of the appearance of the reed both before and after it is cut,

which matches **(A)**. **(B)** is Out of Scope because there is no indication in the stanza that it took great strength for Pan to cut down the reed. **(C)** is also Out of Scope; Pan's preference for a certain length of reed is not discussed anywhere in the poem. **(D)** is Extreme; although Pan is referenced several times throughout the poem as being a "great god," none of the details in the poem suggest that only a great god could do what Pan has done.

28. E

Category: Global

Getting to the Answer: This question asks how the given stanza contributes to the overall theme of the poem. In this stanza, Pan speaks for the first time, and he says that he has done what he has done in order to make music, as gods have always done. For the first time in the poem, Pan is providing his own commentary on his actions, which matches with **(E)**. **(F)** is a Distortion; although Pan is described as laughing while he speaks, there are no details to indicate that he is laughing because he thinks that his actions are funny. **(G)** is Out of Scope; the poem only discusses this particular incident at the river. Pan's words allude to other gods having done something similar in order to make music, but there is no relationship given between those other gods and this particular river. **(H)** is incorrect because a new perspective on Pan's actions is being provided, but it is Pan's perspective, not the narrator's.

29. B

Category: Global

Getting to the Answer: The question asks for the sentence that best describes how the given lines contribute to the development of the ideas in the poem. In this stanza, Pan plays his music by the river. It is described as being "sweet." In fact, the music is so sweet that "the sun on the hill forgot to die," "the lilies revived," and "the dragon-fly came back." The next stanza, however, highlights the lasting implications of Pan's actions. Therefore, **(B)** is correct. **(A)** is Extreme; although the narrator is describing some of the positive effects of Pan's music, there is no indication that the narrator feels that this justifies Pan's actions. **(C)** is incorrect because the assertion that no lasting impact was made is directly contradicted elsewhere in the poem. **(D)** is incorrect because the music did not literally pierce and blind the creatures by the river; rather, the sweetness of the music is described as being piercing and blinding.

30. G

Category: Function

Getting to the Answer: The question asks how the repetition of the given phrase contributes to the development of ideas within the poem. Almost any time that Pan is mentioned by name in the poem, he is referred to as "the great god Pan." At first, it seems acceptable to refer to Pan as being a great god. However, as the poem continues, it becomes apparent that the narrator does not believe that Pan's actions are those that a truly great god would take. Therefore, the phrase is used to contrast with the destructive nature of Pan's actions; **(G)** is correct. **(E)** is incorrect because although his title is "the great god Pan," the narrator sets up the argument throughout the poem that Pan's actions do not match with those that a great god would take, nor give any way to measure Pan's greatness against that of other gods. **(F)** is incorrect because the repetition of the phrase brings attention to its changing meaning throughout the poem, which does contribute meaningfully to the themes present in the poem. **(H)** is incorrect because the narrator directly criticizes Pan's actions at the end of the poem.

PART THREE

SHSAT Math

CHAPTER 12

Introducing SHSAT Math

CHAPTER OBJECTIVES

By the end of this chapter, you will be able to:

- Identify the format and timing of the SHSAT Math section
- Apply tips and strategies to the SHSAT Math questions

Math Overview

The Math section is the second section on the test. It contains 57 questions and accounts for one-half of your total points on the SHSAT. The suggested total time for the section is 90 minutes, or 1 hour and 30 minutes.

Math Subsection	Total Number of Questions	Pacing
Grid-In	5 questions	$1\frac{1}{2}$ minutes per question
Multiple-Choice	52 questions	

The beginning of the Math section will look like this:

PART 2—MATHEMATICS

57 QUESTIONS—SUGGESTED TIMING: 90 MINUTES

IMPORTANT NOTES

1. Definitions and formulas are **not** provided.

2. Diagrams are **not** necessarily drawn to scale, with the exception of graphs.

3. Diagrams are drawn in single planes unless the question specifically states they are not.

4. Graphs are drawn to scale.

5. Simplify all fractions to their lowest terms.

The directions include important information that help you understand what you should expect on Test Day.

1. **Definitions and formulas are not provided.**
   What this means: The Department of Education is not going to provide a reference sheet with common formulas, like how to calculate the area of a parallelogram ($a = b \times h$), so memorize those math formulas.

2. **Diagrams are not necessarily drawn to scale, with the exception of graphs.**
   What this means: You cannot take much for granted about diagrams unless you are specifically told that they are drawn to scale. For example, lines that look parallel may, in fact, not be parallel. Figures that look like squares may not be square. Lines that look like the diameter of a circle may not be the diameter.

3. **Diagrams are drawn in single planes unless the question specifically states they are not.**
   What this means: One thing that you can assume is that diagrams are in one plane. In other words, assume that figures are flat unless you are told otherwise.

4. **Graphs are drawn to scale.**
   What this means: You can use the way graphs look to your advantage. For example, if lines look parallel, you can assume that they are. You can also estimate and label coordinates of points on graphs.

5. **Simplify all fractions to their lowest terms.**
   What this means: If you solve a problem that has a fraction for its answer and you do not simplify the fraction to its lowest terms, you will not find your answer among the choices.

The Question Types

Grid-In Questions

The beginning of the grid-in section will look like this:

GRID-IN QUESTIONS

QUESTIONS 58–62

DIRECTIONS: Answer each question. Write your answer in the boxes at the top of the grid on the answer sheet. Start on the left side of each grid, printing only one number or symbol in each box. **DO NOT LEAVE A BOX BLANK IN THE MIDDLE OF AN ANSWER.** Under each box, fill in the circle that matches the number or symbol you wrote above. **DO NOT FILL IN A CIRCLE UNDER AN UNUSED BOX.**

Multiple-Choice Questions

The multiple-choice section starts like this:

MULTIPLE-CHOICE QUESTIONS

QUESTIONS 63–114

DIRECTIONS: Answer each question, selecting the best answer available. On the answer sheet, mark the letter of each of your answers. You can do your figuring in the test booklet or on paper provided by the proctor.

SHSAT EXPERT NOTE

Save yourself time by knowing what to expect. The directions are not going to change, so learn them now so you can move more quickly through them on Test Day.

How to Approach SHSAT Math

You've most likely been exposed to the majority of the math concepts you'll see on the SHSAT, which include:

- Arithmetic
  - Number properties (odds, evens, positives, negatives)
  - Order of operations
  - Ratios and proportions
- Algebra
  - Expressions
  - Equations
  - Inequalities
- Geometry
  - Angles
  - Polygons
  - Circles
- Statistics and Probability
  - Mean, median, mode, and range
  - Probability of single and compound events

While you likely have seen most, if not all, of these concepts in school, you need to approach SHSAT math differently than you would approach any other math. You don't necessarily have to do the math *differently* than you would in class, it's just that you have to do it very methodically. You are being timed when you take the test, so you'll want to use your time well.

> ### SHSAT EXPERT NOTE
>
> Unlike the math test you take at school, no one is going to check your work. Choose the *fastest* method to solve the problem, even if it's not the way you would do your schoolwork.

Ultimately, the best way to take control of your testing experience is to approach every SHSAT math problem the same way. This doesn't mean that you will solve every *problem* the same way. Rather, it means that you'll use the same *process* to decide how to solve—or whether to solve—each problem.

Read Through the Question

You need to read the entire question carefully before you start solving the problem. When you do not read the question carefully, it's very easy to make careless errors. Consider the following problem:

1. For what negative value of x does $\left|\frac{1}{x}\right| = \frac{1}{4}$?

    A. -4
    B. $-\frac{1}{4}$
    C. $\frac{1}{4}$
    D. 4

It's crucial that you pay close attention to precisely what the question is asking. Question 1 contains a classic trap that's very easy to fall into if you don't read the question carefully. Did you notice how easy it would be to solve for the positive value of x and incorrectly choose **(D)**? When solved correctly, however, the answer is **(A)** because x is equal to -4. This is because the absolute value of $-\frac{1}{4}$ is $\frac{1}{4}$.

There are other reasons to read the whole question before you start solving the problem. One is that you may save yourself some work. If you start to answer too quickly, you may assume that a problem is more difficult than it actually is. Similarly, you might assume that the problem is less difficult than it actually is and skip a necessary step or two.

Decide Whether to Do the Problem or Skip It for Now

Every time you approach a new math problem, you have the option of whether or not to answer the question. Therefore, you have to make a decision about how to best use your time. You have three options:

- If you can solve the problem relatively quickly and efficiently, go ahead and do it.
- If you think you can solve it but it will take you a long time, circle the number in your test booklet and go back to it later.
- If you have no idea what to do, skip the problem and mark it with an X. Save your time for the problems you can do.

> **SHSAT EXPERT NOTE**
>
> Remember that when you go back to the problems you skipped, you still want to fill in an answer even if you have to guess. You'll see more about this later, but you may very well be able to eliminate wrong answers even when you do not know how to solve a problem. Every time you eliminate a wrong answer, you increase your chances of guessing correctly.

2. Tamika, Becky, and Kym were investors in a new restaurant. Tamika and Becky each invested one-half as much as Kym invested. If the total investment made by these three was $5,200, how much did Kym invest?

    E. $900
    F. $1,300
    G. $1,800
    H. $2,600

245 - 253

Different test takers are going to have different reactions to question 2. Some test takers may quickly see the algebra and do the math. Others may see a word problem and want to run screaming from the room. If, despite practice, you know that you habitually have difficulty with algebra word problems, you may choose to save this problem for later or make an educated guess.

Here's the algebra, by the way. Kym, Tamika, and Becky contributed a total of $5,200. You can represent this algebraically as $K + T + B = \$5,200$. Since Tamika and Becky each contributed $\frac{1}{2}$ as much as Kym, you can represent these relationships as follows:

$$T = \frac{1}{2}K$$

$$B = \frac{1}{2}K$$

Now, substitute variables so that you can solve the equation.

$$K + T + B = K + \frac{1}{2}K + \frac{1}{2}K$$

$$K + \frac{1}{2}K + \frac{1}{2}K = \$5,200$$

$$2K = \$5,200$$

$$K = \$2,600 \text{ Choice (H) is correct.}$$

3. Jenna is now x years old, and Amy is 3 years younger than Jenna. In terms of x, how old will Amy be in 4 years?

A. $x - 1$

B. x

C. $x + 1$

D. $x + 4$

Imagine a dialogue between Jenna and Amy:

Jenna: This is an easy problem. If my age is x, then your age, Amy, is $x - 3$ because you're three years younger than me. Therefore, in four years, you'll be $(x - 3) + 4$ or $x + 1$.

Amy: You may be right, but there's a much easier way to figure it out. Let's say you're 10 years old now. That makes me 7 because I'm three years younger. In four years, I'll be 11. Now let's just substitute your age, 10, for x in all the answer choices and see which answer gives us 11. Once you try all the answers, you see that only **(C)**, $x + 1$, works.

Jenna: That's so much extra work. Why not just do the algebra?

Amy: You can do the algebra, but my way feels like less work to me.

Here's the point: Know your strengths and make decisions about how to approach math problems accordingly!

Some people are very good at algebra. Some people have a harder time with it. The same is true for geometry, word problems, and so on. There is often more than one way to do a particular problem. The "best" method is the method that will get you the correct answer accurately and quickly. Know your strengths and use them to your advantage.

Make an Educated Guess

Don't leave any answers blank on the SHSAT. Since there's no penalty for wrong answers, there is no harm in guessing when you don't know the answer. Even if you answer a multiple-choice question randomly, you have a 1 in 4 chance of guessing correctly. Of course, you should still guess strategically whenever possible. Remember, every answer choice you eliminate increases your odds of guessing correctly.

4.   What is the greatest common factor of 95 and 114?

     E. 1
     F. 5
     G. 6
     H. 19

If you looked at this problem and either could not remember how to find the greatest common factor or were running out of time and wanted to save your time for other questions, you should be able to eliminate at least one answer choice pretty easily. Do you see which one?

Since all multiples of 5 end in either 5 or 0, 5 cannot be a factor of 114, so **(F)** can be eliminated.

Grid Strategically

The first five questions in the Math section are grid-in questions that you can either answer first or save for later. There is no wrong answer penalty, so if you do not know the answer to the question, you can—and should—still guess. For every grid-in question, you'll enter your response into a grid that looks like this:

When gridding in your answer, begin on the left. Write only one number or decimal symbol in each box, using the "." symbol if your answer includes a decimal point. Fill in the circle under the box that matches the number or symbol that you wrote. The first column on the left of the grid is only for recording a negative sign, so if your answer is positive, leave the first column blank and begin recording your answer in the second column.

If you are gridding a value that doesn't take up the whole grid, do not leave a box blank in the middle of an answer. If there is a blank column in the middle of your answer, it will be scored as incorrect. If your answer is 50, you will leave the first column—the negative sign—blank, use the next two columns for 5 and 0, and then leave the last two columns blank.

If your answer is a fraction, such as $\frac{3}{4}$, you must first convert the fraction to a decimal because it is not possible to grid in a fraction on the SHSAT. To enter 0.75, the equivalent of $\frac{3}{4}$, fill in the circles under the 0, ".", 7, and 5. You would also receive credit if you entered .75 rather than 0.75 because they represent the same value.

SHSAT EXPERT NOTE

Memorize Common Decimals

The SHSAT does not allow you to grid in fractions, so memorizing common decimal equivalents such as $\frac{1}{4} = 0.25$, $\frac{1}{5} = 0.2$, and $\frac{1}{2} = 0.5$ can save you valuable time.

A repeating decimal can either be rounded or shortened, but it should be entered to as many decimal places as possible. This means it should fill four spaces. For example, you should grid $\frac{1}{6}$ as .166 or .167 rather than .16 or .17.

Note that you cannot grid any value greater than 9,999 or less than −999. If you get an answer that will not fit in the grid, you've made a mistake and should check your work.

Lastly, make sure you fill in the circles that match all parts of your answer, and make sure that there is no more than one value bubbled in for each column. Always double-check the accuracy of your gridding so that you don't make errors that will cost you points.

SHSAT EXPERT NOTE

Practice Grid-In Questions In A Test-Like Manner

Gridding does require some care, so practice gridding in your answers when you complete grid-in questions throughout this book, just as you will do on Test Day.

CHAPTER 13

Math Foundations

CHAPTER OBJECTIVES

By the end of this chapter, you will be able to:

- Efficiently apply the Kaplan Method for SHSAT Math
- Use properties of real numbers to perform basic operations

Math Foundations

The Kaplan Method for SHSAT Math

Step 1	What is the question?
Step 2	What information is provided in the question? In what format do the answers appear?
Step 3	What can I do with the information?

- Picking Numbers
- Backsolving
- Straightforward Math

Step 4	Am I finished?

The Kaplan Method for SHSAT Math helps you organize the information in a question and decide on the best approach to answer the question. This step-by-step approach applies to all multiple choice questions. Let's apply the Kaplan Method to the question that follows:

If $3(x + y) = 12 + 3y$, then $x =$

A. -4

B. -1

C. 1

D. 4

Getting to the Answer: The question asks for the value of x and provides an equation to simplify. Using straightforward math will be the simplest way to solve. Begin by distributing the 3 over the terms inside the parentheses on the left side of the equation. This gives you $3x + 3y = 12 + 3y$. Subtracting $3y$ from both sides results in $3x = 12$. Dividing both sides by 3 gives you $x = 4$. The question asks for the value of x, so you are finished.

Grid-In Questions

The SHSAT Math grid-in section requires you to stay organized as you answer the five grid-in questions you are guaranteed to see on Test Day. Some questions ask for straightforward calculations, while others are more complex. If the question is a word problem, work through the text systematically, breaking sentences into short phrases before calculating.

SHSAT EXPERT NOTE

Grid-In Word Problems with Algebra

Approach these questions strategically:

- If variables are not defined, choose letters that make sense. Be careful not to use the same letter for different variables.
- Translate each phrase into a mathematical expression.
- Put the expressions together to form an equation.

Basic Terms

The SHSAT tests your knowledge of fundamental math concepts and operations. Being comfortable with how numbers look and work can make your life easier on all sorts of math question types on the SHSAT.

Here are some essential rules and definitions to know:

- **Integers** include 0 and negative whole numbers. If a question says "*x* and *y* are integers," it's not ruling out numbers like 0 and −1.

- A **fraction** represents part of a whole. The bottom number (the denominator) indicates how many parts the whole is divided into, and the top number (the numerator) shows how many parts are present.

- The **reciprocal** of a fraction is the inverse of that fraction. For example, the reciprocal of $\frac{2}{3}$ is $\frac{3}{2}$. The reciprocal of a fraction has the same sign as the original fraction. For example, the reciprocal of $-\frac{2}{3}$ is $-\frac{3}{2}$.

- **Evens** and **odds** include 0 and negative whole numbers. 0 and −2 are even numbers; −1 is an odd number. Between 1 and 100, there are 50 even numbers and 50 odd numbers.

- **Consecutive numbers** follow each other in order from smallest to largest, with an equal gap between them. For example, 1, 2, 3, and 4 are consecutive numbers; 2, 4, 6, and 8 are consecutive even numbers; 1, 3, 5, and 7 are consecutive odd numbers; and 3, 6, 9, and 12 are consecutive multiples of 3. Consecutive numbers can be negative, such as −7, −6, −5, and −4.

- A **prime number** is a positive integer greater than 1 that is divisible by only 1 and itself. The smallest prime number is 2, and 2 is the only even prime number.

- A **set** is a collection of distinct elements. For example, {1, 4, 7, 8} and {2, 4, 6, 8, 10} are sets.

Word Problems/Variables in Answer Choices

Translating from English into Math	
English	**Math**
equals, is, equivalent to, was, will be, has, costs, adds up to, the same as, as much as	=
times, of, multiplied by, product of, twice, double, by	×
divided by, per, out of, each, ratio	÷
plus, added to, and, sum, combined, total, increased by	+
minus, subtracted from, smaller than, less than, fewer, decreased by, difference between	−
a number, how much, how many, what	*x*, *n*, etc.

Translation

DIRECTIONS: Translate the following expressions into mathematical operations or equations:

Statement: **Translation:**

A. 2 more than *z* is twice the value of *z* $(z+2)2 = z$

B. 5 fewer than *x* equals *y*

C. The product of 3 and *x* subtracted from 3 $x - 5 = y$

D. What fraction of *x* is *y* ?

E. One-fourth of the sum of 4 and *x* $\frac{1}{4}(4+x) =$

DIRECTIONS: Translate the following equations or operations into words.

Equation or Operation: **Translation:**

F. $3z$ 3 Times z

G. b^2 b multiplied by b

H. $\dfrac{a}{b-c}$ c less then b out of A

I. $8x = \dfrac{x^3}{2}$ 8 by x is equivalent to x cube divided by 2

J. $\dfrac{h}{g} = 4h$ h divided by g is as much as the sum of 4 and h

---

DIRECTIONS: Translate the following more advanced statements into mathematical operations or equations.

Statement: **Translation:**

K. An integer greater than 0, when divided
   by the square of itself equals 2. $\dfrac{x > 0}{x^2} = 2$

L. The product of two distinct real numbers
   is 2 greater than the sum of the numbers. $xy + 2 = x + y$

SHSAT EXPERT NOTE

Keys to Translation Success

1) Learn the common terms for all major operations.

2) Pay close attention to the order of operations when translating.

1. "Seven less than 4 times x is equal to twice x plus 9." Which of the following equations is a mathematical translation of the previous statement?

   A. $4x - 7 = 2 + 9x$

   B. $4x - 7 = 2x + 9$

   C. $7 - 4x = 2 + 9x$

   D. $7 - 4x = 2x + 9$

   $4x - 7 = 2x + 9$

2. Moira had D dollars in her wallet. She withdrew B dollars from the bank. Then she spent S dollars at the store. How many dollars does Moira have now?

   E. $D + B + S$

   F. $D + B - S$

   G. $D - B + S$

   H. $D - B - S$

3. Arwen has half as many pens as Adrienne. Adrienne gives Arwen 3 pens, but still has 6 more than Arwen. How many pens did Arwen have originally?

   A. 12

   B. 15

   C. 21

   D. 24

4. The least of 4 consecutive integers is s, and the greatest is t. What is the value of $\frac{2t + s}{3}$ in terms of s?

   E. $s + 1$

   F. $s + 2$

   G. $s + 3$

   H. $s + 4$

PEMDAS

PEMDAS is an acronym for the order of operations, which is the order in which you must do mathematical calculations. It stands for

P: Parentheses (or other brackets)

E: Exponents

MD: Multiplication and Division (from left to right)

AS: Addition and Subtraction (from left to right)

When you do calculations involving parentheses or other types of brackets, be sure to distribute the term outside of the parentheses, paying close attention to its sign.

   A. $(3 + 2)^2 - 6 \times 2^2 =$

   B. $3 + (2^2 - 6) \times 2^2 =$

5. $\left(\dfrac{1}{3}+\dfrac{2}{5}\right)\div\dfrac{3}{4}=$

    A. $\dfrac{9}{32}$

    B. $\dfrac{1}{2}$

    C. $\dfrac{11}{20}$

    D. $\dfrac{44}{45}$

SHSAT EXPERT NOTE

PEMDAS can be recalled using the expression "Please Excuse My Dear Aunt Sally." You may have heard other expressions for remembering the order of operations. However you remember it, the important thing is to perform the order of operations properly on Test Day. Although the SHSAT will seldom test PEMDAS directly, you will need to follow the order of operations for every calculation.

Number Properties

    A. Odd +/− Odd =

    B. Odd × Odd =

    C. Positive − Negative =

    D. Positive ×/÷ Positive =

    E. Odd +/− Even =

    F. Odd × Even =

    G. Negative − Positive =

    H. Positive ×/÷ Negative =

    I. Even +/− Even =

    J. Even × Even =

    K. Negative + Negative =

    L. Negative ×/÷ Negative =

SHSAT EXPERT NOTE

Positive and negative number properties are always the same in multiplication and division, but not always in addition and subtraction.

Even and odd number properties are always the same for addition, subtraction, and multiplication. Picking any two numbers proves the rule. There are no rules for evens and odds in division.

Zero is an even number.

Adding and Subtracting Variables

A **variable** is a letter that represents an unknown value. For example, x is a variable in the expression $x + 3$.

To **add** or **subtract** variables, **combine like terms**.

$x + x = 2x$

$5x + x = 6x$

$7x - 3x = 4x$

$3 + 3 = 2(3)$

$5(3) + 3 = 6(3)$

$7(3) - 3(3) = 4(3)$

A. $4n + 5n =$

B. $4x + x + 6x =$

C. $8g + 5g =$

D. $d + n + d + 2n =$

E. $8y + 7y =$

F. $5x - 3y + 2x - y =$

6. $5a - 3 + a =$

    E. $3a$

    F. $4a - 3$

    G. $5 + 2a$

    H. $6a - 3$

7. $2xy - y + 7 + xy =$

    A. $xy + 7$

    B. $2xy + x + 7$

    C. $3xy - y + 7$

    D. $2x^2y^3 + 7$

8. $(3d - 7) - (5 - 2d) =$

    E. $d - 12$

    F. $5d - 2$

    G. $5d + 12$

    H. $5d - 12$

9. $15x - 3y - 7x + 4y - 8x + x =$

    A. y

    B. $x + y$

    C. $31x + 7y$

    D. $8x + 7y$

SHSAT EXPERT NOTE

You should collect like terms whenever you are asked to add or subtract variables.

Multiplying and Dividing Variables

To **multiply** variables, multiply the numbers and the variables separately: $2a \times 3b = (2 \times 3)(a \times b) = 6ab$.

$x \times y = xy$

$2x \times 3y = 2 \times 3 \times x \times y = 6xy$

A. $4g \times 6h =$ _____

B. $2(5x \times 3y) =$ _____

C. $\frac{1}{2}x(3y)(4z) =$ _____

Variables or numbers just outside of parentheses are multiplied by each term inside the parentheses.

$4(2x + y) = 8x + 4y$

D. $3(5s - 3r) =$ _____

E. $-b(4 - 3a) =$ _____

F. $-2(3a - 2b) =$ _____

G. $x(a + b - c) =$ _____

To **divide** variables with coefficients, simplify expressions and cancel like terms.

$x \div y = \frac{x}{y}$

$\frac{6x}{3y} = \frac{2x}{y}$

H. $\frac{12r}{4s} =$ _____

I. $\frac{15j}{3k} =$ _____

J. $\frac{21wx}{7} =$ _____

The same number or variable can be divided out from every term and placed outside parentheses.

$8x + 4y = 4(2x + y)$

K. $12x + 9y = $ _____

L. $8ab - 6b + 2bc = $ _____

M. $25g + 15h = $ _____

N. $xy + 3x = $ _____

SHSAT EXPERT NOTE

Work carefully when you distribute negative signs! One of the choices will often entice test takers who neglect the signs.

Always look for common factors and variables to factor out of expressions.

---

10. $5r(3s) + 6r - 2rs = $

   E. $9rs$

   F. $11r + s - 2rs$

   G. $13rs + 6r$

   H. $19rs$

11. $2x(3y) + y = $

   A. $5xy$

   B. $5xy + y$

   C. $6xy$

   D. $6xy + y$

12. $3(x + y) - 3(-x - y) = $

   E. 0

   F. $3x + y$ $3x + 3y$

   G. $6x + 6y$

   H. $3xy$

13. $-5n(3m - 2) = $

   A. $-15mn + 10n$

   B. $15mn - 10n$

   C. $-8mn + 7n$

   D. $8mn + 7n$

14. $\dfrac{25xyz}{5z} =$

    E. xy

    E. $5x$

    F. $5xy$

    G. Cannot be determined from the information given.

15. $a(3b) + b(-3a) =$

    A. 0 $3ab - 3ab$

    B. $-ab$

    C. $6ab$

    D. $a + b - 3$

16. $12cd + 6c =$

    E. $3d(4c + 2)$

    F. $3c(4d + 2c)$

    G. $6c(2d + 1)$

    H. $6d(2c + 1)$

17. $3(x + 2) - (x - 4) =$

    A. $2x - 2$

    B. $2x + 2$ $3x + 6 - x + 4$

    C. $2(x + 5)$

    D. $3x + 10$

Picking Numbers

This strategy relates to questions that include unknown values. This type of question may contain variables or unknown quantities. When you encounter questions with unknown quantities, you can assign variables to the unknowns, such as assigning c to represent an unknown number of cars. Then you can pick numbers to make abstract problems—such as those that involve variables rather than numbers—more concrete. This strategy can be useful when there are **variables in the answer choices.** You may not even need to *solve* for the variables in an SHSAT question but rather determine how the variables would behave if they were real numbers. You simply pick a real number and see for yourself. Follow these guidelines:

    Step 1: Pick a simple number to stand in for a variable, making sure it follows the criteria stated in the question stem. Does the number have to be even or odd? Positive or negative? Be careful when using 0 and 1, as they behave differently than most other numbers. Instead, try to pick easy-to-use numbers.

    Step 2: Solve the *question* using the number(s) you picked.

    Step 3: Test each of the *choices* using the number(s) you picked, eliminating those that give you a result that is different from the one you're looking for.

    Step 4: If more than one choice remains, pick a different set of numbers and repeat steps 1–3 with the choices that remain.

SHSAT EXPERT NOTE

For questions with percents of an unknown number, 100 will almost always be the most manageable number to pick for the unknown number. Use 100 to make your calculations easier.

Picking Numbers is the perfect strategy to apply to story problems that ask for an expression that represents a given scenario. Let's use this strategy to answer the question that follows.

Maggie has at least 10 more toy cars than Ramón has. Which of the following inequalities gives the relationship between Maggie's toy cars (m) and Ramón's toy cars (r) ?

A. $m - 10 \leq r$

B. $m - r \leq 10$

C. $r - m \geq 10$

D. $m - r \geq 10$

Getting to the Answer: If the mere thought of this question gives you a headache, Picking Numbers can provide you with a safe way to quickly get to the answer. The efficient way to answer this question is to choose numbers that make the math easy for you. Because you know Maggie has at least 10 more toy cars than Sam has, you can pick 13 for m and then subtract 11 to get 2 as a possible value for r. Now, plug $m = 13$ and $r = 2$ into the answer choices. Often only one, maybe two, will yield a true statement. If needed, simply pick a second set of numbers.

Choice **(A):** $13 - 10$ is not ≤ 2 Eliminate.

Choice **(B):** $13 - 2$ is not ≤ 10 Eliminate.

Choice **(C):** $2 - 13$ is not ≥ 10 Eliminate.

Choice **(D):** $13 - 2 \geq 10$ Keep.

Only **(D)** works, so it must be correct. A second set of numbers isn't needed.

Questions that involve properties of numbers (even/odd, prime/composite, rational/irrational, etc.) are another example of questions in which Picking Numbers can make your life easier. Let's give the next question a try.

If a is an odd integer and b is an even integer, which of the following must be odd?

E. $2a + b$

F. $a + 2b$

G. ab

H. $a^2 b$

Getting to the Answer: Rather than trying to think this one through abstractly, it may be easier to pick numbers for a and b. There are rules for whether sums, differences, and products of integers are even or odd, but there's no need to memorize those rules.

The question states that a is odd and b is even, so let $a = 3$ (remember, 1 can be used but is not typically helpful) and $b = 2$. Plug those values into the answer choices, and identify any that produce an odd result:

(E) $2a + b = 2(3) + 2 = 8$ Eliminate.

(F) $a + 2b = 3 + 2(2) = 7$ Keep.

(G) $ab = (3)(2) = 6$ Eliminate.

(H) $a^2b = (3)^2(2) = 18$ Eliminate.

(F) is the only odd result when $a = 3$ and $b = 2$, so it *must* be the one that's odd no matter *what* odd number a and even number b actually stand for. Even if you're not positive **(F)** will always be right, you know for a fact that all the others are definitely wrong, which is just as good!

> ### SHSAT EXPERT NOTE
>
> If more than one of the answer choices returned an odd value, then you would simply try another pair of numbers with different properties, such as $a = -5$ and $b = -8$, in the remaining choices. Very rarely would you need to pick more than two sets of numbers before you find the correct answer.

18. Working together, x people earn y dollars per hour. Which of the following represents the number of dollars that z people earn if they work at this rate for 4 hours?

    E. $4xyz$

    F. $xy + 4z$

    G. $\dfrac{4yz}{x}$

    H. $\dfrac{4xy}{z}$

19. Each of the n members of an organization may invite up to 3 guests to a conference. What is the maximum number of members and guests who might attend the conference?

    A. $n + 3$

    B. $3n$

    C. $3n + 4$

    D. $4n$

20. Paolo sold x tickets, and Gina sold y tickets. The number of tickets that Gina sold is 10 less than 3 times as many tickets as Paolo sold. What is the value of y in terms of x ?

    E. $10x - 3$

    F. $10 - 3x$

    G. $3x - 10$

    H. $3(x - 10)$

Backsolving

For the multiple-choice questions on the SHSAT, you know for certain that one of the four answer choices is correct. Therefore, with some SHSAT Math multiple-choice questions, such as the one below, it may actually be easier to try out each answer choice until you find the one that works than to try to solve the problem using straightforward math and then look among the choices for the answer. This approach is called Backsolving.

When Backsolving, it can be helpful to **start with a middle answer choice (B/F or C/G).** The numerical answer choices on the SHSAT are always either in ascending or descending order. If you solve for the one in the middle and it comes out too big, you can eliminate it *and the larger number(s)*, and the same if it's too small. So trying *one* answer choice can eliminate up to three options.

> Suppose 200 tickets were sold for a particular concert. Some tickets cost $10 each, and the others cost $5 each. If total ticket sales were $1,750, how many of the more expensive tickets were sold?
>
> A. 20
>
> B. 75
>
> C. 100
>
> D. 150

There are ways to solve this problem by setting up an equation or two, but if you're not comfortable with the algebraic approach to this one (or even if you are!), you should consider Backsolving. You know one of them will work, and as a bonus, once you find one that works, you can stop. You're done!

Getting to the Answer: Start with **(C).** If 100 tickets were sold for $10 each, then the other 100 have to have been sold for $5 each: 100 at $10 is $1,000, and 100 at $5 is $500, for a total of $1,500—too small. There *must* have been more than 100 tickets sold at the higher price point ($10).

This is great news! If you know it's not **(C)** and you know **(C)** is too small, you can eliminate **(A)** and **(B).** By solving for one value, you've eliminated three answer choices.

If 150 tickets went for $10, then the other 50 went for $5. Do the math: 150 tickets at $10 is $1,500, and 50 tickets at $5 is $250, for a total of $1,750—that's it! The answer is **(D),** so no need to go any further.

Practice Set

Drills

Practice applying the concepts covered in this chapter by answering the following skill-building questions.

1. Which of the following is an integer?

   A. 0.112

   B. 1.12

   C. $\dfrac{11}{2}$

   D. 1,120

Find the reciprocal of each of the following:

2. $1\dfrac{1}{100}$

3. $4\dfrac{9}{10}$

4. $7\dfrac{1}{8}$

Use PEMDAS to solve the following.

5. $3\left(3^2 + 1\right) + 11$

6. $2 + \left(4 - 1\right)^2 - \dfrac{3}{5}$

7. $\dfrac{6^2 - (3 + 5)}{2(-2)}$

8. $-3x + 6y + 4x - 7y =$

9. $5x + 4x + 3x + 2x + x =$

10. $6y - 8y + y =$

11. $9n - 3p - 3n + 3p =$

12. $2y + 3x - 4x + 2y =$

Multiply:

13. $4n(5p + 2) =$

14. $2x(2y + 3) =$

15. $-10(3 - 0.5)^2 + 5 =$

16. $5x(5y + 5z - 5) =$

17. $x(6 - 3y + 2z) =$

18. $-6xy(14z - 7) =$

Grid-In Questions

For test-like practice, give yourself 15 minutes (an average of 1.5 minutes per question) to complete this question set. After you're done, be sure to study the explanations, even for questions you answered correctly. They can be found at the end of this chapter.

> **DIRECTIONS:** Answer each question. Write your answer in the boxes at the top of the grid. Start on the left side of each grid, printing only one number or symbol in each box. **DO NOT LEAVE A BOX BLANK IN THE MIDDLE OF AN ANSWER.** Under each box, fill in the circle that matches the number or symbol you wrote above. **DO NOT FILL IN A CIRCLE UNDER AN UNUSED BOX.**

19. What value of g makes the equation $3(2 + g) = 23.5$ true?

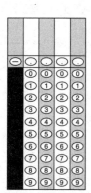

20. In the equation $5f - 45 = 115$, what is the value of f?

21. If $\frac{c}{6} + 8 = 14$, what is the value of c?

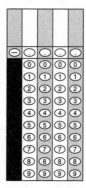

22. If $4b - 12 = 92$, what is the value of b?

23. If $3.45x + 2.1 = 9$, what is the value of x?

24. $\left(3 + |4 - 12| \times 8\right)^2 = ?$

25. What value of m satisfies the equation
$m - 2 = 2 - m$?

26. $\left(\dfrac{1}{2}\right)^3 = ?$

27. $14 - 25 \div 5^2 = ?$

28. If $12\left(2^2 - 3\right)^2 = x$, what is the value of x?

Multiple-Choice Questions

For test-like practice, give yourself 42 minutes (an average of 1.5 minutes per question) to complete this question set. After you're done, be sure to study the explanations, even for questions you answered correctly. They can be found at the end of this chapter.

DIRECTIONS: Answer each question, selecting the best answer available.

---

29. If $5x$ is a positive odd number, how many **even** numbers are between $5x$ and $5x + 6$?

    A. 1

    B. 2

    C. 3

    D. 4

30. If $z - 3$ is an odd number, which one of the following **must** be an odd number?

    E. z

    F. $z - 2$

    G. $z + 3$

    H. $z + 4$

31. On the first 4 of 5 test sections with possible scores between 0 and 20, Jocelyn scored 17, 20, 18, and 19. If she scored an odd number on the final portion of the test, what could have been her total grade?

    A. 88

    B. 91

    C. 94

    D. 99

32. What is the value of $\left(\dfrac{-3(6-2)}{-2}\right) - \left(\dfrac{-6(2-4)}{-3}\right)$?

    E. -10

    F. -2

    G. 2

    H. 10

33. If $x = 4$ and $y = 2$, then $\dfrac{2x - y}{3(y - 4)} =$

    A. -1

    B. $-\dfrac{2}{3}$

    C. $\dfrac{2}{3}$

    D. 1

34. $6 \div 10 \cdot 5 \div 3 =$

    E. $\dfrac{1}{25}$

    F. $\dfrac{3}{5}$

    G. 1

    H. $\dfrac{5}{3}$

35. $\left(\dfrac{3}{4}\right)\left(\dfrac{5}{7}\right) + \left(\dfrac{1}{2}\right)\left(\dfrac{3}{7}\right) =$

    A. $\dfrac{2}{3}$

    B. $\dfrac{3}{4}$

    C. $\dfrac{5}{6}$

    D. $\dfrac{7}{8}$

36. What is the value of $x + y(x + y)$ if $x = 4$ and $y = \frac{1}{2}$?

    E.   2

    F. $6\frac{1}{4}$

    G. $6\frac{1}{2}$

    H.   18

37. If $x = 2$ and $y = 3$, what is the value of $x^2 y^2$?

    A.   25

    B.   36

    C.   49

    D.   64

38. Simplify this expression: $2x \cdot 7 + 2 - 4x$

    E. $9 - 2x$

    F. $9 - 8x^2$

    G. $10x + 2$

    H. $16x$

39. $10^2 \cdot 3^2 + 10 =$

    A.   40

    B.   100

    C.   910

    D.   90,010

40. $\frac{1}{3} - \frac{1}{4} - \frac{1}{9} =$

    E. $-\frac{3}{16}$

    F. $-\frac{1}{10}$

    G. $-\frac{1}{36}$

    H. $\frac{7}{36}$

41. If $\frac{x}{10 + 2 \cdot 7} = 6$, what does x equal?

    A.   4

    B.   24

    C.   144

    D.   504

42. $x + x \cdot y + y =$

    E. xy

    F. $2xy + y$

    G. $4xy$

    H. $x + xy + y$

43. Simplify this expression: $7 + 5 \cdot 3^2$

    A.   37

    B.   52

    C.   108

    D.   1,296

44. $2a(3b - 5b^2) =$

    E. $-4ab^3$

    F. $6ab - 10b^2$

    G. $6ab + 10ab^2$

    H. $6ab - 10ab^2$

45. $4xy\left(\frac{1}{2y} + \frac{3}{2x}\right) =$

    A. $2x + 6y$

    B. $2x + 12y$

    C. $4x + 6y$

    D. $4x + 12y$

46. $3x(y + 4) =$

    E. $3x + 12$

    F. $3xy + 4x$

    G. $3xy + 12x$

    H. $15x + y$

47. $3x(2y - 3x - 2) =$

    A. $3xy - 9x^2 - 6x$

    B. $3xy - 15x$

    C. $6xy - 9x^2 - 6x$

    D. $6xy + 9x^2 - 6x$

48. $4x(4x - 4 - 4x) =$

    E. $-16x$

    F. $16x$

    G. $16x^2 - 16x$

    H. $32x^2 - 16x$

49. Simplify the following: $(3x + 6y) - (4x - 3y)$

    A. $-x + 3y$

    B. $-x + 9y$

    C. $x + 3y$

    D. $x + 9y$

50. If $x = 2$ and $y = -6$, then $2x(x - y) - (3x + y) =$

    E. -38

    F. -16

    G. 20

    H. 32

51. What is the value of $-2(-4 - 6) - 3(6 - 3)$?

    A. -29

    B. -11

    C. -1

    D. 11

52. Kadence is twice as likely to randomly pick a blue marble from a bag as she is to pick a red marble. If there are x red marbles and the bag contains 40 marbles, what is the probability that Kadence will pick a blue marble from the bag?

    E. $\dfrac{16}{40}$

    F. $\dfrac{x}{10}$

    G. $\dfrac{x}{20}$

    H. $\dfrac{x}{40}$

53. Maddie mailed y letters in January. She mailed 3 times as many letters in February. In March, she mailed 10 letters more than half of what she mailed in January and February together. If a letter costs $0.37 to mail, which expression represents the amount of money, in dollars, Maddie spent mailing letters in March?

    A. $1.48y$

    B. $0.74y + 3.7$

    C. $1.48y + 3.7$

    D. $2y + 10$

54. Anne has n pairs of shoes, and Fiona has 3 times as many pairs of shoes. If Fiona gives Anne 6 pairs of shoes, the girls will have an equal number of shoes. How many pairs of shoes did Anne have originally?

    E. 3

    F. 6

    G. 9

    H. 15

Math

55. A pizza is cut into x pieces. Jaylen takes $\frac{1}{4}$ of the total pieces. Maxim takes one piece less than twice the number of pieces Jaylen took. How many pieces of pizza are left?

A. $\frac{1}{4}x$

B. $\frac{1}{4}x + 1$

C. $\frac{1}{2}x + 1$

D. $\frac{3}{4}x - 1$

56. Thermometer A reads $x°$. Thermometer B reads $2°$ below the reading on thermometer A. Thermometers C and D each read $4°$ less than twice the reading on thermometer B. What is the average temperature, in degrees, of the 4 thermometers?

E. $\frac{x - 4}{2}$

F. $x - 4$

G. $\frac{3x - 9}{4}$

H. $\frac{3x - 9}{2}$

Answers and Explanations

Translation

A. $z + 2 = 2z$

B. $x - 5 = y$

C. $3 - 3x$

D. $\dfrac{y}{x}$

E. $\dfrac{1}{4}(4 + x)$

F. The product of 3 and z

G. The square of b

H. a divided by the quantity of b minus c

I. 8 times x is half as large as x cubed

J. The quotient of h and g is equivalent to 4 times the value of h

K. $\dfrac{x}{x^2} = 2$

L. $xy = x + y + 2$

1.   B
Subject: Algebra

Getting to the Answer: Translate from English into math one phrase at a time:

Seven less than 4 times x	$4x - 7$
Is equal to	$4x - 7 =$
Twice x plus 9	$4x - 7 = 2x + 9$

2.   F
Subject: Algebra

Getting to the Answer:

D Dollars	in Moira's wallet
$+ B$ Dollars	withdrawn from bank (added to Moira's wallet)
$- S$ Dollars	spent (subtracted from Moira's wallet)
$D + B - S$	

3.   A
Subject: Algebra

Getting to the Answer: First, set up equations. Arwen (R) has half as many pens as Adrienne (D): $R = \dfrac{1}{2}D$.

Adrienne gives Arwen 3 pens: $D - 3$ and $R + 3$.

Adrienne still has 6 more pens than Arwen: $D - 3 = (R + 3) + 6$.

To find how many pens Arwen had originally, solve $R = \dfrac{1}{2}D$ for D, $D = 2R$, and substitute it into $D - 3 = (R + 3) + 6$:

$$2R - 3 = (R + 3) + 6$$
$$2R - 3 = R + 9$$
$$R = 12$$

4.   F
Subject: Algebra

Getting to the Answer: Since the first integer is s, the second and third integers are $s + 1$ and $s + 2$. Thus, t is the fourth integer or $s + 3$. Substitute $t = s + 3$ into $\dfrac{2t + s}{3}$ and simplify:

$$\frac{2t + s}{3} = \frac{2(s + 3) + s}{3} = \frac{2s + 6 + s}{3} = \frac{3s + 6}{3} = s + 2.$$

PEMDAS

A. $(3 + 2)^2 - 6 \times 2^2 = 1$

B. $3 + (2^2 - 6) \times 2^2 = -5$

5.   D
Subject: Algebra

Getting to the Answer: Follow PEMDAS one step at a time:

$\left(\dfrac{1}{3} + \dfrac{2}{5}\right) \div \dfrac{3}{4} =$	
$\left(\dfrac{5}{15} + \dfrac{6}{15}\right) \div \dfrac{3}{4}$	Add the fractions in parentheses.
$\dfrac{11}{15} \times \dfrac{4}{3} = \dfrac{44}{45}$	To divide fractions, multiply by the reciprocal of the divisor.

Number Properties

A. Even

B. Odd

C. Positive

D. Positive

E. Odd

F. Even

G. Negative

H. Negative

I. Even

J. Even

K. Negative

L. Positive

Adding and Subtracting Variables

A. $9n$

B. $11x$

C. $13g$

D. $2d + 3n$

E. $15y$

F. $7x - 4y$

6. H

Subject: Algebra

Getting to the Answer: Add the a terms you have in the operation: $5a + a = 6a$. Then subtract 3.

7. C

Subject: Algebra

Getting to the Answer: Add like terms; in this case, add the xy terms:

$2xy - y + 7 + xy =$ Combine like terms.

$3xy - y + 7$

8. H

Subject: Algebra

Getting to the Answer:

$(3d - 7) - (5 - 2d) =$ Distribute to get rid of the parentheses.

$3d - 7 - 5 + 2d =$ Combine like terms.

$5d - 12$

9. B

Subject: Algebra

Getting to the Answer: Simplify the equation.

$15x - 3y - 7x + 4y - 8x + x =$ Combine like terms.

$x + y$

Multiplying and Dividing Variables

A. $24gh$

B. $30xy$

C. $6xyz$

D. $15s - 9r$

E. $-4b + 3ab$

F. $-6a + 4b$

G. $xa + xb - xc$

H. $\dfrac{3r}{s}$

I. $\dfrac{5j}{k}$

J. $3wx$

K. $3(4x + 3y)$

L. $2b(4a - 3 + c)$

M. $5(5g + 3h)$

N. $x(y + 3)$

10. G

Subject: Algebra

Getting to the Answer:

$5r(3s) + 6r - 2rs =$ Do the multiplication first.

$15rs + 6r - 2rs =$ Now, combine like terms.

$13rs + 6r$

11. D

Subject: Algebra

Getting to the Answer: Following PEMDAS, multiply first and then add:

$2x(3y) + y = 6xy + y$

12. G

Subject: Algebra

Getting to the Answer:

$3(x + y) - 3(-x - y) =$ Multiply; distribute across parentheses.

$3x + 3y + 3x + 3y =$ Combine like terms.

$6x + 6y$

13. A

Subject: Algebra

Getting to the Answer:

$-5n(3m - 2) =$ Distribute the $5n$ across the parentheses.

$-15mn + 10n$

14. G

Subject: Algebra

Getting to the Answer:

$\dfrac{25xyz}{5z}$ Cancel common factors in the numerator and the denominator.

$5xy$

15. A

Subject: Algebra

Getting to the Answer:

$a(3b) + b(-3a) =$ Do the multiplication first.

$3ab - 3ab =$ Combine like terms.

0

16. G

Subject: Algebra

Getting to the Answer: Pull out the common factors among the two terms in the expression.

$12cd + 6c =$

$6c(2d + 1)$

17. C

Subject: Algebra

Getting to the Answer:

$3(x + 2) - (x - 4) =$ Distribute to get rid of the parentheses.

$3x + 6 - x + 4 =$ Combine like terms.

$2x + 10 =$ Pull out the common factor.

$2(x + 5)$

Picking Numbers

18. G

Subject: Algebra

Getting to the Answer: With variables in the answer choices, pick easy numbers to work with: $x = 2$, $y = 6$ and $z = 3$.

If 2 people work 1 hour, they make 6 dollars, so each person makes $3 an hour. This means that 3 people working 4 hours at that rate will make $3 \times 4 \times \$3 = \$36$.

Now check each answer choice to see which one works out to $36.

(E) $4xyz = 144$

(F) $xy + 4z = 12 + 12 = 24$

(G) $\dfrac{4yz}{x} = \dfrac{72}{2} = 36$

(G) is your answer. You can always check the remaining choice, but be aware of time constraints.

19. D

Subject: Algebra

Getting to the Answer: With variables in the question and the answer choices, you can pick numbers: $n = 5$; this means that if 5 members each brought 3 guests, there are 15 guest attendees plus the original 5 members = 20. Check the choices:

(A) $n + 3 = 8$, which is incorrect.

(B) $3n = 15$, which is also incorrect.

(C) $3n + 4 = 19$, which is also incorrect.

(D) $4n = 20$, which matches your answer above.

20. G

Subject: Algebra

Getting to the Answer: This question will be much easier to solve with real numbers instead of variables. Pick $x = 4$ for Paolo. To find out how many tickets Gina sold, follow the math in the question stem:

$4 \times 3 = 12$ and $12 - 10 = 2$, so $y = 2$.

Now, plug in 4 for x in the answer choices, looking for a value of 2:

(E) $10x - 3 = 37$, which does not work.

(F) $10 - 3x = -2$, which is incorrect.

(G) $3x - 10 = 2$, which matches your choice of $y = 2$.

(G) is correct. You can check the remaining choice, but be aware of your pacing.

Practice Set

1. **D**

2. $\dfrac{100}{101}$

3. $\dfrac{10}{49}$

4. $\dfrac{8}{57}$

5. $3(10) + 11 = 30 + 11 = 41$

6. $2 + (3)^2 - \dfrac{3}{5} = 2 + 9 - \dfrac{3}{5} = 11 - \dfrac{3}{5} = 10\dfrac{2}{5}$

7. $\dfrac{36 - (8)}{-4} = \dfrac{28}{-4} = -7$

8. $x - y$

9. $15x$

10. $-y$

11. $6n$

12. $4y - x$

13. $20np + 8n$

14. $4xy + 6x$

15. -57.5

16. $25xy + 25xz - 25x$

17. $6x - 3xy + 2xz$

18. $-84xyz + 42xy$

19. **5.83**

Subject: Algebra

Getting to the Answer: Start by eliminating the 3 on the left side of the equation. From there, isolate g like you would in any other equation:

$$3(2 + g) = 23.5$$
$$(2 + g) = 7.8\overline{33}$$
$$g = 7.8\overline{33} - 2$$
$$g = 5.8\overline{33}$$

Round the repeating decimal to the nearest hundredth.

20. 32

Subject: Algebra

Getting to the Answer: Solve this equation like you would any other two-step equation. Add 45 to both sides, then divide by 5:

$$5f - 45 = 115$$
$$5f = 160$$
$$f = 32$$

Grid in **32**.

21. 36

Subject: Algebra

Getting to the Answer: Isolate the variable here like you would in any other two-step equation. Subtract 8 from both sides, then multiply the equation by 6 to isolate c:

$$\frac{c}{6} + 8 = 14$$
$$\frac{c}{6} = 6$$
$$c = 36$$

Grid in **36**.

22. 26

Subject: Algebra

Getting to the Answer: Solve this equation like you would any other equation. Add 12 to both sides and divide the equation by 4 to isolate b:

$$4b - 12 = 92$$
$$4b = 104$$
$$b = 26$$

Grid in **26**.

23. 2

Subject: Algebra

Getting to the Answer: Don't let the decimals change your approach! Isolate x as you would in any other equation by subtracting 2.1 from both sides and then dividing by 3.45:

$$3.45x + 2.1 = 9$$
$$3.45x = 6.9$$
$$x = 2$$

Grid in **2**.

24. 4489

Subject: Arithmetic

Getting to the Answer: Knowledge of the order of operations (PEMDAS) will help you answer this question correctly. Start with the subtraction within the absolute value brackets. Proceed to multiplication, then addition, and then finally apply the exponent outside the parentheses.

$$\left(3 + |4 - 12| \times 8\right)^2$$
$$\left(3 + 8 \times 8\right)^2$$
$$\left(3 + 64\right)^2 = 67^2 = 4,489$$

Grid in **4489**.

25. 2

Subject: Algebra

Getting to the Answer: Don't try to take any shortcuts with this equation! Just solve as you would any other equation:

$$m - 2 = 2 - m$$
$$2m = 4$$
$$m = 2$$

Grid in **2**.

26. .125

Subject: Arithmetic

Getting to the Answer: Taking a number to the third power simply means to multiply a number by itself 3 times. Don't let the fraction throw you off:

$$\left(\frac{1}{2}\right)^3 = \frac{1}{2} \times \frac{1}{2} \times \frac{1}{2} = \frac{1}{8}$$

Grid in **.125**, which is equivalent to $\frac{1}{8}$.

27. 13

Subject: Arithmetic

Getting to the Answer: Remembering the order of operations is the key to answering this question correctly. Address the exponent first, then do division, and finish with subtraction:

$$14 - 25 \div 5^2$$
$$14 - 25 \div 25$$
$$14 - 1 = 13$$

Grid in **13**.

28. 12

Subject: Algebra

Getting to the Answer: Even though this question may look like an equation, the order of operations and basic computational skills are all that is necessary to answer this question correctly. Remember to start inside the parentheses, and then follow the order of operations accordingly:

$$12(2^2 - 3)^2$$
$$12(4 - 3)^2$$
$$12(1)^2 = 12$$

Grid in **12**.

29. C

Subject: Arithmetic

Getting to the Answer: This is a great question for Picking Numbers. Let $x = 1$, so $5(1) = 5$ and $5(1) + 6 = 11$. Count the even numbers between 5 and 11: 6, 8, 10. There are 3 even numbers in this range.

30. G

Subject: Arithmetic

Getting to the Answer: You know z must be even if $z - 3$ is odd, because 3 more than an odd number is an even number. This allows you to rule out **(E)**. Knowing that z is an even number allows you to evaluate the remaining answer choices; $z - 2$ and $z + 4$ must also be even, leaving **(G)**, $z + 3$, to be the only answer choice that must be odd.

31. B

Subject: Arithmetic

Getting to the Answer: An odd score on the final test will give you three sections with an odd score. Because the number of odd elements in the sum is odd, the total must also be an odd number. Only **(B)** and **(D)** are odd numbers. Because the maximum possible score on any section is 20 and Jocelyn scored a total of 74 on the previous sections, the only possible answer is **(B)**.

32. H

Subject: Arithmetic

Getting to the Answer: Follow PEMDAS to solve.

$$\left(\frac{-3(6-2)}{-2}\right) - \left(\frac{-6(2-4)}{-3}\right) = \quad \text{Work inside the parentheses first.}$$

$$\left(\frac{-3(4)}{-2}\right) - \left(\frac{-6(-2)}{-3}\right) = \quad \text{Remember your rules for multiplying positive and negative numbers.}$$

$$\left(\frac{-12}{-2}\right) - \left(\frac{12}{-3}\right) = \quad \text{Remember your rules for dividing positive and negative numbers.}$$

$$6 - (-4) = \quad \text{Add the positive.}$$

$$6 + 4 = \quad 10$$

33. A

Subject: Algebra

Getting to the Answer: Substitute the values provided for x and y.

$$\frac{2x - y}{3(y - 4)} =$$

$$\frac{2(4) - (2)}{3(2 - 4)} = \quad \text{Substitute the given values.}$$

$$\frac{8 - 2}{3(-2)} = \quad \text{A positive divided by a negative always equals a negative.}$$

$$\frac{6}{-6} = -1$$

34. G

Subject: Arithmetic

Getting to the Answer: Following PEMDAS, multiply or divide from left to right.

$$6 \div 10 \cdot 5 \div 3 = \frac{6}{10} \times 5 \div 3$$
$$= \frac{30}{10} \div 3$$
$$= 3 \div 3$$
$$= 1$$

35. B

Subject: Arithmetic

Getting to the Answer:

$$\left(\frac{3}{4}\right)\left(\frac{5}{7}\right) + \left(\frac{1}{2}\right)\left(\frac{3}{7}\right) = \frac{15}{28} + \frac{3}{14}$$

Multiply to get the LCM, 28, as the common denominator.

$$= \frac{15}{28} + \frac{3}{14}\left(\frac{2}{2}\right)$$

$$= \frac{15}{28} + \frac{6}{28}$$

$$= \frac{21}{28}$$

Simplify.

$$= \frac{3}{4}$$

36. F

Subject: Algebra

Getting to the Answer: First, substitute the values of x and y into the expression, and then use PEMDAS to evaluate the expression.

$$x + y(x + y) = 4 + \left(\frac{1}{2}\right)\left(4 + \frac{1}{2}\right)$$

$$= 4 + \left(\frac{1}{2}\right)\left(4\frac{1}{2}\right)$$

$$= 4 + 2\frac{1}{4}$$

$$= 6\frac{1}{4}$$

37. B

Subject: Algebra

Getting to the Answer: Substitute the values provided for x and y.

$$2^2 3^2 = (4)(9) = 36$$

38. G

Subject: Algebra

Getting to the Answer: Combine like terms.

$$2x \cdot 7 + 2 - 4x = 14x + 2 - 4x$$

$$= 10x + 2$$

39. C

Subject: Arithmetic

Getting to the Answer:

$$10^2 \cdot 3^2 + 10 = 100 \times 9 + 10$$

$$= 900 + 10$$

$$= 910$$

40. G

Subject: Arithmetic

Getting to the Answer: The least common multiple (LCM) of 3, 4, and 9 is 36, so:

$$\frac{1}{3} - \frac{1}{4} - \frac{1}{9} = \frac{12}{36} - \frac{9}{36} - \frac{4}{36}$$

$$= \frac{3}{36} - \frac{4}{36}$$

Go from left to right when there is only one operation!

$$= -\frac{1}{36}$$

41. C

Subject: Algebra

Getting to the Answer: Begin by simplifying the denominator:

$$\frac{x}{10 + 2 \cdot 7} = 6$$

$$\frac{x}{24} = 6$$

$$x = 6 \cdot 24$$

$$= 144$$

42. H

Subject: Algebra

Getting to the Answer: Distribute:

$$x + x \cdot y + y = x + xy + y$$

43. B

Subject: Arithmetic

Getting to the Answer: Use PEMDAS to solve.

$$7 + 5 \cdot 3^2 = 7 + 5 \times 9$$

$$= 7 + 45$$

$$= 52$$

44. H

Subject: Algebra

Getting to the Answer: Distribute:

$$2a(3b - 5b^2) = 6ab - 10ab^2$$

45. A

Subject: Algebra

Getting to the Answer: Distribute and simplify.

$$4xy\left(\frac{1}{2y} + \frac{3}{2x}\right) =$$

$$\frac{4xy}{2y} + \frac{12xy}{2x}$$

$$2x + 6y$$

46. G

Subject: Algebra

Getting to the Answer: Distribute:

$$3x(y + 4) = 3xy + 12x$$

47. C

Subject: Algebra

Getting to the Answer: Distribute:

$$3x(2y - 3x - 2) = 6xy - 9x^2 - 6x$$

48. E

Subject: Algebra

Getting to the Answer: Distribute:

$$4x(4x - 4 - 4x) = 4x(-4) = -16x$$

49. B

Subject: Algebra

Getting to the Answer: Distribute:

$(3x + 6y) - (4x - 3y)$ Distribute the negative sign properly.

$\quad 3x + 6y - 4x + 3y$ Combine the like terms.

$-x + 9y$

50. H

Subject: Algebra

Getting to the Answer: Plug in the given values for x and y.

$2x(x - y) - (3x + y) =$ Substitute the given values.

$(2(2))(2 - (-6)) - (3(2) + (-6)) =$ Observe the positive/ negative rules.

$\quad\quad 4(2 + 6) - (6 - 6) =$

$\quad\quad\quad 4(8) - 0 = 32$

51. D

Subject: Arithmetic

Getting to the Answer: Apply PEMDAS carefully:

$-2(-4 - 6) - 3(6 - 3) =$ Work out the values inside the parentheses first.

$\quad -2(-10) - 3(3) =$ Remember that a negative times a negative always equals a positive.

$\quad\quad 20 - 9 = \quad 11$

52. G

Subject: Statistics and Probability

Getting to the Answer: Identify the term that represents the blue marbles.

x This is the number of red marbles.

$2x$ Figure out the number of blue marbles.

$\dfrac{2x}{40} = \dfrac{x}{20}$ Compute the probability of picking blue.

53. B

Subject: Algebra

Getting to the Answer: This is a good question for Picking Numbers. Pick a number for y, then compute the values of y and z. Determine the amount spent in March, then use the numbers you picked to find the choice that matches.

$y = 10$ Pick a number for January's letters, y.

$3y = 3(10) = 30$ Compute the number of February's letters.

$\frac{1}{2}(y + 3y) + 10 =$ Compute the number of March's letters.

$\frac{1}{2}(10 + 30) + 10 =$

$\frac{1}{2}(40) + 10 = 30$

$0.37(30) = 11.10$ Calculate the price for March's letters.

$0.74y + 3.7 =$ This matches **(B)**.

$0.74(10) + 3.7 =$

$7.40 + 3.7 = 11.10$

54. F

Subject: Algebra

Getting to the Answer: Assign a variable for the number of pairs of shoes Anne has and write the number of pairs of shoes Fiona has in terms of that variable.

Anne $= n$

Fiona $= 3n$

If Fiona gives Anne 6 pairs of shoes, then they are equal, so set the two new situations equal to one another.

$$3n - 6 = n + 6$$
$$3n = n + 12$$
$$2n = 12$$
$$n = 6$$

Note that if you forget to add 6 pairs to Anne's shoe collection, you will get 3.

55. B

Subject: Algebra

Getting to the Answer: Pick numbers to make this question easier to work with.

$x = 12$ Pick a value for the number of total pieces, x.

$\frac{1}{4}(12) = 3$ Calculate Jaylen's pieces.

$2(3) - 1 = 5$ Calculate Maxim's pieces.

$3 + 5 = 8$ Add the two together.

$12 - 8 = 4$ Calculate the number remaining.

Plug $x = 12$ into each of the answer choices to find which one matches. The only option that equals 4 when $x = 12$ is **(B)**, the correct answer.

56. H

Subject: Algebra

Getting to the Answer: Pick numbers to make this question more manageable.

$x = 30$ Pick a value for x.

$30 - 2 = 28$ Find the temperature on thermometer B.

$2(28) - 4 = 56 - 4 = 52$ Find the temperature for thermometers C and D.

$30 + 28 + 52 + 52 = 162$ Remember to add 52 twice, for C and D.

$\frac{162}{4} = 40.5$ Calculate the average.

Plug $x = 30$ into each of the answer choices to find which one matches. The only expression that equals 40.5 when $x = 30$ is **(H)**, which is the correct answer.

CHAPTER 14

Arithmetic

CHAPTER OBJECTIVES

By the end of this chapter, you will be able to:

- Calculate fractions, decimals, and percents
- Round numbers to specific place values
- Calculate distance on a number line
- Calculate absolute value
- Identify factors and multiples
- Calculate percent change
- Calculate mean, median, mode, and range
- Set up and solve a proportion for a missing value
- Use ratios to perform unit conversions
- Calculate probabilities based on data sets

Arithmetic I

Fraction Operations

Any number that can be expressed as a fraction or a repeating decimal is a **rational number**. This includes numbers like 3, $\frac{2}{5}$, −0.1666, and $0.\overline{3}$.

- The process used to write a fraction in **lowest terms** is called **simplifying**. This simply means dividing out any common multiples from both the numerator and denominator so that the numerator and the denominator are not divisible by any common integer greater than 1. This process is also commonly called **canceling**. For example, the fraction $\frac{3}{6}$ is not in lowest terms because 3 and 6 are both divisible by 3. Simplifying $\frac{3}{6}$ gives $\frac{1}{2}$.

- To add or subtract fractions, first find a **common denominator,** and then add or subtract the numerators. Finding a common denominator often involves multiplying one or more of the fractions by a number so that the denominators will be the same. Note that multiplying both the numerator and denominator of a fraction by the same number is essentially just multiplying by 1, so it does not change the value of the original fraction. For example, $\frac{2}{15} \times \frac{2}{2} + \frac{3}{10} \times \frac{3}{3} = \frac{4}{30} + \frac{9}{30} = \frac{4+9}{30} = \frac{13}{30}$.

- To **multiply fractions**, multiply straight across—numerator times numerator and denominator times denominator. For example, $\frac{5}{7} \times \frac{3}{4} = \frac{5 \times 3}{7 \times 4} = \frac{15}{28}$.

- To **divide fractions**, invert the second fraction (or fraction in the denominator) and multiply:
$\frac{1}{2} \div \frac{3}{5} = \frac{1}{2} \times \frac{5}{3} = \frac{1 \times 5}{2 \times 3} = \frac{5}{6}$.

- To **convert a mixed number**, which is a whole number with a fraction, to an improper fraction, which is a fraction where the numerator is greater than the denominator, multiply the whole number part by the denominator, then add the numerator. The result is the new numerator (over the same denominator). To convert $7\frac{1}{3}$, first multiply 7 by 3, then add 1 to get the new numerator of 22. Put that over the same denominator, 3, to get $\frac{22}{3}$.

- To **convert an improper fraction** to a mixed number, divide the denominator into the numerator, and the remainder will be the numerator of the fraction part with the same denominator. For example, to convert $\frac{108}{5}$, first divide 5 into 108, which yields 21 with a remainder of 3. Therefore, $\frac{108}{5} = 21\frac{3}{5}$.

- The **reciprocal** of a fraction is the inverse of that fraction. To find the reciprocal of a fraction, switch the numerator and the denominator. The reciprocal of $\frac{3}{7}$ is $\frac{7}{3}$. The reciprocal of 5 (or $\frac{5}{1}$ because all whole numbers can be written over 1) is $\frac{1}{5}$. The product of two reciprocals is always 1.

- One way to **compare fractions** is to manipulate them so they have a common denominator. For instance, compare $\frac{3}{4}$ and $\frac{7}{10}$:

$\frac{3}{4} = \frac{30}{40}$ and $\frac{7}{10} = \frac{28}{40}$; $\frac{30}{40}$ is greater than $\frac{28}{40}$, so $\frac{3}{4}$ is greater than $\frac{7}{10}$.

Another way to compare fractions is to convert them both to decimals: $\frac{3}{4}$ converts to 0.75, $\frac{7}{10}$ converts to 0.7, and 0.75 is greater than 0.7.

> **DIRECTIONS:** Use the information in the list above to complete the following fraction operations.

A. Simplify by canceling out common factors on top and bottom.

$$\frac{39}{72} = \underline{\quad} = \underline{\quad}$$

B. Find a common denominator and then add the numerators and simplify.

$$\frac{5}{9} + \frac{2}{6} = \underline{\quad} + \underline{\quad} = \underline{\quad} = \underline{\quad}$$

C. Find a common denominator and then subtract the numerators.

$$\frac{1}{2} - \frac{3}{7} = \underline{\quad} - \underline{\quad} = \underline{\quad}$$

D. Multiply the numerators to get the new numerator and multiply the denominators to get the new denominator.

$$\frac{1}{3} \times \frac{2}{5} = \underline{\quad}$$

E. To divide by a fraction, multiply by the reciprocal.

$$\frac{1}{4} \div \frac{1}{3} = \frac{1}{4} \times \underline{\quad} = \underline{\quad}$$

F. To convert to an improper fraction, multiply the whole number by the denominator, then add the numerator. The resulting value becomes the new numerator (over the same denominator).

$$4\frac{3}{7} = \underline{\quad}$$

G. To convert to a mixed number, divide the denominator into the numerator, and the remainder will be the numerator of the fraction part, with the same denominator.

$$\frac{43}{8} = \underline{\quad}$$

H. Find the reciprocal by switching the numerator and the denominator.

$$\frac{5}{9} = \underline{\quad}$$

I. Manipulate the fractions so they have a common denominator, and determine which value is greater.

$$\frac{2}{5} \text{ compared to } \frac{4}{11}$$

$$\underline{\quad} \text{ compared to } \underline{\quad}$$

$$\underline{\quad} \text{ is greater}$$

J. Convert the fractions to decimals and then determine which value is greater.

$$\frac{6}{8} \text{ compared to } \frac{8}{10}$$

$$\frac{6}{8} = \underline{\quad} . \underline{\quad} \underline{\quad}$$

$$\frac{8}{10} = \underline{\quad} . \underline{\quad}$$

$$\underline{\quad} \text{ is greater}$$

Math

1. What is the value of $2\frac{2}{3} + 3\frac{3}{4} - 1\frac{1}{3} + 3\frac{1}{12}$?

    A. $7\frac{3}{4}$

    B. $7\frac{7}{16}$

    C. $8\frac{1}{12}$

    D. $8\frac{1}{6}$

SHSAT EXPERT NOTE

To add or subtract fractions, the denominators need to be the same.

Converting Fractions, Decimals, and Percents

To convert a fraction to a decimal, divide the numerator by the denominator. For example, to convert $\frac{3}{8}$, divide 3 by 8, which yields 0.375.

$$\frac{3}{8} = 8\overline{)3.000}$$

$$
\begin{array}{r}
0.375 \\
8\overline{)3.000} \\
-2.4 \\
\hline
.60 \\
-.56 \\
\hline
.40 \\
-.40 \\
\hline
0
\end{array}
$$

Often, numbers in the quotient will start repeating, such as with $\frac{1}{6}$. When 1 is divided by 6, the decimal starts repeating almost right away, 0.16666666..., so it can be written as $0.1\overline{66}$ (the line over the 66 means "repeating"). To find a particular digit in a repeating decimal, note the number of digits in the cluster that repeats. If there are two digits in that cluster, then every second digit is the same. For example, for $\frac{23}{99} = 0.\overline{23}$, the second digit, fourth digit, sixth digit, and so on is 3. If there are three digits in that cluster, then every third digit is the same. For example, for $\frac{152}{333} = 0.\overline{456}$, the third digit, sixth digit, ninth digit, and so on is 6. To find the nth digit, divide the number of the digits you are looking for by the number of digits that are repeated in the decimal. The remainder (R) will correspond to the position that digit will hold. For the previous example, since there are 3 digits in the repeating decimal, to find the 13th digit, divide 13 by 3: $\frac{13}{3} = 4$ R1 The remainder of 1 means the 13th digit is the same as the 1st digit, which is 4.

To convert a decimal to a fraction, put each number to the right of the decimal over the power of 10 that corresponds to that number's digit. Note that the number to the left of the decimal is an integer and thus does not need to be converted into a fraction.

For example, to convert 3.246 to a fraction, place 2 over 10, 4 over 100, and 6 over 1000 and then add them using a common denominator.

$$3 + \frac{2}{10} + \frac{4}{100} + \frac{6}{1000} = 3\frac{246}{1000}$$

Then simplify: $3\frac{246}{1000} = 3\frac{123}{500}$

To convert a decimal to a percent, multiply by 100%: Percent = Decimal × 100%. For example, 0.45 as a percent is

$0.45 \times 100\% = 45\%$.

To convert a percent to a decimal, divide by 100%: Decimal $= \frac{\text{Percent}}{100\%}$. For example, 15% as a decimal is $\frac{15\%}{100\%} = 0.15$.

To convert a fraction to a percent, first convert the fraction to a decimal. For example, $\frac{3}{5}$ as a percent is $0.6 \times 100\% = 60\%$.

	Fraction	Decimal	Percent
A.	$\frac{1}{4}$		
B.	$\frac{1}{6}$		
C.			99%
D.		0.35	

2. The decimal 0.16 can be expressed as the fraction $\frac{x}{25}$. What is the value of x?

   E. 2

   F. 4

   G. 8

   H. 16

$$\frac{2}{7} = 0.\overline{285714}$$

3. In the decimal above, 2 is the first digit in the repeating pattern. What is the 415th digit?

   A. 1

   B. 2

   C. 5

   D. 8

SHSAT EXPERT NOTE

The SHSAT will reward you not only for knowing some common equivalences but also for being able to work with them.

To remember how to convert a fraction to a decimal, think of a fraction as an unfinished division problem.

Multiplying and Dividing with Decimals

Multiplying decimals is also a lot like multiplying whole numbers. Multiply each digit in the first number by each digit in the second number. The number of decimal places in the product will equal the total number of decimal places in the original numbers.

For example, to multiply 9.76 by 0.4:

First, multiply the digits as whole numbers.

$$
\begin{array}{r}
976 \\
\times\ 04 \\
\hline
3904
\end{array}
$$

Then find the total number of decimal places.

- There are 2 decimal places in 9.76.
- There is 1 decimal place in 0.4.
- The product must have $2 + 1 = 3$ decimal places. Write 3.904.
  $9.76 \times 0.4 = 3.904$

Dividing decimals is similar to dividing whole numbers.

First, make the divisor (the number doing the dividing) a whole number by multiplying it by a power of 10. Then, multiply the dividend (the number being divided by the divisor) by the same power of 10. For example, to divide 18.93 by 1.5:

Change the divisor to a whole number by multiplying by a power of 10. So, $1.5 \times 10 = 15$.

Multiply the dividend by the same power of 10.
$18.93 \times 10 = 189.3$.

Divide. Line up the decimal point in the quotient.

Continue dividing until there is no amount left over or you see a repeating pattern. You can add zeros to the end of the dividend.

$$
\begin{array}{r}
12.62 \\
15\overline{)189.30} \\
-15 \\
\hline
39 \\
-30 \\
\hline
93 \\
-90 \\
\hline
30 \\
-30 \\
\hline
0
\end{array}
$$

Rounding

To round a number, look at the value to the right of the digit in question. If the number is 4 or less, round down. If the number is 5 or greater, round up. For example, to round 28.935 to the nearest tenth, look at the 3, which is to the right of the tenths place. Since 3 is less than 4, round 28.935 down to 28.9.

Scenarios that involve countable items may also require you to round your answer up or down. For instance, a store does not sell $1\frac{2}{7}$ bags of flour, so a person would need to purchase 2 bags of flour to meet his or her needs. A pitcher containing 100 fluid ounces of lemonade can completely fill 12 8-ounce bottles, since $\frac{100}{8} = 12.5$.

4. Wes is buying plates for a graduation party. The plates are sold 12 in a pack, and there will be 80 guests. How many packs of plates does Wes need to buy in order for each of the guests to have a plate?

    E. 5

    F. 6

    G. 7

    H. 8

Number Lines

Number lines show values placed at intervals. Values may be whole numbers, negatives numbers, fractions, or decimals. As you move to the left, values decrease, and as you move to the right, values increase. For the number line shown, $A < B < C < D$ and $B - A = C - B = D - C$.

The midpoint is the halfway point between two points. If B is halfway between A and C, then B is the midpoint of AC. You can find the midpoint of a line segment on a number line by calculating the average of the two endpoints. If $A = 2$ and $C = 6$, then the midpoint is $\frac{2+6}{2} = \frac{8}{2} = 4$.

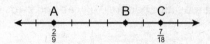

5. The intervals between the tick marks on the number line above are equal. What is the value of point B ?

    A. $\dfrac{1}{18}$

    B. $\dfrac{1}{6}$

    C. $\dfrac{2}{9}$

    D. $\dfrac{1}{3}$

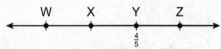

Note: Figure not drawn to scale.

6. On the number line above, $YZ = 2\dfrac{1}{4}$, $WZ = 5\dfrac{1}{10}$, and $WX = 1\dfrac{3}{5}$. What is the value of point X ?

    E. $-2\dfrac{1}{20}$

    F. $-\dfrac{9}{20}$

    G. $\dfrac{11}{20}$

    H. $3\dfrac{1}{20}$

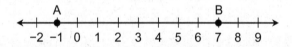

7. On the number line above, Point M (not shown) is the midpoint of line segment AB. What is the location of point M?

    A. 2

    B. 3

    C. 4

    D. 5

8. On a number line, points A, B, C, and D represent -7, -5, -1, and 3, respectively. How many units is the midpoint of $\overline{AB}$ from the midpoint of $\overline{CD}$?

    E. 4

    F. 7

    G. 14

    H. 21

> ## SHSAT EXPERT NOTE
>
> A number line shows the distance between real numbers in a positive or negative direction from a point.
>
> A midpoint is a point that is the same distance from both ends of a line segment.

Absolute Value

The **absolute value** of a number (integers, fractions, and decimals alike) is its distance from zero on the number line, which is why absolute value is greater than or equal to 0. Treat absolute value signs a lot like parentheses: do what's inside them first and then take the absolute value of the result. Don't take the absolute value of each piece between the bars before calculating. In order to calculate $|(-12) + 5 - (-4)| - |5 + (-10)|$, first do what's inside the bars to arrive at $|-3| - |-5|$, which is $3 - 5$, or -2.

A. What is $|3|$?

B. What is $|-3|$?

> ## SHSAT EXPERT NOTE
>
> When applying PEMDAS, absolute value signs should be treated as parentheses.

9. $|9 + (-3.4)| - |(-4) + 1.6| =$

 A. -7

 B. 2

 C. 3.2

 D. 8

Factors and Multiples

A **factor** of an integer is any number that divides precisely into that integer (with no remainder).

A **multiple** of an integer is that integer times any number. In other words, factor × factor = multiple.

> **DIRECTIONS:** For each statement, determine whether the first number is a factor, a multiple, or both a factor and a multiple of the second number.

A. 4 is a factor/multiple of 24.

B. 49 is a factor/multiple of 7.

C. 8 is a factor/multiple of 8.

> ### SHSAT EXPERT NOTE
>
> 2 is the only even prime, and 1 is not a prime number.
>
> There are only a few factors of a number but many multiples.
>
> When a question seems to involve a lot of complex multiplication or division, consider looking at the prime factors to break it down.

To calculate **multiples** of a given number, multiply the number by positive integers. To calculate consecutive multiples, multiply that number by positive integers that increase by 1 each time.

Consecutive Multiples

   A. List the three smallest multiples of both 6 and 8.

   B. Four consecutive multiples of 6 yield a sum of 156. What are these multiples?

   C. Five consecutive multiples of 3 yield a sum that is equal to the product of 7 and 15. What are these multiples?

10. How many positive odd factors of 30 are greater than 3 and less than 30?

   E. 2

   F. 3

   G. 4

   H. 5

11. In the set of consecutive integers from 8 to 25 inclusive, two integers are multiples of both 3 and 4. How many integers in this set are multiples of neither 3 nor 4?

   A. 2

   B. 4

   C. 6

   D. 9

Divisibility Rules

Divisible by:	Rule:	Example:
2	The last digit must be even.	2002
3	The sum of the digits is a multiple of 3.	813
4	The last two digits are a multiple of 4.	456
5	The last digit must be 5 or 0.	705
6	The rules for both 2 and 3 must apply.	924
9	The sum of the digits is a multiple of 9.	891

A. Is 115, 370, 465, or 890 a multiple of 3 ?

B. Is 12,420 or 20,242 a multiple of 6 ?

SHSAT EXPERT NOTE

Knowing these rules by memory will save you time on Test Day. The SHSAT will never explicitly ask you for these definitions, but knowing them will save you a lot of time and calculations on Test Day.

Greatest Common Factor

The **greatest common factor (GCF)** of two numbers is the highest number that divides precisely into each of them without a remainder. To find the greatest common factor, break down both numbers into their prime factorizations and take all the prime factors they have in common. For example, try 36 and 48: $36 = 2 \times 2 \times 3 \times 3$ and $48 = 2 \times 2 \times 2 \times 2 \times 3$. What they have in common is two 2s and one 3, so the GCF is $2 \times 2 \times 3 = 12$.

For a GCF problem, simply check the largest answer choice to see if it divides evenly into both numbers. If not, proceed to the second-largest answer choice. Keep going until you've found the greatest factor of both numbers.

A **prime number** is a positive integer that is divisible without a remainder by only 1 and itself. The number 2 is the smallest prime number and the only even prime number; 1 is not considered prime.

To find the **prime factorization** of an integer, use a factor tree to keep breaking the integer up into factors until all the factors are prime numbers. To find the prime factorization of 36, for example, you could begin by breaking it into 4×9. Then break 4 into 2×2 and break 9 into 3×3. The prime factorization of 36 is $2 \times 2 \times 3 \times 3$.

DIRECTIONS: To find the greatest common factor of 240 and 980, identify all of the prime factors the two have in common.

A. They share a _____, another _____, and a _____.

B. The greatest common factor is _____.

SHSAT EXPERT NOTE

For a GCF or LCM problem with prime factorization, all of the choices are presented in prime factorization. This means there is no need to multiply any of the numbers out!

---

12. What is the greatest common factor of 48 and 180?

    E. 4

    F. 12

    G. 16

    H. 18

Least Common Multiple

The **least common multiple (LCM)** of two numbers is the smallest multiple both of those numbers divide into. To find the LCM of two or more numbers, check out the multiples of the larger number until you find one that's also a multiple of the smaller number. For example, to find the LCM of 12 and 15, identify which multiple of 15 is also a multiple of 12:

$1 \times 15 = 15$ is not divisible by 12; $2 \times 15 = 30$ is not divisible by 12; nor is 45, which is 3×15. But the next multiple of 15, $4 \times 15 = 60$, is divisible by 12, so it's the LCM.

To find the LCM, begin with the smallest answer choice. Check to see if it is a multiple of both numbers. If not, proceed to the second-smallest answer choice. Keep going until you've found the smallest multiple of both numbers.

To find the LCM using prime factorization, write the **prime factorization** of each value, then take out each factor (not just factors common to both numbers), and raise it to the highest power with which it appears.

DIRECTIONS: Use the steps below to find the LCM of 240 and 980.

    A. First of all, what are the distinct factors?

    B. Now raise them to the highest power with which they appear:

13. What is the least common multiple of 12, 4, and 32 ?

    A. 64

    B. 72

    C. 96

    D. 384

Arithmetic II

Percents

Percents are one of the most commonly used mathematical relationships and are quite popular on the SHSAT.

$$\text{Percent} = \frac{\text{Part}}{\text{Whole}} \times 100\%$$

Percent is just another word for *hundredth*. For example, 27% (27 percent) means:

$$27\% = \frac{27}{100} \times 100\%$$

Other ways to express 27% include:

27 hundredths

$\frac{27}{100}$

0.27

27 out of every 100 things

27 parts out of a whole of 100 parts

SHSAT EXPERT NOTE

In percent questions, you can use the same **three-part percent formula** whether you need to find the part, the whole, or the percent: part = percent × whole.

When you work with a percent in a formula, be sure to convert the percent into decimal form:

Example: What is 12% of 25 ?
Setup: Part = 0.12 × 25

Example: 15 is 3% of what number?
Setup: 15 = 0.03 × whole

Example: 45 is what percent of 9 ?
Setup: 45 = percent × 9

Here are some other types of questions that may involve percents:

- To **increase a number by a percent**, add the percent to 100%, convert to a decimal, and multiply. For example, to increase 40 by 25%, add 25% to 100%, convert 125% to 1.25, and multiply by 40. The result is 1.25 × 40 = 50. To decrease, subtract the percent from 100%, convert to a decimal, and multiply. For example, to decrease 40 by 25%, subtract 25% from 100%, convert 75% to 0.75, and multiply by 40 to give 0.75 × 40 = 30.

- To calculate a **percent increase** (or decrease), use the formula:

$$\text{Percent Change} = \frac{\text{Amount of Change}}{\text{Original Amount}} \times 100\%$$

- When there are **multiple percent increases** and/or decreases, and the question asks for the combined percent increase or decrease, the easiest and most effective strategy is to pick 100 for the original value and see what happens in each step.

Example: A price went up 10% one year, and the new price went up 20% the next year. What was the combined percent increase over the two-year period?

Setup: First year: 100 + (10% of 100) = 110. Second year: 110 + (20% of 110) = 132. That's a combined 32% increase (which does not equal 10% + 20% = 30%).

SHSAT EXPERT NOTE

You cannot just add or subtract the percents to get the total percent increase or decrease.

- To find the **original whole before a percent increase or decrease,** set up an equation with a variable in place of the original number. Suppose you have a 15% increase over an unknown original amount, such as x. You would follow the same steps as always: 100% plus 15% is 115%, which is 1.15 when converted to a decimal. Then multiply by the number, which in this case is x, and you get $1.15x$. Finally, set that equal to the new amount.

    Example: After a 5% increase, the population was 59,346. What was the population *before* the increase?

    Setup: $1.05x = 59,346 \rightarrow x = 56,520$

SHSAT EXPERT NOTE

Questions may ask for a part, the whole, or a percent. No matter which of them the question asks for, the question will give you the other two pieces of information you need to find the missing one.

A. Regina wants to donate 15% of her paycheck to charity. If she receives a paycheck of $300, how much money will she donate?

_____

B. Andrew has a coupon for 20% off of the price of any CD. If he purchases a CD originally priced at $16, what will the discounted price be?

Solve the above problem by using decimals.

_____

1. In a certain class, 15 students are seniors. This is 30% of the total number of students in the class. How many students are in the class?

   A. 45

   B. 50

   C. 200

   D. 450

2. A light bulb filament is one-hundredth of an inch thick, with an allowable error of 2 percent. What is the **least** allowable thickness of the filament?

   E. 0.00098 in.

   F. 0.0002 in.

   G. 0.0098 in.

   H. 0.0102 in.

3. A sweater is on sale for 20% less than the original price. Julie has a coupon for an additional 10% off. What discount off the original amount does Julie receive?

   A. 15%

   B. 28%

   C. 30%

   D. 34%

4. Mandy buys a toaster that is on sale for 20% less than the original price, and then she uses a coupon worth an additional 15% off of the sale price. What percentage of the original price has she saved?

   E. 32%

   F. 34%

   G. 35%

   H. 38%

SURVEY OF TABLETS PER HOUSEHOLD

Number of Tablets	Number of Households
0	11
1	60
2	75
3	23

5. The table above gives the number of tablets per household in Sumir's neighborhood. By what percent is the number of households with 2 tablets greater than the number of households with 1 tablet?

A. 15

B. 25

C. 60

D. 80

SHSAT EXPERT NOTE

For any percent problem, you can use the formula, set up two proportions, or use decimals. On Test Day, use the method with which you are most comfortable.

Mean, Median, Mode, and Range

Suppose Jake took five quizzes in an algebra class and earned scores of 85, 92, 85, 80, and 96. Descriptions of three fundamental statistical measures you can find for this data set follow:

- **Mean (also called average):** The sum of the values divided by the number of values. The mean of Jake's quiz scores is $\frac{85 + 92 + 85 + 80 + 96}{5} = \frac{438}{5} = 87.6$.

- **Median:** The value that is in the middle of the set *when the values are arranged in order (ascending or descending)*. The test scores in ascending order are 80, 85, 85, 92, and 96, making the median 85. Be careful: the SHSAT could give you a set of numbers that is not in order. Make sure you properly arrange them before determining the median.

SHSAT EXPERT NOTE

To find the median of a data set that contains an even number of terms, arrange the terms in ascending order, then find the average of the two middle terms.

- **Mode:** The value that occurs most frequently. The score that appears more than any other is 85 (twice vs. once), so it is the mode. If more than one value appears the most often, that's okay: a set of data can have multiple modes. If no value appears the most often because they all appear the same number of times, that's okay, too: a set of data can have no mode.

- **Range:** The difference between the highest and lowest values. In this data set, the lowest and highest values are 80 and 96, respectively, so the range is $96 - 80 = 16$.

> **SHSAT EXPERT NOTE**
>
> The SHSAT won't ask you for these definitions, but you will be expected to know them.

DIRECTIONS: As with the percent formula, if you have two components of the average formula, you can find the missing piece. Use the average formula to answer the following questions.

A. Juan went to the bookstore 3 times. The first time, he bought 3 books. On both of the other trips, he bought 6 books. What is the average number of books he bought per trip?

_____

B. Alyssa has an average of 90 in English class after taking 4 tests. What is the sum of her scores?

_____

C. Muriel makes an average of $30 a day babysitting. If she made $270 in one month, how many days did she work?

_____

6. Zuri bought 4 apples at the farmer's market for a mean price of $1.35 per apple. She bought 5 pears at the local grocery store. If the total price of the apples is equal to the total price of the pears, what was the mean price of the pears?

    E. $1.01

    F. $1.08

    G. $1.21

    H. $1.68

7. A museum records 16 visitors to an exhibit on Monday, 21 on Tuesday, 20 on Wednesday, 17 on Thursday, 19 on Friday, 21 on Saturday, and 17 on Sunday. What is the median number of visitors for the week?

    A. 18.5

    B. 18.75

    C. 19

    D. 19.5

8. The scores of Garrett's last 5 quizzes are 80, 90, 80, 70, and 100. What is Garrett's mode quiz score?

    E. 30

    F. 80

    G. 84

    H. 85

LIFTS IN WEIGHTLIFTING COMPETITION

Class	Lowest Lift	Range
I	55	54
II	58	52
III	61	50

9. At a weightlifting competition, competitors were divided into three weight classes. The table above shows the lowest lift and the range of lifts for each class. What is the overall range of all the lifts in all three weight classes?

A. 50

B. 52

C. 54

D. 56

SHSAT EXPERT NOTE

Don't be intimidated by complex problems. Break them down into manageable pieces.

Rates

Rate Formula: $\text{Rate} = \dfrac{\text{Distance}}{\text{Time}}$

Of course, this formula can be modified to $\text{Rate} = \dfrac{\text{Dollars}}{\text{Hour}}$ or $\text{Rate} = \dfrac{\text{Pages}}{\text{Minute}}$, as needed.

Speed is a measure of distance per time, such as miles per hour or meters per second.

When two objects are moving, their average speed is the *total* distance traveled divided by the *total* time.

SHSAT EXPERT NOTE

As you saw with percent and average, if you have two components of the formula, then you can find the third.

A. Regina drove 325 miles in 5 hours. What was her average speed?

_____

B. Bob produces 70 widgets every hour. If he worked 3.5 hours, how many widgets did he make?

_____

C. A grocery store has salmon on sale for $5.50 per pound. If Andres spent $13.75 on salmon, how many pounds did he buy?

_____

D. A car travels at 20 mph for 1 hour, then at 40 mph for 2 hours. What is the average speed for the entire trip?

_____

10. If Jordan took 3 hours to bike 48 miles, and 1 mile = 5,280 feet, which of the following calculations would give his average speed in feet per second?

    E. $\dfrac{16 \times 60}{5,280}$

    F. $\dfrac{16 \times 3600}{5,280}$

    G. $\dfrac{16 \times 5,280}{3,600}$

    H. $\dfrac{16 \times 5,280}{60}$

11. Henry traveled 225 miles in 5 hours, and Demi traveled 350 miles in 7 hours. How much greater was Demi's mean speed, in miles per hour (mph), than Henry's?

    A. 3

    B. $4\dfrac{1}{2}$

    C. 4

    D. 5

12. Last week, Jennifer babysat on 4 different days for the Fosters. She babysat for $3\dfrac{1}{2}$ hours each day. If her total pay for the week was $77.00, how much was she paid per hour?

    E. $4.75

    F. $5.50

    G. $6.20

    H. $22.00

13. Annaliese can clean 3 fish tanks in 45 minutes. Angelina can clean 3 fish tanks in 54 minutes. What is the total number of fish tanks they can clean in 1.5 hours?

    A. 5

    B. 6

    C. 11

    D. 30

> ### SHSAT EXPERT NOTE
>
> The SHSAT rewards you for being able to manipulate a formula, as opposed to just using it in its most basic form. Be flexible on Test Day!

Ratios and Proportions

A **ratio** expresses the **relationship** between two numbers.

A **ratio** is a comparison of one quantity to another. In a ratio of two numbers, the numerator is often associated with the word *of* and the denominator with the word *to*. For example, the ratio *of* 3 *to* 4 is $\frac{of\ 3}{to\ 4} = \frac{3}{4}$.

A **part-to-part ratio** can be turned into two **part-to-whole ratios** by putting each number in the original ratio over the sum of the parts. If a flower arrangement has two types of flowers, and the ratio of lilies to daisies is 1 to 2, then lilies-to-flowers ratio is $\frac{1}{1+2} = \frac{1}{3}$ and the daisies-to-flowers ratio is $\frac{2}{1+2} = \frac{2}{3}$. This is the same as saying $\frac{1}{3}$ of all the flowers are lilies and $\frac{2}{3}$ are daisies.

A **proportion** is two ratios set equal to each other. Proportions are an efficient way to solve certain problems, but you must exercise caution when setting them up. Watching the units of each piece of the proportion will help you with this. To solve a proportion, cross multiply:

$$\frac{x}{5} = \frac{3}{4}$$
$$4x = 5(3)$$
$$x = \frac{15}{4} \text{ or } 3.75$$

> ### SHSAT EXPERT NOTE
>
> Ratios get reduced to the simplest form the same way that fractions do. In fact, fractions are really just a way to express part-to-whole ratios.

14. If $\frac{36}{8} = \frac{9}{y}$, what is the value of y?

    E. 2

    F. 4

    G. 8

    H. 32

15. There are 60 people in a movie theater. The ratio of people who have seen the movie before to those who haven't seen the movie before is 3:2. How many people have not seen the movie before?

    A.   24
    B.   30
    C.   90
    D.   120

16. Kate began a novel on Monday and read $\frac{1}{4}$ of it. If she reads an additional $\frac{1}{6}$ of the novel on Tuesday, what is the ratio of the amount of the novel she has read to the amount of the novel she has not read?

    E.   1:6
    F.   1:4
    G.   5:12
    H.   5:7

17. Asphalt, by weight, is composed of 5 parts stone, 4 parts gravel, 3 parts sand, and 1 part bitumen. To pave one parking lot, 260 tons of asphalt are needed. How many tons of gravel are needed to pave three parking lots?

    A.   80
    B.   195
    C.   240
    D.   300

18. The sum of the numbers a, b, and c is 110. The ratio of a to c is 1:7, and the ratio of b to c is 3:7. What is the value of c ?

    E.   20
    F.   40
    G.   70
    H.   110

SHSAT EXPERT NOTE

On Test Day, a question may ask for a part-to-part, part-to-whole, or whole-to-part ratio. Pay careful attention to exactly what the question is asking for, and remember that order matters when it comes to ratios.

If you are given a proportion with one missing value, you can cross multiply to solve it.

Conversions

You can set up a proportion to perform unit conversions. This is especially useful when there are multiple conversions or when the units are unfamiliar. For example, there are 8 furlongs in a mile and 3 miles in a league (though these units of measurement are no longer commonly used and may therefore be unfamiliar to you). Say you're asked to convert 4 leagues into furlongs. A convenient way to do this is to set up a proportion so that equivalent units cancel:

$$4 \text{ leagues} \times \frac{3 \text{ miles}}{1 \text{ league}} \times \frac{8 \text{ furlongs}}{1 \text{ mile}} = 4 \times 3 \times 8 \text{ furlongs} = 96 \text{ furlongs}$$

Notice that all the units cancel out except the furlongs, which is the one you want. You need to do this: set up a proportion to make equivalent units cancel. (Keep track of the units by writing them down next to the numbers in the proportion.) You should be left with the units you're converting into.

Learn to look past unfamiliar units to determine what a question is really asking and then solve accordingly.

DIRECTIONS: Use the conversion provided to solve the following questions.

A. 1 calorie = 4.184 joules. How many joules are in 3 calories?

_____

B. 3 slugs = 43.77 kilograms. How many kilograms are in 9 slugs?

_____

1 bushel = 60 pounds of potatoes
1 bushel = 48 pounds of barley

19. Adien has 1,800 pounds of potatoes and 960 pounds of barley. According to the rates above, if he fills bins that hold one bushel each, how many bins will he need?

    A. 20

    B. 30

    C. 50

    D. 108

20. On a map legend, 0.675 inches represents 67.5 miles. How many inches represent 1 mile?

    E. 0.001

    F. 0.01

    G. 10

    H. 100

21. The maximum capacity of a water tower is 4,500,000 liters. The tower is $\frac{3}{5}$ full of water. How many kiloliters need to be added to completely fill the tower?

    A. 900

    B. 1,800

    C. 2,700

    D. 3,600

SHSAT EXPERT NOTE

When converting units, set up proportions such that the units you don't want cancel out and that you're left with the units you want.

Probability

Probability measures the likelihood of an event taking place. It can be expressed as a fraction ("The probability of snow tomorrow is $\frac{1}{2}$"), a decimal ("There is a 0.5 chance of snow tomorrow"), or a percent ("The probability of snow tomorrow is 50%").

To compute a probability, divide the number of desired outcomes by the number of possible outcomes.

$$\text{Probability} = \frac{\text{Number of Desired Outcomes}}{\text{Number of Possible Outcomes}}$$

Example: If you have 12 shirts in a drawer and 9 of them are white, what is the probability of picking a white shirt at random?

Setup: When picking a shirt in this situation, there are 12 possible outcomes, 1 for each shirt. Of these 12 shirts, 9 of them are white, so there are 9 desired outcomes. Therefore, the probability of picking a white shirt at random is $\frac{9}{12} = \frac{3}{4}$. The probability can also be expressed as 0.75 or 75%.

A **probability of 0** means that the event has no chance of happening. A **probability of 1** means that the event will always happen.

Thus, probability is just another ratio, specifically a part-to-whole ratio. How many parts desired? How many total parts? Finding the probability that something *won't* happen is simply a matter of taking the other piece of the pie.

If the probability of picking a white shirt is $\frac{3}{4}$, the probability of not picking a white shirt is $\frac{1}{4}$, or 1 minus the probability that it will happen. These two events are called **complementary events**.

To find the probability that **two separate events** will both occur, *multiply* the probabilities.

A. There are 24 marbles in a bag: 6 green, 8 red, and 10 white. If one marble is chosen at random, what is the probability that it will be green?

_____

What is the probability that it will **not** be red?

_____

B. Express the probabilities in the above questions as decimals.

Will be green: _____

Will **not** be red: _____

C. The probability that a single cookie taken from a jar will be chocolate chip is $\frac{1}{5}$. If there are 6 chocolate chip cookies in the jar, how many are **not** chocolate chip?

_____

SHSAT EXPERT NOTE

Probability can also be expressed as a fraction or a decimal. Convert probability fractions and decimals as you would any other fractions and decimals.

22. In a drawer, there are 6 white socks, 5 blue socks, and 4 black socks. If one sock is pulled out at random, what is the probability that it will **not** be white?

 E. $\frac{4}{15}$

 F. $\frac{1}{3}$

 G. $\frac{2}{5}$

 H. $\frac{3}{5}$

23. There are 10 blue marbles, 4 black marbles, 5 white marbles, and 6 red marbles in a box. If two marbles are drawn at random without replacement, what is the probability that both marbles removed are **not** blue?

 A. $\frac{7}{20}$

 B. $\frac{42}{125}$

 C. $\frac{7}{12}$

 D. $\frac{13}{20}$

Number of Pairs of Shoes	Number of Students
1	6
2	29
3	95
4	68
5 or more	32

24. Lacie surveyed students at her school to determine the number of pairs of shoes they owned. Using the table above, what is the probability that a student surveyed owns at least 4 pairs of shoes?

   E. $\dfrac{34}{115}$

   F. $\dfrac{10}{23}$

   G. $\dfrac{13}{23}$

   H. $\dfrac{99}{115}$

SHSAT EXPERT NOTE

Probability falls between 0 and 1, inclusive (meaning that you can have a probability of 0 or 1). Something with a probability of 0 will *never* happen, and something with a probability of 1 will *always* happen.

Permutations and Combinations

Permutations are sequences in which order matters. Permutation questions ask "how many distinct ways" an element can be arranged. A computer password would be an example of a permutation—even if you have the right numbers, letters, and/or special characters, the password won't work if they're out of order.

   A. How many different ways can Sydney, Jed, Corinne, and Devin stand in a line? _____

Combinations are groups in which order does not matter. Combination questions ask "how many ways" might elements of a set be arranged or "how many arrangements" are possible. Choosing from a selection of ice cream flavors would be an example of a combination—the order in which you choose doesn't change the end result.

B. Amy packed 3 shirts and 4 pairs of pants for her vacation. Assuming that an outfit consists of one shirt and one pair of pants, how many different outfits are possible?

_____

C. Miguel has 4 cans of soda and 6 pieces of fruit. He plans to make himself a snack consisting of one can of soda and one piece of fruit. How many snack possibilities does he have?

_____

The previous two problems deal with the possible arrangements of multiple objects. However, the SHSAT is also known to test the possible arrangements of a single type of object.

D. Anita owns 4 different books and will place one book on her top shelf and one book on her bottom shelf. How many different arrangements are possible?

> **SHSAT EXPERT NOTE**
>
> If the same object cannot be used twice, there are fewer possibilities for the second option than there are for the first.

25. An interior designer plans to place 2 potted plants in 1 of 3 possible locations in the house. There are 6 varieties of plant to choose from. If the designer chooses 2 different varieties, how many different arrangements are possible?

  A. 12

  B. 15

  C. 36

  D. 45

26. Jennifer has 9 cookie cutters but only enough dough left for 2 cookies, both of which she will position side-by-side on the baking sheet. How many different arrangements of cookies on the baking sheet are possible, assuming she uses each cookie cutter no more than once?

  E. 2

  F. 9

  G. 72

  H. 81

27. How many 4-digit numbers can be created using 1, 2, 4, 7, and 9 if each number is used only once?

  A. 20

  B. 30

  C. 60

  D. 120

Practice Set

Drills

Practice applying the concepts covered in this chapter by answering the following skill-building questions.

Which of the following is an integer?

1. A. -2

    B. -0.667

    C. $-\frac{1}{2}$

    D. $-\frac{1}{3}$

2. E. $\frac{4}{40}$

    F. $\frac{1}{4}$

    G. 0.4

    H. 4

Convert mixed numbers to improper fractions:

3. $100\frac{1}{10} =$

4. $1\frac{1}{1000} =$

Convert improper fractions to mixed numbers:

5. $\frac{18}{8}$

6. $\frac{25}{2}$

7. $\frac{9}{5}$

8. $\frac{22}{17}$

Find the reciprocal of each of the following:

9. $\frac{3}{7}$

10. 9

11. $3x$

12. $\frac{2x}{y}$

What is the prime factorization of each number?

13. 144

14. 60

Grid-In Questions

For test-like practice, give yourself 15 minutes (an average of 1.5 minutes per question) to complete this question set. After you're done, be sure to study the explanations, even for questions you answered correctly. They can be found at the end of this chapter.

DIRECTIONS: Answer each question. Write your answer in the boxes at the top of the grid. Start on the left side of each grid, printing only one number or symbol in each box. **DO NOT LEAVE A BOX BLANK IN THE MIDDLE OF AN ANSWER.** Under each box, fill in the circle that matches the number or symbol you wrote above. **DO NOT FILL IN A CIRCLE UNDER AN UNUSED BOX.**

15. $3\left(\dfrac{4}{15}\right) + 1\dfrac{1}{15} - 2\left(\dfrac{3}{5}\right) =$

16. $|6 - (-1.3) + 2| + |4 - 2.8 - 3)| =$

17. In the set of consecutive integers from 15 to 30 inclusive, two integers are multiples of both 3 and 5. How many integers in this set are multiples of neither 3 nor 5 ?

18. Gasol has completed 85% of his homework. His homework is 60 questions long. How many questions does Gasol have left to do?

19. If Matthew scored an average of 15 points per basketball game and played 24 games in one season, how many points did he score in the season?

20. Adam runs for 10 minutes at 30 miles per hour. How far does he run?

21. $(8 \div 2 + 3) - (4 - 2)^2 = ?$

22. A closet of towels contains exactly 10 white towels. The probability of choosing a white towel from the closet is $\frac{2}{5}$. How many of the towels in the closet are **not** white?

23. How many 6-digit numbers can be created using 8, 0, 1, 3, 7, and 5 if each number is used only once?

24. Using 2.2 pounds = 1 kilogram, how many pounds are in 36 kilograms?

Multiple-Choice Questions

For test-like practice, give yourself 30 minutes (an average of 1.5 minutes per question) to complete this question set. After you're done, be sure to study the explanations, even for questions you answered correctly. They can be found at the end of this chapter.

DIRECTIONS: Answer each question, selecting the best answer available.

---

25. What is the value of $3\frac{1}{8} - 2\frac{3}{4} + 4\frac{1}{2} + 1\frac{5}{8}$?

    A. $4\frac{2}{7}$

    B. $5\frac{3}{5}$

    C. $6\frac{1}{2}$

    D. $7\frac{1}{2}$

PRICES FOR LOTS OF FARMLAND

Lot of Farmland	Price
$\frac{1}{4}$ acre	$1,000
$\frac{1}{2}$ acre	$1,750
1 acre	$3,000

26. The table above shows prices for lots of farmland. The Callan family buys an equal number of $\frac{1}{4}$ acre, $\frac{1}{2}$ acre, and 1 acre lots of farmland for a total of $17,250. What is the total number of acres the family bought?

    E. $1\frac{3}{4}$

    F. 3

    G. $5\frac{1}{4}$

    H. 9

27. The decimal 0.55 can be expressed as the fraction $\frac{x}{20}$. What is the value of x ?

    A. 5

    B. 11

    C. 15

    D. 50

$$\frac{2}{13} = 0.\overline{153846}$$

28. In the decimal above, 1 is the first digit in the repeating pattern. What is the 279th digit?

    E. 1

    F. 3

    G. 4

    H. 5

29. Becca's car engine has a capacity of 3.6 quarts and contains 1.2 quarts of engine oil. One bottle of engine oil is 0.5 quart. Approximately how many bottles of engine oil does Becca need to completely fill her car engine?

    A. 4

    B. 5

    C. 6

    D. 7

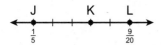

30. The intervals between the tick marks on the number line above are equal. What is the value of point K ?

    E. $\dfrac{1}{20}$

    F. $\dfrac{1}{4}$

    G. $\dfrac{7}{20}$

    H. $\dfrac{3}{4}$

31. $|(-5.6) + 2| + |1 - (-2.7)| =$

    A. 0.1

    B. 5.3

    C. 7.3

    D. 11.3

32. How many positive even factors of 52 are greater than 5 and less than 50 ?

    E. 1

    F. 2

    G. 3

    H. 4

33. What is the greatest common factor of 720 and 756:

    A. 12

    B. 24

    C. 36

    D. 42

34. What is the least common multiple of 8, 9, and 12 ?

    E. 18

    F. 32

    G. 60

    H. 72

35. In a pet store, 9 animals are hamsters. This is 12% of the total number of animals in the pet store. How many animals are in the store?

    A. 25

    B. 63

    C. 75

    D. 108

36. Zelina scored 10% higher on her second quiz than on her first quiz. On her third quiz, Zelina scored 20% higher than on her second quiz. What percent of her first quiz score is her third quiz score?

    E. 15

    F. 28

    G. 30

    H. 32

37. After taking 9 tests, Carol's average grade in her Italian class is 90. Her teacher drops the lowest of the 9 test scores to determine the final grade. If Carol's final grade is 91, what was her lowest test score?

    A. 70

    B. 77

    C. 82

    D. 90

Cost of Headphones	Number of Stores
$13	1
$15	2
$16	1
$20	3

38. The table above shows the cost of headphones at 7 stores. What is the mean price of the headphones at the stores?

    E. $16

    F. $17

    G. $18

    H. $20

39. A motorist travels 90 miles at a rate of 20 miles per hour. If he returns the same distance at a rate of 40 miles per hour, what is the average speed for the entire trip, in miles per hour?

    A. 20

    B. $\dfrac{65}{3}$

    C. $\dfrac{80}{3}$

    D. 30

40. There are 120 people at a polling place. The ratio of people who have voted to those who haven't voted is 1:5. How many people have not voted?

    E. 8

    F. 50

    G. 100

    H. 115

1 gulp = 5 rigs

1 gulp = 0.1 mews

41. Jade has 200 rigs and 10 mews. If she exchanges the rigs and mews for gulps according to the rates above, how many gulps will she receive?

    A. 41

    B. 50

    C. 140

    D. 210

Number of Marbles	Color of Marble
5	red
7	blue
2	green
4	yellow
9	orange
8	purple

42. The marbles in the table above are mixed in a bag. Which color has exactly 1 in 5 chance of being picked at random from the box?

    E. red

    F. blue

    G. green

    H. purple

43. A bag contains 8 white, 4 red, 7 green, and 5 blue marbles. Eight marbles are withdrawn randomly. How many of the withdrawn marbles were white if the chance of withdrawing a white marble is now $\dfrac{1}{4}$?

    A. 0

    B. 3

    C. 4

    D. 6

44. Tristen is packing lunch boxes for the school trip. Each lunch box consists of 1 sandwich, 1 fruit, and 1 drink. Tristen can choose from 3 types of sandwiches, 4 types of fruit, and 2 types of drinks. How many different lunch boxes can Tristen pack?

E.   3
F.   9
G.   24
H.   72

Answers and Explanations

Fraction Operations

A. $\dfrac{39}{72} = \dfrac{3 \times 13}{3 \times 24} = \dfrac{13}{24}$

B. $\dfrac{5}{9} + \dfrac{2}{6} = \dfrac{10}{18} + \dfrac{6}{18} = \dfrac{16}{18} = \dfrac{8}{9}$

C. $\dfrac{1}{2} - \dfrac{3}{7} = \dfrac{7}{14} - \dfrac{6}{14} = \dfrac{1}{14}$

D. $\dfrac{1}{3} \times \dfrac{2}{5} = \dfrac{2}{15}$

E. $\dfrac{1}{4} \div \dfrac{1}{3} = \dfrac{1}{4} \times \dfrac{3}{1} = \dfrac{3}{4}$

F. $4\dfrac{3}{7} = \dfrac{(4 \times 7) + 3}{7} = \dfrac{31}{7}$

G. $\dfrac{43}{8} = \dfrac{(5 \times 8) + 3}{8} = \dfrac{5 \times 8}{8} + \dfrac{3}{8} = 5\dfrac{3}{8}$

H. $\dfrac{9}{5}$

I. $\dfrac{2}{5}$ compared to $\dfrac{4}{11}$

LCD of 5 and 11 is 55

$\dfrac{2 \times 11}{5 \times 11}$ compared to $\dfrac{4 \times 5}{11 \times 5}$

$\dfrac{22}{55}$ compared to $\dfrac{20}{55}$

$\dfrac{22}{55} = \dfrac{2}{5}$ is greater

J. $\dfrac{6}{8}$ compared to $\dfrac{8}{10}$

$\dfrac{6}{8} = \dfrac{3}{4} = 0.75$

$\dfrac{8}{10} = 0.80$

$0.80 = \dfrac{8}{10}$ is greater

1. D

Subject: Arithmetic

Getting to the Answer: To add fractions, you need a common denominator. The lowest common denominator of 3, 4, and 12 is 12. Convert all the fractions so they have a denominator of 12 and then calculate their sum.

$$2\dfrac{2}{3} + 3\dfrac{3}{4} - 1\dfrac{1}{3} + 3\dfrac{1}{12}$$

$$2\dfrac{8}{12} + 3\dfrac{9}{12} - 1\dfrac{4}{12} + 3\dfrac{1}{12}$$

$$(2 + 3 - 1 + 3) + \left(\dfrac{8 + 9 - 4 + 1}{12}\right)$$

$$7 + 1\dfrac{1}{6}$$

$$8\dfrac{1}{6}$$

Note that you could have also converted the mixed numbers to improper fractions:

$$2\dfrac{8}{12} + 3\dfrac{9}{12} - 1\dfrac{4}{12} + 3\dfrac{1}{12}$$

$$\dfrac{32}{12} + \dfrac{45}{12} - \dfrac{16}{12} + \dfrac{37}{12}$$

$$\dfrac{98}{12}$$

$$8\dfrac{1}{6}$$

Converting Fractions, Decimals, and Percents

	Fraction	Decimal	Percent
A.	$\dfrac{1}{4}$	.25	25%
B.	$\dfrac{1}{6}$	$.1\overline{6}$	$16.\overline{6}\%$
C.	$\dfrac{99}{100}$	.99	99%
D.	$\dfrac{7}{20}$	0.35	35%

2.   F

Subject: Arithmetic

Getting to the Answer: Write the decimal as a fraction and then simplify: $0.16 = \frac{16}{100} = \frac{4}{25}$. Thus, the value of x is 4.

3.   B

Subject: Arithmetic

Getting to the Answer: In the repeating decimal (285714), there are 6 digits. Since 2 is the first digit, it will also be the 1st + 6 = the seventh digit,

the 1st + 6 + 6 = the thirteenth digit, and so on. To find the 415th digit, divide 415 by 6:

$$6\overline{)415} \quad 69\,R1$$

The remainder of 1 means the 415th digit is the same as the 1st digit, which is 2.

Rounding

4.   F

Subject: Arithmetic

Getting to the Answer: Divide the number of guests by the number of plates per pack: $\frac{80}{12} = 6.67$. Since Wes cannot buy 0.67 of a package, round up to 7 so there will be enough plates for all the guests.

Number Lines

5.   D

Subject: Arithmetic

Getting to the Answer: To find the value of point B, you need to determine the interval between the tick marks. First, determine the distance between A and C and then divide by the number of sections between A and C. The distance between A and C is $\frac{7}{18} - \frac{2}{9} = \frac{7}{18} - \frac{4}{18} = \frac{3}{18} = \frac{1}{6}$.

There are 6 sections between A and C, so the interval between the tick marks is $\frac{1}{6} \div 6 = \frac{1}{6} \times \frac{1}{6} = \frac{1}{36}$.

B is 4 sections away from A, so the value of point B is $\frac{2}{9} + 4\left(\frac{1}{36}\right) = \frac{2}{9} + \frac{1}{9} = \frac{3}{9} = \frac{1}{3}$.

6.   F

Subject: Arithmetic

Getting to the Answer: To find the value of point X, first use $YZ = 2\frac{1}{4}$ to find the value of Z:

$$Z = \frac{4}{5} + 2\frac{1}{4} = \frac{16}{20} + \frac{45}{20} = \frac{61}{20}.$$

Next, use $WZ = 5\frac{1}{10}$ to find the value of W:

$$W = \frac{61}{20} - \frac{51}{10} = \frac{61}{20} - \frac{102}{20} = -\frac{41}{20}.$$

Then use $WX = 1\frac{3}{5}$ to find the value of X:

$$X = -\frac{41}{20} + \frac{8}{5} = -\frac{41}{20} + \frac{32}{20} = -\frac{9}{20}.$$

Note that you could have also converted the fractions to decimals if you find decimals easier to work with.

7.   B

Subject: Arithmetic

Getting to the Answer: The difference in value between the two endpoints is 8. So, since the midpoint is halfway between the endpoints, it must be four units from each end. Four units to the right of -1 and to the left of 7 puts the midpoint at 3.

8.   F

Subject: Arithmetic

Getting to the Answer: First, find the midpoint of AB and the midpoint of CD:

The midpoint of AB is $\frac{-7 + -5}{2} = \frac{-12}{2} = -6$.

The midpoint of CD is $\frac{-1 + 3}{2} = \frac{2}{2} = 1$.

Thus, the distance between the two midpoints is $1 - (-6) = 7$ units.

Absolute Value

A.   3

B.   3

9.   C

Subject: Arithmetic

Getting to the Answer: Keep in mind what the absolute value symbol affects:

$|9 + (-3.4)| - |(-4) + 1.6| = |5.6| - |-2.4| = 5.6 - 2.4 = 3.2$

Factors and Multiples

A.   factor

B.   multiple

C.   both a factor and multiple

Consecutive Multiples

A.   The first three multiples of both 6 and 8 are 24, 48, 72.

B.   Four multiples of 6 can be expressed as $6x, 6(x+1), 6(x+2)$, and $6(x+3)$.

Adding the multiples and setting equal to 156:

$$6x + 6(x+1) + 6(x+2) + 6(x+3) = 156$$
$$6x + 6x + 6 + 6x + 12 + 6x + 18 = 156$$
$$24x + 36 = 156$$
$$24x = 120$$
$$x = 5$$

Therefore, the multiples are $6(5), 6(5+1),$ $6(5+2), 6(5+3)$, or 30, 36, 42, 48.

C.   Five multiples of 3 can be expressed as:

$3x, 3(x+1), 3(x+2), 3(x+3)$, and $3(x+4)$

The product of 15 and 7 is 105.

Adding the multiples and setting equal to 105:

$$3x + 3(x+1), 3(x+2) + 3(x+3) + 3(x+4) = 105$$
$$3x + 3x + 3 + 3x + 6 + 3x + 9 + 3x + 12 = 105$$
$$15x + 30 = 105$$
$$15x = 75$$
$$x = 5$$

The multiples are $3(5), 3(5+1), 3(5+2),$ $3(5+3), 3(5+4)$, or 15, 18, 21, 24, and 27.

10. E

Subject: Arithmetic

Getting to the Answer: First, list the factors of 30 and then identify how many factors greater than 3 and less than 30 are odd. The positive factors of 30 are 1 and 30, 2 and 15, 3 and 10, and 5 and 6. The factors greater than 3 and less than 30 are 5, 6, 10, and 15. Thus, there are 2 positive odd factors of 30 greater than 3 and less than 30.

11. D

Subject: Arithmetic

Getting to the Answer: To determine which integers are **not** multiples of 3 or 4, list all the numbers in the set and then eliminate those that are multiples of 3 and 4. The set of consecutive integers from 8 to 25 inclusive is [8, 9, 10, 11, 12, 13, 14, 15, 16, 17, 18, 19, 20, 21, 22, 23, 24, 25]. Eliminate the multiples of 3: 9, 12, 15, 18, 21, 24. From the remaining integers in the set, eliminate the multiples of 4: 8, 16, 20.

That leaves [10, 11, 13, 14, 17, 19, 22, 23, and 25]. Thus, there are 9 numbers in the set that are not multiples of 3 or 4.

Divisibility Rules

A.   465

B.   12,420

Greatest Common Factor

A.   2, 2, 5 (Note: $240 = 2 \times 2 \times 2 \times 2 \times 3 \times 5$, and $980 = 2 \times 2 \times 5 \times 7 \times 7$)

B.   20

12. F

Subject: Arithmetic

Getting to the Answer: To determine the greatest common factor, start with the largest answer choice and work your way down.

(H)   This is a factor of 180, but not of 48.

(G)   This is a factor of 48, but not of 180.

(F)   This is a factor of both and therefore the correct answer.

Note that 4, although a factor of both 48 and 180, is not the **greatest** common factor.

Alternatively, you can use prime factorization. The prime factorization of 48 and 180 is

$48 = 2 \times 2 \times 2 \times 2 \times 3$ and $180 = 2 \times 2 \times 3 \times 3 \times 5$.

Thus, the GCF is $2^2 \times 3 = 12$, **(F)**.

Least Common Multiple

A. 2, 3, 5, 7

B. $2^4 \times 3 \times 5 \times 7^2$

13. C
Subject: Arithmetic

Getting to the Answer: Since 12 and 32 are both multiples of 4, you only need to check whether the answer choice is a common multiple of 12 and 32. To find the least common multiple, start with the smallest number and work your way up.

(A) This is a multiple of 32, but not of 12.

(B) This is a multiple of 12, but not of 32.

(C) This is a multiple of both numbers and therefore is the correct answer.

Note that although 384 is also a multiple of both 12 and 32, it is not the **least** common multiple.

Alternatively, you could use prime factorization to determine the LCM of 12 and 32. The prime factorization of 12 and 32 is $12 = 2 \times 2 \times 3$ and $32 = 2 \times 2 \times 2 \times 2 \times 2$. So, the LCM is $2^5 \times 3 = 96$, **(C)**.

Percents

A. $\$300 \times 15\% = \$300 \times 0.15 = \$45$

B. $\$16 - \$16(0.20) = \$16 - \$3.20 = \$12.80$ or $\$16(0.8) = \$12.80$

1. B
Subject: Arithmetic

Getting to the Answer: Plug the known values for part and percent into the $\text{Percent} = \frac{\text{Part}}{\text{Whole}} \times 100\%$ formula to solve for the whole: $30\% = \frac{15}{\text{whole}} \times 100\%$

Divide both sides by 100% and isolate the whole:

$$\frac{30\%}{100\%} = \frac{15}{\text{whole}}$$
$$0.3 \times \text{whole} = 15$$
$$\text{whole} = \frac{15}{0.3}$$
$$\text{whole} = 50$$

2. G
Subject: Arithmetic

Getting to the Answer: First, find 2% of one-hundredth of an inch and then determine the least allowable thickness. One-hundredth of an inch is 0.01, so 2% of 0.01 equals $\frac{2}{100} \times 0.01 = 0.0002$. Thus, the least allowable thickness of the filament would be $0.01 - 0.0002 = 0.0098$ inch.

3. B
Subject: Arithmetic

Getting to the Answer: Pick a value like $100 for the original value. Evaluate each percent discount one at a time. Then calculate the total percent change. Let S represent the sale price.

First, determine the sale price of the sweater: $S = \$100 - 0.2 \times \$100$. So, $S = \$80$.

Next, determine the price Julie paid for the sweater. Let P represent the paid price: $P = \$80 - 0.1 \times \$80$. The price paid is $72.

The question is asking what discount Julie received off of the original price. $\$100 - \$72 = \$28$. $28 out of $100 is 28%.

4. E
Subject: Arithmetic

Getting to the Answer: Picking Numbers is a good approach for questions that ask about a percentage of an unknown number, and the easiest number to pick is 100. If the original price was 100, then:

$\$100 \times 20\% = \$20$

$\$100 - \$20 = \$80$

$\$80 \times 15\% = \$12$ and $\$12 + \$20 = \$32$ less than the original price.

$$\frac{32}{100} = 32\%$$

Math

5. B
Subject: Arithmetic

Getting to the Answer: Calculate the difference between the number of households with 2 tablets and the number of households with 1 tablet and then divide by the number of households with 1 tablet and multiply by 100%.

The difference between the number of households with 2 tablets and the number of households with 1 tablet is $75 - 60 = 15$. Thus, the percent by which the number of households with 2 tablets is greater than the number of households with 1 tablet is:

$$\frac{15}{60} \times 100\% = 25\%$$

Mean

A. Average = $\dfrac{\text{Sum of Terms}}{\text{Number of Terms}}$

$$= \frac{3+6+6}{3}$$

$$= \frac{15}{3}$$

$$= 5$$

B. Average = $\dfrac{\text{Sum of Terms}}{\text{Number of Terms}}$

average $\times$ # of tests = sum of scores

$$90 \times 4 = 360$$

C. Average = $\dfrac{\text{Sum of Terms}}{\text{Number of Terms}}$

average earnings = $\dfrac{\text{total earnings}}{\text{# of days}}$

# of days = $\dfrac{\text{total earnings}}{\text{average earnings}}$

# of days = $\dfrac{\$270}{\$30}$

$$= 9$$

6. F
Subject: Arithmetic

Getting to the Answer: First, determine the total cost of the 4 apples, and then use the average formula

Average = $\dfrac{\text{Sum}}{\text{Number of Items}}$ to calculate the mean price for 5 pears.

The total cost of the 4 apples is $4 \times \$1.35 = \$5.40$.
Therefore, the mean price of 5 pears is $\dfrac{\$5.40}{5} = \$1.08$.

7. C
Subject: Arithmetic

Getting to the Answer: You need to put the numbers in sequential order and determine which is the middle number: 16, 17, 17, 19, 20, 21, 21.

The middle number is 19.

8. F
Subject: Arithmetic

Getting to the Answer: The mode is the number that appears most often. Garrett scored 80 twice, while he scored 70, 90, and 100 only once. Thus, Garrett's mode quiz score is 80.

9. D
Subject: Arithmetic

Getting to the Answer: First calculate the highest lift for each weight class by adding the range to the lowest lift:

Class I: $55 + 54 = 109$

Class II: $58 + 52 = 110$

Class III: $61 + 60 = 111$

The overall lowest lift is 55, and the overall highest lift is 111. Therefore, the overall range of all the lifts is

$111 - 55 = 56$.

Rates

A. $R = \dfrac{d}{t} = \dfrac{325}{5} = 65$ mph

B. # of widgets = (rate)(time) = $70 \times 3.5 = 245$ widgets

C. # of pounds = $\dfrac{\text{total price}}{\text{price per pound}} \dfrac{\$13.75}{\$5.50} = 2.5$ pounds

D. $\dfrac{\text{total number of miles}}{\text{total number of hours}} = \dfrac{20 + 40 + 40}{3} =$

$\dfrac{100}{3} = 33.\overline{3}$ mph

10. H

Subject: Arithmetic

Getting to the Answer: First, determine Jordan's rate in miles per hour, and then convert his speed to feet per minute.

To find Jordan's rate in miles per hour, use the information you have about distance (miles) and time (hours): $\frac{48 \text{ miles}}{3 \text{ hours}} = 16$ miles per hour. Then use 1 mile = 5,280 feet and 1 hour equals 60 minutes to convert miles per hour to feet per minute:

$$\frac{16 \text{ miles}}{\text{hour}} \times \frac{5,280 \text{ feet}}{1 \text{ mile}} \times \frac{1 \text{ hour}}{60 \text{ minutes}}$$
$$= \frac{16 \times 5,280}{60} \text{ feet per minute}$$

11. D

Subject: Arithmetic

Getting to the Answer: First, calculate the mean speeds for Henry and Demi, and then find the difference between their mean speeds.

Henry's mean speed is $\frac{225}{5} = 45$ mph.

Demi's mean speed is $\frac{350}{7} = 50$ mph.

The difference between their mean speeds is $50 - 45 = 5$ mph, so Demi's speed is 5 mph greater than Henry's.

12. F

Subject: Arithmetic

Getting to the Answer: Use Rate $= \frac{\text{Total Pay}}{\text{Total Hours}}$ to calculate the rate.

$$\text{Rate} = \frac{\$77}{4 \times 3\frac{1}{2} \text{ Hours}} = \frac{\$77}{14 \text{ Hours}}$$
$$\text{Rate} = \$5.50/\text{hour}$$

13. C

Subject: Arithmetic

Getting to the Answer: First, determine how many tanks Annaliese and Angelina can each clean in 1.5 hours. Then calculate how many they can clean together.

$$\frac{3}{45} = \frac{x}{90}$$
$$\frac{1}{15} = \frac{x}{90}$$
$$90 = 15x$$
$$6 = x$$

Annaliese can clean 6 tanks in 1.5 hours. Note that reducing the fraction to its lowest terms simplifies the calculations.

$$\frac{3}{54} = \frac{y}{90}$$
$$\frac{1}{18} = \frac{y}{90}$$
$$90 = 18y$$
$$5 = y$$

Angelina can clean 5 tanks in 1.5 hours.

Thus, Annaliese and Angelina can together clean $6 + 5 = 11$ tanks in 1.5 hours.

Ratios and Proportions

14. E

Subject: Arithmetic

Getting to the Answer: Cross multiply to solve for y.

$$\frac{36}{8} = \frac{9}{y}$$
$$36y = 72$$
$$y = 2$$

15. A

Subject: Arithmetic

Getting to the Answer: First, determine the part-to-whole ratio from the given information and then set up a proportion to solve for the number of people who have not seen the movie before, x.

The ratio given is a part-to-part ratio. Since the question gives the total number of people in the movie theater, you need to use the part-to-whole ratio. The number of people who have not seen the movie before to the total number of movie attendees is $\frac{2}{2+3} = \frac{2}{5}$.

Setting up the proportion to solve for x gives:

$$\frac{x}{60} = \frac{2}{5}$$
$$5x = 120$$
$$x = 24$$

16. H

Subject: Arithmetic

Getting to the Answer: First calculate how much of the book Kate has read: $\frac{1}{4}+\frac{1}{6}=\frac{3}{12}+\frac{2}{12}=\frac{5}{12}$. She read 5 parts. Then calculate the amount of the book she has not read: $1-\frac{5}{12}=\frac{7}{12}$. Kate did not read 7 parts. Compare the parts read to the parts unread in a ratio and, in this case, read to unread equals 5:7.

17. C

Subject: Arithmetic

Getting to the Answer: First, determine the whole from the parts. The ratio is 5:4:3:1, so the whole is $5+4+3+1=13$. The fraction of the asphalt that is gravel is $\frac{4}{13}$. Set up a proportion to determine the amount of gravel needed for one parking lot:

$$\frac{4}{13}=\frac{x}{260}$$
$$1,040=13x$$
$$80=x$$

The question asks for the amount of asphalt need for 3 parking lots, so multiply 80 by 3 to get 240 tons.

18. G

Subject: Arithmetic

Getting to the Answer: Since both ratios have a c in common, solve each ratio in terms of c:

$$\frac{a}{c}=\frac{1}{7}$$
$$7a=c$$
$$a=\frac{c}{7}$$
$$\frac{b}{c}=\frac{3}{7}$$
$$7b=3c$$
$$b=\frac{3c}{7}$$

Since $a+b+c=110$, substitute a and b and solve for c.

$$\frac{c}{7}+\frac{3c}{7}+c=110$$
$$\frac{11c}{7}=110$$
$$c=70$$

Conversions

A. $3 \text{ calories} \times \frac{4.184 \text{ joules}}{1 \text{ calorie}} = 3 \times 4.184$ joules so there are 12.552 joules in 3 calories.

B. $9 \text{ slugs} \times \frac{43.77 \text{ kilograms}}{3 \text{ slugs}} = \frac{(9 \times 43.77)}{3}$ kilograms, and since $9 \div 3 = 3$ and $3 \times 43.77 = 131.31$, there are 131.31 kilograms in 9 slugs.

19. C

Subject: Arithmetic

Getting to the Answer: Use proportions to make the conversion from pounds to bushels.

Potatoes:

$$\frac{1,800}{x}=\frac{60}{1}$$
$$1,800=60x$$
$$30=x$$

Barley:

$$\frac{960}{y}=\frac{48}{1}$$
$$960=48y$$
$$20=y$$

Total bushels $= 30 + 20 = 50$

20. F

Subject: Arithmetic

Getting to the Answer: Set up a proportion to solve for the number of inches representing 1 mile. Let x be the number of inches.

$$\frac{x}{1}=\frac{0.675}{67.5}$$
$$67.5x=0.675$$
$$x=0.01$$

21. B

Subject: Arithmetic

Getting to the Answer: First, find the number of liters that need to be added to fill the tower. The tower is $\frac{3}{5}$ full, so it is $\frac{2}{5}$ empty. $\frac{2}{5}\times 4,500,000=1,800,000$. Use the conversion 1 kiloliter = 1,000 liters to calculate the number of kiloliters:

$$\frac{1,800,000}{1,000}=1,800 \text{ kiloliters}$$

Probability

A. The probability of picking a green marble is $\frac{6}{24} = \frac{1}{4}$. There are 8 red out of 24 total marbles, so 16 are not red. The probability of picking a marble that is not red is $\frac{16}{24} = \frac{2}{3}$.

B. probability that it is green = 0.25
probability that it is not red = 0.67

C. $\frac{1}{5}$ of the cookies are chocolate chip. 6 is $\frac{1}{5}$ of 30, so there must be 30 total cookies and, therefore, 24 are not chocolate chip.

22. H

Subject: Statistics and Probability

Getting to the Answer: Use the probability formula, Probability $= \frac{\text{Number of Desired Outcomes}}{\text{Number of Possible Outcomes}}$. The non-white socks are all of the blue and black socks, so there are 9 socks that are not white out of a total of 15 socks.

$$\text{probability} = \frac{9}{15} = \frac{3}{5}$$

23. A

Subject: Statistics and Probability

Getting to the Answer: The total number of marbles is $10 + 4 + 5 + 6 = 25$. The number of marbles that are not blue are $4 + 5 + 6 = 15$.

The probability of the first marble not being blue is $\frac{15}{25}$. Now, there are 14 marbles left that are not blue. The probability of the second marble not being blue is $\frac{14}{24}$. Multiply these two probabilities to get

$$\frac{15}{25} \times \frac{14}{24} = \frac{3}{5} \times \frac{7}{12} = \frac{3 \times 7}{5 \times 12} = \frac{7}{5 \times 4} = \frac{7}{20}.$$

24. F

Subject: Statistics and Probability

Getting to the Answer: First determine the total number of students surveyed:

$6 + 29 + 95 + 68 + 32 = 230$. Then determine the number of students who own at least 4 pairs of shoes. Students who own 4 pairs of shoes (68) + students who own 5 or more (32) $= 68 + 32 = 100$.

The probability of a student who was surveyed owning at least 4 pairs of shoes is $\frac{100}{230} = \frac{10}{23}$.

Permutations and Combinations

A. The total number of ways 4 people can stand in a line is $4 \times 3 \times 2 \times 1 = 24$.

B. For each of the 3 shirts, 4 pairs of pants are possible. That makes 12 total combinations (the product of 3 and 4).

C. For each of the 4 cans of soda, 6 pieces of fruit are possible. That makes 24 total combinations (the product of 4 and 6).

D. For the first shelf there are 4 books available, and for the second shelf there are 3 books available; $4 \times 3 = 12$ arrangements.

25. D

Subject: Statistics and Probability

Getting to the Answer: First, figure out how many different combinations of pairs of plants are possible. Use 1, 2, 3, 4, 5, and 6 to represent the varieties and list the possible pairs:

1, 2; 1, 3; 1, 4; 1, 5; 1, 6

2, 3; 2, 4; 2, 5; 2, 6

3, 4; 3, 5; 3, 6

4, 5; 4, 6

5, 6

There are 15 different possible pairs for one location. Since there 3 possible locations, multiply the total number of combinations by 3 to get the total number of arrangements the designer can create: $3 \times 15 = 45$.

26. G

Subject: Statistics and Probability

Getting to the Answer: For each of the 9 cookie cutters Jennifer could make the first cookie with, she has 8 others left to make the second cookie with. So the total number of cookie arrangements possible on the baking sheet is $9 \times 8 = 72$.

27. D

Subject: Statistics and Probability

Getting to the Answer: Determine the number of choices for each digit and then multiply to get the total number of possibilities. For the first digit, there are 5 choices; for the second digit, there are 4 choices; for the third digit, there are 3 choices; and for the fourth digit, there are 2 choices. The total number of possibilities is thus $5 \times 4 \times 3 \times 2 = 120$.

Practice Set

1. **A**

2. **H**

3. $\dfrac{1,001}{10}$

4. $\dfrac{1,001}{1,000}$

5. $2\dfrac{1}{4}$

6. $12\dfrac{1}{2}$

7. $1\dfrac{4}{5}$

8. $1\dfrac{5}{17}$

9. $\dfrac{7}{3}$

10. $\dfrac{1}{9}$

11. $\dfrac{1}{3x}$

12. $\dfrac{y}{2x}$

13. $2 \cdot 2 \cdot 2 \cdot 2 \cdot 3 \cdot 3$

14. $2 \cdot 2 \cdot 3 \cdot 5$

15. .667

Subject: Arithmetic

Getting to the Answer: To add fractions, you need a common denominator. The lowest common denominator of 15 and 5 is 15. Convert all the fractions so they have a denominator of 15 and then calculate their sum.

$$3\left(\frac{4}{15}\right) + 1\frac{1}{15} - 2\left(\frac{3}{5}\right)$$

$$\frac{12}{15} + \frac{16}{15} - 2\left(\frac{9}{15}\right)$$

$$\frac{12}{15} + \frac{16}{15} - \frac{18}{15}$$

$$\frac{12 + 16 - 18}{15}$$

$$\frac{10}{15}$$

$$\frac{2}{3}$$

Convert $\frac{2}{3}$ into a decimal, and grid in as many spaces as the grid allows, which in this case is **.667**.

16. 11.1

Subject: Arithmetic

Getting to the Answer: Keep in mind what the absolute value symbol affects:

$|6 - (-1.3) + 2| + |4 - 2.8 - 3)| = |9.3| + |-1.8| = 9.3 + 1.8 = 11.1$. Grid in **11.1**.

17. 8

Subject: Arithmetic

Getting to the Answer: To determine which integers are not multiples of 3 or 5, list all the numbers in the set and then eliminate those that are multiples of 3 and 5. The set of consecutive integers from 15 to 30 inclusive is [15, 16, 17, 18, 19, 20, 21, 22, 23, 24, 25, 26, 27, 28, 29, 30]. Eliminate the multiples of 3: 15, 18, 21, 24, 27, 30. From the remaining integers in the set, eliminate the multiples of 5: 20, 25. That leaves [16, 17, 19, 22, 23, 26, 28, 29]. Thus, there are 8 numbers in the set that are not multiples of 3 or 5. Grid in **8**.

18. 9

Subject: Arithmetic

Getting to the Answer: Since Gasol completed 85% of his homework, he has 15% remaining. Plug the known values for part and percent into the Percent $= \dfrac{\text{Part}}{\text{Whole}} \times 100\%$

formula to solve for the whole: $15\% = \dfrac{\text{part}}{60} \times 100\%$

Multiply both sides by 60 and divide both sides by 100% to isolate the part:

$$\frac{15}{100} \times 60 = \text{part}$$

$$\frac{15 \times 60}{100} = \text{part}$$

$$\frac{15 \times 3}{5} = \text{part}$$

$$9 = \text{part}$$

Grid in **9**.

19. 360

Subject: Arithmetic

Getting to the Answer: Use Points $=$ Rate $\times$ Games to calculate the total points: Points $= 15 \times 24 = 360$. Grid in **360**.

20. 5

Subject: Arithmetic

Getting to the Answer: Because your rate is in hours, first convert the time from minutes to hours. Then plug the value into the rate formula and solve for distance.

Converting minutes to hours gives:

$10 \text{ min} \times \dfrac{1 \text{ hour}}{60 \text{ min}} = \dfrac{1}{6}$ hour.

Use Distance $=$ Rate $\times$ Time to solve for distance:

distance $= 30 \times \dfrac{1}{6} = 5$ miles. Grid in **5**.

21. 3

Subject: Arithmetic

Getting to the Answer: Remembering the order of operations is crucial to getting a question like this correct! If you remember PEMDAS, then you should have no problem answering this question correctly:

$$(8 \div 2 + 3) - (4 - 2)^2$$

$$(4 + 3) - (2)^2$$

$$7 - 4 = 3$$

22. 15

Subject: Statistics and Probability

Getting to the Answer: First, set up a proportion to find the total number of towels:

$$\frac{2}{5} = \frac{10}{x}$$

$$2x = 50$$

$$x = 25$$

Since 10 of the 25 towels are white, $25 - 10 = 15$ towels are not white. Grid in **15**.

23. 720

Subject: Statistics and Probability

Getting to the Answer: Determine the number of choices for each digit and then multiply to get the total number of possibilities. For the first digit, there are 6 choices; for the second digit, there are 5 choices; for the third digit, there are 4 choices; for the fourth digit, there are 3 choices; for the fifth digit, there are 2 choices; and for the sixth digit, there is 1 choice. The total number of possibilities is thus $6 \times 5 \times 4 \times 3 \times 2 \times 1 = 720$. Grid in **720**.

24. 79.2

Subject: Arithmetic

Getting to the Answer: Multiply 36 kilograms by the given conversions to find the number of pounds:

$$36 \text{ kilograms} \times \frac{2.2 \text{ pounds}}{1 \text{ kilogram}} = 79.2 \text{ pounds}$$

Grid in **79.2**.

25. C

Subject: Arithmetic

Getting to the Answer: To add fractions, you need a common denominator. The lowest common denominator of 2, 4, and 8 is 8. Convert all the fractions so they have a denominator of 8 and then calculate their sum.

$$3\frac{1}{8} - 2\frac{3}{4} + 4\frac{1}{2} + 1\frac{5}{8}$$

$$3\frac{1}{8} - 2\frac{6}{8} + 4\frac{4}{8} + 1\frac{5}{8}$$

$$(3 - 2 + 4 + 1) + \left(\frac{1 - 6 + 4 + 5}{8}\right)$$

$$6 + \frac{4}{8}$$

$$6\frac{1}{2}$$

Note that you could have also converted the mixed numbers to improper fractions:

$$3\frac{1}{8} - 2\frac{3}{4} + 4\frac{1}{2} + 1\frac{5}{8}$$

$$\frac{25}{8} - \frac{22}{8} + \frac{36}{8} + \frac{13}{8}$$

$$\frac{52}{8}$$

$$6\frac{1}{2}$$

26. G

Subject: Arithmetic

Getting to the Answer: First, determine how many of each lot of land the family bought. The family bought an equal number of each lot (x). Write an equation for the total cost by multiplying the price per lot by x and setting it equal to the total spent:

$$\$1,000x + \$1,750x + \$3,000x = \$17,250$$
$$\$5,750x = \$17,250$$
$$x = 3$$

Note that since x must be a whole number, you could use estimation to solve for x. For example, $\$6,000x = \$18,000$.

The Callan family purchased 3 lots of each farmland, so the total number acres is

$$3 \times \frac{1}{4} \text{ acre} + 3 \times \frac{1}{2} \text{ acre} + 3 \times 1 \text{ acre} = \frac{3}{4} + \frac{3}{2} + 3 = 5\frac{1}{4}.$$

27. B

Subject: Arithmetic

Getting to the Answer: Write the decimal as a fraction and then simplify: $0.55 = \frac{55}{100} = \frac{11}{20}$. Thus, the value of x is 11.

28. F

Subject: Arithmetic

Getting to the Answer: In the repeating decimal (153846), there are 6 digits. Since 1 is the first digit, it will also be the 1st + 6 = 7th digit, the 1st + 6 + 6 = 13th digit, and so on. To find the 277th digit, divide 279 by 6:

$$\begin{array}{r} 46 \text{ R3} \\ 6\overline{)279} \end{array}$$

The remainder of 3 means the 279th digit is the same as the 3rd digit, which is 3.

29. B

Subject: Arithmetic

Getting to the Answer: First, find the number of quarts Becca needs to completely fill her tank:

$3.6 - 1.2 = 2.4$ quarts. Divide the number of quarts by the amount in each bottle: $\frac{2.4}{0.5} = 4.8$. Since 4.8 is closer to 5 than to 4, you need to round up to 5.

30. G

Subject: Arithmetic

Getting to the Answer: To find the value of point K, you need to determine the interval between the tick marks. First, determine the distance between J and L and then divide by the number of sections between J and L. The distance between J and L is $\frac{9}{20} - \frac{1}{5} = \frac{9}{20} - \frac{4}{20} = \frac{5}{20} = \frac{1}{4}$. There are 5 sections between J and L, so the interval between the tick marks is $\frac{1}{4} \div 5 = \frac{1}{4} \times \frac{1}{5} = \frac{1}{20}$.

K is 3 sections away from J, so the value of point K is $\frac{1}{5} + 3\left(\frac{1}{20}\right) = \frac{1}{5} + \frac{3}{20} = \frac{4}{20} + \frac{3}{20} = \frac{7}{20}$.

31. C

Subject: Arithmetic

Getting to the Answer: Keep in mind what the absolute value symbol affects: $|(-5.6) + 2| + |1 - (-2.7)| = |-3.6| + |3.7| = 3.6 + 3.7 = 7.3$.

32. E

Subject: Arithmetic

Getting to the Answer: First, list the factors of 52 and then identify how many factors greater than 5 and less than 50 are even. The positive factors of 52 are 1 and 52, 2 and 26, and 4 and 13. The factors greater than 5 and less than 50 are 13 and 26. Thus, there is 1 positive even factor of 52 greater than 5 and less than 50.

33. C

Subject: Arithmetic

Getting to the Answer: To determine the greatest common factor, start with the largest answer choice and work your way down.

(D)   This is a factor of 756, but not of 720.

(C)   This is a factor of both and the greatest common factor.

(B)   This is a factor of 720, but not of 756.

(A)   This is a factor of both but not the greatest common factor.

Note that you could have stopped at **(C)** once you found the GCF.

Alternatively, you can use prime factorization. The prime factorization of 720 and 756 is $720 = 2 \times 2 \times 2 \times 2 \times 3 \times 3 \times 5$ and $756 = 2 \times 2 \times 3 \times 3 \times 3 \times 7$. Compare the factorizations of the two numbers. The GCF will have all the common primes. Thus, the GCF is $2^2 \times 3^2 = 36$, **(C)**.

34. H

Subject: Arithmetic

Getting to the Answer: Use Backsolving, starting with the smallest value, **(E)**:

(E)   18 is only divisible by 9.

(F)   32 is only divisible by 8.

(G)   60 is only divisible by 12.

(H)   72 is divisible by 8, 9, and 12.

72 is the LCM of 8, 9, and 12.

Alternatively, you could use prime factorization to determine the LCM of 8, 9, and 12. The prime factorization of 8 is $2 \times 2 \times 2$; the prime factorization of 9 is 3×3; and the prime factorization of 12 is $2 \times 2 \times 3$. So the LCM is $2^3 \times 3^2 = 72$, **(H)**.

35. C

Subject: Arithmetic

Getting to the Answer: Plug the known values for part and percent into the $\text{Percent} = \dfrac{\text{Part}}{\text{Whole}} \times 100\%$ formula to solve for the whole. Then divide both sides by 100% and isolate the whole:

$$\frac{12\%}{100\%} = \frac{9}{\text{whole}}$$
$$0.12 \times \text{whole} = 9$$
$$\text{whole} = \frac{9}{0.12}$$
$$\text{whole} = 75$$

36. H

Subject: Arithmetic

Getting to the Answer: Pick a value like 100 for the first quiz score. Evaluate each percent increase one at a time. Then calculate the percent change. Let S represent the quiz score.

First, determine the score of the second quiz: $S = 100 + 0.1 \times 100$. So, $S = 110$.

Next, determine Zelina's third quiz score. Let T represent the third quiz score: $T = 110 + 0.2 \times 110 = 132$.

The question is asking for the percent of the first quiz score, so use

$$\text{Percent Change} = \frac{\text{Amount of Change}}{\text{Original Amount}} \times 100\%$$

$\text{Percent Change} = \dfrac{132 - 100}{100} \times 100\%$. The third quiz score was 32% higher than the first quiz score.

Note that adding the two percents together will lead to a trap answer: $10\% + 20\% = 30\%$.

37. C

Subject: Arithmetic

Getting to the Answer: Plug the information you have for each scenario into the different averages equations and solve for the sum of test scores for each scenario. The difference between the two test score sums will be the lowest test score that was dropped.

$\dfrac{\text{Sum of 9}}{9 \text{ tests}} = 90$. Multiply each side by 9 to give the sum of $9 = 810$.

$\dfrac{\text{Sum of 8}}{8 \text{ tests}} = 91$. Multiply each side by 8 to give the sum of $8 = 728$.

The difference is $810 - 728 = 82$.

38. F

Subject: Arithmetic

Getting to the Answer: First, determine the total price of the headphones at each store by multiplying the price of the headphones by the number of stores that sell the headphones at that price.

Cost of Headphones	Number of Stores	Total Cost
$13	1	$13
$15	2	$30
$16	1	$16
$20	3	$60
		$119

Then add to get the total price of headphones. To calculate the mean price, divide the total price by the number of stores: Average $= \dfrac{\$119}{7} = \$17$. The mean price of the headphones is $17.

39. C

Subject: Arithmetic

Getting to the Answer: During the first part of the trip, the motorist traveled at 20 miles per hour for 90 miles.

This took him $\dfrac{90 \text{ miles}}{20 \text{ mph}} = \dfrac{9}{2}$ hours.

On the way back, he traveled the same distance at 40 miles per hour, so it took him $\dfrac{90 \text{ miles}}{40 \text{ mph}} = \dfrac{9}{4}$ hours.

Total distance: 90 miles + 90 miles = 180 miles

Total time: $\dfrac{9}{2}$ hours $+ \dfrac{9}{4}$ hours $= \dfrac{18}{4} + \dfrac{9}{4} = \dfrac{27}{4}$ hours

Average speed: $\dfrac{180 \text{ miles}}{\frac{27}{4} \text{ hours}} = 180 \times \dfrac{4}{27} = \dfrac{720}{27} = \dfrac{80}{3}$ mph

(G) is the correct answer.

(H), the average of the two speeds, is a trap.

40. G

Subject: Arithmetic

Getting to the Answer: First, determine the part-to-whole ratio from the given information and then set up a proportion to solve for the number of people who have not voted, n.

The ratio given is a part-to-part ratio. Since the question gives the total number of people in the polling place, you need to use the part-to-whole ratio. The number of people who have not voted to the total number of voters is $\dfrac{5}{1+5} = \dfrac{5}{6}$.

Setting up the proportion to solve for n gives:

$$\dfrac{n}{120} = \dfrac{5}{6}$$
$$6n = 600$$
$$n = 100$$

41. C

Subject: Arithmetic

Getting to the Answer: Use proportions to make the conversion from rigs to gulps and from mews to gulps.

Rigs to gulps:

$$\dfrac{200}{x} = \dfrac{5}{1}$$
$$200 = 5x$$
$$40 = x$$

Mews to gulps:

$$\dfrac{10}{y} = \dfrac{0.1}{1}$$
$$10 = 0.1y$$
$$100 = y$$

Total gulps = 40 + 100 = 140.

42. F

Subject: Statistics and Probability

Getting to the Answer: First, determine the total number of marbles in the bag: $5 + 7 + 2 + 4 + 9 + 8 = 35$.

Then set up a proportion to find which color has exactly a 1 in 5 chance of being picked:

$$\dfrac{x}{35} = \dfrac{1}{5}$$
$$5x = 35$$
$$x = 7$$

There are 7 blue marbles in the bag, so a blue marble has a 1 in 5 chance of being randomly selected.

43. C

Subject: Statistics and Probability

Getting to the Answer: If 8 marbles are removed, then 16 are left in the bag. Because you know that the probability of pulling out a white marble is now $\frac{1}{4}$, set up a proportion with remaining white marbles as an unknown, w, and then solve for the remaining white marbles.

$$\frac{1}{4} = \frac{w}{16}$$
$$16 = 4w$$
$$4 = w$$

But you're not done there—subtract the remaining white marbles from the original number of white marbles to determine how many were removed:

$$8 - 4 = 4.$$

44. G

Subject: Statistics and Probability

Getting to the Answer: Multiply the number of types of each item to calculate the total number of combinations. Tristen can pack $3 \times 4 \times 2 = 24$ different lunch boxes.

CHAPTER 15

Algebra

CHAPTER OBJECTIVES

By the end of this chapter, you will be able to:

- Isolate a variable
- Evaluate an algebraic expression
- Solve an inequality for a range of values
- Identify the graph of an inequality or a system of inequalities

Algebra I

Evaluate an Algebraic Expression

Evaluating an expression typically involves substituting a given value (or values) for the variables into the expression and then simplifying. For example, the value of $3x + 4y$ when $x = 5$ and $y = -2$ is $3(5) + 4(-2) = 15 - 8 = 7$.

A. If $a = 3$, then $a(5 - a) =$

B. If $a = 3$, then $a(5) - a =$

C. If $b = -7$, then $4 - b =$

D. If $b = 7$, then $4 - b =$

E. When $c = 3$ and $d = 2$, what is the value of $c^d - d^c$?

F. If $n = 4$, then $2\left(\dfrac{n}{n+1}\right) =$

G. If $x = 2$, then $x(3^x) =$

1. What is the value of $x(y - 2) + xz$ if $x = 2$, $y = 5$, and $z = 7$?

    A. 12

    B. 20

    C. 22

    D. 28

    handwritten: $2(5-2)+14$
    handwritten: 6

2. If $x = 3$, $y = 2$, and $z = 0.5$, then $x^2 - 5yz + y^2 =$

    E. 1

    F. 4

    G. 8

    H. 12

    handwritten: $9 - 5 + 4$
    handwritten: $3^2 - 5(1) + 2^2 =$
    handwritten: $9 - 5 + 4 =$
    handwritten: $4 + 4 = 8$

3. If $a + b = 17$ and $c = 2$, then $ac + bc =$

    A. 17

    B. 18

    C. 34

    D. Cannot be determined from the information given.

Math

> ### SHSAT EXPERT NOTE
>
> You must always follow the order of operations when solving algebraic equations. PEMDAS = Parentheses; Exponents; Multiplication/Division from left to right; Addition/Subtraction from left to right.

Solve Equations with One Variable

To **solve an equation**, isolate the variable. To solve $5x - 12 = -2x + 9$, first get all the x terms on one side by adding $2x$ to both sides: $7x - 12 = 9$. Then add 12 to both sides: $7x = 21$. Finally, divide both sides by 7 to get $x = 3$. As long as you do the same thing to both sides of the equation, the equation is still balanced.

DIRECTIONS: Solve each of the following equations for the variable.

    A. $2x + 4 = 8$

    B. $\frac{x}{3} + 1 = 5$

    C. $x - 5 = 3x - 10$

    D. If $\left(\frac{1}{3}\right)x = 8$, then $\left(\frac{1}{4}\right)x =$

4.   If $0.5n + 2 = 3$, what is the value of n ?

    E. 0.5

    F. 1

    G. 2

    H. 2.5

5.   For what value of x is $2x - 13 = 25$ true?

    A. 6

    B. 6.5

    C. 19

    D. 38

6.   The sum of five consecutive multiples of 2 is 130. What are the five numbers?

    E. 12, 14, 16, 18, 20

    F. 18, 20, 22, 24, 26

    G. 22, 24, 26, 28, 30

    H. 26, 28, 30, 32, 34

> ### SHSAT EXPERT NOTE
>
> When manipulating an equation, always perform the same operation on both sides of the equal sign.

Solve Equations with Two Variables

Equations often contain more than one variable. When two variables are present, solve the equation piece by piece. If you are given a value for one or more variables, substitute the value for its variable. Then isolate the remaining variable and solve.

A. What is the value of a in the equation $3a - 6 = b$ if $b = 18$?

B. If $k = \frac{1}{3}$ in the equation $2m + \frac{1}{3}k = \frac{1}{3}k^2$, then $m =$

C. If $\frac{4a + b}{b} = 7$ and $b = 2$, $a =$

D. If x is a positive odd number less than 10, list all of the potential solutions for y in the following equation:

$$x^2 + 2x + 1 = y$$

x	y

> ### SHSAT EXPERT NOTE
>
> Always set up an equation and write it down rather than trying to work it out in your head.

7. What is the value of x in the equation $5x - 7 = y$ if $y = 8$?

    A. -1
    B. 1
    C. 3
    D. 33

8. If $q \neq 0$, for what value of p is $p(12q) = 6q$?

    E. 0.5
    F. 2
    G. 4
    H. 8

9. If $m = 2$ and $2m(2m - 3n) = 34$, what is the value of n ?

    A. -6
    B. $-\dfrac{3}{2}$
    C. -1
    D. $\dfrac{3}{2}$

$$4(4 - 3n) = 34$$
$$16 - 12n = 34$$
$$-16 \qquad -16$$
$$-12n = 18$$
$$-12 \qquad -12$$

10. If $\dfrac{x}{y} = \dfrac{2}{5}$ and $x = 10$, $y =$

    E. 4
    F. 10
    G. 15
    H. 25

$$\frac{10}{y} \quad \frac{2}{5} \qquad \frac{SO \, 2y}{2y \, SO}$$

11. The set of possible values of a is $\{1, 4, 7\}$. If $3b = 10 - a$, what is the set of possible values of b ?

    A. $\{1, 2, 3\}$
    B. $\{3, 6, 9\}$
    C. $\{6, 12, 18\}$
    D. $\{9, 18, 27\}$

$$b = 3.3 - a$$

SHSAT EXPERT NOTE

Perform only one step at a time. First substitute, then simplify the resulting equation, and then isolate the remaining variable.

Solve for One Variable in Terms of the Other

Even if you aren't given numerical values to substitute, you can still solve for one variable in an equation in terms of the other variable(s).

    A. If $2r + 8s = 24$, then $r =$

    B. Solve for c in the equation $b(a - 1) = \dfrac{bc}{2}$

    C. $3x + 2y + 4z = 12$

    Solve for each of the variables.

    $x =$

    $y =$

    $z =$

SHSAT EXPERT NOTE

When you perform the same operation to both sides of an equation, you are not altering the equation but merely rearranging it.

---

12. If $\dfrac{(a + b)}{2} = 8$, then $a =$

                                 $a + b = 16$
                                    $-c$

    E. $b + 4$

    F. $4 - b$

    G. $16 - b$

    H. $\dfrac{16}{b}$

13. If $3(a - 2) = 5m - 6 + 2a$, what is the value of a in terms of m?

    A. $\dfrac{3m}{2}$
                                $3a - 6 = 5m - 6 + 2a$
                                   $+6 \qquad\qquad +6$

    B. 3

    C. $5m$

    D. $3m - 3$
                                   $a = 3m$

14. If $3(2t + 6) = 12s$, then $t =$

                                  $6t + 18 = 12s$

    E. $2s + 3$
                                     $-18 \qquad -18$

    F. $2s - 3$

    G. $4s$
                                  $\dfrac{6t}{6} = \dfrac{12s - 18}{6}$

    H. $3s - 8$
                                     $t = 2s - 3$

Algebra II

Expressions and Equations

    A. Solve $2(3 + 1)^2 + 5 - 6 \div 3 =$

    B. When $x = 2$, $2x + 3 =$

    C. When $x = \frac{1}{4}$, $y = \frac{1}{5}$, and $z = \frac{1}{6}$, what is the value of $\frac{x}{15} + \frac{y}{6} + \frac{z}{5}$?

    D. What is x when $4x + 3 = 19$?

    E. Solve for x in terms of y: $7xy = 3$

SHSAT EXPERT NOTE

Always perform the same mathematical operation on both sides of an equation.

---

1. If $3x + 7 = 14$, then $x =$

    A. -14

    B. 0

    C. $\frac{7}{3}$

    D. 7

2. If $4z - 3 = -19$, then $z =$

    E. -16

    F. -5

    G. -4

    H. 4

3. For what value of y is $4(y - 1) = 2(y + 2)$?

    A. 0

    B. 2

    C. 4

    D. 6

Math

4. If $5p + 12 = 17 - 4\left(\dfrac{p}{2} + 1\right)$, what is the value of p ?

    E. $\dfrac{1}{7}$

    F. $\dfrac{1}{3}$

    G. $\dfrac{6}{7}$

    H. $1\dfrac{2}{7}$

5. If $-2x + xy = 30$ and $y = 8$, then what is the value of x ?

    A. $-\dfrac{15}{4}$

    B. $-\dfrac{15}{16}$

    C. 3

    D. 5

6. $15 + xy \div 3 = 35$ and $x = 5$. What is the value of y ?

    E. $-\dfrac{2}{3}$

    F. $5\dfrac{1}{4}$

    G. 12

    H. 18

7. If $\dfrac{2x}{5y} = 6$, what is the value of y, in terms of x ?

    A. $\dfrac{x}{15}$

    B. $\dfrac{x}{2}$

    C. $\dfrac{15}{x}$

    D. $15x$

8. If $3ab = 6$, what is the value of a in terms of b ?

    E. 2

    F. $\dfrac{2}{b}$

    G. $2b^2$

    H. $2b$

9. If $2(a + m) = 5m - 3 + a$, what is the value of a, in terms of m ?

    A. $\dfrac{3m}{2}$

    B. 3

    C. $m - 1$

    D. $3m - 3$

SHSAT EXPERT NOTE

Questions that ask for one variable "in terms of" another can also be answered effectively by picking numbers for the variables. Always pick numbers that fit the rules and be sure to check every answer choice.

Standard Inequalities

Solving an inequality means finding the set of all values that satisfy the given statement. They work just like equations: your task is to isolate the variable on one side of the inequality symbol. The only significant difference is that **if you multiply or divide by a negative number, you must reverse the direction** of the inequality symbol.

    A. Solve for a: $4a + 5 > 9a + 15$

    B. Solve for y: $2y - 3 < 9 + y$

    C. Solve for y: $3y - 10 > 11$

    D. Solve for x: $7 - 2x > 3y$

10. Which of the following is equivalent to the inequality $9 > 5x - 6$?

    E. $x > -3$

    F. $x > 3$

    G. $x < 3$

    H. $x > 5$

11. Which of the following is equivalent to $13 - 2y < 7$?

    A. $y < -\dfrac{7}{13}$

    B. $y < 3$

    C. $y > 3$

    D. $y < 10$

12. What is the range of possible values of y when $2y - 3 < 6$?

    E. $y > \dfrac{2}{9}$

    F. $y > \dfrac{3}{2}$

    G. $y < \dfrac{9}{2}$

    H. $y < 6$

SHSAT EXPERT NOTE

Always perform the same operation on both sides of the inequality.

Always reverse the inequality sign when multiplying or dividing by a negative number.

Ranges

Ranges are inequalities with three parts. When you perform a mathematical operation on one part, you have to do the same thing to all three parts.

DIRECTIONS: Find the range of values for each of these variables.

    A. y when $(y - 2)$ is greater than 3 and less than 10
    B. z when $(2z)$ is less than 6 and greater than -2
    C. x^2 when x lies between 8 and 9
    D. a when $-a$ lies between -4 and 7

13. Which of the following is equivalent to the inequality $7 > -3x > -12$?

    A. $-7 < x < 12$

    B. $\dfrac{7}{3} < x < 4$

    C. $-\dfrac{7}{3} < x < 4$

    D. $-4 < x < -\dfrac{7}{3}$

14. Which of the following is equivalent to the inequality $-8 < -2x < 12$?

    E. $-3 < x < 2$

    F. $-4 < x < 6$

    G. $-6 < x < 4$

    H. $-12 < x < 8$

15. The number a is a number less than -3. What is the range of possible values of $\frac{1}{a^2}$?

    A. $\quad \frac{1}{a^2} < -9$

    B. $\quad \frac{1}{a^2} < -3$

    C. $\quad -\frac{1}{9} < \frac{1}{a^2} < \frac{1}{9}$

    D. $\quad 0 < \frac{1}{a^2} < \frac{1}{9}$

SHSAT EXPERT NOTE

When you divide or multiply the parts of a range by a negative number, you must change the direction of the inequality signs.

Number Lines

The solution to an inequality can be represented on a number line. For example, $x > 4$ could be graphed like this:

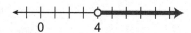

Notice the open dot at 4, indicating that 4 is not a solution to the inequality. This is called a **strict** inequality. By contrast, the graph of $x \le 4$ looks like this:

Notice the closed (solid) dot, indicating that 4 should be included in the solution set for the inequality.

DIRECTIONS: Draw the following ranges on the number lines provided.

    A. $\quad -6 < x < 4$

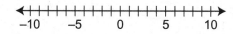

    B. $\quad 4 > -2y > -2$

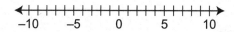

    C. $\quad 3 \le z \le 5$

Math

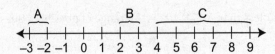

16. The value x^2 is greater than 4 and less than 9. Which region or regions on the number line above represent the range of values for x?

    E. A

    F. B

    G. C

    H. A and B

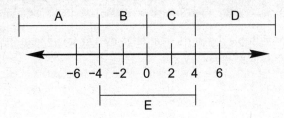

17. Which region(s) on the number line above is the set of all possible values of $-4x$, where $x > 1$?

    A. A

    B. B

    C. C

    D. D and E

SHSAT EXPERT NOTE

When Picking Numbers, be sure to write down what numbers you picked and for which variables. This makes it less likely that you will make a mistake when checking the choices.

Be sure to check every choice. If the number you picked works for more than one choice, you'll need to pick another number.

Practice Set

Drills

Practice applying the concepts covered in this chapter by answering the following skill-building questions.

1. When $x = 0$ and $y = 0$, what is the value of $(3x - 6)(2x + y) + 5$?

2. When $x = 10$ and $y = 20$, what is the value of $\dfrac{1}{2x^2 3y}$?

3. When $x = 75$ and $y = 1$, what is the value of $\dfrac{x}{75} + \dfrac{1}{y}$?

4. When $x = 3$, $y = 4$, and $z = 0$, what is the value of $\dfrac{3x + 2xy + 3y}{6z}$?

5. When $x = 1$, $y = 2$, and $z = 3$, what is the value of $(x - 1)(y - 2)(z - 3)$?

6. When $x = 2$, $y = 2$, and $z = 2$, what is the value of $3xy - 3xz + 3zy$?

7. When $x = 2$, $y = 1$, and $z = 3$, what is the value of $15x^2 + 23y^{10} + z^4$?

8. When $x = 2$, what is the value of $x^5 - 3x^3 + 2x - 7$?

9. When $x = \dfrac{1}{2}$, what is the value of $3x^3$?

10. When $x = 20$, what is the value of $2x^2 - 15$?

11. Solve for x in the following equation:
$$x = \frac{1}{2}\left[(-8)^2 - 4\right]$$

12. Solve for x in the following equation:
$$\frac{2}{3} = \frac{x}{6}$$

13. Solve for x in the following equation:
$$x = -15(-7)$$

14. Solve for x in the following equation:
$$2x = \frac{1}{2}\left(3 + 5^2\right)$$

15. Solve for x in the following equation:
$$x = \frac{1}{2} + \frac{1}{3} + \frac{1}{4}$$

16. Solve for x in the following equation:
$$x + 2 = 14$$

Grid-In Questions

For test-like practice, give yourself 15 minutes (an average of 1.5 minutes per question) to complete this question set. After you're done, be sure to study the explanations, even for questions you answered correctly. They can be found at the end of this chapter.

> **DIRECTIONS:** Answer each question. Write your answer in the boxes at the top of the grid. Start on the left side of each grid, printing only one number or symbol in each box. **DO NOT LEAVE A BOX BLANK IN THE MIDDLE OF AN ANSWER.** Under each box, fill in the circle that matches the number or symbol you wrote above. **DO NOT FILL IN A CIRCLE UNDER AN UNUSED BOX.**

17. What is the value of b in the equation $3b - 14 = -5$?

19. If $0.02a = 2$, what is the value of a ?

18. If $x < 24$ and $2y + 3 < 17$, and x and y are both positive integers, what is the largest possible value of $x + y$?

20. What is the value of b in the equation $4b = 8b - 88$?

21. If $x - 4 \leq 10$ and $x + 2 \geq 6$, and x is an integer, how many possible values of x are there?

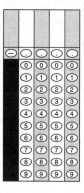

22. If $\frac{1}{3}(6z + 18) = 3z - 9$, what is the value of z?

23. What is the value of the expression $a^2 - 4a + 12$ if $a = -6$?

24. What is the value of z in the equation $4\left(\frac{1}{2}z - 10\right) = 10z + 4$?

25. If $6h + 2 - 5(2h + 4) = 22$, what is the value of h?

26. What is the value of the expression $x - (y + 2) + x^2 - y^2$ if $x = 9$ and $y = 4$?

Multiple-Choice Questions

For test-like practice, give yourself 30 minutes (an average of 1.5 minutes per question) to complete this question set. After you're done, be sure to study the explanations, even for questions you answered correctly. They can be found at the end of this chapter.

DIRECTIONS: Answer each question, selecting the best answer available.

---

27. What is the value of $3x(9 - 9x)$ when $x = \frac{4}{3}$?

    A. -12

    B. -9

    C. 4

    D. 12

$$\frac{11}{4} - a = 3$$

28. What is the value of a in the equation above?

    E. $-\frac{23}{4}$

    F. $-\frac{11}{4}$

    G. $-\frac{1}{4}$

    H. $\frac{1}{4}$

29. What is the value of x in the equation $10 = 5x - 5$?

    A. 2

    B. 3

    C. 5

    D. 7

30. Rachel is now 11 years old. Five years ago, Lily was twice as old as Rachel. How old is Lily now?

    E. 12

    F. 13

    G. 16

    H. 17

31. If n is an integer, which of the following **must** be odd?

    A. $3n - 5$

    B. $3n + 4$

    C. $4n + 10$

    D. $4n - 5$

32. When z is divided by 8, the remainder is 5. What is the remainder when $4z$ is divided by 8?

    E. 1

    F. 3

    G. 4

    H. 5

33. If the price of a stock increases by 40% and then by an additional 25%, by what percentage has the price increased from its original value?

    A. 60%

    B. 62%

    C. 65%

    D. 75%

34. If $a + 2b + 2c = 5$ and $a + 2b + 3c = 5$, what is the value of $a + 2b + 4c$?

    E. 0

    F. 5

    G. 10

    H. 15

35. If $a^2 - 25 = a^2 - b$, then what is the value of b ?

    A. -25

    B. 0

    C. 5

    D. 25

36. A computer programmer receives a salary of $100 a day, plus $0.05 for each line of code that she writes. If this is her only income, which of the following expressions represents the number of dollars she would be paid for a day that she wrote n lines of code?

    E. $100 + n$

    F. $(100 + 0.05)n$

    G. $0.05 + 100n$

    H. $100 + 0.05n$

37. If $6z - 1 = -37$, then $z =$

    A. -6

    B. -5

    C. 5

    D. 6

38. What is the value of $\dfrac{m}{m^2 - m}$ if $m = -5$?

    E. $-\dfrac{1}{6}$

    F. $-\dfrac{1}{20}$

    G. $-\dfrac{1}{30}$

    H. $\dfrac{1}{4}$

39. Which of the following indicates that n is less than double the value of m and that n is greater than 1 ?

    A. $1 > n > \dfrac{m}{2}$

    B. $1 < n < 2m$

    C. $\dfrac{1}{2} < 2n < m$

    D. $1 < 2n < m$

40. If $50 - xy = 75$ and $y = -5$, what is the value of x ?

    E. -25

    F. -5

    G. 5

    H. 25

41. Simplify the following inequality: $x - 20 > 20 - x$

    A. $x > -20$

    B. $x > 10$

    C. $x > 20$

    D. $x < 20$

42. If $a = 4$, $b = -7$, $c = -3$ and $d = -9$, then $|a + b + c + d| - d =$

    E. -4

    F. 6

    G. 15

    H. 24

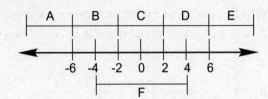

43. Which region on the number line above is the set of all values of $-\frac{x}{3}$, where $-6 < x < 6$?

A. B

B. C

C. D

D. F

$$y\overline{)\,xy-3}^{\,x-1\,\mathrm{R}\,n}$$

44. If $y > 3$, what is the value of n ?

E. 2

F. 3

G. $y-2$

H. $y-3$

45. If $a < b < c < 0$, then which of the following must be true?

    I. $a + b < b + c$

    II. $c - a > 0$

    III. $a < b + c$

A. I only

B. II only

C. I and II only

D. I and III only

46. If $x = 7$, what is the value of $(x-1) + (x-2) + (x-3) + \ldots + (x-x)$?

E.   0

F.   7

G. 14

H. 21

Answers and Explanations

Evaluate an Algebraic Expression

A. $a(5-a) = 3(5-3) = 3(2) = 6$

B. $a(5) - a = 3(5) - 3 = 15 - 3 = 12$

C. $4 - b = 4 - (-7) = 4 + 7 = 11$

D. $4 - b = 4 - 7 = -3$

E. $c^d - d^c = 3^2 - 2^3 = 9 - 8 = 1$

F. $2\left(\dfrac{n}{n+1}\right) = 2\left(\dfrac{4}{4+1}\right) = 2\left(\dfrac{4}{5}\right) = \dfrac{8}{5}$

G. $x(3^x) = 2(3^2) = 2(9) = 18$

1. B

Subject: Algebra

Getting to the Answer: The equation is ready for substitution as it stands. Just substitute:

$x(y-2) + xz =$
$(2)[(5) - 2] + (2)(7) = 6 + 14 = 20$

2. G

Subject: Algebra

Getting to the Answer: Substitute carefully:

$x^2 - 5yz + y^2 =$
$(3)^2 - 5(2)(0.5) + (2)^2 =$
$9 - 5 + 4 = 8$

3. C

Subject: Algebra

Getting to the Answer: Given that you are looking for $ac + bc$, you can simplify by factoring:

$ac + bc = c(a + b)$

You know that $c = 2$ and $a + b = 17$; therefore $c(a+b) = 2(17) = 34$.

Solve Equations with One Variable

A. $2x + 4 = 8$
$2x = 4$
$x = 2$

B. $\dfrac{x}{3} + 1 = 5$
$\dfrac{x}{3} = 4$
$x = 12$

C. $x - 5 = 3x - 10$
$-5 = 2x - 10$
$5 = 2x$
$\dfrac{5}{2} = x$

D. $\left(\dfrac{1}{3}\right)x = 8$
$x = 24$
$\left(\dfrac{1}{4}\right)x = \left(\dfrac{1}{4}\right)(24) = 6$

4. G

Subject: Algebra

Getting to the Answer: You need to isolate the variable:

$0.5n + 2 = 3$
$0.5n = 1$ or $\dfrac{1}{2}n = 1$ Multiply by 2.
$n = 2$

5. C

Subject: Algebra

Getting to the Answer: Isolate the x:

$2x = 13 + 25$
$2x = 38$ Divide by 2.
$x = 19$

6. G

Subject: Algebra

Getting to the Answer: Each multiple of 2 is 2 more than the previous. Let x represent the smallest:

$x + (x+2) + (x+4) + (x+6) + (x+8) = 130$
$5x + 20 = 130$
$5x = 110$
$x = 22$

Thus, 22 is the smallest of the five numbers.

Solve Equations with Two Variables

A. $3a - 6 = b$

$3a - 6 = (18)$

$3a = 24$

$a = 8$

B. $2m + \frac{1}{3}k = \frac{1}{3}k^2$; plug in $k = \frac{1}{3}$

$2m + \frac{1}{3}\left(\frac{1}{3}\right) = \frac{1}{3}\left(\frac{1}{3}\right)^2$

$2m + \frac{1}{9} = \frac{1}{27}$

$2m = -\frac{2}{27}$

$m = -\frac{1}{27}$

C. $\frac{4a + b}{b} = 7$; plug in $b = 2$

$\frac{4a + (2)}{(2)} = 7$

$4a + 2 = 14$

$4a = 12$

$a = 3$

D.

x	y
1	4
3	16
5	36
7	64
9	100

7. C

Subject: Algebra

Getting to the Answer: Plug in the 8 for y and isolate the x:

$5x - 7 = y$

$5x - 7 = (8)$ Substitute $y = 8$.

$5x = 15$ Isolate.

$x = 3$ Simplify.

8. E

Subject: Algebra

Getting to the Answer: Solve for p:

$p(12q) = 6q$

$p = \frac{6q}{12q}$ Divide by $12q$.

$p = \frac{1}{2}$ or 0.5

9. B

Subject: Algebra

Getting to the Answer: Substitute:

$2m(2m - 3n) = 34$

$2(2)[2(2) - 3n] = 34$

$4(4 - 3n) = 34$

$16 - 12n = 34$

$-12n = 18$ Divide by -12.

$n = -\frac{18}{12} = -\frac{3}{2}$

10. H

Subject: Algebra

Getting to the Answer: Cross multiply and then substitute the value given for x.

$\frac{x}{y} = \frac{2}{5}$

$5x = 2y$

$5(10) = 2y$

$50 = 2y$

$25 = y$

11. A

Subject: Algebra

Getting to the Answer: $3b = 10 - a$, so $b = \frac{10 - a}{3}$. Substitute each value of a in the set to find the set of values of b:

$b = \frac{10 - (1)}{3} = 3$

$b = \frac{10 - (4)}{3} = 2$

$b = \frac{10 - (7)}{3} = 1$

The set of possible values of b is $\{1, 2, 3\}$.

Solve for One Variable in Terms of the Other

A. $2r + 8s = 24$

$2r = 24 - 8s$

$r = 12 - 4s$

B. $b(a - 1) = \dfrac{bc}{2}$

$2b(a - 1) = bc$

$2(a - 1) = c$

$2a - 2 = c$

C. $3x + 2y + 4z = 12$

Solving for x:

$3x = 12 - 2y - 4z$

$x = 4 - \dfrac{2}{3}y - \dfrac{4}{3}z$

Solving for y:

$2y = 12 - 3x - 4z$

$y = 6 - \dfrac{3}{2}x - 2z$

Solving for z:

$4z = 12 - 3x - 2y$

$z = 3 - \dfrac{3}{4}x - \dfrac{1}{2}y$

12. G

Subject: Algebra

Getting to the Answer: Keep in mind what question you are answering.

$\dfrac{(a + b)}{2} = 8$

$(a + b) = 16$

$a = 16 - b$

After you have eliminated the fraction, isolate a.

13. C

Subject: Algebra

Getting to the Answer: Simplify and work to isolate a.

$3(a - 2) = 5m - 6 + 2a$ Subtract $2a$.

$3a - 6 = 5m - 6 + 2a$ Add 6.

$a - 6 = 5m - 6$

$a = 5m$

14. F

Subject: Algebra

Getting to the Answer: In this case, you have to distribute through and then isolate:

$3(2t + 6) = 12s$ Divide each side by 6 to

$6t + 18 = 12s$ simplify.

$t + 3 = 2s$

$t = 2s - 3$

Expressions and Equations

A. $2(3 + 1)^2 + 5 - 6 \div 3 =$

$2(4)^2 + 5 - 6 \div 3 =$

$2(16) + 5 - 6 \div 3 =$

$32 + 5 - 6 \div 3 =$

$32 + 5 - 2 =$

$37 - 2 =$

35

B. When $x = 2$, $2x + 3 = 2(2) + 3 = 4 + 3 = 7$

C. When $x = \dfrac{1}{4}$, $y = \dfrac{1}{5}$, and $z = \dfrac{1}{6}$,

$\dfrac{x}{15} + \dfrac{y}{6} + \dfrac{z}{5} =$

$\dfrac{\left(\frac{1}{4}\right)}{15} + \dfrac{\left(\frac{1}{5}\right)}{6} + \dfrac{\left(\frac{1}{6}\right)}{5} =$

$\dfrac{1}{60} + \dfrac{1}{30} + \dfrac{1}{30} =$

$\dfrac{1}{60} + \dfrac{2}{60} + \dfrac{2}{60} =$

$\dfrac{5}{60} = \dfrac{1}{12}$

D. $4x + 3 = 19$

$4x = 16$

$x = 4$

E. $7xy = 3$

$x = \dfrac{3}{7y}$

1.   C

Subject: Algebra

Getting to the Answer: You need to isolate the terms with x in them and then solve:

$$3x + 7 = 14$$
$$3x = 7$$
$$x = \frac{7}{3}$$

2.   G

Subject: Algebra

Getting to the Answer: Solve for z:

$$4z - 3 = -19$$
$$4z = -16$$
$$\frac{4z}{4} = \frac{-16}{4}$$
$$z = -4$$

Once you have the z terms on one side, simplify.

3.   C

Subject: Algebra

Getting to the Answer: The problem is straightforward; distribute and solve:

$$4(y - 1) = 2(y + 2)$$
$$4y - 4 = 2y + 4$$
$$2y = 8$$
$$\frac{2y}{2} = \frac{8}{2}$$
$$y = 4$$

4.   E

Subject: Algebra

Getting to the Answer: Combine like terms:

$$5p + 12 = 17 - 4\left(\frac{p}{2} + 1\right)$$
$$5p + 12 = 17 - 2p - 4$$
$$5p + 12 = 13 - 2p$$
$$7p = 1$$
$$p = \frac{1}{7}$$

5.   D

Subject: Algebra

Getting to the Answer: Substitute 8 for y:

$$-2x + xy = 30$$
$$-2x + x(8) = 30$$
$$6x = 30$$
$$x = 5$$

6.   G

Subject: Algebra

Getting to the Answer: Substitute 5 for x:

$$15 + xy \div 3 = 35$$
$$15 + (5)y \div 3 = 35$$
$$5y \div 3 = 20 \quad \text{Subtract 15 from both sides.}$$
$$5y = 60 \quad \text{Multiply both sides by 3 to isolate the } y \text{ term.}$$
$$y = 12 \quad \text{Divide by 5 to solve for } y.$$

7.   A

Subject: Algebra

Getting to the Answer:

$$\frac{2x}{5y} = 6$$
$$2x = 30y$$
$$\frac{2x}{30} = \frac{30y}{30} \quad \text{After cross multiplying, just simplify the terms.}$$
$$\frac{x}{15} = y$$

8.   F

Subject: Algebra

Getting to the Answer: Isolate the a:

$$a = \frac{6}{3b} \quad \text{Divide by } 3b.$$
$$a = \frac{2}{b} \quad \text{Simplify.}$$

9. D

Subject: Algebra

Getting to the Answer: You'll need to get the *a* terms on one side of the equation:

$2(a + m) = 5m - 3 + a$ — Distribute the 2.

$2a + 2m = 5m - 3 + a$ — Combine like terms.

$a = 3m - 3$

Standard Inequalities

A. $4a + 5 > 9a + 15$

$-10 > 5a$

$-2 > a$

B. $2y - 3 < 9 + y$

$y < 12$

C. $3y - 10 > 11$

$3y > 21$

$y > 7$

D. $7 - 2x > 3y$

$-2x > 3y - 7$

$x < -\dfrac{3y + 7}{2}$

10. G

Subject: Algebra

Getting to the Answer: Go about it like a regular equation:

$$9 > 5x - 6$$
$$9 + 6 > 5x$$
$$15 > 5x$$
$$3 > x$$
$$x < 3$$

11. C

Subject: Algebra

Getting to the Answer: Solve for *y*:

$13 - 2y < 7$

$-2y < -6$

$-y < -3$ — Divide by -2, then reverse the inequality sign.

$y > 3$

12. G

Subject: Algebra

Getting to the Answer: Solve for *y*:

$$2y - 3 < 6$$
$$2y < 9$$
$$y < \frac{9}{2}$$

Ranges

A. $3 < y - 2 < 10$

$5 < y < 12$

B. $-2 < 2z < 6$

$-1 < z < 3$

C. $8 < x < 9$

$64 < x^2 < 81$

D. $-4 < -a < 7$

$4 > a > -7$

$-7 < a < 4$

13. C

Subject: Algebra

Getting to the Answer: Solve for the range of *x*:

$7 > -3x > -12$ — Divide through by -3, and then reverse the signs.

$-\dfrac{7}{3} > x > 4$

$-\dfrac{7}{3} < x < 4$

14. G

Subject: Algebra

Getting to the Answer: Solve for the range of *x*:

$$-8 < -2x < 12$$
$$-4 < -x < 6$$
$$4 > x > -6 \text{ or}$$
$$-6 < x < 4$$

15. D

Subject: Algebra

Getting to the Answer: If a is a number less than -3, to find the range of values for $\frac{1}{a^2}$, you have to plug in values for a starting with -3 and working downward $(-4, -5, \text{etc.})$.

if $a = -3$, then $\frac{1}{a^2} = \frac{1}{9}$. This sets the upper boundary.

if $a = -4$, then $\frac{1}{a^2} = \frac{1}{16}$. If $a = -5$, then $\frac{1}{a^2} = \frac{1}{25}$.

As a gets smaller, the value gets closer to zero but never reaches zero, so 0 is the lower boundary:

$0 < \frac{1}{a^2} < \frac{1}{9}$

Number Lines

A. Put open dots at -6 and 4, then shade between.

B. Simplify the range first by dividing all sides by -2, so that $-2 < y < 1$. Put open dots at -2 and 1, then shade between -2 and 1.

C. Put closed dots at 3 and 5, then shade between.

16. H

Subject: Algebra

Getting to the Answer: First, set up the inequality described in the question stem: x is the square root of x^2, so the parameters of x will be the square roots of the given parameters of x^2.

$$4 < x^2 < 9$$
$$\sqrt{4} < \sqrt{x^2} < \sqrt{9}$$
$$2 < x < 3 \text{ or } -2 > x > -3$$

17. A

Subject: Algebra

Getting to the Answer: Consider the original inequality.

$x > 1$	
$-4x$	Consider what you must do to x to produce the new situation
$(-4)x > 1(-4)$	Multiply both sides of the inequality by -4. Remember to change the sign.
$-4x < -4$	Look for the values that are less than -4.

Practice Set

1. 5

2. $\frac{1}{12,000}$

3. 2

4. undefined

5. 0

6. 12

7. 164

8. 5

9. $\frac{3}{8}$

10. 785

11. 30

12. 4

13. 105

14. 7

15. $1\frac{1}{12}$

16. 12

17. 3

Subject: Algebra

Getting to the Answer: Solve this equation as you would any other equation. Add 14 to both sides and divide by 3 to isolate the variable:

$$3b - 14 = -5$$
$$3b = 9$$
$$b = 3$$

Grid in **3**.

18. 29

Subject: Algebra

Getting to the Answer: Begin by simplifying the second inequality. The second inequality simplifies to $y < 7$. You know that $x < 24$ and $y < 7$, and both numbers are integers. To maximize $x + y$, you want the largest possible values of the two numbers. The largest possible values of x and y are 23 and 6, respectively, and $23 + 6 = 29$. Grid in **29**.

19. 100

Subject: Algebra

Getting to the Answer: Simply divide both sides by 0.02 to isolate a. Dividing by 0.02 is like multiplying by 50, so $a = 100$. Grid in **100**.

20. 22

Subject: Algebra

Getting to the Answer: Start by subtracting the $8b$, then divide both sides by -4:

$$4b = 8b - 88$$
$$-4b = -88$$
$$b = 22$$

Grid in **22**.

21. 11

Subject: Algebra

Getting to the Answer: Start by solving both inequalities. Doing this tells you that x must be greater than or equal to 4 and less than or equal to 14. There are 11 integers between and including 4 and 14, so grid in **11**.

22. 15

Subject: Algebra

Getting to the Answer: Start by distributing the fraction on the left side of the equation. From there, combine like terms and solve for z:

$$\frac{1}{3}(6z + 18) = 3z - 9$$
$$2z + 6 = 3z - 9$$
$$15 = z$$

Grid in **15**.

23. 72

Subject: Algebra

Getting to the Answer: Simply substitute -6 for a in the given expression and simplify. Don't forget what happens to negative numbers multiplied by other negative numbers:

$$a^2 - 4a + 12$$
$$(-6)^2 - 4(-6) + 12$$
$$36 + 24 + 12 = 72$$

Grid in **72**.

24. −5.5

Subject: Algebra

Getting to the Answer: Start by distributing the 4 on the left side of the equation. From there, solve as you would any other equation:

$$4\left(\frac{1}{2}z - 10\right) = 10z + 4$$
$$2z - 40 = 10z + 4$$
$$-8z = 44$$
$$z = -5.5$$

Don't forget the negative sign! Grid in **−5.5**.

25. −10

Subject: Algebra

Getting to the Answer: Follow PEMDAS to solve for h.

$$6h + 2 - 5(2h + 4) = 22$$
$$6h + 2 - 10h - 20 = 22$$
$$-4h - 18 = 22$$
$$-4h = 40$$
$$h = -10$$

Grid in −**10**.

26. 68

Subject: Algebra

Getting to the Answer: Begin by substituting 9 and 4 for x and y, respectively. Then follow PEMDAS to simplify:

$$x - (y + 2) + x^2 - y^2$$
$$9 - 6 + (9)^2 - (4)^2$$
$$3 + 81 - 16$$
$$3 + 81 - 16 = 68$$

Grid in **68**.

27. A

Subject: Algebra

Getting to the Answer: Substitute:

$$3 \times \frac{4}{3}\left(9 - 9 \times \frac{4}{3}\right) =$$
$$4(9 - 12) =$$
$$4(-3) =$$
$$-12$$

28. G

Subject: Algebra

Getting to the Answer: Isolate a:

$$\frac{11}{4} - a = 3$$
$$-a = 3 - \frac{11}{4}$$
$$-a = \frac{12}{4} - \frac{11}{4} \qquad \text{Combine the fractions,}$$
$$-a = \frac{1}{4} \qquad\qquad \text{simplify, and divide by } -1.$$
$$a = -\frac{1}{4}$$

29. B

Subject: Algebra

Getting to the Answer: Isolate x:

$$10 = 5x - 5$$
$$10 + 5 = (5x - 5) + 5$$
$$15 = 5x \qquad\qquad \text{Add 5 to both sides.}$$
$$\frac{15}{5} = \frac{5x}{5} \qquad\qquad \text{Divide both sides by 5.}$$
$$3 = x$$

30. H

Subject: Algebra

Getting to the Answer: Take the problem step by step. If Rachel is now 11 years old, then 5 years ago she was $11 - 5 = 6$ years old. If Lily was twice as old then as Rachel was, then Lily was $2 \times 6 = 12$ years old, and therefore *now*, 5 years later, she is $12 + 5 = 17$ years old.

31. D

Subject: Algebra

Getting to the Answer: Pick numbers to plug into each answer choice. Because you want the choice that **must** be odd, check all choices. In this case, choosing an odd number and an even number makes sense. Try each choice with both numbers; 1 and 2 work nicely:

(A) If $n = 1$, then $3n - 5 = -2$. If $n = 2$, then $3n - 5 = 1$.

(B) If $n = 1$, then $3n + 4 = 7$. If $n = 2$, then $3n + 4 = 10$.

(C) If $n = 1$, then $4n + 10 = 14$. If $n = 2$, then $4n + 10 = 18$.

(D) If $n = 1$, then $4n - 5 = -1$. If $n = 2$, then $4n - 5 = 3$.

Therefore, the answer is **(D)**, which will always be an odd integer.

32. G

Subject: Algebra

Getting to the Answer: Because you always want to pick the easiest numbers to work with, using the divisor $8\left(\frac{8}{8} = 1\right)$ plus the remainder 5 works best. $z = 8 + 5 = 13$. Therefore, $4z = 52$, and $\frac{4z}{8} = \frac{52}{8} = 6$ R 4.

33. D

Subject: Algebra

Getting to the Answer: Use $100 as the original price of the stock. If the stock increases by 40%, then $100 \times 40\% = \$40$ increase. $\$100 + \$40 = \$140$ is the new price. If the stock then increases by 25%, $\$140 \times 25\% = \$35$ increase. $\$140 + \$35 = \$175$ new price. The change in price is $\$175 - \$100 = \$75$. The percent increase is $\frac{\$75}{\$100} = 75\%$.

34. F

Subject: Algebra

Getting to the Answer: Ordinarily you would not be able to solve for three variables with only two equations. In this case however, what can you deduce from the fact that both equations are identical except for the coefficient of c? By subtracting the first equation from the second, you will see that $c = 0$. This is the only way that both $a + 2b + 2c$ and $a + 2b + 3c$ can equal 5. Therefore, $a + 2b = 5$ and $a + 2b + 4c = a + 2b + 0 = 5$.

35. D

Subject: Algebra

Getting to the Answer:

$$a^2 - 25 = a^2 - b$$
$$-25 = -b \quad \text{Subtract } a^2 \text{ from both}$$
$$25 = b \qquad \text{sides.}$$

36. H

Subject: Algebra

Getting to the Answer: Think about each part of the programmer's salary, then put it together. She gets $100 a day for showing up. She gets $0.05 per line of code, so if she writes n lines, she earns $0.05n$. So her total salary is $100 + 0.05n$ dollars.

37. A

Subject: Algebra

Getting to the Answer: You're given the equation, so just solve for z.

$$6z - 1 = -37$$
$$6z = -36 \qquad \text{Add 1 to both sides.}$$
$$z = -6 \qquad \text{Divide both sides by 6 to solve for } z.$$

38. E

Subject: Algebra

Getting to the Answer: Plug in -5 for m then solve.

$$\frac{(-5)}{(-5)^2 - (-5)} =$$
$$\frac{-5}{25 + 5} =$$
$$-\frac{5}{30} = -\frac{1}{6}$$

39. B

Subject: Algebra

Getting to the Answer: Carefully translate the words into math.

"n is less than double the value of m" $\rightarrow n < 2m$

"n is greater than 1" $\rightarrow 1 < n$

combined $\rightarrow 1 < n < 2m$

40. G

Subject: Algebra

Getting to the Answer: Substitute -5 for y:

$$50 - (-5)x = 75$$
$$50 + 5x = 75 \quad \text{Cancel out the negative signs.}$$
$$5x = 25 \quad \text{Subtract 50 from both sides to simplify.}$$
$$x = 5 \quad \text{Divide by 5 to solve for } x.$$

41. C

Subject: Algebra

Getting to the Answer:

$$x - 20 > 20 - x \qquad \text{Add } x \text{ and 20 to both sides}$$
$$2x > 40 \qquad \text{to isolate the } x \text{ term.}$$
$$x > 20 \qquad \text{Divide both sides by 2 to solve for } x.$$

42. H

Subject: Algebra

Getting to the Answer: Plug in the given values for a, b, c, and d, then solve:

$$|(4) + (-7) + (-3) + (-9)| - (-9) =$$
$$|4 - 7 - 3 - 9| + 9 =$$
$$|-15| + 9 = 15 + 9 = 24$$

43. B

Subject: Algebra

Getting to the Answer: Consider the original inequality.

$-6 < x < 6$

$-6 < x \quad x < 6$ — Split the inequality into separate parts.

$-\dfrac{x}{3}$ — Consider what you must do to x to produce the new situation (multiply by $-\dfrac{1}{3}$).

$\left(-\dfrac{1}{3}\right)(-6) > \left(-\dfrac{1}{3}\right)x \quad \left(-\dfrac{1}{3}\right)x > 6\left(-\dfrac{1}{3}\right)$ — Do that to both sides of both inequalities. Remember to change the signs.

$2 > -\dfrac{x}{3} \quad -\dfrac{x}{3} > -2$ — Now merge the two back together.

$2 > -\dfrac{x}{3} > -2$ — Look for values between -2 and 2.

44. H

Subject: Algebra

Getting to the Answer: Pick numbers ($x = 7$, $y = 4$)

$$\begin{array}{r} 7 - 1\,\text{R}\,n \\ 4\overline{)(7 \cdot 4) - 3} \end{array}$$

$$\begin{array}{r} 6\,\text{R}\,1 \\ 4\overline{)25} \end{array}$$

The remainder is 1, so $n = 1$. This is not an answer choice, so try the choices with variables: **(G)** $y - 2 = 4 - 2 = 2$, and **(H)** $y - 3 = 4 - 3 = 1$.

Pick different numbers ($x = 8$, $y = 10$)

$$\begin{array}{r} 8 - 1\,\text{R}\,n \\ 10\overline{)(8 \cdot 10) - 3} \end{array}$$

$$\begin{array}{r} 7\,\text{R}\,7 \\ 10\overline{)77} \end{array}$$

(G) $y - 2 = 10 - 2 = 8$, and **(H)** $y - 3 = 10 - 3 = 7$. **(H)** is therefore correct.

The remainder each time is different, so you must consider which variable answer fits the remainder each time. Just plug the value into each to find the answer as done above.

45. C

Subject: Algebra

Getting to the Answer: Pick numbers: $a = -3$, $b = -2$, $c = -1$

Substitute:

   I. $-3 + (-2) < -2 + (-1)$

       $-5 < -3$ True.

  II. $-1 - (-3) > 0$

       $2 > 0$ True.

 III. $-3 < -2 + (-1)$

       $-3 < -3$ False.

I and II are true, so **(C)** is correct.

46. H

Subject: Algebra

Getting to the Answer:

Plug in 7 for x:

$(7 - 1) + (7 - 2) + (7 - 3) + (7 - 4) + (7 - 5) + (7 - 6) + (7 - 7) =$

$6 + 5 + 4 + 3 + 2 + 1 + 0 = 21$

Geometry

Math

Geometry I

Lines and Angles

Angles are formed by two line segments that begin at the same point. Adjacent angles can be added to find the measure of a larger angle. The following diagram demonstrates this.

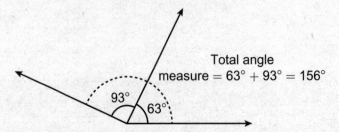

There are 180 degrees in a straight line, and 90 degrees in a right angle. Two angles that sum to 180° are called supplementary angles. Two angles that sum to 90° are called complementary angles.

DIRECTIONS: Use the information provided to solve for the angle measures.

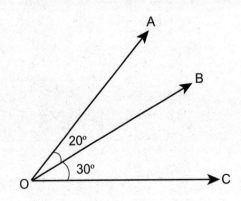

A. ∠AOC =

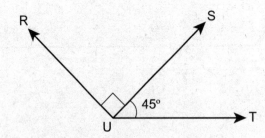

B. ∠RUT =

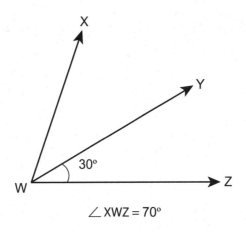

$\angle$ XWZ = 70°

C. $\angle$XWY =

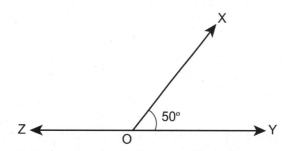

D. $\angle$XOZ =

SHSAT EXPERT NOTE

Figures on the SHSAT may not necessarily be drawn to scale. Don't guess solely based on how a figure looks.

When two lines intersect, adjacent angles are supplementary because they add up to 180 degrees, and **vertical** angles (two angles opposite a vertex) are equal, or **congruent**.

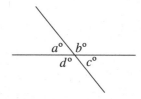

The angles marked $a°$ and $b°$ are supplementary; therefore, $a° + b° = 180°$. The angle marked $a°$ is vertical (and thus equal) to the one marked $c°$, so $a° = c°$.

DIRECTIONS: Use the information provided to solve for the missing angle measures.

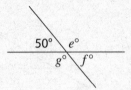

E. $e =$

F. $f =$

G. $g =$

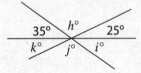

H. $h =$

I. $i =$

J. $j =$

K. $k =$

When two parallel lines are intersected by another line (called a **transversal**), all acute angles are equal, and all obtuse angles are equal. Additionally, **corresponding angles** are angles that are in the same position but on different parallel lines/transversal intersections; they are also equal. Furthermore, **alternate interior angles** and **alternate exterior angles** are equal. Alternate interior angles are angles that are positioned between the two parallel lines on opposite sides of the transversal, whereas alternate exterior angles are positioned on the outside of the parallel lines on opposite sides of the transversal. Consider the following figure:

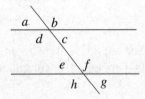

- Angles *a, c, e,* and *g* are acute and equal.
- Angles *b, d, f,* and *h* are obtuse and equal.
- Angle pairs (*b* and *f*), (*c* and *g*), (*a* and *e*), and (*d* and *h*) are corresponding angles.
- Angle pairs (*a* and *g*) and (*b* and *h*) are alternate exterior angles.
- Angle pairs (*d* and *f*) and (*c* and *e*) are alternate interior angles.

SHSAT EXPERT NOTE

Having the rules for parallel lines memorized for Test Day will translate to easy points!

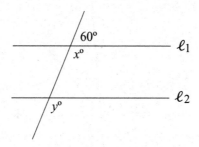

$$\ell_1 \parallel \ell_2$$

L. $\angle x =$

M. $\angle y =$

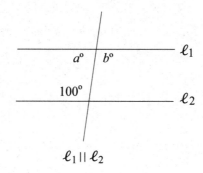

$$\ell_1 \parallel \ell_2$$

N. $\angle a =$

O. $\angle b =$

Math

Math

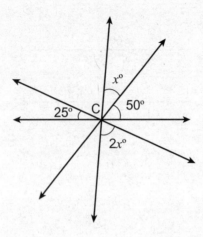

1. In the figure above, four straight lines intersect at point C. What is the value of x ?

    A. 25
    B. 35
    C. 75
    D. 105

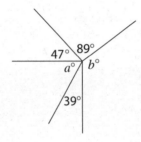

2. In the figure above, what is the value of $a + b$?

    E. 145
    F. 175
    G. 185
    H. 275

SHSAT EXPERT NOTE

Two intersecting lines create two sets of congruent angles called vertical angles.

If two lines intersect at a 90° angle, they are perpendicular. If one intersection is 90°, then all four angles are 90°.

If a question asks for the value of $a + b$, see if you can find the answer without solving for a and b separately.

Perimeter and Area of Quadrilaterals

Perimeter and area are basic properties that all two-dimensional shapes have. The **perimeter** of a quadrilateral can be calculated by adding the lengths of all its sides. **Area** is the amount of two-dimensional space a shape occupies. The most common shapes for which you'll need these two properties on Test Day are squares, rectangles, parallelograms, and trapezoids.

The area (A) of a **square** is given by $A = s^2$, where s is the side of the square. To find the area of a **rectangle**, multiply the length by the width. **Parallelograms** are quadrilaterals with two pairs of parallel sides. Rectangles and squares are subsets of parallelograms. You can find the area of a parallelogram using $A = bh$. As with triangles, you can use any side of a parallelogram as the base; in addition, the height is still perpendicular to the base. Use the side perpendicular to the base as the height for a rectangle or square; for any other parallelogram, the height (or enough information to find it) will be given. A **trapezoid** is a quadrilateral with only one set of parallel sides. Those parallel sides form the two bases. To find the area, average those bases and multiply by the height.

Scaling involves changing the size of one or more sides of a shape and then evaluating the difference in the new shape's area or perimeter.

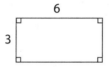

A. Perimeter =

B. Area =

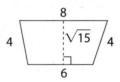

C. Perimeter =

D. Area =

E. Perimeter =

F. Area =

G. Draw a rectangle with an area of 40, labeling the sides. What is the perimeter?

H. A fence surrounds a rectangular field whose length is 3 times its width. If the entire length of the fence is 240 meters, what is the width of the field?

I. How much will the area change when the side lengths of a square with an area of 16 are doubled?

3. A rectangular doormat that is 1 foot by 2 feet is placed on a square porch that has a perimeter of 16 feet. What is the area, in square feet, of the porch **not** covered by the doormat?

    A. 4
    B. 8
    C. 14
    D. 16

SHSAT EXPERT NOTE

The SHSAT will test your ability to handle geometry problems that do not have a diagram. Be sure to draw your own diagram if none is provided on Test Day.

---

4. The length of a rectangle is 56 centimeters. The ratio of the length to the width is 7:4. What is the perimeter of the rectangle?

    E. 32 cm
    F. 88 cm
    G. 176 cm
    H. 1,792 cm

SHSAT EXPERT NOTE

Be careful to answer exactly what the question asks. If a question asks for the area, the perimeter is often among the wrong answers and vice versa.

Perimeter and Area of Triangles

Perimeter of a triangle: The perimeter of a triangle is the distance around the triangle. In other words, the perimeter is equal to the sum of the lengths of the sides.

An **isosceles** triangle is a triangle that has at least two sides of equal length. The two equal sides are called the legs, and the third side is called the base. Because the two legs have the same length, the two angles opposite the legs must have the same measure.

An **equilateral triangle** is a triangle that has three equal sides. Because all the sides are equal, all the angles are also equal. All three angles in an equilateral triangle measure 60°, regardless of the lengths of the sides. All equilateral triangles are also isosceles, but not all isosceles triangles are equilateral.

A **right triangle** has one interior angle of 90°. The longest side, which lies opposite the right angle, is called the **hypotenuse**. The other two sides are called the **legs**.

Area of a triangle: The area of a triangle refers to the space it takes up. The area of a triangle is $\frac{1}{2} \times$ base $\times$ height.

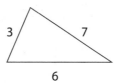

A. Perimeter = _____

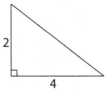

B. Area = _____

C. Area = _____

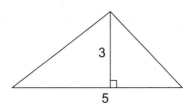

D. Area = _____

SHSAT EXPERT NOTE

The height of a triangle is the perpendicular distance from any side chosen as the base to the opposite vertex.

5. A square sandwich that is 4 inches wide is diagonally cut in half, and half of the sandwich is placed on a square napkin that is 5 inches wide. What is the area of the napkin **not** covered by half of the sandwich?

    A.   9 sq in.
    B.   16 sq in.
    C.   17 sq in.
    D.   25 sq in.

6. The perimeter of an isosceles triangle is 50 centimeters. The ratio of the two equal sides to the third side is 3:4. What are the dimensions of the triangle?

    E.   3 cm × 3 cm × 4 cm
    F.   6 cm × 6 cm × 8 cm
    G.   15 cm × 15 cm × 20 cm
    H.   18 cm × 18 cm × 30 cm

Degrees of Triangles and Quadrilaterals

The interior angles of any triangle sum to 180°.

The interior angles of any quadrilateral sum to 360°.

For parallelograms, opposite angles are equal and adjacent angles add up to 180°. A diagonal of a parallelogram separates it into two congruent triangles.

For any polygon, the total degrees of the interior angles = 180°($n - 2$), where n is the number of sides.

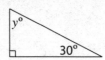

A. $y =$ _____

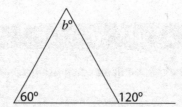

B. $b =$ _____

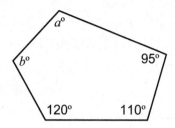

C. $a + b =$ _____

D. A quadrilateral has angles measuring 56°, 78°, and 90°. How large is the missing angle?
_____

E. The measure of one angle in a parallelogram is 46°. What is the measure of the adjacent angle?

SHSAT EXPERT NOTE

For Test Day, you must know that the interior angles of a triangle sum to 180° and the interior angles of a quadrilateral sum to 360°.

Math

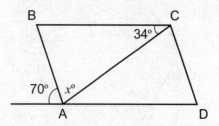

7. In the given figure, ABCD is a parallelogram. What is the value of x ?

    A. 36
    B. 56
    C. 66
    D. 76

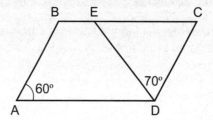

8. In the given figure, ABCD is a parallelogram. The measure of $\angle BAD$ is 60°, and the measure of $\angle EDC$ is 70°. What is the measure of $\angle CED$?

    E. 50°
    F. 60°
    G. 70°
    H. 80°

Circumference and Area of Circles

A circle's **perimeter** is known as its **circumference** (C) and is found using $C = 2\pi r$, where r is the radius (distance from the center of the circle to its edge). The lowercase Greek letter π (pronounced "pie") is approximately $\frac{22}{7}$ or 3.14. One revolution of a wheel equals the circumference of the wheel. The **area** of a circle is given by $A = \pi r^2$.

DIRECTIONS: Find the missing measurement for each circle.

A. Radius $= 8$

Circumference $=$

B. Radius $= 5$

Area $=$

C. Area $= 16\pi$

Radius $=$

D. Circumference $= 6\pi$

Area $=$

9. Six circular lights, each with a circumference of 10π inches, are installed in a ceiling that is 11 feet by 20 feet. What is the area of the ceiling **not** covered by the lights?

A. $62 - 25\pi$ sq ft

B. $62 - 150\pi$ sq ft

C. $220 - 25\pi$ sq ft

D. $220 - 150\pi$ sq ft

10. A bicycle travels 22 feet per minute. If the radius of each wheel is 12 inches, how many revolutions does one wheel make in 1 hour? $\left(\pi \approx \frac{22}{7}\right)$

E. $\dfrac{7}{2}$

F. $\dfrac{44}{7}$

G. 17.5

H. 210

SHSAT EXPERT NOTE

Identify whether the question asks you to calculate the actual area or circumference or whether the answer is expressed in terms of π.

Geometry II

Figures in the Coordinate Plane

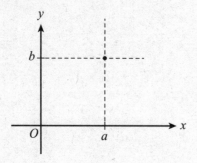

The horizontal line is the *x*-axis.

The vertical line is the *y*-axis.

The two dotted lines meet at the point (*a*, *b*).

A location is given by two numbers in parentheses.

    The first is the *x*-coordinate.

    The second is the *y*-coordinate.

If you start at the origin and move:

    To the right, *x* is positive.

    Up, *y* is positive.

SHSAT EXPERT NOTE

Understanding the basics of the coordinate grid will help you unlock more difficult problems and get more points on Test Day!

For some questions, you'll have to combine what you know about different geometric figures with what you know about the coordinate plane.

DIRECTIONS: Find the areas of the shapes graphed below.

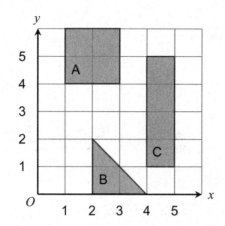

A. A = _____

B. B = _____

C. C = _____

SHSAT EXPERT NOTE

Often, coordinate plane questions ask you to use your knowledge of basic shapes as well as your understanding of the coordinate plane.

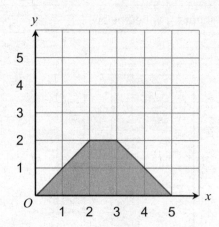

1. In the graph above, what is the area of the shaded region?

    A. 4 sq units

    B. 6 sq units

    C. 8 sq units

    D. 12 sq units

SHSAT EXPERT NOTE

To find the length of a line segment that is parallel to either axis, take the absolute value of the difference between the coordinates that are at either end of the line segment.

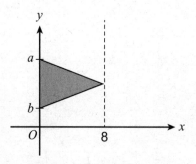

2. In the figure above, what is the area of the shaded triangle?

    E. $\frac{1}{2}(a - b)$

    F. $2(a - b)$

    G. $4(a - b)$

    H. $8(a - b)$

Complex Figures

Many geometry questions combine two or more common shapes. You must understand the relationships between the shapes to answer the questions correctly.

When you encounter questions with multiple figures, look for the connections between the shapes.

DIRECTIONS: Use the steps below to solve the following test-like problem.

In the figure above, a circle is inscribed within a square. If the area of the circle is 25π, what is the perimeter of the shaded region?

  A. First, determine the connection between the shapes:

  B. Next, decide what information you need to find and solve for unknown variables:

  C. Finally, solve the question:

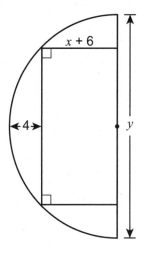

3.   In the figure above, what is y in terms of x ?

  A. $x + 10$

  B. $2x + 10$

  C. $2x + 20$

  D. $4x + 24$

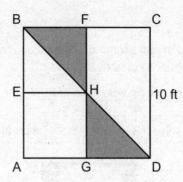

4.   In the figure above, E, F, and G are midpoints of the sides of square ABCD, and H is the center of square ABCD. What is the total area, in square feet, of the shaded portions?

E.   12.5

F.   25

G.   50

H.   100

Three-Dimensional Shapes

Three-dimensional (3D) shapes are also called solids. The following diagram shows the basic anatomy of a 3D shape:

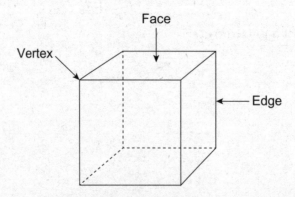

A **face** (or **surface**) is a two-dimensional (2D) shape that acts as one of the sides of the solid. Two faces meet at a line segment called an **edge**, and three faces meet at a single point called a **vertex**.

Commonly tested three-dimensional shapes on the SHSAT are prisms, which have two parallel faces, and pyramids, which have a base and three or more triangular faces that meet at a point. Note that a cube is a rectangular prism with all sides equal.

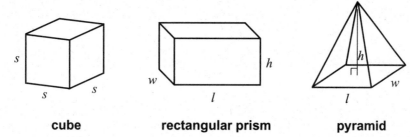

| cube | rectangular prism | pyramid |

Volume is the amount of 3D space occupied by a solid. Volume is analogous to the area of a 2D shape. You can find the volume of prisms by finding the area of the base and multiplying it by the height: $(V = A_{base} \times h)$.

When you are not explicitly given the area of the base of a 3D shape, you'll need to rely on your two-dimensional geometry knowledge to find it before calculating the volume of the prism.

Surface area is the sum of the areas of all faces of a solid. To calculate the surface area of a solid, simply find the area of each face using your 2D geometry skills, then add them all together.

You might think that finding the surface area of a solid with many sides, such as a square pyramid, is a tall order. However, you can save time by noticing a vital trait: such a pyramid has four identical triangular faces and one square base. Don't waste time finding the area of each of the surfaces. Find the area of one triangular face and one rectangular base only. Then multiply the area of the triangular face by 4 and add it to the area of the rectangular base, and you're done. The same is true for other 3D shapes.

Because formulas are not given on the SHSAT, you will need to memorize the ones that will help you most. Be smart when you memorize—sometimes you can break up a solid into polygons with area formulas you already know.

Shape	Surface Area	Volume
Cube	$6s^2$	s^3
Rectangular Prism	$2lw + 2hw + 2lh$ Think: find the area of each rectangle, then add.	$l \times w \times h$ Think: area of the base times the height.
Pyramid	$\frac{1}{2} \times$ base area $\times$ perimeter $\times$ slant length	$\frac{1}{3} \times$ base area $\times$ height

A. A rectangular prism is 5 inches long, 3 inches wide, and 2 inches high. What is the volume of the prism, in cubic inches?

B. A cube has a surface area of 294 square centimeters. What is the length of each edge of the cube, in centimeters?

Math

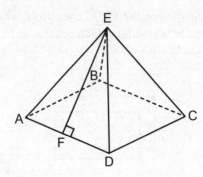

5. In the figure above, the areas of each triangular face are equal, and the sides of the square base ABCD are each 4 inches. If EF = 6 inches, what is the surface area of the pyramid **including** the base?

A. 48 sq in.

B. 52 sq in.

C. 60 sq in.

D. 64 sq in.

SHSAT EXPERT NOTE

To calculate the surface area of a three-dimensional shape, find the sum of the areas of each face. Save time by identifying identical faces and multiplying the area of that face by the number of identical faces.

---

6. A storage bench has a rectangular base. The length of the base is three times the width of the base. The height is equal to the width of the bench. If the length of the bench is 120 centimeters, what is the volume of the chest?

E. 43,200 cu cm

F. 192,000 cu cm

G. 576,000 cu cm

H. 728,000 cu cm

SHSAT EXPERT NOTE

You can calculate the volume of prisms by finding the area of the base and multiplying it by the height: $(V = A_{base} \times h)$.

Practice Set

Drills

Practice applying the concepts covered in this chapter by answering the following skill-building questions.

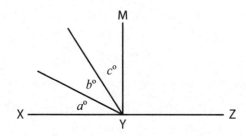

1. In the figure above, Y is a point on XZ. If $\angle$XYM is a right angle and $a = b = c$, then what is the value of b ?

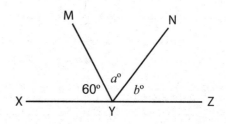

4. In the figure above, Y is a point on line XZ. If NY bisects angle MYZ, what is the value of b ?

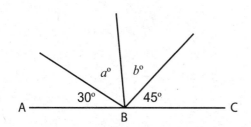

2. In the figure above, B is a point on line AC. If $b = 50°$, what is the value of a ?

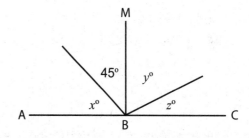

5. In the figure above, B is a point on line AC. If $x° + y° = 110°$, what is the value of z ?

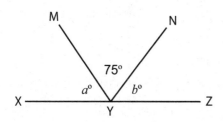

3. In the figure above, Y is a point on line XZ. What is the value of $a + b$?

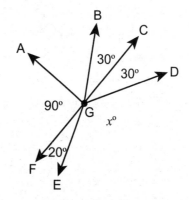

6. If $\angle$AGB $= 60°$, what is the value of x ?

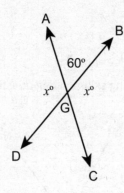

7. Two straight lines intersect at point G, as shown in the diagram above. What is the measure of ∠CGD?

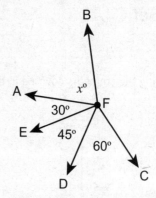

10. If ∠BFC = 2x°, what is the measure of ∠BFA?

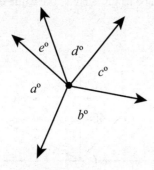

8. In the diagram above, a° + b° = 210° and c° + d° = 120°. What is the value of e ?

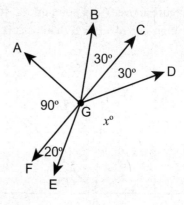

11. If ∠AGB = 60°, what is the measure of ∠FGD?

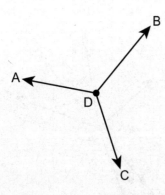

9. In the diagram above, ∠ADC ≅ ∠BDC ≅ ∠ADB. What is the measure of each angle?

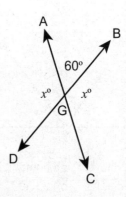

12. Two straight lines intersect at point G, as shown in the diagram above. What is the value of x ?

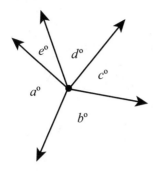

13. In the diagram above, $a° + b° = 210°$ and $c° + d° = 120°$. What is the value of $a° + b° + e°$?

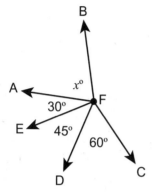

14. If $\angle BFC = 2x°$, what is the measure of $\angle BFA$?

15. What is the area of a rectangle with a length of 20 inches and a width of 3 inches?

16. What is the perimeter of a rectangle with a length of 6 meters and a width of 9 meters?

17. If a square of side length x is cut in half horizontally, what is the perimeter of one of the resultant halves?

18. If the sides of a square increase by a factor of 3, by what factor does the area of the square increase?

19. If the length of a rectangle is $x + 4$ and the width is $3x − 5$, what is the perimeter?

20. A rectangle has a width that is 5 greater than its length. If the perimeter of that rectangle is 22, what is its area?

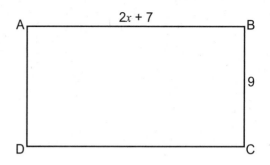

21. Look at the diagram above. If ABCD is a rectangle with an area of 153, then what is the value of x?

22. A triangle has sides measuring 5 cm, 7 cm, and 3 cm. What is the perimeter?

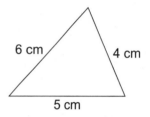

23. What is the perimeter of the above triangle?

24. What is the perimeter of a triangle with sides measuring 10 cm, 11 cm, and 15 cm?

25. A triangle has a base of 10 cm and a height of 5 cm. What is the area?

26. What is the area of a triangle with a height of 12 cm and a base of 5 cm?

27. What is the area of a triangle with a height of 9 cm and a base of 6 cm?

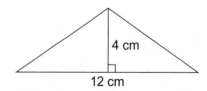

28. What is the area of the above triangle?

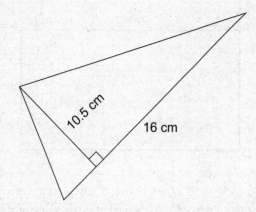

29. What is the area of the above triangle?

30. If the radius of a circle is 13 inches, what is its area?

Multiple-Choice Questions

For test-like practice, give yourself 30 minutes (an average of 1.5 minutes per question) to complete this question set. After you're done, be sure to study the explanations, even for questions you answered correctly. They can be found at the end of this chapter.

> **DIRECTIONS:** Answer each question, selecting the best answer available.

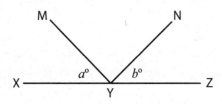

31. In the figure above, Y is a point on line XZ, and ∠MYN is a right angle. What is the value of $a° + b°$?

    A. 30°

    B. 45°

    C. 60°

    D. 90°

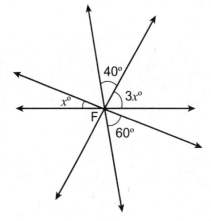

33. In the figure above, four straight lines intersect at point F. What is the value of x ?

    A. 20°

    B. 30°

    C. 45°

    D. 60°

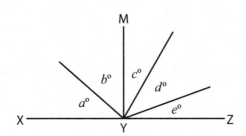

32. In the figure above, XZ is a line, ∠MYZ is a right angle, and $a° = d°$. What is the value of $a° + c° + e°$?

    E. 60°

    F. 75°

    G. 90°

    H. 115°

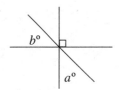

34. In the figure above, $a + b =$

    E. 70

    F. 80

    G. 90

    H. 100

35. A rectangle has a length of 12 and a width of $2x$. If the area of the rectangle is 72, what is the rectangle's perimeter?

 A. 6

 B. 18

 C. 36

 D. 72

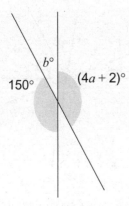

36. In the figure above, what is the value of $a - b$?

 E. 7

 F. 30

 G. 37

 H. 107

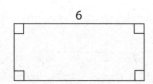

37. If the perimeter of the rectangle above is 20, what is its area?

 A. 4

 B. 8

 C. 12

 D. 24

38. Four rectangular placemats, each with a perimeter of 36 inches, are on a square table that is 4 feet long. If a placemat is 12 inches long, what is the area of the table **not** covered by the four placemats?

 E. 2 sq ft

 F. 4 sq ft

 G. 8 sq ft

 H. 14 sq ft

39. The length of a rectangle is three times its width. If the area of the rectangle is 48, what is its length?

 A. 4

 B. 8

 C. 12

 D. 16

40. A square has a length of $5x$ and a width of $2y$. If $y = 5$, find the area of the square.

 E. 10

 F. 25

 G. 50

 H. 100

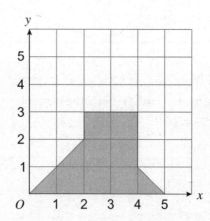

41. In the graph above, what is the area of the shaded region?

 A. 5.5 sq units

 B. 8.5 sq units

 C. 9 sq units

 D. 11 sq units

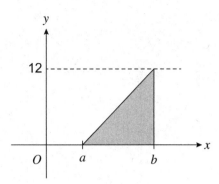

42. In the figure above, what is the area of the shaded triangle in terms of a and b?

    E. $\frac{1}{2}(b-a)$

    F. $2(b-a)$

    G. $6(b-a)$

    H. $12(b-a)$

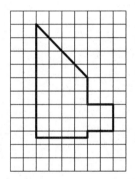

Scale: 1 inch = 6 feet

43. The grid above is made up of 1-inch squares. Approximately how many square **yards** are contained in the figure above?

    A.   30

    B.   60

    C.   120

    D.   180

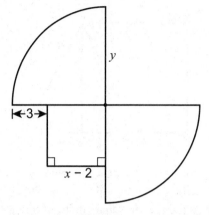

44. In the figure above, what is y in terms of x ?

    E. $x-5$

    F. $x-1$

    G. $x+1$

    H. $x+5$

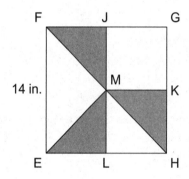

45. In the figure above, J, K, and L are midpoints of the sides of square EFGH, and M is the center of square EFGH. What is the total area, in square inches, of the shaded portions?

    A.   24.5

    B.   49

    C.   73.5

    D.   98

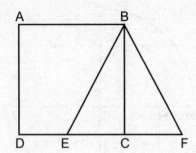

46. A square and a triangle are drawn together as shown above. The area of the square is 64, and DC = EF. What is the area, in square units, of triangle BEF?

    E. 32

    F. 64

    G. 128

    H. Cannot be determined from the information given.

47. If the area of the square in the figure above is 36 square meters, what is the circumference in meters of the circle?

    A. 6π

    B. 9π

    C. 12π

    D. 15π

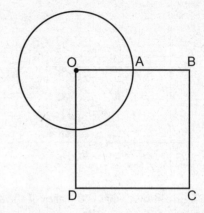

48. In the figure above, O is the center of the circle, and OBCD is a square where OA = AB. If the area of the square is 64 square feet, what is the area of the circle?

    E. 4π sq ft

    F. 8π sq ft

    G. 16π sq ft

    H. 64π sq ft

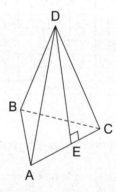

49. In the figure above, the sides of the equilateral triangle base ABC are each 3 inches. If ED = 4 inches, what is the surface area of the pyramid **excluding** the base?

    A. 6 sq in.

    B. 18 sq in.

    C. 24 sq in.

    D. 30 sq in.

50. A rectangular pool has a perimeter of 40 feet. The length of the pool is 12 feet, and the width is twice the depth of the pool. What is the volume of the pool?

    E. 384 cu ft

    F. 576 cu ft

    G. 768 cu ft

    H. 1,536 cu ft

Answers and Explanations

Lines and Angles

A. $\angle AOC = 50°$

B. $\angle RUT = 90° + 45° = 135°$

C. $\angle XWY = 70° - 30° = 40°$

D. $\angle XOZ = 180° - 50° = 130°$

E. $e = 180° - 50° = 130°$

F. $f = 50°$

G. $g = 130°$

H. $h = 180° - 60° = 120°$

I. $i = 35°$

J. $j = 120°$

K. $k = 25°$

L. $x = 120°$

M. $y = 120°$

N. $a = 80°$

O. $b = 100°$

1. B

Subject: Geometry

Getting to the Answer: Let y represent the missing angle in the top half of the figure. The sum of the top four angles is equal to 180°: $x° + y° + 25° + 50° = 180°$.

Since y is vertical to $2x$, $y = 2x$. Use that to solve for x:

$$x° + 2x° + 25° + 50° = 180°$$
$$3x° + 75° = 180°$$
$$3x° = 105°$$
$$x° = 35°$$

2. G

Subject: Geometry

Getting to the Answer: Angles around a single point total 360°, so set up an equation with what you know. Then solve for $a + b$.

$$a° + 47° + 89° + b° + 39° = 360°$$
$$a° + b° + 175 = 360°$$
$$a° + b° = 185°$$

Perimeter and Area of Quadrilaterals

A. $2(6 + 3) = 2(9) = 18$

B. $6 \times 3 = 18$

C. 22

D. $\frac{1}{2}\sqrt{15}(8 + 6) = 7\sqrt{15}$

E. 20

F. 25

G. The perimeter depends on knowing the side lengths of the rectangle. Since we only know the area is 40, we do not know the exact dimensions. To see that we get different perimeters, let's pick values based on having an area of 40. If we pick sides 4 and 10, the perimeter is $2(4 + 10) = 28$. If we pick sides 20 and 2, the perimeter is $2(20 + 2) = 44$.

H. Label the width x and the length $3x$. The problem provides the total length of the fence, so use the perimeter equation: $x + 3x + x + 3x = 240$. Simplify: $8x = 240, x = 30$.

I. $A = 16 \rightarrow$ side $= 4$

Then, double the side length to get the new side length, 8.

$$A = 8^2 = 64$$

$$\frac{64}{16} = 4$$

Therefore, the new area is 4 times larger.

3.   C

Subject: Geometry

Getting to the Answer: Drawing your own diagram may seem like it will take up valuable time, but it will actually prevent you from making careless errors on Test Day.

Calculate the area of the doormat using the dimensions of the doormat: $A = l \times w = 1$ ft $\times 2$ ft $= 2$ sq ft.

Use the perimeter of the porch to find the side length of the porch. Then use the side length to calculate the area the porch. Since $P = 4s$ and $P = 16$ ft, then 16 ft $= 4s$ and 4 ft $= s$.

Thus, the area is $A = s^2 = 4^2 = 16$ sq ft.

Subtract the area of the doormat from the area of the porch: $16 - 2 = 14$ sq ft.

4.   G

Subject: Geometry

Getting to the Answer: Set up a proportion to find the width of the rectangle. Let w represent the width.

$$\frac{56}{w} = \frac{7}{4}$$
$$224 = 7w$$
$$32 = w$$

Thus, the perimeter is $2 \times 56 + 2 \times 32 = 176$ centimeters.

Perimeter and Area of Triangles

A.   Perimeter $= 16$

B.   Area $= 4$

C.   Area $= 6$

D.   Area $= 7.5$

5.   C

Subject: Geometry

Getting to the Answer: First, calculate the area of the napkin: $A = s^2 = 5^2 = 25$ sq in. Then calculate the area of half of the sandwich. Diagonally cutting the square sandwich in half creates two triangular halves that each have a base of 4 inches and a height of 4 inches. Thus, the area of half of the sandwich is $\frac{1}{2}bh = \frac{1}{2}(4)(4) = 8$ sq in. Subtract the area of the half sandwich from the area of the napkin: $25 - 8 = 17$ sq in.

6.   G

Subject: Geometry

Getting to the Answer: Let $3x$, $3x$, and $4x$ represent the sides of the triangle. The perimeter is $3x + 3x + 4x = 50$, $10x = 50$, $x = 5$. So, the sides of the triangle are $3 \times 5 = 15$, 15, and $4 \times 5 = 20$ centimeters.

Degrees of Triangles and Quadrilaterals

A. $y = 60$

B. $b = 60$

C.   Total degrees in polygon $= (n-2)(180°)$
For 5 sides: $(5-2)(180°) = 540°$
$95 + 110 + 120 + a + b = 540$
$a + b = 215$

D.   Quadrilaterals have 360° inside
$56° + 78° + 90° = 224°$
Missing angle $= 360° - 224° = 136°$

E.   Adjacent angles in a parallelogram add up to 180°. $180° - 46° = 134°$.

7.   D

Subject: Geometry

Getting to the Answer: Remember, the diagonal of a parallelogram divides it into two congruent triangles. Thus, $\angle BCA = \angle CAD = 34°$. The sum of the angles that form a line is 180°, so $70° + x° + 34° = 180°$. Solve for x: $x° = 180° - 70° - 34° = 76°$.

8.   E

Subject: Geometry

Getting to the Answer: In a parallelogram, opposite angles are equal, so $\angle ECD = \angle BAD = 60°$. Since the sum of the interior angles of a triangle is 180°, $\angle CED + 60° + 70° = 180°$. Thus, $\angle CED = 50°$.

Circumference and Area of Circles

A. Circumference $= 16\pi$

B. Area $= 25\pi$

C. Radius $= 4$

D. Area $= 9\pi$

9. D

Subject: Geometry

Getting to the Answer: First, use the circumference of one light to find the radius of one light.

$$C = 2\pi r$$
$$10\pi = 2\pi r$$
$$5 = r$$

Then use the radius to calculate its area:

$$A = \pi r^2$$
$$= \pi (5)^2$$
$$= 25\pi$$

Multiply by 6 to get the area of the 6 lights: $6 \times 25\pi = 150\pi$ sq in.

Next, use the dimensions of the ceiling to find its area.

$$A = l \times w$$
$$= 11 \times 20$$
$$= 220$$

Subtract the area of the ceiling from the area of the 6 lights: $220 - 150\pi$ sq ft.

10. H

Subject: Geometry

Getting to the Answer: One revolution equals the circumference of the wheel. Note the radius in feet is 1 foot.

$$C = 2\pi r = 2\left(\frac{22}{7}\right)(1) = \frac{44}{7} \text{ feet}$$

Since the bicycle travels 22 feet per minute, the number of revolutions one wheel makes is

$22 \div \frac{44}{7} = 22 \times \frac{7}{44} = \frac{7}{2}$ revolutions per minute. Multiply

by 60 minutes to get $\frac{7}{2} \times 60 = 210$ revolutions per hour.

Figures in the Coordinate Plane

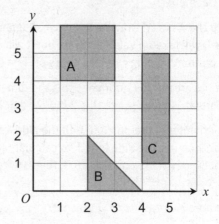

A. $A = 4$ square units

B. $B = 2$ square units

C. $C = 4$ square units

1. B

Subject: Geometry

Getting to the Answer: The shaded region is a trapezoid. The length of the top side is 1 unit, the length of the base is 5 units, and the height is 2 units. Thus, the area is $\frac{1}{2}(1 + 5) \times 2 = 6$ square units. Alternatively, you can divide the trapezoid into two right triangles and one rectangle, which gives an area of $2 \times \frac{1}{2}(2 \times 2) + 1 \times 2 = 4 + 2 = 6$ square units.

2. G

Subject: Geometry

Getting to the Answer: Recall the area of a triangle is $\frac{1}{2}bh$. The length of the base of the triangle is $a - b$, and the height of the triangle is 8 units. Thus, the area is $\frac{1}{2}(a - b)8 = 4(a - b)$.

Complex Figures

A. Since the circle is inscribed in a square, the circle's diameter is equal to the length of a side of the square.

B. Here, the perimeter of the square provides the outside perimeter of the shaded area, and the circumference of the circle provides the inside perimeter. Add them together to find the total perimeter. Since the area of the circle is 25π, the radius is 5. The diameter and length of a side of the square is 10.

C. The circumference of the circle is 10π. The perimeter of the square is $4(10) = 40$. Add these together to get the total perimeter of the shaded area: $40 + 10\pi$.

3. C

Subject: Geometry

Getting to the Answer: In the figure, the diameter is y and the radius is $(x + 6) + 4$. Since the diameter is twice the radius, set $y = 2[(x + 6) + 4]$ and solve for y:

$$y = 2(x + 10)$$
$$= 2x + 20$$

4. F

Subject: Geometry

Getting to the Answer: The length of the side of the square is 10 ft. Since E, F, and G are midpoints and H is the center, then **BF, FH, GH**, and **GD** all equal 5 ft. The two shaded triangles, BFH and HGD, are right triangles, so the area of one of the triangles is $\frac{1}{2}(5)(5) = \frac{25}{2}$. The sum of the areas is $\frac{25}{2} + \frac{25}{2} = \frac{50}{2} = 25$ sq ft.

Three-Dimensional Shapes

A. Volume $= l \times w \times h = 5 \times 3 \times 2 = 30$

B. Surface area of a cube $= 6s^2 = 294$
$$s^2 = 49$$
$$s = 7$$

5. D

Subject: Geometry

Getting to the Answer: The height of triangle AED is EF $= 6$. The length of AD is 4. Thus, the area is $\frac{1}{2}bh = \frac{1}{2}(4)(6) = 12$ sq in. The base of the pyramid is $A = s^2 = 4^2 = 16$. Since there are 4 congruent triangular faces, the total surface area of the pyramid is $4 \times 12 + 16 = 64$ sq in.

6. F

Subject: Geometry

Getting to the Answer: First, use the length of the bench to find the width and height of the chest. Then use the dimensions to calculate the volume.

The length is three times the width of the bench: $l = 3w$. Since the length is 120 centimeters, the width of the base is $\frac{120}{3} = 40$ cm. The height equals the width, so the height is also 40 cm. Thus, the volume of the chest is $l \times w \times h = 120 \times 40 \times 40 = 192,000$ cu cm.

Practice Set

1. $30°$
2. $55°$
3. $105°$
4. $60°$
5. $25°$
6. $130°$
7. $60°$
8. $30°$
9. $120°$
10. $75°$
11. $150°$
12. $120°$
13. $240°$
14. $75°$
15. 60 square inches
16. 30 meters
17. $3x$
18. 9
19. $8x - 2$
20. 24
21. 5

22. **15 cm**

23. **15 cm**

24. **36 cm**

25. **25 sq cm**

26. **30 sq cm**

27. **27 sq cm**

28. **24 sq cm**

29. **84 sq cm**

30. **169π square inches**

31. **D**

Subject: Geometry

Getting to the Answer: Line XZ forms an angle of 180°, so if the measure of $\angle$MYN is 90°, then $a° + b° = 180° - 90° = 90°$.

32. **G**

Subject: Geometry

Getting to the Answer: XZ is 180°, and $c + d + e = 90°$. Because $a° = d°$, $a° + c° + e°$ also equals 90°.

33. **A**

Subject: Geometry

Getting to the Answer: Let y represent the missing angle in the top half of the figure. The sum of the top four angles is equal to 180°: $x° + y° + 40° + 3x° = 180°$.

Since y is vertical to 60° then $y = 60°$. Use that to solve for x:

$$x° + 60° + 40° + 3x° = 180°$$
$$4x° + 100° = 180°$$
$$4x° = 80°$$
$$x° = 20°$$

34. **G**

Subject: Geometry

Getting to the Answer: Because vertical angles are equal, the angle to the right of b must have a value of $a°$. Since the angle in the upper right is 90°, all four angles created by the vertical and horizontal lines must be 90°. Therefore, $a° + b° = 90°$.

35. **C**

Subject: Geometry

Getting to the Answer:

Area of a rectangle $= lw$
$$72 = (12)(2x)$$
$$72 = 24x$$
$$x = 3$$
Perimeter of a rectangle $= 2l + 2w$

$$P = 2(12) + 2(6)$$

$$P = 36$$

36. **E**

Subject: Geometry

Getting to the Answer:

$$150° + b° = 180°$$
$$b° = 30°$$

Vertical angles are equal, so $150° = (4a + 2)°$.

$$150 = 4a + 2$$
$$148 = 4a$$
$$37 = a$$

Thus, $a - b = 37 - 30 = 7$, and **(E)** is correct. Be sure you answer the right question: **(F)** is b and **(G)** is a, but neither of those is what you are looking for.

37. **D**

Subject: Geometry

Getting to the Answer: If you cannot calculate the answer directly, start by making any deductions you can from the information you do have. To determine the area of the rectangle, you need to know the length and the width. You can use the information you are given about the length and the perimeter to figure out the width, then you can multiply length times width to determine the area.

$P = 2l + 2w$ $20 = 12 + 2w$	Use what you know to find the width.
$2w = 8$ $w = 4$	Then use the width to find the area.
$A = l \times w = 6 \times 4 = 24$	

38. H

Subject: Geometry

Getting to the Answer: Calculate the area of the square table using the dimensions of the table: $A = s^2 = 4^2 = 16$ sq ft.

Use the length and perimeter of one placemat to find the width of a placemat. Convert inches to feet to simplify calculations: 12 inches = 1 foot, and $36 \text{ inches} \times \dfrac{1 \text{ foot}}{12 \text{ inches}} = 3$ feet.

$$P = 2l + 2w$$
$$3 = 2(1) + 2w$$
$$1 = 2w$$
$$\tfrac{1}{2} = w$$

Then use the dimensions of the length and width of a placemat to calculate the area: $A = l \times w = 1\left(\tfrac{1}{2}\right) = \tfrac{1}{2}$ sq ft. Multiply the area of one placemat by 4 to get the area of 4 placemats: $4 \times \tfrac{1}{2} = 2$ sq ft. Subtract the area of the four placemats from the area of the table: $16 - 2 = 14$ sq ft.

39. C

Subject: Geometry

Getting to the Answer: Set up an area equation expressing length as three times width.

$$l = 3w$$
$$3w \times w = A = 48$$
$$3w^2 = 48$$
$$w^2 = 16 \qquad \text{Solve for width.}$$
$$w = 4 \qquad \text{Then use width to solve for}$$
$$l = 3(4) = 12 \quad \text{length.}$$

40. H

Subject: Geometry

Getting to the Answer: Since $y = 5$, and the width is $2y$, the side length of this square is $2 \times 5 = 10$. Then, since the area of a square is equal to side length squared, the square's area is $10^2 = 100$.

41. B

Subject: Geometry

Getting to the Answer: The shaded region is composed of two right triangles and a rectangle. The first right triangle has a base of 2 units and a height of 2 units. The rectangle has a width of 2 units and a height of 3 units. The second right triangle has a base of 1 unit and a height of 1 unit. Thus, the total area of the shaded region is $\tfrac{1}{2}(2 \times 2) + (2 \times 3) + \tfrac{1}{2}(1 \times 1) = \tfrac{1}{2}(4) + 6 + \tfrac{1}{2} = 8\tfrac{1}{2}$ or 8.5 square units.

42. G

Subject: Geometry

Getting to the Answer: Recall the area of a triangle is $\tfrac{1}{2}bh$. The length of the base of the triangle is $b - a$, and the height of the triangle is 12 units. Thus, the area is $\tfrac{1}{2}(b - a)12 = 6(b - a)$.

43. C

Subject: Geometry

Getting to the Answer: The side of each square in the grid is equivalent to 6 feet, or 2 yards. Remember, calculate everything in yards from the beginning. Break up the complex shape into three simple shapes: a triangle on top with a base of 8 yards and height of 8 yards, a 9 × 8 yard rectangle below, and a 4 × 4 yard square on the right. Calculate the areas of these simple shapes individually. Then add them up, and you've got the area of the complex shape.

$$\left(\tfrac{1}{2}bh\right) + (l \times w) + (s^2) = \left(\tfrac{1}{2} \times 8 \times 8\right) + (9 \times 8) + (4^2)$$
$$= 32 + 72 + 16 = 120 \text{ square yards}$$

44. G

Subject: Geometry

Getting to the Answer: In the figure above, the radius is y, and the radius is also $(x - 2) + 3$. Set $y = (x - 2) + 3$ and simplify: $y = x + 1$.

45. C

Subject: Geometry

Getting to the Answer: The length of the side of the square is 14 in. Since J, K, and L are midpoints and M is the center, then FJ, JM, KM, LM, and EL all equal 7 inches. The three shaded triangles, FJM, MKH, and MLE, are right triangles, so the area of one of the triangles is $\frac{1}{2}(7)(7) = \frac{49}{2}$ sq in. The sum of the areas is $\frac{49}{2} + \frac{49}{2} + \frac{49}{2} = \frac{147}{2} = 73.5$ sq in.

46. E

Subject: Geometry

Getting to the Answer: Take what you are given in the question stem and go from there. The area of the square is 64; therefore, the sides of the square are 8. Thus, DC and BC are 8 because they are sides of the square. You are given that DC = EF, so EF = 8, and it is the base of the triangle. BC = 8 and is the height. Finally, the area is $\frac{1}{2} \times 8 \times 8 = 32$.

47. A

Subject: Geometry

Getting to the Answer: The square has an area of 36 square meters; therefore, it has sides of 6 meters. This is the diameter of the circle. The circumference is the diameter times π. Therefore, the circumference is 6π.

48. G

Subject: Geometry

Getting to the Answer: The figure may seem imposing; just use the knowledge you have of each individual shape. This answer takes two separate calculations. If the area of the square is 64 square feet, then the sides have to be 8 feet. Therefore, OB = 8, and OA and AB both must equal half of 8, or 4. OA is the radius of the circle, and the formula for the area of the circle is $A = \pi r^2 = \pi 4^2 = 16\pi$ sq ft.

49. B

Subject: Geometry

Getting to the Answer: The height of triangle ADC is DE = 4 inches. The length of AC is 3 inches. Thus, the area is $\frac{1}{2}bh = \frac{1}{2}(3)(4) = 6$ sq in. Since there are 3 congruent triangular faces, the total surface area of the pyramid, excluding the base, is $3 \times 6 = 18$ sq in.

50. E

Subject: Geometry

Getting to the Answer: The perimeter of the pool is $2l + 2w = 40$ ft. Substitute $l = 12$ into the equation and solve for w: $w = \frac{40 - 2(12)}{2} = \frac{16}{2} = 8$ ft. The width is twice the depth of the pool, so $d = \frac{8}{2} = 4$ ft. Then use the dimensions to calculate the volume. Thus, the volume of the chest is $l \times w \times h = 12 \times 8 \times 4 = 384$ cu ft.

CHAPTER 17

Word Problems

By the end of this chapter, you will be able to:

- Translate word problems into mathematical terms
- Solve SHSAT word problems

Word Problems

Arithmetic

The ratio of *a* to *b* can be written as *a:b* or as $\frac{a}{b}$.

A. A grocery store stocks 3 apples for every 4 oranges. What is the ratio of apples to oranges?

B. If the store has 28 pieces of fruit and they are all either apples or oranges, how many apples are there?

$$\text{Percent} = \frac{\text{Part}}{\text{Whole}} \times 100\% \quad \text{Percent change} = \frac{\text{Change}}{\text{Original}} \times 100\%$$

C. What percentage of 50 is 35?

D. 12 is 20% of what number?

Common rate equations:

$$\text{Rate} = \frac{\text{distance}}{\text{time}}, \text{Distance} = \text{time} \times \text{rate}, \text{Time} = \frac{\text{distance}}{\text{rate}}$$

E. John travels 80 miles in 2 hours. What is his average speed?

F. Mary makes \$72 on Friday. If she works for 8 hours, how much does she make per hour?

SHSAT EXPERT NOTE

As with all translation questions, first translate the English into equations. Only when you are sure you have the translation correct should you begin the actual math.

---

1. If the price of a stock decreases by 20%, and then by an additional 25%, by what percentage has the price decreased from its original value?

   A. 40

   B. 45

   C. 50

   D. 55

2. At Mattress Shop, 75% of the mattresses are memory foam and 20% of the mattresses are extra firm. Of the total mattresses at Mattress Shop, 12% are extra firm memory foam mattresses. What percentage of the total mattresses are **not** extra firm non-memory foam mattresses?

   E. 8

   F. 17

   G. 63

   H. 80

3. In a piggy bank, there are 12 bills. Of the four types of coins, 42 coins are pennies. The bill-to-coin ratio for the piggy bank is 1 to 25. What is the total number of nickels, dimes, and quarters in the piggy bank?

   A. 258

   B. 300

   C. 342

   D. 479

4. Three students are each giving a slide show presentation with 12 slides each. Astrid presents 1 slide every 3 minutes. Steven presents 1 slide every 8 minutes, and Anna presents 1 slide every 4 minutes. How many minutes did the three students spend giving their presentations?

   E. 48

   F. 96

   G. 180

   H. 210

5. At Eddie's convenience store, 2 of every 21 items purchased are returned. If 441 items are purchased, how many items will be returned?

   A. 24
   B. 28
   C. 36
   D. 42

6. A sheet of one-ply paper towel has a thickness of 0.2 millimeters, with an error of 5%. What is the least thickness of a sheet of one-ply paper towel?

   E. 0.01
   F. 0.1
   G. 0.19
   H. 0.9

7. Ken turned on his oven at noon to bake a casserole. The starting temperature of the oven was 195°F. The temperature increased 10 degrees every minute. How long did it take the oven to reach 375°F?

   A. 12
   B. 14
   C. 18
   D. 20

SHSAT EXPERT NOTE

Picking Numbers often works well when a question includes variables in the answer choices, percentages, number properties, or unknown values.

Algebra

Label your own variables to translate problems in which the variables you're trying to solve for aren't explicitly labeled.

> **DIRECTIONS:** Identify the variable(s) in each of the phrases below, and translate the statements into appropriate equations:

Statement: Translation:

   A. Martha is 3 times as old as Ann.

   B. There are 5 more orange marbles than blue marbles in a bag.

   C. There are 3 empty boxes for every full box.

SHSAT EXPERT NOTE

When translating, try to avoid using o, l, s, and z if you can. These letters can be easily confused with numbers. If those variables are already included in a question, take care to keep your numbers and letters straight.

A linear model is generally defined by two parameters: the rate of change, or slope, and the initial value, or y-intercept. Real-world scenarios that involve a constant rate of change—such as the position of a car moving at a constant speed—can be represented by linear models.

> **DIRECTIONS:** Write a linear equation for each of the following scenarios.

Scenario: Equation:

   D. A fitness club has 45 members and plans to increase membership by 4 members every month.

   E. The cost of a pizza starts at $5, and each additional topping costs $1.

   F. The value of a car initially is $22,500 and declines by $2,000 a year.

8. Anna is now y years old, and Marco is 3 years younger. In terms of y, how old was Marco 5 years ago?

    E. $y - 2$

    F. $y - 3$

    G. $y - 5$

    H. $y - 8$

9. Cade's age now is two times Taylor's age. If Taylor will be 15 in three years, how old was Cade two years ago?

    A. 10

    B. 18

    C. 22

    D. 23

10. Christopher is at least 7 years younger than Lillian. Which of the following inequalities represents the relationship between Christopher's age (c) and Lillian's age (l) ?

    E. $c + l \leq 7$

    F. $c + l \geq 7$

    G. $7 + c \geq l$

    H. $7 + c \leq l$

11. A tank when full can hold 16 gallons. There are g gallons in the tank. If 2 gallons are used, the tank would be a quarter full. What is the value of g ?

    A. 4

    B. 6

    C. 10

    D. 12

12. Levi has a phone plan that charges $20 per month plus $6 per 1 gigabyte of data. Jayden has a phone plan that charges $44 per month for unlimited data. At the end of the month, Levi's charges are equal to Jayden's charges. How many gigabytes of data did Levi use?

    E. 4

    F. 7

    G. 10

    H. 12

13. Dylan rented a studio for four years. He paid a one-time security deposit of $250 and an additional $875 per month for the full four years. What is the total amount Dylan paid for renting the studio for four years?

   A. $3,750

   B. $12,875

   C. $41,750

   D. $42,250

14. The monthly expenses for Addison's music shop are $360. It costs Addison $290 to build a guitar, and she sells each guitar for $510. What is Addison's profit if she builds and sells 6 guitars in 1 month?

   E. $220

   F. $960

   G. $1,320

   H. $2,770

15. Mason bought 3 apples for $1.29 each and 2 pounds of salmon. His total purchase for these items, not including tax, was $24.95. What was the price per pound of the salmon?

   A. $7.46

   B. $10.54

   C. $11.83

   D. $21.08

16. To make lemonade, Skylar could buy a bag of lemons for $5.40, or she could buy x individual lemons for $0.60 each. What is the largest value of x that would make buying individual lemons less expensive than buying the bag?

   E. 7

   F. 8

   G. 9

   H. 10

SHSAT EXPERT NOTE

Problems with numbers in the answer choices are often solved quickly with Kaplan's Backsolving strategy.

Geometry

Translation of geometry problems typically involves putting information from the question directly into the given diagram or, occasionally, drawing a brand new figure.

A. If the width of a rectangle is 4 and the length is twice the width, what is the area?

B. ABC is an isosceles triangle. Sides AB and AC are 7 units each, and side BC is 3 units. The measure of angle ABC is 78°. What is the measure of angle CAB?

C. Six bridges are connected at points A, B, C, D, E, and F, in a hexagon. The points appear clockwise when viewed from above, from A to F. If Jenny starts at point A and walks 725 bridges in a clockwise direction, at what point will she be when she has stopped?

17. A cup with a circumference of 2π inches is placed in the center of a circular coaster that has a radius of 2 inches. What is the area of the coaster **not** covered by the bottom of the cup, in square inches?

    A. π

    B. 3π

    C. 4π

    D. 5π

18. A toy chest has a rectangular base. The length of the base is four times the width of the base. The height of the chest is one-half the length of the base. If the height of the chest is 10 inches, what is the volume of the chest, in cubic inches?

    E. 400

    F. 500

    G. 1,000

    H. 8,000

19. A right triangle in a diagram has a base of 3 centimeters and a height of 4 centimeters. A copy machine enlarges the diagram. The base of the enlarged triangle is 9 centimeters. What is the area of the triangle in the enlarged diagram, in square centimeters?

    A. 12

    B. 21

    C. 54

    D. 108

20. A rope with a specific length is used to measure a horizontal distance of 39 yards. The same rope is also used to measure a distance of 45 yards. What is the greatest possible length, in yards, of the rope?

    E. 3

    F. 6

    G. 9

    H. 18

21. The perimeter of a rectangle is 32 inches. The ratio of the length to the width is 5:3. What is the area of the rectangle?

    A. 52

    B. 56

    C. 60

    D. 64

Statistics and Probability

- **Mean (or average):**

$$\text{Average} = \frac{\text{Sum of Items}}{\text{Number of Items}}$$

- **Median:** Middle value in a data set when values are in ascending or descending order.
- **Mode:** Most frequent value in a data set (can have multiple modes).
- **Range:** The highest value in a data set minus the lowest value.

Xiaomei ran 5 laps. The times of each lap are 4.0, 4.8, 4.2, 4.5, and 4.0 minutes.

    A. What is the average time it took Xiaomei to complete one lap?
    B. What is Xiaomei's median lap time?
    C. What is the mode of Xiaomei's lap time?
    D. What is the range of Xiaomei's lap time?

Probability:

$$\text{Probability} = \frac{\text{Number of Desired Outcomes}}{\text{Number of Possible Outcomes}}$$

Jean spins a prize wheel that is divided into 6 even slices that are colored red, orange, yellow, green, blue, and purple.

    E. What is the probability of landing on the green slice?
    F. What is the probability of landing on the green or blue slice?
    G. What is the probability of not landing on the green or blue slice?

22. Rishi received a mean score of 88 per quiz for his first four quizzes in physics. On his 5th quiz, he scored 93. What is his mean quiz score for the first 5 quizzes?

   E. 89
   F. 90
   G. 91
   H. 92

23. Kelsey bought 5 pairs of pants at the department store for a mean price of $24 per pair of pants. She bought 2 pairs of shoes at the footwear store. If the total price of the pants equals the total price of the shoes, what was the mean price of the shoes?

   A. $56
   B. $60
   C. $64
   D. $72

24. A zoo records 127 visitors to an exhibit on Monday, 178 on Tuesday, 112 on Wednesday, 103 on Thursday, 196 on Friday, 271 on Saturday, and 217 on Sunday. What is the median number of visitors for the week?

   E. 103
   F. 172
   G. 178
   H. 271

25. The average weight of Jake, Ken, and Larry is 60 kilograms. If Jake and Ken each weigh 50 kilograms, how much does Larry weigh, in kilograms?

   A. 40
   B. 50
   C. 60
   D. 80

26. The high temperature on Monday, measured in degrees Fahrenheit, was 34°. If the low temperature was 3° below zero, what was the range of temperatures on Monday?

    E. $-3°$

    F. $31°$

    G. $34°$

    H. $37°$

27. On a shelf, there are 7 comic books, 3 joke books, and 5 space books. If one book is pulled out at random, what is the probability that it will **not** be a comic book?

    A. $\dfrac{1}{5}$

    B. $\dfrac{7}{15}$

    C. $\dfrac{8}{15}$

    D. $\dfrac{4}{5}$

28. There are 2 red scarves, 7 purple scarves, 6 yellow scarves, and 3 green scarves in a hat. If two scarves are drawn at random without replacement, what is the probability that both scarves removed are **not** purple?

    E. $\dfrac{55}{153}$

    F. $\dfrac{121}{153}$

    G. $\dfrac{70}{153}$

    H. $\dfrac{98}{153}$

Practice Set

Grid-In Questions

For test-like practice, give yourself 15 minutes (an average of 1.5 minutes per question) to complete this question set. After you're done, be sure to study the explanations, even for questions you answered correctly. They can be found at the end of this chapter.

DIRECTIONS: Answer each question. Write your answer in the boxes at the top of the grid. Start on the left side of each grid, printing only one number or symbol in each box. **DO NOT LEAVE A BOX BLANK IN THE MIDDLE OF AN ANSWER.** Under each box, fill in the circle that matches the number or symbol you wrote above. **DO NOT FILL IN A CIRCLE UNDER AN UNUSED BOX.**

---

1. A trail mix contains nuts, granola, and fruit in the ratio 2:3:5. If there are 27 ounces of granola in the mix, how many ounces of fruit are in the mix?

2. Mark is 5 years less than 3 times Jessica's age. If Mark is 25 years old, what is Jessica's age?

3. Alex, Brian, Chandler, Doug, and Eve all ate pizza at a pizza party. Alex ate 3 slices of pizza, Brian and Chandler each ate 4 slices of pizza, Doug ate 5 slices of pizza, and Eve ate 2 slices of pizza. If a pizza contains 8 slices, how many pizzas did they eat?

4. Bruce and Robin went on a scavenger hunt. Bruce collected 10 fewer than four times the number of items that Robin collected. If Bruce and Robin collected a combined 50 items, how many items did Bruce collect?

5. The mean number of bacterial colonies on Richa's first three petri dishes was 67. On her fourth petri dish, there were 55 colonies. What is the mean bacterial colony count for the four petri dishes?

7. A grocery store sells cartons of orange juice. Each carton contains 40 ounces of juice. If Roberta pays $15 for three cartons of orange juice, what is the cost of orange juice per ounce? Express your answer in cents.

6. Azuka bought 3 boxes of nails at the hardware store for a mean price of $2.80 per box. In a second transaction, he bought 5 boxes of screws. If the total price of the nails is equal to the total price of the screws, what was the mean price of the screws?

8. A wagon has a rectangular base. The length of the wagon is 4 times the width of the wagon. The height is one-fourth the width of the wagon. If the width is 8 inches, what is the volume of the wagon?

9. The bottom of a shoe is used to measure a distance of 98 inches. The same shoe is also used to measure a distance of 70 inches. What is the longest possible length, in inches, of the shoe?

10. To make tomato soup, Sebastian could buy a case of t tomatoes for $7.59, or he could buy t individual tomatoes for $0.69 each. What is the smallest value of t that would make buying the case of tomatoes less expensive than buying individual tomatoes?

Multiple-Choice Questions

For test-like practice, give yourself 33 minutes (an average of 1.5 minutes per question) to complete this question set. After you're done, be sure to study the explanations, even for questions you answered correctly. They can be found at the end of this chapter.

> **DIRECTIONS:** Answer each question, selecting the best answer available.

11. Meghan has $100 more than Andrew. After Meghan spends $20 on groceries, she will have 5 times as much money as Andrew. How much money does Andrew have?

   A. $20
   B. $30
   C. $40
   D. $50

12. The original price of an item is reduced by 40% for a sale. After two weeks, the sale price is reduced by an additional 25%. The final price is what percentage less than the original price?

   E. 45%
   F. 50%
   G. 55%
   H. 60%

13. Thirty percent of high school senior boys at a certain high school play in the school band. If the high school has 60 senior boys, how many boys play in the school band?

   A. 12
   B. 18
   C. 22
   D. 30

14. A bag of dominoes contains red dominoes and blue dominoes in the ratio of 4:7. If there are 42 blue dominoes in a bag, how many total dominoes are in the bag, assuming red and blue are the only two colors of dominoes?

   E. 24
   F. 42
   G. 66
   H. 90

15. An electronic tablet has a thickness of 0.75 centimeters, with an error of 0.1%. What is the greatest thickness of the tablet?

   A. 0.074925
   B. 0.075075
   C. 0.74925
   D. 0.75075

16. A class of 30 is divided into 2 groups such that the size of the smaller group is $\frac{2}{3}$ the size of the larger group. How large is the smaller group?

   E. 10
   F. 12
   G. 18
   H. 20

17. Three people are fishing on a boat. Chad caught 10 fish every 40 minutes. Stephanie caught 6 fish every half hour, and Manny caught 15 fish every 1.5 hours. How many fish did the three people catch in one hour?

    A. 30

    B. 33

    C. 35

    D. 37

18. A promotion offers $5 off for every $75 spent. Cynthia received $15 off her purchase. How much was the total cost of her purchase?

    E. $200

    F. $225

    G. $250

    H. $275

19. A school records the number of students late for school each day of the school week. The number of late students was 6 on Monday, 2 on Tuesday, 2 on Wednesday, 4 on Thursday, and 5 on Friday. What is the median number of late students for the week?

    A. 2

    B. 4

    C. 5

    D. 6

20. There are 5 discs, 6 jump ropes, 3 balls, and 12 pieces of sidewalk chalk in a bin. If two items are drawn at random without replacement, what is the probability that both items removed are **not** jump ropes?

    E. $\frac{49}{169}$

    F. $\frac{100}{169}$

    G. $\frac{38}{65}$

    H. $\frac{42}{65}$

21. A library records the number of attendees to their weekly programs. The number of attendees was 48 on Monday, 39 on Tuesday, 40 on Wednesday, 22 on Thursday, 53 on Friday, 90 on Saturday, and 85 on Sunday. What is the median of this week's attendees?

    A. 22

    B. 40

    C. 48

    D. 85

22. Riley's Windows and Company manufactures windowpanes. The minimum thickness of a windowpane is $\frac{3}{32}$ inches. The maximum thickness of a windowpane is $\frac{1}{8}$ inches. What is the range, in inches, of windowpane thickness?

    E. $\frac{1}{32}$

    F. $\frac{1}{16}$

    G. $\frac{7}{64}$

    H. $\frac{3}{8}$

23. Ron is 3 years older than Sherry, who is 4 years less than twice as old as John. Which of the following represents Ron's age, if J = John's age?

    A. $J - 1$

    B. $J + 3$

    C. $2J - 1$

    D. $2J - 4$

24. If the average height of a group of 5 people is 67 inches, what is the total height, in inches, of the people?

    E. 305

    F. 320

    G. 335

    H. 365

25. Two square photographs, each with a perimeter of 20 inches, are pinned to a rectangular board that is 12 inches by 16 inches. What is the area, in square inches, of the board **not** covered by the two photographs?

    A. 25

    B. 50

    C. 142

    D. 192

26. Nathan subscribed to cable for five years. He paid a one-time registration fee of $100, and an additional $70 per month for the full five years. What is the total amount Nathan paid for his cable subscription for five years?

    E. $450

    F. $570

    G. $4,200

    H. $4,300

27. Lincoln bought 6 ears of corn for $0.50 each and 3 pounds of potatoes. The cost for these items, not including tax, was $6.99. What was the price per pound of the potatoes?

    A. $0.92

    B. $1.33

    C. $2.16

    D. $3.99

28. The width of a rectangle is one-half of its length. If the area of the rectangle is 18, what is its length?

    E. 3

    F. 4

    G. 5

    H. 6

29. A large circular clock with a circumference of 3π feet is hung on a rectangular wall that is 4 feet by 14 feet. What is the area, in square feet, of the wall **not** covered by the clock?

    A. $36 - \dfrac{3}{2}\pi$

    B. $56 - \dfrac{3}{2}\pi$

    C. $36 - \dfrac{9}{4}\pi$

    D. $56 - \dfrac{9}{4}\pi$

30. A box with a square base has a height that is half the width of the base. The length of the base is 30 centimeters. What is the volume of the box, in cubic centimeters?

    E. 6,750

    F. 13,500

    G. 27,000

    H. 108,000

31. A triangle has an area of 15 cm^2 and a base of 5 cm. If a circle is drawn with a diameter equal to the length of the triangle's height, what is the area of the circle, in square centimeters?

    A. 6π

    B. 9π

    C. 12π

    D. 36π

32. A rectangle has a length of 6 inches and an area of 18 inches. If the radius of a circle is equal to the width of the rectangle, what is the area of the circle, in square inches?

    E. $2\frac{1}{4}\pi$

    F. $4\frac{1}{4}\pi$

    G. 6π

    H. 9π

Answers and Explanations

Arithmetic

A. 3 apples : 4 oranges

B. 12 apples because 3 apples + 4 oranges = 7 pieces of fruit, which means the ratio of apples to fruit is 3:7. Set up a proportion and solve:

$$\frac{3}{7} = \frac{x}{28}$$
$$7x = 84$$
$$x = 12$$

C. $\dfrac{\text{part}}{\text{whole}} \times 100\% = \dfrac{35}{50} \times 100\% = \dfrac{70}{100} \times 100\% = 70\%$

D. 12 = 20% of x

$$12 = .2x$$
$$\frac{12}{.2} = \frac{.2x}{.2}$$
$$60 = x$$

E. Rate (speed) $= \dfrac{\text{Distance}}{\text{Time}} = \dfrac{80 \text{ miles}}{2 \text{ hours}}$
$$= 40 \text{ miles per hour}$$

F. Rate $= \dfrac{\text{Total \$ Earned}}{\text{Time}} = \dfrac{\$72}{8 \text{ hours}} = \$9 \text{ per hour}$

1. A

Subject: Arithmetic

Getting to the Answer: Since the original price of the stock is not given, use the Picking Numbers strategy. Picking 100 for percent problems simplifies the calculations.

Price of the stock = $100

$100 − ($100 × 0.20) = $100 − $20 = $80

$80 − ($80 × 0.25) = $80 − $20 = $60

$100 − $60 = $40

$\dfrac{40}{100} = 40\%$ Always divide the difference by the original number to find the percent change.

2. F

Subject: Arithmetic

Getting to the Answer: Solve this problem step by step. Put all the given information into a table and determine the unknown information.

	Memory Foam	Non-memory Foam	TOTAL
Extra firm	12%	20% − 12% = 8%	20%
Not extra firm	75% − 12% = 63%	80% − 63% = 17%	100% − 20% = 80%
TOTAL	75%	25%	100%

17% of the mattresses at Mattress Shop are not extra firm non-memory foam mattresses.

3. A

Subject: Arithmetic

Getting to the Answer: Let x represent the number of nickels, dimes, and quarters. Set up a proportion and solve for x:

$$\frac{1}{25} = \frac{12}{42 + x}$$
$$42 + x = 300$$
$$x = 258$$

4. G

Subject: Arithmetic

Getting to the Answer: Calculate the number of minutes each student spent presenting. Astrid spent 12 × 3 = 36 minutes, Steven spent 12 × 8 = 96 minutes, and Anna spent 12 × 4 = 48 minutes. The total time is 36 + 96 + 48 = 180 minutes.

5. D

Subject: Arithmetic

Getting to the Answer: Let r represent the number of items returned. Set up a proportion and solve for r.

$$\frac{r}{441} = \frac{2}{21}$$
$$21r = 882$$
$$r = 42$$

6. G

Subject: Arithmetic

Getting to the Answer: First, find 5% of 0.2 millimeters and then determine the least thickness. 5% of 0.2 millimeters equals 0.01 millimeters. Thus, the least thickness of the paper towel would be 0.2 − 0.01 = 0.19 millimeters.

7. C

Subject: Arithmetic

Getting to the Answer: Find the difference between the starting temperature and final temperature: 375°F − 195°F = 180°F. Use the rate of 10° per minute to calculate the number of minutes.

$$180° \times \frac{1\,\text{min}}{10°} = 18\,\text{min}$$

Algebra

A. $M = 3A$

B. $O = B + 5$

C. $E = 3F$

D. $N = 4M + 45$

E. $C = 1T + 5$

F. $V = 22{,}500 − 2{,}000y$

8. H

Subject: Algebra

Getting to the Answer: Assign a variable for Anna's age and write Marco's age as an expression with that variable. Then pick a number for Anna's age and solve for Marco's age 5 years ago.

Anna's age $= y$

Marco's age $= y − 3$

Let $y = 20$

Marco's age $= 20 − 3 = 17$

Marco's age 5 years ago $= 17 − 5 = 12$

Find the answer choice that matches.

(E) $y − 2 = 20 − 2 = 18$. Eliminate it.

(F) $y − 3 = 20 − 3 = 17$. Eliminate it.

(G) $y − 5 = 20 − 5 = 15$. Eliminate it.

(H) $y − 8 = 20 − 8 = 12$. This is the answer.

9. C

Subject: Algebra

Getting to the Answer: Let $C =$ Cade's age now and let $T =$ Taylor's age now.

$T + 3 = 15$ so $T = 12$ (Taylor's age now)

$C = 2T$

$C = 2(12) = 24$ (Cade's age now)

$C − 2 = 24 − 2 = 22$ (Cade's age now)

10. H

Subject: Algebra

Getting to the Answer: Translate "Christopher is at least 7 years younger than Lillian": $c \leq l − 7$.

Rewrite the inequality to find the match among the answer choices: $7 + c \leq l$.

11. B

Subject: Algebra

Getting to the Answer: First, determine how many gallons are in the tank when a quarter full. Since a full tank is 16 gallons, one-quarter of 16 is 4. Then determine the number of gallons initially in the tank: $g − 2 = 4$, so $g = 6$.

12. E

Subject: Algebra

Getting to the Answer: Let d represent the number of gigabytes of data Levi used. Levi's monthly charges were $\$20 + \$6d$. Set Levi's charges equal to Jayden's charges and solve for d:

$$\$20 + \$6d = \$44$$
$$\$6d = \$24$$
$$d = 4$$

Levi used 4 gigabytes of data.

13. D

Subject: Algebra

Getting to the Answer: First, determine the number of months in four years. Since there are 12 months in a year, there are 12 × 4 = 48 months in four years. Write an expression to calculate the total amount Dylan paid: $250 + $875(48) = $42,250.

14. F

Subject: Algebra

Getting to the Answer: First, calculate the profit Addison makes from one guitar. Each guitar costs Addison $290 to build, and she sells the guitar for $510. Thus, her profit equals the selling price minus the cost: $510 − $290 = $220. If Addison builds and sells 6 guitars in a month, her initial profit is 6 × $220 = $1,320. However, she has monthly expenses of $360, so her final profit is $1,320 − $360 = $960.

15. B

Subject: Algebra

Getting to the Answer: First, assign a variable for the price per pound of salmon, s. Then set up an equation for the total cost.

$$3(\$1.29) + 2s = \$24.95$$
$$\$3.87 + 2s = \$24.95$$
$$2s = \$21.08$$
$$s = \$10.54$$

16. F

Subject: Algebra

Getting to the Answer: Set up an inequality:

$$\$0.60x \le \$5.40$$
$$x \le 9$$

Thus, 9 lemons would cost $5.40, so 8 is the greatest number of individual lemons that Skylar could buy that would be less expensive than the bag.

Geometry

A. $w = 4, l = 8$, Area $= 4 \times 8 = 32$

B.   Draw an isosceles triangle with A at the apex. Side AB = side AC = 7, and base BC = 3. ∠ACB must be equal to ∠CBA (78°), since they are opposite equal sides.
∠CAB = 180° − 78° − 78° = 24°

C.   Draw a regular hexagon. Label the points A … F. Since she walks over 725 bridges, divide by 6 to find how many times she goes all the way around the hexagon.

$$\frac{725}{6} = 120 \text{ R5}$$

Her final trip around will take her over 5 bridges. Jenny stops at bridge F.

17. B

Subject: Geometry

Getting to the Answer: Use the circumference of the cup to first find the radius of the cup.

$$C = 2\pi r$$
$$2\pi r = 2\pi r$$
$$1 = r$$

Then use the radius to calculate the area of the bottom of the cup: $A = \pi r^2 = \pi(1)^2 = \pi$ sq in.

Next use the radius of the coaster to calculate the area of the coaster: $A = \pi(2)^2 = 4\pi$ sq in.

Subtract the area of the bottom of the cup from the area of the coaster: $4\pi − \pi = 3\pi$ sq in.

18. G

Subject: Geometry

Getting to the Answer: First, use the height of the chest to find the length and width of the base. Then use the dimensions to calculate the volume.

The height is one-half the length of the base. Since the height is 10 inches, the length of the base is 2 × 10 = 20 inches. The length is four times the width of the base, so the width is 20 ÷ 4 = 5 inches.

Thus, the volume of the chest is $l \times w \times h = 20 \times 5 \times 10 = 1,000$ in³.

19. C

Subject: Geometry

Getting to the Answer: First, calculate the height of the larger triangle. If the enlarged base is 9, the triangle tripled in size. Multiply 4×3 to find the new height: 12. Then, calculate the area of the enlarged triangle.

$$A = \frac{1}{2}bh = \frac{1}{2}(9)(12) = 54 \text{ cm}^2$$

20. E

Subject: Geometry

Getting to the Answer: The length of the rope is the greatest common factor (GCF) of 39 and 45. The factors of 39 are 1, 3, 13, and 39. The factors of 45 are 1, 3, 5, 9, 15, and 45. The GCF is 3. The rope is 3 yards long.

Note that you could also determine the GCF from the prime factors. The prime factorization of 39 is 3×13, and the prime factorization of 45 is $3 \times 3 \times 5$. The prime factor that 39 and 45 have in common is 3, so the GCF is 3.

21. C

Subject: Geometry

Getting to the Answer: Let $5x$ represent the length and $3x$ represent the width. The perimeter is $2(5x) + 2(3x) = 32$

$$10x + 6x = 32$$
$$16x = 32$$
$$x = 2$$

So, the sides of the rectangle are $5 \times 2 = 10$ and $3 \times 2 = 6$.

The area of the rectangle is $10 \times 6 = 60$ sq in.

Statistics and Probability

A. $\frac{21.5}{5} = 4.3$

B. 4.2

C. 4.0

D. 0.8

E. $\frac{1}{6}$

F. $\frac{2}{6} = \frac{1}{3}$

G. $1 - \frac{1}{3} = \frac{2}{3}$

22. E

Subject: Statistics and Probability

Getting to the Answer: Use the average formula to calculate the mean score of the first 5 quizzes. Rishi scored a mean of 88 points per quiz on the first 4 quizzes, so he earned a total of $4 \times 88 = 352$ points. Thus, the sum of the 5 quizzes is $352 + 93 = 445$, and the mean score of the 5 games is Average $= \frac{445}{5} = 89$.

23. B

Subject: Statistics and Probability

Getting to the Answer: First, determine the total cost of the 6 pairs of pants. Then use the average formula, Average $= \frac{\text{Sum}}{\text{Number of Items}}$, to calculate the mean price for 2 pairs of shoes.

The total cost of the 5 pairs of pants is $5 \times \$24 = \$120$. Therefore, the mean price of 2 pairs of shoes is $\frac{\$120}{2} = \$60$.

24. G

Subject: Statistics and Probability

Getting to the Answer: You need to put the numbers in sequential order and determine which is the middle number: 103, 112, 127, 178, 196, 217, 271.

The middle number is 178.

25. D

Subject: Statistics and Probability

Getting to the Answer: You can always use Backsolving if you cannot find the answer algebraically. Use the average formula to find the sum: $\frac{(\text{Jake} + \text{Ken} + \text{Larry})}{3} = 60$. So, Jake + Ken + Larry = 180.

If Jake and Ken each are 50, then

$$50 + 50 + \text{Larry} = 180$$
$$100 + \text{Larry} = 180$$
$$\text{Larry} = 80$$

26. H

Subject: Statistics and Probability

Getting to the Answer: To find the range, subtract the lowest temperature from the highest temperature. Since 3° below zero is $-3°$, the range is $34° - (-3°) = 37°$.

27. C

Subject: Statistics and Probability

Getting to the Answer: Use the probability formula:

$\text{Probability} = \frac{\text{Number of Desired Outcomes}}{\text{Number of Possible Outcomes}}$. The non-comic books are all of the joke and space books, so there are eight books that are not comic books out of a total of 15 books.

$\text{Probability} = \frac{8}{15}$.

28. E

Subject: Statistics and Probability

Getting to the Answer: The total number of scarves is $2 + 7 + 6 + 3 = 18$. The number of scarves that are not purple are $2 + 6 + 3 = 11$.

The probability of the first scarf not being purple is $\frac{11}{18}$. Now there are 10 scarves left that are not purple. The probability of the second scarf not being purple is $\frac{10}{17}$. Multiply these two probabilities to get

$\frac{11}{18} \times \frac{10}{17} = \frac{11 \times 10}{18 \times 17} = \frac{11 \times 5}{9 \times 17} = \frac{55}{153}$.

Practice Set

1. 45

Subject: Arithmetic

Getting to the Answer: Only use the information that is relevant to the question! You are asked how many ounces of fruit are needed for the trail mix, and you are given an amount of granola. The amount of nuts is not needed, so don't use it: The ratio of granola to fruits is 3:5 and there are 27 ounces of granola, so the following proportion can be written:

$$\frac{3}{5} = \frac{27}{x}$$

Cross multiplication gives $3x = 135$, so $x = 45$. Grid in **45**.

2. 10

Subject: Algebra

Getting to the Answer: Translate the given information into an equation using m for Mark's age and j for Jessica's age. Plug in Mark's age, $m = 25$, and solve for Jessica's age, j.

$$m = 3j - 5$$
$$(25) = 3j - 5$$
$$30 = 3j$$
$$10 = j$$

Since Jessica's age is 10, grid in **10**.

3. 2.25

Subject: Arithmetic

Getting to the Answer: Start by computing the total number of pieces that the five of them ate: $3 + 4 + 4 + 5 + 2 = 18$ slices. There are 8 slices in an entire pizza, so they ate 2 pizzas, with 2 slices left over. Two slices is one quarter of a pizza, so they ate $2\frac{1}{4}$ pizzas, or 2.25 pizzas. Grid in **2.25**.

4. 38

Subject: Algebra

Getting to the Answer: Begin by translating the question to algebra. Let r represent the number of items that Robin collected. If Bruce collected 10 less than four times this number, Bruce collected $4r - 10$ items. Since together they collected 50 items, you can create the equation $r + (4r - 10) = 50 \Rightarrow 5r - 10 = 50$. Adding 10 to both sides and dividing by 5 gives $r = 12$. However, you aren't done yet! The question asks you for the number of items that Bruce collected, which is $4(12) - 10 = 48 - 10 = 38$. Grid in **38**.

5. 64

Subject: Statistics and Probability

Getting to the Answer: Use the average formula to calculate the mean bacterial colony count of the first 4 petri dishes. The mean colony count per petri dish for the first 3 petri dishes was 67 points, so there was a total of $3 \times 67 = 201$ colonies. Thus, the sum of the colonies on the 4 petri dishes is $201 + 55 = 256$, and the mean colony count of the first 4 petri dishes is: average $= \frac{256}{4} = 64$. Grid in **64**.

6. 1.68

Subject: Statistics and Probability

Getting to the Answer: First, determine the total cost of the 3 boxes of nails. Then use the average formula, Average $= \frac{\text{Sum}}{\text{Number of Items}}$, to calculate the mean price for 5 boxes of screws.

The total cost of the 3 boxes of nails is $3 \times \$2.80 = \$8.40$. Therefore, the mean price of 5 boxes of screws is $\frac{\$8.40}{5} = \$1.68$. Grid in **1.68**.

7. 12.5

Subject: Algebra

Getting to the Answer: You know that 3 cartons of orange juice cost $15. That means that one carton of orange juice costs $5. If there are 40 ounces of orange juice in a carton, then the cost per ounce would be $5 divided by 40. This operation yields 0.125. Since the question asks for the cost per ounce in cents, convert this value to cents by multiplying by 100. This gives 12.5, so grid in **12.5**.

8. 512

Subject: Geometry

Getting to the Answer: First, use the width of the base to find the length and height of the wagon. Then use the dimensions to calculate the volume.

Since the length is 4 times the width, it is $4 \times 8 = 32$ inches. The height is one-fourth the width or $\frac{1}{4} \times 8 = 2$ inches. Thus, the volume of the wagon is $l \times w \times h = 32 \times 8 \times 2 = 512$ cu in. Grid in **512**.

9. 14

Subject: Geometry

Getting to the Answer: The length of the shoe is the greatest common factor (GCF) of 98 and 70. The factors of 98 are 1, 2, 7, 14, 49, and 98. The factors of 70 are 1, 2, 5, 7, 10, 14, 35, and 70. The GCF is 14. The shoe is 14 inches long.

Note that you could also determine the GCF from the prime factors. The prime factorization of 98 is $2 \times 7 \times 7$, and the prime factorization of 70 is $2 \times 5 \times 7$. The prime factors that 98 and 70 have in common are 2 and 7, so the GCF is $2 \times 7 = 14$. Grid in **14**.

10. 12

Subject: Algebra

Getting to the Answer: Set up an inequality:

$$\$0.69t \geq \$7.59$$
$$t \geq 11$$

Thus, 11 tomatoes would cost $7.59, so 12 is the smallest number of tomatoes that would make buying a case of tomatoes less expensive than buying individual tomatoes. Grid in **12**.

11. A

Subject: Algebra

Getting to the Answer: Translate the given information into math. Meghan has $100 more than Andrew, so $m = a + 100$. After spending $20, Meghan has five times as much money as Andrew, so $m - 20 = 5a$. The question is asking you to find a, so substitute $a + 100$ into the second equation for m, and solve for a.

$$m - 20 = 5a$$
$$(a + 100) - 20 = 5a$$
$$80 = 4a$$
$$a = 20$$

Andrew has $20, so **(A)** is correct.

12. G

Subject: Arithmetic

Getting to the Answer: Let 100 be the original price.

$$100 - 40\% = 100 - (100 \times 0.40) = 100 - 40 = 60$$
$$60 - 25\% = 60 - (60 \times 0.25) = 60 - 15 = 45$$
$$\frac{(100 - 45)}{100} = \frac{55}{100} = 55\%$$

13. B

Subject: Arithmetic

Getting to the Answer: Set up a ratio and solve for the unknown, x.

$$\frac{30}{100} = \frac{x}{60}$$
$$100x = 1,800$$
$$x = 18$$

14. G

Subject: Arithmetic

Getting to the Answer: Use the information given in the question to form a proportion. You know that the ratio of red to blue dominoes is 4:7 and there are 42 blue dominoes. This gives a proportion that can be used to solve for the number of red dominoes:

$$\frac{4}{7} = \frac{x}{42}$$
$$7x = 168$$
$$x = 24$$

There are 24 red dominoes, but don't select **(E)**! The question asks you for the number of total dominoes, which is $42 + 24 = 66$, **(G)**.

15. D

Subject: Arithmetic

Getting to the Answer: First, find 0.1% of 0.75 centimeters and then determine the greatest thickness. 0.1% of 0.75 centimeters equals 0.00075 centimeters. Thus, the greatest thickness of the tablet would be $0.75 + 0.00075 = 0.75075$ centimeters, **(D)**.

16. F

Subject: Arithmetic

Getting to the Answer: Let a represent the larger group and write an expression.

$$a + \frac{2}{3}a = 30$$
$$\frac{3}{3}a + \frac{2}{3}a = 30$$
$$\frac{5}{3}a = 30$$
$$a = 30\left(\frac{3}{5}\right)$$
$$a = 18$$

Since the larger group is a, the smaller group is $\frac{2}{3}(18) = 12$. Note that this is a great question for the Kaplan Backsolving strategy.

17. D

Subject: Arithmetic

Getting to the Answer: Set up proportions to determine the number of fish each caught in 1 hour.

Chad

$$\frac{10}{40} = \frac{c}{60}$$
$$600 = 40c$$
$$15 = c$$

Stephanie

$$\frac{6}{30} = \frac{s}{60}$$
$$360 = 30s$$
$$12 = s$$

Manny

$$\frac{15}{90} = \frac{m}{60}$$
$$900 = 90m$$
$$10 = m$$

Together, they caught $15 + 12 + 10 = 37$ fish in one hour, **(D)**.

18. F

Subject: Arithmetic

Getting to the Answer: Let p represent the total cost of Cynthia's purchase. Set up a proportion and solve for p.

$$\frac{5}{75} = \frac{15}{p}$$
$$5p = 1,125$$
$$p = 225$$

19. B

Subject: Statistics and Probability

Getting to the Answer: You need to put the numbers in sequential order and determine which is the middle number: 2, 2, 4, 5, 6.

The middle number is 4, **(B)**.

20. G

Subject: Statistics and Probability

Getting to the Answer: The total number of items in the bin is $5 + 6 + 3 + 12 = 26$. The number of items that are not jump ropes is $5 + 3 + 12 = 20$.

The probability of the first item not being a jump rope is $\frac{20}{26} = \frac{10}{13}$. Now there are 19 items left that are not jump ropes. The probability of the second item not being a jump rope is $\frac{19}{25}$. Multiply these two probabilities to get

$$\frac{10}{13} \times \frac{19}{25} = \frac{10 \times 19}{13 \times 25} = \frac{2 \times 19}{13 \times 5} = \frac{38}{65}, \textbf{(G)}.$$

21. C

Subject: Statistics and Probability

Getting to the Answer: You need to put the numbers in sequential order and determine which is the middle number: 22, 39, 40, 48, 53, 85, 90.

The middle number is 48, **(C)**.

22. E

Subject: Statistics and Probability

Getting to the Answer: The range is the difference between the highest and lowest values. Since the minimum is $\frac{3}{32}$ inches and the maximum is $\frac{1}{8}$ inches, the range is $\frac{1}{8} - \frac{3}{32} = \frac{1}{32}$ inches.

23. C

Subject: Algebra

Getting to the Answer: Assign a variable to John's age. Then, write an expression for Sherry's and Ron's ages in terms of John's age if John's age $= J$.

Sherry's age $= 2J - 4$

Ron's age $= (2J - 4) + 3$

Simplifying Ron's age produces $2J - 1$, **(C)**.

24. G

Subject: Statistics and Probability

Getting to the Answer: Use the average formula to calculate the average height of the group:

$$\text{Average} = \frac{(\text{total height of the group})}{5}$$
$$67 = \frac{(\text{total height of the group})}{5}$$
$$335 = \text{total height of the group}$$

25. C

Subject: Geometry

Getting to the Answer: Use the perimeter of one photograph to first find the side length of the square. Then use the side length to calculate the area of one photograph. Multiply by 2 to find the area of the two photographs.

$$P = 4s$$
$$20 = 4s$$
$$5 = s$$

$A = s^2 = 5^2 = 25$ sq in.

Area of the two photographs $= 2 \times 25 = 50$ sq in.

Next, use the dimensions of the board to find its area.

$A = l \times w = 12 \times 16 = 192$ sq in.

Subtract the area of the two photographs from the area of the board:

$192 - 50 = 142$ sq in.

26. H

Subject: Algebra

Getting to the Answer: First, determine the number of months in five years. Since there are 12 months in a year, there are $12 \times 5 = 60$ months in five years. Write an expression to calculate the total amount Nathan paid: $100 + \$70(60) = \$4,300$, **(H)**.

27. B

Subject: Algebra

Getting to the Answer: First, assign a variable for the price per pound of potatoes, p. Then set up an equation for the total cost:

$$6(\$0.50) + 3p = \$6.99$$
$$\$3.00 + 3p = \$6.99$$
$$3p = \$3.99$$
$$p = \$1.33$$

28. H

Subject: Geometry

Getting to the Answer: Write width in terms of length. Plug that into the area formula, along with the given area, to solve for length.

$$\text{Area} = \text{Length} \times \text{Width}$$
$$\text{Width} = \tfrac{1}{2} \text{ length}$$
$$\text{Area} = \text{length} \times \tfrac{1}{2} \text{ length}$$
$$18 = \tfrac{1}{2} \text{ length} \times \text{length}$$
$$36 = \text{length}^2$$
$$6 = \text{length}$$

29. D

Subject: Geometry

Getting to the Answer: Use the circumference of the clock to first find the radius of the clock. Then use the radius to calculate the area.

$$C = 2\pi r$$
$$3\pi = 2\pi r$$
$$\frac{3}{2} = r$$

$$A = \pi r^2 = \pi \left(\frac{3}{2}\right)^2 = \frac{9}{4}\pi \text{ sq ft.}$$

Next use the dimensions of the wall to find its area:
$A = l \times w = 4 \times 14 = 56$ sq ft.

Subtract the area of the clock from the area of the wall:
$56 - \frac{9}{4}\pi$ sq ft. The correct answer is **(D)**.

30. F

Subject: Geometry

Getting to the Answer: First, use the length of the base to find the width and height of the box. Then use the dimensions to calculate the volume.

Since the base is square, the width equals the length. The length of the base is 30 cm, so the width of the base is also 30 cm. The height is half the width: $\frac{1}{2} \times 30 = 15$ cm.

Thus, the volume of the box is $l \times w \times h = 30 \times 30 \times 15 = 13,500$ cu cm. The correct answer is **(F)**.

31. B

Subject: Geometry

Getting to the Answer: Because the triangle has an area of 15, $15 = \frac{1}{2} \times 5 \times$ height. Therefore, height $= 6$. Because the diameter is equal to the height of the triangle, the radius is equal to half of that. $\left[\left(\frac{1}{2}(6) = 3\right)\right]$ and its area is $\pi r^2 = \pi 3^2 = 9\pi$ cm^2.

32. H

Subject: Geometry

Getting to the Answer: A rectangle with an area of 18 and a length of 6 has a width $= \frac{18}{6} = 3$. A circle with a radius of 3 has an area $= \pi r^2 = \pi 3^2 = 9\pi$ sq in.

Math

CHAPTER 18

Advanced Math

CHAPTER OBJECTIVES

By the end of this chapter, you will be able to:

- Draw inferences about data presented in a variety of graphical formats
- Draw inferences about surveys and data samples

Advanced Math

Charts and Data Interpretation

To excel at data interpretation, you must recognize the many ways that charts communicate information. The most common types of charts and graphs include pie charts, line graphs, bar graphs, and pictographs.

Favorite Color Distribution

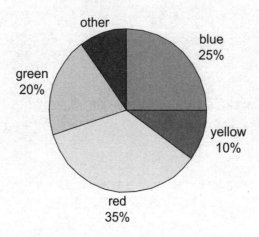

A. What conclusions can you draw from the circle graph above?

_____

B. What's missing from the circle graph?

_____

C. If 200 people were surveyed, how many more people picked red than picked yellow as their favorite color?

_____

SHSAT EXPERT NOTE

Before working on data interpretation questions, briefly study the graph, table, or chart and determine what it represents and what patterns are apparent in the data.

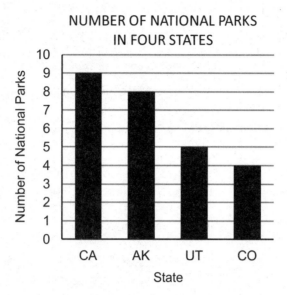

NUMBER OF NATIONAL PARKS
IN FOUR STATES

1. The graph above shows the number of national parks for four states. CA has 10 million visitors per park per year, and AK has 2.8 million visitors per park per year. UT and CO each have 4.5 million visitors per park per year. Which of the states has the **least** number of national park visitors per year?

   A. CA

   B. AK

   C. UT

   D. CO

SHSAT EXPERT NOTE

When tackling charts and graphs, first identify the title and what the chart represents. Next, determine what the *x*-axis represents and what the *y*-axis represents. Your success will be determined by your ability to keep track of different pieces of information.

Data Tables

Questions with data tables usually ask about percent, average, range, and probability.

A **frequency distribution** shows the number of times each value appears in the data set.

- To find the mean, multiply each value by the number of times it occurs, add all these products, then divide by the total number of values.
- To find the median, add the frequencies to find the number of values, then determine which group the middle value falls into.

Practice

Value	Frequency
4	5
5	2
6	4
7	4
8	6

A. What is the mean of the data in the table above?

_____

B. What is the median of the data in the table above?

_____

SHSAT EXPERT NOTE

The mean is the average of the values in a data set. The median is the value in the middle when the terms are arranged in order. The mode is the value that occurs most frequently in the data set. The range of a data set is the difference between the largest and smallest values in the set.

Number of Framed Artworks	Percent of Rooms
1	12%
2	60%
3	25%
4 or more	3%

2. A study reported the number of framed artworks in a hotel room. The table above shows the percent distribution for 500 rooms. How many of the 500 rooms had at **least** 2 framed artworks?

    E. 60
    F. 140
    G. 300
    H. 440

Number of Notebooks	Number of Backpacks
0	8
1	10
2	25
3	11
4	3
5	3

3. The table above shows the number of notebooks that students on campus carried in their backpacks. What is the mean number of notebooks per backpack?

    A. 1
    B. 2
    C. 3
    D. 4

Team	Lowest Score	Range
Portal	1,850	98
J & J	1,733	101
Danger	1,910	68
Bots	1,512	215

4. Four teams participated at a cybersecurity competition. The table above shows the lowest score and the range of scores for each team. What is the overall range of all the scores for all four teams?

   E. 147

   F. 215

   G. 398

   H. 466

Number of Pieces	Color on Piece
6	blue
9	green
4	white
2	yellow
3	purple

5. A box contains jigsaw pieces. Using the table above, which color has exactly a 1 in 6 chance of being selected at random from the box?

   A. blue

   B. green

   C. white

   D. purple

Surveys with Two Responses

For questions that involve a survey with two responses (A and B), the total number surveyed is the number of responses for A plus the number of responses for B minus the number of responses for A and B plus the number of responses for neither A nor B. In other words, the total is the union minus the intersection.

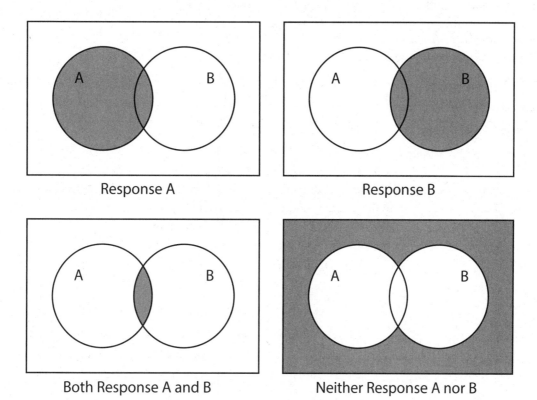

Response A

Response B

Both Response A and B

Neither Response A nor B

A survey polled students to determine whether they liked the summer or winter season. Below are the results of the survey:

- 50 students answered summer.
- 40 students answered winter.
- 15 students said both summer and winter.
- 20 students said neither summer nor winter.

A. How many students answered summer and winter?

_____

B. How many students answered summer or winter?

_____

C. How many students were surveyed?

_____

A survey polled customers to determine what type of detergent they use. The following statements are the results of the survey.

- 15 customers use liquid detergent.
- 25 customers use detergent pods.
- 4 customers use both liquid detergent and detergent pods.
- 2 customers use neither liquid detergent nor detergent pods.

6. How many customers were surveyed?

    E. 38

    F. 40

    G. 42

    H. 46

7. At a restaurant, a survey asked two "yes" or "no" questions. Of the 290 diners who responded to the survey, 220 answered "yes" to the first question, and 150 answered "yes" to the second question. What is the **least** possible number of diners who answered "yes" to both questions?

    A. 50

    B. 60

    C. 70

    D. 80

Practice Set

Multiple-Choice Questions

For test-like practice, give yourself 33 minutes (an average of 1.5 minutes per question) to complete this question set. After you're done, be sure to study the explanations, even for questions you answered correctly. They can be found at the end of this chapter.

DIRECTIONS: Answer each question, selecting the best answer available.

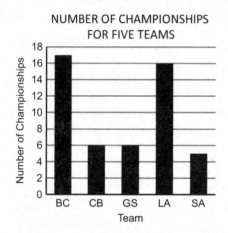

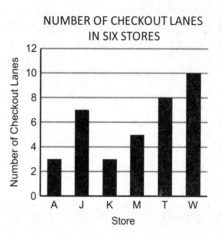

1. The graph above shows the number of championships for five teams. BC had 18,600 attendees per game. CB and SA each had 20,000 attendees per game. GS has 16,500 attendees per game, and LA had 17,900 attendees per game. Which of the teams has the **least** number of total championship game attendees?

    A. CB
    B. GS
    C. LA
    D. SA

2. The graph above shows the number of checkout lanes for six stores. A and J had 600 customers per checkout lane per day. K had 800 customers per checkout lane per day. M and W had 325 customers per checkout lane per day, and T had 490 customers per checkout lane per day. Which of the stores has the **greatest** number of total customers per day?

    E. J
    F. M
    G. T
    H. W

Number of Bicycles	Percent of Bike Racks
1	3%
2	5%
3	18%
4	29%
5 or more	45%

Number of Calories Per Serving	Number of Entrees
200	2
250	4
300	1
350	5

3. The number of bicycles parked in bike racks on a college campus was recorded. The table above shows the percent distribution for 50 bike racks. How many of the 50 bike racks had at **least** 4 parked bicycles?

A. 15

B. 23

C. 28

D. 37

5. The cafeteria serves 12 entrees for lunch. The table above shows the number of entrees that have 200, 250, 300, and 350 calories per serving. What is the mean number of calories per entree?

A. 91.7

B. 170.5

C. 275

D. 287.5

Weight (grams)	Number of Apples
70	7
80	17
90	10
100	6

Driver	Highest Tip	Range
Carlos	$10	$8
Alec	$5	$1
Miles	$15	$12

4. What is the mean weight of apples in the table above?

E. 80

F. 81.25

G. 83.75

H. 85

6. Three drivers received tips throughout the day. The table above shows the highest tip and the range of tips for each driver. What is the overall range of all the tips for all three drivers?

E. $10

F. $11

G. $13

H. $14

Combo Number	Number of Times Ordered
#1	65
#2	39
#3	60
#4	31
#5	45

7. The table above shows the number of times a combo on the menu was ordered in a day. What is the probability of a customer ordering combo #3 ?

   A. 15%
   B. 20%
   C. 25%
   D. 30%

Number of Phone Calls	Number of Classmates
0	7
1	11
2	9
3 or more	23

8. Karen conducted a survey to determine the number of phone calls her classmates made a day. The results are shown in the table above. What is the probability that a classmate who participated in the survey made at **most** 1 phone call per day?

   E. $\frac{11}{50}$
   F. $\frac{9}{25}$
   G. $\frac{16}{25}$
   H. $\frac{39}{50}$

9. A survey recorded whether shoppers used paper or plastic bags. The following statements are the results of the survey.

   - 41 shoppers used paper bags.
   - 77 shoppers used plastic bags.
   - 23 shoppers used both paper and plastic bags.
   - 19 shoppers used neither paper nor plastic bags.

   How many customers were surveyed?

   A. 114
   B. 118
   C. 137
   D. 160

10. At a doctor's office, patients were asked two "yes" or "no" questions. Of the 216 patients who responded to the questions, 160 answered "yes" to the first question, and 104 answered "yes" to the second question. What is the **least** possible number of patients who answered "yes" to both questions?

    E. 22
    F. 34
    G. 48
    H. 64

Number of Restrooms	Percent of Floors
1	2%
2	28%
3	8%
4	52%
5 or more	10%

Length (inches)	Number of Salmon
55	5
56	5
57	3
58	1

11. The number of restrooms on each floor of a skyscraper was recorded. The table above shows the percent distribution for 60 floors. How many of the 60 floors had at **least** 3 restrooms?

A. 5

B. 18

C. 31

D. 42

13. What is the mean length of salmon in the table above, in inches?

A. 54

B. 54.5

C. 56

D. 56.5

12. A career fair surveyed 600 attendees to determine their major. Of the attendees, 350 were engineering majors, and 275 were liberal arts majors. Of the attendees, 75 double majored in engineering and liberal arts. How many attendees had a major other than engineering and liberal arts?

E. 10

F. 25

G. 50

H. 75

Number of Packages per Week	Number of Houses
0	0
1	10
2	15
3	10

14. The table above shows the number of packages delivered per week to houses in a residential neighborhood. What is the mean number of packages per house per week?

E. 0

F. 1

G. 2

H. 3

Number of Spectators	Number of Games
62	4
65	2
71	4
74	1
80	7
83	0

Computer	Number of Times Used
#1	19
#2	22
#3	11
#4	28

15. The table above shows the number of spectators that attended lacrosse games during the season. What is the mean number of spectators per game?

   A. 71
   B. 72
   C. 73
   D. 74

17. The table above shows the number of times a computer was used at the library in a day. What is the probability of a person using computer #2 ?

   A. 13.75%
   B. 23.75%
   C. 27.5%
   D. 35%

Racer	Fastest Lap Time (seconds)	Range
Dana	91	4
Anthony	87	12
Katie	74	6

Number of Credit Cards	Number of People
0	9
1	33
2	15
3 or more	3

16. Three racers raced around a track five times. The table above shows the fastest lap time and the range of times for each racer. What is the overall range of all the times for all three racers?

   E. 8
   F. 13
   G. 23
   H. 25

18. Anya conducted a survey to determine the number of credit cards customers carried. The results are shown in the table above. What is the probability that a person who participated in the survey carried at least 2 credit cards?

   E. $\frac{1}{4}$
   F. $\frac{3}{10}$
   G. $\frac{7}{10}$
   H. $\frac{3}{4}$

Number of Postage Stamps	Picture on Postage Stamp
18	flag
6	flower
6	animal
4	star
2	bell

19. A sheet contains postage stamps. Based on the table above, which postage stamp picture has exactly a 1 in 9 chance of being selected at random from the sheet?

A. flag

B. flower

C. star

D. bell

20. A survey recorded whether people folded or hung their clothes. The following statements are the results of the survey:

- 85 people folded their clothes.
- 56 people hung their clothes.
- 40 people both folded and hung their clothes.
- 2 people neither folded nor hung their clothes.

How many people were surveyed?

E. 103

F. 143

G. 156

H. 183

21. At a party, guests were asked two "true" or "false" questions. Of the 300 guests who responded to the questions, 270 answered "true" to the first question, and 240 answered "true" to the second question. What is the least possible number of guests who answered "true" to both questions?

A. 30

B. 60

C. 210

D. 255

22. A class was surveyed to determine what vegetables students like. The results indicated that 12 students like broccoli, 10 students like cauliflower, and 14 students like neither. If there are 30 students in the class, how many students like both broccoli and cauliflower?

E. 2

F. 4

G. 6

H. 8

Answers and Explanations

Charts and Data Interpretation

A. The greatest number of people chose red, then blue, then green.

B. No percentage given for "other."

C. First, find how many people picked red and yellow if 200 people were surveyed. $200 \times 0.35 = 70$ picked red; $200 \times 0.10 = 20$ picked yellow. Then subtract $70 - 20 = 50$ more picked red.

1. D

Subject: Statistics and Probability

Getting to the Answer: The question asks for the state with the least number of national park visitors a year, so you only need to perform calculations for UT and CO, which have a smaller number of visitors than CA and AK. The bar graph shows UT has 5 national parks, and CO has 4 national parks. Thus, UT has $5 \times 4.5 = 22.5$ million visitors a year, and CO has $4 \times 4.5 = 18$ million visitors a year. CO has the least number of national park visitors a year.

Data Tables

A. The sum of the products is $4(5) + 5(2) + 6(4) + 7(4) + 8(6) = 20 + 10 + 24 + 28 + 48 = 130$. The number of data points is $5 + 2 + 4 + 4 + 6 = 21$. Now divide: the mean is $\frac{130}{21} \approx 6.2$.

B. Since there are 21 values, the 11th value is the median. The 8th through 11th values are all 6, so the median is 6.

2. H

Subject: Arithmetic

Getting to the Answer: Add the percentage of rooms that have 2, 3, and 4 or more framed artworks: $60\% + 25\% + 3\% = 88\%$.

Multiply that percentage by the total number of rooms to calculate the number of rooms that had at least 2 framed artworks: $500 \times 0.88 = 440$ rooms.

Alternatively, you could find the number of rooms with 1 framed artwork and then subtract it from the total: $500 - 0.12(500) = 440$.

3. B

Subject: Statistics and Probability

Getting to the Answer: First, determine the total number of notebooks by multiplying the number of notebooks by the number of students.

Number of Notebooks	Number of Backpacks	Total Number of Notebooks
0	8	0
1	10	10
2	25	50
3	11	33
4	3	12
5	3	15
		120

Then add to get the total number of notebooks. To calculate the mean, divide the total number of notebooks by the number of backpacks: average $= \frac{120}{60} = 2$. The mean number of notebooks per backpack is 2.

4. H

Subject: Arithmetic

Getting to the Answer: First calculate the highest score for each team by adding the range to the lowest score:

Portal: $1,850 + 98 = 1,948$

J & J: $1,733 + 101 = 1,834$

Danger: $1,910 + 68 = 1,978$

Bots: $1,512 + 215 = 1,727$

The overall lowest score is 1,512, and the overall highest score is 1,978. Therefore, the overall range of all the scores is $1,978 - 1,512 = 466$.

5. C

Subject: Statistics and Probability

Getting to the Answer: First determine the total number of jigsaw pieces in the box: $6 + 9 + 2 + 4 + 2 + 3 = 24$.

Then set up a proportion to find which color has exactly a 1 in 6 chance of being picked:

$$\frac{x}{24} = \frac{1}{6}$$
$$6x = 24$$
$$x = 4$$

There are 4 white pieces in the box, so a white piece has a 1 in 6 chance of being randomly selected.

Surveys with Two Responses

    A. 15
    B. $50 + 40 = 90$
    C. $50 + 40 - 15 + 20 = 95$

6. E

Subject: Statistics and Probability

Getting to the Answer: Let $x =$ the number of customers who only use liquid detergent. Let $y =$ the number of customers who only use detergent pods. Use the given information to calculate x and y: There are 15 customers who use liquid detergent, 4 of whom use both liquid detergent and detergent pods. So, $x = 15 - 4 = 11$. There are 25 customers who use detergent pods, 4 of whom use both liquid detergent and detergent pods. So, $y = 25 - 4 = 21$.

The total number of customers surveyed is the number of customers who only use liquid detergent (11) plus the number of customers who only use detergent pods (21) plus the number of customers who use both (4) plus the number of customers who use neither (2): $11 + 21 + 4 + 2 = 38$.

7. D

Subject: Geometry

Getting to the Answer: Seventy ($290 - 220$) of the diners answered "no" to the first question, so 70 diners could not have answered "yes" to both questions. Therefore, the least possible number of diners who answered "yes" to both questions is $150 - 70 = 80$.

Alternatively, the number of diners that answered "yes" to either question is $220 + 150 = 370$. Given there were 290 diners surveyed, the least possible number of diners that answered "yes" to both questions is $370 - 290 = 80$.

Practice Set

1. B

Subject: Statistics and Probability

Getting to the Answer: The question asks for the team with the least number of championship game attendees, so you only need to perform calculations for CB, GS, and SA, which according to the graph had fewer championships. The bar graph shows CB and GS each had 6 championships, and SA had 5 championships. Thus, CB has $6 \times 20,000 = 120,000$ championship game attendees, GS has $6 \times 16,500 = 99,000$ attendees, and SA has $5 \times 20,000 = 100,000$. GS has the least number of championship game attendees.

2. E

Subject: Statistics and Probability

Getting to the Answer: The question asks for the store with the greatest number of customers per day. For the stores listed in the answer choices, multiply the number of checkout lanes by the number of customers per checkout lane per day to calculate the total number of customers per day.

J: $7 \times 600 = 4,200$

M: $5 \times 325 = 1,625$

T: $8 \times 490 = 3,920$

W: $10 \times 325 = 3,250$

J has the greatest number of customers per day.

3. D

Subject: Statistics and Probability

Getting to the Answer: Add the percentage of bike racks that have 4 and 5 or more parked bicycles: 29% + 45% = 74%.

Multiply that percentage by the total number of bike racks to calculate the number of bike racks that had at least 4 parked bicycles: 50 × 0.74 = 37.

4. G

Subject: Statistics and Probability

Getting to the Answer: Multiply the number of apples by the weight and add them together to get the sum. Then divide by the total number of apples to find the mean weight of the apples: Average = $\frac{70(7) + 80(17) + 90(10) + 100(6)}{7 + 17 + 10 + 6}$ = $\frac{3,350}{40}$ = 83.75.

5. D

Subject: Statistics and Probability

Getting to the Answer: Multiply the number of calories by the number of entrees and add them together to get the sum. Then divide by the total number of entrees to find the mean number of calories per entree: Average = $\frac{200(2) + 250(4) + 300(1) + 350(5)}{2 + 4 + 1 + 5}$ = $\frac{3,450}{12}$ = 287.5.

6. G

Subject: Statistics and Probability

Getting to the Answer: First, calculate the lowest tip for each driver by subtracting the range from the highest tip:

Carlos: $10 − $8 = $2

Alec: $5 − $1 = $4

Miles: $15 − $12 = $3

The overall highest tip is $15, and the overall lowest tip is $2. Therefore, the overall range of all the tips is $15 − $2 = $13.

7. C

Subject: Statistics and Probability

Getting to the Answer: The total number of combos ordered is 65 + 39 + 60 + 31 + 45 = 240. Thus, the probability of a customer ordering combo #3 is $\frac{60}{240} = \frac{1}{4}$ = 25%.

8. F

Subject: Statistics and Probability

Getting to the Answer: First, determine the total number of classmates. Then add the number of classmates who made 0 phone calls a day to the number of classmates who made 1 phone call per day to get the number of students who made at most 1 phone call a day. The probability is $\frac{7 + 11}{50} = \frac{18}{50} = \frac{9}{25}$.

9. A

Subject: Statistics and Probability

Getting to the Answer: Let x = the number of shoppers who only used paper bags. Let y = the number of shoppers who only used plastic bags. Use the given information to calculate x and y: There are 41 shoppers who used paper bags, 23 of whom used both paper and plastic bags. So, x = 41 − 23 = 18. There are 77 shoppers who used plastic bags, 23 of whom used both paper and plastic bags. So, y = 77 − 23 = 54.

The total number of shoppers surveyed is the number of shoppers who only used paper bags (18) plus the number of shoppers who only used plastic bags (54) plus the number of shoppers who used both (23) plus the number of customers who used neither (19): 18 + 54 + 23 + 19 = 114.

10. G

Subject: Statistics and Probability

Getting to the Answer: Fifty-six (216 − 160) of the patients answered "no" to the first question, so 56 patients could not have answered "yes" to both questions. Therefore, the least possible number of patients who answered "yes" to both questions is 104 − 56 = 48.

Alternatively, the number of patients that answered "yes" to either question is 160 + 104 = 264. Given there were 216 patients, the least possible number of patients that answered "yes" to both questions is 264 − 216 = 48.

11. D

Subject: Statistics and Probability

Getting to the Answer: Add the percentage of floors that have 3, 4, and 5 or more restrooms: 8% + 52% + 10% = 70%.

Multiply that percentage by the total number of floors to calculate the number of floors that had at least 3 restrooms: $60 \times 0.7 = 42$ restrooms.

12. G

Subject: Statistics and Probability

Getting to the Answer: The number of attendees who major in engineering and/or liberal arts is 350 + 275 = 625. To find the number of attendees who major in engineering or liberal arts, subtract the number of attendees that major in both engineering and liberal arts: 625 − 75 = 550. Thus, the number of attendees that had a major other than engineering and liberal arts is 600 − 550 = 50.

13. C

Subject: Statistics and Probability

Getting to the Answer: Multiply the number of salmon in each row by the length in each row and add them together to get the sum. Then divide by the total number of salmon to find the mean length of the salmon:

$$\text{Average} = \frac{55(5) + 56(5) + 57(3) + 58(1)}{5 + 5 + 3 + 1} = \frac{784}{14} = 56.$$

14. G

Subject: Statistics and Probability

Getting to the Answer: Multiply the number of packages by the number of houses and add them together to get the sum. Then divide by the total number of packages to find the mean number of packages per house per week:

$$\text{Average} = \frac{0(0) + 1(10) + 2(15) + 3(10)}{0 + 10 + 15 + 10} = \frac{70}{35} = 2.$$

15. B

Subject: Statistics and Probability

Getting to the Answer: First determine the total number of spectators by multiplying the number of spectators by the number of games.

Number of Spectators	Number of Games	Total Number of Spectators
62	4	248
65	2	130
71	4	284
74	1	74
80	7	560
83	0	0
		1,296

Then add to get the total number of spectators. To calculate the mean, divide the total number of spectators by the number of games: average $= \frac{1{,}296}{18} = 72$. The mean number of spectators per game is 72.

16. H

Subject: Statistics and Probability

Getting to the Answer: First, calculate the slowest lap for each racer by adding the range to the fastest lap:

Dana: 91 + 4 = 95

Anthony: 87 + 12 = 99

Katie: 74 + 6 = 80

The overall fastest lap is 74, and the overall slowest lap is 99. Therefore, the overall range of all the laps is 99 − 74 = 25.

17. C

Subject: Statistics and Probability

Getting to the Answer: The total number of computers used is 19 + 22 + 11 + 28 = 80. Thus, the probability of a person using computer #2 is $\frac{22}{80} = \frac{11}{40} = 27.5\%$.

18. F

Subject: Statistics and Probability

Getting to the Answer: First, determine the total number of people surveyed. Then add the number of people who carried 2 credit cards to the number of people who carried 3 or more credit cards. The probability is
$\frac{15+3}{60} = \frac{18}{60} = \frac{3}{10}$.

19. C

Subject: Statistics and Probability

Getting to the Answer: First, determine the total number of postage stamps on the sheet: $18 + 6 + 6 + 4 + 2 = 36$.

Then set up a proportion to find which picture has exactly a 1 in 9 chance of being selected:

$$\frac{x}{36} = \frac{1}{9}$$
$$9x = 36$$
$$x = 4$$

There are 4 star stamps on the sheet, so a star stamp has a 1 in 9 chance of being randomly selected.

20. E

Subject: Statistics and Probability

Getting to the Answer: Let $x =$ the number of people who only folded their clothes. Let $y =$ the number of people who only hung their clothes. Use the given information to calculate x and y: There are 85 people who folded their clothes, 40 of whom also hung their clothes. So, $x = 85 - 40 = 45$. There are 56 people who hung their clothes, 40 of whom also folded their clothes. So, $y = 56 - 40 = 16$.

The total number of people surveyed is the number of people who only folded their clothes (45) plus the number of people who only hung their clothes (16) plus the number of people who both folded and hung their clothes (40) plus the number of people who neither folded nor hung their clothes (2): $45 + 16 + 40 + 2 = 103$.

21. C

Subject: Statistics and Probability

Getting to the Answer: Thirty $(300 - 270)$ of the guests answered "false" to the first question, so 30 guests could not have answered "yes" to both questions. Therefore, the least possible number of guests who answered "yes" to both questions is $240 - 30 = 210$.

Alternatively, the number of guests who answered "true" to either question is $270 + 240 = 510$. Given there were 300 guests who responded to the questions, the least possible number of guests who answered "true" to both questions is $510 - 300 = 210$.

22. G

Subject: Statistics and Probability

Getting to the Answer: Since there are 30 students in the class and 14 students do not like broccoli or cauliflower, then 16 students in the class like broccoli and/or cauliflower. Add the number of students who like broccoli to the number of students who like cauliflower to get the number of students who like broccoli or cauliflower: $12 + 10 = 22$. Then subtract that from the number of students in the class who like broccoli or cauliflower to find the number of students who like both broccoli and cauliflower is $22 - 16 = 6$.

Note that the total number of students in the class equals the number of students who like only broccoli plus the number of students who like only cauliflower plus the students who like both broccoli and cauliflower plus the number of students who like neither broccoli nor cauliflower.

PART FOUR

Ready, Set, Go!

CHAPTER 19

Countdown to the Test

CHAPTER OBJECTIVES

By the end of this chapter, you will be able to:

- Recall important information for Test Day success
- Identify what to do the week before, the night before, and the morning of the test

---

Countdown to the Test

It's normal to have some pre-test nervousness. This chapter provides a helpful plan for the week before Test Day, so that you can feel prepared and confident.

The Week Before the Test

- Focus on pacing and strategy.
- Decide how you are going to approach each section and question type.
- Sit down and do practice problems in the Practice Sets or complete extra drills you skipped the first time through.
- Practice waking up early and eating breakfast on the weekend so that you will be alert on Test Day.

Two Days Before the Test

Do your last studying—a few more practice problems—and then relax. Don't start making hundreds of flash cards or take practice test after practice test.

The Night Before the Test

Do NOT study. Instead, get together the following items:

- Your admission/registration ticket
- Your ID
- A watch (choose one that is easy to read)
- Slightly dull No. 2 pencils (so they fill in the ovals faster)
- A pencil sharpener
- Erasers
- The clothes you will wear (layers)
- Snacks (easy to open and eat quickly)
- Money
- A packet of tissues

Know exactly where you're going and exactly how you're getting there.

Relax the night before the test and get a good night's sleep. Go to bed at a reasonable hour and leave yourself extra time in the morning.

The Morning of the Test

Eat breakfast. Make it something substantial and nutritious, but don't deviate too much from your everyday pattern.

Dress in layers so that you can adjust to the temperature of the test room. The climate at the test location may vary, as may your body temperature. Make sure you can warm up or cool down easily.

Be sure to get there early. Leave enough time to allow for traffic, mass transit delays, getting lost on the way, or any other snag that could slow you down.

Don't stress! Check out the next chapter for more information on how to manage your stress before and during the test.

Strategic Review: Reading

The Kaplan Method for Reading Comprehension

Step 1: Read actively

Step 2: Examine the question stem

Step 3: Predict and answer

Actively read the following passage, taking notes to create a Roadmap. Be sure to write down the topic of each paragraph and the main idea of the passage.

Daniel Webster

1   Though he later became known as one of the greatest orators of his time, the prominent attorney and statesman Daniel Webster suffered from a debilitating fear of public speaking in his youth. Webster was the son of a farmer, born in New Hampshire in 1782 and brought up in a large family. As a boy, he was encouraged to read and had a strong natural intellect and a passion for learning that convinced his parents to prioritize a formal education for him. Unfortunately, when he was 14 years old, Webster's introduction to schooling at the prestigious Phillips Exeter Academy was nothing short of traumatic for him. A significant curricular requirement for students of the Academy was "declamation," the act of public speaking. Historical records indicate that Webster became so petrified when asked to speak in front of an audience that he simply refused to stand up in front of his classmates, retreating to his room in fear.

2   Although Webster's time at Exeter Academy was short-lived, it is not known whether he left school due to the trauma of the educational model employed there or for other reasons, perhaps financial. In any case, just a year later, Webster enrolled at Dartmouth College where he was able to finally overcome this powerful phobia. Webster dealt with his fear of public speaking, technically termed glossophobia, by plunging himself into activities that demanded he speak before an audience. He became an active member of the United Fraternity where he was required to deliver many speeches. He relied on his other great skills, such as his remarkable memory and writing talent, to enhance his performance in public debates. When he graduated from Dartmouth in 1801, Webster was already so polished a speaker that he was invited to deliver the Independence Day oration on campus.

3   After graduating from college, Webster began his career as a teacher before ultimately finding his calling in the practice of law. Webster, known for his relentless determination and lofty aspirations, was not satisfied with merely giving speeches for colleagues at annual holiday parties. He soon opened his own law practice in Portsmouth in 1807. His reputation as a lawyer grew rapidly, and he quickly rose to prominence. Webster took an active interest in the political landscape of the time, expressing criticism of the Jefferson administration's actions leading up to the War of 1812. In fact, it was in 1812 that Webster officially entered politics with his election to the U.S. House of Representatives. Historians credit Webster's fervently articulated opposition to the War of 1812 as the reason for his successful entree into political office.

4   Webster's political career is marked by an interesting shift from being an advocate of states' rights, to that of a staunch nationalist championing the importance of a unified nation without international influences and entanglements. He served as a U.S. congressman and senator from Massachusetts, did a stint as U.S. secretary of state under President William Harrison, and even made a bid for president. Perhaps his most influential role continued to be that of debater, as Webster argued many important cases in front of the Supreme Court that influenced judicial decision-making. Under Chief Justice John Marshall, Webster's arguments helped shape policy that fostered a strong federal government and powerful judicial branch.

5   As an orator, Daniel Webster had no equal. He spoke with eloquence and dramatic expression. His talent for persuasion is legendary. It is remarkable indeed that such great triumphs can be traced back to that young student who found himself literally sick with fear, attempting to address his classmates. Webster's accomplishments powerfully demonstrate that talent can evolve, that tapping into one's other strengths can help overcome adversity, and that even the most intense of fears can be overcome through concerted effort.

FAMOUS PEOPLE WITH GLOSSOPHOBIA[1]

Name	Profession	Born
Demosthenes	Greek Politician	384 B.C.E.
Thomas Jefferson	U.S. Politician	1743
Daniel Webster	U.S. Politician	1782
Mahatma Gandhi	Activist	1869
Maya Angelou	Poet	1928
Warren Buffet	Investor	1930
Harrison Ford	Actor	1942
Ricky Williams	Football Player	1977
Adele	Singer	1988

[1]The fear of public speaking

Global

    A.   What is the subject of the passage?

    B.   What does the author say about that subject?

1.   Which statement best describes the central idea of the passage?

    A.   Webster was scared of speaking before a large audience for much of his life.

    B.   Webster laid his phobias to rest and became the most effective politician of his time.

    C.   Webster's lofty aspirations for the presidency were never fulfilled.

    D.   Webster overcame his aversion to public speaking to become a successful politician.

Detail

    C.   Where in the passage are Webster's skills as a public speaker addressed?

    D.   Based on the information in the passage, what is a good prephrase, or prediction, for the answer to the question below?

2.   Which sentence best explains why Webster was able to become such an effective public speaker?

    E.   "Webster was the son of a farmer, born in New Hampshire in 1782 and brought up in a large family." (paragraph 1)

    F.   "He relied on his other great skills, such as his remarkable memory and writing talent, to enhance his performance in public debates." (paragraph 2)

    G.   "After graduating from college, Webster began his career as a teacher before ultimately finding his calling in the practice of law." (paragraph 3)

    H.   "Under Chief Justice John Marshall, Webster's arguments helped shape policy that fostered a strong federal government and powerful judicial branch." (paragraph 4)

Function

    E.   Why does the author begin the passage with a discussion of Webster's fear of public speaking?

    F.   Why does the author characterize Webster's phobia as "powerful" in paragraph 2?

3.   Read the sentence from paragraph 2.

> **In any case, just a year later, Webster enrolled at Dartmouth College where he was able to finally overcome this powerful phobia.**

The author most likely uses the word "powerful" in order to

    A.   highlight that Webster's ability to overcome such an all-consuming fear was impressive.

    B.   foreshadow Webster's eventual failure within the political sphere.

    C.   assert that Webster was regarded as a particularly effective lawyer.

    D.   introduce the idea that Webster's efforts to overcome his considerable fear were ineffective.

Inference

    G. What does the passage say about "giving holiday speeches" specifically?

    H. Based on the information in the passage, what is a good prephrase, or prediction, for the answer to the question below?

4. What is the most likely reason the author mentions that Webster "was not satisfied with merely giving speeches for colleagues at annual holiday parties"? (paragraph 3)

    E. Webster was famous for his determination.

    F. Webster refused future invitations to speak in front of colleagues.

    G. Webster was driven by passionate nationalism.

    H. Webster's ambition led to his rise as a prominent statesman.

Infographic

    I. What does the table below the passage show?

    J. How does this information relate to the passage as a whole?

5. The table below the passage contributes to the development of the topic of the passage by

    A. suggesting that Webster was inspired to overcome glossophobia by other famous people who overcame their fear of public speaking.

    B. implying that Webster was only one person among many famous people, past and present, affected by glossophobia.

    C. comparing Webster's accomplishments with those of other famous people who suffered from glossophobia.

    D. proving that overcoming a fear of public speaking through facing the fear has been common from ancient times to the present.

Strategic Review: Revising/Editing

The Kaplan Method for Revising/Editing Text

Step 1: Examine the question

Step 2: Read the text

Step 3: Select the most correct, concise, and relevant choice

---

REVISING/EDITING Part A

DIRECTIONS: Answer the following questions, recognizing and correcting errors so that the sentences or paragraphs are grammatically correct. Re-read relevant parts of the text before choosing the best answer for each question.

---

1. Read this paragraph.

> A new music class, eagerly anticipated by new <u>students,</u> <u>includes</u> exercises for developing vocal range and for making musical notation understandable to beginner <u>musicians. The</u> course provides instruction in a variety of topics, such as tonality and <u>harmony,</u> <u>formal</u> and contemporary styles of music are also part of the curriculum. Students will explore the interaction of theory and technique as well as how these features apply to rhythm, scales, improvisation, and creative <u>expression</u>. <u>The</u> class culminates in a highly anticipated concert at the end of the semester.

Which revision corrects the error in sentence structure in the paragraph?

A. students. Includes

B. musicians; the

C. harmony. Formal

D. expression, the

2. Read this paragraph.

> (1) Built in 1889 for the World's Fair, the Eiffel Tower was almost destroyed due to Parisians' dislike of this architectural wonder. (2) Fortunately, the tower became home to a radio antenna in 1909 and has since had over 200 million visitors who have taken the elevator to the top level. (3) Visitors might notice that every seven years the tower receives a new coat of paint, which takes 15 months to apply to its network of beams. (4) While taking a sightseeing tour of Paris, the Eiffel Tower is often a tourist's first stop.

Which sentence contains an error in its construction and should be revised?

E. sentence 1

F. sentence 2

G. sentence 3

H. sentence 4

3. Read this paragraph.

> (1) Canada's ten provinces and two territories cover an extremely large portion of North America. (2) The country includes forests, mountains, rivers, and grasslands, which can be influenced by extreme seasonal temperatures. (3) Canadians speak English and French, and tend to live in the southern part of the country, where they generally inhabiting urban locations. (4) Since it shares a long border with America, Canada has developed trading arrangements and various shared interests with the United States.

Which revisions correct the errors in the paragraph?

A. Sentence 1: Insert a comma after **provinces**, AND change **cover** to **covers**.

B. Sentence 2: Delete the comma after **grasslands**, AND change **can be** to **are**.

C. Sentence 3: Delete the comma after **French**, AND change **inhabiting** to **inhabit**.

D. Sentence 4: Insert a comma after **Canada**, AND change **developed** to **develop**.

4. Read these sentences.

> (1) The first magnetic resource imaging (MRI) scan was completed on July 3, 1977.
> (2) An MRI scan creates detailed images of the organs and tissues within the body that help physicians diagnose a variety of medical conditions.

What is the best way to combine the sentences to clarify the relationship between the ideas?

E. Even though the first magnetic resource imaging (MRI) scan was completed on July 3, 1977, MRI scans create detailed images of the organs and tissues within the body that help physicians diagnose a variety of medical conditions.

F. An MRI scan, the first of which was completed on July 3, 1977, creates detailed images of the organs and tissues within the body that help physicians diagnose a variety of medical conditions.

G. Today, an MRI scan creates detailed images of the organs and tissues within the body that help physicians diagnose a variety of medical conditions, but the first magnetic one was completed on July 3, 1977.

H. While the first magnetic resource imaging (MRI) scan was completed on July 3, 1977, MRI scans create detailed images of the organs and tissues within the body that help physicians diagnose a variety of medical conditions.

5. Read this sentence.

> During the pivotal moment in the murder mystery novel, the main character—a highly-respected detective—talked to people who seemed to be lying about some things.

Which revision uses the most precise language for "talked to people who seemed to be lying about some things"?

A. questioned the two main suspects

B. spoke to a few untrustworthy people

C. discussed the case with suspects

D. yelled loudly at the criminals

REVISING/EDITING Part B

DIRECTIONS: Read the passage and answer the questions following it, improving the writing quality and correcting grammatical errors. Re-read relevant parts of the text before choosing the best answer for each question.

Milton Hershey

(1) Who has not enjoyed a Hershey Bar or a Hershey Kiss? (2) Both were created by master confectioner Milton Hershey, born into a Pennsylvania farm family in 1857. (3) His education was limited—he went only as far as the fourth grade—and after a disastrous first apprenticeship to a printer, his mother arranged for his training with a local caramel candy maker. (4) Hershey not only learned his craft but also began a lifelong dedication to quality ingredients. (5) In 1883, Hershey opened the highly successful Lancaster Caramel Company, which packaged caramels in bulk. (6) This was a new and profitable innovation.

(7) Hershey's interest in chocolate was sparked by his 1893 visit to the World's Columbian Exposition. (8) He sold the caramel company and used the money to open the Hershey Chocolate company. (9) Because of its location near the farmland of Lancaster, Pennsylvania, Hershey was able to buy fresh milk. (10) At the time, it was considered a luxury product, but the mass production of the Hershey products made chocolate more popular. (11) This purchase was strategic, since he was able to incorporate it into his own milk chocolate recipe.

(12) In 1905, Hershey's huge new factory opened and became the center of a town that grew up around it. (13) With his workers in mind, Hershey oversaw the construction of houses, schools, churches, public transportation, and even a zoo. (14) Today the town is a tourist attraction, popularly called Chocolatetown, USA; Hershey called it "the sweetest place on Earth." (15) It is one of several locations named after their founders, such as Disneyland.

(16) Hershey and his wife Catherine had no children, so they focused a great deal of their attention to philanthropic endeavors. (17) Their best known project was an orphanage, called the Hershey Industrial School (later renamed the Milton Hershey School). (18) In 1918, Hershey put all his shares of the Hershey's Chocolate Company into a trust for the school, which today provides an excellent education for children from troubled backgrounds. (19) Milton Hershey died peacefully in 1945 at the age of 88, having happily given away most of his money in his lifetime.

6. Which is the best way to combine sentences 5 and 6 to clarify the relationship between ideas?

    E. In 1883, Hershey opened the highly successful Lancaster Caramel Company, packaging caramels in bulk, this was a new and profitable innovation.

    F. In 1883, Hershey opened the highly successful Lancaster Caramel Company, packaging caramels in bulk, however this was a new and profitable innovation.

    G. In 1883, Hershey opened the highly successful Lancaster Caramel Company, packaging caramels in bulk, a new and profitable innovation.

    H. In 1883, Hershey opened the highly successful Lancaster Caramel Company, packaging caramels in bulk, starting a new and profitable innovation.

7. Which transition should be added to the beginning of sentence 8?

    A. Nonetheless

    B. Even so

    C. Unfortunately

    D. Afterward

8. Which revision of sentence 10 uses the most precise language?

    E. At the time, chocolate was considered a luxury product, but the mass production of the Hershey Bar, introduced in 1903, and Hershey's Kisses, first sold in 1907, made chocolate widely available and affordable.

    F. During that period in the United States, milk was considered a luxury product, but the mass production of the Hershey products, made chocolate widely available and affordable.

    G. At the time, chocolate was considered a product, but the mass production of the Hershey Bar, introduced in 1903, and Hershey's Kisses, first sold in 1907, made chocolate widely available and affordable.

    H. Milk, being a luxury product, was first introduced in 1903, and Hershey's Kisses, first sold in 1907, made chocolate widely available and affordable.

9. Where should sentence 11 be moved to improve the organization of the second paragraph (sentences 7−11)?

    A. to the beginning of the paragraph (before sentence 7)

    B. between sentences 7 and 8

    C. between sentences 8 and 9

    D. between sentences 9 and 10

10. Which sentence presents information that shifts away from the main topic of the third paragraph (sentences 12−15) and should be removed?

    E. sentence 12

    F. sentence 13

    G. sentence 14

    H. sentence 15

11. Which sentence would best follow and support sentence 16?

    A. Indeed, Milton Hershey is in the Philanthropy Hall of Fame.

    B. The two were equal partners in philanthropic contributions.

    C. Not every married couple without children gives to charity, though.

    D. Their contributions went to all manner of charitable organizations.

Ready, Set, Go!

Strategic Review: Math

The Kaplan Method for SHSAT Math

Step 1: What is the question?

Step 2: What information is provided in the question? In what format do the answers appear?

Step 3: What can I do with the information?

- Picking Numbers
- Backsolving
- Straightforward math

Step 4: Am I finished?

1. Points A, B, and C are on a number line. A is between B and C. $\overline{AC} = \frac{2}{3}\overline{BA}$, and $\overline{BA} = 15$ units. What is the distance between points B and C?

   A. 20 units

   B. 22.5 units

   C. 25 units

   D. 30 units

2. How many positive odd factors of 60 are greater than 2 and less than 20 ?

   E. 1

   F. 3

   G. 5

   H. 7

Minimum Wage	Number of States
$7.25	16
$8.25	3
$13.25	1

3. What is the mean minimum wage of the 20 states in the table above?

   A. $7.19

   B. $7.70

   C. $8.75

   D. $9.58

4. A package of cups contains exactly 6 blue cups. The probability of choosing a blue cup from the package is $\frac{3}{5}$. How many of the cups in the package are **not** blue?

   E. 4

   F. 10

   G. 12

   H. 16

5. An air mattress is partially filled with *a* liters of air. Gwen adds 80 liters of air to the air mattress, such that it is 80% inflated. If Gwen adds 30 more liters of air, the air mattress will be 90% full. What is the value of *a* ?

   A. 100

   B. 121

   C. 160

   D. 209

6. Which of the following number lines shows the solution set for $4x + 1 \leq y$ or $y < 2x - 5$ when $y = 2$?

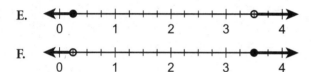

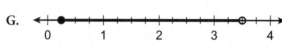

7. Today, Weiwei is half as old as Caleb. In 3 years, Weiwei will be $\frac{2}{3}$ as old as Caleb. How old is Caleb today?

   A. 3

   B. 6

   C. 9

   D. 12

8. Ester and Noel each rented a 20-cubic foot dumpster for 2 weeks. The total cost of Ester's dumpster rental was $365 plus $1.25 per pound over 3,000 pounds. Noel paid a flat fee of $430 for his dumpster rental. If Ester's and Noel's total costs were identical, how many pounds over 3,000 pounds did Ester go?

   E. 52

   F. 65

   G. 82

   H. 292

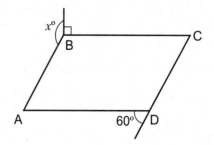

9. In the figure above, ABCD is a parallelogram. What is the value of *x* ?

   A. 110

   B. 120

   C. 140

   D. 150

10. A truck travels 88 inches per second. If the diameter of each tire is 20 inches, how many revolutions does one tire make in 1 minute? $\left(\pi \approx \frac{22}{7} \right)$

   E. $\frac{7}{5}$

   F. 43

   G. $\frac{440}{7}$

   H. 84

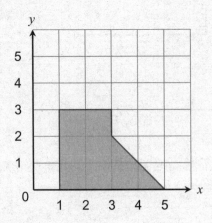

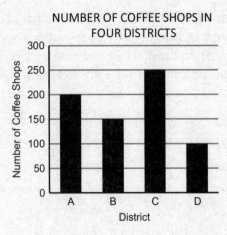

11. In the graph above, what is the area of the shaded region?

   A. 8

   B. 10

   C. 11

   D. 13

12. The graph above shows the number of coffee shops for four districts. Districts A and B each have 150 patrons per coffee shop. Districts C and D each have 100 patrons per coffee shop. Which of the districts has the **greatest** number of coffee shop patrons?

   E. District A

   F. District B

   G. District C

   H. District D

Strategic Review: Math Grid-In Questions

When answering SHSAT grid-in questions, the goal is to stay organized. Work quickly but carefully through the questions that require straightforward calculations. If the question is a word problem, break the sentences into short phrases before calculating.

DIRECTIONS: Answer each question. Write your answer in the boxes at the top of the grid. Start on the left side of each grid, printing only one number or symbol in each box. **DO NOT LEAVE A BOX BLANK IN THE MIDDLE OF AN ANSWER.** Under each box, fill in the circle that matches the number or symbol you wrote above. **DO NOT FILL IN A CIRCLE UNDER AN UNUSED BOX.**

$$6 + 4 \div |-2| + (-4)^3 \times \frac{1}{2}$$

1. What is the value of the expression shown above?

2. Solve for x:

    $$8x + 2 - 4(x + 4) = 6$$

3. In the equation $\frac{h}{12} - 10 = -6$, what is the value of h?

4. What is the value of the expression $2(a - 5)^2 + 3a \div 4$ if $a = 8$?

5. If Maria ran 2.1 miles on Monday, 6 miles on Tuesday, and 4.2 miles on Wednesday, what is the mean number of miles she ran over the course of three days?

6. In a cupboard with only red and blue cups, the ratio of red cups to blue cups is 3:4. If there are 48 red cups, how many total cups are in the cupboard?

7. Mark paints houses as part of his job. In a given week, he has 28 houses to paint. If he paints $\frac{1}{4}$ of these houses on Monday and $\frac{1}{7}$ of the remaining houses on Tuesday, how many houses does Mark still have to paint after Tuesday?

8. A magazine pays authors by the word for essays that are submitted. Authors are paid $0.10 per word for the first 250 words and $0.05 per word for every word after 250 words. Sam submitted three essays: a 300-word essay, a 400-word essay, and a 500-word essay. How much did the magazine pay Sam for his three essays?

9. What number is halfway between −5 and 23 on a number line?

10. An art instructor is buying tubes of paint and paint-brushes for an upcoming class. If a tube of paint costs $5 and a paintbrush costs $1.50, how much does the instructor spend if the class has 8 students and each student needs 5 tubes of paint and a paintbrush?

11. Maria recently took a nonstop flight from Miami, Florida, to Quito, Ecuador. If the airplane flew at a constant speed of 436 miles per hour and the flight took 4.5 hours, what is the distance from Miami to Quito?

12. William is enrolled in a book-of-the-month club. This club sends members leather-bound editions of classic books the same day each month. As a reward for loyalty, William receives a free book at the end of each year. If William pays $468 per year for the club, what is the average price he pays for each book?

13. Danielle and Emma participated in a book-reading contest over the summer. Danielle read 13 books, and Emma read 15 fewer than 3 times the number of books that Danielle read. How many books did Danielle and Emma read over the summer?

14. Patricia ate lunch at a restaurant yesterday. She ordered three items: a salad, a bowl of soup, and a glass of iced tea. The salad cost $3, the soup cost $4, and the iced tea cost $1. If there is a 6% tax on food but not on drinks, how much did Patricia pay for lunch?

15. A recipe calls for $1\frac{2}{3}$ cups of water, $\frac{1}{2}$ cup of oil, and $\frac{5}{6}$ cup of milk. If these are the only three liquids used in the recipe, then how many total cups of liquid are used?

16. Krista and Dana are both avid tea drinkers and have many different tea mugs. Dana has 4 more than half the number of mugs that Krista has, and together they have 19 tea mugs. How many tea mugs does Krista have?

17. Plow trucks are used to clear snow off highways after snowstorms, as well as to spread anti-skid material on the road to help snow melt and give drivers more traction. A certain anti-skid material is 3 parts gravel to 2 parts salt. If 300 tons of salt were used in this material last year, how many total tons of anti-skid material were used?

LAST YEAR'S TOTAL SALES

Bicycle Type	Number
Road	600
Mountain	900
Hybrid	1,200
Total	2,700

18. The table above shows the number of each type of bicycle sold at a local shop last year. If 300 bikes will be sold next month, what is the best estimate (based on last year's sales) of the number of mountain bicycles that will be sold?

19. Elli opens an account with a deposit of $1,200. This account earns 4% simple interest annually. How many years will it take for her $1,200 deposit to earn $432 interest?

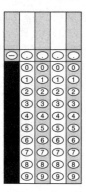

20. A camp counselor has 54 paintbrushes, 72 tubes of paint, and 90 sheets of paper to distribute to the children in the camp. If each child receives an equal number of each item and there are no items remaining, what is the greatest possible number of children in the camp?

Answers and Explanations

Strategic Review: Reading Comprehension

Global

A. Daniel Webster was one of the most outspoken politicians of his time.

B. Webster overcame a huge fear of public speaking in order to achieve his goals.

1. D

Category: Global

Getting to the Answer: If you have already identified the main idea on your own, you will have a much easier time finding the correct answer choice. Remember, the correct choice will match both the tone and the scope of the passage. **(D)** does this best. **(A)** is a Misused Detail; the passage discusses Webster's fear, but it is how he overcomes his fear that is the focus. **(B)** is Extreme; the passage does not say that Webster was the "most effective" politician of his time. **(C)** is a Misused Detail; the author mentions that Webster did not become president, but it is not the primary idea of the passage.

Detail

C. Paragraph 2

D. Webster used his great memory and writing skills to do well in public debates.

2. F

Category: Detail

Getting to the Answer: Paragraph 2 tells you that Webster used his memory and skills as a writer to excel at public debate, which matches **(F)**. **(E)**, **(G)**, and **(H)** are Misused Details; they are mentioned in the passage, but they do not specifically answer the question.

Function

E. To provide information about a fear that Webster was eventually able to overcome

F. To show that Webster's fear was considerable, which makes it all the more admirable that he was able to move past it

3. A

Category: Function

Getting to the Answer: The author describes Webster's fear of public speaking as greatly affecting his life before he courageously overcame it, which matches **(A)**. **(B)** is a Distortion. While Webster did not become president, the author does not characterize his political career as a failure. **(C)** is incorrect because Webster's success as a lawyer is mentioned in paragraph 3, not paragraph 2. **(D)** is Opposite; Webster did, in fact, overcome his fear.

Inference

G. Webster wanted to do more than speak in front of colleagues at holiday parties.

H. Webster did more than give holiday speeches; he became a lawyer and politician.

4. H

Category: Inference

Getting to the Answer: Paragraph 3 discusses Webster's pursuit of political esteem. The phrase "merely giving speeches for colleagues" introduces the idea that Webster wished to fulfill greater goals—in this case, a political career, which matches **(H)**. While **(E)** and **(G)** may be true, the primary purpose of the phrase is to point out that Webster had goals that extended beyond practicing law. The passage does not include information to support the idea that Webster refused to give speeches in front of coworkers, so **(F)** is incorrect.

Infographic

I. The table shows additional famous people over time and in different professions who had or have a fear of public speaking.

J. The main idea of the passage is that Daniel Webster overcame his fear of public speaking and became a great orator, and, according to the table, there are many other famous people who suffered from a fear of public speaking.

5. B

Category: Infographic

Getting to the Answer: Daniel Webster was greatly affected by his fear of public speaking, and other famous people such as Mahatma Gandhi and Maya Angelou have had to overcome glossophobia too; **(B)** is correct. **(A)** and **(D)** are Out of Scope because the passage does not say that Webster was inspired by others, and it does not provide information to support the idea that glossophobia is common. **(C)** is incorrect because the table does not provide specific information about the accomplishments of the famous people listed; it provides only names, professions, and years of birth.

Strategic Review: Revising/Editing

1. C

Category: Sentence Structure

Getting to the Answer: The question indicates that there is an error that needs to be fixed. Check each underlined segment systematically to locate the issue. The second sentence of the paragraph is a run-on because both clauses—"The course provides instruction in a variety of topics, such as tonality and harmony" and "formal and contemporary styles of music are also part of the curriculum"—are independent clauses. **(C)** fixes this error with a period. **(A)**, **(B)**, and **(D)** are incorrect because they do not address the original error, and they each create a new issue.

2. H

Category: Sentence Structure

Getting to the Answer: Modifying words and phrases must be properly placed to accurately reflect the author's intended meaning. As written in sentence 4, it is "the Eiffel Tower" that is "taking a . . . tour of Paris," which is not logical; **(H)** is correct. Eliminate **(E)**, **(F)**, and **(G)** because they are grammatically correct sentences.

3. C

Category: Punctuation & Usage

Getting to the Answer: The question indicates that the paragraph includes two errors. In sentence 3, the comma after "French" is unnecessary and must be deleted, and

"inhabiting" should be "inhabit" to keep it consistent with the verbs "speak" and "tend"; **(C)** is correct. Eliminate **(A)**, **(B)**, and **(D)** because they are grammatically correct.

4. F

Category: Organization

Getting to the Answer: When combining two sentences, determine the relationship between the two. The first sentence states when the first MRI scan was conducted and the second sentence provides details about what an MRI scan does and how it is used. **(F)** correctly reflects the relationship between the two by putting the information from the first sentence between two commas, which indicates that the two ideas are closely related. **(E)**, **(G)**, and **(H)** are incorrect because they use the contrast transitions "Even though," "but," and "While," which do not accurately reflect the writer's intention to express two pieces of related information about a single topic.

5. A

Category: Knowledge of Language

Getting to the Answer: The question asks you to use precise, or specific, language to express the phrase "talked to people who seemed to be lying about some things". **(A)** precisely states the detective's action ("questioned") as well as with whom the detective spoke ("the two main suspects"). **(B)** and **(C)** do not provide specific information about exactly what the detective was doing, and **(D)** adds information that the writer may not have intended to include. Be sure to eliminate any choices that change the original meaning of the text.

6. G

Category: Organization

Getting to the Answer: Since both sentences are about packaging in bulk, the two can logically be joined by making the second sentence dependent and adding it to the first with a comma. **(G)** is correct. **(E)** incorrectly joins two independent clauses with a comma, and **(F)** incorrectly contrasts the two sentences, whereas one is a continuation of the other. **(H)** is redundant; both "new" and "innovation" imply "starting."

7.   D

Category: Organization

Getting to the Answer: In context, it can be inferred that after visiting the exposition and becoming interested in chocolate, Hershey sold the caramel company to make chocolate candies instead. The best word to describe this change of events is **(D)**, "Afterward." **(A)** and **(B)** are contrast words, which do not convey the intended meaning, and **(C)** adds a point of view that the author doesn't state.

8.   E

Category: Knowledge of Language

Getting to the Answer: "It" does not provide specific details, but **(E)** makes the sentence clear: it was chocolate that was considered a luxury product until Hershey began to mass produce it. **(F)** and **(H)** refer to the wrong product—milk instead of chocolate—and **(G)** omits the important word "luxury."

9.   D

Category: Organization

Getting to the Answer: When relocating a sentence, look for context clues that indicate where it must be placed to make the paragraph as logical as possible. Sentence 11 uses the phrase "This purchase" to refer to how Hershey was able to buy fresh milk, which is first mentioned in sentence 9; sentence 11 should be placed directly after this reference, so **(D)** is correct. **(A)**, **(B)**, and **(C)** place the sentence in locations that do not make logical sense given the information provided in sentence 11.

10. H

Category: Topic Development

Getting to the Answer: The entire passage is about Milton Hershey, including the fact that the town he built is named after him. It's true that this is just one example of towns or other locations named after their founders, but that is irrelevant in a passage about a specific person. **(H)** is correct. All other sentences make sense in the passage.

11. D

Category: Topic Development

Getting to the Answer: The previous sentence introduces the Hersheys' charity work, and **(D)** provides a logical transition from the introduction of this philanthropy to the example provided in sentence 16. None of the other answers provides a supporting example of sentence 16.

Strategic Review: Math

1.   C

Subject: Arithmetic

Getting to the Answer: First, use $\overline{BA} = 15$ units and $\overline{AC} = \frac{2}{3}\overline{BA}$ to find the distance between A and C.

$\overline{AC} = \frac{2}{3}\overline{BA} = \frac{2}{3}(15) = 10$ units.

Since points A, B, and C are on a number line, and A is between B and C, then $\overline{BC} = \overline{BA} + \overline{AC}$. Thus, $\overline{BC} = 15 + 10 = 25$ units.

2.   F

Subject: Arithmetic

Getting to the Answer: First list the factors of 60 and then identify how many factors greater than 2 and less than 20 are odd. The positive factors of 60 are 1 and 60, 2 and 30, 3 and 20, 4 and 15, 5 and 12, and 6 and 10. The factors greater than 2 and less than 20 are 3, 4, 5, 6, 10, 12, and 15. Thus, there are 3 positive odd factors of 60 greater than 2 and less than 20.

3.   B

Subject: Arithmetic

Getting to the Answer: Use $\text{Average} = \frac{\text{Sum}}{\text{Number of Items}}$ to find the mean. To calculate the sum, first multiply the number of states by the minimum wage for each row and then add them together.

$$\text{Average} = \frac{16(\$7.25) + 3(\$8.25) + 1(\$13.25)}{20}$$
$$= \frac{\$154}{20}$$
$$= \$7.70$$

4. F

Subject: Statistics and Probability

Getting to the Answer: Let c be the total number of cups in the package. Set up a proportion to find c.

$$\frac{3}{3+5} = \frac{6}{c}$$
$$48 = 3c$$
$$16 = c$$

If there are 16 total cups and 6 are blue, there are 10 cups that are not blue.

5. C

Subject: Algebra

Getting to the Answer: Let t be the total number of liters the air mattress can hold, and use Percent $= \frac{\text{Part}}{\text{Whole}}$ to write two equations: $\frac{a+80}{t} = 80\%$ and $\frac{a+80+30}{t} = 90\%$.

Solve each equation for t:

Equation 1:

$$\frac{a+80}{t} = \frac{80}{100}$$
$$\frac{a+80}{t} = \frac{4}{5}$$
$$5(a+80) = 4t$$
$$\frac{5a+400}{4} = t$$

Equation 2:

$$\frac{a+80+30}{t} = \frac{90}{100}$$
$$\frac{a+110}{t} = \frac{9}{10}$$
$$10(a+110) = 9t$$
$$\frac{10a+1{,}100}{9} = t$$

Set the two equations equal to each other and solve for a:

$$\frac{5a+400}{4} = \frac{10a+1{,}100}{9}$$
$$9(5a+400) = 4(10a+1{,}100)$$
$$45a+3{,}600 = 40a+4{,}400$$
$$5a = 800$$
$$a = 160$$

6. E

Subject: Algebra

Getting to the Answer: Solve each side of the inequality separately. Then substitute $y = 2$ and solve for x:

Left side of the inequality:

$$4x+1 \leq y$$
$$4x+1 \leq 2$$
$$4x \leq 1$$
$$x \leq \frac{1}{4}$$

Right side of the inequality:

$$y < 2x-5$$
$$2 < 2x-5$$
$$7 < 2x$$
$$\frac{7}{2} < x$$

The solution set is $x \leq \frac{1}{4}$ or $3\frac{1}{2} < x$, which matches **(E)**.

7. B

Subject: Algebra

Getting to the Answer: Let W represent Weiwei's age and C represent Caleb's age today. Set up equations expressing the relationship between Weiwei's age and Caleb's age today and in 3 years: $W = \frac{1}{2}C$ and $W+3 = \frac{2}{3}(C+3)$.

Substitute W, and solve for C:

$$\frac{1}{2}C+3 = \frac{2}{3}(C+3)$$
$$\frac{1}{2}C+3 = \frac{2}{3}C+2$$
$$1 = \frac{2}{3}C - \frac{1}{2}C$$
$$1 = \frac{4}{6}C - \frac{3}{6}C$$
$$1 = \frac{1}{6}C$$
$$6 = C$$

8. E

Subject: Algebra

Getting to the Answer: Let p be the number of pounds Ester went over 3,000 pounds. Ester's total cost is $\$365 + \$1.25p$. Noel's total cost is identical to Ester's, so $\$365 + \$1.25p = \$430$. Solving for p gives:

$$\$365 + \$1.25p = \$430$$
$$\$1.25p = \$65$$
$$p = 52$$

Ester went 52 pounds over 3,000 pounds.

9. D

Subject: Geometry

Getting to the Answer: Angle ADC and 60° add up to 180° because they form a straight line. Therefore, $\angle ADC = 180° - 60° = 120°$. Remember, corresponding angles are equal. Thus, $\angle ABC = \angle ADC = 120°$. The sum of the angles around B is 360°, so $x° + 120° + 90° = 360°$. Solving for x gives $x = 150$.

10. H

Subject: Geometry

Getting to the Answer: One revolution equals the circumference of the tire. The radius is half the diameter, or 10 inches.

$$C = 2\pi r = 2\left(\frac{22}{7}\right)(10) = \frac{440}{7} \text{ inches}$$

Since the truck travels 88 inches per second, the number of revolutions one tire makes is $88 \div \frac{440}{7} = 88 \times \frac{7}{440} = \frac{7}{5}$ revolutions per second. Multiply by 60 seconds to get $\frac{7}{5} \times 60 = 84$ revolutions in 1 minute.

11. A

Subject: Geometry

Getting to the Answer: The shaded region is composed of one rectangle and one right triangle. The rectangle has a width of 2 units and a height of 3 units. The right triangle has a base of 2 units and a height of 2 units. Thus, the total area of the shaded region is $(2 \times 3) + \frac{1}{2}(2 \times 2) = 6 + 2 = 8$ square units.

12. E

Subject: Statistics and Probability

Getting to the Answer: Multiply each district's number of coffee shops by the number of patrons. Note that since Districts A and B have the same number of patrons, you only need to calculate the number of patrons for District A, which has a greater number of coffee shops. Similarly, since Districts C and D have the same number of patrons, you only need to calculate the number of patrons for District C, which has a greater number of coffee shops.

District A: $200 \times 150 = 30,000$

District C: $250 \times 100 = 25,000$

District A has the greatest number of patrons.

Strategic Review: Math Grid-In Questions

1. −24

Subject: Arithmetic

Getting to the Answer: Apply the order of operations, or PEMDAS, and calculate carefully:

$$6 + 4 \div |-2| + (-4)^3 \times \frac{1}{2}$$
$$6 + 4 \div 2 + (-4)^3 \times \frac{1}{2}$$
$$6 + 4 \div 2 + -64 \times \frac{1}{2}$$
$$6 + 2 + (-32) = -24$$

Grid in −**24**.

2. 5

Subject: Algebra

Getting to the Answer: Solve this question as you would any other equation. Isolate the variable by subtracting 16 from both sides, then dividing by −4:

$$8x + 2 - 4(x + 4) = 6$$
$$8x + 2 - 4x - 16 = 6$$
$$4x - 14 = 6$$
$$4x = 20$$
$$x = 5$$

Grid in **5**.

3.   48

Subject: Algebra

Getting to the Answer: To solve this equation, begin by adding 10 to both sides. The final step is to multiply both sides by 12 to undo the fraction.

$$\frac{h}{12} - 10 = -6$$
$$\frac{h}{12} = 4$$
$$h = 48$$

Grid in **48**.

4.   24

Subject: Algebra

Getting to the answer: Substitute 8 in for a everywhere it appears in the given expression. Compute and simplify, keeping in mind the correct rules for the order of operations, or PEMDAS:

$$2(a - 5)^2 + 3a \div 4$$
$$2((8) - 5)^2 + 3(8) \div 4$$
$$2(3)^2 + 24 \div 4$$
$$18 + 6 = 24$$

Grid in **24**.

5.   4.1

Subject: Statistics and Probability

Getting to the Answer: To find the mean, or average, distance that Maria ran over the three days, add the three distances and divide by the number of days:

$2.1 + 6 + 4.2 = 12.3$ miles

12.3 miles $\div$ 3 days $= 4.1$ miles per day

Grid in **4.1**.

6.   112

Subject: Algebra

Getting to the Answer: First, create a proportion that expresses the given information. You know that the ratio of red cups to blue cups is 3:4 and there are 48 red cups:

$$\frac{3}{4} = \frac{48}{x}$$
$$3x = 192$$
$$x = 64$$

Don't grid in 64, though! You are asked how many total cups there are, so add 48 and 64 together to get 112. Grid in **112**.

7.   18

Subject: Arithmetic

Getting to the Answer: On Monday, Mark paints one-fourth of the 28 houses, or 7 houses. On Tuesday, he paints one-seventh of the remaining 21 (not 28!) houses, which is 3 houses. This means that he paints $7 + 3 = 10$ houses on Monday and Tuesday, leaving 18 houses for the rest of the week. Grid in **18**.

8.   97.5

Subject: Arithmetic

Getting to the Answer: Start by calculating how much Sam was paid for each essay. Essay 1 was 300 words, so he received $250(\$0.10) + 50(\$0.05) = \$25 + \$2.50 = \$27.50$. Essay 2 was 400 words, so he received $250(\$0.10) + 150(\$0.05) = \$25 + \$7.50 = \$32.50$. Essay 3 was 500 words, so he received $250(\$0.10) + 250(\$0.05) = \$25 + \$12.50 = \$37.50$. Together, Sam was paid $\$27.50 + \$32.50 + \$37.50 = \$97.50$. Grid in **97.5**.

9.   9

Subject: Arithmetic

Getting to the Answer: Finding the halfway point between two numbers is the same as finding the midpoint of two numbers. To find the midpoint, add the two numbers together and divide by 2. This yields $\frac{-5 + 23}{2} = \frac{18}{2} = 9$. Grid in **9**.

10.   212

Subject: Arithmetic

Getting to the Answer: Each of the 8 students needs a paintbrush, so the cost of 8 paintbrushes is $8 \times \$1.50 = \$12$. Each student needs 5 tubes of paint, meaning that $8 \times 5 = 40$ tubes of paint are needed. 40 tubes of paint cost $40 \times \$5 = \$200$. Thus, the instructor spends $\$12 + \$200 = \$212$ on supplies, so grid in **212**.

11. 1,962

Subject: Arithmetic

Getting to the Answer: If an airplane flies 436 miles per hour and the flight takes 4.5 hours, then the distance the airplane flies is simply 436 × 4.5, using $d = rt$. This product is 1,962, meaning the distance between Miami and Quito is 1,962 miles. Grid in **1,962**.

12. 36

Subject: Statistics and Probability

Getting to the Answer: The question tells you that the book club sends William a book each month, which would be 12 books over the course of a year. However, don't forget about the free book! If William receives a free book at the end of the year, then he receives 13 books total for the year. If you are computing the average price per book, you need to consider all 13 books. The answer, then, will simply be $468 divided by 13, which is $36. Grid in **36**.

13. 37

Subject: Arithmetic

Getting to the Answer: You know that Danielle read 13 books, and that Emma read 15 fewer than 3 times this amount. Here, that means that Emma read 15 fewer than 3(13) books, or $3(13) - 15 = 24$ books. The question asks for the number of books that Danielle and Emma read combined, which would be $13 + 24 = 37$ books, so grid in **37**.

14. 8.42

Subject: Arithmetic

Getting to the Answer: First, consider which items are taxed and which aren't. The question tells you that food is taxed, so the salad and the soup will be taxed at 6%. Thus, these two items cost $3 + $4 = $7, but you also need to consider the tax, which is $7(0.06) = $0.42. Including tax, these two items cost $7.42. You also need to include the cost of the iced tea, which is $1, giving you a total of $8.42. Grid in **8.42**.

15. 3

Subject: Arithmetic

Getting to the Answer: To determine how much liquid is used, simply add the three numbers together. Remember to use a common denominator when adding or subtracting fractions. Also, converting mixed numbers to improper fractions first is usually a good idea.

$$\frac{5}{3} + \frac{1}{2} + \frac{5}{6} \Rightarrow \frac{10}{6} + \frac{3}{6} + \frac{5}{6} = \frac{18}{6} = 3$$

Grid in **3**.

16. 10

Subject: Algebra

Getting to the Answer: Let t be the number of tea mugs that Krista has. If Dana has four more than half of this number of mugs and they have a total of 19 mugs, then the following equation can be constructed:

$$t + \frac{1}{2}t + 4 = 19$$
$$\frac{3}{2}t + 4 = 19$$
$$\frac{3}{2}t = 15$$
$$t = 10$$

The question asks for the number of mugs that Krista has, so grid in **10**.

17. 750

Subject: Algebra

Getting to the Answer: Start by calculating how much gravel was used in the anti-skid material last year. You know that the ratio of gravel to salt was 3:2 and 300 tons of salt were used, so the following proportion can be set up: $\frac{3}{2} = \frac{x}{300}$. Multiplying by 2 and dividing by 3 will give you 450, so 450 tons of gravel were used. This isn't the correct answer, though! The question asks how much total material was used, so add up both numbers to get $300 + 450 = 750$ tons of material. Grid in **750**.

18. 100

Subject: Algebra

Getting to the Answer: Let m represent the number of mountain bicycles that will be sold next month. Use the information in the table to set up a proportion:

$$\frac{m}{300} = \frac{900}{2,700}$$
$$2,700m = 900(300)$$
$$m = \frac{900(300)}{2,700}$$
$$m = 100$$

Grid in **100**.

19. 9

Subject: Arithmetic

Getting to the Answer: Calculate simple interest by multiplying the initial deposit (p), the interest rate (r), and the number of years (t) together and set that equal to the interest earned:

$$(p)(r)(t) = \text{Interest Earned}$$
$$(1{,}200)(0.04)t = 432$$
$$48t = 432$$
$$t = 9$$

Grid in **9**.

20. 18

Subject: Arithmetic

Getting to the Answer: The greatest possible number of children in the camp is equal to the greatest common factor (GCF) of 72, 60, and 84. Write the prime factorization of each number to find the factors that all three have in common:

$$54 = 2 \times 3^3$$
$$72 = 2^3 \times 3^2$$
$$90 = 2 \times 3^2 \times 5$$

The factors they have in common are 2, 3, and 3. Multiply those together to find the GCF: $2 \times 3 \times 3 = $ **18**.

CHAPTER 20

Stress Management

Make the Most of Your Prep Time

The countdown to the SHSAT has begun. Your test date is looming on the horizon, and your anxiety is probably on the rise. Your stomach may feel twisted, or your thinking may be getting cloudy. You might be worried that you won't be ready in time. Worst of all, you may not be sure of what to do about these feelings.

First, don't panic! It is possible to conquer that anxiety and stress—both before and during the test. Lack of control is a common cause of stress. Research shows that if you don't have a sense of control over what's happening in your life, you can easily end up feeling helpless and hopeless. This means that just having specific things to do and to think about may help reduce your stress. This chapter discusses how to take control, including stress management strategies for both your remaining time leading up to the test and for the SHSAT itself.

SHSAT EXPERT NOTE

Avoid Must-y Thinking

Let go of "must-y" thoughts: those notions that you must do something in a certain way. For example, thoughts like "I must get a great score, or else!" or "I must meet everyone's expectations!" can have a negative influence on your actions.

Identify the Sources of Stress

In the space provided, jot down anything you identify as a source of your test-related stress. The idea is to pin down as much free-floating anxiety as possible so that you can take control of it. Here are some common examples to get you started:

- I always freeze up on tests.
- I'm nervous about the English Language Arts section.
- I'm never any good at math.
- I need a good/great score to go to Brooklyn Tech.
- My older brother/sister/best friend got in. I need to get in, too.
- People will be really disappointed if I don't get in.
- I'm afraid of losing my focus and concentration.
- I'm afraid that I'm not spending enough time preparing.
- I study like crazy, but nothing seems to stick.
- I always run out of time and get nervous or anxious during the test.

Sources of Stress

_____

_____

_____

_____

Take a few minutes to think about the sources of stress you've just written down. Then, rewrite them, listing the statements that contribute most to your stress first and putting the least stressful items last. Chances are, the top of the list is a fairly accurate description of your test anxiety, both physically and mentally. The items at the bottom of the list usually describe your more general fears. As you write the list, you're creating a prioritized list of sources of stress so that you can start by dealing with the sources that affect you most. Often, taking care of the most stressful sources at the top of the list goes a long way toward relieving overall testing anxiety, and you may not even need to bother with the worries you placed last.

SHSAT EXPERT NOTE

Create a study space. Don't study in a messy, cramped, or loud area if at all possible. Before you sit down to work, clear yourself an uncluttered space. Make sure you have whatever tools you will need—such as books, pencils, or highlighters—within easy reach before you sit down to study. Put your phone on silent and turn it over so that you're not tempted by notifications. Set up a study space that allows you to focus on your work with minimal distractions.

Know Your Strengths

Research shows that reframing your thoughts in a positive way can actually influence how you act; reflecting on positive experiences can influence positive behaviors. The following exercise is most effective when completed multiple times, so you should plan to complete it at least once before you take the SHSAT. First, spend one minute listing the areas of the test that you are good at. These areas can be general ("reading") or specific ("math grid-in questions"). Write down as many as you can think of and, if possible, write for the entire minute. If you have trouble brainstorming, think about more than just the SHSAT: In which areas have you succeeded recently in school?

Strong Subjects

_____
_____
_____
_____

Next, spend one minute listing the areas of the test you're not so good at yet. Again, keep it to one minute, but do your best to continue writing until you reach the cutoff. Don't be afraid to identify and write down your weak spots; everyone has them! In all probability, as you do both lists, you'll find that you are strong in some areas and not so strong in others. Taking note of both your strengths and your areas of opportunity boosts your confidence and focuses your studying.

Areas of Opportunity

_____
_____
_____
_____

Identifying your areas of opportunity gives you some distinct advantages over those who choose to only focus on their strengths. First, doing this helps you to determine where you need to spend extra effort, especially if you have a lot of time to study. Increased exposure to tough material makes it feel more familiar and less intimidating, so reviewing a topic, even if you don't feel that you have time to master it, can reduce your stress level when you encounter a question with that topic on Test Day. Also, you'll feel better about your own progress because you'll be dealing directly with areas of the test that bring on your anxiety. It's easier to feel confident when you know you're actively strengthening your chances of earning a higher overall test score.

Now that you have identified both your strengths and your areas of opportunity, go back to your list of strengths and expand on it for two minutes. Start with the general items on that first list and make them more specific. If anything new comes to mind, jot it down. For now, focus all of your attention and effort on your strengths. Don't underestimate yourself or your abilities; at the same time, don't list strengths you don't really have.

Expanding from general to specific might go like this: If you listed "reading" as a broad topic you feel strong in, you would then narrow your focus to include the parts of reading about which you are particularly knowledgeable. Your areas of strength related to "reading" might include identifying the main idea of a passage, locating key details, being able to answer complicated questions about a passage, etc.

Strong Subjects: An Expanded List

_____

_____

_____

_____

After you've stopped, check your time. Did you find yourself going beyond the two minutes allotted? Did you write down more things than you thought you knew? Is it possible you know more than you've given yourself credit for?

Here's another way to think about this type of exercise: every area of strength and confidence you can identify is like having a reserve of solid gold in a safe, protected place. You can then use these reserves to solve difficult questions, maintain confidence, and keep test stress and anxiety at a distance. The most encouraging part is that every time you recognize another area of strength, succeed at coming up with a solution, or get a good score on a test, you increase your reserves, and there is absolutely no limit to how much self-confidence you can have or how good you can feel about yourself.

> ### SHSAT EXPERT NOTE
>
> Just by completing these brief exercises, you have taken an active step toward helping yourself. Notice any increased feelings of confidence? Enjoy them: you've earned it!

Imagine Yourself Succeeding

These two exercises are both physical and mental. For both exercises, you will want to find a comfortable chair and get yourself into a comfortable sitting position in a quiet setting. Wear loose clothes. If you wear glasses, take them off.

Start by closing your eyes and breathing in a deep, satisfying breath of air. Really fill your lungs until your rib cage is fully expanded and you feel like you can't take in any more. Hold your breath for a moment, and then, slowly exhale the air completely. Imagine you're blowing out a candle with your last little puff of air. Do this two or three more times, filling your lungs to their maximum and emptying them totally. Keep your eyes closed comfortably but not tightly. Let your body sink deeper into the chair as you become even more comfortable.

With your eyes shut, you may notice something very interesting. When you sit comfortably, close your eyes, and focus on your breathing; you're no longer focusing on the world outside of you. Now, you can concentrate on what happens _inside_ you. The more you recognize your own physical reactions to stress and anxiety, the more you can do about them. You might not realize it, but as this happens, you're beginning to regain a sense of being in control.

Once you've settled into a relaxed, comfortable breathing pattern, imagine yourself in a relaxing situation. Your situation might take place in a special place you've visited before or it can be one you've only heard about. It can even be a fictional location that you create in your imagination, but a real-life memory of a place or situation you know usually requires less effort. Imagine the scene with as much detail as possible, and notice as much as you can about it. Once you feel that you have noticed everything there is to notice about the situation, allow the first relaxing situation to fade away and another to take its place. Do what you can to allow the images to come easily and naturally; don't force them.

Stay focused on these images as you sink farther back into your chair. Breathe easily and naturally. You might have the sensation of stress or tension draining from your muscles and flowing downward, out your feet, and away from you. If you're having trouble seeing anything, that's okay. Focus on your relaxed breathing, noticing how you feel as you breathe in and out. If an image comes to mind, examine it. If not, just keep breathing.

After two or three images (or approximately 20–30 breaths), take a moment to check how you're feeling. Notice how comfortable you've become, and imagine how much easier it would feel if you could take the test feeling this comfortable. If you were successful, you've coupled the images of your special place with sensations of comfort and relaxation. You've also found a way to become relaxed simply by visualizing your own safe, special place. If you weren't successful, that's okay . . . try again tomorrow!

Once you've completed this relaxation exercise, close your eyes and start remembering a real-life situation in which you did well on a test. If you can't come up with one, remember a situation in which you did something (academic or otherwise) that you were really proud of—just make sure that it's a genuine accomplishment.

Now, make this memory as detailed as possible. Think about the sights, the sounds, the smells, even the tastes associated with this memory. Remember how confident and motivated you felt as you accomplished your goal. Now, start thinking about the upcoming SHSAT. Keep your thoughts and feelings in line with that successful experience. Don't try to make comparisons between them. Instead, focus on imagining yourself taking the upcoming test with the same feelings of confidence and relaxed control.

These two exercises are a great way to manage your stress, especially stress related to the SHSAT. You should practice them often, especially whenever the prospect of taking the exam starts to stress you out. The more you practice, the more effective these exercises will be for you.

> ### SHSAT EXPERT NOTE
>
> Your school likely has counseling available. If you've tried multiple strategies for conquering test stress on your own and don't feel like you're making progress, make an appointment with your counselor for one-on-one support.

Get Active

Whether your choice is walking, jogging, biking, dance, push-ups, or even a pickup basketball or baseball game, physical exercise is a very effective way to stimulate both your mind and body and to improve your ability to think and concentrate. Also, it's a medical fact that sedentary people get less oxygen to the blood, and, therefore, to the head, than active people. You can live fine with a little less oxygen, but you definitely can't think as well. Ironically, a surprising number of students get out of the habit of regular exercise because they're spending so much time prepping for exams. In the long term, however, making time for exercise will pay off as part of your stress management efforts.

When you're in the middle of studying and start feeling tired, take a short, brisk walk. Breathe deeply and swing your arms as you walk to clear your mind.

There's something else that happens when students don't make exercise an integral part of their test preparation. Like all natural things, you operate best if all your "energy systems" are in balance. Studying uses a lot of energy, but that energy is (usually) only mental energy. When you take a study break, try to do something active (instead of scrolling through social media or trying to take a very short nap). Set a timer, and take a five- to ten-minute movement break for every hour that you study.

Need some inspiration? A quick internet search should pull up some easy activities for short movement breaks. The physical exertion helps use up your physical energy, which helps to keep your mind and body in sync. Then, when you finish studying for the night and go to bed, it's less likely that you will lie there tense and unable to sleep because your head is overtired and your body wants to get out and do something.

One warning about physical activity: it's not a good idea to exercise vigorously during the hour or two before you go to bed. It takes some time for your body to relax after physical activity, so doing so could easily cause sleep problems. For the same reason, it's also not a good idea to study right up to bedtime. Make time for a "buffer period" for 30 to 60 minutes before you go to bed that's designed to help you transition from being awake to being asleep.

Here's another natural route to relaxation and invigoration. It's an exercise that you can do whenever you get stressed out—including right before the test begins or even *during* the test. It's very simple and takes just a few minutes.

First, close your eyes. Start with your eyes, and—without holding your breath—gradually tighten every muscle in your body (noticeably, but not to the point of pain) in the following sequence:

1. Close your eyes tightly.

2. Squeeze your nose and mouth together so that your whole face is scrunched up. (If it makes you self-conscious to do this in the test room, skip the face-scrunching part.)

3. Pull your chin into your chest, and pull your shoulders together.

4. Tighten your arms to your body, and then clench your hands into tight fists.

5. Pull in your stomach.

6. Squeeze your thighs together and tighten your calves.

7. Stretch your feet, and then curl your toes (watch out for cramping in this part).

At this point, every muscle should be tightened. Now, relax your body, one part at a time, *in reverse order*, starting with your toes. Let the tension drop out of each muscle. The entire process might take five minutes from start to finish when you are not in a timed situation (but probably only a minute or two during the test). This clenching and unclenching exercise should help you to feel very relaxed.

Keep Breathing

Dedicated attention to breathing is an excellent way of managing stress. Often, those who are struggling (either with physical or mental stress) end up taking shallow breaths. They breathe using only their upper chest and shoulder muscles, and they may even hold their breath for long periods of time. Conversely, those who experience stress while continuing to breathe normally and rhythmically are more likely to be relaxed and in control during the entire experience. This means that now is the time to get used to the practice of relaxed breathing. Practice the next exercise to learn to breathe in a natural, easy rhythm.

With your eyes still closed, breathe in slowly and *deeply* through your nose. Hold the breath for a bit and then release it through your mouth. The key is to breathe slowly and deeply by using your diaphragm (the big band of muscle that spans your body just above your waist) to draw air in and out naturally and effortlessly. Breathing deeply with your diaphragm (as opposed to your shoulders and chest) encourages relaxation and helps minimize tension. Try it, and notice how relaxed and comfortable you feel, especially compared to breathing more shallowly.

This is yet another stress management technique you can use during the test to collect your thoughts and ward off excess stress. The entire exercise should take no more than three to five minutes. Again, though, this is suggested timing while you are in an untimed situation; during the test, you should plan to spend a minute or less on this activity at any one time.

Handling Stress During the Test

The biggest stress generator is often the test itself. Fear not; there are methods designed to reduce your stress during the test.

- Remind yourself to keep moving forward instead of getting bogged down in a difficult question. Remember, you don't have to get everything right to achieve a good score. The best test takers skip difficult material temporarily (sometimes permanently!) in search of the easier questions. They mark the questions that require extra time and thought, and they strategically skip questions if doing so increases the number of questions they can answer correctly. This strategy buys time and builds confidence so they can handle the tough questions later, and you can use this strategy regardless of how much content you have mastered.

- Keep breathing! Test takers often tend to forget to breathe properly as the test proceeds. They may start holding their breath without realizing it, or they may breathe erratically. Improper breathing interferes with clear thinking, so use the breathing exercises from this chapter to help you overcome mid-test stress.

- Some quick, small physical activity during the test—especially if your concentration is wandering or energy is waning—can help. Try this: put your palms together and press intensely for a few seconds. Concentrate on the tension you feel through your palms, wrists, forearms, and up into your biceps and shoulders. Then, quickly release the pressure. Feel the difference as you let go. Focus on the warm relaxation that floods through the muscles. Now you're ready to return to the task.

- Here's another quick activity that will relieve tension in both your neck and eye muscles. Slowly rotate your head from side to side, turning your head and eyes to look as far back over each shoulder as you can. Feel the muscles stretch on one side of your neck as they contract on the other. Repeat five times in each direction.

- If it feels like something is going really wrong, don't panic. If the test booklet is defective—two pages are stuck together or the ink has run—stay calm. Raise your hand to tell the proctor you need a new book. If you accidentally skip a page and realize you have more questions left than you originally thought, just work through each question strategically and be sure to fill in an answer for every question even if it's a complete guess.

- Don't be thrown if other test takers seem to be working faster or with more exertion than you are. Continue to spend your time working systematically through your answers; this process leads to better results. Don't mistake the other test takers' activity as a sign of progress and higher scores.

- If you find yourself starting to worry, remind yourself of how well you've prepared. Try to change your mindset: think of any nerves as excitement for being able to prove what you know. You know the structure of the test, you know the instructions, and you've studied for every question type. You've got this!

PART FIVE

SHSAT Practice Tests and Explanations

SHSAT Practice Test 1

SHSAT Practice Test 1
ANSWER SHEET

Scan Code

Please use this Answer Sheet only if the test will be scored via a webgrid/online scoring process. This Answer Sheet will NOT work if the test will be scanned.

For scanned exams, please refer to the Kaplan Answer Grid (which requires the use of a No. 2 pencil and is formatted for scanning machines).

Enrollment ID

PART 1—ENGLISH LANGUAGE ARTS

1. Ⓐ Ⓑ Ⓒ Ⓓ
2. Ⓔ Ⓕ Ⓖ Ⓗ
3. Ⓐ Ⓑ Ⓒ Ⓓ
4. Ⓔ Ⓕ Ⓖ Ⓗ
5. Ⓐ Ⓑ Ⓒ Ⓓ
6. Ⓔ Ⓕ Ⓖ Ⓗ
7. Ⓐ Ⓑ Ⓒ Ⓓ
8. Ⓔ Ⓕ Ⓖ Ⓗ
9. Ⓐ Ⓑ Ⓒ Ⓓ
10. Ⓔ Ⓕ Ⓖ Ⓗ

11. Ⓐ Ⓑ Ⓒ Ⓓ
12. Ⓔ Ⓕ Ⓖ Ⓗ
13. Ⓐ Ⓑ Ⓒ Ⓓ
14. Ⓔ Ⓕ Ⓖ Ⓗ
15. Ⓐ Ⓑ Ⓒ Ⓓ
16. Ⓔ Ⓕ Ⓖ Ⓗ
17. Ⓐ Ⓑ Ⓒ Ⓓ
18. Ⓔ Ⓕ Ⓖ Ⓗ
19. Ⓐ Ⓑ Ⓒ Ⓓ
20. Ⓔ Ⓕ Ⓖ Ⓗ

21. Ⓐ Ⓑ Ⓒ Ⓓ
22. Ⓔ Ⓕ Ⓖ Ⓗ
23. Ⓐ Ⓑ Ⓒ Ⓓ
24. Ⓔ Ⓕ Ⓖ Ⓗ
25. Ⓐ Ⓑ Ⓒ Ⓓ
26. Ⓔ Ⓕ Ⓖ Ⓗ
27. Ⓐ Ⓑ Ⓒ Ⓓ
28. Ⓔ Ⓕ Ⓖ Ⓗ
29. Ⓐ Ⓑ Ⓒ Ⓓ
30. Ⓔ Ⓕ Ⓖ Ⓗ

31. Ⓐ Ⓑ Ⓒ Ⓓ
32. Ⓔ Ⓕ Ⓖ Ⓗ
33. Ⓐ Ⓑ Ⓒ Ⓓ
34. Ⓔ Ⓕ Ⓖ Ⓗ
35. Ⓐ Ⓑ Ⓒ Ⓓ
36. Ⓔ Ⓕ Ⓖ Ⓗ
37. Ⓐ Ⓑ Ⓒ Ⓓ
38. Ⓔ Ⓕ Ⓖ Ⓗ
39. Ⓐ Ⓑ Ⓒ Ⓓ
40. Ⓔ Ⓕ Ⓖ Ⓗ

41. Ⓐ Ⓑ Ⓒ Ⓓ
42. Ⓔ Ⓕ Ⓖ Ⓗ
43. Ⓐ Ⓑ Ⓒ Ⓓ
44. Ⓔ Ⓕ Ⓖ Ⓗ
45. Ⓐ Ⓑ Ⓒ Ⓓ
46. Ⓔ Ⓕ Ⓖ Ⓗ
47. Ⓐ Ⓑ Ⓒ Ⓓ
48. Ⓔ Ⓕ Ⓖ Ⓗ
49. Ⓐ Ⓑ Ⓒ Ⓓ
50. Ⓔ Ⓕ Ⓖ Ⓗ

51. Ⓐ Ⓑ Ⓒ Ⓓ
52. Ⓔ Ⓕ Ⓖ Ⓗ
53. Ⓐ Ⓑ Ⓒ Ⓓ
54. Ⓔ Ⓕ Ⓖ Ⓗ
55. Ⓐ Ⓑ Ⓒ Ⓓ
56. Ⓔ Ⓕ Ⓖ Ⓗ
57. Ⓐ Ⓑ Ⓒ Ⓓ

PART 2—MATHEMATICS

58.   59.   60.   61.   62.

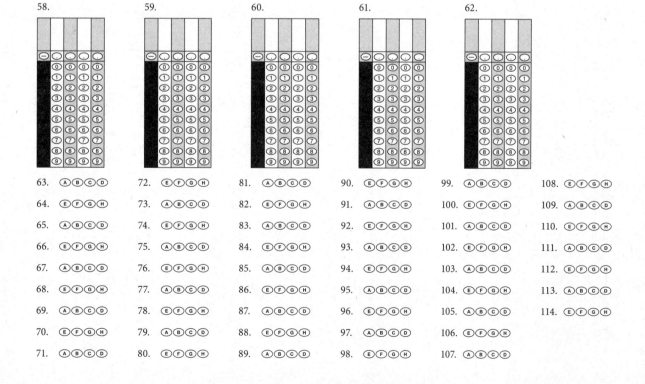

63. Ⓐ Ⓑ Ⓒ Ⓓ
64. Ⓔ Ⓕ Ⓖ Ⓗ
65. Ⓐ Ⓑ Ⓒ Ⓓ
66. Ⓔ Ⓕ Ⓖ Ⓗ
67. Ⓐ Ⓑ Ⓒ Ⓓ
68. Ⓔ Ⓕ Ⓖ Ⓗ
69. Ⓐ Ⓑ Ⓒ Ⓓ
70. Ⓔ Ⓕ Ⓖ Ⓗ
71. Ⓐ Ⓑ Ⓒ Ⓓ

72. Ⓔ Ⓕ Ⓖ Ⓗ
73. Ⓐ Ⓑ Ⓒ Ⓓ
74. Ⓔ Ⓕ Ⓖ Ⓗ
75. Ⓐ Ⓑ Ⓒ Ⓓ
76. Ⓔ Ⓕ Ⓖ Ⓗ
77. Ⓐ Ⓑ Ⓒ Ⓓ
78. Ⓔ Ⓕ Ⓖ Ⓗ
79. Ⓐ Ⓑ Ⓒ Ⓓ
80. Ⓔ Ⓕ Ⓖ Ⓗ

81. Ⓐ Ⓑ Ⓒ Ⓓ
82. Ⓔ Ⓕ Ⓖ Ⓗ
83. Ⓐ Ⓑ Ⓒ Ⓓ
84. Ⓔ Ⓕ Ⓖ Ⓗ
85. Ⓐ Ⓑ Ⓒ Ⓓ
86. Ⓔ Ⓕ Ⓖ Ⓗ
87. Ⓐ Ⓑ Ⓒ Ⓓ
88. Ⓔ Ⓕ Ⓖ Ⓗ
89. Ⓐ Ⓑ Ⓒ Ⓓ

90. Ⓔ Ⓕ Ⓖ Ⓗ
91. Ⓐ Ⓑ Ⓒ Ⓓ
92. Ⓔ Ⓕ Ⓖ Ⓗ
93. Ⓐ Ⓑ Ⓒ Ⓓ
94. Ⓔ Ⓕ Ⓖ Ⓗ
95. Ⓐ Ⓑ Ⓒ Ⓓ
96. Ⓔ Ⓕ Ⓖ Ⓗ
97. Ⓐ Ⓑ Ⓒ Ⓓ
98. Ⓔ Ⓕ Ⓖ Ⓗ

99. Ⓐ Ⓑ Ⓒ Ⓓ
100. Ⓔ Ⓕ Ⓖ Ⓗ
101. Ⓐ Ⓑ Ⓒ Ⓓ
102. Ⓔ Ⓕ Ⓖ Ⓗ
103. Ⓐ Ⓑ Ⓒ Ⓓ
104. Ⓔ Ⓕ Ⓖ Ⓗ
105. Ⓐ Ⓑ Ⓒ Ⓓ
106. Ⓔ Ⓕ Ⓖ Ⓗ
107. Ⓐ Ⓑ Ⓒ Ⓓ

108. Ⓔ Ⓕ Ⓖ Ⓗ
109. Ⓐ Ⓑ Ⓒ Ⓓ
110. Ⓔ Ⓕ Ⓖ Ⓗ
111. Ⓐ Ⓑ Ⓒ Ⓓ
112. Ⓔ Ⓕ Ⓖ Ⓗ
113. Ⓐ Ⓑ Ⓒ Ⓓ
114. Ⓔ Ⓕ Ⓖ Ⓗ

PRACTICE TEST 1

Directions: Mark your answers on the separate sheet provided. You will receive credit only for answers marked on the answer grid. **DO NOT MAKE ANY STRAY MARKS ON THE ANSWER GRID.** You can write in the test booklet, or use the paper provided for scratchwork.

Marking Your Answers

Each question has only one correct answer. Select the **best** answer for each question. Your score is determined by the number of questions you answered correctly. **It is to your advantage to answer every question, even though you may not be certain which choice is correct.**

Planning Your Time

You have 180 minutes to complete the entire test. How you split the time between the English Language Arts and Mathematics sections is up to you. **If you begin with the English Language Arts section, you may go on to the Mathematics section as soon as you are ready. If you begin with the Mathematics section, you may go on to the English Language Arts section as soon as you are ready.** It is recommended that you do not spend more than 90 minutes on either section. If you complete the test before the allotted time (180 minutes) is over, you may go back to review questions in either section.

Work as rapidly as you can without making mistakes. Don't spend too much time on a difficult question. Return to it later if you have time. If time remains, you should check your answers.

Part 1—English Language Arts

57 QUESTIONS—SUGGESTED TIMING: 90 MINUTES

REVISING/EDITING

QUESTIONS 1–11

IMPORTANT NOTE

The Revising/Editing section includes Part A and Part B.

REVISING/EDITING Part A

DIRECTIONS: Answer the following questions, recognizing and correcting errors so that the sentences or paragraphs are grammatically correct. Re-read relevant parts of the text before choosing the best answer for each question, but be mindful of time. You may write in your test booklet to take notes.

1. Read this paragraph.

> Capable of reaching a weight of up to 100 <u>tons, the great</u> blue whale is the largest animal currently in <u>existence. Adult</u> females, which are larger than males, can each measure approximately 100 feet long. Despite their enormous size, these impressive creatures eat some of the smallest marine <u>life, using</u> baleen to filter their food from the water, blue whales can consume several tons of krill and other small sea animals per <u>day. The blue</u> whale's great size has not protected it from human hunters, however, and it is considered an endangered species.

Which revision corrects the error in sentence structure in the paragraph?

A. tons. The great
B. existence; adult
C. life. Using
D. day, the blue

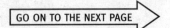
GO ON TO THE NEXT PAGE

Practice Tests

2. Read this paragraph.

> (1) Benjamin Franklin was not the first person to need glasses for seeing both near and far, but he has been the first to actually create a pair of bifocals. (2) The lenses on these glasses were designed to have upper and lower areas, with two focuses in each area. (3) Franklin also invented a type of clock, a chair with special folding parts, and a musical instrument called a glass armonica. (4) This scientist, revolutionary, businessman, and writer also designed improvements for sailing vessels attempting to improve their safety and convenience.

Which pair of revisions needs to be made in the paragraph?

E. Sentence 1: change *has been* to *was*.
   Sentence 3: remove the comma after *parts*.

F. Sentence 1: change *has been* to *was*.
   Sentence 4: insert a comma after *vessels*.

G. Sentence 2: change *were* to *are*.
   Sentence 3: remove the comma after *parts*.

H. Sentence 2: change *were* to *are*.
   Sentence 4: insert a comma after *vessels*.

3. Read this sentence.

> After her recent visit to Costa Rica, Zoe said that something she liked a lot was taking in the scenery.

Which revision uses the most precise language for the words *something she liked a lot was taking in the scenery*?

A. one good part was taking time to look at and really enjoy the pretty landscapes

B. she enjoyed visiting one of the national parks and seeing beautiful things

C. she really did enjoy the vistas in the mountains because of the nice scenery

D. her favorite memory was the view from the summit of Turrialba Volcano

4. Read this sentence.

> Able to change not only its color but also its shape and even its texture, predators are often fooled by the advanced camouflage skills of the octopus.

How should the sentence be revised?

E. Able to change not only its color but also its shape and even its texture, the octopus uses its advanced camouflage skills to elude predators.

F. Using advanced camouflage skills, including the ability to change not only its color but also its shape and even its texture, predators cannot spot the octopus.

G. Able to change not only its color but also its shape and even its texture, the advanced camouflage skills of the octopus help it evade predators.

H. The octopus, able to change not only its color but also its shape and even its texture, hides from predators with advanced camouflage skills.

GO ON TO THE NEXT PAGE

Practice Tests

Vaccines

(1) Vaccination has become one of the most important and most widely used tools of modern medicine. (2) However, very few people know the history of vaccines and how they were developed. (3) The idea of immunization goes back more than 500 years—a time when doctors still scoffed at the practice of washing their hands between patients—and found its inspiration in both traditional medicine and folklore. (4) Today, a wide variety of dangerous diseases can be prevented using vaccines.

(5) Smallpox was among the first diseases people sought to immunize against. (6) The earliest recorded success came in China in the fifteenth century. (7) There, medical practitioners employed what is now called "variolation," a process by which uninfected patients were exposed to smallpox to infect them with a mild form of the disease. (8) Much later, in the eighteenth century, the English doctor Edward Jenner began to examine a local legend that held that milkmaids who were exposed to cowpox became immune to the more dangerous smallpox. (9) Variolation, however, still posed a risk of a potentially fatal, full-scale smallpox infection. (10) Experimentation soon proved folklore correct: the relatively safe, related virus could protect patients from the deadlier illness. (11) Administering a cowpox vaccine became the standard method of inoculating against smallpox.

(12) The cowpox vaccine developed from Jenner's work set the standard for vaccines—to find a "safe" virus that confers immunity without the risks of full-blown infection. (13) Later, the French scientist Louis Pasteur discovered that ineffective, outdated disease cultures could still confer immunity and could do so without causing infection. (14) The technique of using "dead" viruses soon became an important method for developing new vaccines. (15) Vaccines using dead viruses include diphtheria, flu, and the injected polio vaccine. (16) Polio has been almost completely eliminated throughout the world by use of the Salk vaccine, an injection using a dead virus, as well as by the live but weakened Sabin vaccine given by mouth. (17) The Sabin vaccine substitutes 57 nucleotides and produces a mutation in the internal ribosome entry site. (18) Between the two, the World Health Organization reports that the worldwide incidence of polio went from 350,000 in 1988 to 74 in 2015.

5.   Which sentence should replace sentence 4 to best introduce the main topic of the passage?

   A.   From there, medical understanding of immunization expanded through both experimentation and accident.

   B.   The first vaccine was important both in its own right and because it provided the foundation for many others to follow.

   C.   Many doctors and scientists contributed to the development of better vaccines and better methods for creating vaccines.

   D.   The effectiveness of vaccines in preventing viral illnesses has been proven repeatedly in the centuries since they were invented.

6. Where should sentence 8 be moved to improve the organization of the second paragraph (sentences 5–11)?

    E. to the beginning of the paragraph (before sentence 5)

    F. between sentences 6 and 7

    G. between sentences 9 and 10

    H. between sentences 10 and 11

7. Which transition should be added to the beginning of sentence 11?

    A. However

    B. Furthermore

    C. Thus

    D. For example

8. Which sentence would best follow sentence 13 and support the ideas in the third paragraph (sentences 12–18)?

    E. He used this technique to develop a vaccine for rabies in 1885.

    F. He also developed a technique for preventing bacterial contamination in milk.

    G. He coined the word "vaccine" based on the scientific name for cowpox, vaccinia.

    H. He hypothesized that exposure to oxygen weakened diseases.

9. What is the best way to combine sentences 14 and 15 to clarify the relationship between ideas?

    A. While the technique of using "dead" viruses soon became an important method for developing new vaccines, diphtheria, flu, and the injected polio vaccine were just a few of those created using dead viruses.

    B. Thus, scientists invented an important method for developing new vaccines by using "dead" viruses, including diphtheria, flu, and the injected polio vaccine.

    C. By using "dead" viruses, the technique that became important for developing new vaccines included diphtheria, flu, and the injected polio vaccine.

    D. The technique of using "dead" viruses soon became an important method for developing new vaccines, including diphtheria, flu, and the injected polio vaccine.

10. Which sentence presents information that shifts away from the main topic of the third paragraph (sentences 12–18) and should be removed?

    E. sentence 12

    F. sentence 13

    G. sentence 16

    H. sentence 17

GO ON TO THE NEXT PAGE ⟶

11. Which concluding sentence would best follow sentence 18 and support the topic presented in the passage?

   A. The World Health Organization hopes that with more work, this disease will be completely eradicated, just as smallpox was decades ago.

   B. Because of the efforts of many dedicated professionals, people around the world are now healthier than they have ever been before.

   C. Scientists are still developing new vaccines, working to immunize people against diseases from malaria to HIV.

   D. Vaccines have made once-feared diseases nearly unheard of today and continue to improve the lives and health of people around the world.

READING COMPREHENSION

QUESTIONS 12–57

DIRECTIONS: Read the six passages and answer the corresponding questions. Re-read relevant parts of the text before choosing the best answer for each question, but be mindful of time. Base your answers only on the content within each passage. You may write in your test booklet to take notes.

Coral Islands

1 The lovely islands of the Maldives, found off the southern coasts of India and Sri Lanka in the Indian Ocean, are a favored spot for tropical vacations. It may be hard to believe that a tiny creature less than one-tenth of an inch long is responsible for building these islands; however, as the Maldives are coral islands, that is precisely their origin story. Coral islands are usually small, rise only a few feet above sea level, and comprise just a small visible part of the coral reef ecosystem. Beneath the waves, below the level of the water reached during high tides, however, the coral reefs supporting the islands are a fantastic and very beautiful world, depending entirely upon a complex web of interrelationships between plants, animals, and climatic conditions.

2 The structure of the coral reef is formed over thousands of years by the deposition of thin layers of material during the life cycles of vast numbers of coral animals, or polyps. The main architect of the reef is the stony coral, a relative of the sea anemone that lives in tropical climates and secretes a skeleton of almost pure calcium carbonate. Its partner is the green algae, a tiny unicellular plant, which lives within the tissues of the coral and is responsible for the color of the coral. The two organisms coexist in a mutually beneficial relationship, with the algae consuming carbon dioxide given off by the coral, and the coral thriving in the abundant oxygen produced photosynthetically by the algae. When the coral dies, its skeleton is left, and other organisms grow on top of it. Over the years, the sheer mass of coral skeletons, together with those of associated organisms, provides an environment conducive to the existence of a wide variety of sea creatures, including sponges, fish, mollusks, turtles, crustaceans, and dolphins. Only tropical rainforests can compete with coral reefs when it comes to the diversity of species found in, and supported by, these ecosystems.

3 Scientists classify coral reefs into four categories, depending on the proximity of the reefs to associated land masses. Fringing reefs are very close to, or attached to, non-reef islands. Many of the reefs found in the Caribbean are fringing reefs. Barrier reefs are also associated with non-reef islands but are separated from the land mass by channels or lagoons of deep water. The reef of the northeastern coast of the continent of Australia, perhaps the most famous in the world, is fringed by coral communities that have gradually grown into vast ribbons of barrier reefs. Atolls are rings of circular-shaped reefs without a central land mass and are found primarily in the Pacific and Indian Oceans. Platform, or patch, reefs form on the continental shelves, usually on those in the Pacific and Indian Oceans, and spread outward relatively evenly from their point of origin.

4 Two processes are involved in the formation of coral islands: uplift or accretion. Uplift islands are the result of shifts in the plates of the earth's crust that push the reefs above sea level. If the reef was originally an atoll, the ring may still be visible, although water in the center may be much shallower or even completely drained away. Accretion islands are formed when pieces of a coral reef are dislodged by waves, storms and, most notably, by cyclones. The reef fragments accumulate in shallower water, and other material is added by wind and wave action. Since these fragments are almost pure calcium carbonate, the exposed fragments dissolve in rain and gradually cement the structure together, making it possible for animals and plants to become established. The Maldives are examples of accretion coral islands, a bountiful and beautiful habitat for humans thanks to thousands of years and billions of coral polyps.

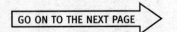

12. Which statement best describes the central idea of the passage?

    E. Coral reefs are home to a variety of unusual animal life.

    F. Coral islands can be formed by uplift or accretion.

    G. Coral reefs have complex biological and geological features.

    H. Coral reefs are characterized by profound physical beauty.

13. With which of the following would the author most likely agree?

    A. Tropical rainforests contain a greater diversity of animal species than coral reefs.

    B. Tropical rainforests are more popular tourist destinations than coral reefs.

    C. Tropical rainforests are under threat due to increasing deforestation.

    D. Tropical rainforests shelter a similar amount of biological diversity to coral reefs.

14. The skeleton of the stony coral is mostly made up of what?

    E. cartilage

    F. stone

    G. calcium carbonate

    H. carbon dioxide

15. How does paragraph 2 fit into the overall structure of the passage?

    A. It introduces stony coral as necessary to the existence of non-reef islands.

    B. It provides a transition from the discussion of stony coral's importance in reef formation to a discussion of theories about how coral reefs form into islands.

    C. It elaborates on the theories of coral island formation.

    D. It explains the importance of animals in the formation of coral reefs.

16. What geological feature of coral reefs is discussed in this passage?

    E. their evolution into islands

    F. their ability to support diverse communities of life

    G. the ease with which they withstood the destructive effects of the last Ice Age

    H. their evolution from isolated reefs into great land masses

17. Which of the following is usually close to land masses?

    A. barrier reefs

    B. atolls

    C. fringing reefs

    D. barrier islands

18. What does the passage suggest about coral islands?

    E. They are the most beautiful natural phenomena in the world.

    F. Fringing reefs are more popular than atolls.

    G. The diversity of animal life is exaggerated by divers with rich imaginations.

    H. They can be truly appreciated only from an underwater perspective.

19. What is the most likely reason the author uses the word "architect" in paragraph 2?

    A. to argue that the original designer of the reef is the stony coral

    B. to show that a building company was employed to build the reef

    C. to emphasize that the stony coral is a major component of the reef

    D. to prove that a relative of the sea anemone invented the skeleton of the reef

20. How does the author's use of chronological structure contribute to the development of ideas in the passage?

    E. It explains the formation of coral reefs before discussing the formation of coral islands from those coral reefs.

    F. It shows how coral reefs form in the Caribbean and in Australia before expanding to the Pacific and Indian Oceans.

    G. It describes how stony coral must form before green algae can be produced.

    H. It identifies the desire for tropical vacation destinations as the guiding force behind the creation of the Maldives.

Excerpt from *Gulliver's Travels*
by Jonathan Swift

1   One morning, about a fortnight after I had obtained my liberty, Reldresal, principal secretary (as they style him) for private affairs, came to my house attended only by one servant. He ordered his coach to wait at a distance, and desired I would give him an hours audience; which I readily consented to, on account of his quality and personal merits, as well as of the many good offices he had done me during my solicitations at court. I offered to lie down that he might the more conveniently reach my ear, but he chose rather to let me hold him in my hand during our conversation.

2   He began with compliments on my liberty; said "he might pretend to some merit in it;" but, however, added, "that if it had not been for the present situation of things at court, perhaps I might not have obtained it so soon. For," said he, "as flourishing a condition as we may appear to be in to foreigners, we labour under two mighty evils: a violent faction at home, and the danger of an invasion, by a most potent enemy, from abroad. As to the first, you are to understand, that for about seventy moons past there have been two struggling parties in this empire, under the names of Tramecksan and Slamecksan, from the high and low heels of their shoes, by which they distinguish themselves. [. . .] The animosities between these two parties run so high, that they will neither eat, nor drink, nor talk with each other. We compute the Tramecksan, or high heels, to exceed us in number; but the power is wholly on our side. We apprehend his imperial highness, the heir to the crown, to have some tendency towards the high heels; at least we can plainly discover that one of his heels is higher than the other, which gives him a hobble in his gait.

3   Now, in the midst of these intestine disquiets, we are threatened with an invasion from the island of Blefuscu, which is the other great empire of the universe, almost as large and powerful as this of his majesty. For as to what we have heard you affirm, that there are other kingdoms and states in the world inhabited by human creatures as large as yourself, our philosophers are in much doubt, and would rather conjecture that you dropped from the moon, or one of the stars; because it is certain, that a hundred mortals of your bulk would in a short time destroy all the fruits and cattle of his majesty's dominions: besides, our histories of six thousand moons make no mention of any other regions than the two great empires of Lilliput and Blefuscu. Which two mighty powers have, as I was going to tell you, been engaged in a most obstinate war for six-and-thirty moons past.

4   It began upon the following occasion. It is allowed on all hands, that the primitive way of breaking eggs, before we eat them, was upon the larger end; but his present majesty's grandfather, while he was a boy, going to eat an egg, and breaking it according to the ancient practice, happened to cut one of his fingers. Whereupon the emperor his father published an edict, commanding all his subjects, upon great penalties, to break the smaller end of their eggs.

5   The people so highly resented this law, that our histories tell us, there have been six rebellions raised on that account; wherein one emperor lost his life, and another his crown. These civil commotions were constantly fomented by the monarchs of Blefuscu; and when they were quelled, the exiles always fled for refuge to that empire. It is computed that eleven thousand persons have at several times suffered death, rather than submit to break their eggs at the smaller end.

6   Many hundred large volumes have been published upon this controversy: but the books of the Big-endians have been long forbidden, and the whole party rendered incapable by law of holding employments. During the course of these troubles, the emperors of Blefusca did frequently expostulate by their ambassadors,

GO ON TO THE NEXT PAGE

accusing us of making a schism in religion, by offending against a fundamental doctrine of our great prophet Lustrog, in the fifty-fourth chapter of the Blundecral (which is their Alcoran). This, however, is thought to be a mere strain upon the text; for the words are these: 'that all true believers break their eggs at the convenient end.' And which is the convenient end, seems, in my humble opinion to be left to every man's conscience, or at least in the power of the chief magistrate to determine.

7 Now, the Big-endian exiles have found so much credit in the emperor of Blefuscu's court, and so much private assistance and encouragement from their party here at home, that a bloody war has been carried on between the two empires for six-and-thirty moons, with various success; during which time we have lost forty capital ships, and a much a greater number of smaller vessels, together with thirty thousand of our best seamen and soldiers; and the damage received by the enemy is reckoned to be somewhat greater than ours. However, they have now equipped a numerous fleet, and are just preparing to make a descent upon us; and his imperial majesty, placing great confidence in your valour and strength, has commanded me to lay this account of his affairs before you."

8 I desired the secretary to present my humble duty to the emperor; and to let him know, "that I thought it would not become me, who was a foreigner, to interfere with parties; but I was ready, with the hazard of my life, to defend his person and state against all invaders."

21. Which sentence from the excerpt best describes the extreme consequences of an absurd argument?

   A. "Which two mighty powers have, as I was going to tell you, been engaged in a most obstinate war for six-and-thirty moons past." (paragraph 3)

   B. "[B]ut his present majesty's grandfather, while he was a boy, going to eat an egg, and breaking it according to the ancient practice, happened to cut one of his fingers." (paragraph 4)

   C. "It is computed that eleven thousand persons have at several times suffered death, rather than submit to break their eggs at the smaller end." (paragraph 5)

   D. "[H]is imperial majesty, placing great confidence in your valour and strength, has commanded me to lay this account of his affairs before you." (paragraph 7)

22. Read this sentence from paragraph 6.

> **Many hundred large volumes have been published upon this controversy: but the books of the Big-endians have been long forbidden, and the whole party rendered incapable by law of holding employments.**

This sentence highlights the author's view that

   E. the citizens of Lilliput and Blefuscu have taken their quarrel too far, tying up the resources of society at a significant cost.

   F. the Big-endians are absurd for refusing to work because of this controversy.

   G. the issues involved in the dispute among the Lilliputians are very serious and important to their society.

   H. the issues involved in this dispute are just and worth dying for.

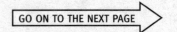

23. Which sentence from the excerpt best conveys the notion that "a bloody war has been carried on between the two empires for six-and-thirty moons" (paragraph 7)?

    A. "It began upon the following occasion. It is allowed on all hands, that the primitive way of breaking eggs, before we eat them, was upon the larger end;" (paragraph 4)

    B. "The people so highly resented this law, that our histories tell us, there have been six rebellions raised on that account;" (paragraph 5)

    C. "[F]or the words are these: 'that all true believers break their eggs at the convenient end.'" (paragraph 6)

    D. "However, they have now equipped a numerous fleet, and are just preparing to make a descent upon us;" (paragraph 7)

24. What impact do the words "you," "I," and "us" have on the meaning of the excerpt?

    E. Swift is encouraging the reader to get personally engaged with the debate in the story, take a position on the topic, and care about the result of the battle.

    F. Swift is bringing the reader into the story, hoping they will see it as satire and find parallels to things that are relevant to their own experiences.

    G. They are a storytelling device intended to make the events more emotional and meaningful for the reader.

    H. These terms are intended to catch the reader off guard, adding an element of confusion to the recounting of the tale.

25. Read the following from paragraph 6.

    > [T]he emperors of Blefusca did frequently expostulate by their ambassadors, accusing us of making a schism in religion, by offending against a fundamental doctrine of our great prophet Lustrog, in the fifty-fourth chapter of the Blundecral . . .

    How does this selection and its references to religion emphasize a central theme of the excerpt?

    A. by suggesting the dispute is something sacred and should be taken seriously by the reader

    B. by suggesting that the dispute is a matter of etiquette and that the situation could have been resolved by not offending the other party

    C. by emphasizing the absurdity of the situation in showing that it has led to religious fervor

    D. by showing that the issues of law involved are complex and not susceptible to easy remedy

26. Which of the following best expresses what the Big-endians are willing to fight and die for?

   E. They want all citizens to be forced to break their eggs at the small end.

   F. They want the citizens of Blefuscu to be forced to break their eggs at the large end.

   G. They want the right to break their eggs at the convenient end.

   H. They want to prevent others from breaking their eggs in the primitive way according to ancient practice.

GO ON TO THE NEXT PAGE

"The Landlord's Tale: Paul Revere's Ride"

by Henry Wadsworth Longfellow

Listen, my children, and you shall hear
Of the midnight ride of Paul Revere,
On the eighteenth of April, in Seventy-Five:
Hardly a man is now alive
5 Who remembers that famous day and year.

He said to his friend, "If the British march
By land or sea from the town to-night,
Hang a lantern aloft in the belfry-arch
Of the North-Church-tower, as a signal-light,—
10 One if by land, and two if by sea;
And I on the opposite shore will be,
Ready to ride and spread the alarm
Through every Middlesex village and farm,
For the country-folk to be up and to arm."

15 Then he said "Good night!" and with muffled oar
Silently rowed to the Charlestown shore,
Just as the moon rose over the bay,
Where swinging wide at her moorings lay
The Somerset, British man-of-war:
20 A phantom ship, with each mast and spar
Across the moon, like a prison-bar,
And a huge black hulk, that was magnified
By its own reflection in the tide.

27. The description in the first stanza (lines 1–5) helps establish a central idea of the poem by

   A. contrasting the children listening with the men who remember that famous day.

   B. foreshadowing the fame and significance of Paul Revere's midnight ride.

   C. showing how the perception of historical events often differs from the reality.

   D. suggesting that Paul Revere did not take his role seriously.

28. Which of the following supports what is indicated by the term "signal-light" in line 9?

   E. "He said to his friend, 'If the British march" (line 6)

   F. "And I on the opposite shore will be," (line 11)

   G. "Ready to ride and spread the alarm" (line 12)

   H. "Through every Middlesex village and farm," (line 13)

29. What impact do the phrases "like a prison-bar" (line 21) and "huge black hulk" (line 22) have on the meaning of the poem?

   A. The phrases serve as a reminder of the danger Paul Revere is in.

   B. The phrases emphasize the colonists' dominance.

   C. The phrases function as a symbol of hope and inspiration.

   D. The phrases encourage the colonists to fight back should the British invade.

30. How do lines 15–16 contribute to the development of ideas in the third stanza?

   E. The lines illustrate Revere's concern and worry over the colonists' plan.

   F. The lines portray Revere as multi-talented in his intelligence and rowing skills.

   G. The lines function as Revere's next step in the scheme to wait for the signal.

   H. The lines emphasize Revere's need to not disturb any sleeping animals at night.

31. The second stanza helps develop a theme of the poem by suggesting that

   A. Revere will not offer help to the country-folk.

   B. any colonist who sees the British invading must hang lanterns.

   C. the British will prove a more challenging opponent if coming by sea.

   D. Revere will be responsible for alerting those in the countryside.

GO ON TO THE NEXT PAGE

32. How does the form of the poem contribute to its meaning?

    E. The pastoral style offers the perspective of the average countryman.

    F. The narrative structure places a historical event into the form of a story.

    G. The fable structure teaches children the importance of being prepared with a plan.

    H. The ode format makes the poem more memorable by suggesting a tune.

33. Which line from the poem best supports the idea that the story takes place in a past time within living memory?

    A. "Listen, my children, and you shall hear" (line 1)

    B. "Of the midnight ride of Paul Revere," (line 2)

    C. "Hardly a man is now alive" (line 4)

    D. "Just as the moon rose over the bay," (line 17)

34. Which detail from the poem reflects the speaker's view that Paul Revere is on a dangerous mission?

    E. "Hardly a man is now alive" (line 4)

    F. "Hang a lantern aloft in the belfry-arch" (line 8)

    G. "And I on the opposite shore will be," (line 11)

    H. "Silently rowed to the Charlestown shore," (line 16)

The Moons of Jupiter

1   The four brightest moons of Jupiter were the first objects in the solar system discovered through the use of the telescope. Both Galileo Galilei, an Italian astronomer, and Simon Marius, working in Germany, independently identified these moons in 1610. As the first objects to be observed orbiting a body other than Earth, their proven existence played a central role in Galileo's famous argument in support of the Copernican model of the solar system, in which the planets are described as revolving around the Sun.

2   Despite the early discovery of these moons, scientific understanding of them increased fairly slowly over the next several centuries. Observers on Earth named the moons Io, Europa, Ganymede, and Callisto after Jupiter's lovers in Greco-Roman mythology, and these scientists succeeded in measuring their approximate diameters, their relative densities, and eventually some of their light-reflecting characteristics. However, it wasn't until 1979, when a spectacular series of photographs was sent back by the Voyager missions, that our impressions of these bodies were forever changed.

3   The Voyager photographs revealed that all four of the moons probably experienced early, heavy asteroid bombardment. The moon furthest from Jupiter, Callisto, has a very ancient surface that has changed little since the moon's formation, primarily due to Callisto's distance from Jupiter's magnetic field and radiation belt. Callisto is the most heavily cratered body known in the solar system and, thus, is of great interest to scientists. The next closest moon to Jupiter is Ganymede, the largest of the four moons and the only one of Jupiter's moons with its own gravitational field. Ganymede's younger surface shows more variety, featuring distinctive light and dark areas. Ancient craters dot the dark areas, while the light areas are crisscrossed by ridges and grooves that resulted from more recent ice flows. The smallest of the four moons is Europa, whose surface is entirely covered in vast oceans of ice which have almost obliterated all impact craters. The extensive surface ice makes this moon highly reflective and one of the brightest moons in the solar system. Europa is the object of intensive study because of the possibility that extensive oceans below the surface ice may harbor life.

4   Perhaps the biggest surprise of the Voyager mission was the discovery of intense volcanic or geyser-like activity on Io, the moon closest to Jupiter. Eruptions first recognized as plumes of dust and gas were immediately noticeable on the Voyager photographs. Further inspection revealed at least seven such events occurring all at once on Io's otherwise frigid surface—massive plumes of material were being ejected from the surface of the satellite to form clouds 500 kilometers high. This makes Io the only object in the solar system, other than Earth, known to have active volcanoes. At other points on the surface, scientists detected three hot spots believed to be ponds of molten lava, sulfur, or sodium overlain by a crust. The largest of these hot lakes was estimated to have a greater surface area than the state of Hawaii.

5   Although they have been observed for over four centuries, these moons continue to fascinate scientists. Because of Voyager's intriguing discoveries, many other missions have been sent to Jupiter's moons in the last decades. Just as Voyager did, these later missions have both added to our knowledge and generated new questions to be answered.

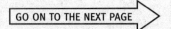

OBSERVED* VOLCANIC ACTIVITY ON LO, 1979–2018

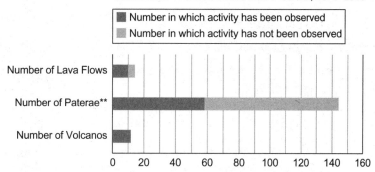

■ Number in which activity has been observed
■ Number in which activity has not been observed

*Observations from the Voyager missions, the Galileo, New Horizons, and Juno missions, as well as telescopic observations from Earth.
**Paterae: crater-like planetary features, most often caused by volcanic activity.

35. Which statement best describes the central idea of the passage?

    A. Galileo invented the telescope to enable the discovery of moons in the solar system.

    B. The discovery of ice on Europa was groundbreaking in the field of astronomy.

    C. Our current scientific understanding of Jupiter would be minimal without the help of Galileo and Marius.

    D. Scientists knew little about Jupiter's four brightest moons before Voyager's photographs of them in 1979.

36. This passage suggests that Galileo was one of the first scientists to

    E. attack the Copernican theory of the solar system.

    F. make accurate measurements of the diameters of Jupiter's moons.

    G. engage in studies of stars.

    H. make important use of the telescope.

37. How does paragraph 2 fit into the overall structure of the passage?

    A. It presents the discovery of Jupiter's four brightest moons and discusses Galileo's role in this breakthrough.

    B. It explains Greco-Roman mythology's advances in astronomy before introducing modern science's discoveries.

    C. It emphasizes the impact of Voyager on the naming of Jupiter's moons.

    D. It introduces the main idea of the passage by discussing science's limited knowledge of Jupiter's moons before the Voyager missions.

38. The geologic features found in the light areas of Ganymede were most likely formed

    E.   after the features found in Ganymede's dark areas.

    F.   in an earlier period than those in the dark areas.

    G.   at about the same time as the features in the dark areas.

    H.   mainly by ancient bombardment.

39. How does the graph provide additional support to the central idea of paragraph 4?

    A.   It emphasizes the number of Io's surface features in which scientists have observed volcanic activity.

    B.   It explains the three main types of volcanic features that scientists found on Io.

    C.   It shows that a large proportion of Io's volcanic features have no recorded activity.

    D.   It proves that the Voyager 1 mission recorded activity in at least 80 surface features on Io out of a total of 170 features.

40. What was the most unexpected fact to emerge from the Voyager photographs?

    E.   the size of Io's molten lakes

    F.   the disappearance of impact sites on Europa

    G.   the discovery of volcanic activity on Io

    H.   the evidence of asteroid bombardment on all four moons

41. The moons of Jupiter were named after

    A.   Copernicus's discovery.

    B.   the geologic features of the moons.

    C.   mythical lovers of Jupiter.

    D.   the Voyager mission.

42. It can be inferred that from 1610 until 1979

    E.   scientists turned their attention to other planets in the solar system.

    F.   scientific understanding of Jupiter's moons made some progress.

    G.   the Copernican model of planetary rotation was discredited.

    H.   asteroid bombardment of Jupiter's moons increased.

The Eradication of Smallpox

1 For thousands of years, smallpox was one of the world's most dreaded diseases. An acutely infectious illness spread by a virus, smallpox was the scourge of medieval Europe, where, due to its symptoms of extreme fever and disfiguring red rash, it was known as "the invisible fire." In many outbreaks, mortality rates were higher than 25 percent. Ancient Chinese medical texts show that the disease was known as long ago as 1122 B.C.E., but even as recently as 1967, more than 2 million people died of smallpox in one year.

2 Because of the virulence of smallpox, physicians have long sought an effective method to impede its transmission. The first effort to combat smallpox was an attempt to immunize healthy patients. In a procedure called variolation, known since the ninth century, a healthy patient's skin was deliberately scratched with infectious material from a person with a mild case of smallpox. If the treatment was successful, the patient suffered a mild smallpox infection and then became immune to the disease. By the eighteenth century, when smallpox epidemics were regular occurrences, variolation was a common practice among the wealthy and aristocratic classes, but unfortunately, variolation sometimes led to severe, even fatal, infections. Moreover, even if the procedure was successful, the patient could still spread smallpox to others.

3 A safer method of conferring immunity was discovered in 1796 by an English doctor named Edward Jenner. Jenner, who had himself undergone the variolation process as a child, was fascinated by the fact that people who caught cowpox, a mild disease spread by cattle, became immune to smallpox. To test whether this immunity could be replicated, Jenner inoculated a young boy with infectious matter taken from a child who had cowpox, and the boy developed a minor infection. Later, Jenner inoculated the boy with smallpox matter and discovered that no disease developed. Jenner wrote a paper describing his results, but the Royal Society of Physicians, who were skeptical about his unconventional approach, rejected it. Jenner published his findings independently, and his paper became a bestseller. Within a matter of years, the new procedure, known as vaccination, was in widespread use throughout Europe and the United States, and the effective fight against smallpox was underway.

4 In an unprecedented effort, the World Health Organization launched a worldwide campaign in 1966 with the goal of wiping out smallpox altogether. It was an immense project that involved thousands of health workers deployed under the direction of WHO teams that moved from country to country, locating every case of active smallpox and vaccinating all potential contacts. In 1977, the last active case of smallpox was found and eliminated. Since there are no animal carriers of smallpox, the WHO was able to declare in 1980 that the dreaded killer had been conquered, and that, for the first time in the history of medicine, a disease had been completely destroyed.

5 Today, although there are no longer any natural sources of smallpox, the virus is retained in two government laboratories, one in the United States and one in Russia, for ongoing research. The United States continues to maintain sufficient reserves of inoculant to immediately treat every person in the country in the unlikely event that it should ever again become necessary.

43. Which statement best describes the central theme of the passage?

    A. Viral diseases can be treated in a variety of ways, depending on how they are spread.

    B. The dangers of variolation are not well-known, and the results often vary.

    C. Edward Jenner discovered vaccination by accident while studying variolation.

    D. The fight against smallpox is one of success through progressive stages.

44. When was a method of immunizing against smallpox first developed?

    E. 1122 B.C.E.

    F. the ninth century C.E.

    G. 1796

    H. 1966

45. As discussed in this passage, one disadvantage of variolation was that

    A. the inoculated patient could still spread smallpox.

    B. variolation did not give immunity to cowpox.

    C. immunity wore off after a time.

    D. variolation was hard to carry out.

46. The passage implies that Jenner began to experiment with vaccination because he

    E. was suffering from a mild case of smallpox himself.

    F. had noticed a relationship between two diseases.

    G. wanted to be accepted into the Royal Society of Physicians.

    H. had attempted variolation without success.

47. The words "scourge," "virulence," and "dreaded killer" affect the tone of the passage because they

    A. demonstrate the author's personal contempt for smallpox.

    B. depict smallpox as a particularly deadly disease that humanity fought.

    C. emphasize the WHO's hatred of diseases.

    D. represent the Royal Society of Physicians' view of Edward Jenner.

48. The passage implies that smallpox was not eliminated before 1966 because

    E. vaccination did not prevent all forms of the disease.

    F. not enough was known about immunity to disease.

    G. there was no effective protection against animal carriers.

    H. there had never been a coordinated worldwide vaccination campaign.

GO ON TO THE NEXT PAGE ⟹

49. The author uses the word "scourge" in paragraph 1 in order to

    A.   indicate that smallpox was linked to uncleanliness.

    B.   imply that smallpox was more deadly than chickenpox.

    C.   emphasize the suffering smallpox caused.

    D.   underscore the importance of ancient Chinese medical texts.

50. The early use of variolation and later use of vaccination suggest that

    E.   protection against disease was ineffective until the discovery of vaccination.

    F.   it is medically possible to provide protection against disease.

    G.   all deadly epidemics have been wiped out.

    H.   the incidence of smallpox was vastly minimized by Jenner's discovery.

An Engineering Disaster

1   For four months in the fall of 1940, citizens of the Puget Sound area of Washington traversed—both by car and on foot—one of the most famous, and most dangerous, suspension bridges ever built. Although the Tacoma Narrows Bridge, or "Galloping Gertie," had a relatively short life compared to similar structures in the United States, in its short career "Gertie" taught important lessons on what to do—and what not to do—when building a suspension bridge.

2   The plan for the bridge was conceived because state officials in Washington saw a need to connect the city of Tacoma, on the mainland, with the Olympic Peninsula on the other side of Puget Sound. The closest point between the two was the Tacoma Narrows, a windy, 2,800-foot gap that, at the time, appeared to be the ideal place for a suspension bridge. Designed by New York native Leon Moisseiff, a world-renowned bridge engineer, the bridge was a state-of-the-art structure that embraced the architectural trends of the period. The Tacoma Narrows Bridge emphasized slim, streamlined forms and slender structures: the towers were sleek and tall, and its pencil-thin roadway appeared to float delicately above the water, hanging gracefully from the light, airy cables. The engineers saw a bridge that was light, beautiful, and sturdy and would stand the test of time.

3   Construction began in November of 1938, at a cost of $6 million, and the bridge was officially opened on July 1, 1940. However, in early May 1940, when the bridge's roadbed was installed, the problem that gave the bridge its ominous nickname emerged. The roadbed, or deck, of the bridge began to wave, or bounce, in the strong winds that rushed through the Tacoma Narrows. Moisseiff was consulted, and he admitted that two of his bridges of similar design were having the same problem, though not as severely as the Tacoma Narrows Bridge. Because the roadbed was made of solid, stiffening plate girders, it could not absorb the winds of the Sound. Instead, the roadway acted as a giant sail, collecting the force of the wind gusts. The narrowness of the roadway—it was only two lanes wide—made it extremely flexible. Therefore, on any windy day, the roadway buckled and flexed, or "galloped"—hence, its nickname.

4   State officials sprang into action in an attempt to solve the problem, commissioning engineering Professor F. Bert Farquharson at the University of Washington, who immediately began studying a scale model of the bridge in a wind tunnel. In an attempt to stabilize the deck and reduce the size and speed of the waves, workers installed tie-down cables that connected the roadbed to the supporting structures on land. In the fall of 1940, the Tacoma Narrows bridge successfully weathered several storms, enduring wind speeds of over 50 miles per hour. Farquharson and the bridge designers believed the problem was solved, although Farquharson continued to monitor the wind speed, wind direction, and the bridge's movements. In some of his wind tunnel studies, he had been able to create conditions that caused the model to twist wildly, and Farquharson believed that if those conditions ever occurred, the Tacoma Narrows Bridge would not withstand the severe gyrations. He recommended that either the stiffening girders be perforated to allow the wind to flow through them, or special deflectors be constructed to direct the wind flow around them.

5   Unfortunately, just days after state officials accepted Farquharson's recommendations, but before the modifications could be built, a strong storm swept in from the southwest on November 7, 1940, replicating the catastrophic conditions Farquharson had created in his laboratory. That was the day "Gertie" galloped its last. After an hour of contortions, the bridge collapsed into Puget Sound. Because the twisting motions gradually built up during that time, several vehicles were lost, but, fortunately, everyone on the bridge had time to escape.

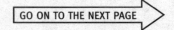

6 News crews had time to assemble as well, and the dramatic footage chronicling the collapse of the bridge remains a part of many college engineering and physics classes. The bridge is treated as a case study, and students investigate the interrelationships of the forces that brought Galloping Gertie to its spectacular end. The failure of the bridge also spurred research into bridge aerodynamics and aeroelasticity, affecting the design of every long-span bridge built afterward.

51. The author's main purpose in writing this passage is to

   A. discuss how the Tacoma Narrows Bridge acquired the nickname "Galloping Gertie."
   B. illustrate the use of aerodynamics in suspension bridges.
   C. detail why building the Tacoma Narrows Bridge was necessary.
   D. describe the history and features of the Tacoma Narrows Bridge.

52. The statement that the Tacoma Narrows Bridge "had a relatively short life" in paragraph 1 suggests that

   E. "Galloping Gertie" had a longer career than other bridges.
   F. most bridges last more than four months.
   G. the Tacoma Narrows was a difficult place to build a suspension bridge.
   H. the bridge's span was too long for the construction methods of the time.

53. According to the passage, what was the reason for building the bridge?

   A. Washington wanted to build the third-largest span in the world.
   B. Officials wanted to connect Tacoma to Puget Sound.
   C. The state required a bridge that could cross the sound at its widest point.
   D. State officials wanted to connect the Olympic Peninsula with the mainland.

54. The author most likely includes the engineers' opinion of the bridge in paragraph 4 in order to

   E. explain how the bridge acquired its nickname.
   F. show the genius of the bridge's designers.
   G. contrast their professional opinion with the bridge's ultimate result.
   H. emphasize the long-lasting nature of the bridge.

55. The phrase "acted as a giant sail" (paragraph 3) conveys that

   A. the bridge's web truss roadway absorbed all the energy of the wind.
   B. the bridge's roadway was perfect for sailing ships.
   C. the roadway collected all the force of the wind.
   D. only flexible roadways collect wind forces.

56. Which provides the strongest evidence for the claim that engineers learned a lesson from "Galloping Gertie"?

    E. No people were injured in the collapse of the bridge.

    F. Professor Farquharson created a model of the bridge for further study.

    G. Physics and engineering students still study the bridge today.

    H. Puget Sound was deemed uncrossable after 1940.

57. The author uses the word "spectacular" in paragraph 6 in order to

    A. highlight the dramatic result of poor engineering.

    B. praise the magnificent design of the original bridge.

    C. acknowledge the excitement the collapse evoked.

    D. point out that the end result was truly tragic.

Part 2—Mathematics

57 QUESTIONS—SUGGESTED TIMING: 90 MINUTES

IMPORTANT NOTES

1. Definitions and formulas are **not** provided.

2. Diagrams are **not** necessarily drawn to scale, with the exception of graphs.

3. Diagrams are drawn in single planes unless the question specifically states they are not.

4. Graphs are drawn to scale.

5. Simplify all fractions to lowest terms.

GRID-IN QUESTIONS

QUESTIONS 58–62

DIRECTIONS: Answer each question. Write your answer in the boxes at the top of the grid on the answer sheet. Start on the left side of each grid, printing only one number or symbol in each box. **DO NOT LEAVE A BOX BLANK IN THE MIDDLE OF AN ANSWER.** Under each box, fill in the circle that matches the number or symbol you wrote above. **DO NOT FILL IN A CIRCLE UNDER AN UNUSED BOX.**

---

58. Jada has completed 24 pages in her vocabulary workbook. This is 30% of the pages in the workbook. How many pages are in the workbook?

    80

59. What is the value of z in the equation $\frac{z}{3} - 35 = -10$?

     79

    $\cdot 3 \qquad \cdot 3$
    $\frac{z}{3} - 35 = -30$

60. A survey asked students whether they would like a drama club, a step team, both clubs, or neither club. The results are below:

    - 34 students would like a drama club.
    - 27 students would like a step team.
    - 14 students would like both.
    - 13 students would like neither.

    How many students were surveyed?

     60

61. Jayden and Bailey collect comic books. Bailey has 2 more than 3 times the number of comic books that Jayden has. They have a total of 50 comic books. How many comic books does Jayden have?

    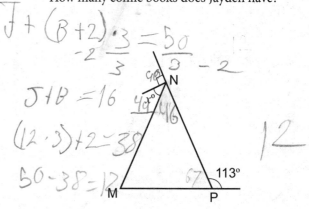

    $J + (B+2) \cdot 3 = 50$
    $-2 \quad \frac{3}{3} \quad \frac{50}{3} - 2$
    $J + B = 16$
    $(12 \cdot 3) + 2 = 38$
    $50 - 38 = 12$
    12

62. In the figure above, MNO is an isosceles triangle with MN = NP. What is the value of x ?

    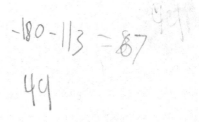

    $180 - 113 = 87$
    49

> ## MULTIPLE-CHOICE QUESTIONS
>
> ### QUESTIONS 63–114
>
> **DIRECTIONS:** Answer each question, selecting the best answer available. On the answer sheet, mark the letter of each of your answers. You can do your figuring in the test booklet or on paper provided by the proctor.

63. A certain city garden has 64 flowers and 24 decorative shrubs planted. The garden planner wants to plant more flowers until the ratio of flowers to shrubs is 12:1. How many more flowers will the garden planner need?

   A. 224

   B. 264

   C. 288

   D. 312

(handwritten: 58; 2)

(handwritten: $24 \cdot 12 = 288$)

(handwritten: $288 - 64 = 224$)

64. What is the value of c in the equation $2a + 3b + 5 = c$ if $a = 3$ and $b = -3$?

   E. −7

   F. −5

   G. 1

   H. 2

(handwritten: $6 + -9 + 5 = c$)

65. What is the value of x if $4(6x - x) = -10$?

   A. −2

   B. $-\dfrac{1}{2}$

   C. 0

   D. $\dfrac{1}{2}$

(handwritten: $\dfrac{20x}{20} = \dfrac{-10}{20}$)

(handwritten: $x = -\dfrac{1}{2}$)

66. Volunteering at the library, Ji-hu can shelve 8 books in 15 minutes, working at a constant rate. Sebastian can shelve 6 books in 10 minutes, working at his own constant rate. What is the total number of books the two of them can shelve in one **hour**?

   E. 14

   F. 56

   G. 68

   H. 84

67. Three apples cost as much as 4 pears. Three pears cost as much as 2 oranges. How many apples cost as much as 72 oranges?

   A. 36

   B. 48

   C. 64

   D. 81

```
      J          K  L              M
 <--------------|--|----------|--------->
    -19                       0  5
```

68. On the number line above, points J, K, L, and M are integers, and JK:KL:KM = 2:1:3. What is the value of KM?

   E. 8

   F. 12

   G. 16

   H. 24

GO ON TO THE NEXT PAGE ⟹

69. Fran has a drawer containing 4 black T-shirts, 3 orange T-shirts, and 5 blue T-shirts. If these are the only T-shirts in the drawer and she picks one at random, what is the probability that it will **not** be orange?

A. $\frac{1}{4}$

B. $\frac{1}{3}$

C. $\frac{5}{12}$

D. $\frac{3}{4}$

70. If 65% of x is 130, what is the value of x?

E. 84.5

F. 130

G. 165

H. 200

PRACTICE 5K TIMES

Name	Fastest Time	Range
Krisanta	31:16	4:37
Lindsey	33:02	2:29
Tara	29:48	3:35

71. Three friends are preparing to run a 5K together. They all use the same route for practice. The table above shows each friend's fastest time on the practice route and her range of times across all practice runs. What is the **overall** range for all three girls?

A. 4:38

B. 5:43

C. 6:05

D. 7:51

72. After a 5-hour flight from Newark, Harry arrived in Denver at 2:30 pm. If the time in Newark is 2 hours later than the time in Denver, what was the time in Newark when Harry began the flight?

E. 10:30 am

F. 11:30 am

G. 12:30 pm

H. 3:30 pm

73. If q and r are integers, in which of the following equations **must** q be positive?

A. $qr^2 = 1$

B. $q - r = 1$

C. $qr = 1$

D. $q^2 r = 1$

FAVORITE SPORTS IN MURPHYSBORO

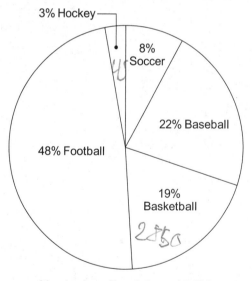

Murphysboro Population = 15,000

74. In Murphysboro, how many more people choose basketball than hockey as their favorite sport?

E. 2,400

F. 2,850

G. 3,300

H. 3,750

GO ON TO THE NEXT PAGE

75. A delivery service charges $25 per pound for making a delivery. If there is an additional 8% sales tax, what is the cost of delivering an item that weighs $\frac{4}{5}$ of a pound?

A. $20.00
B. $21.60
C. $22.60
D. $24.00

76. A rectangular mural covers a total area of 132 sq ft. If the mural is 12 feet high, what is its perimeter?

E. 44 feet
F. 46 feet
G. 48 feet
H. 88 feet

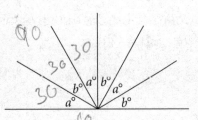

77. In the figure above, what is the sum of $a + b$?

A. 45
B. 60
C. 75
D. 90

78. How many five-digit numbers can be created using the digits 2, 3, 4, 7, 8, and 9 without repeating any digits in that five-digit number?

E. 20
F. 30
G. 720
H. 1,296

79. If $x = \frac{1}{8}$, what is the value of y when $\frac{2}{x} = \frac{y}{4}$?

A. $\frac{1}{4}$
B. 1
C. 4
D. 64

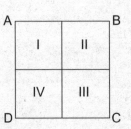

80. In the figure above, square ABCD is made up of 4 smaller, equal squares. If the perimeter of ABCD is 16, what is the sum of the perimeters of squares I, II, III, and IV ?

E. 16
F. 24
G. 32
H. 48

81. Kimiko is filling boxes with scented soap that she made as gifts for her friends. A full box holds 24 bars of soap. If Kimiko made 200 bars of soap, how many bars will she have left over if she fills as many boxes as she can?

A. 0
B. 4
C. 8
D. 10

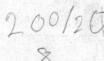

GO ON TO THE NEXT PAGE

82. A bowl contains three types of fruit: 7 apples, 8 oranges, and 3 pears. What is the probability that a piece of fruit chosen at random is **not** an orange?

    E. $\frac{1}{6}$

    F. $\frac{7}{18}$

    G. $\frac{4}{9}$

    H. $\frac{5}{9}$

83. Yamila had an average score of 4 strokes on the first 6 holes of a mini-golf course. On the 7th hole, she scored 11 strokes. What was her mean score for the first 7 holes?

    A. 4

    B. 5

    C. 6

    D. 7

84. In a sample of 60 ties at a local clothing store, there are 8 purple ties and 32 striped ties. Of the 8 purple ties, 5 have stripes. If a tie is selected at random from the given sample, what is the probability that **both** of the following are true: the tie is **not** purple and does **not** have stripes?

    E. $\frac{1}{12}$

    F. $\frac{1}{3}$

    G. $\frac{5}{12}$

    H. $\frac{9}{20}$

85. A marker is chosen at random from a box that contains 21 black markers, 6 red markers, and 9 blue markers. What is the probability that the marker selected is blue?

    A. $\frac{1}{12}$

    B. $\frac{1}{6}$

    C. $\frac{1}{4}$

    D. $\frac{7}{12}$

86. Mai bought 1.25 gallons of paint at $20.00 per gallon. If there was a 6% sales tax, what was the total cost of the paint?

    E. $25.00

    F. $26.50

    G. $28.20

    H. $31.80

87. Here are two ways to add numbers:

    Abe's method: Round the numbers to the nearest integer and add.

    Ben's method: Add the numbers, then round the result to the nearest integer.

    What is the difference between Abe's method and Ben's method when adding 6.4 and 3.3 ?

    A. 0

    B. 0.7

    C. 1.0

    D. 1.7

R   T

$3\frac{5}{12}$

88. On the number line above, RT = $\frac{1}{6}$. Point S (not shown) is located between point R and point T. Which value below is a possible value for point S?

    E. $\frac{1}{12}$

    F. $3\frac{1}{12}$

    G. $3\frac{1}{2}$

    H. $3\frac{11}{12}$

89. Devin prepares for a multi-day hike by packing his backpack with food, water, bedding, and emergency supplies. He tracks how many pounds of each he's carrying and finds the ratio of their respective weights is 2:3:1:4. If the total weight of his supplies is 35 pounds, how many pounds of water is Devin carrying?

    A.   7

    B.   10.5

    C.   13.5

    D.   14

90. Three students work together to make paper flowers to decorate a school dance. Mia takes 3 minutes to make one flower, Robinson takes 4 minutes, and Vessa takes 6 minutes. If all three students start at the same time and work continuously, how many flowers will Mia have made by the time all three students are once again beginning a new flower at the same time?

    E.   3

    F.   4

    G.   12

    H.   24

91. If $x = -3$, what is the value of $\frac{1}{2}|2x - 2|$?

    A.   −2

    B.   2

    C.   3

    D.   4

$1/2(8+2) = 4$

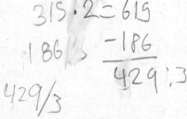

92. Circle O above has a diameter of 6, an area of b square units, and a circumference of c units. What is the value of $b + c$?

    E. 15π

    F. 18π

    G. 36π

    H. 48π

93. A 19th-century express train could travel 186 miles in 3 hours. A modern bullet train can travel 315 miles in 1.5 hours. How much faster, in miles per hour, is the modern bullet train?

    A.   62 mph

    B.   129 mph

    C.   148 mph

    D.   210 mph

$315 \cdot 2 = 615$

$186/3$ $\frac{-186}{429/3}$

$429/3$

94. Juan is practicing archery using a simple circular target with a radius of 18 inches. The target's bullseye has a circumference of 18π inches. What is the area of the portion of the target that is **not** part of the bullseye?

    E. 81π sq in

    F. 243π sq in

    G. 324π sq in

    H. 405π sq in

Practice Tests

GO ON TO THE NEXT PAGE ⟹

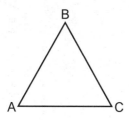

95. Triangle ABC above is an equilateral triangle with a height of 7. If its perimeter is 24, what is its area?

    A. 8
    B. 14
    C. 24
    D. 28

96. A fish tank has a small leak such that, if it is not refilled, the amount of water left in the tank at the end of each week is 10% less than the amount at the beginning of that same week. If the fish tank is not refilled, what percent of the original amount of water will remain in the tank after two weeks?

    E. 19%
    F. 20%
    G. 81%
    H. 90%

SANDWICH CHOICES

Sandwich	Number of Times Ordered
Turkey Club	42
BLT	36
Hummus Veggie	23
Roast Beef	39

97. The table above shows the number of times that different sandwiches were ordered at a restaurant. Based on this information, what is the probability of a customer ordering a turkey club sandwich?

    A. 30%
    B. 35%
    C. 40%
    D. 42%

98. Jeremiah must type 70 pages. He wants to type $\frac{1}{5}$ of the pages tomorrow morning, $\frac{1}{7}$ of the remaining pages tomorrow afternoon, and the rest of the pages tomorrow evening. How many pages does Jeremiah intend to type tomorrow evening?

    E. 28
    F. 40
    G. 46
    H. 48

99. What is the value of $\dfrac{8(y+5)}{3(3y+7)}$ if $y = 3$?

    A. $\frac{1}{3}$
    B. $\frac{4}{3}$
    C. $\frac{3}{2}$
    D. $\frac{5}{3}$

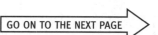GO ON TO THE NEXT PAGE

Practice Tests

100. The set of possible values of r is $\{5, 8, 14\}$. What is the set of possible values for q if $3q = r + 4$?

    E. $\{2, 3, 5\}$

    F. $\{3, 4, 6\}$

    G. $\{5, 8, 14\}$

    H. $\{9, 12, 18\}$

101. If n is an integer, which of the following **must** be odd?

    A. $n + 1$

    B. $2n + 1$

    C. $3n + 2$

    D. n^2

102. When a number, x, is multiplied by 5, the result is 8 less than the result of multiplying a number, y, by 3. Which of the following equations correctly expresses the relationship between x and y?

    E. $5x = 24y$

    F. $5x - 8 = 3y$

    G. $5x + 8 = 3y$

    H. $5x + 3y = 8$

103. If Tony bought z trading cards and Jason bought 3 more than 5 times the number of trading cards Tony bought, what is the total number of trading cards they both bought?

    A. $4z$

    B. $5z$

    C. $5z + 3$

    D. $6z + 3$

Number of Pets	Number of Students
0	5
1	3
2	7
3	6
4	2
5	1

104. There are 24 students in a class. The frequency table above shows the number of students in the class who have 0, 1, 2, 3, 4, or 5 pets. What is the mean number of pets per student in this class?

    E.   1.5

    F.   2

    G.   2.5

    H.   4

105. Today, Austin's age is $\frac{1}{4}$ of Stephanie's age. In 4 years, Austin's age will be $\frac{2}{5}$ of Stephanie's age. How old is Stephanie today?

    A.   4

    B.   6

    C.   16

    D.   24

106. A square with a side length of 4 inches is divided into squares with side lengths of 1 inch. Three of the small squares are labeled A, 5 are labeled B, 4 are labeled C, 2 are labeled D, and the remainder are labeled E. If one small square is then chosen at random, what is the chance it's labeled E?

    E.   1 in 8

    F.   3 in 16

    G.   1 in 4

    H.   1 in 2

GO ON TO THE NEXT PAGE

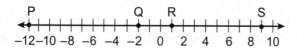

107. What is the distance from the midpoint of PQ to the midpoint of RS in the number line above?

    A. 12
    B. 14
    C. 16
    D. 18

108. Four consecutive even numbers have a sum of 28. What is the **largest** of these numbers?

    E. 10
    F. 12
    G. 14
    H. 18

    28/4

    7·2

109. Vincent ate $\frac{1}{5}$ of a protein bar. Austin ate 3 times as much of the same protein bar as Vincent ate. What is the ratio of the amount of the protein bar both of them ate to the amount of the protein bar remaining?

    A. 1:1
    B. 1:4
    C. 4:5
    D. 4:1

110. What is the value of $10(c + 3) + 6(c - 5)$ in terms of d if $c = 2d$?

    E. 4d
    F. 8d
    G. 16d
    H. 32d

    10(2D+3)+6(2D-5)

    20D+30+12D-30

    20D+12D

111. The perimeter of a rectangle is 208 inches. The ratio of its length to its width is 5:3. What are the dimensions of this rectangle?

    A. 60 in by 44 in
    B. 65 in by 39 in
    C. 68 in by 36 in
    D. 72 in by 32 in

112. A certain basket maker can make 150 baskets with 20 bundles of reed. Approximately how many bundles of reed would she need to make 250 baskets?

    E. 30
    F. 34
    G. 35
    H. 39

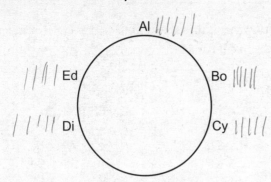

113. Five people are seated at a round table as shown above. If 52 cards are dealt to the five people beginning with Al and continuing clockwise (alphabetically), who gets the last card?

A. Al
B. Bo
C. Cy
D. Di

114. A granola recipe requires $\frac{3}{5}$ of an ounce of vanilla extract. How many batches of granola can be made using a package containing 60 ounces of vanilla extract?

E. 36
F. 48
G. 80
H. 100

60/5=12

×3=36

THIS IS THE END OF THE TEST. IF TIME REMAINS, YOU MAY CHECK YOUR ANSWERS. BE SURE THAT THERE ARE NO STRAY MARKS, PARTIALLY FILLED ANSWER CIRCLES, OR INCOMPLETE ERASURES ON YOUR ANSWER SHEET.

518 K

Practice Tests

Answer Key

PART 1—ENGLISH LANGUAGE ARTS

1. C	16. E	31. D	46. F
2. F	17. C	32. F	47. B
3. D	18. H	33. C	48. H
4. E	19. C	34. H	49. C
5. B	20. E	35. D	50. F
6. G	21. C	36. H	51. D
7. C	22. E	37. D	52. F
8. E	23. B	38. E	53. D
9. D	24. F	39. A	54. G
10. H	25. C	40. G	55. C
11. D	26. G	41. C	56. G
12. G	27. B	42. F	57. A
13. D	28. G	43. D	
14. G	29. A	44. F	
15. D	30. G	45. A	

PART 2—MATHEMATICS

58. 80	73. A	88. G	103. D
59. 75	74. E	89. B	104. F
60. 60	75. B	90. F	105. C
61. 12	76. F	91. D	106. E
62. 44	77. B	92. E	107. A
63. A	78. G	93. C	108. E
64. H	79. D	94. F	109. D
65. B	80. G	95. D	110. H
66. G	81. C	96. G	111. B
67. D	82. H	97. A	112. F
68. G	83. B	98. H	113. B
69. D	84. G	99. B	114. H
70. H	85. C	100. F	
71. C	86. F	101. B	
72. F	87. C	102. G	

Answers and Explanations

PART 1—ENGLISH LANGUAGE ARTS

1. C

Category: Sentence Structure

Getting to the Answer: When the paragraph presents a long, complex sentence, it may be a run-on. Here, both "these impressive creatures eat . . . life" and "blue whales can . . . day" are independent clauses separated only by commas. **(C)** separates these two into their own complete sentences and is correct. **(A)** is incorrect because it introduces an error in a sentence that was correct as written; "Capable of . . . tons" is not an independent clause, so it cannot stand on its own as a complete sentence. **(B)** is incorrect because although connecting two sentences with a semicolon is fine, it doesn't fix an error. **(D)** is incorrect because it creates an even longer run-on by connecting another sentence with a comma.

2. F

Category: Usage and Punctuation

Getting to the Answer: When a question has two different issues, look at each one individually. You can use the answer choices here to help guide your examination of the paragraph. First, verb tenses: the paragraph as a whole is in past tense, so changing "were" to "are" would be incorrect; eliminate **(G)** and **(H)**. Sentence 1 changes verb form from "was" to "has been" midway through without any context to show a reason for changing verb tense, so that should be corrected, as in **(E)** and **(F)**. Second, punctuation: removing the comma after "parts" would make the punctuation in the list incorrect, so eliminate **(E)**. "Attempting to improve their safety and convenience" is extra information that should be set off from the sentence with a comma, so **(F)** is correct.

3. D

Category: Knowlege of Language

Getting to the Answer: Precise language means language that is specific or detailed. **(A)** is no more specific than the original, so eliminate it. "National parks" in **(B)** and "vistas in the mountains" in **(C)** are both more specific, but neither is as specific or detailed as "the view from the summit of Turrialba Volcano" in **(D)**. Additionally, "her favorite memory" is more specific

than the original or any of the other answer choices; **(D)** is correct.

4. E

Category: Sentence Structure

Getting to the Answer: A modifying phrase should be right next to what it is describing. The introductory phrase "Able to change . . . texture" ought to be describing "the octopus," but the sentence, as it is originally written, describes "predators" instead. **(E)** fixes this by making "the octopus" the subject of the sentence and is correct. **(F)** is incorrect because, although the sentence has been rearranged, the descriptive phrases about camouflage are still next to "predators." **(G)** is incorrect because in it, "Able to change . . . texture" now describes "advanced camouflage skills." This may be tempting, but it is not the skills themselves that change shape or color—the skills allow the octopus to do so. Finally, **(H)** is incorrect because although "able to change . . . texture" *is* next to "the octopus," "with advanced camouflage skills" is now describing "the predators," creating a new error.

5. B

Category: Topic Development

Getting to the Answer: Think about the main topic of the passage. It discusses the historical development of vaccines; paragraph 2 is about the development of the smallpox vaccine, which was the first vaccine, and paragraph 3 is about later vaccines that were developed using the first one as a standard. This fits with **(B)**. **(A)** is incorrect because the passage rarely discusses *how* understanding was expanded, except in the case of Edward Jenner. **(C)** is incorrect because, although the passage does talk about several people who contributed to developing vaccines, that is not the main topic of the passage. Likewise, **(D)** is incorrect because the effectiveness of vaccines is not the passage's main focus.

6. G

Category: Organization

Getting to the Answer: Look for clues to where the sentence would best fit in the paragraph. Sentence 8 begins with the transition "Much later, in the eighteenth century" and goes on to describe a story that cowpox could inoculate against smallpox. Sentence 5, the first sentence in the paragraph, states that smallpox was among the first diseases people tried to immunize against; a sentence about something "much later" would not fit before this, so eliminate **(E)**. Putting it between sentences 6 and 7, **(F)**, would interrupt the discussion of earlier efforts in China. Sentence 10, however, says that "experimentation proved folklore correct" and that a safe, related disease could inoculate people against a more dangerous one. This connects well to sentence 8. The story needs to be explained before it is proven correct, so sentence 8 should come before sentence 10; **(G)** is correct. **(H)** is incorrect because it places sentence 8 after sentence 10, which does not flow logically.

7. C

Category: Organization

Getting to the Answer: When a question asks you to add a transition, look at the sentences being connected to determine the relationship between ideas. Sentence 10 says that the relatively safe cowpox could protect people from the deadlier smallpox, and sentence 11 says this method of inoculation became standard. A cause-and-effect transition would make sense here, so **(C)** is correct. **(A)** indicates a contrast between ideas that is not present. **(B)** treats sentence 11 as if it were an addition to the information of sentence 10 rather than a result. **(D)** incorrectly identifies the sentence as an illustration.

8. E

Category: Topic Development

Getting to the Answer: Sentence 13 tells that Louis Pasteur discovered weakened diseases could inoculate without infection, and the paragraph as a whole is about the vaccines developed based on the cowpox vaccine and Pasteur's dead virus technique. The correct answer will relate to these concepts. **(E)** works well; it discusses a vaccine developed using the technique described in sentence 13. **(F)** simply gives further information about Louis Pasteur's non-vaccine discoveries, which does not support the topic of the paragraph. **(G)** may be tempting because it discusses Pasteur, vaccines, and cowpox, but it's about the word "vaccines" rather than the development of actual vaccines. Similarly, **(H)** discusses Pasteur's theory about how weakening diseases works, but that is not the focus of the paragraph.

9. D

Category: Organization

Getting to the Answer: For a question like this, first determine the relationship between the ideas. Sentence 15 provides examples of vaccines developed using the technique described in sentence 14. **(D)** shows this clearly and is correct. **(A)** is incorrect because "While" introduces a contrast between the sentences. **(B)** is incorrect because the sentence structure suggests that "diphtheria, flu, and the injected polio vaccine" were examples of dead viruses, not new vaccines created from them. **(C)** is incorrect because (in addition to being awkward) it suggests that the *technique* included diphtheria, etc.

10. H

Category: Topic Development

Getting to the Answer: The third paragraph is focused on additional discoveries about vaccines and their results. Sentence 12, **(E)**, is the topic sentence of the paragraph, so deleting it would not make sense. Sentence 13, **(F)**, describes a discovery that led to many additional vaccines, as discussed in sentences 14 and 15, so it fits well and ought to be kept. Sentence 16, **(G)**, further describes the results of certain vaccines, which supports the paragraph topic. Sentence 17, **(H)**, does talk about a vaccine, but the sentence is much more focused on technical details than the rest of the paragraph, which is primarily concerned with broad strokes of what was discovered and its impact. Therefore, sentence 17 should be removed; **(H)** is correct.

11. D

Category: Topic Development

Getting to the Answer: For a question like this, you need to consider not only the sentence it follows but also the passage as a whole. The previous sentence describes the decrease in polio cases after the introduction of vaccines for it, and the passage as a whole is about the development and importance of vaccines. **(D)** incorporates both and is correct. **(A)** connects well to the previous sentence but is too narrowly focused on outcomes for two specific diseases to be a good concluding sentence. On the other hand, **(B)** is too broad and vague; "healthier than they have ever been" could be describing many topics besides the impact of vaccines. **(C)** is about developing vaccines, but it doesn't relate to the previous sentence or address the importance of vaccines.

Passage Analysis: This is a science passage about coral reefs. Paragraph 1 introduces the main idea, which focuses on "the complex web of interrelationships between plants, animals, and climatic conditions." Paragraph 2 describes how reefs are formed out of green algae and the skeletons of stony coral. Paragraph 3 discusses the different classifications of coral reefs. Paragraph 4 details several theories about how coral reefs are transformed into islands.

12. G

Category: Global

Getting to the Answer: To find which choice best describes the whole passage, focus on the paragraph topics. Paragraph 2 discusses the animals involved in reef formation, and paragraph 4 describes how reefs become islands. **(G)** summarizes the passage best since both biological and geological issues are repeatedly discussed. The incorrect choices are all too narrow: animal life, **(E)**, is discussed only in paragraph 2; the formation of coral islands, **(F)**, appears only in paragraph 4; and physical beauty, **(H)**, is simply a happy consequence of the deeper biological and geological processes involved in reef formation.

13. D

Category: Inference

Getting to the Answer: Tropical rainforests are mentioned at the very end of the second paragraph. The author states that "Only tropical rainforests can compete with coral reefs when it comes to the diversity of species found in, and supported by, these ecosystems." This means that the biological diversity in these two ecosystems is roughly equivalent; **(D)** is correct. **(A)** is a Distortion; tropical rainforests have a comparable, not greater, amount of biological diversity. **(B)** is Out of Scope; the passage does not say anything about rainforests' popularity with tourists. **(C)** also lacks support from the passage.

14. G

Category: Detail

Getting to the Answer: Paragraph 2 is the only place where the stony coral is discussed. The second sentence of the paragraph indicates that the stony coral's skeleton is composed of "almost pure calcium carbonate." The correct answer is **(G)**. **(E)** is Out of Scope; cartilage is never mentioned in the passage. **(F)** is also Out of Scope; stone is never associated with the skeleton of the stony coral. **(H)** is a Distortion; paragraph 2 says that stony coral gives off carbon dioxide, not that its skeleton is made of carbon dioxide.

15. D

Category: Global

Getting to the Answer: Paragraph 2 outlines the relationship between the coral and the algae. The animals are described as partners that "coexist in a mutually beneficial relationship." The paragraph notes the "vast numbers of coral animals" that help to form the coral reef's structure. Thus, **(D)**, which mentions animals' importance to reef formation, is correct. **(A)** places emphasis on non-reef islands, which are not of importance to paragraph 2. **(B)** incorrectly depicts paragraph 2 as a transition from a discussion of animals' importance in reef formation, which itself is the topic of paragraph 2, to a discussion of coral island formation, which is actually the topic of paragraph 4. **(C)** is more properly a description of paragraph 4 and is incorrect.

16. E

Category: Detail

Getting to the Answer: Paragraph 3 details the different types of coral reefs, and paragraph 4 describes how they transform into islands. **(E)** is correct. **(F)** is certainly mentioned in the passage, but this is a *biological* feature of reefs, not a *geological* one. **(G)** is Out of Scope; the destructive effects of the last Ice Age are not discussed. **(H)** is a Distortion; the passage talks about islands, not "great land masses."

17. C

Category: Detail

Getting to the Answer: Paragraph 3 discusses the various types of coral reefs. The passage states, "Fringing reefs are very close to, or attached to, non-reef islands." Thus, **(C)** is correct. Barrier reefs are "also associated with non-reef islands but are separated from the land mass by channels or lagoons of deep water," so **(A)** is incorrect. **(B)** is wrong because atolls are "rings of circular-shaped reefs without a central land mass." Finally, **(D)** is Out of Scope; "barrier islands" are not mentioned in the passage.

18. H

Category: Inference

Getting to the Answer: The passage states that coral islands are popular vacation destinations but that the islands themselves rise only a few feet above sea level. "Beneath the waves," however, coral islands are "fantastic and very beautiful." The correct answer is **(H)**. **(E)** is Extreme; while reefs are certainly beautiful, the author does not claim that they are the "most beautiful" in the world. The passage never compares the relative popularity of different types of reefs, so **(F)** is Out of Scope. **(G)** is also Out of Scope; the author never suggests that divers are waging a disinformation campaign about coral islands.

19. C

Category: Function

Getting to the Answer: In paragraph 2, the author uses the word "architect" to emphasize that the stony coral is a major component of the reef's structure; **(C)** is correct. While the primary definition of "architect" is "designer," a stony coral lacks the intellectual capacity to consciously design a structure; **(A)** is incorrect. **(B)** is incorrect because coral reefs are not built by construction companies. The stony coral is indeed a relative of the sea anemone, but **(D)** is incorrect for the same reason as **(A)**; these are creatures of instinct, not abstract thought.

20. E

Category: Function

Getting to the Answer: Paragraph 2 discusses the process by which coral reefs are formed and then proceeds to discuss the processes by which coral

islands can form from coral reefs, so **(E)** is correct. The passage mentions the Caribbean and Australia before the Pacific and Indian Oceans, but this is just happenstance, as there is no chronological relationship between these areas or locations, so **(F)** is incorrect. **(G)** suggests that coral must form before algae, which is not supported by the passage. **(H)** incorrectly claims that the Maldives were artificially created as vacation destinations.

Passage Analysis: The author, Jonathan Swift, was a noted satirist who viewed human nature with amusement. The passage begins with a visit from the principal secretary, who informs the narrator of two major conflicts facing the nation. Paragraph 1 describes the secretary's arrival, and paragraph 2 discusses a conflict between the Tramecksan and the Slamecksan parties. Paragraphs 3 and 4 describe an external threat from Blefuscu and how the simple act of breaking an egg was regarded as a major philosophical and religious event, worthy of years of warfare. Paragraphs 5 and 6 discuss the consequences of the continuing dispute between Lilliput and Blefuscu. Paragraph 7 talks about the latest developments of the conflict, which include an attack the Blefuscu fleet is planning to wage on Lilliput, and paragraph 8 notes the narrator's response to the secretary's news.

21. C

Category: Detail

Getting to the Answer: A central theme of the passage is the absurdity of the law dictating how to break an egg and the dire consequences of disobeying that law. Actually being willing to die rather than break their eggs in the manner the law dictates is absurd and extreme, making **(C)** the correct answer. **(A)** is incorrect because it concerns the consequences, but not the absurdity, of the situation. **(B)** is incorrect because it speaks to a detail underlying the events that unfold but does not itself suggest anything absurd or dire. The last sentence of the passage is focused on the narrator and listener and does not speak to the larger themes of the passage; **(D)** is incorrect.

22. E

Category: Function

Getting to the Answer: Swift tells us these details so that we can see what extreme lengths these societies were willing to go to in order to continue their ridiculous fight. That clearly matches **(E)**. While the author is interested in the absurdity of the quarrel, the facts are wrong. The Big-endians are not refusing to work; they are being prevented from working. So, **(F)** is incorrect. **(G)** is a Distortion; the dispute is not among the Lilliputians, but between them and the citizens of Blefuscu. While the dispute was certainly serious to these characters, Swift does not say that the egg-breaking cause is just and worth dying for; **(H)** is incorrect.

23. B

Category: Detail

Getting to the Answer: In Swift's language, time passes in terms of "moons." We don't know exactly how long that is but can infer that it is some extended period of time. The passage describes a "bloody war" that has been "carried on" for 36 "moons." Thus, **(B)** is a good match. It underscores a lengthy state of fighting, telling us that "histories" report that the fighting happened over six rebellions. **(A)** is incorrect because it focuses on the touchstone event, but not upon the length of the dispute. **(C)** is simply Out of Scope, giving a detail about how certain citizens break their eggs. While **(D)** is tempting—dealing with a battle being fought—it suggests a single focused, present event and not a protracted dispute.

24. F

Category: Function

Getting to the Answer: Swift was a satirist, interested in enduring and universal aspects of human nature. His story about the absurd dispute between the citizens of these fictional empires can be seen as a way to comment on the disputes between nations that are relevant to his readers. He likely wrote in these personal terms in order to engage directly with his audience, to make the story seem more real and, though completely implausible in exact context, possible in parallel. As such, **(F)** fits and is correct. **(E)** and **(G)** are incorrect because Swift finds the debate absurd and does not want his reader to take it seriously, either by taking sides or by finding it emotionally resonant. The writing

may be challenging to follow for a modern audience, but there is no suggestion that Swift is intentionally attempting to add confusion; **(H)** is incorrect.

25. C

Category: Global

Getting to the Answer: Swift's satire exposes the absurdity of the debate, given that it is over how to crack an egg. Thus, **(C)** is correct. **(A)** is tempting because the residents of these societies do find the debate extremely important. However, Swift discusses religion in paragraph 6 not to introduce the spirituality of these societies, but rather their politics. The reference is to a "schism," or division, in the system of belief. Thus, Swift's central theme deals with social and political systems entangled in the absurdity of this situation. **(B)** and **(D)** are incorrect because they suggest that the dispute could be addressed via etiquette or law.

26. G

Category: Detail

Getting to the Answer: It's important to separate and understand each voice in a fiction passage. The question asks about the point of view of the Big-endians. We know that everyone originally cracked eggs on the larger end. Then, an unfortunate incident happened with a royal child doing so and cutting himself. The boy's father declared that everyone should henceforth crack their eggs on the small end instead. The Big-endians, as their name suggests, were in favor of continuing to crack eggs on the larger end and did not wish to be told that they must crack on the small end. The key to what the Big-endians actually want comes toward the end paragraph 6: that people should be allowed to crack their eggs at "the convenient end"—in other words, it should be left to each person's own "conscience" how they crack their eggs. This matches **(G)**. **(E)** is incorrect because Big-endians do not want citizens to be forced to crack eggs at the small end. They are in favor of free choice on the issue, but favor the big end themselves. **(F)** is incorrect because the Big-endians don't want anyone required to crack their eggs on the large end, least of all the Blefuscu citizens. They are in favor of citizens being allowed to crack their eggs on the end they choose. **(H)** is not correct; Big-endians wouldn't want to prevent anyone from cracking eggs in the "primitive" way, because the primitive way is at the big end, their preferred end.

Poem Analysis: Written in 1861, Longfellow's famous poem tells of the events on the night of April 18, 1775. The Revolutionary War is about to begin, and patriot Paul Revere anticipates that the British troops now stationed in Boston will soon be on the move throughout the Middlesex countryside. He must warn the citizens. In the first stanza of this excerpt from the longer poem, the narrator introduces the story. The second stanza relates a conversation between Revere and a friend, setting up the warning system—lighting one lantern if the British are coming by land, two if by sea. In the third stanza, Revere crosses the river to await the signal and sees a British war ship, dark and ominous.

27. B

Category: Global

Getting to the Answer: You may know that the American Revolutionary War began the day after Paul Revere's ride, on April 19, 1775. Thus, this action takes place on the eve of the war. Even if you do not know the dates, clearly this poem describes a courageous and heroic event: Paul Revere's alerting the Boston countryside to an impending invasion. This matches **(B)**. **(A)** is incorrect because the first stanza's mentioning that "Hardly a man is now alive; Who remembers that famous day and year" (lines 4–5) establishes that this is a very significant historical event and does not directly contrast the men remembering with the children listening. **(C)** and **(D)** are incorrect because there is no indication that the perception of historical events differs from reality or that Paul Revere did not take his role seriously.

28. G

Category: Detail

Getting to the Answer: Focus on the second stanza, which describes how Revere intends to let others know of the arrival of the British. The "signal-light" (line 9) indicates that the British are indeed invading. Likewise, Revere being "ready to ride and spread the alarm" (line 12) demonstrates the use of the "signal-light"; **(G)** is correct. Line 6 introduces Revere's discussion with his friend but does not explain what the "signal-light" means; **(E)** is incorrect. **(F)** is incorrect because this simply describes Revere's location prior to seeing one or two lanterns, and **(H)** is incorrect because this notes where Revere will travel to spread the news.

29. A

Category: Function

Getting to the Answer: The phrases "like a prison-bar" and "huge black hulk" both describe the British ship called Somerset. With the moon's light behind them, the mast and spar look "like a prison-bar," and the "huge black hulk" is reflected in the water, magnifying its size. Both phrases serve as a symbol of British dominance and also show how Paul Revere is indeed placing himself in danger; **(A)** is correct and **(C)** is incorrect. These phrases act as symbols of Britain's dominance; **(B)** is incorrect. **(D)** is incorrect because these phrases do not call for the colonists to fight back; rather, they act as a reminder of the danger in battling the British.

30. G

Category: Function

Getting to the Answer: Lines 15–16 describe Revere's move to his position where he will await the signal that the British are invading; **(G)** is correct. These lines do not emphasize Revere's concern or doubt regarding the plan, making **(E)** incorrect. **(F)** is incorrect because these lines represent Revere's fulfillment of the next steps in the colonists' plan rather than an indication of his talents. **(H)** is incorrect because Revere's main objective is to row to Charlestown undetected, not to refrain from disturbing sleeping animals.

31. D

Category: Global

Getting to the Answer: In the second stanza, Paul Revere and his friend set the plan; the friend will light one signal lantern if the British are coming by land, and two if they are coming by sea (lines 6–10). This stanza sets Revere up as the responsible party for alerting those in the countryside; **(D)** is correct. The second stanza states that Revere will notify those in the countryside that the British are coming and to be alert and armed; **(A)** is incorrect. **(B)** is incorrect because Revere tells one friend to hang the lanterns. **(C)** is incorrect because there is no indication that the British will be more challenging opponents if they arrive by sea as opposed to by land.

32. F

Category: Function

Getting to the Answer: Because the poem presents Paul Revere's ride as a story with characters and quotes, it is considered a narrative; **(F)** is correct. **(E)** is incorrect because the story does not focus on shepherds or rural life. Fables are typically fictitious stories that emphasize a moral; the poem is based on a historical event, and there is no central moral for children, making **(G)** incorrect. While there are songs about Paul Revere's famous midnight ride, **(H)** is incorrect because this poem was not written to be sung.

33. C

Category: Detail

Getting to the Answer: The narrator comments that there is almost no one left who personally remembers the ride of Paul Revere in line 3, saying "Hardly a man is now alive." Because this is qualified as *almost* no one, the implication is that there may be at least one living person who remembers these events. That makes **(C)** the right answer. **(A)** is incorrect because it does not give a time reference. **(B)** and **(D)** are incorrect because neither demonstrates a relationship to a set time in the past.

34. H

Category: Detail

Getting to the Answer: Line 16, "Silently rowed to the Charlestown shore," suggests that Paul Revere is in danger of being caught on his mission; **(H)** is correct. Line 4 refers to how long ago these events occurred, not how many people survived, making **(E)** incorrect. While hanging a lantern will trigger a set of dangerous events, the actual hanging of the lantern does not suggest the level of danger Revere is in; **(F)** is incorrect. **(G)** is incorrect because this line notes Revere's initial location to watch for the lantern and does not indicate how dangerous the mission is.

Passage Analysis: This is a science passage about four of Jupiter's moons. Paragraph 1 relates the moons' discovery and their role in early debates about the nature of the solar system. Paragraph 2 introduces the main idea—scientists didn't know much about these moons until the 1979 Voyager missions provided data.

Paragraphs 3 and 4 describe what the scientists learned about each of the four moons.

35. D

Category: Global

Getting to the Answer: Remember that the main idea of the passage is the choice that describes the whole passage. Since the passage discusses both how Jupiter's moons were discovered and what scientists learned about them from the Voyager missions, **(D)** is correct. **(A)** is not mentioned in the passage. **(B)** refers to a detail in the passage. **(C)** is too broad; this passage isn't about Jupiter as a whole and is more concerned with Voyager than Galileo.

36. H

Category: Inference

Getting to the Answer: Paragraph 1 contains the answer to this question. It says that the Galilean moons were the "first objects in the solar system discovered through the use of the telescope" and that Galileo's discovery played a central role in a famous debate about the nature of the solar system. You can infer from this that Galileo was one of the first to "make important use of the telescope." **(H)** is correct. **(E)** is incorrect because Galileo supported Copernicus. **(F)** is incorrect because accurate measurements of the moons didn't come until centuries later. **(G)** is incorrect because many other people studied stars before Galileo.

37. D

Category: Global

Getting to the Answer: Paragraph 2 presents the passage's main idea, which is Voyager's impact on our knowledge of Jupiter's four brightest moons. **(D)**, therefore, is correct. **(A)** is a better description of paragraph 1's role in the passage. **(B)** incorrectly suggests that Greco-Roman mythology made scientific advances in astronomy. **(C)** wrongly claims that Voyager influenced the naming of Jupiter's moons, which were named prior to Voyager.

38. E

Category: Inference

Getting to the Answer: This question asks about Ganymede's light areas, discussed in Paragraph 3. The passage states that "*ancient* craters dot the dark areas, while the light areas are crisscrossed by ridges and grooves that resulted from *more recent* ice flows." From this, you can infer that the light areas were formed *later* than the dark areas. **(E)** is correct. **(F)** is Opposite. **(G)** and **(H)** are contradicted by the phrase "more recent ice flows."

39. A

Category: Infographic

Getting to the Answer: Paragraph 4 describes the surprising discovery of volcanic activity on Io. The graph shows the number of features that have had observed volcanic activity from both the Voyager mission and post-Voyager observations. Look for the choice that relates observations of volcanic activity to the description of the volcanic activity in the text; **(A)** is correct. **(B)** is incorrect because the graph does not explain the types of volcanic features; it just describes the number that have recorded activity. Eliminate **(C)** because, while the graph does show that some features have had no recorded activity, that is not the central idea of the paragraph. The graph includes observations from the Voyager missions as well as missions since then, so **(D)** must be incorrect.

40. G

Category: Detail

Getting to the Answer: In very beginning of paragraph 4, the author expresses surprise at "the discovery of intense volcanic or geyser-like activity on Io." The answer is **(G)**. **(E)**, **(F)**, and **(H)** are all discoveries made by Voyager, but there is no indication that the author finds any of them surprising.

41. C

Category: Detail

Getting to the Answer: Paragraph 2 states that Jupiter's four moons were named after four of the Roman god's mythological lovers (Callisto, Ganymede, Io, and Europa), so **(C)** is the correct answer. All other answers are mentioned in the passage but are not relevant to the question. When researching a Detail question, be sure to focus on precisely what the question is asking for.

42. F

Category: Inference

Getting to the Answer: The passage states that Jupiter's moons were discovered in 1610, and that the Voyager mission sent back revealing photos in 1979. The question asks for an inference about what happened between those centuries. Paragraph 2 states that in those years "scientific understanding of them increased fairly slowly." Although new knowledge came slowly, it did come, as evidenced by the several facts detailed in the paragraph. **(F)** is correct. Scientists may also have been interested in other planets, **(E)**, but they kept learning about Jupiter. There is no evidence in the passage for either **(G)** or **(H)**.

Passage Analysis: This is a social studies passage about smallpox, "one of the world's most dreaded diseases." Paragraph 1 gives some historical background on the disease. Paragraph 2 describes one of the first attempts to protect people against the disease, a process called "variolation." Paragraph 3 details Edward Jenner's discovery of a superior method—the process of vaccination. Paragraph 4 tells the story of the WHO's successful effort to wipe out the disease altogether. Paragraph 5 reveals that the smallpox virus is still kept in certain government laboratories.

43. D

Category: Global

Getting to the Answer: The bulk of the passage is concerned with the fight against smallpox from the ninth century into the 1970s. **(D)** is correct. **(A)** is too broad—the passage isn't about *all* infectious or viral diseases. **(B)** and **(C)** relate only to paragraphs 2 and 3, respectively.

44. F

Category: Detail

Getting to the Answer: The second paragraph indicates that variolation, the first known immunization process, was known since the ninth century C.E. The correct answer is **(F)**. **(E)** is incorrect because it describes the earliest recorded instances of the disease. **(G)** dates Jenner's discovery of vaccination, but variolation came before this. **(H)** dates the first worldwide immunization campaign, not the first-ever immunization process.

45. A

Category: Detail

Getting to the Answer: According to paragraph 2, variolation patients were sometimes fatally infected, and they could spread the disease to others even when successfully inoculated. **(A)** summarizes this second disadvantage and is therefore the correct answer. Cowpox, **(B)**, was a part of Jenner's treatment discussed in paragraph 3. No description of variolation wearing off, **(C)**, or being difficult to carry out, **(D)**, is given.

46. F

Category: Inference

Getting to the Answer: Paragraph 3 indicates that Jenner became "fascinated" by the fact that having had cowpox somehow immunized people to smallpox and tried to see "whether this immunity could be replicated." Since he had noticed a relationship between cowpox and smallpox, **(F)** is correct. **(E)** is never stated. Although Jenner probably wanted his vaccination work to be recognized by the Royal Society of Physicians, there is no evidence that his motivation was to be accepted into the society, **(G)**. Jenner underwent variolation as a boy, but the passage never indicates that he attempted to work with variolation himself, **(H)**.

47. B

Category: Global

Getting to the Answer: **(B)** is correct—the words suggest the deadliness of the disease. **(A)** and **(C)** are Out of Scope and not relevant to the terminology used. **(D)** is incorrect because the words describe smallpox, not the Royal Society of Physicians' skeptical view of Jenner's work.

48. H

Category: Inference

Getting to the Answer: Paragraph 4 describes the massive effort involved in wiping out smallpox altogether—every active case of the disease in the world had to be found and isolated. You can infer from this that it was the difficulty of coordinating such an effort that had prevented the elimination of the disease, not a problem with the inoculation process itself. The correct answer is **(H)**. The passage does not suggest that the disease could take on other forms, so eliminate **(E)**. Immunization through variolation was known as early as the ninth century C.E., making **(F)** incorrect. In paragraph 4, the

passage states that "there are no animal carriers of smallpox," so **(G)** is also incorrect.

49. C

Category: Function

Getting to the Answer: Since smallpox was "one of the world's most dreaded diseases," killing more than 25 percent of those infected, it certainly caused great suffering. **(C)** is correct. The word "scourge" looks similar to the word "scour," which means "to clean by rubbing hard," but they are not synonyms; thus, **(A)** is incorrect. **(B)** is Out of Scope because the author does not mention chickenpox. **(D)** links the word to ancient Chinese medical texts, to which there is only a distant and flimsy connection.

50. F

Category: Inference

Getting to the Answer: Both variolation and vaccination are immunizations against smallpox, and both are the product of medical actions against the disease. **(F)** is correct. **(E)** is Extreme; though variolation was not always effective and had its own dangers, it was "a common practice," so it must have worked in at least some cases. **(G)** uses the word "all," so it is also Extreme. **(H)** is contradicted by the information in paragraph 1 that "more than 2 million people died of smallpox" in 1967, almost 200 years after Jenner's discovery.

Passage Analysis: The passage tells the history and flaws of the Tacoma Narrows Bridge, also known as "Galloping Gertie." Paragraph 1 introduces the bridge and tells of its eventual collapse. Paragraph 2 talks about the site planning and describes the bridge's appearance and structure. Paragraph 3 discusses the construction of the bridge and how it began to buckle. Paragraph 4 details Professor Farquharson's recommendations. Paragraph 5 describes the strong storm that collapsed the bridge. Paragraph 6 discusses the bridge's engineering legacy.

51. D

Category: Global

Getting to the Answer: For Global questions, look at your Roadmap to find the main idea. According to the Roadmap, the main idea is the construction, features, and flaws of the Tacoma Narrows Bridge. **(D)** is correct. **(A)** is a Misused Detail; the bridge's nickname is mentioned in paragraph 1, but is not the main idea of the passage. **(B)** is another Misused Detail; the use of aerodynamics is only discussed in reference to the Tacoma Narrows Bridge during paragraph 3. **(C)**, again, is a Misused Detail; the reasons for the bridge's construction are stated in paragraph 2 but are not the main idea of the passage.

52. F
Category: Inference

Getting to the Answer: When given a line reference, always read the surrounding text to get a sense of the context. Here, the rest of the sentence states that the bridge had a relatively short life compared to other bridges of the period. Thus, other bridges lasted longer; **(F)** is correct. **(E)** is Opposite; "Galloping Gertie" had a shorter career than other bridges. **(G)** is a Distortion; the passage actually states that the Tacoma Narrows was a natural place for a bridge. **(H)** is Out of Scope; while the passage does discuss certain aspects of the construction methods, nothing suggests that the bridge's span was the problem.

53. D
Category: Detail

Getting to the Answer: Always note the location of details in the passage so that you can quickly find them when confronted with a Detail question. Paragraph 2 says that state officials wanted to connect Tacoma on the mainland with the Olympic Peninsula. **(D)** is correct. **(A)** is Out of Scope; the passage never says that the state wanted to build the third-largest span in the world. **(B)** is a Distortion; officials wanted to connect Tacoma to the Olympic Peninsula. **(C)** is Opposite; the bridge was designed to cross the sound at its narrowest point.

54. G
Category: Function

Getting to the Answer: Usually, the author's reasoning for including specific information is to enhance or refute an idea expressed in the passage. In this case, the positive opinions of the engineers are contrasted with the negative realities of the bridge as shown in paragraphs 3 and 5. **(G)** is correct. **(E)** is a Distortion; the acquisition of the nickname is not explained by the engineers' opinion. **(F)** is Extreme/Opposite; the word

"genius" is too strong, and in fact the opposite is true: the bridge's calamitous fate did not show the genius of the designers. **(H)** is also Opposite; the opinion is stated to emphasize the brief life of the bridge.

55. C
Category: Inference

Getting to the Answer: Phrases are often used either to advance or rebut an idea expressed in the text. Here, "acted as a giant sail" is explained in paragraph 3: the roadway collected the force from the wind gusts. **(C)** is correct. **(A)** is a Distortion; the bridge did not have a web truss roadway. **(B)** is irrelevant; ships cannot sail on roadways. **(D)** is Out of Scope; the passage never states that only flexible roadways collect wind forces.

56. G
Category: Detail

Getting to the Answer: Always look for evidence from the passage to support your answer choice, but do not get attached to the exact wording of the text. Paragraph 6 states that the bridge is still used as a case study in college physics and engineering classes. **(G)** is correct. **(E)** is Out of Scope; injuries from the collapse are not mentioned; the passage states only that "everyone on the bridge had time to escape." **(F)** is a Misused Detail. Professor Farquharson made his model while the bridge was still standing; his goal was to prevent the bridge from collapsing, not to study it for its own sake. **(H)** is Extreme and Out of Scope; the passage never states or suggests that Puget Sound was deemed uncrossable after 1940.

57. A
Category: Function

Getting to the Answer: This passage is about a failed bridge, and the word "spectacular" precedes the word "end." Predict that the "spectacular" collapse of the bridge was "like a spectacle" or "a major event noticed by many." **(A)** is correct. **(B)** is Opposite; although "magnificent" is a common synonym for "spectacular," the bridge's failure was not striking in a beautiful way. **(C)** is Opposite; the passage never states that the bridge's failure caused positive emotions, such as excitement or enthusiasm. **(D)** is Extreme; while the bridge's fate is unfortunate, there were no deaths associated with it, and the passage does not depict it as a tragedy.

PART 2—MATHEMATICS

58. 80

Subject: Arithmetic

Getting to the Answer: Remember that *of* means multiply, and *is* means equals. Use these to set up an equation: 24 *is* 30% of the total pages, so $24 = 0.30x$. Divide both sides by 0.3 to get $x = 80$.

59. 75

Subject: Algebra

Getting to the Answer: Although the variable in a fraction may look intimidating at first, you can solve this equation like you would any other two-step equation. First, add 35 to both sides, and then multiply by 3:

$$\frac{z}{3} - 35 = -10$$
$$\frac{z}{3} = 25$$
$$z = 75$$

60. 60

Subject: Statistics and Probability

Getting to the Answer: Be careful not to count any students twice when finding your total. Students who would like both activities are included in the totals for both drama and step. First, find the number of students interested *only* in drama: $34 - 14 = 20$. Next, find the number of students interested *only* in step: $27 - 14 = 13$. Finally, add the totals for students interested only in drama (20), students interested only in step (13), students interested in both (14), and students interested in neither (13): $20 + 13 + 14 + 13 = 60$.

61. 12

Subject: Algebra

Getting to the Answer: When translating a word problem into an equation, pick variables that will be easy to connect back to what they represent. Let j represent the number of comic books Jayden has. Bailey has two more than three times the number of comic books that Jayden has, or $3j + 2$ comic books. Together, they have a total of 50 comic books. This gives the equation $j + 3j + 2 = 50$, which simplifies to $4j + 2 = 50$. Subtracting 2 from both sides and dividing by 4 yields $j = 12$. The questions asks for the number of comic books Jayden has, so grid in 12.

62. 44

Subject: Geometry

Getting to the Answer: When working on a geometry problem, write down any new information you figure out directly on the figure to help you keep track of it. Here, you can use the given angle measure of 113° to find the measure of $\angle MPN$: $180° - 113° = 67°$. Since the triangle is isosceles, $\angle NMP$ must also equal 67°. If you remember the rule that any external angle of a triangle is equal to the two opposite internal angles added together, you can find the total measure of the external angle that includes x by adding the matching angles: $67° + 67° = 134°$. (If you don't remember this rule, you can still find the angle measure by finding m$\angle MNP$ [46°] and subtracting from 180°.) Then, subtract the right angle to find the value of x. $134° - 90° = 44°$.

63. A

Subject: Arithmetic

Getting to the Answer: When dealing with ratios, be sure to keep track of which part is which. Here, you first need to find the total number of flowers the garden planner needs. Since the ratio of flowers to shrubs is 12:1, you can simply multiply the number of shrubs by 12 to find the total number of flowers: $24 \times 12 = 288$. The question asks how many *more* flowers the garden planner needs, so subtract the number of flowers already in the garden: $288 - 64 = 224$.

64. H

Subject: Algebra

Getting to the Answer: Plug in the values you have for a and b. Since $a = 3$ and $b = -3$, the equation reads $2(3) + 3(-3) + 5 = c$. After doing the multiplication, you have $6 + (-9) + 5 = c$. And after doing this addition, you get $2 = c$.

65. B

Subject: Algebra

Getting to the Answer: Solve for x according to PEMDAS: $4(5x) = -10$; thus, $20x = -10$. Dividing both sides by 20, you get $x = -\frac{1}{2}$.

66. G

Subject: Arithmetic

Getting to the Answer: Watch out for changing units. Here, the problem gives two different rates using minutes, but asks the question using hours. Use 60 minutes to correctly set up the proportion for each boy's total books shelved. First, Ji-hu's total (j):

$$\frac{8}{15} = \frac{j}{60}$$
$$15j = 480$$
$$j = 32$$

Then, Sebastian's total (s):

$$\frac{6}{10} = \frac{s}{60}$$
$$10s = 360$$
$$s = 36$$

Finally, add the two together: $32 + 36 = 68$.

67. D

Subject: Arithmetic

Getting to the Answer: The key to this problem is to start at the end. Because 3 pears cost the same as 2 oranges, set up the proportion $\frac{3}{2} = \frac{x}{72}$, where x is the number of pears that costs as much as 72 oranges. Cross multiply and solve for x: $2x = 3(72)$, so $2x = 216$ and $x = 108$. Now you can set up another proportion from the other relationship described in the question: $\frac{3}{4} = \frac{y}{108}$, where y is the number of apples that costs as much as 108 pears. Cross multiply and solve for y: $3(108) = 4y$, so $4y = 324$ and $y = 81$. Therefore, 81 apples cost the same as 72 oranges. Note that this problem could also be solved by picking a number for the cost of an orange, solving for the cost of a pear, and then solving for the cost of an apple.

68. G

Subject: Arithmetic

Getting to the Answer: In ratio problems, be clear on whether you have a part-to-part or part-to-whole ratio. In this problem, you are given a part-to-part ratio and a number line that allows you to find the length of the whole line segment. Find the whole of the ratio by adding the parts together: $2 + 1 + 3 = 6$. The problem asks for the value of KM, which includes both KL and LM, so make a new part-to-whole ratio with those two parts: $(1 + 3):6$, or $4:6$, which simplifies to $2:3$. Next, use the number line to find the length of the whole line segment. $5 - (-19) = 5 + 19 = 24$. Finally, set up a proportion using your part-to-whole ratio and cross multiply to solve.

$$\frac{2}{3} = \frac{x}{24}$$
$$3x = 48$$
$$x = 16$$

69. D

Subject: Statistics and Probability

Getting to the Answer: The probability of an event occurring is a fraction: the number of possible outcomes in which the event can occur divided by the total number of possible outcomes. The question asks for the probability of picking a non-orange shirt, which would be a blue or black shirt: $4 + 5 = 9$ non-orange shirts. This means there are 9 possible successful outcomes. The total number of shirts to choose from, including the orange shirts, is 12, so there are 12 possible outcomes. Thus, the probability of Fran picking a non-orange shirt is $\frac{9}{12}$, which can be simplified to $\frac{3}{4}$. Alternatively, the probability of an event NOT occurring is 1 minus the probability of the event occurring $\left(1 - \frac{3}{12} = \frac{9}{12} \text{ or } \frac{3}{4}\right)$.

70. H

Subject: Arithmetic

Getting to the Answer: Remember: *of* means multiply, and *is* means equals. Here, you need to set up the following equation: $\frac{65}{100}x = 130$. Multiply both sides by $\frac{100}{65}$ to get $x = (130)\left(\frac{100}{65}\right) = 200$.

71. C

Subject: Statistics and Probability

Getting to the Answer: This question asks for the *overall* range for the friends, meaning the difference between the slowest time and fastest time among all three of them. The fastest time is Tara's, at 29:48. Next, find the slowest time among the three girls. Krisanta's is $31:16 + 4:37 = 35:53$, and Lindsey's is $33:02 + 2:29 = 35:31$. Since Tara's range is smaller than Krisanta's and her best time is faster, she cannot have the slowest time, so there's no need to calculate hers. The slowest time is Krisanta's (35:53), so subtract Tara's fastest time: $35:53 - 29:48 = 6:05$.

72. F

Subject: Arithmetic

Getting to the Answer: Draw a chart or table to help organize the information. Newark's time is two hours later than Denver's time, so if the time in Denver when Harry arrives is 2:30 pm, then the time in Newark when he arrives in Denver is 4:30 pm. The flight takes 5 hours, so the time he began in Newark is 5 hours earlier than 4:30 pm, or 11:30 am.

73. A

Subject: Algebra

Getting to the Answer: When you see variables in the answer choices, Picking Numbers may be a helpful strategy. Try each answer choice and see if the statement can be true with a negative q. Pick a simple number for q; since all of the answer choices equal 1, $q = -1$ will work well.

(A): $(-1) \times r^2 = 1$. Therefore, r^2 would have to equal -1, which is impossible. Keep.

(B): $-1 - r = 1$. Therefore, $r = -2$. Eliminate.

(C): $-1r = 1$. Therefore, $r = -1$. Eliminate.

(D): $(-1)^2 r = 1$. Therefore, $r = 1$. Eliminate.

All of the answer choices can work with a negative q except for **(A)**, which is correct.

74. E

Subject: Arithmetic

Getting to the Answer: When you need to find the difference between amounts in a percent problem, subtract the percents first before finding the amounts in order to save a step. According to the graph, basketball is the favorite sport of 19% of people in Murphysboro, and hockey is the favorite of 3%. $19\% - 3\% = 16\%$ more people favor basketball. There are 15,000 people in Murphysboro, so find 16% of 15,000: $0.16 \times 15,000 = 2,400$.

75. B

Subject: Arithmetic

Getting to the Answer: When solving a word problem, break the problem down into small pieces and go step by step. The charge for delivering one pound is $25, so the charge for delivering $\frac{4}{5}$ of a pound is $\frac{4}{5}$ of $25, or $\frac{4}{5} \times \$25$ which is $20. The tax is 8% of $20, or $0.08 \times \$20$ which is $1.60. The total cost of delivering the item is $20 + $1.60 which is $21.60.

76. F

Subject: Geometry

Getting to the Answer: Since the mural is rectangular, its area is base times height. You are given that the height is 12 feet and the area is 132 square feet, so you can express this in an equation: $132 = 12 \times$ base. If you divide both sides by 12, you find that the base is equal to $132 \div 12$, or 11 feet. The perimeter of a rectangle is the sum of the lengths of the four sides, so the perimeter of this mural is $11 + 12 + 11 + 12$, or 46 feet.

77. B

Subject: Geometry

Getting to the Answer: You don't have enough information to figure out what a or b is individually, but you can figure out what the sum of a and b is. Altogether, the three angles marked a and the three angles marked b add up to make a straight line, or a 180° angle. This can be represented by the equation $3a + 3b = 180$. Divide both sides by 3 and find that $a + b = 180 \div 3$, or 60.

78. G

Subject: Statistics and Probability

Getting to the Answer: If you can't repeat digits, you have 6 options for the first digit, 5 options for the second, 4 options for the third, 3 options for the fourth, and 2 options for the fifth. $6 \times 5 \times 4 \times 3 \times 2 = 720$.

79. D

Subject: Algebra

Getting to the Answer: In order to avoid a fraction in the denominator, begin by cross multiplying: $8 = xy$. Next, substitute $\frac{1}{8}$ for x. This gives $8 = \frac{1}{8}y$. Multiply both sides of this equation by 8 to get $64 = y$.

80. G

Subject: Geometry

Getting to the Answer: With a perimeter of 16, each side of square ABCD has a length of $\frac{16}{4} = 4$, and thus each small square has a side length of 2. Hence, each small square has a perimeter of 8, so the 4 small squares have a total perimeter of $(4)(8) = 32$.

81. C

Subject: Arithmetic

Getting to the Answer: How many times does 24 go into 200? Calculate $200 \div 24 = 8$ with a remainder of 8, so Kimiko can fill 8 boxes of soap with 8 bars of soap left over.

82. H

Subject: Statistics and Probability

Getting to the Answer: To find the probability that something does *not* happen, find the probability that it *does* happen and subtract from one whole. There are 18 pieces of fruit in all, and 8 of them are oranges, so the probability of selecting an orange at random is $\frac{8}{18}$, or $\frac{4}{9}$. The probability of choosing a *different* fruit is $1 - \frac{4}{9} = \frac{5}{9}$.

83. B

Subject: Statistics and Probability

Getting to the Answer: Remember that for three-part formulas, if you have any two parts, you can always find the third. Since Average $= \frac{\text{Sum}}{\text{Number}}$, you can find the sum of Yamila's scores for the first several holes by multiplying her average score by the number of holes: $4 \times 6 = 24$. The average of her scores for the first 7 holes is $\frac{24 + 11}{7}$, or 5 strokes.

84. G

Subject: Statistics and Probability

Getting to the Answer: There's a lot of information in this problem, so break it down piece by piece. In order to find the probability the question asks for, you need to find the number of non-purple unstriped ties. Find the number of purple or striped ties and subtract from 60. 8 purple + 32 striped = 40 ties. You might be tempted to go ahead and subtract from 60 now (which would give a probability of $\frac{20}{60}$, or $\frac{1}{3}$), but remember that 5 ties

are *both* purple and striped. You don't want to count those twice, so subtract them: $40 - 5 = 35$. Now you can subtract from 60 to get 25 ties that are neither purple nor striped. The probability of selecting one of these ties is $\frac{25}{60}$, or $\frac{5}{12}$.

85. C

Subject: Statistics and Probability

Getting to the Answer: Remember that probability is just the number of desired outcomes out of the total number of possible outcomes. Here, the question asks for a blue marker. There are 9 blue markers and 36 total markers, so the probability of choosing a blue one at random is $\frac{9}{36}$, or $\frac{1}{4}$.

86. F

Subject: Arithmetic

Getting to the Answer: First, find the cost of the paint before tax. $1.25 \times 20 = \$25$. Next, calculate how much tax cost: 6% of $25 = .06 \times 25$, or $1.50. Finally, add the tax on to find the total cost: $\$25 + \$1.50 = \$26.50$.

87. C

Subject: Arithmetic

Getting to the Answer: Abe's method yields $6 + 3 = 9$, and Ben's method yields $6.4 + 3.3 = 9.7$, rounded $= 10$. Hence, the difference is 1.

88. G

Subject: Arithmetic

Getting to the Answer: First, find point T: $\frac{1}{6} = \frac{2}{12}$, so T is at $3\frac{7}{12}$. Next, find an answer choice that falls between $3\frac{5}{12}$ and $3\frac{7}{12}$. Using a common denominator of 12, you can determine that $3\frac{1}{2}$ is the same as $3\frac{6}{12}$, which is exactly halfway between points R and T. **(G)** is correct.

89. B

Subject: Arithmetic

Getting to the Answer: To answer this question, you need to find the ratio of water weight to total weight. Add all the parts of the ratio to find the whole: $2 + 3 + 1 + 4 = 10$. The ratio of water to total is 3:10. Now, set up a proportion using the total weight and cross multiply to solve.

$$\frac{3}{10} = \frac{w}{35}$$
$$10w = 105$$
$$w = 10.5$$

90. F

Subject: Arithmetic

Getting to the Answer: This problem rewards careful reading of the question. It doesn't ask how long before all three students are starting a new flower together again, but *how many flowers Mia makes* in that time. To find the amount of time, find the least common multiple of 3, 4, and 6, which is 12. Notice that this is among the answer choices—but you're not done just yet. To find how many flowers Mia can make in 12 minutes, divide: $12 \div 3 = 4$ flowers.

91. D

Subject: Algebra

Getting to the Answer: Substitute -3 for x in the given expression:

$$\frac{1}{2}\left|2(-3) - 2\right|$$
$$\frac{1}{2}\left|-6 - 2\right|$$
$$\frac{1}{2}\left|-8\right|$$
$$\frac{1}{2}(8) = 4$$

Remember that when working with absolute value, the result of the expression within the bars must become nonnegative when the bars are removed.

92. E

Subject: Geometry

Getting to the Answer: Given a diameter of 6, the radius must equal 3. The area formula gives you $\pi r^2 = \pi(3)^2 = 9\pi$. Next, the circumference $= 2\pi r = 2\pi(3) = 6\pi$. Adding these two values together results in $9\pi + 6\pi = 15\pi$.

93. C

Subject: Arithmetic

Getting to the Answer: For this problem, the DiRT equation will be useful: Distance = Rate $\times$ Time, which can be rearranged (by dividing both sides by Time) to Rate $= \frac{\text{Distance}}{\text{Time}}$. The 19th-century train's speed is $\frac{186}{3}$, or 62 miles per hour. The modern train's speed is $\frac{315}{1.5}$, or 210 miles per hour. The difference in their speeds is 210 mph $-$ 62 mph $=$ 148 mph.

94. F

Subject: Geometry

Getting to the Answer: When a geometry problem does not give you a diagram, draw one yourself to help you visualize the problem. Here, you will need to subtract the area of the bullseye from the target's total area to find the portion of the target that *isn't* in the bullseye. To find the target's total area, plug the target's radius into the circle area formula: $A = \pi r^2 = \pi(18)^2 = 324\pi$ sq in. Next, find the area of the bullseye. Since the problem doesn't give you its radius, use the circumference formula to find it. $C = 2\pi r$, so $18\pi = 2\pi r$, and $r = 9$. This gives the bullseye an area of $\pi(9)^2$, or 81π sq in. Now you can subtract. $324\pi - 81\pi = 243\pi$ sq in.

95. D

Subject: Geometry

Getting to the Answer: The test does not provide formulas, so you need to have the area formula for triangles memorized: $\frac{1}{2}(\text{Base} \times \text{Height})$. The problem provides the height (7), but you will need to use the perimeter to find the base. Since this is an equilateral triangle, all sides are equal, so each side is $24 \div 3 = 8$. Plug these values into the area formula to get $\frac{1}{2}(8 \times 7) = 28$.

96. G

Subject: Arithmetic

Getting to the Answer: When a question asks you to find a percent but doesn't give you any amounts to work with, like this one, Picking Numbers is a useful strategy. The easiest number to pick for any percent problem is 100. Also, note that the question asks for the percent of water that *remains*, not the percent that has leaked out. If 10% leaks out, 90% must remain. Calculating what remains directly instead of calculating what leaks out and then subtracting will save steps and time. After one week, $100 \times 0.90 = 90$ units of water remain. The tank starts the second week with 90 units of water, and at the end of the second week, $90 \times 0.90 = 81$ units of water remain. 81 out of 100 is simply 81%.

97. A

Subject: Statistics and Probability

Getting to the Answer: Probability is the number of desired outcomes divided by the number of possible outcomes. According to the table, the number of customers ordering a turkey club is 42. The total number of customers isn't listed, so add the number of people ordering each sandwich to get the total: $42 + 36 + 23 + 39 = 140$. The probability of a customer ordering a turkey club is $\frac{42}{140}$, which simplifies to $\frac{3}{10}$. However, the answer choices are in the form of percents. Knowing common fraction/percent equivalents is helpful here, or you can convert: $\frac{3}{10}$ is equal to $\frac{30}{100}$, or 30%.

98. H

Subject: Arithmetic

Getting to the Answer: There are several ways to solve this problem. One way is to figure out how many pages Jeremiah plans to type in the morning and afternoon. In the morning, he plans to type $\frac{1}{5}$ of 70, or $\frac{1}{5} \times 70$ which is 14. Thus, Jeremiah plans to type 14 pages in the morning, leaving $70 - 14 = 56$ pages left to type. He plans to type $\frac{1}{7}$ of the remaining pages in the afternoon. Since $\frac{1}{7}$ of 56 is 8, Jeremiah plans to type 8 pages in the afternoon, leaving $56 - 8 = 48$ pages for him to type in the evening.

99. B

Subject: Algebra

Getting to the Answer: Substitute the number 3 for each y in this expression. The numerator of the fraction becomes $8(3 + 5)$, and the denominator becomes $3[(3 \times 3) + 7]$. Now, follow the order of operations (PEMDAS). In the numerator, $3 + 5$ is 8, and 8×8 is 64, so the numerator is 64. In the denominator, 3×3 is 9, $9 + 7$ is 16, and 3×16 is 48, making the denominator 48. The fraction is now $\frac{64}{48}$, which can be reduced to $\frac{4}{3}$.

100. F

Subject: Algebra

Getting to the Answer: The wording "set of possible values" just signals a different approach to a substitution problem. You know what r equals and how q relates to r. Therefore, simply plug the values of r given into the equation and solve for q:

$$3q = 5 + 4$$
$$3q = 9$$
$$q = 3$$

At this point, eliminate both **(G)** and **(H)**, since neither includes 3 as a possible value for q. You may also have spotted that 3 must be the *smallest* value of q, so **(F)** must be correct. If you didn't, though, just plug in another value of r:

$$3q = 8 + 4$$
$$3q = 12$$
$$q = 4$$

(F) is the only answer choice that includes both 3 and 4 as values of q.

K

101. B

Subject: Algebra

Getting to the Answer: To solve this problem, pick numbers to plug in for n and try them in each answer choice. First, try $n = 2$.

(A): $2 + 1 = 3$. Keep.

(B): $2(2) + 1 = 5$. Keep.

(C): $3(2) + 2 = 8$. Eliminate.

(D): $2^2 = 4$. Eliminate.

Two answer choices are still possible, so pick a new number to try. Since the previous number was even, choose an odd number: $n = 3$.

(A): $3 + 1 = 4$. Eliminate.

Since all but one answer choice has now been eliminated, you don't need to check **(B)**. It must be correct.

102. G

Subject: Algebra

Getting to the Answer: This is a translation problem. "A number, x, is multiplied by 5," can be represented as $5x$. "The result is" is represented by an equal sign. "8 less than the result of multiplying a number, y, by 3" means $3y - 8$. The entire sentence can be written as $5x = 3y - 8$. This does not match any of the answer choices, but if 8 is added to both sides, you get $5x + 8 = 3y$.

103. D

Subject: Algebra

Getting to the Answer: Since Tony bought z trading cards, 5 times the number of trading cards Tony bought is $5z$ trading cards. The amount that Jason bought is 3 more than this: $5z + 3$. The total that both bought is $5z + 3 + z$, which simplifies to $6z + 3$.

You could also solve this problem by Picking Numbers: if Tony bought 2 trading cards, Jason bought $5(2) + 3 = 13$ trading cards, and Tony and Jason together bought 15. When you plug 2 in for z in the answer choices, you'll find that only **(D)** gives you 15.

104. F

Subject: Statistics and Probability

Getting to the Answer: You may be tempted to simply find the mean of the numbers in the left column of the table, but be careful—this would not take into account the fact that some quantities of pets are more common than others. In order to find the mean number of pets per student, first find the total number of pets owned by all students in the class: $5(0) + 3(1) + 7(2) + 6(3) + 2(4) + 1(5) = 0 + 3 + 14 + 18 + 8 + 5 = 48$ pets total. Then, divide by the number of students in the class: $48 \div 24 = 2$ pets per student.

105. C

Subject: Algebra

Getting to the Answer: This problem will be easiest to solve by Backsolving. Be smart about approaching the answer choices: since the question asks for Stephanie's age, and Stephanie is older than Austin, start with one of the larger numbers. Try **(C)**. If Stephanie is 16 today, then Austin is $\frac{1}{4} \times 16 = 4$. In 4 years, Stephanie will be $16 + 4 = 20$ and Austin will be $4 + 4 = 8$. $\frac{2}{5}$ of 20 is 8, as the problem says, so **(C)** checks out.

106. E

Subject: Geometry

Getting to the Answer: Draw a diagram here. You will find that there are 16 squares—3 are labeled A, 5 are labeled B, 4 are labeled C, and 2 are labeled D. This accounts for 14 of the 16 squares. This leaves 2 squares to be labeled E. The probability of an event occurring is a fraction—here the probability is $\frac{2}{16}$, which can be simplified to $\frac{1}{8}$, or 1 in 8.

107. A

Subject: Geometry

Getting to the Answer: To find the midpoint of a segment on the number line, you add the coordinates of the two endpoints and then divide the sum by 2. So, the midpoint of PQ is $\frac{(-12) + (-2)}{2} = \frac{-14}{2} = -7$. The midpoint of RS is $\frac{1 + 9}{2} = \frac{10}{2} = 5$. The distance between the two points is the positive difference between their coordinates, or $5 - (-7) = 12$.

108. E
Subject: Arithmetic

Getting to the Answer: Call the first number x. Then, the second consecutive even number is $x + 2$, the third consecutive even number is $x + 4$, and the fourth consecutive even number is $x + 6$. The sum of these numbers is represented as $x + x + 2 + x + 4 + x + 6$. Combining like terms gives $4x + 12$. The sum of these four numbers is 28, so $4x + 12 = 28$. The next step is to solve for x. First, subtract 12 from both sides: $4x = 28 - 12$, or $4x = 16$. Now, divide both sides by 4 and find that $x = 16 \div 4$, or 4. Since $x = 4$ and the largest number is $x + 6$, the largest number must be $4 + 6$, or 10.

109. D
Subject: Arithmetic

Getting to the Answer: Identify the type of ratio you are looking for. In this case, it is a part:part. You need to decide which parts you have. First, figure out how much Austin ate: $\frac{1}{5} \times 3 = \frac{3}{5}$. Now find how much they ate together: $\frac{1}{5} + \frac{3}{5} = \frac{4}{5}$. Figure out how much is left: $1 - \frac{4}{5} = \frac{5}{5} - \frac{4}{5} = \frac{1}{5}$.

Last, take the two parts you need: [what they both ate]:[what is left].

$\frac{4}{5} : \frac{1}{5} = 4 : 1$.

110. H
Subject: Algebra

Getting to the Answer: Plug $2d$ in for c. The expression becomes $10(2d + 3) + 6(2d - 5)$. You can't add $2d$ and 3 or subtract 5 from $2d$, so the next step is to multiply using the distributive property. This gives $(10 \times 2d) + (10 \times 3) + (6 \times 2d) + [6 \times (-5)]$, which simplifies to $20d + 30 + 12d + (-30)$. Because $30 + (-30) = 0$, you are left with $20d + 12d$, or $32d$.

111. B
Subject: Geometry

Getting to the Answer: Since you know that the rectangle's perimeter is 208, you can use the ratio of length to width and the perimeter formula to set up a proportion. $P = 2(l + w)$, so proportionate to the length and width, the perimeter is $2(5 + 3) = 16$. Set up a proportion using the length and the perimeter, then cross multiply and divide to solve:

$$\frac{5}{16} = \frac{l}{208}$$
$$16l = 1{,}040$$
$$l = 65$$

Note that the lengths and widths in the answer choices are all different, so you only need to find one of them to find the answer. **(B)** is correct.

112. F
Subject: Arithmetic

Getting to the Answer: You can simplify the ratio the problem gives you to make the math easier. $150{:}20 = 15{:}2$. Then, set up a proportion with the new number of baskets and cross multiply to solve:

$$\frac{15}{2} = \frac{250}{r}$$
$$15r = 500$$
$$r = 33.\overline{3}$$

The question asks *approximately* how many bundles of reed she would need, so look for the answer closest to the value you found, which is **(F)**.

113. B
Subject: Arithmetic

Getting to the Answer: Five people are being dealt 52 cards, so divide 52 by 5: $52 \div 5 = 10$ (remainder 2). Since Al receives the first card, after dealing 5 cards, Al will receive the sixth card, and so on for every multiple of 5. After 50 cards, Al will receive the 51st card, and Bo gets the 52nd card.

114. H
Subject: Arithmetic

Getting to the Answer: To answer this question, you have to figure out how many times $\frac{3}{5}$ goes into 60. Since you're dividing by a number smaller than 1, the result must be more than 60, so eliminate **(E)** and **(F)**. The equation is $60 \div \frac{3}{5} = \frac{60}{1} \times \frac{5}{3}$. Canceling will make the multiplication easier: $\frac{60}{1} \times \frac{5}{3} = \frac{20}{1} \times \frac{5}{1}$, which equals 20×5, or 100.

SHSAT Practice Test 2

SHSAT Practice Test 2
ANSWER SHEET

Scan Code

Enrollment ID

Please use this Answer Sheet only if the test will be scored via a webgrid/online scoring process. This Answer Sheet will NOT work if the test will be scanned.

For scanned exams, please refer to the Kaplan Answer Grid (which requires the use of a No. 2 pencil and is formatted for scanning machines).

PART 1—ENGLISH LANGUAGE ARTS

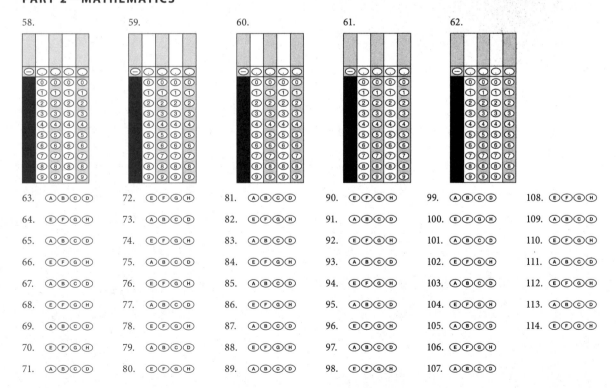

PART 2—MATHEMATICS

PRACTICE TEST 2

Directions: Mark your answers on the separate sheet provided. You will receive credit only for answers marked on the answer grid. **DO NOT MAKE ANY STRAY MARKS ON THE ANSWER GRID.** You can write in the test booklet, or use the paper provided for scratchwork.

Marking Your Answers

Each question has only one correct answer. Select the **best** answer for each question. Your score is determined by the number of questions you answered correctly. **It is to your advantage to answer every question, even though you may not be certain which choice is correct.**

Planning Your Time

You have 180 minutes to complete the entire test. How you split the time between the English Language Arts and Mathematics sections is up to you. **If you begin with the English Language Arts section, you may go on to the Mathematics section as soon as you are ready. If you begin with the Mathematics section, you may go on to the English Language Arts section as soon as you are ready.** It is recommended that you do not spend more than 90 minutes on either section. If you complete the test before the allotted time (180 minutes) is over, you may go back to review questions in either section.

Work as rapidly as you can without making mistakes. Don't spend too much time on a difficult question. Return to it later if you have time. If time remains, you should check your answers.

Part 1—English Language Arts

57 QUESTIONS—SUGGESTED TIMING 90 MINUTES

REVISING/EDITING

QUESTIONS 1–11

IMPORTANT NOTE

The Revising/Editing section includes Part A and Part B.

REVISING/EDITING Part A

DIRECTIONS: Answer the following questions, recognizing and correcting errors so that the sentences or paragraphs are grammatically correct. Re-read relevant parts of the text before choosing the best answer for each question, but be mindful of time. You may write in your test booklet to take notes.

---

1. Read this sentence.

> That the Superbowl was the most highly rated television show last week coming as no surprise to the sponsors whose commercials aired during the broadcast.

Which edit should be made to correct this sentence?

A. Change *was* to **being**.

B. Insert a comma after *week*.

C. Change *coming* to **came**.

D. Insert a comma after *aired*.

2. Read this sentence.

> The rock group attracts a multifarious audience; a surprisingly diverse group of people flock to their sold-out concerts.

Which edit should be made to correct this sentence?

E. Change *attracts* to **attract**.

F. Change *flock* to **flocks**.

G. Change *their* to **there**.

H. Change *concerts* to **concert**.

3. Read this paragraph.

> (1) James D. Watson studied biology as a graduate student at Indiana University, but the scientists there inspired him to pursue the fields of genetics and biochemistry instead. (2) In Copenhagen, he conducted research on DNA for his postdoctoral studies but became discouraged due to his lack of success. (3) After hearing a speech by Maurice Wilkins, Watson renewed his interest in DNA and then collaborated in England with a biologist named Francis Crick to research and study the structure of the DNA molecule. (4) Rosalind Franklin's X-ray images of DNA helped Watson, Crick, and Wilkins earn the Nobel Prize in 1962.

How should the paragraph be revised?

A. Sentence 1: Change *genetics and biochemistry* to **genetics**.

B. Sentence 2: Change *postdoctoral studies* to **studies**.

C. Sentence 3: Change *research and study* to **research**.

D. Sentence 4: Change *Nobel Prize in 1962* to **Nobel Prize**.

4. Read this paragraph.

> The Siberian husky's good-natured temperament, speed, and eagerness to <u>cooperate make</u> it a valuable dog in the Arctic regions. In addition to running for hundreds of miles in dogsled <u>competitions the</u> outgoing huskies have readily helped people in need. For example, through the efforts of 20 heroic, courageous dogsled teams, a life-saving serum was relayed across the 674 miles of frigid <u>Alaskan wilderness</u> from Nenana to Nome in 1925 to save a town stricken with diphtheria. In addition, during World War II, Siberian huskies served in the Army's Arctic <u>Search and</u> Rescue Unit.

Which revision corrects the error in sentence structure in the paragraph?

E. cooperate, make

F. competitions, the

G. Alaskan, wilderness

H. Search, and

REVISING/EDITING Part B

DIRECTIONS: Read the passage and answer the questions following it, improving the writing quality and correcting grammatical errors. Re-read relevant parts of the text before choosing the best answer for each question, but be mindful of time. You may write in your test booklet to take notes.

Helium

(1) Pierre-Jules César Janssen first obtained evidence for the existence of the new element helium when studying a total solar eclipse in 1868. (2) He detected a yellow line on his spectroscope while observing the Sun, and realized that, because of its wavelength, it could not be the result of any element known at the time. (3) Janssen's experiment was repeated by Norman Lockyer, who also concluded that no known element produced such a line. (4) However, other scientists were dubious, finding it unlikely that an element existed only on the Sun. (5) In 1895, William Ramsay isolated helium by treating cleveite—a uranium mineral—with mineral acids. (6) Ramsay sent samples of the resulting gas to Norman Lockyer. (7) Lockyer identified it conclusively as the missing element helium. (8) It was Lockyer who named the element "helium," from the Greek word "helios," meaning "sun."

(9) The relatively recent discovery of this new element is ironic, considering that helium is the second most abundant element in the universe (hydrogen being the first). (10) However, helium does not bind to Earth by gravitation and is thus found mostly in space. (11) On Earth, it is created by the decay of radioactive elements, such as uranium and thorium. (12) Helium becomes trapped in natural gas deposits and can then be extracted for commercial use. (13) Helium is a nonrenewable resource. (14) Once extracted, it quickly returns to space.

(15) Since its discovery, helium has become a helpful resource in several industries. (16) The most common application for liquid helium is in cryogenics, a branch of physics that studies very low temperatures. (17) Among other uses, helium is employed to cool superconducting magnets in devices such as MRI scanners. (18) It is also used to grow crystals for silicon wafers. (19) In non-scientific endeavors, helium is the gas that makes balloons and blimps rise. (20) Until recently, scientist's had been concerned that helium are in very short supply.

5. Which sentence presents information that shifts away from the main topic of the first paragraph and should be removed?

   A.   sentence 4

   B.   sentence 5

   C.   sentence 6

   D.   sentence 7

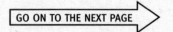

6. Which sentence should replace sentence 8 to best introduce the main claim of the passage?

    E. In addition to his work in chemistry, Lockyer founded the prestigious scientific journal *Nature*.

    F. Today, helium is prized for its valuable commercial and industrial applications, but it is considered relatively rare.

    G. Helium is the lightest and simplest of the Noble Gases, but is by no means the least important.

    H. Helium is both colorless and odorless, which partly explains why it took so much time and effort to discover.

7. Which sentence would best follow and support sentence 11?

    A. When these elements break down, they release helium.

    B. Uranium is also widely used in nuclear power plants.

    C. Scientists measure the rate of decay of radioactive elements using *half-life*.

    D. When handling radioactive elements, it is important to take proper safety precautions.

8. What is the best way to combine sentences 13 and 14 to clarify the relationship between ideas?

    E. Helium is a nonrenewable resource, so once extracted, it quickly returns to space.

    F. Helium quickly returns to space after having been extracted and because of this is a nonrenewable resource.

    G. Because helium quickly returns to space once extracted, it is a nonrenewable resource.

    H. Helium is a nonrenewable resource, although it quickly returns to space after extraction.

9. What transition should be added to the beginning of sentence 19?

    A. Similarly

    B. In contrast

    C. It has also been known that

    D. In addition

10. What edit is necessary to correct sentence 20?

    E. Change *Until* to **Before** AND *scientist's* to **scientists**.

    F. Change *scientist's* to **scientists** AND *are* to **is**.

    G. Change *scientist's* to **scientists'** AND *had been* to **has been**.

    H. Change *concerned* to **unconcerned** AND *that* to **because**.

11. Which sentence would best follow and support sentence 20?

    A. However, new research indicates that it is possible for helium to be collected in large quantities.

    B. In fact, there have been frequent scientific discussions about this concern, and future research will likely be conducted.

    C. Happily, the concern is unwarranted, so people having parties with lots of balloons don't have to worry.

    D. In reality, there is enough helium on the Sun to fill Earth's needs, but there is no way to harness it.

READING COMPREHENSION

QUESTIONS 12–57

DIRECTIONS: Read the six passages and answer the corresponding questions. Re-read relevant parts of the text before choosing the best answer for each question, but be mindful of time. Base your answers only on the content within each passage. You may write in your test booklet to take notes.

The Origins of Basketball

1   It was a particularly cold winter in Springfield, Massachusetts when Luther Gulick, head of the Physical Education department at the School for Christian Workers, faced a rowdy class of young men. Gulick was frustrated. There had to be something he could do to keep the boys engaged and allow them to blow off some steam. He made a fateful decision when he called teacher James Naismith to his office to talk over the problem. The conversation that followed would change the future of sports.

2   At his wit's end, Gulick ordered Naismith to invent a game that could be played indoors and that would provide an "athletic distraction" for the eighteen members of this especially rambunctious student body. This was a tall order, made yet taller by the two-week deadline Gulick gave Naismith. Naismith's initially decided to simply adapt another known outdoor game, like soccer, to the indoors. Ultimately, Naismith was not satisfied with just reworking something that had already been done. As the deadline drew closer, Naismith recalled a game from his childhood in Canada that required skill and precision, teamwork and athleticism. This was just the kind of activity the situation called for. By adopting some of the ideas from this childhood game (Duck on a Rock) and incorporating elements from other popular games of the era, Naismith created a new game that maximized appropriate play and safety for schoolboys: basketball. He gathered his students in the gymnasium to premiere the game with equipment that consisted of two peach baskets and a soccer ball. The date was December 21, 1891.

3   The original thirteen rules included elements, such as tackling, that have since become obsolete in modern basketball and did not yet include elements that have now become game staples, such as dribbling. Still, in many ways, that inaugural game of basketball would be recognizable today. From its humble beginnings, the game caught on quickly, assisted by the YMCA organization. Although that first basketball game was played by a group of men, women also quickly became interested in the new sport. A few weeks after basketball's introduction, the first women's basketball team began at a nearby school, whose teachers saw Naismith's students playing. By the next year, the first women's college team was formed at Smith College in Northampton, Massachusetts.

4   Soon the sport became more organized with the formation of the National Basketball League, and play became popularized; troops in World War I even played the game overseas. In general, basketball was played mostly for recreation until 1946, when the owners of the United States' biggest arenas began to consider the idea of professional basketball. The Basketball Association of America—the precursor to today's NBA—was formed, in part, to fill arena seats on days when there were no professional hockey or college basketball matches.

5   Basketball is now played in every corner of the world, though the United States remains its most significant stronghold. It has become an extremely popular sport in America, both for spectators and as something played by everyday Americans. Though its rules have changed over the years, the game of basketball has stayed close to the one envisioned by its creator over one hundred years ago.

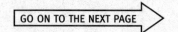
GO ON TO THE NEXT PAGE

12. Which statement best describes the central idea of this passage?

   E. The modern sport of basketball began in 1861, when it was invented by James Naismith as a way for young men to exercise indoors during a particularly cold winter.

   F. James Naismith included elements of a game from his childhood when he invented basketball, and the rules of the game have continued to evolve until the present day.

   G. Early basketball games included rules that are no longer used, and modern basketball has added different skills to the game.

   H. James Naismith's invention of basketball has evolved and spread all over the world in a variety of formats.

13. The phrase "blow off some steam" in paragraph 1 conveys the idea that

   A. basketball not only required teamwork, but was physically and mentally challenging.

   B. Gulick believed additional exercise would improve the behavior of the boys in his school.

   C. the boys at the School for Christian Workers were inclined to fight with each other.

   D. the "athletic distraction" of basketball was a useful addition to the Physical Education classes.

14. Which detail provides support for the author's statement about the rules for basketball in paragraph 5?

   E. the rapid expansion of basketball to include women's teams

   F. the establishment of the Basketball Association of America

   G. the loss of tackling and the addition of dribbling

   H. the spread of basketball internationally during World War I

15. Based on the passage, what is the most likely reason that Luther Gulick wanted James Naismith to create a new game?

   A. Gulick wanted a game that spectators would come to watch in his arena.

   B. Gulick thought outdoor games like soccer had become too commonplace.

   C. Gulick was inspired by a childhood game.

   D. Gulick wanted his students to channel their energy in a healthy direction.

16. What evidence best indicates the reason basketball became a professional sport?

   E. the availability of arenas where games could be played

   F. the official rules established by the National Basketball League

   G. the international popularity of basketball following World War One.

   H. the widespread popularity of basketball as a recreational sport

17. What is the primary role of paragraph 3 in the structure of the passage?

   A. It explains how the rules of basketball have changed since its invention.

   B. It connects the game played at the School for Christian Workers to modern basketball.

   C. It describes the formation of a national organization for professional basketball.

   D. It provides details on the start of women's basketball.

18. Which conclusion is best supported by the information in paragraph 5?

   E. Basketball is played more often in the United States than in any other country.

   F. Basketball today does not resemble the original game invented by James Naismith.

   G. Basketball for recreation will become more popular internationally.

   H. In the United States, basketball is played for recreation more often than it is played professionally.

GO ON TO THE NEXT PAGE ⇒

Early Artistic Expression

1   For the great bulk of human prehistory, there was no art. That is, there is no convincing evidence that our distant ancestors engaged in any form of artistic expression until quite recently. Of course, it is possible that our remote ancestors created performance art, decorated their bodies, or indulged in other art forms that did not survive to the present era, but nothing can be confirmed until the Paleolithic era, when art clearly blossomed. Interestingly, the oldest traces of works of art appeared almost simultaneously in a variety of locations in Europe, Africa, and Australia. This early art assumed many forms, including wood and bone carving, engraving, bas relief and three-dimensional sculpture, painting, and music. What compelled the human spirit to so fully engage with artistic expression at a single point in time may never be fully understood, but there is much we can learn about past cultures by studying the art that they left behind.

2   One of the most impressive and best-known caches of art from this time period can be found in the cave paintings of the Cro-Magnon people from France and Spain, who lived from about 40,000 to 10,000 years ago. Modern people may associate "cave art" with "cavemen," a term that immediately evokes images of hairy brutes, partly draped in animal furs, using caves for shelter in a limited crude life. But in fact, the Cro-Magnons lived a more sophisticated and expressive life than one might expect, with territory that ranged far from the caves in which their art is found. Cro-Magnon people are associated with caves simply because that is where the best-preserved evidence of their lives and culture has been found.

3   A great deal can be inferred about the Cro-Magnons from what was preserved in these caves. From their garbage, their burials, and their art, we know that they had needles, buttons, and sewn clothing; we know that they buried their dead sensitively, in elaborate rituals with ornaments and decorations; we know that they were skilled toolmakers and even made and played musical instruments. But the most significant contribution may come from their stunning cave art. The drawings found within the caves are delicate and nuanced, almost coming alive with movement. The caves provide evidence not only of Cro-Magnon artistry, but also of their expectation that it would be shared with others. For instance, they actually marked their caves with trail signs called "claviforms," apparently used to direct people to the right-hand side of wide passages, to point out art in concealed niches, or to avoid hazards. The footprints of the makers are still visible on the cave floors, their handprints and scaffolding marks still on the cave walls. These traces provide a vivid impression of the artists as people.

4   But why did the Cro-Magnons create cave art in the first place? Archaeologists used to debate various interpretations: that the paintings represented mindless copies of nature by savage people, or magical rites to ensure success at hunting, or depictions of myths, and so on. Such theories became less popular when anthropologists began to ask present-day tribal Australian Aborigines and African Bushmen why they create their own rock art. The reasons turned out to bear little resemblance to archaeologists' guesses. The same image—for example, a fish painted by aboriginal Australians—has been painted for different reasons on different occasions. Some fish paintings served to mark tribal territory, others to tell a story ("I caught this big fish"), and yet others to convey religious significance. It shouldn't surprise us that the Cro-Magnons' motives may have been equally varied, given all the modern evidence for their mentality. The ways of this well-rounded group, with its nuanced culture, may not ever be neatly and simply summed up. But the more we study the art left behind by the Cro-Magnons—and by other ancient artists—the more modern scholars can learn about humanity itself.

GO ON TO THE NEXT PAGE

19. Which statement best describes the central idea of the passage?

    A. Present-day tribal people can provide information about humans in the prehistoric era.

    B. Early humans were not that different in their lifestyle and technology from present-day Australian Aborigines.

    C. The art and artifacts left behind by early humans provide important insights into their lives and culture.

    D. The artistic creations of the cave dwellers included not only paintings, but also crafts, tools, sculpture, and music.

20. How does paragraph 2 contribute to the passage?

    E. It describes many forms of early art.

    F. It discusses the debate surrounding the interpretations of art created by the Cro-Magnons.

    G. It suggests that the Cro-Magnons may have had varying motives for creating art.

    H. It introduces Cro-Magnon art as a significant example of ancient art.

21. What is the most likely reason that more Cro-Magnon artifacts have been found in caves than in other locations?

    A. Although they had large territories, Cro-Magnon people usually lived in caves.

    B. Artifacts in other locations are more likely to have decayed.

    C. Claviform trail signs led archaeologists to many cave sites.

    D. Caves were located at the center of Cro-Magnon territories.

22. Which statement describes how the author's response to "Such theories" in paragraph 4 contributes to the development of ideas in the passage?

    E. Modern Australian Aborigines and African Bushmen indicate that the rock art produced today is used for different purposes, so these theories have become more popular.

    F. Because modern Australian Aborigines and African Bushmen indicate that the rock art produced today is used for different purposes, these theories are weakened.

    G. Since the rock art produced by modern Australian Aborigines is different from that produced by African Bushmen, these theories are weakened.

    H. Because modern Australian Aborigines and African Bushmen use similar symbols to depict similar meanings, these theories have become more popular.

23. Which excerpt from the passage supports the idea that Cro-Magnons used markings to communicate information to others?

    A. "From their garbage, their burials, and their art, we know that they had needles, buttons, and sewn clothing; we know that they buried their dead sensitively, in elaborate rituals with ornaments and decorations; we know that they were skilled toolmakers and even made and played musical instruments." (paragraph 3)

    B. "The drawings found within the caves are delicate and nuanced, almost coming alive with movement." (paragraph 3)

    C. "For instance, they actually marked their caves with trail signs called 'claviforms,' apparently used to direct people to the right-hand side of wide passages, to point out art in concealed niches, or to avoid hazards." (paragraph 3)

    D. "The footprints of the makers are still visible on the cave floors, their handprints and scaffolding marks still on the cave walls." (paragraph 3)

24. Read this sentence from paragraph 4.

    > The ways of this well-rounded group, with its nuanced culture, may not ever be neatly and simply summed up.

    The words "well-rounded" and "nuanced" convey a

    E. sense of respect for the diversity and depth of Cro-Magnon culture.

    F. sense of concern for the difficulty of learning about Cro-Magnon culture

    G. feeling of excitement about future archaeological discoveries.

    H. feeling of appreciation for the difficulties faced by archaeologists.

25. How does paragraph 1 fit into the overall structure of the passage?

    A. It describes how ancient art was created.

    B. It provides a history of ancient art.

    C. It shows the variety of ancient art.

    D. It explains why ancient art is important.

26. Which detail about Cro-Magnon art provides support for the author's opinion in paragraph 2?

    E. its location in caves

    F. its early appearance in human history

    G. its variety and complexity

    H. its similarity to that of modern groups

"The Song of Wandering Aengus"

by William Butler Yeats

I went out to the hazel wood,
Because a fire was in my head,
And cut and peeled a hazel wand,
And hooked a berry to a thread;
5   And when white moths were on the wing,
And moth-like stars were flickering out,
I dropped the berry in a stream
And caught a little silver trout.

When I had laid it on the floor
10 I went to blow the fire a-flame,
But something rustled on the floor,
And someone called me by my name:
It had become a glimmering girl
With apple blossom in her hair
15 Who called me by my name and ran
And faded through the brightening air.

Though I am old with wandering
Through hollow lands and hilly lands,
I will find out where she has gone,
20 And kiss her lips and take her hands;
And walk among long dappled grass,
And pluck till time and times are done,
The silver apples of the moon,
The golden apples of the sun.

27. How does the form of "The Song of Wandering Aengus" contribute to its meaning?

A. Each stanza presents the viewpoint of a different narrator.

B. Each stanza indicates a change in the season of the year.

C. The events of each stanza occur in different locations.

D. The events of each stanza occur in chronological order.

GO ON TO THE NEXT PAGE ⇨

28. Read line 2.

> **Because a fire was in my head,**

How does this line contribute to the development of a central idea of the poem?

- **E.** It explains that Aengus has a headache.
- **F.** It indicates that Aengus was very hot.
- **G.** It introduces Aengus's intense desire for love.
- **H.** It describes Aengus's sorrow over the loss of his love.

29. Read lines 5–6.

> **And when white moths were on the wing,**
> **And moth-like stars were flickering out,**

These lines help develop the theme of the poem by suggesting that Aengus

- **A.** was disturbed by the presence of many flying insects.
- **B.** was fishing at a stream close to his home.
- **C.** knows that love is only a fleeting experience.
- **D.** is about to enter a new period in his life.

30. Which line from the poem best supports the idea that Aengus is a mortal human being?

- **E.** "And moth-like stars were flickering out," (line 6)
- **F.** "Though I am old with wandering" (line 17)
- **G.** "And pluck till time and times are done," (line 22)
- **H.** "The silver apples of the moon," (line 23)

31. Which detail from the poem reflects the poet's view that, once recognized, love may be elusive?

- **A.** "I went to blow the fire a-flame,/But something rustled on the floor," (lines 10–11)
- **B.** "And someone called me by my name:/It had become a glimmering girl" (lines 12–13)
- **C.** "Who called me by my name and ran/And faded through the brightening air." (lines 15–16)
- **D.** "I will find out where she has gone/And kiss her lips and take her hands;" (lines 19–20)

32. Read lines 17 and 18.

> Though I am old with wandering
>
> Through hollow lands and hilly lands,

What impact do the phrases "hollow lands" and "hilly lands" have on the meaning of the poem?

E. They suggest that it may be necessary to search widely in order to find love.

F. They describe the landscape of Ireland, the setting for the poem.

G. They imply that the search for love has caused the narrator to grow old.

H. They point to the most likely locations where the narrator may find love.

33. With which statement would the author of this poem most likely agree?

A. Because everyone's path in life is different, it is important to be true to yourself.

B. Even if the search is unsuccessful, a life spent looking for love is worthwhile.

C. Life may involve disappointments, but to reach your goal you must persevere.

D. Life is uncertain, so take action as soon as an opportunity becomes available.

34. Which detail from the poem reflects the idea of love slipping away?

E. "I went to blow the fire a-flame," (line 10)

F. "But something rustled on the floor," (line 11)

G. "It had become a glimmering girl" (line 13)

H. "And faded through the brightening air." (line 16)

GO ON TO THE NEXT PAGE

Practice Tests

How World War I Began

1 Most scholars agree that, due to the political climate in Europe in the period leading up to World War I, a conflict of some kind was inevitable. Several circumstances contributed long-term to the breakout of war, though only serving to set the stage. The missing ingredient was a spark that would ignite the volatile situation. It came in the form of an assassin's bullet on June 28, 1914.

2 At that time, Bosnia-Herzegovina was a province of Austria-Hungary. It had been recently annexed by that empire against not only its own wishes but also the wishes of many in the region, Serbia in particular. Serbia was a country with which Austria-Hungary had very tense relations. The set of circumstances, including Bosnians' resentment of Austrian rule and desire for independence, as well as unrest and mistrust toward Austria-Hungary among Serbians and many others in the Baltic Region, created a precarious situation. Thus, when Archduke Franz Ferdinand, the heir to the Austro-Hungarian throne, announced plans to visit Bosnia, many people were upset. While the Archduke himself may not have been a key political player at this time, he represented Austria-Hungary's control over Bosnia-Herzegovina's imperialism, and the pressures of his empire's incursions in the region were reaching a boiling point. A terrorist organization known as the Black Hand made plans to strike out in a symbolic fashion and assassinate the Archduke.

3 Several assassins were trained and outfitted in Serbia for this task, and their actions were hardly kept secret. In fact, many warnings reached the Archduke in Austria-Hungary. The Archduke's decision to visit Bosnia was, by all accounts, foolhardy, since there were such clear threats and many believed he would become an assassin's target. However, the visit went forward as planned. As Ferdinand's entourage arrived at the Sarajevo train station, members of the Black Hand were already lining the path to City Hall, his destination. Surprisingly, even though there had been threats, the security detail for this visit was scant; there were few officers providing protection, and the route had even been published in advance. As the motorcade passed the central police station, Black Hand member Nedeljko Cabrinovic tossed a grenade at the Archduke's vehicle. When the driver of the car carrying the Archduke saw an object coming toward him, he accelerated and drove off. Meanwhile, the grenade rolled under the next car where it exploded, injuring several people. The Archduke's driver quickly sped the rest of the way so that none of the terrorists were able to attack the Archduke's vehicle, and Ferdinand made it safely through this gauntlet.

4 Perhaps surprisingly, even after the assassination attempt, Ferdinand was as determined in continuing the visit as he had been in deciding to make it. He actually attended the official reception at City Hall that had been planned. Afterward, however, when he found out that passengers in the second car had been badly injured, the Archduke insisted on visiting the hospital where they were being cared for, overruling arguments that it might still be dangerous for him in the city. On the way to the hospital, the driver, whose quick thinking had saved the Archduke's life earlier in the day, took a fateful wrong turn. The mistake was quickly realized and the motorcade began reversing, but the damage was done. Just at that moment, one of the conspirators, Gavrilo Princip, happened to be walking down the same road. As the Archduke's car slowly reversed, it came within five feet of Princip, who saw his opportunity and fired twice into the car, instantly killing the Archduke and his wife.

5 This was the spark needed to ignite the tense situation in Europe. A misguided attempt to reach resolution failed when Austria-Hungary presented Serbia with an unreasonable list of demands and those demands were rejected wholesale. The two nations declared war. That triggered other alliances, and tensions in Europe quickly escalated out of control. Within months, the entire continent would be engulfed in war.

GO ON TO THE NEXT PAGE

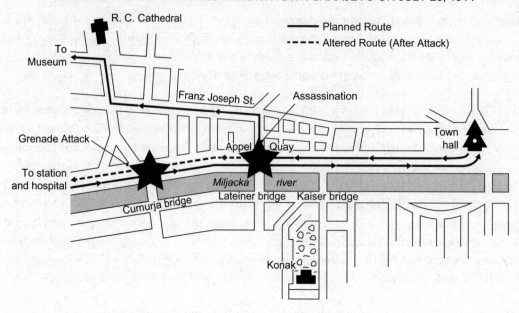

FRANZ FERDINAND'S ROUTES IN DOWNTOWN SARAJEVO ON JULY 28, 1914

35. Which of the following best describes the goal of the Black Hand?

A. to free Bosnia-Herzegovina from the control of Serbia

B. to assassinate Archduke Ferdinand

C. to kindle the outbreak of World War I

D. to reunite Bosnia-Herzegovina with Serbia

36. Which statement describes how paragraph 4 contributes to the overall structure of the passage?

E. It outlines the detailed preparations the Black Hand made prior to the Archduke's visit.

F. It demonstrates that, if better protection had been provided to the Archduke, the assassination may have been prevented.

G. It provides historical background to the events leading up to the Archduke's visit.

H. It shows that an unplanned mistake, as well as the Archduke's own decisions, contributed to the start of World War I.

37. Which sentence from the passage indicates that the assassination of Archduke Ferdinand might have been avoided?

A. "When the driver of the car carrying the Archduke saw an object coming toward him, he accelerated and drove off." (paragraph 3)

B. "He actually attended the official reception at City Hall that had been planned." (paragraph 4)

C. "On the way to the hospital, the driver, whose quick thinking had saved the Archduke's life earlier in the day, took a fateful wrong turn." (paragraph 4)

D. "A misguided attempt to reach resolution failed when Austria-Hungary presented Serbia with an unreasonable list of demands and those demands were rejected wholesale." (paragraph 5)

GO ON TO THE NEXT PAGE

38. Read this sentence from paragraph 1.

> **The missing ingredient was a spark that would ignite the volatile situation.**

The sentence contributes to the overall structure of the excerpt by

    E. shifting the focus of the text from the broad reasons for tensions in Europe to the specific event that led to the start of World War I.

    F. highlighting the political, economic, and geographic reasons that World War I started between Bosnia-Herzegovina and Austria-Hungary.

    G. revealing information about the political systems in Europe prior to the start of World War I.

    H. introducing the reason why the Black Hand would prepare to assassinate Archduke Ferdinand.

39. Based on the passage, what is the most likely reason "many people were upset" (paragraph 2) when Archduke Ferdinand decided to visit Bosnia?

    A. Archduke Ferdinand was a powerful political leader.

    B. There was not enough time to make the arrangements to guarantee his safety.

    C. The Baltic region was under Serbian control.

    D. Austria-Hungary was invading surrounding territories.

40. Read this sentence from paragraph 5.

> **A misguided attempt to reach resolution failed when Austria-Hungary presented Serbia with an unreasonable list of demands and those demands were rejected wholesale.**

The words "misguided," "unreasonable," and "wholesale" most clearly convey the idea that

    E. other countries would soon take sides and enter the dispute.

    F. the negotiations were time-consuming and unimportant.

    G. the two countries should not have tried to reach an agreement.

    H. both Austria-Hungary and Serbia did not expect that the negotiations would be successful.

41. How does the map provide additional support for the central idea of the passage?

A. It shows how the Black Hand outsmarted the shrewd travel plans of Franz Ferdinand and his advisors in order to carry out the assassination.

B. It illustrates how Franz Ferdinand's route through the city set the stage for the Black Hand attacks.

C. It reveals how tragic the driver's decision to reverse after taking a wrong turn was, since it led to the assassination.

D. It highlights how the confusing nature of the roads in Sarajevo made Franz Ferdinand's decision to visit Sarajevo irresponsible.

42. What is the primary role of paragraph 2 in the structure of the passage?

E. It provides background for the event described in the first paragraph.

F. It details examples that support the main idea of the first paragraph.

G. It states a theory that will be supported by the third paragraph.

H. It outlines the main idea of the passage that will be developed in the following paragraphs.

Excerpt from "The Masque of the Red Death"
by Edgar Allan Poe

1   The "Red Death" had long devastated the country. No pestilence had ever been so fatal, or so hideous. Blood was its Avatar and its seal—the madness and the horror of blood. There were sharp pains, and sudden dizziness, and then profuse bleeding at the pores, with dissolution. The scarlet stains upon the body and especially upon the face of the victim, were the pest ban which shut him out from the aid and from the sympathy of his fellow-men. And the whole seizure, progress, and termination of the disease, were incidents of half an hour.

2   But Prince Prospero was happy and dauntless and sagacious. When his dominions were half depopulated, he summoned to his presence a thousand hale and light-hearted friends from among the knights and dames of his court, and with these retired to the deep seclusion of one of his castellated abbeys. This was an extensive and magnificent structure, the creation of the prince's own eccentric yet august taste. A strong and lofty wall girdled it in. This wall had gates of iron. The courtiers, having entered, brought furnaces and massy hammers and welded the bolts.

3   They resolved to leave means neither of ingress nor egress to the sudden impulses of despair or of frenzy from within. The abbey was amply provisioned. With such precautions the courtiers might bid defiance to contagion. The external world could take care of itself. In the meantime it was folly to grieve or to think. The prince had provided all the appliances of pleasure. There were buffoons, there were improvisatori, there were ballet-dancers, there were musicians, there was Beauty, there was wine. All these and security were within. Without was the "Red Death."

4   It was toward the close of the fifth or sixth month of his seclusion that the Prince Prospero entertained his thousand friends at a masked ball of the most unusual magnificence. [. . .]

5   And the revel went whirlingly on, until at length there commenced the sounding of midnight upon the clock. And then the music ceased, as I have told; and the revolutions of the waltzers were quieted; and there was an uneasy cessation of all things as before. But now there were twelve strokes to be sounded by the bell of the clock; and thus it happened, perhaps, that more of thought crept, with more of time, into the meditations of the thoughtful among those who reveled. And thus too, it happened, that before the last echoes of the last chime had utterly sunk into silence, there were many individuals in the crowd who had found leisure to become aware of the presence of a masked figure which had arrested the attention of no single individual before. And the rumor of this new presence having spread itself whisperingly around, there arose at length from the whole company a buzz, or murmur, of horror, and of disgust.

6   In an assembly of phantasms such as I have painted, it may well be supposed that no ordinary appearance could have excited such sensation. In truth the masquerade license of the night was nearly unlimited; but the figure in question had out-Heroded Herod, and gone beyond the bounds of even the prince's indefinite decorum. There are chords in the hearts of the most reckless which cannot be touched without emotion. Even with the utterly lost, to whom life and death are equally jests, there are matters of which no jest can be made. The whole company, indeed, seemed now deeply to feel that in the costume and bearing of the stranger neither wit nor propriety existed. The figure was tall and gaunt, and shrouded from head to foot in the habiliments of the grave. The mask which concealed the visage was made so nearly to resemble the

GO ON TO THE NEXT PAGE

countenance of a stiffened corpse that the closest scrutiny must have had difficulty in detecting the cheat. And yet all this might have been endured, if not approved, by the mad revellers around. But the mummer had gone so far as to assume the type of the Red Death. His vesture was dabbled in blood—and his broad brow, with all the features of the face, was besprinkled with the scarlet horror.

7 When the eyes of the Prince Prospero fell upon this spectral image (which, with a slow and solemn movement, as if more fully to sustain its role, stalked to and fro among the waltzers) he was seen to be convulsed, in the first moment with a strong shudder either of terror or distaste; but, in the next, his brow reddened with rage.

43. How does paragraph 1 contribute to the plot of the excerpt?

    A. It offers a historical context for how others have avoided the Red Death.

    B. It describes the symptoms of a disease that is no longer cause for concern.

    C. It introduces a disease that a country tries unsuccessfully to avoid.

    D. It illustrates how the courtiers plan to eliminate the spread of the disease.

44. Which sentence from the excerpt best supports the idea that the country over which Prince Prospero rules has suffered major losses?

    E. "And the whole seizure, progress, and termination of the disease, were incidents of half an hour." (paragraph 1)

    F. "When his dominions were half depopulated, he summoned to his presence a thousand hale and light-hearted friends…" (paragraph 2)

    G. "They resolved to leave means neither of ingress nor egress to the sudden impulses of despair or of frenzy from within." (paragraph 3)

    H. "And the rumor of this new presence having spread itself whisperingly around, there arose at length from the whole company a buzz, or murmur, of horror, and of disgust." (paragraph 5)

45. Read this sentence from paragraph 1.

> The scarlet stains upon the body and especially upon the face of the victim, were the pest ban which shut him out from the aid and from the sympathy of his fellow-men.

This sentence indicates that a person who shows symptoms of the Red Death is

    A. carefully tended to by others.

    B. gravely ill but likely to recover.

    C. shunned by all.

    D. sick for a long time.

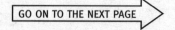

46. Read this text from paragraph 2.

> A strong and lofty wall girdled it in. This wall had gates of iron. The courtiers, having entered, brought furnaces and massy hammers and welded the bolts.

These details convey a central idea in the excerpt by showing that the courtiers are hoping to

E. secure the abbey from attack since it was a building that was particularly vulnerable to assault.

F. keep out any rival princes and other dignitaries from both nearby and remote provinces.

G. separate themselves from the common people who were considered to be of lower status.

H. ensure that no one entered or left, thus preventing the Red Death from spreading to them.

47. Read this text from paragraph 3.

> The external world could take care of itself. In the meantime it was folly to grieve or to think. The prince had provided all the appliances of pleasure.

How do these sentences contribute to the development of the plot?

A. They illustrate that the prince is unconcerned for his people's welfare outside of the abbey.

B. They show that the prince is focused on remaining humble and frugal.

C. They explain that the prince is resigned to give up his pleasure-seeking ways.

D. They note that the prince is secure in his ability to meet all of his people's needs.

48. Read this text from paragraph 4.

> It was toward the close of the fifth or sixth month of his seclusion that the Prince Prospero entertained his thousand friends at a masked ball of the most unusual magnificence.

Which statement best describes how the sentence fits into the overall structure of the excerpt?

E. It indicates a shift to the realization that the Red Death is already present within the abbey.

F. It emphasizes a shift from analysis of the courtiers' behavior to the behavior of the prince.

G. It introduces the idea that time has passed while foreshadowing a momentous event.

H. It provides a transition to the observation that the courtiers dislike being secluded.

49. In paragraph 4, how do the words "uneasy," "silence," and "masked figure" contribute to the meaning of the excerpt?

   A. They illustrate a sense of anger.

   B. They highlight a sense of foreboding.

   C. They demonstrate a sense of revelry.

   D. They allude to a sense of disdain.

50. How does paragraph 5 contribute to the central idea of the excerpt?

   E. It condemns those who try to protect themselves against a fatal disease.

   F. It discusses the medical symptoms of the Red Death.

   G. It highlights the inevitability of death.

   H. It emphasizes the foolishness of revelry.

GO ON TO THE NEXT PAGE

Orwell: Overcoming Adversity

1   Although it took the publication of his now-famous novel *Animal Farm* in 1945 to finally establish British writer George Orwell's reputation for shrewd political commentary, this well-known satire did not mark the beginning of Orwell's writing career. Indeed, by the time Orwell achieved fame, he had already been writing seriously for nearly fifteen years. In the decade preceding his completion of *Animal Farm*, Orwell struggled to make ends meet as a writer. He managed to scrape by, subsisting on writing assignments that paid his bills but lacked creative possibilities. In fact, right up to his final, bedridden days, much of Orwell's life was marked by a struggle of one kind or another.

2   Born in 1903 to a lower-middle-class father who was a British civil servant in India[1], Orwell moved to England with his parents when he was just eight years old. He was sent away to boarding school and then educated at Eton College, where he first began to write. He was distinguished among his classmates by his brilliance and his relative poverty, both of which affected his life and his choices. Orwell's talent won him recognition and the opportunity to publish his essays in school periodicals. But feeling that he did not fit in, Orwell ultimately returned to India—following in his father's footsteps—rather than study further in England.

3   In India, he became an administrator for the Indian Imperial Police. Again, Orwell struggled, this time with the clash between his responsibilities as a bureaucrat of the British government and his growing disillusionment with the concept of imperialism[2]. In fact, it was during these years that Orwell first began to feel the intense disenchantment with large state bureaucracies that fills the pages of his later, and most popular, literary works.

4   Upon his return to England in 1928, Orwell wrote a series of essays exploring this discontent. Then, in 1930, he began his literary career in earnest. Immersing himself in the slums of London, Orwell attempted to fully experience the everyday adversity of poverty. This research resulted in the acclaimed 1933 book *Down and Out in Paris and London*. In late 1936, already a committed socialist, Orwell was sent to Spain to report on the civil war. Once there, however, he quickly abandoned his responsibilities as a journalist and joined the communist Republican Army in its struggle against the Nationalists. After more than 100 days on the front lines, Orwell was promoted to second lieutenant, given command of more than 30 men—and wounded by a sniper. During this time, thrust into violent clashes, Orwell again found his political identity changing.

5   By the time he returned to England in 1938, he had grown cynical about communism, a change that alienated his left-wing publishers. Nevertheless, the ideological shift inspired his crowning literary achievement, the wholly pessimistic and satirical novel *Nineteen Eighty-Four*, which depicts the threat of political tyranny in the future. Unfortunately, Orwell would not live to experience the tremendous impact of this final work, as one last struggle—this time with tuberculosis—claimed his life just months after the novel's release in 1949.

[1] British rule was in effect on the Indian subcontinent from 1858 to 1947.

[2] Rule over other nations or territories, often by force.

Practice Tests

51. The use of chronological structure contributes to the development of the ideas in the passage by

    A. explaining why Orwell struggled during his experiences abroad in India and Spain.

    B. showing the process by which Orwell finally became an enormously successful writer.

    C. illustrating the reasons why Orwell found little success as a writer early in his career.

    D. showing how the events in Orwell's life contributed to the themes of his literature.

52. How does paragraph 1 introduce the idea that George Orwell was not immediately successful as a writer?

    E. through describing his early writings as lacking creative opportunities

    F. through mentioning the struggles at the end of his life

    G. by stating that Orwell's income from writing was insufficient to meet his needs

    H. by noting that *Animal Farm* established his reputation as a shrewd political commentator

53. Read this sentence from paragraph 2.

    > **But feeling that he did not fit in, Orwell ultimately returned to India—following in his father's footsteps—rather than study further in England.**

    The sentence contributes to the development of ideas in the passage by

    A. showing that Orwell longed to return to the land of his childhood.

    B. revealing that Orwell accepted British domination over India.

    C. demonstrating Orwell's interest in continuing his father's work.

    D. illustrating Orwell's desire to work instead of continuing his education.

54. Read this sentence from paragraph 4.

    > **After more than 100 days on the front lines, Orwell was promoted to second lieutenant, given command of more than 30 men—and wounded by a sniper.**

    How does the author's use of the dash at the end of the sentence contribute to the development of ideas in the passage?

    E. It provides another example of the struggles in Orwell's life that were introduced in the first paragraph.

    F. It emphasizes the rapid progress Orwell made during this time of his life.

    G. It describes an event that reinforced the ideas that were guiding Orwell's life.

    H. It suggests a contributing factor to the shift in Orwell's thinking mentioned in the next sentence.

GO ON TO THE NEXT PAGE

55. Which sentence from the passage best supports the idea that Orwell's books reflect his personal beliefs?

    A. "He was distinguished among his classmates by both his brilliance and his relative poverty, both of which affected his life and his choices." (paragraph 2)

    B. "Again, Orwell struggled, this time with the clash between his responsibilities as a bureaucrat of the British government and his growing disillusionment with the concept of imperialism." (paragraph 3)

    C. "Once there, however, he quickly abandoned his responsibilities as a journalist and joined the communist Republican Army in its struggle against the Nationalists." (paragraph 4)

    D. "Nevertheless, the ideological shift inspired his crowning literary achievement, the wholly pessimistic and satirical novel *Nineteen Eighty-Four*, which depicts the threat of political tyranny in the future." (paragraph 5)

56. How do the details of the decade of Orwell's life described in paragraph 4 convey a central idea of the passage?

    E. by suggesting that if Orwell had continued as a journalist, he would have succeeded

    F. by connecting Orwell's experiences to the themes he presents in his literary works

    G. by outlining the steps Orwell took to reach the pinnacle of his success as an author

    H. by showing how Orwell's time as a soldier in the communist army confirmed his beliefs

57. With which statement would the author of the passage most likely agree?

    A. Orwell's continued efforts in the face of difficulties contributed to his success.

    B. Living in two different countries as a child made Orwell the distinguished author he became.

    C. Publishing his first stories in his school magazine made Orwell's later literary career possible.

    D. Because he changed his way of thinking so often, Orwell struggled to clearly express his ideas.

Practice Tests

Part 2—Mathematics

57 QUESTIONS—SUGGESTED TIMING: 90 MINUTES

IMPORTANT NOTES

1. Definitions and formulas are **not** provided.

2. Diagrams are **not** necessarily drawn to scale, with the exception of graphs.

3. Diagrams are drawn in single planes unless the question specifically states they are not.

4. Graphs are drawn to scale.

5. Simplify all fractions to lowest terms.

GRID-IN QUESTIONS

QUESTIONS 58–62

DIRECTIONS: Answer each question. Write your answer in the boxes at the top of the grid on the answer sheet. Start on the left side of each grid, printing only one number or symbol in each box. **DO NOT LEAVE A BOX BLANK IN THE MIDDLE OF AN ANSWER.** Under each box, fill in the circle that matches the number or symbol you wrote above. **DO NOT FILL IN A CIRCLE UNDER AN UNUSED BOX.**

---

58. A bin in the gym holds 40 balls, which are a mix of basketballs, soccer balls, and dodgeballs. The ratio of basketballs to soccer balls is 3:1. The ratio of soccer balls to dodgeballs is 1:4. How many basketballs are in the bin?

59. If $\frac{2}{3} = \frac{21}{x}$, what is the value of x?

60. If x is a positive, even integer and $2x + 8 < 22$, how many possible values of x are there?

61. A certain game gives scores between 0 and 5. Trinity played 6 times and her mean score was 4.5. Jayden played 4 times. If both players have the same sum of scores, what was Jayden's mean score?

62. Denise drives to and from work every day. The distance from her house to her work is 3.7 miles. If Denise works 5 days per week, how many miles does she drive in total between her house and work in a week?

GO ON TO THE NEXT PAGE

MULTIPLE-CHOICE QUESTIONS

QUESTIONS 63–114

DIRECTIONS: Answer each question, selecting the best answer available. On the answer sheet, mark the letter of each of your answers. You can do your figuring in the test booklet or on paper provided by the proctor.

63. The sum of a number and 6 is twice as great as the number itself. What is the number?

   A.   3

   B.   6

   C.   9

   D.   12

64. What is the value of $2(5b - 7)$ in terms of y if $b = 3y$?

   E. $30y$

   F. $30y + 7$

   G. $30y - 7$

   H. $30y - 14$

65. Sienna, Rhys, and Micah are all reading the same book for school. Sienna has read 40% as far as Rhys has, and Rhys has read 40% as far as Micah has. If Sienna has read 60 pages, how many pages has Micah read?

   A.   150

   B.   300

   C.   375

   D.   500

66. Points X, Y, and Z are on a straight line, and Z is between X and Y. The length of $\overline{XZ}$ is $\frac{1}{3}$ the length of $\overline{YZ}$, and the length of $\overline{YZ} = 27$ meters. How long is $\overline{XY}$?

   E.   9

   F.   18

   G.   36

   H.   81

67. The decimal 0.55 can be written as the fraction $\frac{x}{20}$. What is the value of x?

   A.   5

   B.   9

   C.   11

   D.   55

GO ON TO THE NEXT PAGE

SURVEY OF DOG OWNERSHIP

Number of Dogs	Number of Families
0	45
1	38
2	27
3 or more	10

68. The table above shows the number of dogs per family in 120 households in a certain neighborhood. By what **percentage** is the number of families with 2 dogs less than the number of families with no dogs?

E. 15%

F. 18%

G. 30%

H. 40%

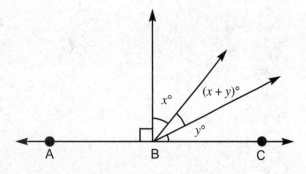

69. In the figure above, B is a point on line AC. What is the value of $x° + y°$?

A. $x°$

B. $y°$

C. $45°$

D. $90°$

70. Dominic buys a new suit that is on sale for 20% off the original price, and he uses a coupon to get an additional 20% off. Not including sales tax, what percent of the original price of the suit did Dominic pay?

E. 36%

F. 40%

G. 60%

H. 64%

71. At basketball practice, Keira has attempted 25 free throws so far, and 36% of her shots made it in. If she attempts 125 **more** free throws, with the same amount of accuracy, by the end of practice, how many free throws will she have made in total?

A. 9

B. 36

C. 45

D. 54

72. In a certain tourism destination, 28% of the city's residents work in the hospitality industry. 55% of residents are age 40 or younger, and 15% of residents are people age 40 or younger who work in the hospitality industry. What percentage of the employed population are people older than 40 who do **not** work in the hospitality industry?

E. 13%

F. 17%

G. 32%

H. 45%

GO ON TO THE NEXT PAGE

73. Point P is **not** on line *m*. How many lines can be drawn through P that form a 90° angle with line *m*?

    A. 0

    B. 1

    C. 2

    D. Cannot be determined from the information given.

74. Carson took his turkey out of the freezer at 7:00 a.m. The thermometer on the turkey read −6°F, and Carson needed the turkey to be 30°F before he could cook it. If the temperature of the turkey rose 4°F per hour, at what time could Carson start to cook his turkey?

    E. 1:00 p.m.

    F. 2:30 p.m.

    G. 4:00 p.m.

    H. 7:30 p.m.

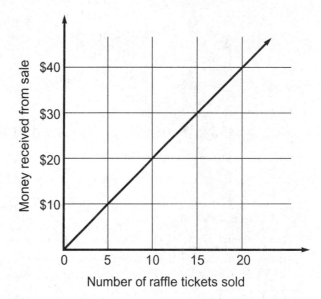

75. The graph above shows the relationship between the number of raffle tickets sold and the amount of money received from the sale. What is the price of two tickets?

    A. $2.00

    B. $3.00

    C. $4.00

    D. $10.00

76. The product of two consecutive integers is 72. Which of the following could be their sum?

    E. −17

    F. −1

    G. 1

    H. 18

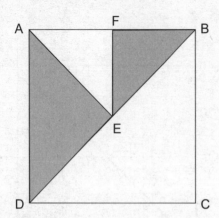

77. In the figure above, ABCD is a square, where E is the midpoint of the diagonal and F is the midpoint of $\overline{AB}$. If the perimeter is 16, what is the area of the shaded region?

    A.   4

    B.   6

    C.   8

    D. 24

78. Which of the following is equivalent to the inequality $7 > 2x - 5 > -7$?

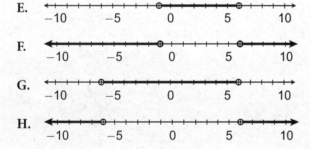

79. The restaurant Casa Felisa spends $7 of every $12 it earns on rent. If the restaurant makes $34,800 in a month, how much does its monthly rent cost?

    A. $1,540

    B. $2,900

    C. $12,270

    D. $20,300

80. A certain test track for new car models is 6,720 meters long. If a car is currently $\frac{2}{3}$ of the way down the track, how many more **kilometers** must it travel to reach the end?

    E.   2.24

    F.   4.48

    G.   6.72

    H. 10.08

81. A box of crayons contains exactly 10 blue crayons. The probability of choosing a blue crayon from the box is $\frac{2}{9}$. How many of the crayons in the box are **not** blue?

    A.   7

    B. 35

    C. 38

    D. 45

82. A man is walking 3 miles per hour toward point B from point A. At the same time, a woman is running 6 miles per hour toward point A from point B. If point A and point B are 15 miles apart, how far from point B will they meet?

    E.   5 miles

    F.   6 miles

    G.   9 miles

    H. 10 miles

GO ON TO THE NEXT PAGE

Practice Tests

83. In a sample of 16 mini-golf balls, 6 are yellow and 10 are pink. If 2 balls are selected at random from the sample, one at a time without replacement, what is the probability that both balls are **not** pink?

A. $\dfrac{1}{8}$

B. $\dfrac{9}{64}$

C. $\dfrac{17}{24}$

D. $\dfrac{3}{4}$

VOCABULARY QUIZ SCORES

Score	Number of Students
90	5
80	9
70	4
60	2

84. What is the mean score of the 20 students in the table above?

E. 15

F. 75

G. 78.5

H. 82.5

85. There are 1,000 horses on a ranch in random pens. In one pen are 25 brown horses, 20 black horses, and 15 white horses. If there are only black, brown, and white horses, what is the best estimate of the number of white horses on the ranch?

A. 100

B. 150

C. 250

D. 400

86. The perimeter of a rectangle is 24 inches. If the length is 5 times the width, what is the area, in square inches?

E. 8

F. 16

G. 20

H. 32

87. Monty has to make his own dinner. He chooses 1 vegetable, 1 meat, and 1 drink. He has 3 vegetables to choose from, 3 meats, and 2 drinks. How many different dinner combinations can there be?

A. 10

B. 12

C. 16

D. 18

HOUSEHOLD POPULATIONS IN CENSUS

Number of People in Household	Percent of Households
1	18%
2	26%
3	31%
4	19%
5 or more	6%

88. A census-taker recorded the number of people living in each household in a certain town and reported the percent distribution in the table above. If the town has 540 households, how many of them hold **at least** 4 people?

E. 103

F. 135

G. 180

H. 196

Practice Tests

89. What is the value of $(x + y)(y - x)$ when $x = 10.5$ and $y = 9.5$?

   A. -400

   B. -20

   C. 0

   D. 20

90. The difference between Yu-Chen's age and Adele's age is no more than 4 years, and Adele is older than Yu-Chen. Which of the following inequalities gives the relationship between Yu-Chen's age (y) and Adele's age (a) ?

   E. $a - y \leq 4$

   F. $a - y \geq 4$

   G. $4 - a \geq y$

   H. $4 - y \geq a$

91. There are 5 different colored markers in a box. Amaia will choose 2 of these markers to make a poster with. How many different pairs of 2 markers can she choose from the 5 ?

   A.   5

   B.   10

   C.   15

   D.   20

$$m = 3 \times 5 \times 7$$

$$n = 3 \times 3 \times 5 \times 7 \times 11$$

92. What is the least common multiple of m and n ?

   E.   3

   F. $3 \times 5 \times 7 \times 11$

   G. $3 \times 3 \times 5 \times 7 \times 11$

   H. $3 \times 3 \times 3 \times 5 \times 5 \times 7 \times 7 \times 11$

93. A model fire truck is built to a scale of 1 to 16 (model to real). If the model is 6 inches wide, how many **feet** wide is the real fire truck?

   A.   2 ft

   B.   4 ft

   C.   8 ft

   D.   16 ft

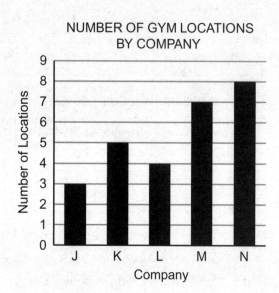

NUMBER OF GYM LOCATIONS
BY COMPANY

94. The graph above shows the number of gym locations per company for five different gym companies. Companies J and K each have 600 customers per location. Companies L and M each have 400 customers per location. Company N has 300 customers per location. Which company has the **most** customers?

   E.   Company J

   F.   Company K

   G.   Company M

   H.   Company N

95. x, y, and z are consecutive even integers, counting from smallest to largest. What is $x + z$ in terms of y ?

   A. y

   B. $y + 4$

   C. $y - 4$

   D. $2y$

GO ON TO THE NEXT PAGE

Practice Tests

96. A box contains 6 red index cards, 3 yellow index cards, and 4 green index cards. If Gabriella pulls out 2 cards at random from this box, without replacement, what is the probability that both cards are **not** green?

    E. $\frac{16}{169}$

    F. $\frac{4}{39}$

    G. $\frac{6}{13}$

    H. $\frac{81}{169}$

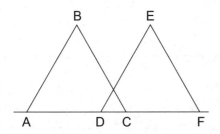

97. In the figure above, the two triangles have the same height. In addition, angles BCF and ADE are equal. What can you conclude about angles BCD and CDE?

    A. They are equal.

    B. They add up to 90°.

    C. m∠BCD is larger than m∠CDE.

    D. m∠CDE is larger than m∠BCD.

98. A siren will go off when the temperature in a certain engine reaches 205% of the maximum allowable temperature. If the maximum allowable temperature is 180°F, at what temperature will the siren go off?

    E. 185°F

    F. 288°F

    G. 346°F

    H. 369°F

99. Jaxon answered 9 out of 60 questions on a test incorrectly. What percentage of the questions did he answer correctly?

    A. 85%

    B. 72%

    C. 24%

    D. 15%

100. If $x = 4$ and $y = 2$, what is the value of $\frac{x^2}{y^5}$?

    E. $\frac{1}{4}$

    F. $\frac{1}{2}$

    G. $\frac{3}{4}$

    H. $\frac{4}{5}$

101. A dyer mixes three pigments, L, M, and N, in a large tub. The amount of L is 6 times the amount of M, and the amount of N is $\frac{1}{4}$ the amount of M. What is the ratio of the amount of N to the amount of L?

    A. 1:24

    B. 2:3

    C. 3:2

    D. 24:1

102. This week, Joshua earned twice as much as Alison earned. Noah earned $50 more than twice what Alison earned. If Noah earned $250, how much did Joshua earn?

    E. $100

    F. $150

    G. $200

    H. $250

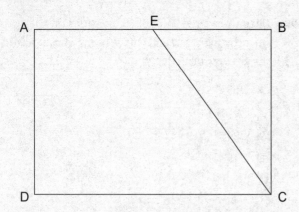

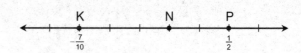

Note: Figure not drawn to scale.

103. In the rectangle above, AB = 8 and BC = 6. If E is the midpoint of AB, then what is the area of AECD?

A. 24

B. 32

C. 36

D. 48

105. On the number line above, $AC = 8\frac{5}{6}$, $AD = 10\frac{1}{2}$, and $BD = 4\frac{5}{12}$. What is the position of point B?

A. $2\frac{2}{3}$

B. $2\frac{3}{4}$

C. $2\frac{5}{6}$

D. $3\frac{1}{2}$

104. Last week, Breanna read 29% of her entire book. This week, she read 36% of her entire book. In simplest form, what fraction of the book is left for her to read?

E. $\frac{3}{10}$

F. $\frac{7}{20}$

G. $\frac{13}{20}$

H. $\frac{7}{10}$

106. The hash marks on the number line above are evenly spaced. What is the coordinate of point N?

E. $-\frac{11}{50}$

F. $\frac{1}{50}$

G. $\frac{6}{25}$

H. $\frac{13}{50}$

107. Adrienne took 3 hours and 20 minutes to complete an 18-kilometer hike. At that rate, how many **meters** does she hike per minute?

A. 0.09

B. 90

C. 900

D. 9,000

GO ON TO THE NEXT PAGE

108. From her drawer containing 3 pairs of black socks, 6 pairs of blue socks, 4 pairs of yellow socks, and 10 pairs of green socks, Sadie removes 1 pair of black socks, 1 pair of yellow socks, and 2 pairs of green socks. If she removes 1 more pair at random, what is the probability that it will be green?

E. $\dfrac{8}{23}$

F. $\dfrac{10}{23}$

G. $\dfrac{6}{19}$

H. $\dfrac{8}{19}$

109. How many positive, even integers satisfy the inequality $4n + 13 \leq 69$?

A. 1

B. 2

C. 5

D. 7

110. A recipe calls for $1\dfrac{1}{2}$ teaspoons of cinnamon and $\dfrac{1}{8}$ teaspoon of nutmeg. What is the ratio of nutmeg to cinnamon in this recipe?

E. 1:12

F. 1:8

G. 1:4

H. 1:3

111. A contractor pours a layer of cement 6 inches deep to form the foundation of a house. If the house is a rectangle with dimensions of 24 feet by 30 feet, what is the volume of the foundation in cubic **feet**?

A. 360

B. 540

C. 720

D. 4,320

112. Sam can run 2 miles in $\dfrac{1}{3}$ of an hour. How far can he run in $\dfrac{4}{5}$ of an hour?

E. $2\dfrac{1}{2}$ miles

F. 3 miles

G. 4 miles

H. $4\dfrac{4}{5}$ miles

113. Sanzhar, Isabella, Zachary, and Ksenia are running laps for a charity fundraiser. Sanzhar ran $2\dfrac{3}{4}$ laps, Isabella ran $3\dfrac{1}{2}$, Zachary ran $4\dfrac{3}{8}$, and Ksenia ran $5\dfrac{1}{4}$. How many laps did the four of them run all together?

A. 14

B. $14\dfrac{7}{8}$

C. 15

D. $15\dfrac{7}{8}$

114. The average test score of 15 students was 85. One score was dropped, changing the mean of the remaining scores to 86. What score was dropped?

E. 70

F. 71

G. 80

H. 85

Answer Key

PART 1—ENGLISH LANGUAGE ARTS

1. C	16. E	31. C	46. H
2. F	17. B	32. E	47. A
3. C	18. E	33. B	48. G
4. F	19. C	34. H	49. B
5. A	20. H	35. B	50. G
6. F	21. B	36. H	51. D
7. A	22. F	37. C	52. G
8. G	23. C	38. E	53. B
9. D	24. E	39. D	54. H
10. F	25. D	40. H	55. D
11. A	26. G	41. B	56. F
12. H	27. D	42. E	57. A
13. B	28. G	43. C	
14. G	29. D	44. F	
15. D	30. F	45. C	

PART 2—MATHEMATICS

58. 15	73. B	88. F	103. C
59. 31.5	74. G	89. B	104. F
60. 3	75. C	90. E	105. B
61. 6.75	76. E	91. B	106. F
62. 37	77. B	92. G	107. B
63. B	78. E	93. C	108. H
64. H	79. D	94. F	109. D
65. C	80. E	95. D	110. E
66. G	81. B	96. G	111. A
67. C	82. H	97. A	112. H
68. H	83. A	98. H	113. D
69. C	84. G	99. A	114. F
70. H	85. C	100. F	
71. D	86. G	101. A	
72. G	87. D	102. G	

Answers and Explanations

PART 1—ENGLISH LANGUAGE ARTS

1. C
Category: Sentence Structure

Getting to the Answer: As written, this sentence is a fragment because "coming" is the incorrect verb form. **(C)** fixes this problem, so it is correct. **(A)** introduces a new error by creating another incorrect *-ing* verb form. **(B)** and **(D)** introduce unnecessary commas.

2. F
Category: Usage

Getting to the Answer: The subject of a verb is not always the noun closest to it. The subject of the second clause is "group," not "people." The group is singular, even though it includes multiple people. Therefore, the second clause requires the singular verb "flocks." **(F)** is correct. **(E)** incorrectly changes the singular verb "attracts" into a plural verb. **(G)** incorrectly uses the word "there," which shows a place instead of possession. **(H)** changes the sentence's meaning by making it sound like the rock group performed only one concert.

3. C
Category: Knowledge of Language

Getting to the Answer: "Research" and "study" mean the same thing, so sentence 3 should be revised. **(C)** is correct. **(A)**, **(B)**, and **(D)** are incorrect because they alter the writer's intended meaning by removing relevant information from the paragraph.

4. F
Category: Sentence Structure

Getting to the Answer: In sentence 2, a comma should be placed after "competitions" to separate the introductory phrase from the rest of the sentence. **(F)** is correct. **(E)**, **(G)**, and **(H)** are incorrect because they add unnecessary punctuation.

5. A
Category: Topic Development

Getting to the Answer: This paragraph discusses how helium was discovered. Sentence 4 is off-topic because it describes how people reacted to the discovery rather than how the discovery was made. Therefore, **(A)** is correct. **(B)**, **(C)**, and **(D)** all contribute essential information.

6. F
Category: Topic Development

Getting to the Answer: When you are asked to introduce the main claim of a passage, do a quick scan of the remaining paragraphs to determine what the passage is about. Paragraph 2 discusses how helium is abundant in space but relatively rare on Earth. Paragraph 3 lists various uses for helium. **(F)** is correct, since it bridges the gap between helium's discovery and its applications. **(E)** and **(G)** are irrelevant. **(H)** may be tempting, since it transitions well into the first sentence of paragraph 2. However, it has no bearing on the ideas mentioned in the rest of the passage and is thus incorrect.

7. A
Category: Topic Development

Getting to the Answer: When you are asked to find a sentence that would follow and support, read the surrounding text for additional context. Sentence 11 describes how helium comes from radioactive elements. **(A)** relates directly to this and is correct. **(B)**, **(C)**, and **(D)** all introduce irrelevant ideas.

8. G

Category: Organization

Getting to the Answer: When combining sentences, think about how the ideas in the sentences connect to one another. In this case, sentence 13 states that helium is a nonrenewable resource, and sentence 14 tells the reason why. The combined sentence should thus show the cause-and-effect relationship between the ideas. **(G)** does so and is correct. **(E)** may be tempting, but it reverses the cause and the effect. **(F)** correctly sets up the relationship, but it is unnecessarily wordy. **(H)** incorrectly shows a contrast relationship between the ideas in the sentence.

9. D

Category: Organization

Getting to the Answer: This sentence gives another example of the non-scientific uses of helium. Thus, it requires a continuation phrase such as "In addition"; **(D)** is correct. Although **(A)** is a continuation word, it is illogical to say that using helium to grow crystals for silicon wafers is similar to using helium in blimps and balloons. **(B)** is a contrast phrase, and **(C)** is wordy.

10. F

Category: Punctuation

Getting to the Answer: As written, this sentence has two problems: "scientist's" should be a plural noun, not a possessive noun, and the verb "are" should be singular because "helium" is singular. **(F)** corrects both mistakes. **(E)** creates the idiomatically incorrect phrase "before recently" and does nothing to address the verb issue. **(G)** makes "scientists" into a plural possessive noun and merely changes the tense, not the number, of the verb. **(H)** dramatically changes the meaning of the sentence.

11. A

Category: Topic Development

Getting to the Answer: Sentence 20 starts with the words "Until recently," which hint that something new has changed scientists' thinking. A concluding sentence describing that new event is needed to bring the thought to a logical end. **(A)** supplies that conclusion and is correct. **(B)** does not make sense with the "Until recently" phrase in sentence 20. Without additional information, there is no support for **(C)**, and it does not fit within the tone of the passage. **(D)** is also unsupported.

Passage Analysis: This passage describes how basketball was created and follows the pathway it took to become the game it is today. The first paragraph sets the stage for basketball's creation: Gulick wanted to keep a rowdy class busy. Paragraph 2 explains how Naismith adapted a game from his youth, which became basketball. The third paragraph describes the game's introduction to colleges and women's teams. Paragraph 4 discusses how professional basketball was used as a backup for other sports. Paragraph 5 details how basketball has continued to change.

12. H

Category: Global

Getting to the Answer: The passage discusses basketball from its invention until the present day. Only **(H)** is broad enough to include the entire passage, and is the correct answer. **(E)** is incorrect because the passage discusses more than the invention of basketball. **(F)** is also too narrow; more than the rules are discussed in the latter paragraphs. **(G)** is incorrect since only a small part of the passage discusses the changes in the rules.

13. B

Category: Inference

Getting to the Answer: The circumstances behind the invention of basketball are discussed in paragraph 1, where the phrase in question, "blow off some steam," is found. Look at the surrounding sentences for context. It was a very cold winter and the young men were "rowdy." At the start of paragraph 2, Gulick wanted an "athletic distraction" for "especially rambunctious" students. These statements indicate "blow off some steam" means an activity that will use up some of the extra energy the students had, and matches **(B)**. **(A)** is a correct detail describing basketball, but is not connected to "blowing off steam." **(C)** goes beyond what is stated in the text. There is no mention of the boys fighting. **(D)** is incorrect because the phrase "blow off some steam" was used to describe why basketball was invented, not any potential results it had.

14. G

Category: Detail

Getting to the Answer: Return to paragraph 5 and identify the author's statement about the rules for basketball. That author states that despite some changes in the rules, basketball today is similar to the game when it was invented. **(G)** is a detail that supports the idea that the rules of basketball have indeed changed over the years and is the correct answer. **(E)** is incorrect because the expansion of basketball to include women is not connected to any rules in the passage. **(F)** is also incorrect because the passage discusses the Basketball Association of America in relation to the start of professional basketball, not to the rules. **(H)** is also incorrect because the international spread of basketball is not connected to the rules of the game.

15. D

Category: Inference

Getting to the Answer: Paragraph 2 says that Gulick wanted an "athletic distraction" for a rowdy group of students, so **(D)** is correct. **(A)** is incorrect since the passage does not refer to Gulick as an arena owner. **(B)** is incorrect because outdoor games could not be played because of the weather, not because of their commonplace nature. **(C)** is incorrect since the only childhood game mentioned in the passage served to inspire Naismith, not Gulick.

16. E

Category: Inference

Getting to the Answer: Basketball as a professional sport is discussed in paragraph 4, so return there to look up the answer. The text says that owners wanted to "fill arena seats on days when there were no professional…matches." So, there were arenas that were idle, which means that **(E)** is correct. **(F)** is incorrect because the passage states the National Basketball League "organized" basketball, but not that it established official rules. **(G)** and **(H)** are incorrect since the passage does not connect professional basketball with either its international or recreational popularity.

17. B

Category: Function

Getting to the Answer: Review your notes and predict your answer before reading the choices. The first two paragraphs describe why and how basketball was invented, and the fourth paragraph describes the establishment of professional basketball. **(B)** is correct because paragraph 3 logically connects the main ideas of paragraphs 2 and 4. **(A)** and **(D)** are incorrect because they are too narrow. Both are correct details from the paragraph but do not express the complete purpose of paragraph 3. **(C)** is incorrect because it describes the function of paragraph 4, not paragraph 3.

18. E

Category: Detail

Getting to the Answer: Match the choices to paragraph 5, and be sure you can prove your answer from the passage. **(E)** is correct, because the passage states that even though basketball is popular all over the world, "the United States remains its most significant stronghold." The emphasis keyword "most" means no country outstrips the United States. **(F)** is incorrect because the passage says modern basketball does resemble the original game. **(G)** and **(H)** are not mentioned in the passage and are incorrect. The author neither discusses any aspect of the future of basketball nor compares American recreational and professional basketball.

Passage Analysis: This passage explores the creation of art by early peoples and explains that as we learn more about ancient peoples, we learn more about ourselves. Paragraph 1 opens with a discussion of the oldest known art that appeared at about the same time in widely dispersed locations. Paragraph 2 explains when and where early art was created, focusing on Cro-Magnon art. Paragraph 3 refutes popular misconceptions about prehistoric peoples, showing that they had more skills and resources than many believe. Paragraph 4 explores reasons why early art may have been created, suggesting that Australian Aborigines and African Bushmen may provide information: that art is created for a variety of reasons.

19. C
Category: Global

Getting to the Answer: The information in each of the four paragraphs (the emergence of ancient art, where and when ancient art was made, that it includes a variety of forms in addition to paintings, and that paintings can have various meanings) all contribute to the point made in the last sentence of the passage that much can be learned from studying ancient art. **(C)** is correct. **(A)** is too narrow and distorts information in the passage. Although the passage uses the examples of collecting information from Australian Aborigines and African Bushmen, the text states only that this information *may* provide insight into the motivations of prehistoric humans, not that it *does*. In addition, this choice does not include any of the ideas from the earlier paragraphs. **(B)** is not mentioned in the passage, and is incorrect. No comparison is made between the lives of early humans and those of Australian Aborigines. **(D)** is a detail that appears only in paragraph 3 and is too narrow to describe the entire passage.

20. H
Category: Function

Getting to the Answer: Use your notes and predict an answer before you look at the choices. After a general introduction to ancient art in the first paragraph, in paragraph 2 the author introduces the early art created by the Cro-Magnons. **(H)** is correct. The first paragraph considers the many forms of early art in a broad sense, making **(E)** incorrect. **(F)** and **(G)** are incorrect because the fourth paragraph discusses the debate surrounding the interpretations of art created by the Cro-Magnons and suggests that the Cro-Magnons may have had varying motives for creating art.

21. B
Category: Inference

Getting to the Answer: This question asks you to find the reason most Cro-Magnon artifacts have been found in caves. Match the choices to the passage until you find the one you can prove from the text. Paragraph 2 is where you can find where early art was created, so begin your search there. The last sentence says, "caves...[are] where the best-preserved evidence of their lives and culture has been found." If the "best-preserved" evidence is found in caves, evidence in other locations will not be as well preserved. **(B)** is correct. The author says that Cro-Magnons lived both in caves and far from them; she says nothing

about where they "usually" lived; **(A)** is incorrect. Paragraph 3 says archaeologists found trail signs *inside* caves, not leading to them, which eliminates **(C)**. The author says nothing about the exact locations of the caves within Cro-Magnon territories, so **(D)** is also incorrect.

22. F
Category: Function

Getting to the Answer: Start by identifying "Such theories"; they are mentioned in the third sentence of paragraph 4 but described in the previous sentence. The theories are archaeologists' guesses for the reasons Cro-Magnons produced cave drawings. The third sentence mentions that these theories have become "less popular," and the reason follows later in the paragraph. Scientists have discovered that similar paintings made by Aborigines and Bushmen are made for a variety of reasons; thus, **(F)** is correct. **(E)** and **(H)** are incorrect because they say the theories are more popular. In addition, **(H)** makes a comparison between the Aborigines and the Bushmen that is not mentioned in the passage. **(G)** correctly identifies the theories as weakened, but for the wrong reason, and so it is also incorrect. The text never compares the art of the Aborigines and Bushmen.

23. C
Category: Detail

Getting to the Answer: All the choices are from paragraph 3, so look for evidence Cro-Magnons used markings to communicate. Since "'claviforms'...[were] used to direct people...," the correct answer is **(C)**. **(A)** describes many types of Cro-Magnon art forms, but does not say any of them were used to communicate to others, and is incorrect. Similarly, **(B)** and **(D)** are incorrect because neither the drawings or the prints are said to communicate information.

24. E
Category: Inference

Getting to the Answer: Return to paragraph 4 to determine the context of the sentence. The "group" is the Cro-Magnons, so that is who the adjectives are describing. The main idea of the passage is that recent discoveries indicate that the Cro-Magnon were a complex culture, so the correct answer is **(E)**. Although the sentence indicates that we may never have complete knowledge of the Cro-Magnon, the words do not indicate concern. Eliminate **(F)**. **(G)** and **(H)** describe the archaeologists, not the Cro-Magnon, and so are incorrect.

SHSAT Practice Test 2

25. D

Category: Global

Getting to the Answer: Look over your notes, and think about the main idea of the whole passage. Then, determine how the first paragraph helped the author to reach that main idea. The main idea of the passage is that studying ancient art contributes to the study of humanity, and this idea is introduced in the last sentence of paragraph 1. Thus, **(D)** is correct. **(A)** and **(C)** are incorrect because, although these are correct details from the paragraph, the passage does not continue to explore how art is created **(A)** or the variety of art **(C)**, but how art can be used to learn more about ancient peoples and about ourselves. **(B)** is incorrect because there is no history of ancient art described. The paragraph simply states when the oldest known art appeared.

26. G

Category: Detail

Getting to the Answer: Since the question asks for evidence that supports the author's opinion, return to the second paragraph to identify the author's point. The first sentence presents a fact, and the second sentence presents the opinion of "Modern people," not the author. The third sentence, introduced with the opinion keywords "But in fact" indicates the author believes the Cro-Magnon "lived a . . . sophisticated and expressive life." Complex and varied art is evidence of that type of life, and **(G)** is the correct answer. **(E)** and **(F)** include details about Cro-Magnon art, but do not support the idea that Cro-Magnon life was sophisticated. **(H)** is a Misused Detail. Researchers spoke to modern groups about the meaning of their art, but the passage never states that the art of those groups was similar to Cro-Magnon art.

Poem Analysis: Published in 1899, "The Song of Wandering Aengus" has several themes, but overall, it is a love story. In Celtic mythology, Aengus is the god of love and beauty, but in this poem, he seems to be a love-struck mortal. The first stanza introduces the narrator, Aengus, going into the woods on a fishing trip, during which he lands "a little silver trout." The second stanza describes the startling transformation of the trout into a beautiful girl, who calls his name and then

immediately runs away. In the third stanza, Aengus describes his futile search for the girl, even into his old age, and his hopes for when—and if—he ever finds her. The moon and sun signify the passing days, and the apples give a sense of the magic of nature.

27. D

Category: Global

Getting to the Answer: The form of the poem is three stanzas, each with eight verses. The first sets the scene, the second describes what happens, and the third relates the result of the events of the second stanza. **(D)** is correct. The poem only has one narrator, so **(A)** is incorrect. **(B)** is incorrect because there are no images in the poem that relate to the seasons of the year. **(C)** is incorrect because the events of the first two stanzas occur in the same location.

28. G

Category: Global

Getting to the Answer: Keep the overall theme in mind. The entire poem is describing Aengus's pursuit of love, so the fire must refer to love, foreshadowing the progression of the poem. **(G)** is correct. **(E)** and **(F)** are too literal and have no connection to the overall theme, making them incorrect. **(H)** is incorrect because the fire in Aengus's head is described before Aengus meets the girl, so he has yet to experience the sorrow of lost love.

29. D

Category: Global

Getting to the Answer: When do moths fly away and stars flicker out? At dawn, when night changes to day. Keep the theme of the poem in mind. Aengus goes fishing and meets a girl who changes his life forever. The poet uses the image of dawn to hint at the change that is about to enter Aengus's life. **(D)** is correct. **(A)** and **(B)** are too literal and do not contribute to the overall theme of the poem and so are incorrect. **(C)** is incorrect because this image appears well before the girl runs away, so Aengus does not yet know he will lose love.

30. F

Category: Detail

Getting to the Answer: In the third stanza, Aengus notes that his wandering has aged him, which indicates his mortality. Thus, **(F)** is correct. **(E)** is incorrect because the stars flickering out describes the time of day, not Aengus's mortality. **(G)** and **(H)** are incorrect because lines 22–23 describe actions that Aengus plans to do once he finds the girl.

31. C

Category: Detail

Getting to the Answer: The first stanza and the first half of the second stanza describe the events that lead up to Aengus's discovery of love. **(C)** is correct because the first verse describes Aengus recognized by love, and the second describes the girl disappearing. Eliminate **(A)**, which describes Aengus preparing to cook the trout, **(B)**, which describes Aengus's first look at the girl, and **(D)**, which describes Aengus's plans once he finds the girl.

32. E

Category: Inference

Getting to the Answer: You likely have never heard of "hollow lands" so consider the context: Aengus is now "old with wandering," so he's spent many, many years searching for the girl, and has likely traveled to many places. "Hollow lands" are contrasted with "hilly lands," so "hollow lands" are the valleys surrounding the hills. The image conveys that Aengus has looked everywhere for the girl, who represents love. **(E)** is correct. **(F)** may be factually true, but the poem is not discussing the Irish landscape, so this is incorrect. **(G)** is a distortion of the idea in the verse and is incorrect. The poem says Aengus has aged *during* the long time he's searched for love, but not *because* he's been searching. **(H)** is incorrect because the main idea of the poem is Aengus's lifelong search for love, not the exact places where he might find it.

33. B

Category: Inference

Getting to the Answer: Keep the main theme and the tone of the poem in mind. The main theme is Aengus's lifelong, and ultimately unsuccessful, search for the girl. Although Aengus is unsuccessful, the tone of the last stanza is serene and focused on beautiful natural images. **(B)** is correct. **(A)** is incorrect because Aengus is

the only person whose path in life is discussed. Aengus never reaches his goal, making **(C)** incorrect. The poem does not mention the uncertainty of life, so **(D)** is also incorrect.

34. H

Category: Detail

Getting to the Answer: The girl "faded through the brightening air" (line 16) after running away. Later in the third stanza, Aengus is still searching for her, making **(H)** correct. **(E)** is incorrect because Aengus had not yet met the girl in line 10. This line describes him making a fire to cook the trout. **(F)** and **(G)** are incorrect because these two lines signal the transformation of the trout into the "glimmering girl" who had not yet run away, so they do not convey the idea of love slipping away.

Passage Analysis: This passage describes the events that led to the beginning of World War I. Paragraph 1 states that the world was already on the brink of war when an assassination set it off in 1914. Paragraph 2 explains the political situation in Bosnia-Herzegovina, where the Black Hand was making plans to assassinate Archduke Ferdinand. Paragraph 3 details the preparations made in Serbia for the assassination, and the unsuccessful first attempt. Paragraph 4 describes how the Archduke's car took a wrong turn and a member of the Black Hand, Princip, shot and killed the Archduke. Paragraph 5 details how this event led to the start of World War I.

35. B

Category: Detail

Getting to the Answer: The Black Hand is first mentioned at the end of the second paragraph, and the last sentence of that paragraph says "the 'Black Hand' made plans to strike out in a symbolic fashion and assassinate the Archduke." **(B)** is correct. **(A)** is incorrect because, according to the passage, Bosnia-Herzegovina was under the control of Austria-Hungary, not Serbia. **(C)** is a Distortion and is incorrect. Although the passage describes the actions of the Black Hand leading to the start of World War I, the text does not say that this was the group's goal. **(D)** is incorrect since the text never identifies this as a goal of the Black Hand.

36. H

Category: Global

Getting to the Answer: Since the question asks about the "overall structure" of the passage, the correct answer will include the main idea—how the assassination of Archduke Ferdinand led to the start of World War I. **(H)** is the only answer consistent with the passage and is correct. The paragraph shows how the Archduke's decision not to leave the city, even after the attack on his car, as well as his driver's wrong turn, led to his assassination and thus the start of the war. **(E)** and **(G)** are incorrect; they describe correct details from the passage, but not how paragraph 4 contributes to the main idea. **(F)** is incorrect because it goes beyond what is stated in the text. The passage only states that adequate protection was not provided, and doesn't speculate about what may have happened if the Archduke had been protected.

37. C

Category: Detail

Getting to the Answer: **(C)** is correct because the word "fateful" indicates that the driver's mistake was the reason the Archduke was close enough to Princip to be killed. If the driver had not made a wrong turn, perhaps Ferdinand would not have been assassinated. **(A)** describes how the Archduke was saved in the first attempt on his life, **(B)** describes how he followed his original plan, and **(D)** describes the breakdown of the talks designed to prevent the outbreak of the war after the assassination. None of these relate to preventing the assassination, so all are incorrect.

38. E

Category: Global

Getting to the Answer: The question asks how a sentence serves the purpose of the passage, so look at your notes for paragraph 1 and then read a little before and after the sentence. Identify why the author included the sentence. **(E)** is correct; before the sentence, the passage describes the unsettled political situation, and following the sentence, the events that led to the start of World War I are described. **(F)**, **(G)**, and **(H)** are incorrect, because although they are all mentioned in the text, none of them specifically describe why the author included the sentence.

39. D

Category: Inference

Getting to the Answer: The statement that "many people were upset" is made toward the end of the second paragraph. Immediately following this statement are the reasons why they were upset: the Archduke represented Austria-Hungary's unwelcome control of Bosnia-Herzegovina and other "incursions" in the area. **(D)** is thus correct. **(A)** is incorrect because it distorts information from the passage. Although the Archduke would have eventually ruled Austria-Hungary, the text describes says he was "not a key political player at this time." **(B)** is a distortion of the information in the text and is incorrect. People were not upset that the trip happened too quickly for the security arrangements to be made. **(C)** is incorrect because the issue was that the area was under the control of Austria-Hungary, not Serbia.

40. H

Category: Inference

Getting to the Answer: Review paragraph 5 where these words appear. The passage map states that this paragraph describes the start of World War I. **(H)** is correct because Austria-Hungary was "misguided" in presenting "unreasonable" demands that were rejected "wholesale," or completely, leading to the start of the war. The strong language indicates that the author does not think that either side was willing to take action to avoid the war. **(E)** is incorrect because, although it is a correct detail from the passage, it has no connection to the specific, negative words in the question. **(F)** and **(G)** are never mentioned in the text and are incorrect.

41. B

Category: Infographic

Getting to the Answer: Both the passage and the map describe the events on the day of Franz Ferdinand's assassination, and the map provides additional information about how Franz Ferdinand's route through the city affected those events. **(B)** most accurately reflects this connection. Using the word "shrewd," which means "smart," to refer to Franz Ferdinand and his advisors is completely contradictory to the passage, which characterized Franz Ferdinand's decision to visit Bosnia as "foolhardy" (paragraph 3) and described how Franz Ferdinand overruled his staff when deciding to visit the hospital despite the dangers. These were not "shrewd" travel plans, so **(A)** is incorrect. Eliminate

(C) and **(D)**, since the focus of the passage with the map is not on the "tragic" nature of the driver's decision nor how the "confusing" nature of the roads affected any of Franz Ferdinand's decisions, but instead on how the routes affected the events of that day.

42. E

Category: Function

Getting to the Answer: Review the passage notes and describe how the information in paragraph 2 contributes to the main idea. The author introduces the "circumstances...[that] set the stage" for the start of World War I in the first paragraph, and the second paragraph describes those circumstances. **(E)** is correct. Paragraph 2 does not contain examples, **(F)**, or a theory, **(G)**. The main idea is stated in paragraph 1, so **(H)** is also incorrect.

Passage Analysis: In this cautionary horror story by Edgar Allan Poe, a thousand of Prince Prospero's titled friends gather in his locked, fortified abbey. They are attempting to shield themselves from contact with the fatal Red Death disease. Paragraph 1 describes the scourge of the Red Death and how quickly and ruthlessly it kills its victims. Paragraph 2 introduces the happy Prince Prospero, the light-hearted friends at his abbey, and how the abbey is bolted shut. Paragraph 3 describes the joys and frivolities the Prince provides within the abbey and the courtiers' determination to make merry, while outside, the Red Death continues to rage. Paragraph 4 introduces one of the Prince's parties—an unusually magnificent one. Paragraph 5 introduces the appearance of a a masked figure at midnight. Paragraph 6 describes the masked figure, and paragraph 7 discusses the prince's reaction. It can be inferred from the horrified response of the revelers and the prince's anger that they all recognize this figure as the Red Death. All their precautions have failed.

43. C

Category: Global

Getting to the Answer: The first paragraph introduces a disease called the Red Death, along with its symptoms. The paragraph describes the prince's country attempting to avoid the Red Death and ultimately failing; **(C)** is correct. **(A)** is incorrect because the first paragraph does not explain how others have avoided the Red Death.

While the first paragraph explains the disease's symptoms, it does not suggest that it is no longer a cause for concern; **(B)** is incorrect. Paragraphs 2 and 3, not paragraph 1, illustrate how the courtiers intend to stop the spread of the Red Death; **(D)** is incorrect.

44. F

Category: Detail

Getting to the Answer: The second paragraph mentions that the Red Death has caused the prince's dominions to be "half depopulated," suggesting massive numbers of his citizens have died; **(F)** is correct. **(E)** is incorrect because this statement notes only how the symptoms of the Red Death progress, not how many people suffer from it. **(G)** is incorrect because this sentence details the courtiers locking themselves in the abbey as a means of preventing anyone from entering or exiting. Finally, **(H)** is incorrect because these lines illustrate the reaction of the courtiers to the presence of the Red Death, not the devastating toll the disease has taken on the prince's country.

45. C

Category: Detail

Getting to the Answer: In paragraph 1, "shut him out from the aid and from the sympathy of his fellow-men" means that the victim was left to suffer and die alone; **(C)** is correct. **(A)** is incorrect because the passage states that a victim of the Red Death is *not* cared for by others. **(B)** is incorrect because it is contradicted by the statement "No pestilence had ever been so fatal." (paragraph 1) **(D)** is incorrect because paragraph 1 states that the entire incident would last half an hour: "And the whole seizure, progress, and termination of the disease, were incidents of half an hour."

46. H

Category: Global

Getting to the Answer: Upon entering, the courtiers "welded the bolts," essentially locking themselves in the abbey, to shield themselves from the Red Death; **(H)** is correct. Both **(E)** and **(F)** are incorrect because there is no attack and no rival princes are mentioned. Since the guests were the "knights and dames of his court," it is likely true that they did not mix with the common people, but this is not the reason they secluded themselves in the abbey; **(G)** is incorrect.

47. A

Category: Function

Getting to the Answer: The prince's notion that "the external world could take care of itself" shows that he is unconcerned with the people outside of the abbey; **(A)** is correct. The excerpt states that the prince "provided all the appliances of pleasure," which offers no evidence that the prince is humble or frugal, that he has given up his pleasure-seeking ways, or that he can meet all of his people's needs. Thus, **(B)** and **(C)** are incorrect. **(D)** is incorrect because the prince seems to be concerned only with some of his people—those that were invited into the abbey—not all of his people.

48. G

Category: Global

Getting to the Answer: The fourth paragraph begins by stating how many months the courtiers have been secluded and also foreshadows the masked ball to come; therefore, **(G)** is correct. **(E)** is incorrect because the Red Death does not make an appearance until later in paragraph 4. **(F)** is incorrect because the prince's behavior was analyzed in paragraph 2. There is no indication that the courtiers dislike being secluded, so **(H)** is incorrect.

49. B

Category: Function

Getting to the Answer: These words used in paragraph 4—"uneasy," "silence," and "masked figure"—combine to create a sense of horror and foreboding; something terrible is going to happen. Thus, **(B)** is correct. Nowhere is anger mentioned or implied; eliminate **(A)**. **(C)** is incorrect because revelry (noisy festivities) is opposite of the tone. **(D)** is incorrect because Poe describes the characters as happy, sagacious, and light-hearted, but not disdainful.

50. G

Category: Global

Getting to the Answer: In paragraph 5, Poe writes that "the music ceased" and "there were many individuals in the crowd who had found leisure to become aware of the presence of a masked figure." These lines show that even with all of their precautions, the courtiers could not

escape death; **(G)** is correct. Poe is not generally condemning people who try to protect themselves against disease; **(E)** is incorrect. **(F)** is incorrect because the medical symptoms of the Red Death are discussed in paragraph 1, not paragraph 5, and they are not a central idea of the excerpt. While the prince and revelers are foolish to think they can avoid the plague, their mistake is only in relation to the Red Death, not to revelry in general; **(H)** is incorrect.

Passage Analysis: The main idea of this passage is that struggles marked and shaped George Orwell's life and efforts to become a successful writer. Paragraph 1 suggests that Orwell struggled in his life and as a writer long before the publication of his enormously successful novel *Animal Farm*. Paragraph 2 describes Orwell's background and the beginning of his writing career. Paragraph 3 describes his early career as a British government official in India. Paragraph 4 describes his first literary success, his changing beliefs, and the next stage of his life in Spain. Paragraph 5 relates the growing disillusionment with communism that inspired Orwell's final and most popular novel and the events surrounding his death.

51. D

Category: Global

Getting to the Answer: First, identify a common theme running through the entire passage. In this case, each paragraph focuses in one way or another on the struggles Orwell experienced in his life and how those experiences were reflected in his writing. Look for an answer choice that best captures this focus. **(D)** is correct. **(A)** is a Misused Detail; this passage describes Orwell's struggles abroad in India and Spain, but this is not the focus of the passage as a whole. **(B)** is a Distortion. The passage builds toward Orwell's ultimate success but does not describe the process, or the steps he took, to become successful. **(C)** is not discussed in the text; the passage never explores *why* Orwell's early literary efforts failed to establish a successful career for him.

52. G

Category: Function

Getting to the Answer: By the end of paragraph 1, you likely knew Orwell wasn't immediately successful. Look back at the paragraph and identify how the author conveyed that idea. Towards the middle of the paragraph, the author states, "... Orwell struggled to make ends meet as a writer..." This means he had trouble living on the money he was paid for writing, so **(G)** is correct. Although the passage mentions that Orwell sought "creative possibilities," his lack of success is not connected in the passage to the lack of creative opportunities. Thus, **(E)** is incorrect. **(F)** is also mentioned in paragraph 1, but the end of Orwell's life is not the reason he wasn't successful at the start of his writing career. **(H)** is mentioned in paragraph 1 as well, but is connected to Orwell's later success, not his early struggles.

53. B

Category: Function

Getting to the Answer: When asked how a feature contributes to the passage, start by thinking of the main idea: Orwell's struggles shaped his beliefs and his literature. Keep this idea in mind, and work through the choices by elimination. Eliminate **(A)** because the text never indicates any interest in Orwell returning to the land where he was born; rather, he went because he felt he didn't belong in England. Orwell's political sentiments are not specifically mentioned in paragraph 2, but the author states that Orwell experienced a "growing disillusionment with the concept of imperialism"; this information, coupled with the fact that Orwell had volunteered for service in the Indian Imperial Police, suggests that before he went to India, Orwell did not have significant problems with British imperialism. **(B)** is correct. His later struggles with imperialism eventually surfaced in his books. **(C)** is incorrect because there's no indication that he was continuing his father's work; the passage does not even specify what his father's actual job was. **(D)** is incorrect because Orwell's decision to work rather than study is a fact from the passage, but does not significantly contribute to the main idea.

54. H

Category: Function

Getting to the Answer: Although you may not be able to clearly grasp the author's meaning behind the use of the dash simply by reading the sentence, use the context in the passage for clarification. In this case, the sentence that follows the cited one states that "Orwell found his political identity changing," so look for an answer choice that takes this information into account. **(H)** does so and is therefore correct. **(E)** is a Misused Detail; Orwell's injury was a struggle, but the *reason* the author uses the dash is to indicate the change of direction in the sentence, mirroring the change of direction in Orwell's life. **(F)** is also a Misused Detail; Orwell did make rapid progress during his short military career, but the point of the phrase is to indicate his changed thinking. **(G)** is Opposite. The dash and the phrase indicate that Orwell's ideas are shifting, not being supported.

55. D

Category: Detail

Getting to the Answer: Look for a choice that clearly connects Orwell's beliefs with his writings; **(D)** is correct, because it describes Orwell's changed thinking, an "ideological shift," as the inspiration for *Nineteen Eighty-Four*. **(A)**, **(B)**, and **(C)** are incorrect because although these are examples that indicate Orwell's beliefs, they are not directly connected to his literature.

56. F

Category: Global

Getting to the Answer: First, refresh your memory of the main idea from your passage notes: Orwell's struggles throughout his life shaped his literature. Paragraph 4 opens with accounts of Orwell's writing following his disillusionment in India, continues with his experiences living in the slums of London, and concludes with his military experience in Spain that causes another change in his beliefs. **(F)** is correct. **(E)** is a Distortion; the text never guesses what might have happened if Orwell had continued as a journalist. **(G)** is incorrect because the paragraph describes his experiences in life, not the steps Orwell took to become successful. **(H)** is a Distortion, and too narrow; the paragraph discusses more than Orwell's military career—an experience that turned him away from communism, not confirmed his belief.

57. A

Category: Inference

Getting to the Answer: Look back at your passage notes and keep the main idea—Orwell's struggles marked and shaped his literature—in mind and work by elimination. **(A)** matches the main idea and the author's respectful tone, and is correct. **(B)** is too narrow. The text describes many more struggles than simply those of his early life. **(C)** and **(D)** are not mentioned in the text and are incorrect. There is no evidence that the author believes either of these are true.

PART 2—MATHEMATICS

58. 15

Subject: Arithmetic

Getting to the Answer: Remember that when given a part:part ratio, you can always find the whole by adding all of the parts. Here, you are given two separate ratios. Since both ratios include soccer balls, and soccer balls are represented by the same value (1) in both ratios, you can easily combine these into one: basketballs to soccer balls to dodgeballs = 3:1:4. Add the parts of the ratio to get the whole: $3 + 1 + 4 = 8$. The question asks for the number of basketballs and gives you the total number of balls, so use the part representing basketballs and the whole to make a new ratio, 3:8. Now you can set up a proportion: $\frac{3}{8} = \frac{b}{40}$. Since $40 = 8 \times 5$, b must equal 3×5, or 15.

59. 31.5

Subject: Algebra

Getting to the Answer: Begin by cross multiplying this proportion. From there, divide both sides of the resulting equation by 2 to find the value of x:

$$\frac{2}{3} = \frac{21}{x}$$
$$2x = 63$$
$$x = 31.5$$

60. 3

Subject: Algebra

Getting to the Answer: Start by simplifying the inequality. First, subtract 8 from both sides, then divide by 2:

$$2x + 8 < 22$$
$$2x < 14$$
$$x < 7$$

The problem says that x is a positive, even integer, which means that x can be 2, 4, or 6. There are three possible values, so grid in 3.

61. 6.75

Subject: Statistics and Probability

Getting to the Answer: Though the problem does not give Trinity's exact scores, you can still find the sum of her scores by plugging her mean and number of times played into the average formula: $\text{Average} = \frac{\text{Sum}}{\text{Number}}$, so $4.5 = \frac{\text{Trinity's sum}}{6}$. Therefore, Trinity's sum $= 6 \times 4.5$, or 27. Jayden's sum is the same, so divide by the number of times he played to find his mean score: $27 \div 4 = 6.75$.

62. 37

Subject: Arithmetic

Getting to the Answer: The question states that Denise drives 3.7 miles from her home to her work. Thus, she will make this trip twice in one day (once from home to work, once from work to home). In a 5-day work week, this means Denise will make this drive a total of 10 times. $3.7 \times 10 = 37$ miles, so grid in 37.

63. B

Subject: Algebra

Getting to the Answer: When translating from words to math, go phrase by phrase. Let x represent the number. "The sum of a number and six" means $x + 6$, "is" means equals, and "twice as great as the number" means $2x$. Put it all together and you get $x + 6 = 2x$. Simply subtract x from both sides to get $6 = x$.

64. H

Subject: Algebra

Getting to the Answer: You can begin by distributing to get rid of the parentheses: $2(5b - 7) = 2(5b) - 2(7) = 10b - 14$. When you substitute $3y$ in for b, you get $10(3y) - 14 = 30y - 14$.

65. C

Subject: Algebra

Getting to the Answer: You can re-word the information in this problem to help you set up the math: Sienna *is* 40% *of* Rhys, and Rhys *is* 40% *of* Micah. Since Sienna has read 60 pages, Rhys has read $60 \div 0.40 = 150$ pages. That means Micah has read $150 \div 0.40 = 375$ pages.

66. G

Subject: Geometry

Getting to the Answer: Break this geometry word problem down piece by piece, and draw out what you know to help you visualize it. $\overline{XZ} = \frac{1}{3}\overline{YZ}$, and $\overline{YZ} = 27$, so $\overline{XZ} = \frac{1}{3}(27) = 9$. Since $\overline{XY}$ is made up of $\overline{XZ}$ and $\overline{YZ}$ together, $\overline{XY} = 9 + 27 = 36$.

67. C

Subject: Arithmetic

Getting to the Answer: The decimal 0.55 is fifty-five hundredths, or $\frac{55}{100}$. Simplify this fraction to match the one in the problem: $\frac{55 \div 5}{100 \div 5} = \frac{11}{20}$, so $x = 11$.

68. H

Subject: Arithmetic

Getting to the Answer: Read carefully to identify the "whole" value for this problem. In this case, the question asks for the difference *from* families with no dogs, so that value represents the whole. There are 45 families with no dogs, and $45 - 27 = 18$ fewer families with 2 dogs. Plug these values into the percent formula: $\frac{18}{45} \times 100 = 40\%$.

69. C

Subject: Geometry

Getting to the Answer: Remember that a straight line has 180°. Since the diagram shows a right angle on the line, the remaining angles together must equal 90°:

$$180° = 90° + (x + y)° + x° + y°$$
$$90° = x° + y° + x° + y°$$
$$90° = 2x° + 2y°$$
$$90° = 2(x° + y°)$$
$$45° = x° + y$$

70. H

Subject: Arithmetic

Getting to the Answer: When a percent problem gives you no amount to work with, it's helpful to pick the number 100 for the amount. Say that Dominic's suit originally cost $100. The suit was on sale for 20% off, but since the question asks for how much Dominic paid rather than how much he saved, focus on the 80% cost rather than the 20% discount. Before the coupon, Dominic paid 80% of $100, or $0.8 \times \$100 = \$80$. Next, apply the coupon: Dominic got 20% off, so he paid 80% of $80, or $0.8 \times \$80 = \$64$. $64 out of $100 is 64%.

71. D

Subject: Arithmetic

Getting to the Answer: The question asks for her *total* number of shots, so first find her total number of shots: $25 + 125 = 150$ shots. 36% of 150 is 0.36×150, or 54.

72. G

Subject: Arithmetic

Getting to the Answer: Read word problems carefully to sort through the information they give you. Here, the question asks for residents older than 40 who do *not* work in hospitality. First, find the percent of residents older than 40: the problem tells you the percent of residents age 40 or younger (55%), so you can subtract from 100 to get 45% of the population older than 40. To find how many of these residents *don't* work in hospitality, you need to know how many *do*, which the problem doesn't tell you. However, it does tell how many total residents work in hospitality (28%) and how many of those are 40 or younger (15%), so you can subtract to find residents over 40 who work in hospitality:

28% − 15% = 13%. Finally, subtract over-40 residents in hospitality from all over-40 residents: 45% − 13% = 32% of residents are older than 40 and *don't* work in hospitality.

73. B

Subject: Geometry

Getting to the Answer: Draw a picture to better visualize the situation.

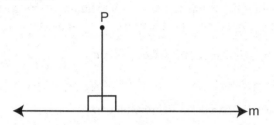

As you can see, a line drawn from P perpendicular to line *m* will create two 90° angles. However, a line drawn anywhere else will no longer be perpendicular and therefore will not create any 90° angles, so only one line meets the conditions of the question.

74. G

Subject: Arithmetic

Getting to the Answer: First, determine how many degrees the temperature needs to increase: 30° − (−6°) = 36°. Next, find out how many hours this will take by dividing by the degree increase per hour: 36° ÷ 4° = 9 hours. Count 9 hours from 7:00 a.m. From 7:00 a.m. to noon is 5 hours, and in 4 more hours the turkey would be ready to cook, at 4:00 p.m.

75. C

Subject: Arithmetic

Getting to the Answer: Divide a known amount received ($10) by its corresponding number of tickets sold (5) to get the individual price of a ticket: $10 ÷ 5 = $2 per ticket. Don't forget that you are looking for the value of *two* tickets: $2 × 2 = $4.

76. E

Subject: Arithmetic

Getting to the Answer: Notice that this question says the integers must be *consecutive*, that is, one right after the other. 72 has many factors, but only two that are consecutive: 8 and 9. 8 + 9 = 17, which isn't an answer choice. However, −17 is, and −8 and −9 are also consecutive integers with a product of 72. **(E)** is correct.

77. B

Subject: Geometry

Getting to the Answer: Don't be afraid to write what you know about the drawing on the figure itself. If the perimeter of the square is 16, then each side is 4 and the area is 16. The area of the shaded region is the area of △ADB − the area of △AFE. The area of △ADB is half of the square, or 8. Algebraically, the area of △AFE is $\frac{1}{2}b \times h$ or $\frac{1}{2}(\overline{AF})(\overline{FE})$: $\frac{1}{2}(2)(2) = 2$. Thus, the area of the shaded region is 8 − 2 = 6.

78. E

Subject: Algebra

Getting to the Answer: Remember that for three-part inequalities, whenever you make a change to one part, you must make it to all three parts. So, to solve for *x*, first add 5 to all three parts of the inequality, then divide all three parts by 2:

$$7 > 2x - 5 > -7$$
$$12 > 2x > -2$$
$$6 > x > -1$$

Find the number line in the answer choices in which *x* is less than 6 and greater than −1: **(E)**.

79. D

Subject: Arithmetic

Getting to the Answer: Though the large numbers may be intimidating here, the math is straightforward. $7 out of $12 is just $\frac{7}{12}$, and to find the amount of Casa Felisa's profits spent on rent, you simply need to multiply: $\frac{7}{12} \times \$34,800 = \$20,300$. Note that estimation is also an effective way to get to this answer: since $\frac{7}{12}$ is slightly more than one half, the correct answer must be slightly more than half of $34,800, and $20,300 is the only choice that's large enough.

80. E

Subject: Arithmetic

Getting to the Answer: Since one kilometer is 1,000 meters, you can simply move the decimal three places to convert units: the track is 6.72 km long. This means you can eliminate both **(G)**, which is the length of the whole track, and **(H)**, which is *longer* than the whole track. The car has already gone $\frac{2}{3}$ of the way, so it has $\frac{1}{3}$ to go. Of the two remaining answers, **(F)** is more than half the length of the track, so it's too large to be $\frac{1}{3}$ of 6.72. **(E)** must be correct. You'll get the same result if you multiply: $\frac{1}{3} \times 6.72 = 2.24$.

81. B

Subject: Statistics and Probability

Getting to the Answer: Remember that probability is equal to the number of *desired* outcomes out of the number of *total* possible outcomes. For the given probability, that means blue crayons out of total crayons. You can use a proportion to find the total number of crayons: $\frac{2}{9} = \frac{10}{\text{total}}$. Since $2 \times 5 = 10$, there must be $9 \times 5 = 45$ crayons in the box. Subtract the blue crayons to find the number that *aren't* blue: $45 - 10 = 35$.

82. H

Subject: Arithmetic

Getting to the Answer: Try to visualize this problem as two people moving toward each other on a number line. Each hour, these two people move 9 miles closer to each other, so if you divide the total distance of 15 miles by 9, you get the time it takes for them to meet: $\frac{15}{9} = \frac{5}{3} = 1\frac{2}{3}$ hours. To determine the distance from point B, see how far the person beginning at point B travels in that time: $6\left(1\frac{2}{3}\right) = 10$ miles.

You could also Backsolve this problem. To do so, choose an answer and determine how long it would take the woman beginning at point B to travel that distance. Then, find how far the man beginning at point A could travel in that same time. If the two distances add up to 15, then the answer is correct.

83. A

Subject: Statistics and Probability

Getting to the Answer: To find the probability of two separate events happening, you need to find the probability of each and then multiply the two probabilities. Since there are only two ball colors, the probability that a ball taken at random is *not* pink is the same as the probability that it is yellow: $\frac{6}{16}$, or $\frac{3}{8}$. The first ball is not put back, so the numbers change for the second draw. There are now 5 yellow balls out of 15 total balls: $\frac{5}{15}$, or $\frac{1}{3}$. Now, multiply: $\frac{\overset{1}{\cancel{3}}}{8} \times \frac{1}{\cancel{3}_1} = \frac{1}{8}$.

84. G

Subject: Statistics and Probability

Getting to the Answer: When finding mean (average) from a table, remember that you need to add the scores of every individual student, not just the values of the scores themselves. Multiplication will make this more efficient: $5(90) + 9(80) + 4(70) + 2(60) = 1,570$. Then divide by the total number of students to find the mean score: $1,570 \div 20 = 78.5$.

85. C

Subject: Algebra

Getting to the Answer: The problem says that the horses are penned randomly, so each pen would represent a random sample. Of the 60 total horses in the pen, 15 horses, or 25 percent, are white. Therefore, 25% of 1,000, or 250, is the best estimate of the number of white horses.

86. G

Subject: Geometry

Getting to the Answer: Draw a diagram to help you visualize the question. If the perimeter is 24 inches, the length and width add up to 12 inches (half the perimeter). A 5:1 ratio of length to width is 10 to 2. The area is $10 \times 2 = 20$ square inches.

87. D

Subject: Statistics and Probability

Getting to the Answer: There are 3 choices of vegetables, 3 of meats, and 2 of drinks; thus, there are $3 \times 3 \times 2 = 18$ ways to make his dinner.

88. F

Subject: Statistics and Probability

Getting to the Answer: When a problem gives you a graph or table with a lot of information, read the question to find out what to focus on. Here, the question asks for how many households have *at least* 4 people, so you don't need to pay attention to any of the smaller households. 19% have 4 people and 6% have 5 or more people, so 25% have at least 4. Since 25% is the same as $\frac{1}{4}$, you can simply divide: $540 \div 4 = 135$ households.

89. B

Subject: Algebra

Getting to the Answer: Watch your signs and variable substitution to ensure that your calculations are correct. Not carrying your negative signs properly throughout the calculations could lead to an incorrect answer choice like **(D)**. Plug in the values the problem gives you for x and y, and solve using PEMDAS:

$(x + y)(y - x) =$
$(10.5 + 9.5)(9.5 - 10.5) =$
$(20)(-1) =$
-20, **(B)**

90. E

Subject: Algebra

Getting to the Answer: To translate words into algebra, break the information down phrase by phrase. "The difference between" means subtraction. "No more than 4" means it *cannot be greater than* 4, which means it can be less than 4 *or* equal to 4: ≤ 4. Since "Adele is older," a is larger than y and will come first when you subtract. Put it all together: $a - y \leq 4$. You can also solve this problem by picking numbers for the two variables and plugging them in to the answer choices to see which is accurate.

91. B

Subject: Algebra

Getting to the Answer: The most efficient way to reach the answer here is to list the possible pairs, being careful not to repeat combinations. Label the markers A, B, C, D, and E. Amaia could choose:

AB, AC, AD, AE
BC, BD, BE
CD, CE
DE

Count the listed pairs: there are 10 possible marker pairs.

92. G

Subject: Arithmetic

Getting to the Answer: Make sure that you know how to find the LCM using prime factorization. The LCM is the product of the factors for m and n, each raised to the *highest* power with which it appears: $LCM = 3 \times 3 \times 5 \times 7 \times 11$.

93. C

Subject: Arithmetic

Getting to the Answer: Be careful whenever a problem changes units. The model is 6 inches wide, or $\frac{1}{2}$ foot. Since the scale is 1 to 16, multiply this width by 16 to get the width of the full-sized truck: $\frac{1}{2} \times 16 = 8$ feet.

94. F

Subject: Arithmetic

Getting to the Answer: (H) may be tempting, since Company N has the most locations, but it also has the fewest customers per location. Calculate the actual number of customers for the different locations. You can skip Company J since it has the same number of customers per location as Company K (but with fewer locations), and Company L since it isn't among the answer choices.

Company K: $5 \times 600 = 3,000$ customers
Company M: $7 \times 400 = 2,800$ customers
Company N: $8 \times 300 = 2,400$ customers

Company K has the most customers.

95. D

Subject: Algebra

Getting to the Answer: Put all the multiples in terms of y to start, then plug the new values into the expression $x + z$ and simplify:

$$x = y - 2$$
$$y = y$$
$$z = y + 2$$
$$x + z = (y - 2) + (y + 2)$$
$$x + z = 2y$$

Note that you can also Pick Numbers to solve this problem by choosing even numbers for x, y, and z, adding $x + z$, and plugging y into the answer choices to see which gives you a matching result.

96. G

Subject: Statistics and Probability

Getting to the Answer: Remember that "without replacement" means Gabriella will not put the first card she drew back before she pulls out a second one, so the probabilities will be different for each draw. At first, there are 13 index cards, and 9 are not green. After one card is drawn, there are 12 cards, and 8 are not green. You need to multiply to find the probability of both events occurring: $\frac{9}{13} \times \frac{8}{12}$. Cross canceling simplifies this to $\frac{3}{13} \times \frac{2}{1} = \frac{6}{13}$.

97. A

Subject: Geometry

Getting to the Answer: Go through the problem and mark on the diagram what you know and what you can infer. If angles BCF and ADE are equal, then their supplements must be equal. The supplements of $\angle$BCF and $\angle$ADE are $\angle$BCD and $\angle$CDE, respectively. They must be equal.

98. H

Subject: Arithmetic

Getting to the Answer: If you're unsure how to set up a percent problem, you can phrase it as "what is x percent of y" to help you. Here, you need to find what is 205% of 180, so convert 205% to a decimal and multiply: $2.05 \times 180 = 369°F$. You can also estimate; 205% of 180 will be little more than $2 \times 180 = 360$, and **(H)** is the only choice that's greater than 360.

99. A

Subject: Arithmetic

Getting to the Answer: Make sure you answer what the question asks for. To find the percent of questions Jaxon answered *correctly*, first find the percent he answered *incorrectly*: $\frac{9}{60} = \frac{3}{20} = \frac{15}{100}$, or 15%. Then, subtract from 100%: $100 - 15 = 85\%$ correct.

100. F

Subject: Algebra

Getting to the Answer: Substitute the values into the expression and simplify:

$$\frac{x^2}{y^5} = \frac{4^2}{2^5} = \frac{16}{32} = \frac{1}{2}$$

101. A

Subject: Arithmetic

Getting to the Answer: With ratios, remember to pay careful attention to order. The ratio of L:M is 6:1, and M:N is $1:\frac{1}{4}$. Though normally you wouldn't put a fraction in a ratio, here it will help you combine the ratios using M as a common term: L:M:N $= 6:1:\frac{1}{4}$. Since the question isn't concerned with M, take out the middle term to get L:N, then multiply the whole ratio by 4 to get rid of the fraction: L:N $= 24:1$. The question asks for N:L, so swap the order to get 1:24.

You can also reach this answer by Picking Numbers. Since both L and N are related to M in the problem, pick a simple number for M. Because of the division, 4 will work well. If M is 4, then L is $6 \times 4 = 24$, and N is $\frac{1}{4} \times 4 = 1$. Thus, N:L $= 1:24$.

102. G

Subject: Algebra

Getting to the Answer: When you need to translate words to math, read slowly and break the problem down piece by piece:

$$N = 2A + \$50$$
$$\$250 = 2A + \$50$$
$$\$200 = 2A$$
$$\$100 = A$$

$$J = 2A$$
$$J = 2(\$100)$$
$$J = \$200$$

103. C

Subject: Geometry

Getting to the Answer: The area of the whole rectangle is $l \times w = 6 \times 8 = 48$. Because E is the midpoint of AB, you know that $AE = EB = 4$. So the area of $\triangle EBC = \frac{1}{2}bh = \frac{1}{2} \times 4 \times 6 = 12$. Subtracting the triangle from the rectangle will give you the area of trapezoid AECD: $48 - 12 = 36$. Alternatively, you could have used the trapezoid area formula: Area $= \frac{1}{2}$ (Sum of the Lengths of the Parallel Sides)(Height). The two parallel sides are AE and CD. Since ABCD is a rectangle, CD is the same length as AB, or 8, and AD, of length 6, is a height of the trapezoid. Plug these numbers into the formula: Area $= \frac{1}{2}(8 + 4)(6) = \frac{1}{2}(72) = 36$.

104. F

Subject: Arithmetic

Getting to the Answer: First, determine how much of the book Breanna has read all together: $29 + 36 = 65\%$ read. Next, find what percent she *hasn't* yet read: $100 - 65 = 35\%$ unread. As a fraction, this is $\frac{35}{100}$, or $\frac{7}{20}$.

105. B

Subject: Arithmetic

Getting to the Answer: Since you will have to add and subtract several fractions in this problem, it will be useful to put everything in terms of a common denominator from the beginning. Point C is at $5\frac{6}{12}$, $AC = 8\frac{10}{12}$, $AD = 10\frac{6}{12}$, and $BD = 4\frac{5}{12}$. Now you can more easily do the fraction operations. Because the problem does not give you the value of BC, which would allow you to find B directly, you will have to use the other points to find B:

Point A: $5\frac{6}{12} - 8\frac{10}{12} = -3\frac{4}{12}$

Point D: $-3\frac{4}{12} + 10\frac{6}{12} = 7\frac{2}{12}$.

Point B: $7\frac{2}{12} - 4\frac{5}{12} = 2\frac{9}{12}$, or $2\frac{3}{4}$.

106. F

Subject: Arithmetic

Getting to the Answer: Considering the large fraction denominators in the answer choices, it may be easier to do this problem with decimals and then convert back to fractions at the end. $-\frac{7}{10}$ is -0.7, and $\frac{1}{2}$ is 0.5; the distance between them is $0.5 - (-0.7) = 1.2$. Since the hash marks are evenly spaced, each one is $1.2 \div 5 = 0.24$. Point N is two hash marks less than point P, so N is at $0.5 - 2(0.24) = 0.02$. As a fraction, this is $\frac{2}{100}$, or $\frac{1}{50}$.

107. B

Subject: Arithmetic

Getting to the Answer: Remember that Rate $= \frac{\text{Distance}}{\text{Time}}$. Find Adrienne's distance and time in the appropriate units: $18 \text{ km} \times 1,000 \text{ m/km} = 18,000 \text{ m}$, and $(3 \text{ hr} \times 60 \text{ min/hr}) + 20 \text{ min} = 200 \text{ min}$. In meters per minute, Adrienne's hiking rate is $\frac{18,000}{200}$, or 90 meters per minute.

108. H

Subject: Statistics and Probability

Getting to the Answer: First, remember that when items are removed, the whole changes. Consider how many are now in the whole: 23 pairs of socks were originally in the drawer $-$ 4 pairs of socks removed $= 19$ pairs of socks. Now, consider how many green socks are left: 10 pairs of green socks originally $-$ 2 pairs of green socks removed $= 8$ pairs of green socks. Therefore, the probability of choosing a green pair is now $\frac{8}{19}$.

109. D

Subject: Algebra

Getting to the Answer: First, solve for n:

$$4n + 13 \leq 69$$
$$4n \leq 56$$
$$n \leq 14$$

There are 7 positive, even integers that could make this statement true: 2, 4, 6, 8, 10, 12, and 14.

110. E

Subject: Arithmetic

Getting to the Answer: First, convert to like denominators: $1\frac{1}{2} = 1\frac{4}{8}$. Next, convert to an improper fraction to help you compare amounts: $1\frac{4}{8} = \frac{12}{8}$. The ratio of nutmeg to cinnamon is $\frac{1}{8} : \frac{12}{8}$, or simply 1:12.

111. A

Subject: Geometry

Getting to the Answer: The test will not give you a formula sheet, so you need to remember the volume formula for a rectangular prism: $V = l \times w \times h$. Convert 6 inches to 0.5 feet and plug the dimensions into the formula to get $V = 30 \times 24 \times 0.5 = 360$ cubic feet.

112. H

Subject: Arithmetic

Getting to the Answer: For rate problems, remember the DiRT formula: Distance = Rate × Time. For Sam, that's $2 = R\left(\frac{1}{3}\right)$, so Sam runs 6 miles per hour. In $\frac{4}{5}$ of an hour, Sam can run $6 \times \frac{4}{5} = \frac{24}{5}$ miles, or $4\frac{4}{5}$ miles.

113. D

Subject: Arithmetic

Getting to the Answer: Though the fractions may look intimidating, you simply need to convert them to like denominators and add:

$$2\frac{6}{8} + 3\frac{4}{8} + 4\frac{3}{8} + 5\frac{2}{8} = 15\frac{7}{8}$$

114. F

Subject: Arithmetic

Getting to the Answer:

Find the sum of all 15 scores.	$15 \times 85 = 1{,}275$
Find the sum of the remaining 14 scores.	$14 \times 86 = 1{,}204$
The difference is the dropped score.	$1{,}275 - 1{,}204 = 71$

SHSAT Practice Test 3

SHSAT Practice Test 3
ANSWER SHEET

Scan Code

Enrollment ID

Please use this Answer Sheet only if the test will be scored via a webgrid/online scoring process. This Answer Sheet will NOT work if the test will be scanned.

For scanned exams, please refer to the Kaplan Answer Grid (which requires the use of a No. 2 pencil and is formatted for scanning machines).

PART 1—ENGLISH LANGUAGE ARTS

1. Ⓐ Ⓑ Ⓒ Ⓓ	11. Ⓐ Ⓑ Ⓒ Ⓓ	21. Ⓐ Ⓑ Ⓒ Ⓓ	31. Ⓐ Ⓑ Ⓒ Ⓓ	41. Ⓐ Ⓑ Ⓒ Ⓓ	51. Ⓐ Ⓑ Ⓒ Ⓓ
2. Ⓔ Ⓕ Ⓖ Ⓗ	12. Ⓔ Ⓕ Ⓖ Ⓗ	22. Ⓔ Ⓕ Ⓖ Ⓗ	32. Ⓔ Ⓕ Ⓖ Ⓗ	42. Ⓔ Ⓕ Ⓖ Ⓗ	52. Ⓔ Ⓕ Ⓖ Ⓗ
3. Ⓐ Ⓑ Ⓒ Ⓓ	13. Ⓐ Ⓑ Ⓒ Ⓓ	23. Ⓐ Ⓑ Ⓒ Ⓓ	33. Ⓐ Ⓑ Ⓒ Ⓓ	43. Ⓐ Ⓑ Ⓒ Ⓓ	53. Ⓐ Ⓑ Ⓒ Ⓓ
4. Ⓔ Ⓕ Ⓖ Ⓗ	14. Ⓔ Ⓕ Ⓖ Ⓗ	24. Ⓔ Ⓕ Ⓖ Ⓗ	34. Ⓔ Ⓕ Ⓖ Ⓗ	44. Ⓔ Ⓕ Ⓖ Ⓗ	54. Ⓔ Ⓕ Ⓖ Ⓗ
5. Ⓐ Ⓑ Ⓒ Ⓓ	15. Ⓐ Ⓑ Ⓒ Ⓓ	25. Ⓐ Ⓑ Ⓒ Ⓓ	35. Ⓐ Ⓑ Ⓒ Ⓓ	45. Ⓐ Ⓑ Ⓒ Ⓓ	55. Ⓐ Ⓑ Ⓒ Ⓓ
6. Ⓔ Ⓕ Ⓖ Ⓗ	16. Ⓔ Ⓕ Ⓖ Ⓗ	26. Ⓔ Ⓕ Ⓖ Ⓗ	36. Ⓔ Ⓕ Ⓖ Ⓗ	46. Ⓔ Ⓕ Ⓖ Ⓗ	56. Ⓔ Ⓕ Ⓖ Ⓗ
7. Ⓐ Ⓑ Ⓒ Ⓓ	17. Ⓐ Ⓑ Ⓒ Ⓓ	27. Ⓐ Ⓑ Ⓒ Ⓓ	37. Ⓐ Ⓑ Ⓒ Ⓓ	47. Ⓐ Ⓑ Ⓒ Ⓓ	57. Ⓐ Ⓑ Ⓒ Ⓓ
8. Ⓔ Ⓕ Ⓖ Ⓗ	18. Ⓔ Ⓕ Ⓖ Ⓗ	28. Ⓔ Ⓕ Ⓖ Ⓗ	38. Ⓔ Ⓕ Ⓖ Ⓗ	48. Ⓔ Ⓕ Ⓖ Ⓗ	
9. Ⓐ Ⓑ Ⓒ Ⓓ	19. Ⓐ Ⓑ Ⓒ Ⓓ	29. Ⓐ Ⓑ Ⓒ Ⓓ	39. Ⓐ Ⓑ Ⓒ Ⓓ	49. Ⓐ Ⓑ Ⓒ Ⓓ	
10. Ⓔ Ⓕ Ⓖ Ⓗ	20. Ⓔ Ⓕ Ⓖ Ⓗ	30. Ⓔ Ⓕ Ⓖ Ⓗ	40. Ⓔ Ⓕ Ⓖ Ⓗ	50. Ⓔ Ⓕ Ⓖ Ⓗ	

PART 2—MATHEMATICS

58.   59.   60.   61.   62.

63. Ⓐ Ⓑ Ⓒ Ⓓ	72. Ⓔ Ⓕ Ⓖ Ⓗ	81. Ⓐ Ⓑ Ⓒ Ⓓ	90. Ⓔ Ⓕ Ⓖ Ⓗ	99. Ⓐ Ⓑ Ⓒ Ⓓ	108. Ⓔ Ⓕ Ⓖ Ⓗ
64. Ⓔ Ⓕ Ⓖ Ⓗ	73. Ⓐ Ⓑ Ⓒ Ⓓ	82. Ⓔ Ⓕ Ⓖ Ⓗ	91. Ⓐ Ⓑ Ⓒ Ⓓ	100. Ⓔ Ⓕ Ⓖ Ⓗ	109. Ⓐ Ⓑ Ⓒ Ⓓ
65. Ⓐ Ⓑ Ⓒ Ⓓ	74. Ⓔ Ⓕ Ⓖ Ⓗ	83. Ⓐ Ⓑ Ⓒ Ⓓ	92. Ⓔ Ⓕ Ⓖ Ⓗ	101. Ⓐ Ⓑ Ⓒ Ⓓ	110. Ⓔ Ⓕ Ⓖ Ⓗ
66. Ⓔ Ⓕ Ⓖ Ⓗ	75. Ⓐ Ⓑ Ⓒ Ⓓ	84. Ⓔ Ⓕ Ⓖ Ⓗ	93. Ⓐ Ⓑ Ⓒ Ⓓ	102. Ⓔ Ⓕ Ⓖ Ⓗ	111. Ⓐ Ⓑ Ⓒ Ⓓ
67. Ⓐ Ⓑ Ⓒ Ⓓ	76. Ⓔ Ⓕ Ⓖ Ⓗ	85. Ⓐ Ⓑ Ⓒ Ⓓ	94. Ⓔ Ⓕ Ⓖ Ⓗ	103. Ⓐ Ⓑ Ⓒ Ⓓ	112. Ⓔ Ⓕ Ⓖ Ⓗ
68. Ⓔ Ⓕ Ⓖ Ⓗ	77. Ⓐ Ⓑ Ⓒ Ⓓ	86. Ⓔ Ⓕ Ⓖ Ⓗ	95. Ⓐ Ⓑ Ⓒ Ⓓ	104. Ⓔ Ⓕ Ⓖ Ⓗ	113. Ⓐ Ⓑ Ⓒ Ⓓ
69. Ⓐ Ⓑ Ⓒ Ⓓ	78. Ⓔ Ⓕ Ⓖ Ⓗ	87. Ⓐ Ⓑ Ⓒ Ⓓ	96. Ⓔ Ⓕ Ⓖ Ⓗ	105. Ⓐ Ⓑ Ⓒ Ⓓ	114. Ⓔ Ⓕ Ⓖ Ⓗ
70. Ⓔ Ⓕ Ⓖ Ⓗ	79. Ⓐ Ⓑ Ⓒ Ⓓ	88. Ⓔ Ⓕ Ⓖ Ⓗ	97. Ⓐ Ⓑ Ⓒ Ⓓ	106. Ⓔ Ⓕ Ⓖ Ⓗ	
71. Ⓐ Ⓑ Ⓒ Ⓓ	80. Ⓔ Ⓕ Ⓖ Ⓗ	89. Ⓐ Ⓑ Ⓒ Ⓓ	98. Ⓔ Ⓕ Ⓖ Ⓗ	107. Ⓐ Ⓑ Ⓒ Ⓓ	

PRACTICE TEST 3

Directions: Mark your answers on the separate sheet provided. You will receive credit only for answers marked on the answer grid. **DO NOT MAKE ANY STRAY MARKS ON THE ANSWER GRID.** You can write in the test booklet, or use the paper provided for scratchwork.

Marking Your Answers

Each question has only one correct answer. Select the **best** answer for each question. Your score is determined by the number of questions you answered correctly. **It is to your advantage to answer every question, even though you may not be certain which choice is correct.**

Planning Your Time

You have 180 minutes to complete the entire test. How you split the time between the English Language Arts and Mathematics sections is up to you. **If you begin with the English Language Arts section, you may go on to the Mathematics section as soon as you are ready. If you begin with the Mathematics section, you may go on to the English Language Arts section as soon as you are ready.** It is recommended that you do not spend more than 90 minutes on either section. If you complete the test before the allotted time (180 minutes) is over, you may go back to review questions in either section.

Work as rapidly as you can without making mistakes. Don't spend too much time on a difficult question. Return to it later if you have time. If time remains, you should check your answers.

Part 1—English Language Arts

57 QUESTIONS—SUGGESTED TIMING: 90 MINUTES

REVISING/EDITING

QUESTIONS 1–11

IMPORTANT NOTE

The Revising/Editing section includes Part A and Part B.

REVISING/EDITING Part A

DIRECTIONS: Answer the following questions, recognizing and correcting errors so that the sentences or paragraphs are grammatically correct. Re-read relevant parts of the text before choosing the best answer for each question, but be mindful of time. You may write in your test booklet to take notes.

1. Read this paragraph.

> (1) Substantial similarities exist between the behavior of wild and domestic cats for example, when threatened or frightened, a lion flattens its ears against its head, just as a cat does. (2) These creatures share many instincts, which are inborn promptings or reactions. (3) Even when cats are not hungry, they can't resist stalking and catching prey. (4) In addition, wild and domestic cats share the ability to land on their feet, do to an excellent sense of balance.

Which revisions correct the errors in the paragraph?

A. Sentence 1: Insert a semicolon before *for example*.
   Sentence 4: Change *do* to **due**.

B. Sentence 2: Insert a comma after *promptings*.
   Sentence 3: Delete the comma after *hungry*.

C. Sentence 1: Insert a semicolon before *for example*.
   Sentence 3: Delete the comma after *hungry*.

D. Sentence 2: Insert a comma after *promptings*.
   Sentence 4: Change *do* to **due**.

GO ON TO THE NEXT PAGE

2. Read this paragraph.

> (1) Mountain climbers are eager to reach the peak of Mt. Everest because it is higher than that of any other mountain. (2) This popular mountain, located in Nepal, attracts hundreds of climbers every year. (3) Despite facing extreme challenges—such as having low levels of oxygen mountain climbers continue to test their abilities. (4) The climbers use bottled oxygen as they tackle Mt. Everest's peak.

Which edit should be made to correct the paragraph?

- **E.** Insert a comma after *Everest*.
- **F.** Delete the comma after *Nepal*.
- **G.** Insert a dash between *oxygen* and *mountain*.
- **H.** Insert a dash between *oxygen* and *as*.

3. Read this sentence.

> To promote her new book, a book signing will be held by Lola on Friday.

How should the sentence be revised?

- **A.** To promote her new book, on Friday a book signing will be held by Lola.
- **B.** To promote her new book, Lola will hold a book signing on Friday.
- **C.** On Friday to promote her new book, a book signing will be held my Lola.
- **D.** Lola, on Friday to promote her new book, will hold a book signing.

4. Read this sentence.

> If you want to write an interesting short story for the magazine contest, one has to use vivid, descriptive language.

Which edit should be made to correct this sentence?

- **E.** Change *you want* to **someone wants**.
- **F.** Change *you want* to **a person wants**.
- **G.** Change *one has* to **you have**.
- **H.** Change *one has* to **they have**.

REVISING/EDITING Part B

DIRECTIONS: Read the passage and answer the questions following it, improving the writing quality and correcting grammatical errors. Re-read relevant parts of the text before choosing the best answer for each question, but be mindful of time. You may write in your test booklet to take notes.

Jazz Saxophone

(1) Until last year, playing in our school's jazz band was not very popular. (2) This was because only the guitar and drums were seen as being cool instruments. (3) Rock and dance were the most popular kinds of music, but I play jazz on my saxophone.

(4) Last year my music teacher told some of us in the jazz band that he could get us jobs. (5) For example, parents of students at the school like to support student activities. (6) He chose a small group to play and earn a little money playing at various events.

(7) One evening, we were going to play for the whole school at an alumni reunion. (8) I was very nervous. (9) Lots of my classmates were going to be there. (10) There would also be important people. (11) Even one professional musician. (12) He used to go to our school.

(13) I was playing well, so the music teacher told me to take a solo. (14) Terrified, I thought my hands would slip off the keys from shaking so much. (15) I played my very best, and afterward everybody said how much they liked it, even the professional. (16) Jazz may not be as popular as rock or dance music, but playing in the jazz band can still be a positive experience. (17) And it can make you popular, too.

(18) The principal liked our playing so much that he invited us to play next month at a school party to celebrate the retirement of one of the school's most popular teachers, Mrs. Callahan. (19) Since she teaches French, we're learning a bunch of traditional French songs, like "Frère Jacques" and "Sur le Pont d'Avignon." (20) These are really easy songs to play, so I think maybe I can make them more fun by playing them in a jazz style. (21) I may also learn to play the trumpet. (22) I don't know if our music teacher will let me play jazzy French songs, but I think Mrs. Callahan would like it. (23) I would play the song the original way, then maybe do a jazz solo. (24) If my music teacher lets me do this, I bet my friends would be impressed, and I'll get even more popular.

5. What is the best way to combine sentences 1 and 2 to clarify the relationship between ideas?

   A. Playing in our school's jazz band is not very popular because, unlike playing guitar or drums, it was not considered cool.

   B. Until last year, playing in our school's jazz band was not very popular because, unlike playing guitar or drums, it was not considered cool.

   C. Until last year, playing in our school's jazz band was popular because, unlike playing guitar or drums, it was considered cool.

   D. Unlike playing guitar or drums, playing in our school's jazz band was not very popular, until last year, because it was not considered cool.

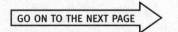
GO ON TO THE NEXT PAGE

6. Which sentence should follow sentence 3 to best state the main claim in the passage?

    E. Sticking only to what is popular is not a good way to enjoy the variety life can offer, however.

    F. I used to agree with this difference in popularity until my mind was changed.

    G. Some people like jazz bands and even particularly enjoy the saxophone.

    H. Over the course of the year, however, I was able to become more popular with my instrument.

7. Where should sentence 6 be moved to improve the organization of the second and third paragraphs (sentences 4–12)?

    A. to the beginning of the second paragraph (before sentence 4)

    B. between sentences 4 and 5

    C. to the beginning of the third paragraph (before sentence 7)

    D. between sentences 11 and 12

8. What is the best way to combine sentences 10 through 12 to clarify the relationship between ideas?

    E. There would be even one important professional musician who used to go to our school.

    F. Having gone to our school, a professional musician would be there along with other important people.

    G. Even one professional musician would be among the important people who used to go to our school.

    H. There would also be important people, including a professional musician who used to go to our school.

9. Which transition should be added to the beginning of sentence 15?

    A. Currently

    B. Nevertheless

    C. Since

    D. To clarify

10. Which sentence would best follow and support sentence 16?

    E. The saxophone is much more difficult to play than either guitar or drums.

    F. From it, I learned that even an instrument like the saxophone can be both fun and profitable.

    G. Many of the students knew my name after that night, and I became very popular.

    H. My solo was the best part of the whole school year.

11. Which sentence should replace sentence 21 to best follow and support sentence 20?

    A. French music often includes instruments such as the trumpet, which we have in our school jazz band.

    B. Jazz music is much more popular and well-known in France.

    C. Furthermore, many French songs lend themselves to being played in a jazz style.

    D. Adapting songs into different styles is common for talented musicians.

READING COMPREHENSION

QUESTIONS 12–57

DIRECTIONS: Read the six passages and answer the corresponding questions. Re-read relevant parts of the text before choosing the best answer for each question, but be mindful of time. Base your answers only on the content within each passage. You may write in your test booklet to take notes.

"Work Gangs"
by Carl Sandburg

Box cars run by a mile long.
And I wonder what they say to each other
When they stop a mile long on a sidetrack.
Maybe their chatter goes:
5 I came from Fargo with a load of wheat up to the
danger line.
I came from Omaha with a load of shorthorns and
they splintered my boards.
I came from Detroit heavy with a load of flivvers.
10 I carried apples from the Hood river last year and this
year bunches of bananas from Florida; they look for
me with watermelons from Mississippi next year.

Hammers and shovels of work gangs sleep in shop
corners
15 when the dark stars come on the sky and the night
watchmen walk and look.

Then the hammer heads talk to the handles,
then the scoops of the shovels talk,
how the day's work nicked and trimmed them,
20 how they swung and lifted all day,
how the hands of the work gangs smelled of hope.
In the night of the dark stars
when the curve of the sky is a work gang handle,
in the night on the mile long sidetracks,
25 in the night where the hammers and shovels sleep
in corners,
the night watchmen stuff their pipes with dreams—
and sometimes they doze and don't care for nothin',
and sometimes they search their heads for meanings,
30 stories, stars.
The stuff of it runs like this:
A long way we come; a long way to go; long rests and
long deep sniffs for our lungs on the way.
Sleep is a belonging of all; even if all songs are old
35 songs and the singing heart is snuffed out like a

GO ON TO THE NEXT PAGE

switchman's lantern with the oil gone, even if we
forget our names and houses in the finish, the secret
of sleep is left us, sleep belongs to all, sleep is the first
and last and best of all.

40 People singing; people with song mouths connecting
with song hearts; people who must sing or die; people
whose song hearts break if there is no song mouth;
these are my people.

12. Which line from the poem best supports the idea that the narrator identifies with the working class?

    E.   "how the hands of the work gangs smelled of hope." (line 21)

    F.   "the night watchmen stuff their pipes with dreams—" (line 27)

    G.   "people who must sing or die;" (line 41)

    H.   "these are my people." (line 43)

13. Read lines 5–12 from the first stanza.

> **I came from Fargo with a load of wheat up to the danger line.**
>
> **I came from Omaha with a load of shorthorns and they splintered my boards.**
>
> **I came from Detroit heavy with a load of flivvers.**
>
> **I carried apples from the Hood river last year and this year**
>
> **bunches of bananas from Florida; they look for me with**
>
> **watermelons from Mississippi next year.**

These lines help develop the theme of the poem by suggesting that the workers

    A.   have divisions among them due to being from different regions.

    B.   have traveled long distances.

    C.   dream of traveling around the country for leisure.

    D.   take pride in the job they do to earn a living.

14. The author uses personification when describing the box cars and tools in order to

    E.   allow them to relate the stories of how they all met their demise.

    F.   narrate the journeys that all of them have taken across the country.

    G.   establish the varied jobs of the working class.

    H.   highlight how they are mishandled and abused.

GO ON TO THE NEXT PAGE

15. The discussion of sleep in lines 34–39 helps show that the common people

    A. share a fulfilling rest after their daily labor.

    B. reject sleep because of their work ethic.

    C. cannot sleep because they still have a long distance to travel.

    D. are exhausted from having to sing all day.

16. Read lines 24–27 from the third stanza.

> **in the night on the mile long sidetracks,**
>
> **in the night where the hammers and shovels sleep in corners,**
>
> **the night watchmen stuff their pipes with dreams—**

How do the lines contribute to the development of ideas in the stanza?

    E. The lines establish a parallel structure with the daytime activities described earlier.

    F. The lines reveal that the conversations are imagined by the night watchmen.

    G. The lines highlight the fact that the night watchmen sleep on the job.

    H. The lines offer a contrast between the work that happens at night versus during the day.

17. Read lines 40–43 from the poem.

> **People singing; people with song mouths connecting**
>
> **with song people who must sing or die; people**
>
> **whose song hearts break if there is no song mouth;**
>
> **these are my people.**

Which of the following best supports the narrator's connection with the working class?

    A. "Hammers and shovels of work gangs sleep in shop corners" (line 13)

    B. "the night watchmen stuff their pipes with dreams—" (line 27)

    C. "A long way we come; a long way to go; long rests and long deep sniffs" (lines 32–33)

    D. "sleep is the first and last and best of all." (lines 38–39)

18. The description in the fourth stanza suggests that the common people

    E. are on the verge of a violent revolution.

    F. are essentially different from the poem's narrator.

    G. sing because it is one aspect of their job.

    H. are virtuous laborers who take pride in their work.

19. Read lines 17–21 from the poem.

> **Then the hammer heads talk to the handles,**
>
> **then the scoops of the shovels talk,**
>
> **how the day's work nicked and trimmed them,**
>
> **how they swung and lifted all day,**
>
> **how the hands of the work gangs smelled of hope.**

What impact do the phrases "lifted all day" and "smelled of hope" have on the meaning of the poem?

A. They suggest that the effortless nature of the workers' tasks gives them a sense of peace and comfort.

B. They contrast the hard daily work with the workers' hopeful spirit.

C. They imply that if the workers continue this heavy labor, they will eventually give up hope.

D. They confirm that the workers would have had better lives if they had selected other careers.

Alchemy: The Ancient Science of Transmutation

1 Alchemy is the name given to the attempt to change lead, copper, or other metals into silver or gold. Today, alchemy is regarded as a pseudoscience because its associations with astrology and the occult suggest primitive superstition to the modern mind. If mentioned at all, the alchemist is generally portrayed as a charlatan obsessed with dreams of impossible wealth. For many centuries, however, alchemy was a highly respected art. Indeed, in the search for the elusive secret to making gold, alchemists helped to develop many of the apparatuses and procedures that are used in laboratories today, and the results of their experiments laid the basic conceptual framework for much of the modern science of chemistry.

2 The philosophy underlying the practice of alchemy emerged in similar forms in ancient China, India, and Greece around the start of the Common Era. The alchemists believed that all matter consisted of various combinations of five elements—air, water, earth, fire, and space—and that there were correspondences among the elements, the planets, and metals. They regarded gold as the "purest" and "noblest" of all metals and believed that "base" metals such as copper and lead were only imperfectly developed forms of gold. The base metals were said to contain impurities that "weighed down" their perfect qualities. Thus, under certain astrological conditions, the alchemists believed that these metals could be purified through long heating or other treatments.

3 Since they believed in the interrelationship between the natural world and the human world, this "purification" process had a profound significance for the alchemists. With purification, the alchemists believed, base metals attained a state of perfection, just as human souls attained a perfect state in heaven.

4 In the twelfth century, translations of Arabic works on alchemy started to become available in Europe, generating a new wave of European interest in the art. In this period, alchemists made many important chemical discoveries, such as mineral acids and alcohol. As late as the seventeenth century, that supreme genius of rationalism, Sir Isaac Newton, devoted 30 years to the study of alchemy. By the early nineteenth century, practitioners of the new discipline of chemistry began to differentiate their research and experiments from those of alchemists, who were defined as those only searching to transmute other elements into gold. Although the possibility of making gold from other elements was conclusively disproved later in the nineteenth century, this belief provided the basis for some of the most fascinating chapters in the history of science and produced a legacy of imagery that persists in modern psychology and literature.

20. Which statement best describes the central theme of the passage?

    E.   Alchemy has an interesting and important history, even though it is not highly regarded now.

    F.   The alchemists were able to manufacture gold from the elements.

    G.   The practice of alchemy was connected to spirituality.

    H.   Modern chemistry evolved from alchemy.

21. What impact does the word "pseudoscience" have in paragraph 1?

    A.   It demonstrates that alchemy should be considered an extremely valuable science.

    B.   It proves that alchemy serves as the foundation of chemistry.

    C.   It shows that alchemy is indeed a pure science.

    D.   It emphasizes that alchemy is considered a type of false science.

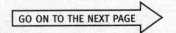
GO ON TO THE NEXT PAGE

22. According to the passage, why are the alchemists not favorably regarded today?

    E. Their secret techniques have mostly been forgotten.

    F. The results of all their experiments were disproved.

    G. The Europeans were not interested in an Eastern art form.

    H. Their use of astrology seems superstitious to scientists.

23. What did the alchemists believe about copper and lead?

    A. They were imperfect forms of gold.

    B. They were the noblest of all metals.

    C. They consisted primarily of air and water.

    D. They were heavier than other metals.

24. How does paragraph 3 fit into the overall structure of the passage?

    E. It demonstrates the significance of base metals to alchemy.

    F. It connects alchemy and astrology.

    G. It shows the alchemists' belief in a parallel between alchemy and spirituality.

    H. It establishes the intricacies of the human soul.

25. The words "charlatan" and "obsessed" in paragraph 1 affect the tone of the paragraph by

    A. conveying the negative light in which the alchemists are viewed by many people today.

    B. depicting the alchemists as shrewd businessmen with great ambitions.

    C. showing the widespread criticism of the alchemists at the time in which they were most active.

    D. relating the alchemists to others who live a simplistic life with few luxuries.

26. With which of the following statements about alchemy would the author of this passage most likely agree?

    E. Belief in alchemy delayed scientific progress for centuries.

    F. Some of the principles of alchemy are still valid today.

    G. Modern chemistry owes nothing to the achievements of the alchemists.

    H. Alchemy is an important part of scientific history.

27. Which sentence best supports the idea that some beliefs are common to many different people?

    A. "The philosophy underlying the practice of alchemy emerged in similar forms in ancient China, India, and Greece around the start of the Common Era." (paragraph 2)

    B. "The alchemists believed that all matter consisted of various combinations of five elements." (paragraph 2)

    C. "In the twelfth century, translations of Arabic works on alchemy started to become available in Europe, generating a new wave of European interest in the art." (paragraph 4)

    D. "By the early nineteenth century, practitioners of the new discipline of chemistry began to differentiate their research and experiments from those of alchemists." (paragraph 4)

Life without Photosynthesis

1   Most life is fundamentally dependent on photosynthetic organisms that store radiant energy from the Sun. In almost all the world's ecosystems and food chains, photosynthetic organisms such as plants and algae are eaten by other organisms, which are then consumed by still others. The existence of organisms that are not dependent on the Sun's light has long been established, but until recently they were regarded as anomalies. Over the last 20 years, however, research in deep-sea areas has revealed the existence of entire ecosystems in which the primary producers of food are chemosynthetic bacteria, bacteria that are dependent on energy from within the earth itself. Indeed, growing evidence suggests that these ecosystems may model the way in which life first came about on this planet.

2   The first of these unique chemosynthetic ecosystems was discovered in 1977 by a small research submarine investigating the Galapagos Rift, a volcanically active area 7,000 feet below the surface of the eastern Pacific Ocean. At a boundary between adjacent plates in the earth, scientists found a surprisingly congenial environment for life. They discovered that water was seeping down through cracks in the ocean floor, being heated by the volcanic rocks, and rising again to create an oasis of warmth in the near-freezing waters. Moreover, under conditions of extreme heat and pressure, chemical reactions were taking place that supplied sufficient energy for the chemosynthetic bacteria to develop. In this ecosystem and others discovered since, bacteria become the primary producers in the ecosystem by transforming chemicals into compounds that can serve as nourishment for more complex forms of life.

3   What do these underwater worlds look like? More than a dozen of these warm-water oases have been discovered in the Pacific so far, and the specific life forms that arise in them vary according to whichever species first colonizes the site. The inhabitants of these deep-sea communities can include clams, mussels, crabs, and octopods, and, as the technology to research these inaccessible sites has only been available recently, over 300 new species have been discovered. The environment often produces sights that are spectacular to behold—clams measuring some 20 centimeters can cover the ocean floor. One oasis, ironically known as the Garden of Eden, is populated by huge tube worms that lack mouths and digestive tracts and obtain their energy instead from bacteria living in their tissues. The tube worms are able to reach an incredible size, sometimes over two meters tall, because their environment is so rich in nutrients.

4   While organisms that do not rely on photosynthesis have long been regarded as mere anomalies, recent research shows several chemosynthetic organisms exist. The deep sea is a vast frontier that is bound to reveal new species and further insight into chemosynthesis and the species that rely upon it. Researchers will continue to use new technologies to discover other species that operate within chemosynthetic ecosystems.

28.   Which statement best describes the central idea of the passage?

    E.   Photosynthesis is integral to the origin of life on Earth.

    F.   Most animals are now known to be chemosynthetic.

    G.   Deep-sea exploration is bound to provide spectacular sights.

    H.   Chemosynthetic ecosystems play a more significant role in the animal world than previously thought.

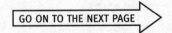

GO ON TO THE NEXT PAGE

29. How does paragraph 2 fit into the overall structure of the passage?

    A. It disproves the importance of sunlight to organisms.

    B. It details the voyage of the submarine exploring the Galapagos Rift.

    C. It introduces the unusually large inhabitants of deep-water environments.

    D. It describes the discovery and ecology of bacteria-driven ecosystems.

30. With which statement would the author of this passage most likely agree?

    E. Most life is ultimately dependent upon deep-sea hot springs.

    F. Most life is ultimately dependent upon the world's oceans.

    G. Most life is ultimately dependent upon bacterial microorganisms.

    H. Most life is ultimately dependent upon light from the Sun.

31. Why is the ecosystem described in this passage called "unique" (paragraph 2)?

    A. It thrives in the absence of sunlight.

    B. It exists in airless, waterless surroundings.

    C. It is infested by dangerous octopods.

    D. It is the only ecosystem found in deep ocean water.

32. Which statement best describes the effect of the phrase "a surprisingly congenial environment for life" (paragraph 2) in the passage?

    E. It demonstrates that chemosynthetic bacteria do not generally provide life-sustaining nourishment.

    F. It explains how searches of the Galapagos Rift had not revealed the presence of any ecosystems.

    G. It shows that tube worms found there are larger than any known to exist on dry land.

    H. It portrays the scientists as having unexpectedly found life in volcanically active underwater areas.

33. According to the passage, the term "primary producers" (paragraph 2) refers to

    A. producers of new and exciting scientific discoveries.

    B. organisms that serve as the first link in an ecosystem's food chain.

    C. organisms that consume other organisms in a food chain.

    D. simple chemicals that can be transformed into more complex compounds.

34. Which of the following conclusions about photosynthetic and chemosynthetic organisms is supported by this passage?

    E. Both perform similar functions in different food chains.

    F. Both are known to support communities of higher organisms at great ocean depths.

    G. Sunlight is a basic source of energy for both.

    H. Chemosynthetic organisms are less nourishing than photosynthetic organisms.

Martha Graham: A Pioneer of Modern Dance

1 The dancer and choreographer Martha Graham is regarded as one of the outstanding innovators in the history of dance. In a career that lasted over 70 years, Graham created more than 170 works ranging from solos to large-scale pieces, danced in most of them herself, and developed a new type of dance—the Graham technique. She was the first dancer to perform for the president at the White House and received the prestigious Presidential Medal of Freedom with Distinction, the highest civilian honor that can be bestowed on a United States citizen.

2 Born in 1894 and raised in a comfortable home in Pennsylvania, Graham never saw a dance performance until her family moved to California when she was fourteen years old. In 1911, at Los Angeles' Mason Opera House, Graham saw her first dance performance, and her life, as well as a new direction in the history of dance, truly began. Graham began training at the Denishawn School of Dancing and Related Arts, the first dance school in the United States to produce a professional dance company, and studied with founders Ruth St. Denis and Ted Shawn until 1923.

3 Although it incorporated dance styles considered innovative at the time such as Cambodian dance, Hawaiian hula, and Japanese sword dancing, the Denishawn School firmly grounded its training in the rigid traditions of classical ballet. When Graham left, she set out to break away from these strictures to create dance forms and movements that would better reflect the full complement of human emotions and experiences and not simply entertain audiences. She developed movements based on the actions of natural breath, contraction and release, and created a distinctive, weighted, and grounded style that directly opposed traditional ballet's illusion of weightlessness.

4 Graham opened the Martha Graham Center of Contemporary Dance in 1926 and showcased 18 of her choreographed works in her first production later that year. Her early dances reflect her innovations and distinctively American spirit. In addition to her new dance techniques, Graham avoided decorative sets and costumes and used an all-female dance troupe. In addition, her productions used music purely as an accompaniment to dance rather than as an elaborate showpiece in itself.

5 At first, the critics and the public understood little of Graham's break with tradition, reacting only to the unfamiliar and original dance movements and not to the feelings and ideas the movements were designed to express. Responding to the criticisms, Graham denied that she was experimenting merely for the sake of being different. Her new style, she said, "was not done perversely to dramatize ugliness, or to strike at sacred tradition. The point was that the old forms could not give voice to the fully awakened man."

6 As the decades passed, Graham's work found wider acceptance, but success did not weaken her desire to experiment. She continued to revise her ideas throughout her career, incorporating men into her company and broadening her subject matter to include sources from Greek mythology and the Old Testament. By continuing to explore the essence of human conflicts and emotions through her dances, Graham created a monumental body of work that not only is performed to this day but also became a point of departure for many of the most illustrious modern choreographers such as Merce Cunningham, Pearl Lang, and Paul Taylor. Her school, the longest continually operating school of dance in the United States, continues to train dancers in the Graham technique for professional roles in the Martha Graham Dance Company, other professional dance companies, and Broadway productions.

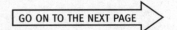

GO ON TO THE NEXT PAGE

35. Which statement best describes the central idea of the passage?

   A. There were drastic changes in the art world during the 1920s.

   B. The revolution in classical ballet impacted most forms of dance.

   C. Graham's role and purpose as an innovator involved revolutionary approaches to dance that were ultimately more widely accepted.

   D. The critical reception of Graham's early works was a great obstacle for her.

36. Martha Graham introduced new dance techniques in order to

   E. attract attention for her all-female troupe.

   F. visually dramatize the ugliness of life.

   G. express the changed mood of her time.

   H. strike a blow to the traditions of classical ballet.

37. How does the author's use of chronological structure contribute to the development of ideas in the passage?

   A. It clarifies the relationship between Graham's tutelage under Ruth St. Denis and Ted Shawn and her receipt of the Presidential Medal of Freedom.

   B. It explains how Graham developed natural breathing techniques before she mastered Japanese sword dancing.

   C. It conveys how the Denishawn School of Dancing ultimately prepared Graham for the Mason Opera House in Los Angeles.

   D. It demonstrates how the public initially rejected Graham's revolutionary art but eventually came to view it in higher regard.

38. With which statement would the author of the passage most likely agree?

   E. Classical ballet was loose and formless.

   F. Classical ballet was disliked by critics and the public.

   G. Classical ballet sought to dramatize ugliness.

   H. Classical ballet employed elaborate sets and costumes.

39. Critics and the public did not understand the universality of Graham's early work because they

   A. rejected the appropriateness of an all-female troupe.

   B. failed to appreciate the spirit of the postwar era.

   C. were distracted by the novelty of the dance movements.

   D. tried to fit her work into the traditions of classical ballet.

40. Which statement best describes the effect of the phrase "not simply entertain" (paragraph 3) in the passage?

    E.   It depicts dance as an art form from which audiences should learn about human emotion and experience.

    F.   It shows that dance music ignores the rules of harmony and emphasizes dissonance and ugly sounds.

    G.   It presents a movement in fiction that focuses on the gritty aspects of everyday life rather than its beautiful aspects.

    H.   It encourages a new trend in theatrical performance that becomes immensely popular and is not soon forgotten.

41. How does paragraph 3 fit into the overall structure of the passage?

    A.   It outlines Graham's early career.

    B.   It shows Graham's break from the rigid traditions of classical ballet.

    C.   It describes Graham's earliest achievements in dance.

    D.   It depicts the reactions of audiences to her revolutionary dance performances.

42. Which statement describes the effect of the phrase "used music purely as an accompaniment to dance" (paragraph 4) in the passage?

    E.   It pits music as the central focus of Graham's work.

    F.   It suggests that Graham used only the purest music in her ballets.

    G.   It puts the music in Graham's ballets on an equal footing with ballet itself.

    H.   It shows that the music used by Graham was secondary to the dancers' moves.

Excerpt from "The Bride Comes to Yellow Sky"
by Stephen Crane

1   The great Pullman was whirling onward with such dignity of motion that a glance from the window seemed simply to prove that the plains of Texas were pouring eastward. Vast flats of green grass, dull-hued spaces of mesquite and cactus, little groups of frame houses, woods of light and tender trees, all were sweeping into the east, sweeping over the horizon, a precipice.

2   A newly married pair had boarded this coach at San Antonio. The man's face was reddened from many days in the wind and sun, and a direct result of his new black clothes was that his brick-colored hands were constantly performing in a most conscious fashion. From time to time he looked down respectfully at his attire. He sat with a hand on each knee, like a man waiting in a barber's shop. The glances he devoted to other passengers were furtive and shy.

3   The bride was not pretty, nor was she very young. She wore a dress of blue cashmere, with small reservations of velvet here and there and with steel buttons abounding. She continually twisted her head to regard her puff sleeves, very stiff, straight, and high. They embarrassed her. It was quite apparent that she had cooked, and that she expected to cook, dutifully. The blushes caused by the careless scrutiny of some passengers as she had entered the car were strange to see upon this plain, under-class countenance, which was drawn in placid, almost emotionless lines.

4   They were evidently very happy. "Ever been in a parlor-car before?" he asked, smiling with delight.

5   "No," she answered, "I never was. It's fine, ain't it?"

6   "Great! And then after a while we'll go forward to the diner and get a big layout. Finest meal in the world. Charge a dollar."

7   "Oh, do they?" cried the bride. "Charge a dollar? Why, that's too much—for us—ain't it, Jack?"

8   "Not this trip, anyhow," he answered bravely. "We're going to go the whole thing."

9   Later, he explained to her about the trains. "You see, it's a thousand miles from one end of Texas to the other, and this train runs right across it and never stops but four times." He had the pride of an owner. He pointed out to her the dazzling fittings of the coach, and in truth, her eyes opened wider as she contemplated the sea-green figured velvet, the shining brass, silver, and glass, the wood that gleamed as darkly brilliant as the surface of a pool of oil. At one end a bronze figure sturdily held a support for a separated chamber, and at convenient places on the ceiling were frescoes in olive and silver.

10   To the minds of the pair, their surroundings reflected the glory of their marriage that morning in San Antonio. This was the environment of their new estate, and the man's face in particular beamed with an elation that made him appear ridiculous to the porter. This individual at times surveyed them from afar with an amused and superior grin. On other occasions he bullied them with skill in ways that did not make it exactly plain to them that they were being bullied. He subtly used all the manners of the most unconquerable kind of snobbery. He oppressed them, but of this oppression they had small knowledge, and they speedily forgot that infrequently a number of travelers covered them with stares of derisive enjoyment. Historically there was supposed to be something infinitely humorous in their situation.

11 "We are due in Yellow Sky at 3:42," he said, looking tenderly into her eyes.

12 "Oh, are we?" she said, as if she had not been aware of it. To evince surprise at her husband's statement was part of her wifely amiability. She took from a pocket a little silver watch, and as she held it before her and stared at it with a frown of attention, the new husband's face shone.

13 "I bought it in San Anton' from a friend of mine," he told her gleefully.

14 "It's seventeen minutes past twelve," she said, looking up at him with a kind of shy and clumsy coquetry. A passenger, noting this play, grew excessively sardonic, and winked at himself in one of the numerous mirrors.

15 At last they went to the dining-car. Two rows of waiters, in glowing white suits, surveyed their entrance with the interest and also the equanimity of men who had been forewarned. The pair fell to the lot of a waiter who happened to feel pleasure in steering them through their meal. He viewed them with the manner of a fatherly pilot, his countenance radiant with benevolence. The patronage, entwined with the ordinary deference, was not plain to them. And yet, as they returned to their coach, they showed in their faces a sense of escape.

43. In paragraph 1, how does the repetition of the word "sweeping" contribute to the meaning of the excerpt?

    A. It highlights the descriptions of the Texas landscape.

    B. It emphasizes the great speed of the train.

    C. It illustrates the unusual view the couple enjoys.

    D. It indicates how frightful the train's speed is.

44. In paragraph 2, what does the phrase "brick-colored hands" convey about the husband?

    E. He prefers his usual city living to life in rural Texas.

    F. He owns the train yet does not seem to belong aboard.

    G. He looks uncomfortable in his usual threadbare suit.

    H. He works outdoors and not indoors.

45. The phrase "It was quite apparent that she had cooked, and that she expected to cook, dutifully" (paragraph 3) supports the idea that the bride

    A. had previously worked in a restaurant and is now a homemaker.

    B. stoically paid the price for wearing a fancy dress in hot weather.

    C. enjoyed the fashions reserved to an upper-class lady like herself.

    D. was surprised by the luxurious quality of the train's dining-car.

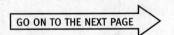
GO ON TO THE NEXT PAGE

46. Read this sentence from paragraph 4.

> **They were evidently very happy.**

Which statement best describes how the sentence fits into the overall structure of the excerpt?

E. It indicates a shift from the description of the couple as awkward individuals in a crowd to that of a pair that is comfortable with one another.

F. It provides a shift from the couple jointly staring out the window of the train to having a happy conversation about the train's attributes.

G. It introduces a transition from awkward silence to the wife excitedly explaining the construction of the train to her husband.

H. It emphasizes that the husband and wife are so in love with each other that they don't pay any attention to the people around them on the train.

47. The idea that the train is very "fine, ain't it?" (paragraph 5) is conveyed mainly through the

A. imagery of the green grass, woods, and other landscape elements speeding by out the window.

B. clothing worn by the couple and their fellow passengers.

C. description of the fittings, velvet, wood, glass, and other physical elements.

D. pride the husband takes in owning the train.

48. Read this sentence from paragraph 8.

> **"Not this trip, anyhow," he answered bravely.**

How does the sentence contribute to the development of the plot?

E. It reveals that the husband is rich from his share in the railroad company.

F. It highlights how the couple is leaving Texas for good.

G. It emphasizes how this couple is celebrating a special occasion.

H. It shows that the wife is careless with the couple's spending.

49. Which sentence from the excerpt best supports the idea that the man's clothes were both new and formal?

A. "From time to time he looked down respectfully at his attire." (paragraph 2)

B. "A newly married pair had boarded this coach at San Antonio." (paragraph 2)

C. "She wore a dress of blue cashmere..." (paragraph 3)

D. "They embarrassed her." (paragraph 3)

50. The author's primary purpose in writing the dialogue between Jack and his bride is to

    E. highlight the joys of train travel.

    F. describe the grandeur of the train's coach car.

    G. describe the bride's cautiousness with her husband.

    H. portray a new couple getting to know each other.

GO ON TO THE NEXT PAGE

The Sherpa People

1   The Sherpas of the Himalayas are famous all over the world as the reliable porters who guide mountaineers to the peaks of the highest mountains. The Sherpas, a group of 50,000 Buddhists who live mainly in the Hindu kingdom of Nepal, seem perfectly adapted to the dangerous slopes that they navigate. First impressions can be misleading, however. Before Western expeditions to the Himalayas began in the early 1900s, no Sherpas were climbers. Instead, the Sherpas treated the mountains with fear and respect, believing that the snowy peaks were the homes of the gods.

2   The Sherpas originally came from a land in eastern Tibet called Kham, migrating south in the sixteenth century to their current location in the lofty, exposed terrain of the Khumbu area. Here the Sherpas raised yaks and traded, and, in the lower, more southern Solu region, they farmed the hillsides for buckwheat, rice, and corn. Living between Nepal and Tibet, the Sherpas were able to survive for centuries in a state of independence, which allowed their language and customs to flourish. When the British colonized India in the 1800s, however, many Sherpas migrated into India to work in British military posts, and Sherpa culture came under the sway of the first of many Western influences.

3   The story of the modern Sherpa begins in the 1920s, when the British hired Sherpas as porters for the first expeditions attempting to reach the top of Mt. Everest, the loftiest peak in the Himalayas and the highest mountain in the world at 29,028 feet. Early expeditions were hampered by laws that prohibited trespassing in the Kingdom of Nepal, forcing climbers to approach the mountain from the more difficult Tibetan side. In 1949, however, the Kingdom of Nepal opened its borders, enabling climbers to trek straight through Khumbu to reach Mt. Everest. Because the Sherpa had lived at these high altitudes for generations, they were remarkably adapted to the lower levels of oxygen found in the air at high altitudes. Once Western explorers discovered this fact, they recruited Sherpas to assist in transporting the vast amount of provisions and equipment that are required to attempt the summit of Mt. Everest. In 1953, New Zealander Edmund Hillary and Sherpa guide Tenzing Norgay were the first to stand on the top of the world.

4   Some feared that their achievement would end mountaineering in the Himalayas. In fact, news of the spectacular feat only attracted more tourists and mountaineers to the region, changing the economy of the Sherpa people forever. Today, more than half of the Sherpa population works in trekking, mountaineering, or some related job, and those who staff climbing expeditions as guides and cooks are among the best-paid people in Nepal. Sherpas who are qualified to work at the highest altitudes earn monthly salaries several times that of the prime minister.

5   As knowledge of the remarkable physical adaptations of the Sherpa spread, scientists began work to document this unique community. Ongoing scientific research studies have not only quantified remarkable Sherpa adaptation to the severe environmental conditions in which they live, but also continue to delve ever more deeply into the basic physiological changes that have brought about their heightened ability to effectively process the small amount of oxygen available in the air.

6   The cultural changes have also been profound, due to the proximity of disparate cultures united in a common, dangerous goal. During the climbing season, the Sherpa live and work with the European and American expedition managers and assume the responsibility for the lives and safety of the expeditions' climbing customers. The two groups usually value the background and assets of the other: the Western customers must rely on the Sherpas' physical abilities and local expertise, and the Sherpas respect their Western charges' education, technology, and organization skills.

GO ON TO THE NEXT PAGE →

7   Interestingly, although the Sherpa appreciate the economic opportunities brought by the climbing and tourism industries, even the most highly-skilled and veteran climbers would not choose to work in such a dangerous job if other occupations were available. Many young Sherpas climb for a few seasons to earn enough money to provide for their families and educate their children, in the hopes that their children will be able to pursue safer, more conventional careers.

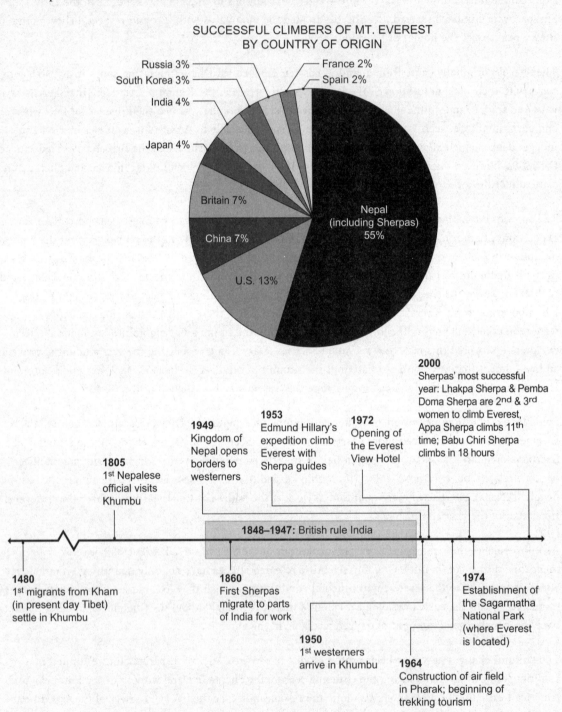

SUCCESSFUL CLIMBERS OF MT. EVEREST
BY COUNTRY OF ORIGIN

Russia 3%
South Korea 3%
India 4%
Japan 4%
Britain 7%
China 7%
U.S. 13%
France 2%
Spain 2%
Nepal (including Sherpas) 55%

1805 1st Nepalese official visits Khumbu

1480 1st migrants from Kham (in present day Tibet) settle in Khumbu

1949 Kingdom of Nepal opens borders to westerners

1953 Edmund Hillary's expedition climb Everest with Sherpa guides

1972 Opening of the Everest View Hotel

2000 Sherpas' most successful year: Lhakpa Sherpa & Pemba Doma Sherpa are 2nd & 3rd women to climb Everest, Appa Sherpa climbs 11th time; Babu Chiri Sherpa climbs in 18 hours

1848–1947: British rule India

1860 First Sherpas migrate to parts of India for work

1950 1st westerners arrive in Khumbu

1964 Construction of air field in Pharak; beginning of trekking tourism

1974 Establishment of the Sagarmatha National Park (where Everest is located)

51. How does the pie chart contribute to the central idea of paragraph 1?

   A. It illustrates that Westerners make up only one-fourth of the successful climbers of Mt. Everest, which compares poorly with success of the Nepalese.

   B. It shows how the Sherpas have begun climbing Mt. Everest in order to adapt to the increased modernization of the world.

   C. It reveals that more Nepalese, which includes Sherpas, have successfully climbed Mt. Everest than other nationalities, helping to earn their reputation as skilled guides.

   D. It illustrates that a surprising 55% of successful climbers of Mt. Everest are Nepalese, which is more than four times as many Americans.

52. From the sixteenth century to the beginning of the nineteenth century, the Sherpas lived mainly in

   E. Kham.

   F. Khumbu and Solu.

   G. western Tibet.

   H. eastern Nepal.

53. How does the timeline provide additional support for the central idea of the passage?

   A. It illustrates how the evolution of the Sherpas as respected climbing guides occurred.

   B. It provides evidence of the astonishing climbing achievements of the Sherpas from the 1400s.

   C. It casts doubt on how significant Edmund Hillary and Tenzing Norgaya's successful climb of Mt. Everest was in Sherpa history.

   D. It suggests that modern development of Mt. Everest tourism could occur only after Mt. Everest was successfully climbed.

54. How does paragraph 6 fit into the overall structure of the passage?

   E. It explains why Sherpas avoided climbing for religious reasons.

   F. It conveys the economic benefits of mountaineering for the Sherpas.

   G. It depicts the Sherpas as skilled mountaineers who take pride in their work.

   H. It shows the impact of increased interest in Mt. Everest on the Sherpas' culture.

55. In paragraph 5, how does the phrase "delve ever more deeply into the basic physiological changes" affect the tone of the passage?

   A. It describes the severity of the medical complications of the Sherpas after working in the mountaineering business.

   B. It depicts the Sherpas' physiological adaptation for mountaineering as being significant enough to be worthy of scientific inquiry.

   C. It shows the scientists' fixation on and baseless curiosity in minor changes in the Sherpas' physiology.

   D. It accentuates the issues of mental well-being for the Sherpas who take up mountaineering jobs.

Practice Tests

56. Which of the following best summarizes the effect of the Everest expedition of 1953?

    E. It discouraged many people from mountaineering.

    F. It provided a massive boost to the economy of the region.

    G. It caused many Sherpas to change their religious beliefs.

    H. It changed the Sherpas' traditional ways of life forever.

57. Which of the following most clearly conveys how Sherpas responded to the changes that were brought about by the expedition of 1953?

    A. Sherpas accepted the meager salaries tourism afforded them.

    B. Sherpas reluctantly abandoned their traditional customs.

    C. Sherpas demanded a stronger adherence to the Buddhist faith.

    D. Sherpas balanced modernization and traditional customs.

Part 2—Mathematics

57 QUESTIONS—SUGGESTED TIMING: 90 MINUTES

IMPORTANT NOTES

1. Definitions and formulas are **not** provided.

2. Diagrams are **not** necessarily drawn to scale, with the exception of graphs.

3. Diagrams are drawn in single planes unless the question specifically states they are not.

4. Graphs are drawn to scale.

5. Simplify all fractions to lowest terms.

GRID-IN QUESTIONS

QUESTIONS 58–62

DIRECTIONS: Answer each question. Write your answer in the boxes at the top of the grid on the answer sheet. Start on the left side of each grid, printing only one number or symbol in each box. **DO NOT LEAVE A BOX BLANK IN THE MIDDLE OF AN ANSWER.** Under each box, fill in the circle that matches the number or symbol you wrote above. **DO NOT FILL IN A CIRCLE UNDER AN UNUSED BOX.**

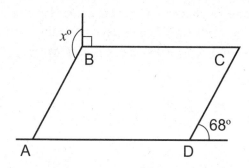

58. In the quadrilateral above, AB is parallel to CD and AD is parallel to BC. What is the value of x ?

59. Today Nia completed her sixth hour of training, which represents 7.5% of the total number of hours in the training. How many hours will Nia spend in training in all?

60. If $x = -4$, what is the value of y if $|x - 3.6| + |5 - 2| - |7.3 + x| = y$?

61. The sum of two consecutive odd integers is 44. If the larger integer is multiplied by 3 and the smaller integer is divided by 3, what is the **difference** of the two resulting integers?

62. For what value of s is $\dfrac{249 - s}{14} = 17$?

GO ON TO THE NEXT PAGE

MULTIPLE-CHOICE QUESTIONS

QUESTIONS 63–114

DIRECTIONS: Answer each question, selecting the best answer available. On the answer sheet, mark the letter of each of your answers. You can do your figuring in the test booklet or on paper provided by the proctor.

63. Marcus had three times as much money as José. Marcus gives José $5.30, but he still has $10 more than José. How much money do the two boys have in all?

    A. $10.30
    B. $30.90
    C. $33.60
    D. $41.20

$$Q = \frac{R}{3} = S - 6 = 7T = \frac{U}{10} > 0$$

64. According to the statement above, which variable has the **least** value?

    E. R
    F. S
    G. T
    H. U

65. John gets paid $6 for each of the first 40 toy cars he makes in a week. For any additional toy cars beyond 40, his pay increases by 50%. How much does John get paid in a week in which he makes 48 toy cars?

    A. $288
    B. $300
    C. $312
    D. $321

66. If $b = 2$ and $c = 3$, what is the value of a in the equation $a = 2b + 3c - 8$?

    E. 2
    F. 3
    G. 4
    H. 5

67. Two large servings of lemonade contain the same amount of liquid as three medium servings of lemonade. Two medium lemonades contain the same amount of liquid as three small lemonades. How many small lemonades contain the same amount of liquid as eight large lemonades?

    A. 12
    B. 16
    C. 18
    D. 24

68. $-2[(-18.75) \div 6.25] - 5[8.46 \div (-4.23)] =$

    E. -4
    F. 4
    G. 12
    H. 16

GO ON TO THE NEXT PAGE ⇨

69. Henry has 4 apples, 3 bananas, and 12 strawberries in his fruit basket. If he picks one piece of fruit at random, what is the probability that it is a banana?

A. $\dfrac{3}{19}$

B. $\dfrac{4}{19}$

C. $\dfrac{3}{7}$

D. $\dfrac{12}{19}$

70. The area of a rectangle is 48, and its length is 7.5. What is the perimeter of this rectangle?

E. 13.9

F. 27.8

G. 30

H. 56.25

Equivalent Currencies (May 2019)	
U.S. Dollar	1
Euro	0.9
Botswana Pula	10.75
Kuwaiti Dinar	0.3

71. Using the table of equivalent currencies above, how many euros must be exchanged for 43 dinars and 10 U.S. dollars?

A. 138

B. 129

C. 53

D. 22.9

72. In the number 258,546, each digit 5 is replaced with the digit 7. How many odd numbers are between the original number and resulting number?

E. 2,200

F. 10,099

G. 10,100

H. 20,200

73. Amalie has a pocket full of change. She has 7 quarters, 2 dimes, 9 nickels, and 14 pennies. What is the probability that a coin pulled out at random will **not** be a penny?

A. $\dfrac{1}{2}$

B. $\dfrac{15}{32}$

C. $\dfrac{7}{16}$

D. $\dfrac{9}{16}$

	Temperature °F				
	30°	20°	10°	0°	−10°
10	15	0	−10	−20	−35
20	5	−10	−25	−40	−50
30	0	−20	−35	−50	−65

Wind Speed mph

Wind Chill Factor Chart

74. The chart above gives wind chill factors for certain temperature-wind speed combinations. If $D = 5$, then for how many wind chill factors (C) is the statement $\dfrac{25}{D} \geq C > -30 + D$ true?

E. 5

F. 6

G. 7

H. 8

75. Points A and C are on a straight line, and point B is located between A and C. If the length of $\overline{AB} = \frac{5}{7}\,\overline{AC}$ and the length of $\overline{BC} = 14$, how long is $\overline{AC}$?

   A. 14
   B. 35
   C. 49
   D. 63

76. If x and y are negative integers, which of the following expressions **must** be negative?

   E. $x + y$
   F. $x - y$
   G. $x^2 + y^2$
   H. $x^2 - y^2$

77. Chen bought $2\frac{3}{5}$ yards of rope at $5.00 per yard. If there was a 8% sales tax, what was the total cost of the rope?

   A. $10.08
   B. $11.70
   C. $14.04
   D. $15.12

78. The average of five consecutive multiples of 5 is 20. What is the **largest** of these numbers?

   E. 25
   F. 30
   G. 35
   H. 50

79. On the number line above, $AB = 3\frac{7}{8}$. What is the position of point A?

   A. $2\frac{1}{8}$
   B. $-1\frac{1}{4}$
   C. $1\frac{1}{4}$
   D. $2\frac{1}{8}$

80. A grocer sells eggs in boxes of 8, and each box of 8 eggs sells for $2.35. He cannot sell boxes that aren't completely filled. If he starts with 175 eggs, what's the most amount of money can he make?

   E. $47.25
   F. $49.35
   G. $51.70
   H. $411.25

GO ON TO THE NEXT PAGE

Practice Tests

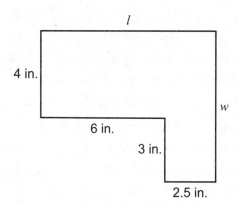

81. Students in Ms. Bonn's class drew a scale drawing, pictured above, of the new school garden that they want to install. In the drawing, the length is represented by l, the width is represented by w, and all angles are right angles. The actual space available is a square of ground that is 25.5 feet on a side. What is the **maximum** width of the actual garden?

    A. 7 feet

    B. 12 feet

    C. 21 feet

    D. 25.5 feet

82. A jar can hold 960 grams of candy when it is completely full. If the jar is $\frac{5}{6}$ full now, how many **kilograms** need to be added in order to fill the jar completely?

    E. 0.08

    F. 0.16

    G. 1.6

    H. 8.0

Number of Soccer Games	Goals Scored
4	0
3	1
5	2
5	3
2	4

83. The Lions soccer team tabulated the number of goals they scored in their last 19 games on the table above. Tomorrow is their last game of the season. How many goals do they have to score tomorrow to have a mean of **at least** 2 goals per game over the whole season?

    A. 1

    B. 2

    C. 3

    D. 4

84. An animal sanctuary that cares for lions, tigers, and bears has 45 caretakers, and the ratio of caretakers to animals is 5:9. If there are 15 bears and at least 1 lion, what is the **maximum** number of tigers?

    E. 9

    F. 25

    G. 65

    H. 81

85. If 25% of x is 120, what is the value of x ?

    A. 30

    B. 120

    C. 145

    D. 480

86. An oatmeal raisin protein bar recipe calls for 2 cups of raisins per batch of dough, and 1 batch of dough makes 5 dozen bars. If 1 cup = 48 teaspoons, which of the following calculations would give the number of teaspoons of raisins per bar in 1 batch?

    E. $\dfrac{2 \times 48}{60}$

    F. $\dfrac{2 \times 48}{5}$

    G. $\dfrac{2 \times 5}{60}$

    H. $\dfrac{2 \times 60}{48}$

87. The least of a set of 4 consecutive multiples of 3 is L, and the greatest is G. What is the value of $\dfrac{2G + L}{3}$ in terms of G?

    A. $G - 3$

    B. $3 - 2G$

    C. $\dfrac{2}{3}G + \dfrac{4}{3}$

    D. $\dfrac{3}{2}G + 1$

88. Elijah's age is $\dfrac{2}{3}$ of Alyssa's age today, but in 4 years, Elijah will be $\dfrac{4}{5}$ of Alyssa's age. How old is Alyssa today?

    E. 4

    F. 6

    G. 8

    H. 10

89. Tam has picked up 5 different books that interest him in the school library, but he can only check out a maximum of 3. How many different combinations can he check out?

    A. 8

    B. 10

    C. 12

    D. 20

90. Kaya and Robert are washing dishes. Working together, they can wash 15 dishes in 10 minutes. Robert working by himself can wash dishes at twice the rate of Kaya working by herself. How many dishes can Robert wash working by himself in 20 minutes?

    E. 5

    F. 10

    G. 20

    H. 30

91. What is the value of $(-ab)(a)$ when $a = -\dfrac{4}{9}$ and $b = 4\dfrac{1}{2}$?

    A. $-\dfrac{8}{9}$

    B. $-\dfrac{8}{81}$

    C. $\dfrac{8}{81}$

    D. $\dfrac{8}{9}$

92. If the circumference of a circle is 10π, what is its area?

    E. 5π

    F. 10π

    G. 25π

    H. 50π

GO ON TO THE NEXT PAGE

93. Suppose $R = \dfrac{a}{b}$ and $S = \dfrac{a+1}{b+1}$, and a and b do not equal -1 or 0. What is $\dfrac{R}{S}$ in terms of a and b?

   A. $\dfrac{2a+b}{2b+b}$

   B. $\dfrac{2a+1}{2b+1}$

   C. 1

   D. $\dfrac{ab+a}{ab+b}$

94. Each square in the grid above has a side length of 4. What is the area of the shaded triangle?

   E.   3

   F.   24

   G.   48

   H.   96

95. If $x = \dfrac{1}{2}$, what is the value of y when $\dfrac{x}{3} = \dfrac{4}{y}$?

   A.   4

   B.   6

   C.   12

   D.   24

96. A sandbox has a rectangular base that measures $4\frac{1}{2}$ feet by 4 feet. The height is $\frac{1}{3}$ of the length of the longest side of the base. How many cubic feet of sand can the sandbox hold?

   E.   12 cu ft

   F.   18 cu ft

   G.   24 cu ft

   H.   27 cu ft

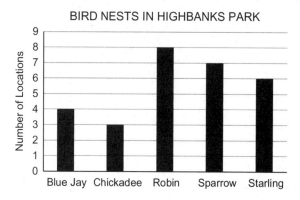

97. The graph above shows the number of nests of different bird species in Highbanks Park. On average, robins lay 3 eggs per nest, sparrows lay 4 eggs per nest, blue jays and starlings each lay 5 eggs per nest, and chickadees lay 7 eggs per nest. Which of the five species of birds has the **least** number of eggs expected in the park?

   A.   blue jays

   B.   chickadees

   C.   robins

   D.   sparrows

98. If $z = 9$, what is the value of $\dfrac{9(3+z)}{5z}$?

   E. $\dfrac{9}{5}$

   F. $\dfrac{12}{5}$

   G. $\dfrac{81}{25}$

   H. $\dfrac{18}{5}$

99. A rectangle with a length of 9 inches and a width of 8 inches is divided into squares, each of which has sides measuring 1 inch. One-third of these squares are painted red. Then, $\frac{1}{8}$ of the remaining squares are painted green, and the others are left unpainted. How many squares are left unpainted?

   A.   24

   B.   33

   C.   36

   D.   42

 GO ON TO THE NEXT PAGE

$$\frac{y}{w} = z(w + x)$$

100. In the equation above, the value of w is -1 and x, y, and z are greater than 0. What is the value of x in terms of y and z?

  E. $\dfrac{-y - z}{z}$

  F. $\dfrac{1 - y}{z}$

  G. $\dfrac{y - z}{z}$

  H. $\dfrac{z - y}{z}$

101. If N is an odd integer, which of the following **must** be even?

  A. $2N - 1$

  B. $3N + 2$

  C. $4N$

  D. $N^2 + 2N$

102. Frank has x shells, and Darnell has 8 more than 7 times the number of shells Frank has. In terms of x, how many shells do Frank and Darnell have in total?

  E. $8x$

  F. $7x + 8$

  G. $8x + 7$

  H. $8x + 8$

103. Five less than 4 times the number n is 2 more than 3 times the number m. Which of the following expresses this relationship?

  A. $5 + 4n = 2 - 3m$

  B. $5 - 4n = 2 + 3m$

  C. $4n - 5 = 3m + 2$

  D. $4(n - 5) = 3(m + 2)$

Position at Kool Klothing	Highest Salary (in thousands)	Range of Salaries (in thousands)
Managers	35	5
Assistant Managers	28	4
Sales Associates	23	8
Cashiers	20	3

104. The CEO of Kool Klothing, Inc. is analyzing the salaries that employees are paid in Kool Klothing stores. The table above shows both the highest salary for each position and the range of salaries for each position. Which of the following expresses the correct **overall** range (r) of all salaries for all four salaries, in thousands?

  E. $15 \le r \le 40$

  F. $17 \le r \le 35$

  G. $17 \le r \le 40$

  H. $15 \le r \le 35$

105. Which number line below shows the range of values that satisfy the inequality $-(a + 5) < \dfrac{b}{-2} \le -3 - a$ when $b = 4$?

  A.

  B.

  C.

  D.

GO ON TO THE NEXT PAGE

106. There are 4 green chips, 6 black chips, and 8 red chips in a bin. If 1 chip is chosen at random from the bin, what is the probability that a red chip is **not** chosen?

E. $\dfrac{4}{9}$

F. $\dfrac{5}{9}$

G. $\dfrac{5}{8}$

H. $\dfrac{4}{5}$

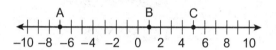

107. What is the distance from the midpoint of AB to point C?

A. 4

B. 6

C. 7

D. 8

108. If the decimal 2.024 is equivalent to the fraction $\dfrac{x+2}{125}$, then what is the value of x ?

E. 1

F. 3

G. 251

H. 253

Number of Responses	Favorite Sport
4	Volleyball
22	Swimming
34	Soccer
20	Basketball

109. Mr. Perez's class conducted a survey of students in seventh grade. Each student was asked to name a favorite sport, and the results were tabulated in the table above. Suppose the surveyor asks a random seventh grader the survey question. Which sport has exactly a 1 out of 4 chance of being the student's favorite sport?

A. volleyball

B. swimming

C. soccer

D. basketball

110. If $3 = \dfrac{9b}{a}$, what is $\dfrac{a}{b}$ equal to?

E. 3

F. $3a$

G. $3ab$

H. 27

GO ON TO THE NEXT PAGE

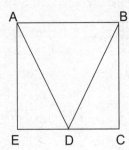

111. In the figure above, triangle ABD is isosceles and has an area of 18. What is the area of square ABCE?

    A. 18
    B. 36
    C. 48
    D. 64

112. If 1 lept = 2.4 munts and 21.6 kants = 2 lepts, how many kants equal 1 munt?

    E. 0.1
    F. 0.2
    G. 4.5
    H. 9

113. A cat is fed $\frac{3}{8}$ of a pound of cat food every day. For how many days will 60 pounds of this cat food feed the cat?

    A. 160
    B. 180
    C. 240
    D. 360

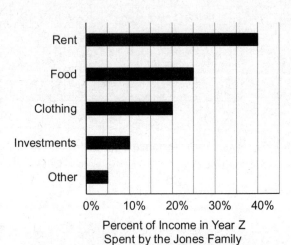

Percent of Income in Year Z
Spent by the Jones Family

114. The table above shows how the Jones family spent their annual income of $60,000 in year Z. Approximately how many more dollars did the Jones family spend on food than on clothing in year Z according to the above graph?

    E. 3,000
    F. 5,000
    G. 12,000
    H. 15,000

**THIS IS THE END OF THE TEST. IF TIME REMAINS, YOU MAY CHECK YOUR ANSWERS.
BE SURE THAT THERE ARE NO STRAY MARKS, PARTIALLY FILLED ANSWER CIRCLES, OR
INCOMPLETE ERASURES ON YOUR ANSWER SHEET.**

STOP

Practice Tests

Answer Key

PART 1—ENGLISH LANGUAGE ARTS

1. A	16. E	31. A	46. E
2. G	17. C	32. H	47. C
3. B	18. H	33. B	48. G
4. G	19. B	34. E	49. A
5. B	20. E	35. C	50. H
6. H	21. D	36. G	51. C
7. B	22. H	37. D	52. F
8. H	23. A	38. H	53. A
9. B	24. G	39. C	54. H
10. F	25. A	40. E	55. B
11. C	26. H	41. B	56. F
12. H	27. A	42. H	57. D
13. D	28. H	43. B	
14. G	29. D	44. H	
15. A	30. H	45. A	

PART 2—MATHEMATICS

58. 158	73. D	88. F	103. C
59. 80	74. G	89. B	104. H
60. 7.3, 7.30	75. C	90. G	105. B
61. 62	76. E	91. A	106. F
62. 11	77. C	92. G	107. D
63. D	78. F	93. D	108. G
64. G	79. A	94. G	109. D
65. C	80. F	95. D	110. E
66. H	81. C	96. H	111. B
67. C	82. F	97. A	112. G
68. H	83. D	98. F	113. A
69. A	84. G	99. D	114. E
70. F	85. D	100. H	
71. A	86. E	101. C	
72. G	87. A	102. H	

Answers and Explanations

PART 1—ENGLISH LANGUAGE ARTS

1.   A

Category: Usage

Getting to the Answer: Although each answer choice has a different pair of changes, there are only four total changes. Check each change, and cross out any choice that either does not include a needed change or includes unnecessary changes. **(A)** is correct because it fixes the run-on in sentence 1 and also changes the incorrect "do" to "due." There is no need for a comma after "promptings," so **(B)** and **(D)** are incorrect, and **(C)** is incorrect because the comma after "hungry" is necessary.

2.   G

Category: Punctuation

Getting to the Answer: A pair of commas, dashes, or parentheses are needed when setting off nonessential information in the middle of a sentence. Sentence 3 is missing the second dash needed to set off the nonessential phrase "such as having low levels of oxygen." **(G)** corrects this issue. **(E)** and **(H)** both add unnecessary punctuation, and **(F)** deletes the second comma that is needed to set off the nonessential "located in Nepal."

3.   B

Category: Sentence Structure

Getting to the Answer: The pronoun "her" indicates that Lola is promoting the book, but the introductory phrase "To promote her new book" is closest to "book signing." **(B)** is the correct answer because it changes the order of the sentence so that the phrase modifies Lola. **(A)** and **(C)** do not correct the modifier error. **(D)** is incorrect because "on Friday to promote her new book" interrupts the main clause.

4.   G

Category: Usage

Getting to the Answer: Pronouns must be consistent; a writer may address the reader either as "you" or "one," but not "you" and "one." By changing "one has" to "you have," the writer consistently addresses the reader as "you." **(G)** is correct. **(E)**, **(F)**, and **(H)** do not fix the error in pronoun agreement.

5.   B

Category: Organization

Getting to the Answer: Any revision must keep the author's original meaning and avoid creating new errors. **(B)** correctly combines the two sentences. **(A)** and **(C)** both change the author's meaning. **(A)** gets rid of the phrase "until last year," changing the meaning of the sentence, and **(C)** changes "unpopular" to "popular." **(D)** introduces a confusing sentence structure.

6.   H

Category: Topic Development

Getting to the Answer: When looking for the main claim of a passage, consider what the different parts of the passage are about. Paragraphs 2–4 describe how the writer played the saxophone for wider groups of people and how the audience appreciated the performances and the instrument. Paragraph 5 describes how the writer looks forward to playing more and getting even more people to like it. **(H)** expresses this well, including using the contrast word "however" to show the difference from the unpopularity described in the first paragraph. **(E)** is Out of Scope because it introduces an idea that is not supported in the essay. **(F)** is not specific enough; it shows a contrast but does not introduce the main point of the passage. **(G)** does not summarize the topic of the entire passage.

7.   B

Category: Organization

Getting to the Answer: As written, it is unclear whom the pronoun "he" in sentence 6 refers to; there is no individual person in sentence 5 that could be "he." Since the person chose some students to play and make money, it makes sense that "he" is the music teacher. **(B)** correctly moves sentence 6 to follow a sentence about the music teacher. **(A)** moves sentence 6 to before the music teacher is mentioned, which makes the flow of ideas in the second paragraph illogical. **(C)** recreates the original error. **(D)** attaches "he" to the professional musician, which is incorrect.

8.   H

Category: Organization

Getting to the Answer: Currently, sentence 11 is a fragment, and sentences 10 and 12 discuss different people. The correct answer needs to fix the fragment while providing a connection between the people in sentences 10 and 12 and the rest of the paragraph. **(H)** correctly makes a good transition from sentence 9 and reflects the writer's intended meaning. **(E)** is concise, but it loses some of the writer's original purpose, while **(F)** distorts the meaning. **(G)** also changes the meaning, and it does not make a good transition from sentence 9.

9.   B

Category: Organization

Getting to the Answer: Sentence 15 provides an outcome that is the opposite of the idea in sentence 14. **(B)** correctly provides a transition that shows a contradiction. **(A)** incorrectly suggests a sequence of events, **(C)** a cause and effect, and **(D)** an example.

10.   F

Category: Topic Development

Getting to the Answer: Sentence 16 emphasizes that even though jazz is a less popular type of music, playing in a jazz band was a positive experience for the writer. The new sentence should reinforce this idea. **(F)** does so by describing the experience as "fun and profitable." **(E)** does not show a positive side of the writer's jazz band experience. **(G)** says the same thing as sentence 17, causing a redundancy. **(H)** does not provide a good transition to the rest of the paragraph.

11.   C

Category: Topic Development

Getting to the Answer: In this paragraph the author writes about another performance the band will give and his suggestion for French music in a jazz style. The correct answer needs to develop this idea. **(C)** is correct because it connects the idea of the jazz style and playing French music. **(A)** retains ideas about the trumpet, which does not fit the topic of the paragraph. **(B)** and **(D)** introduce off–topic subjects.

Poem Analysis: "Work Gangs" celebrates common working men, their dreams, and their "songs." In the first stanza, the narrator imagines what box cars that are carrying different kinds of freight might say to each other. The second stanza introduces working tools and night watchmen. The third stanza imagines what the tools might say to each other at night, the musings of the night watchmen, and the joy of sleep after a long, hard day. The final stanza glorifies the voice and spirit of the common people.

12.   H

Category: Detail

Getting to the Answer: The narrator's oneness with the working class is stated in the very last words: "these are my people" (line 43). Who are those people? They are the common working men, who work with shovels, hammers, the freight brought in by box cars from all over the country—even the box cars themselves, which are analogous to the men. This focus is reflected in **(H)**. Although the reference to workers' hands smelling of hope shows positive emotion, it does not directly connect the narrator with the working class, so **(E)** is incorrect. Likewise, the discussion of the night watchmen in **(F)** showcases admiration on the narrator's part, but it is still not an outright statement of solidarity with the workers. **(G)** is incorrect because it is not directly connected to the narrator's identification with the working class.

13.   D

Category: Inference

Getting to the Answer: The poem glorifies the work ethic of working-class laborers, and emphasizes the commonalities they have. The box cars represent the workers themselves, who have pride in their jobs in common regardless of where they come from. Thus, **(D)** is correct and **(A)** is incorrect. While the box cars have traveled from across the country, **(B)** does not accurately summarize the theme of the poem that the lines are supporting. **(C)** is Out of Scope because the poem does not discuss the workers wanting to travel for leisure.

14. G

Category: Function

Getting to the Answer:

As befits a poem about the voice of the common man, "Work Gangs" focuses on the everyday jobs that workers participate in. The personification of the box cars and tools is one way that the author highlights these jobs; **(G)** is correct. Nothing meets its demise in the poem, and there is no indication that the box cars and tools are mistreated; any scratches on the tools show that they are proud to be used often. Thus, **(E)** and **(H)** are incorrect. **(F)** is incorrect because it is only a partial answer, addressing the traveling box cars but not the tools used by the work gangs.

15. A

Category: Detail

Getting to the Answer: The poem describes how even if workers' spirits are snuffed out like lanterns without oil, or they're too tired to remember their names, they can still enjoy sleep. It is "a belonging of all" regardless of any one person's state of being. Thus, **(A)** is the correct answer. **(B)** is Out of Scope; the poem does not mention workers rejecting sleep. **(C)** is a Distortion; the lines leading up to the cited section mention that the workers still have a long way to go, but hits does not mean they cannot sleep. **(D)** is also a Distortion; it is the labor that tires them, not the singing itself.

16. E

Category: Function

Getting to the Answer: Lines 24–27 function as a way to establish a parallel structure with the daytime activities mentioned earlier in the poem. The repetition of "in the night" echoes the earlier repetition of "how the" tools described their day in the workers' hands. The repetition connects the work happening during the day to the work occurring at night. Thus, **(E)** is correct and **(H)** is incorrect. **(F)** is incorrect because the night watchmen are not described as imagining the conversation amongst the box cars and the tools. **(G)** is incorrect because it is the tools that sleep, not the night watchmen.

17. C

Category: Inference

Getting to the Answer: In lines 40–43, the narrator conveys the upbeat spirit of the common people, and he concludes with a declaration that the workers are his people. **(C)** is the best support for that sentiment, as the narrator strongly implies his own connection with the common people by using "we" in describing how far everyone has come and still has to go. The lines in **(A)** and **(B)** describe the work of the night watchmen specifically; they do not support the connection the narrator feels with the working class as a whole. Similarly, **(D)** is too narrowly focused on sleep to be the correct answer.

18. H

Category: Inference

Getting to the Answer: The fourth and final stanza glorifies the voice and spirit of the common people. A process of elimination approach can help you find the choice that matches this best. There is nothing in the fourth stanza to support the idea that the common people are on the verge of a violent revolution, especially as the rest of the poem conveys a hopeful quality of workers who are content with their positive lives; eliminate **(E)**. The author's declaration that "these are my people" (line 43) suggests that the narrator feels empathy and solidarity with the common people, so eliminate **(F)**. The poem never indicates that singing is a requirement of their job, so **(G)** is also incorrect. This leaves **(H)**, the correct answer.

19. B

Category: Function

Getting to the Answer: The third stanza describes tools that are recounting their day, including pointing out that, even though the laborers' jobs demand considerable time and effort, the workers are still hopeful; **(B)** is correct. **(A)** is incorrect because the poem clearly describes the work as demanding, not effortless. **(C)** and **(D)** are Out of Scope because the poem does not imply that the workers will give up hope or that they would have had better lives if they had chosen other lines of work.

Passage Analysis: This is a social studies passage about alchemy, the ancient science of trying to turn different metals into gold. Paragraph 1 emphasizes the historical importance of alchemy: even though it seems ridiculous to the modern mind, alchemy helped lay the basic framework for the science of chemistry. Paragraph 2 describes the philosophy behind alchemy, and paragraph 3 introduces an analogy between alchemy and spirituality. Paragraph 4 supplies some more history behind alchemy and the fascination with it.

20. E

Category: Global

Getting to the Answer: This passage discusses alchemy's historical importance, the theories behind alchemy, and alchemy's development in Europe from the twelfth century onward. This matches the correct answer, **(E)**. **(F)** is incorrect because the alchemists never actually managed to make gold, despite centuries of trying. **(G)** and **(H)** are minor details from the passage, not its main point.

21. D

Category: Function

Getting to the Answer: In paragraph 1, the author states that alchemy, a pseudoscience, suggests "primitive superstition" and that the alchemist is "a charlatan obsessed with dreams of impossible wealth." This implies that there is no scientific reality in alchemy. Thus, **(D)** is correct and **(C)** is incorrect. **(A)** is incorrect, as both the word pseudoscience and the tone of the passage do not support the view of alchemy as extremely valuable. While paragraph 1 states that the results of the alchemists' "experiments laid the basic conceptual framework for much of the modern science of chemistry," the author uses this detail to contrast how alchemy had been respected for centuries with how it is viewed as pseudoscience today; **(B)** is incorrect.

22. H

Category: Detail

Getting to the Answer: Paragraph 1 describes the reputation of alchemists today—the author states that alchemy's associations with astrology suggest "primitive superstition" to the modern mind. **(H)** is correct. **(E)** goes against the gist of the passage, which suggests that

historians know a lot about alchemy. **(F)** is a Misused Detail from paragraph 4, where it is explained that the alchemists' idea of making gold was disproven. But that just stopped people from trying to make gold; it wasn't responsible for the unfavorable reputation of alchemists today. **(G)** is contradicted in paragraph 4.

23. A

Category: Detail

Getting to the Answer: Copper and lead are discussed in paragraph 2, which indicates that the alchemists believed that they were "only imperfectly developed forms of gold." **(A)** is correct. **(B)** is incorrect because gold, not copper or lead, was the "noblest" metal. There is no support for **(D)**, and **(C)** is a Distortion; though alchemists believed that all matter was composed of five basic elements, including air and water, there is no indication that lead and copper were composed primarily of air and water.

24. G

Category: Global

Getting to the Answer: The "purification" process is described in paragraph 3 as having a "profound significance for the alchemists"—metals attained a state of perfection just as souls attained a state of perfection in heaven. You can infer from this that the alchemists regarded the process as parallel to a spiritual experience, **(G)**. **(E)** is discussed in paragraphs 1 and 2. **(F)** is mentioned just prior to paragraph 3. **(H)** is Out of Scope.

25. A

Category: Global

Getting to the Answer: You do not need to know every word in a question stem in order to get the answer. Go back to paragraph 1, which explains that the alchemists are now viewed as upholding "primitive superstition" and as being "charlatan(s)," whereas they were once viewed as practitioners of "a highly respected art." **(A)** is correct. **(B)** and **(C)** are Distortions of the ideas conveyed by the cited words. **(D)** is Out of Scope and not supported in the passage.

26. H

Category: Inference

Getting to the Answer: The author sums up her point of view on alchemy at the end of the passage. Though not practiced today, alchemy "provided the basis for some of the most fascinating chapters in the history of science" (paragraph 4). The correct answer is **(H)**. **(E)** and **(G)** are incorrect because the passage argues that alchemy actually did contribute to the development of science. **(F)** is a Distortion of the claims made in paragraph 1; although the alchemists left us some valuable apparatuses and procedures, their basic principles have been disproved.

27. A

Category: Detail

Getting to the Answer: Each answer choice must be evaluated individually to determine whether it matches the idea mentioned in the question. **(A)** suggests that people from different countries all developed the underlying principles of alchemy independently around the same time and, thus, is correct. **(B)** depicts one specific group of people as having similar beliefs and, thus, is much weaker than the previous option in showing that "many different people" share the same belief. **(C)** suggests that more than one group of people began to use the same texts but not that they shared the same belief. If anything, **(D)** is Opposite.

Passage Analysis: This is a science passage about underwater ecosystems. Paragraph 1 explains that most ecosystems on our planet depend upon the light of the Sun, which provides energy for plants and algae, which in turn provide energy for animals higher up the food chain. Toward the end of the paragraph, however, it is stated that a new type of ecosystem has been discovered in deep-sea areas, where the first link in the food chain is provided by bacteria that are dependent on energy from within the earth itself. Paragraph 2 describes how these "chemosynthetic" bacteria develop. Paragraphs 3 and 4 describe the sea life that inhabit these deep-sea oases and the chemosynthesis they use.

28. H

Category: Global

Getting to the Answer: The passage is about the newly discovered "chemosynthetic" ecosystems described in paragraphs 2 and 3. **(H)** is correct. **(E)** is much too broad. The origins of life on Earth are briefly mentioned at the end of paragraph 1, but the passage does not thoroughly investigate this difficult topic. **(F)** is a Distortion, as it is an exaggeration of the claim that chemosynthesis is more important than scientists previously believed. **(G)** is Out of Scope.

29. D

Category: Global

Getting to the Answer: Paragraph 2 describes how the chemosynthetic ecosystem was discovered by a research ship and the characteristics of this bacteria-driven system. **(D)** is correct. **(A)** is incorrect because the discovery of organisms not dependent on sunlight doesn't disprove the importance of light to other organisms; indeed, paragraph 1 emphasizes this fact. **(B)** is only a detail of the paragraph, not its main idea. The large creatures in some deep-water environments are described in paragraph 3, making **(C)** a Misused Detail.

30. H

Category: Inference

Getting to the Answer: Paragraph 1 states that "most life is fundamentally dependent on photosynthetic organisms that store radiant energy from the Sun." Thus, light from the Sun powers most life on Earth, and **(H)** is correct. **(E)**, **(F)**, and **(G)** are all Misused Details.

31. A

Category: Detail

Getting to the Answer: Paragraph 1 describes the contrast that makes the chemosynthetic ecosystems "unique"— most life on Earth depends on the Sun's energy, but chemosynthetic ecosystems depend on energy from within the Earth itself. **(A)** is correct. **(B)** is illogical—these deep-sea ecosystems are certainly not waterless. **(C)** is not mentioned as a feature that makes chemosynthetic ecosystems unique. Finally, the passage does not state whether these are the only ecosystems found at these depths, **(D)**.

32. H

Category: Function

Getting to the Answer: The keyword here is "surprisingly." In 1977, scientists in a submarine found something they weren't looking for—namely, a unique, previously unknown ecosystem, 7,000 feet underwater in a volcanically active area. Thus, **(H)** is correct. **(E)** is contradicted by the final sentence of paragraph 2. **(F)** and **(G)** are not mentioned in the passage.

33. B

Category: Detail

Getting to the Answer: The phrase "primary producers" occurs at the end of paragraph 2, where chemosynthetic bacteria are described as primary producers because they "[transform] chemicals into compounds that can serve as nourishment for more complex forms of life." Since the bacteria's fundamental role is to provide food for other animals, **(B)** is correct. **(D)** is incorrect because the bacteria are described as "transforming chemicals into compounds," so the bacteria themselves aren't the simple chemicals in this process. **(C)** is the opposite of how the bacteria in paragraph 2 are described. **(A)** is not supported by the passage.

34. E

Category: Global

Getting to the Answer: Photosynthetic organisms, such as plants and algae, convert the Sun's energy into energy for other animals in their food chain (paragraph 1). Chemosynthetic bacteria do the same sort of thing by converting the earth's energy into energy for the deep-sea animals that consume them. **(E)** is correct; both types of organisms perform similar functions in their different food chains. **(F)** applies to chemosynthetic organisms only. **(G)** is false; only photosynthetic organisms use sunlight as a basic source of energy. **(H)** is not supported anywhere in the passage.

Passage Analysis: Paragraph 1 introduces American dancer Martha Graham and outlines the scope of her career. Paragraph 2 describes her early life and training. Paragraph 3 explains how she wanted to break away from the rigid forms of classical ballet. Paragraph 4 describes some of Graham's first performances and early innovations. Paragraph 5 details the negative reaction of both critics and audiences to her early work. Paragraph 6 states that Graham gradually found more success but continued to experiment, and that her influence is still felt today.

35. C

Category: Global

Getting to the Answer: This passage describes Graham's career, revolutionary style, and reputation with the critics. **(C)** is correct. **(A)** and **(B)** are too broad, and do not encompass the entire main idea of the passage. **(D)** only describes paragraph 5, and is therefore too specific for a Global question.

36. G

Category: Detail

Getting to the Answer: Paragraph 3 puts Graham's approach in context—she wanted "to create dance forms and movements that would better reflect the full complement of human emotions and experiences." Additionally, in paragraph 5, she says that "the old forms could not give voice to the fully awakened man." **(G)** is the correct answer. **(E)** is only a minor element of Graham's style. **(F)** is Opposite; Graham herself states that her new work "was not done perversely to dramatize ugliness." **(H)** exaggerates Graham's reaction against classical ballet; Graham herself was dissatisfied with classical ballet, but she didn't set out to destroy the whole tradition.

37. D

Category: Function

Getting to the Answer: Read each answer choice to determine which one uses chronological structure to great effect. Paragraph 6 begins with "As the decades passed," suggesting chronologically significant information. Paragraph 5 discusses the initially negative reaction of the public to Graham's performances, and paragraph 6 discusses their gradual acceptance and praise of her work. Thus, **(D)** is correct. Graham's Presidential Medal of Freedom, which seems to have been awarded after Graham's many other accomplishments, is mentioned before Denis and Shawn, so the relationship is not made any clearer by the structure. **(A)** is incorrect. **(B)** and **(C)** both suggest that something mentioned later in the passage influenced something mentioned earlier in the passage, which contradicts the chronological structure here.

38. H

Category: Inference

Getting to the Answer: Paragraph 4 contrasts classical ballet with Graham's new style of dance and states that she "avoided decorative sets and costumes." Since Graham was rebelling against the artistic trends of her time, you can infer that classical ballet of this period *did* employ elaborate sets and costumes. **(H)** is correct. **(E)** is Out of Scope; nothing suggests that Graham's style was loose or formless. **(F)** and **(G)** describe critical reactions to Graham's new style.

39. C

Category: Detail

Getting to the Answer: Paragraph 5 says that critics "react[ed] only to the unfamiliar and original dance movements and not to the feelings and ideas the movements were designed to express." **(C)** rephrases this key idea. There is no evidence in the passage to support **(A)**, **(B)**, or **(D)**.

40. E

Category: Function

Getting to the Answer: Read the lines surrounding the quotation. Immediately prior to the quotation, Paragraph 3 states that Graham seeks "to create dance forms and movements that would better reflect the full complement of human emotions and experiences."

Thus, Graham desires her audience to take away more than just mere entertainment; the audience should be exposed to a more complete picture of human emotions and experiences. **(E)** matches this idea and is correct. **(F)** and **(G)** are Distortions. **(H)** is much too broad.

41. B

Category: Global

Getting to the Answer: Paragraph 3 states that Graham wanted "to break away from the strictures" of classical ballet, so **(B)** is correct. **(A)** is better suited as a description of paragraph 2. **(D)** is discussed in paragraph 5. **(C)** is described earlier in the passage.

42. H

Category: Function

Getting to the Answer: Music is discussed in paragraph 4, where the author writes that Graham's "productions used music purely as an accompaniment to dance rather than as an elaborate showpiece in itself." In other words, it was the dance, not the music, that was the focus of the production. **(H)** is correct. **(E)** and **(G)** are Opposite. There is no support for **(F)**.

Passage Analysis: "The Bride Comes to Yellow Sky" is an 1898 story by Stephen Crane. The excerpt from that story describes a newly married couple taking a train trip through Texas. Paragraph 1 relates the scenery that the train is passing by. Paragraph 2 introduces the couple. The husband, Jack, is described as somewhat uncomfortable in his clothes. Paragraph 3 describes his unnamed wife, who is equally uncomfortable. A conversation in paragraphs 4–8 indicates that the husband and wife are happy with one another and that the train trip is a new experience for the bride. They decide to celebrate with a meal that is, by their standards, expensive. Paragraphs 9 and 10 illustrate the couple's delight with both the train and their marriage. The couple is unaware that the porter and the other passengers view them with disdain. Paragraphs 11–14 feature a lighthearted discussion between the couple. Paragraph 15 describes the couple's experience in the dining-car.

43. B

Category: Function

Getting to the Answer: The repetition of the word "sweeping" emphasizes the great speed of the train, as the vast Texan landscape is described but then quickly brushed aside as the train zips onward. Thus, **(B)** is correct. Although the description of the Texan landscape is a key component of the repetition of "sweeping," the focus is on the train, not Texas. For example, the remainder of the excerpt takes place on the train, and the final paragraph describes the wife drinking in the details of the train car's interior; **(A)** and **(C)** are incorrect. There is nothing in the excerpt to indicate the couple is afraid of the train; **(D)** is incorrect. On the contrary, they find it pleasant.

44. H

Category: Detail

Getting to the Answer: Though the author does not describe Jack fully, he does write that Jack's "face was reddened from many days in the wind and sun" (paragraph 2), indicating that he works outdoors. Jack's "brick-colored hands" call back to that description. Thus, **(H)** is correct. Given that he seems to work outdoors in the sun, it is unlikely that Jack lives in a city. Likewise, his discomfort with his formal clothing indicates that he wears more casual attire for his job. Thus, **(E)** is incorrect. While Jack lovingly describes the train at length, he is merely described as having "the pride of an owner." Jack does not actually own the train; **(F)** is incorrect. **(G)** is incorrect because the excerpt explicitly describes Jack's suit as his "new black clothes," and not as a threadbare suit.

45. A

Category: Detail

Getting to the Answer: Note how the author describes the bride: plain, placid, neither pretty nor young. The impression is of a woman who, prior to marriage, had fended for herself. As the author states, she was used to cooking—a form of work—and expected to continue to cook, now for her husband. Thus, **(A)** is correct. **(B)** is tempting, given the previous description of Jack's skin being reddened from working outdoors, but those details were in regard to his economic class. There is nothing in the excerpt to indicate that the train was warm or that it was a hot day. Instead, like Jack, the point is that the bride's discomfort is rooted in dressing

more formally than she usually does. **(C)** is incorrect given the wife's later shock at spending a dollar in the lunch car and her use of slang like "ain't." **(D)** is incorrect because the idea that she expected to cook doesn't support the idea of being impressed.

46. E

Category: Function

Getting to the Answer: "They were evidently very happy" functions as a pivot in the excerpt, shifting the focus from showing the newly wedded couple awkwardly being mindful of other passengers to a personal conversation between the couple; **(E)** is correct. While the couple does discuss the train's attributes, that comes toward the end of the excerpt, not near this pivot point. In addition, the text does not describe the couple jointly staring out the window. Instead, they seem to be paying attention to the other passengers; **(F)** is incorrect. Talk of the train comes later, and **(G)** incorrectly reverses the roles of which spouse does the explaining. While the newly wedded couple does seem to find great comfort in one another, they are nevertheless described as being mindful of their fellow passengers; **(H)** is incorrect.

47. C

Category: Function

Getting to the Answer: The fine quality of the train is relayed to the reader through the extensive descriptions provided through the wife's perspective at the end of the excerpt. Thus, **(C)** is correct. **(A)** incorrectly describes the Texas landscape, not the train. Although the clothing worn by the couple is described in detail, we are given no indication about how the other passengers are dressed. So, **(B)** is incorrect. Finally, while the husband does talk up the train's qualities at length, his pride is only compared to someone who might own the train. Jack does not really own the train; **(D)** is incorrect.

48. G

Category: Global

Getting to the Answer: When Jack insists that spending a lot of money by the couple's standards is okay for "this trip," it emphasizes how the couple is celebrating a special occasion, likely their marriage or honeymoon. Thus, **(G)** is correct. Jack does not own the train, and his sunburnt skin indicates that he likely works outdoors; **(E)** is incorrect. While the couple is clearly traveling across Texas, there is nothing in the text to indicate that they are leaving it for good; **(F)** is incorrect. In paragraph 7, the wife expresses shock at spending so much money, which indicates that she is far from careless with their spending; **(H)** is incorrect.

49. A

Category: Detail

Getting to the Answer: The passage makes it clear that the man's clothes were new and formal, given that Jack keeps glancing at his own attire as if to check to see if it is real, and he does so in a respectful fashion. **(A)** is correct. **(B)** is incorrect because it merely relates that the pair is newly married, not how they are dressed. Although **(C)** is tempting because it relates details of the woman's clothing, it merely conveys the idea that they are nice formal clothes, not that they are new clothes. **(D)**, likewise, is tempting because it indicates the clothes are likely new, given the woman's discomfort, but on its own, the sentence tells us nothing about how fine her clothes are.

50. H

Category: Global

Getting to the Answer: Consider the tone of the conversation—happy but also exploratory, as the characters get to know each other. For example, Jack doesn't know if his bride has been in a parlor-car before, and she is surprised to learn that Jack will spend money on an expensive meal. In other words, they are learning new things about each other, which matches **(H)**. **(E)** and **(F)** are both incorrect because they focus on the train, not the couple, and **(G)** is not supported by the text. Indeed, the author describes them as "happy."

Passage Analysis: This is a social studies passage about the Sherpas of the Himalayas. Paragraph 1 gives some background on the Sherpa people, describing them as "the reliable porters who guide mountaineers to the peaks of the highest mountains." Paragraph 2 describes the origins of the Sherpas and their migration to their current location. Paragraph 3 traces the evolution of today's Sherpas, from their first expeditions as porters to their roles as equal partners in the scaling of Mt. Everest. Paragraph 4 discusses the economic impact of mountaineering on the Sherpa people. Paragraph 5 describes how scientists are interested in studying Sherpas' ability to thrive with very little oxygen. Paragraph 6 discusses the cultural changes brought about by the increasing interest in Mt. Everest. Paragraph 7 states that, although climbing is a lucrative profession, most Sherpas would prefer a less hazardous occupation.

51. C

Category: Infographic

Getting to the Answer: Paragraph 1 introduces Sherpas as the topic of the passage, describing their reputation as "reliable porters" for mountaineers. The pie chart shows that more successful climbers are Nepalese (of which Sherpas are a part) than other nationalities put together. Look for the choice that connects these two ideas. **(C)** correctly characterizes the comparison made by the pie chart and connects it to the idea that Sherpas are climbing experts. **(A)** is a Distortion because the main idea of the paragraph is centered on Sherpas, not Westerners. **(B)** is a Misused Detail; how Sherpas have coped with the modernization of the world appears in paragraph 4, not paragraph 1. Though the chart does show that 55% of successful climbers of Mt. Everest are Nepalese, **(D)** is also a Misused Detail because itndoes not connect that idea to the topic of paragraph 1.

52. F

Category: Detail

Getting to the Answer: In paragraph 2, the author states that the Sherpas migrated into the Khumbu area in the sixteenth century and lived there and in the Solu region until the British colonized India in the 1800s. **(F)** is correct. **(E)** and **(G)** are Distortions; Kham is where the Sherpas lived prior to the sixteenth century, and while the author states that the Sherpas migrated southward from eastern Tibet, there is no mention of them ever living in western Tibet. **(H)** is Out of Scope; their exact location within Nepal is not given.

53. A

Category: Infographic

Getting to the Answer: The Main Idea of the passage is the history of the Sherpa people and how they came to be respected porters to mountaineers today, and the timeline details events from both the periods before the Sherpas started climbing and after. Predict that the timeline shows how the history of the Sherpa people led to their current reputation; **(A)** is correct. **(B)** directly contradicts paragraph 1, which states that the Sherpas did not climb mountains before the 1900s, so eliminate it as an Opposite choice. The timeline does not cast doubt on any aspect of the Sherpa history, so **(C)** is incorrect. Mt. Everest tourism and how it was or was not affected by the first successful climb is Out of Scope, so eliminate **(D)**.

54. H

Category: Function

Getting to the Answer: Paragraph 6 discusses the cultural effects of mountaineering on the Sherpas, so **(H)** is correct. **(E)** is discussed in paragraph 1, and **(F)** is the main idea of paragraph 4. **(G)** is not supported by the passage.

55. B

Category: Global

Getting to the Answer: Paragraph 5 explains that scientists studied the physiological changes that occurred in the Sherpas as a result of working at extremely high altitudes. **(B)** is correct. **(A)** and **(C)** are Distortions. **(D)** is Out of Scope.

56. F

Category: Detail

Getting to the Answer: Paragraph 4 summarizes the effect of the Everest expedition. Far from discouraging mountaineers, the expedition attracted more tourists and mountaineers to the region. **(F)** is correct, and **(E)** is incorrect. **(G)** and **(H)** are Distortions; the Sherpas' religious beliefs about the mountains were apparently changed before the Everest trip, and paragraph 4 focuses on the Sherpa economy, not their traditional ways of life.

57. D

Category: Inference

Getting to the Answer: Paragraph 6 discusses the interactions between Western climbers and native Sherpas, stating that "the two groups usually value the background and assets of the other." Indeed, the Westerners trust their Sherpa guides with their lives, and Sherpas, in turn, are impressed by the organization and technology of the Westerners. **(D)** is correct. **(A)** and **(B)** are Opposite; Sherpas are among the best-paid people in Nepal and retain many of their customs. **(C)** is a Distortion; the passage mentions that the Sherpas are Buddhists in paragraph 1, but it never states that the increasing presence of Westerners affected their religious beliefs in any way.

PART 2—MATHEMATICS

58. 158

Subject: Geometry

Getting to the Answer: Because the sum of the angles around a single point must equal 360, $x = 360 - 90 - m \angle B$. Notice ABCD is a parallelogram, which means that $\angle B \cong \angle D$. To find the measure of $\angle D$ (and thus $\angle B$), subtract its supplementary angle of 68 from 180, which results in 112. Plugging 112 into the original expression gives $x = 360 - 90 - 112 = 158$.

59. 80

Subject: Arithmetic

Getting to the Answer: Use the three-part percent formula $Percent \times Whole = Part$, plugging in 6 for the *Part*. Convert 7.5% to 0.075 and plug in for the *Percent*. Solve for the total training hours.

$$0.075 \times \text{Total hours} = 6$$
$$\text{Total hours} = \frac{6}{0.075} = 80$$

60. 7.3, 7.30

Subject: Arithmetic

Getting to the Answer: Plug in -4 for x and use PEMDAS to simplify. Remember that absolute value bars act as parentheses, so simplify inside them first.

$$|(-4) - 3.6| + |5 - 2| - |7.3 + (-4)| = y$$
$$|-7.6| + |3| - |3.3| = y$$
$$7.6 + 3 - 3.3 = y$$
$$7.3 = y$$

Grid in 7.3 or 7.30.

61. 62

Subject: Algebra

Getting to the Answer: Because the integers are unknown, let x be the smaller integer and $x + 2$ be the larger integer. Their sum can then be represented as $x + (x + 2) = 44$. Solve for x:

$$x + (x + 2) = 44$$
$$2x + 2 = 44$$
$$2x = 42$$
$$x = 21$$

If the smaller integer is 21, then the larger integer must be 23. Next, transform the integers as the problem instructs: multiply the larger integer by 3 to get 69 and divide the smaller integer by 3 to get 7. Finally, the question asks for the difference, so subtract: $69 - 7 = 62$.

62. 11

Subject: Algebra

Getting to the Answer: Isolate the variable, paying careful attention to signs.

$$\frac{249 - s}{14} = 17$$
$$249 - s = 238$$
$$-s = -11$$
$$s = 11$$

63. D

Subject: Algebra

Getting to the Answer: First, set up an equation to represent the initial situation. Marcus (M) has three times as much money as José (J): $M = 3J$. Next, set up an equation for the new situation. Marcus gives José $5.30, so $M - 5.30$ and $J + 5.30$. Marcus still has $10 more than José, so $M - 5.30 = (J + 5.30) + 10$. Simplify to get $M = J + 20.6$. From the first equation, you know M is equal to $3J$, so set $3J$ equal to $J + 20.60$ and solve for J.

$$3J = J + 20.6$$
$$2J = 20.6$$
$$J = 10.3$$

José started out with $10.30, which means Marcus started out with $3 \times 10.60 = 30.90$. Be careful! The question asks how much the boys have in sum, so add $10.60 + 30.90 = 41.20$.

Practice Tests

64. G

Subject: Algebra

Getting to the Answer: Because it's easiest to compare these quantities if you have numbers instead of variables, pick a simple number to substitute for Q, like 2. Take each piece of the equation at a time and solve for each of the answer choices:

$$Q = \frac{R}{3} \Rightarrow 2 = \frac{R}{3} \Rightarrow R = 6$$

$$Q = S - 6 \Rightarrow 2 = S - 6 \Rightarrow S = 8$$

$$Q = 7T \Rightarrow 2 = 7T \Rightarrow T = \frac{2}{7}$$

$$Q = \frac{U}{10} \Rightarrow 2 = \frac{U}{10} \Rightarrow U = 20$$

The only fraction and thus the smallest number is T.

65. C

Subject: Arithmetic

Getting to the Answer: First, notice that there are two rates at which John gets paid: one for the first 40 cars ($6 per car) and a different rate for all other cars after those first 40 ($6 per car plus 50% of $6, which is $6 + $3, or $9 per car). Since he makes 48 cars, he gets paid $6 × 40 cars ($240) plus 8 extra cars at $9 per car ($72) which totals $312.

66. H

Subject: Algebra

Getting to the Answer: Plug the values given for b and c into the equation $a = 2b + 3c - 8$. Then $a = (2 \times 2) + (3 \times 3) - 8$, or $a = 4 + 9 - 8$, so $a = 5$.

67. C

Subject: Algebra

Getting to the Answer: This problem sets up relationships among large, medium, and small lemonades: 2 large (L) lemonades are equal to 3 medium (M), and 2 medium lemonades are equal to 3 small (S): $2L = 3M$ and $2M = 3S$. To find the relationship between L and S, you need to equate them using a common term, M, so M needs to have the same coefficient in both. Therefore, multiply both sides of the first equation by 4, getting $8L = 12M$, and then multiply the second equation by 6, resulting in $12M = 18S$. Combining these two using the matching term $12M$ gives $8L = 12M = 18S$.

68. H

Subject: Arithmetic

Getting to the Answer: Remember PEMDAS to answer this question correctly. Operations inside parentheses come first, so $-2[(-18.75) \div 6.25]$ becomes $-2(-3)$, and $5[8.46 \div (-4.23)]$ becomes $5(-2)$. The full expression now reads $-2(-3) - 5(-2)$, or $6 - (-10)$, which is $6 + 10$, or 16.

69. A

Subject: Statistics and Probability

Getting to the Answer: First, determine how many pieces of fruit there are in all by adding all the numbers: $4 + 3 + 12 = 19$. Since there are only 3 bananas, the probability of Henry getting one is 3 out of 19, or $\frac{3}{19}$.

70. F

Subject: Arithmetic

Getting to the Answer: If the area is 48, the length is 7.5, and Area = Length (l) × Width (w), then $48 = 7.5 \times w$, and $w = 6.4$. The perimeter is $2 \times l + 2 \times w$, which is $2 \times 7.5 + 2 \times 6.4$, or $15 + 12.8 = 27.8$.

71. A

Subject: Arithmetic

Getting to the Answer: Proportions are the key to conversion questions like this. First, set up a proportion of euros to dinars, letting e be the unknown number of euros: $\frac{0.9}{e} = \frac{0.3}{43}$. You could cross multiply to get $0.3e = 38.7$ and solve for e. However, it is faster to notice that $0.9 \div 3$ would result in 0.3, so $e \div 3$ would have to result in 43. So 129 euros are needed to exchange for 43 dinars.

Don't forget that you also need to convert dollars! Set up a proportion of euros to dollars, letting e be the unknown number of euros: $\frac{0.9}{e} = \frac{1}{10}$. Cross multiplying here is fastest, resulting in $e = 9$. Add $129 + 9 = 138$ euros.

72. G

Subject: Arithmetic

Getting to the Answer: The number 258,546 becomes 278,746. Find how many numbers are between them by subtracting the two numbers: $278,746 - 258,546 = 20,200$. Both original numbers are even and the target number is odd, so exactly half of those numbers will be odd: $20,200 \div 2 = 10,100$.

73. D

Subject: Statistics and Probability

Getting to the Answer: Probability is computed by dividing the number of desired outcomes by the total number of outcomes. In this question, the total number of outcomes is the sum of all of the coins in the pocket: $7 + 2 + 9 + 14 = 32$. There are $32 - 14 = 18$ coins that are not pennies. Thus, the probability is $\frac{18}{32} = \frac{9}{16}$.

74. G

Subject: Algebra

Getting to the Answer: First, plug $D = 5$ into the inequality: $\frac{25}{5} \geq C > -30 + 5$ or $5 \geq C > -25$. This statement, when translated into English, means that you need to look for all of the wind chill factors in the chart less than or equal to 5 and greater than -25. The correct answer is 7.

75. C

Subject: Arithmetic

Getting to the Answer: Drawing the line is helpful in number line problems. Notice that $\overline{BC}$ must be $1 - \frac{5}{7} = \frac{2}{7}$ of $\overline{AC}$, and also $\overline{BC} = 14$. So $14 = \frac{2}{7}\overline{AC}$. Solving for $\overline{AC}$ gives 49.

76. E

Subject: Algebra

Getting to the Answer: Use Picking Numbers for number property questions. Pick easy negative numbers to plug in for x and y, like $x = -2$ and $y = -3$. Then plug these values in for each answer choice to see which must result in a negative number:

(E) $x + y = -2 + -3 = -5$. Keep.

(F) $x - y = -2 - (-3) = 1$. Eliminate.

(G) $x^2 + y^2 = (-2)^2 + (-3)^2 = 4 + 9 = 13$. Eliminate.

(H) $x^2 - y^2 = (-2)^2 - (-3)^2 = 4 - 9 = -5$. Keep.

To decide between **(E)** and **(H)**, try plugging in another pair of numbers that might result in one of them producing a positive answer. In this case, simply switching x and y such that $x = -3$ and $y = -2$ in **(H)** gives $x^2 - y^2 = (-3)^2 - (-2)^2 = 9 - 4 = 5$. Eliminate it, and only **(E)** is left.

77. C

Subject: Arithmetic

Getting to the Answer: First, calculate the total cost of the rope: $2\frac{3}{5} \times 5 = \frac{13}{5} \times 5 = 13$. Next, calculate the sales tax, which is represented by 0.08 in decimal form. You can multiply 13 by 0.08 and then add the result to 13, or more efficiently, multiply 13 by 1.08. Either procedure will result in $14.04.

78. F

Subject: Statistics and Probability

Getting to the Answer: The average of a set of evenly-spaced numbers is equal to the median (middle number) of the set. Since the average of five consecutive multiples of 5 is 20, the median equals 20: __, __, 20, __, __. Adding 5 twice to 20 will give you the largest of these numbers, which is 30.

79. A

Subject: Arithmetic

Getting to the Answer: Point A is computed by subtracting the length of AB from the position of point B.

$$A = 1\frac{3}{4} - 3\frac{7}{8}$$
$$A = \frac{7}{4} - \frac{31}{8}$$
$$A = \frac{14}{8} - \frac{31}{8}$$
$$A = -\frac{17}{8}$$

Change the result to a mixed number. The answer is $-2\frac{1}{8}$.

80. F

Subject: Arithmetic

Getting to the Answer: First, compute how many boxes the grocer can completely fill with 175 eggs: $175 \div 8 = 21$ with a remainder of 7. The grocer cannot sell a partial box of eggs, so compute the amount from selling just the 21 boxes for $2.35 each: $21 \times 2.35 = \$49.35$.

81. C

Subject: Geometry

Getting to the Answer: First, compute the length l and width w of the drawing by using the measurements of the parallel sides in the drawing: $l = 6 + 2.5 = 8.5$ in. and $w = 4 + 3 = 7$ in. If the actual space available is a square, then the longest side (the length) can be no greater than 25.5 ft, and the width, which is shorter, must be less than 25.5 ft. Remember that you have to find the actual width, not the length; however, use this information about the actual length to set up a proportion: $\frac{8.5}{7} = \frac{25.5}{w}$. Solve for w by cross multiplying, or by noticing that since $25.5 = 8.5 \times 3$, then w must equal $7 \times 3 = 21$.

82. F

Subject: Arithmetic

Getting to the Answer: First, notice that the jar is $\frac{1}{6}$ empty, since it is $\frac{5}{6}$ full. If it was full, the jar would hold 960 grams, so next compute $\frac{1}{6}$ of 960: $\frac{1}{6} \times 960 = 160$ grams needed to fill the jar. Since the question asks for kilograms, use the conversion 1,000 g = 1 kg and divide 160 by 1,000 to get 0.16.

83. D

Subject: Arithmetic

Getting to the Answer: First, recall that the mean (average) is the total number of the goals over all the games divided by the total number of games. Since there will be a total of 20 games played and the mean must be at least 2 goals per game, the total number of goals must be 40 because 40 total goals ÷ 20 total games = 2 goals per game.

Adding lots of numbers is time-consuming, so to be most efficient, multiply the number of games by the number of goals for each row to get the total number of goals scored: $4(0) + 3(1) + 5(2) + 5(3) + 2(4) = 36$ total goals for the first 19 games. The Lions need $40 - 36 = 4$ goals in the last game to get an average of at least 2 goals per game.

84. G

Subject: Algebra

Getting to the Answer: You must first find the total number of animals so that you can subtract the number of bears and lions to find the number of tigers. So let a represent all the lions, tigers, and bears. Set up a proportion using the given ratio of caretakers to animals: $\frac{5}{9} = \frac{45}{a}$. Cross multiply and then divide by 5 to get $a = 81$. The question asks for the maximum number of tigers if there are 15 bears and at least 1 lion, so subtract $81 - 15 - 1 = 65$ tigers.

85. D

Subject: Algebra

Getting to the Answer: Remember, "of" means multiply and "is" means equals. This gives $\frac{25}{100}x = 120$. Simplify $\frac{25}{100}$ to $\frac{1}{4}$. Now the equation is $\frac{1}{4}x = 120$, so you can multiply both sides of the equation by 4, leaving $x = 120(4) = 480$.

86. E

Subject: Arithmetic

Getting to the Answer: The question asks the amount of raisins per bar, so divide the amount of raisins by the total number of bars. Multiply 2 cups × 48 teaspoons to get the total amount of raisins. Eliminate **(G)** and **(H)**, because the numerator does not match that calculation. The number of bars in 1 batch of dough is $5 \times 12 = 60$ bars, so eliminate **(F)** and choose **(E)**.

87. A

Subject: Algebra

Getting to the Answer: The greatest multiple is G, so the next greatest multiple must be $G - 3$, then $G - 6$, and fourth and last, $G - 9$. Thus, $G - 9$ must be equal to the least value of the set, L. Plug in $G - 9$ for L in the expression and simplify.

$$\frac{2G + L}{3}$$
$$\frac{2G + (G - 9)}{3}$$
$$\frac{3G - 9}{3}$$
$$\frac{\cancel{3}(G - 3)}{\cancel{3}}$$
$$G - 3$$

Alternatively, use Picking Numbers to solve. Choose a set of 4 consecutive multiples of 3, such as 3, 6, 9, and 12. Plug in 3 for L and 12 for G in the original expression such that $\frac{2(12) + 3}{3} = \frac{27}{3} = 9$. The correct choice will result in 9 when 12 is plugged in for G, and the only choice to do so is **(A)**.

88. F

Subject: Algebra

Getting to the Answer: For questions that don't give enough information to figure out the age of at least one person, use the answer choices to your advantage. For each choice, ask yourself, "If Alyssa was this age today, what age would Elijah have to be? In 4 years, will Elijah be $\frac{4}{5}$ of Alyssa's age?" and eliminate accordingly:

(E) Alyssa's age today: 4

Elijah's age today: $\frac{2}{3}$ (Alyssa's age) $= \frac{2}{3}(4) \approx 2\frac{2}{3}$

Alyssa's age in 4 years: $4 + 4 = 8$

Elijah's age in 4 years: $2\frac{2}{3} + 4 = 6\frac{2}{3}$, which <u>is not</u> $\frac{4}{5}$ of 8. Eliminate.

(F) Alyssa's age today: 6

Elijah's age today: $\frac{2}{3}$ (Alyssa's age) $= \frac{2}{3}(6) = 4$

Alyssa's age in 4 years: $6 + 4 = 10$

Elijah's age in 4 years: $4 + 4 = 8$, which <u>is</u> $\frac{4}{5}$ of 10. Keep.

At this point, you do not have to test the rest of the choices, because the constraints of the question are met if Alyssa is 6 today.

89. B

Subject: Statistics and Probability

Getting to the Answer: Create a list of the different books, using a systematic approach so that you don't accidentally end up missing a possibility or counting a possibility twice. A possible system is to start with the first book and list all possible combinations with the second book, then do the same with the second book, leaving out any possibilities listed previously, and so on. Label the books A, B, C, D, and E:

ABC	ABD	ABE
ACD	ACE	
ADE		
BCD	BCE	
BDE		
CDE		

The answer is 10.

90. G

Subject: Arithmetic

Getting to the Answer: First, notice that the question asks for how many dishes Robert washes in 20 minutes, but the total rate given is for 10 minutes. Both people working together would be able to wash twice as many dishes in twice the time, so the rate of both working together for 20 minutes is 30 dishes per 20 minutes.

There are many avenues to the correct answer from here, but testing each answer choice is a helpful strategy. Using the fact that Robert washes twice as many dishes as Kaya, test each to see if using that choice for Robert's rate results in both people washing 30 dishes in 20 minutes:

(E) If Robert washes 5 dishes, then Kaya must wash 2.5: $5 + 2.5 = 7.5$, which is not 30. Eliminate.

(F) If Robert washes 10 dishes, then Kaya must wash 5: $10 + 5 = 15$, which is not 30. Eliminate.

(G) If Robert washes 20 dishes, then Kaya must wash 10: $20 + 10 = 30$. Keep.

(H) If Robert washes 30 dishes, then Kaya must wash 15: $30 + 15 = 45$, which is not 30. Eliminate.

Only **(G)** works.

91. A

Subject: Algebra

Getting to the Answer: Convert $4\frac{1}{2}$ into an improper fraction. Then substitute the values given for a and b into the expression and simplify:

$$\left(-\left(-\frac{4}{9}\right)\times\frac{9}{2}\right)\times\left(-\frac{4}{9}\right)=(2)\times\left(-\frac{4}{9}\right)=-\frac{8}{9}$$

92. G

Subject: Geometry

Getting to the Answer: To find the area of a circle, you need the radius. Use the formula for the circumference of a circle ($C = 2\pi r$) to find it. Plug in the given circumference for C and solve for r: $10\pi = 2\pi r$. Divide both sides by 2π and get $r = 5$. Next, use the formula for the area of a circle, which is $A = \pi r^2$. Thus, $A = \pi(5^2) = \pi(25) = 25\pi$.

93. D

Subject: Algebra

Getting to the Answer: Substitute the values of R and S into the fraction $\frac{R}{S}$ and simplify:

$$\frac{R}{S} = \frac{\dfrac{a}{b}}{\dfrac{a+1}{b+1}}$$

$$= \frac{a}{b}\div\frac{a+1}{b+1}$$

$$= \frac{a}{b}\times\frac{b+1}{a+1}$$

$$= \frac{a(b+1)}{b(a+1)}$$

Distribute a and b to get $\frac{ab+a}{ab+b}$.

94. G

Subject: Geometry

Getting to the Answer: This triangle has a height of 8 (each box counts as 4) and a base of 12. The area of a triangle is

$$\frac{1}{2}(\text{Base})(\text{Height}) = \frac{1}{2}(12)(8) = 48.$$

95. D

Subject: Algebra

Getting to the Answer: In order to avoid a messy denominator, begin by cross multiplying the given equation: $xy = 12$. Next, substitute $\frac{1}{2}$ for x : $\frac{1}{2}y = 12$. Solve for y by multiplying both sides by 2. This leaves $y = 24$.

96. H

Subject: Geometry

Getting to the Answer: A sandbox is a rectangular prism, and the volume for that shape is found using length × width × height. Since the height is $\frac{1}{3}$ of the longest side of the base, convert $4\frac{1}{2}$ into an improper fraction to multiply: $\frac{1}{3}\times\frac{9}{2}=\frac{9}{6}=\frac{3}{2}$. Now plug this height into the volume formula and solve: $\frac{9}{2}\times4\times\frac{3}{2}=\frac{108}{4}=27$ cubic feet.

97. A

Subject: Statistics and Probability

Getting to the Answer: To find the number of eggs expected for a bird species, multiple the average number of eggs per nest by the number of nests in the park.

Blue Jays: $5 \times 4 = 20$

Chickadees: $7 \times 3 = 21$

Robins: $3 \times 8 = 24$

Sparrows: $4 \times 7 = 28$

Blue jays have the least number of eggs.

98. F

Subject: Algebra

Getting to the Answer: Plug in the number 9 for each z in the expression. This yields 9×12 in the numerator and 5×9 in the denominator. The 9s cancel, leaving you with $\frac{12}{5}$.

99. D

Subject: Geometry

Getting to the Answer: First, find the total area: $8 \times 9 = 72$. One-third of that is red $\left(\frac{1}{3}\times72=24\right)$. $72 - 24 = 48$ squares remain, of which $\frac{1}{8}$ are green, so there are 6 green squares. That leaves 42 uncolored squares.

100. H

Subject: Algebra

Getting to the Answer: Plug in -1 for w and then isolate x. Beware of careless errors with the negatives.

$$\frac{y}{-1} = z(-1 + x)$$

$$\frac{1}{z}(-y) = \not{z}(-1 + x)\left(\frac{1}{\not{z}}\right)$$

$$-\frac{y}{z} = -1 + x$$

$$-\frac{y}{z} + 1 = x$$

Now that x is isolated, manipulate the expression until you have matched an answer choice:

$$-\frac{y}{z} + 1 = -\frac{y}{z} + \frac{z}{z} = \frac{-y + z}{z} = \frac{z - y}{z}.$$

Alternatively, after isolating x, use Picking Numbers to solve. Choose easy numbers for y and z, like $y = 4$ and $z = 2$, since you know you need to divide them. Plug them in the expression such that $-\frac{4}{2} + 1 = -2 + 1 = -1$. Now plug in the y and z values into each answer choice. The correct choice will also result in -1.

101. C

Subject: Algebra

Getting to the Answer: This is a perfect problem for Picking Numbers. Pick a simple number for N, like 3. Then plug it into the answer choices and see which one is correct.

(A) $2(3) + 1 = 6 - 1 = 5$. Eliminate.

(B) $3(3) + 2 = 9 + 2 = 11$. Eliminate.

(C) $4(3) = 12$. Keep.

(D) $(3)^2 + 2(3) = 9 + 6 = 15$. Eliminate.

Only **(C)** works.

102. H

Subject: Algebra

Getting to the Answer: Translate English into math. If Frank has x shells, then "8 more than 7 times x" translates to $8 + 7x$. Since the question asks how many shells Frank and Darnell have in total, add x to $8 + 7x$ like so $x + 8 + 7x$. Combine like terms to get $8x + 8$.

103. C

Subject: Algebra

Getting to the Answer: Translate English to math one piece at a time. "Five less than" means $- 5$. "4 times the number n" means $4n$. "Is" always means equals. So the left side of the equation is $4n - 5$.

Since only **(C)** has $4n - 5$, you could stop here. But if you need to, then translate the right side. "Two more than" means $+ 2$. "3 times the number m" means $3m$. So the right side of the equation is "$2 + 3m$" or "$3m + 2$" (since order doesn't matter with addition). The full equation is $4n - 5 = 3m + 2$.

104. H

Subject: Statistics and Probability

Getting to the Answer: A overall range is the difference between the lowest and highest salaries. Notice that the highest salary according to the table is that of managers, which is 35. Eliminate **(E)** and **(G)**. To find the lowest salary, subtract the range from each of the highest salaries:

Managers: $35 - 5 = 30$

Assistant Managers: $28 - 4 = 24$

Sales Associates: $23 - 8 = 15$

Cashiers: $20 - 3 = 17$

The lowest salary is 15, so the answer is **(H)**.

105. B

Subject: Algebra

Getting to the Answer: Separate the compound inequality into two pieces: $-(a + 5) < \frac{b}{-2}$ and $\frac{b}{-2} \le -3 - a$. Then plug in -4 for b and solve each inequality for a. Be careful to flip the sign when multiplying or dividing both sides by a negative number.

$$-(a + 5) < \frac{4}{-2} \qquad\qquad \frac{4}{-2} \le -3 - a$$
$$-a - 5 < -2 \qquad\qquad -2 \le -3 - a$$
$$-a < 3 \qquad\qquad\qquad 1 \le -a$$
$$a > -3 \qquad\qquad\qquad -1 \ge a$$

In English, a is greater than -3 and less than or equal to -1, so the number line that matches is **(B)**.

106. F

Subject: Statistics and Probability

Getting to the Answer: Remember that probability is the number of desired outcomes (the "not red" chips) divided by the number of total outcomes. In this case, the total number of outcomes is the total of all chips: $4 + 6 + 8 = 18$. Then compute the number of "not red" chips: $4 + 6 = 10$. So the probability of choosing a chip that is not red is $\frac{10}{18} = \frac{5}{9}$.

107. D

Subject: Geometry

Getting to the Answer: The most efficient way to find a midpoint on a number line is to find the average of the points (since midpoint is the same as the average). So take the average of A (-7) and B (1), which is $\frac{(-7)+1}{2}$ or -3. Once you've found this point, find the distance from -3 to 5, which is $5 - (-3)$, or 8.

108. G

Subject: Arithmetic

Getting to the Answer: First, translate the given information into an equation: $2.024 = \frac{x+2}{125}$. Notice that 2.024 can be rewritten as a fraction so that $\frac{2024}{1000} = \frac{x+2}{125}$. You could cross multiply, but it is more efficient to simplify the left side such that the denominators match: $\frac{253}{125} = \frac{x+2}{125}$. For these fractions to be equal, 253 must be equal to $x + 2$. Thus, x must be 251.

109. D

Subject: Statistics and Probability

Getting to the Answer: Start by computing the total number of surveyed students in the seventh grade: $14 + 18 + 28 + 20 = 80$. One-fourth of the 80 students answered with a particular sport, so $\frac{1}{4} \times 80 = 20$ students must have picked the correct answer. That matches with basketball.

110. E

Subject: Algebra

Getting to the Answer: Manipulate with algebra until $\frac{a}{b}$ is isolated. Multiply both sides of $3 = \frac{9b}{a}$ by a to get $3a = 9b$. Divide both sides by 3 to get $a = 3b$, and divide both sides by b to get $\frac{a}{b} = 3$.

111. B

Subject: Geometry

Getting to the Answer: Geometry problems will almost never give you extraneous information. Focus on what's being asked in the question, and use all the clues you're given to find a solution. The formula for finding the area of a triangle is $\frac{1}{2}$ Base $\times$ Height. Because the height of the triangle is the same as the height of the square and the base of the triangle is the same as the base of the square, simply multiply the area of the triangle by 2 to get the area of the square: $2 \times 18 = 36$.

112. G

Subject: Arithmetic

Getting to the Answer: First, notice that you can figure out how many kants are in 1 lept and by doing so, you will have a common conversion between kants and munts. Thus, $21.6 \div 2 = 10.8$ kants are in 1 lept. Since you know that 2.4 munts are also in 1 lept, you can conclude that 2.4 munts = 10.8 kants. Use this to set up a proportion to calculate the number of kants (k) in 1 munt.

$$\frac{2.4}{10.8} = \frac{1}{k}$$
$$2.4k = 10.8$$
$$k = 4.5$$

Thus, there are 4.5 kants in 1 munt.

113. A

Subject: Arithmetic

Getting to the Answer: This a division problem. Divide 60 by $\frac{3}{8}$ and you get 160.

114. E

Subject: Arithmetic

Getting to the Answer: You know from the graph that approximately 20% was spent on clothing and 25% was spent on food. The most efficient strategy is to find the difference first. Subtract $25\% - 20\% = 5\%$, and then compute 5% of 60,000: $0.05 \times 60,000 = 3,000$.